Introduction

Time Out's London's Best Restaurants is the most authoritative and comprehensive guide to good restaurants, gastropubs and cafés in the capital. This is not just because we have a great passion for food, and for finding the best places to eat and drink in London. What you have in your hands is the only London guide for which anonymous critics pay for their meal and drinks just like a regular customer (Time Out then reimburses their expenses). We do not tell the restaurants we are coming, nor do we reveal who we are after the meal. Restaurants can exert no pressure on us as to the content of their reviews, and do not pay to be included in the guide. Our editors select all the establishments featured on merit and interest alone.

We want our readers to know just what the experience of eating at each restaurant might be like for them, and take pains to ensure that our reviewers remain totally objective on your behalf. Our insistence on undercover reporting means that our experience is much more likely to reflect your experience. This can't be said of well-known newspaper restaurant columnists: they often receive preferential treatment from restaurant kitchens who have their photographs pinned up to ensure the critics do not go unrecognised (and those critics are inclined to feel insulted or ill-treated if they are not recognised, adding further bias to their reviews).

Many of our reviewers have extraordinary expertise in specialist areas. Several are trained cooks or former chefs, others are well-established food and/or wine authors, and some are simply dedicated enthusiasts who have lived abroad and learned much about a particular region's cuisine. Our contributors include chefs who have worked in the grand hotels of India and in kaiseki restaurants of Japan, expert bakers and baristas, award-winning wine writers, and food lovers hailing from Iran, Russia and Malaysia.

For the weekly *Time Out London* magazine alone, our reviewers visit around 200 new places every year. Their better discoveries are then included in this guide. Reviewers also check other new openings as well as revisiting places included in previous editions. We also take in feedback and recommendations from users of the Time Out website (www.timeout.com/restaurants). Then we eliminate the also-rans to create the list of London's best eateries that this guide represents. We hope you find it useful, and that it helps you get more enjoyment from eating out in the capital.

Published by

Time Out Guides Limited
Universal House
251 Tottenham Court Road
London W1T 7AB
Tel +44 (0)20 7813 3000
Fax +44 (0)20 7813 6001
email guides@timeout.com
www.timeout.com

Editorial

Editor Jenni Muir
Deputy Editors Cath Phillips, Phil Harriss
Group Food & Drink Editor Guy Dimond
Listings Editors William Crow, Gemma Pritchard
Proofreader John Pym

Managing Director Peter Fiennes
Editorial Director Sarah Guy
Series Editor Cath Phillips
Business Manager Daniel Allen
Editorial Manager Holly Pick
Assistant Management Accountant Ija Krasnikova

Design

Art Director Scott Moore
Art Editor Pinelope Kourmouzoglou
Senior Designer Kei Ishimaru
Guides Commercial Designer Jodi Sher

Picture Desk

Picture Editor Jael Marschner
Picture Desk Assistant/Researcher Ben Rowe
Acting Deputy Picture Editor Liz Leahy

Advertising

New Business & Commercial Director Mark Phillips
Magazine & UK Guides Commercial Director St John Betteridge
Account Managers Jessica Baldwin, Michelle Daburn, Ben Holt
Production Controller Chris Pastfield
Copy Controller Alison Bourke

Marketing

Sales & Marketing Director, North America & Latin America Lisa Levinson
Group Commercial Art Director Anthony Huggins
Circulation & Distribution Manager Dan Collins
Marketing Co-ordinator Alana Benton

Production

Group Production Director Mark Lamond
Production Manager Brendan McKeown
Production Controller Katie Mulhern

Time Out Group

Director & Founder Tony Elliott
Chief Executive Officer David King
Group Financial Director Paul Rakkar
Group General Manager/Director Nichola Coulthard
Time Out Communications Ltd MD David Pepper
Time Out International Ltd MD Cathy Runciman
Time Out Magazine Ltd Publisher/MD Mark Elliott
Group Commercial Director Graeme Tottle
Group IT Director Simon Chappell

Sections in this guide were written by
African & Caribbean Jenni Muir, Nana Ocran. **The Americas** (North American) Jenni Muir (Latin American) Chris Moss, Patrick Welch. **Brasseries & Cafés** Euan Ferguson, Jenni Muir. **British** Sarah Guy. **Chinese** Phil Harriss, Charmaine Mok, Jeffrey Ng, Sally Peck. **East European** Katrina Kollegaeva. **Fish** Jenni Muir, Emma Perry. **French** Nicola Evans, Sarah Guy, Jenni Muir, Amanda Nicolas. **Gastropubs** Simon Coppock, Charmaine Mok, Jenni Muir. **Greek** Alexi Duggins. **Hotels & Haute Cuisine** Richard Ehrlich, Euan Ferguson, Roopa Gulati, Jenni Muir, Jeffrey Ng. **Indian** Guy Dimond, Roopa Gulati, Phil Harriss, Charmaine Mok, Jenni Muir. **Italian** Simon Coppock, Jenni Muir. **Japanese** Charmaine Mok, Jeffrey Ng, Celia Plender. **Jewish** Judy Jackson. **Korean** Charmaine Mok. **Malaysian, Singaporean & Indonesian** Jeffrey Ng. **Middle Eastern** Phil Harriss, Ros Sales, Cyrus Shahrad. **Modern European** Sarah Guy, Jenni Muir, Nick Rider, Ros Sales. **North African** Janet Zmroczek. **Pan-Asian & Fusion** Clarie Fogg, Jenni Muir, Celia Plender. **Spanish & Portuguese** Caroline Hire, Chris Moss, Nora Ryan, Elizabeth Winding. **Thai** Charmaine Mok, Sally Peck. **Turkish** Euan Ferguson, Jenni Muir. **Vegetarian** Natasha Polyviou. **Vietnamese** Euan Ferguson, Charmaine Mok. **Wine Bars** Richard Ehrlich.

Additional reviews by Ramona Andrews, Jessica Cargill Thompson, Simon Coppock, Silvija Davidson, Guy Dimond, Alexi Duggins, Richard Ehrlich, Lewis Esson, Nicola Evans, Euan Ferguson, Peter Fiennes, Roopa Gulati, Sarah Guy, Phil Harriss, Caroline Hire, Ruth Jarvis, Susan Low, Andrea McGinniss, Charmaine Mok, Chris Moss, Jenni Muir, Amanda Nicolas, Tom Olsen, Sally Peck, Emma Perry, Cath Phillips, Natasha Polyviou, Nick Rider, Ros Sales, Cyrus Shahrad, Eleanor Smallwood, Caroline Stacey, Elizabeth Winding, Yolanda Zappaterra.

The Editor would like to thank Charmaine Mok.

Maps JS Graphics (john@jsgraphics.co.uk). Maps 1-18 and 24 are based on material supplied by Alan Collinson and Julie Snook through Copyright Exchange. London Underground map supplied by Transport for London.

Photography by pages 1 (left), 3 (top left), 33, 58, 74 (left), 79 (left & middle), 85, 165 (middle), 191 (right), 221 (left), 239 (left), 267 (left) Michelle Grant; 1 (middle), 3 (bottom row), 30 (middle), 52 (middle), 53, 63, 72, 79 (right), 81 (bottom), 84, 87 (middle), 100, 121 (right), 122, 123, 125, 133 (right), 136, 149, 165 (left), 166, 167, 176 (left), 177, 186, 190, 191 (left), 193, 194, 208, 220, 218 (right), 222, 238, 247, 257 (left), 253 (middle), 262 (left), 263, 266 Ming Tang-Evans; 1 (right), 65, 68, 99, 101, 112, 117 (right), 120, 155, 162, 196, 197 Britta Jaschinski; 3 (top row, middle left), 117 (middle), 201, 218 (middle), 219, 227 (middle) Olivia Rutherford; 3 (top row, middle right), 7 (top), 8, 12, 13, 41 (left), 42, 54, 57, 87 (left), 98, 100 (right), 106, 161, 183, 223, 257 (right), 259 Rob Greig; 3 (top right), 40, 63 (left), 67, 75, 83, 114 (left), 121 (left), 176 (right), 201 (left), 239 (right), 241, 262 (middle) Heloise Bergman; 3 (bottom row, middle right), 24, 81 (top & middle), 133 (middle), 191 (middle), 218 (left), 200, 221 (middle), 227 (left), 248, 252, 257 (middle) Jitka Hynkova; 6 (top), 7 (bottom), 31, 41 (right), 47, 48, 87 (right), 92, 117 (left), 126, 134, 159, 217, 227 (right) Michael Franke; 6 (bottom), 12, 52 (left), 59 Scott Wishart; 10, 89 Jason Lowe; 18, 25, 73, 138, 180 (left), 180 (right) Tricia de Courcy Ling; 20, 24 (middle), 29, 39, 41 (middle), 43, 135, 253 (left), 256 Alys Tomlinson; 30 (left), 150, 213, 233, 239 (middle) Ed Marshall; 30 (right) Tove K Breitstein; 51, 74, 80, 121 (middle), 133 (left), 141, 147, 149 (middle), 164, 165 (right), 170, 175, 176 (middle), 178, 180 (middle), 181, 202 Jonathan Perugia; 52 (right) Marzena Zoladz; 88 Ben Rowe; 95, 114 (left) Oliver Knight; 112 Simon Leigh; 186 (right) Christina Theisen; 187 Kate Peters; 221 (right), 226 Nerida Howard; 245 Gemma Day; 246 Marc Rogoff; 253 (right) Thomas Skovsende; 258 Tom Baker; 263 (right) Hayley Harrison.

The following images were provided by the featured establishments: pages 12 (right), 14, 103, 109, 131, 228, 229.

Printer St Ives (Peterborough) Ltd, Storeys Bar Road, Eastern Industry, Peterborough, Cambs PE1 5YS.
Time Out Group uses paper products that are environmentally friendly, from well-managed forests and mills that used certified (PEFC) Chain of Custody pulp in their production.

ISBN 978-1-9054-4247-0
ISSN 1750-4643
Distribution by Comag Specialists (01895 433 800). For further distribution details, see timeout.com.

London's Best Restaurants
Contents

timeout.com/restaurants

100% INDEPENDENT

The reviews in *London's Best Restaurants* are based on the experiences of Time Out restaurant reviewers. All restaurants, gastropubs and cafés are visited anonymously, and Time Out pays the bill. No payment of any kind has secured or influenced a review.

About the guide

LISTED BY AREA

The restaurants in this guide are listed by cuisine type: British, Chinese, Indian, Middle Eastern etc. Then, within each chapter, they are listed by geographical area: ten main areas (in this example, East), then by neighbourhood (Mile End). If you are not sure where to look for a restaurant, there are two indexes at the back of the guide to help: an A-Z Index (starting on p308) listing restaurants by name, and an Area Index (starting on p292), where you can see all the places we list in a specific neighbourhood.

TIME OUT HOT 50

The **HOT 50** symbol means the venue is among what we consider to be London's top 50 iconic eating and drinking experiences. For details of the complete 50, see p16.

AWARD NOMINEES

Winners and runners-up in Time Out's Eating & Drinking Awards 2010. For more information on the awards, see p12.

OPENING HOURS

Times given are for last orders rather than closing times (except in cafés and bars).

PRICES

We have listed the cheapest and most expensive main courses available in each restaurant. In the case of many oriental restaurants, prices may seem lower – but remember that you often need to order several such dishes to have a full meal.

COVER CHARGE

An old-fashioned fixed charge may be imposed by the restaurateur to cover the cost of rolls and butter, crudités, cleaning table linen and similar extras.

MAP REFERENCE

All restaurants that appear on our street maps (starting on p268) are given a reference to the map and grid square where they can be found.

Anonymous, unbiased reviews

The reviews in *London's Best Restaurants* are based on the experiences of Time Out restaurant reviewers. Venues are always visited anonymously, and Time Out pays the bill. No payment or PR invitation of any kind has secured or influenced a review. The editors select which places are listed in this guide, and are not influenced in any way by the wishes of the restaurants themselves. Restaurants cannot volunteer or pay to be listed; we list only those we consider to be worthy of inclusion. Advertising and sponsorship has no effect whatsoever on the editorial content of *London's Best Restaurants*. An advertiser may receive a bad review, or no review at all.

East

Mile End

Caffè Bazza **HOT 50**
2010 RUNNER-UP BEST NEW CAFÉ
555 Wombat Way, E3 6JM (9876 4321). Mile End tube.
Open sparrow's fart-5pm Mon-Fri; 9am-4pm Sat, Sun.
Main courses £2.50-£7.50. **Cover** £1. **Credit** MC, V.
Celebrity barista Barry Hogan has been on a caffeine-fuelled career high since his ejection from the second round of *MasterChef*, and has opened this bonza bijou spot just a tinnie's chuck from the Blackwall Tunnel. Take a seat at one of the specially imported black stumps, to enjoy schooners and midis of coffee and a wide-ranging menu of well-crafted snacks (meat pies, battered savs, friands), all served with a slice of beetroot. The menthol kick of caramel eucalyptus macchiato contrasted perfectly with a pumpkin and wattleseed muffin. Fusion-style sarnies tend to suffer from one ingredient too many – thai prawn and feta panini really didn't need its layer of Vegemite. Pineapple meringue 'chiko' roll was dry as a drover's dog too. The welcome is matey enough, but service is rather too laconic: we would have ordered another round of drinks, but staff clearly didn't give a XXXX.
Babies and children welcome: high chairs; nipper-changing facilities. Disabled: dunny. Tables outdoors (3, under coolabah tree). Tuckerbag service.
Map 6 S4.

SERVICES

These are listed below the review.
Babies and children We've tried to reflect the degree of welcome extended to babies and children in restaurants. If you find no mention of either, take it that the restaurant is unsuitable.
Disabled: toilet means the restaurant has a specially adapted toilet, which implies that customers with walking disabilities or wheelchairs can get into the restaurant. However, we recommend phoning to double-check.
Vegetarian menu Most restaurants claim to have a vegetarian dish on the menu. We've highlighted those that have made a more concerted effort to attract and cater for vegetarian (and vegan) diners.

Busaba Eathai

106–110 Wardour St
London W1F 0TR
Phone 020-7255 8686

22 Store Street
London WC1E 7DF
Phone 020-7299 7900

35 Panton Street
London SW1Y 4EA
Phone 020-7930 0088

8–13 Bird Street
London W1U 1BU
Phone 020-7518 8080

313–319 Old Street
London EC1V 9LE
Phone 020-7729 0808

Opening soon in
Westfield and
Bicester Village

www.busaba.com
Take away available

The year that was

Guy Dimond looks back over the key trends in London's eating and drinking scene in the past year.

The recession of 2009-10 didn't take as big a bite out of London's restaurant scene as expected. The anticipated fallout that should have resulted from cautious spending and diners tightening their belts did not result in the wave of high-profile closures that some predicted – in fact, restaurants and cafés just kept opening at the same rate they ever did.

What did change was the attitude to the capital's expensive and occasionally overpriced restaurants. You only needed to follow comments on Twitter, check blog reports or – if you're still a follower of traditional media – read the reviews of professional critics to see that the tide of opinion has turned against pricey, unexciting and absentee-celeb chef restaurants. Gordon Ramsay Holdings' Pétrus, for example, was received with comments such as 'bland', 'beige', 'dull at worst, inoffensive at best', while Michel Roux Jr's Roux at Parliament Square was criticised for, among other things, 'being as much fun as a day spent transcribing John Redwood interviews'. (The chef present in the first two months has since left.) In contrast, it's been the year of affordable neighbourhood cafés and bistros, which have been prospering and growing in number.

Hello

Here are some of the more notable openings of the past year.

Antelope
Proof that there's life in the gastropub yet, especially when it produces an appealing, affordable menu in a lovely barn of a pub in Tooting. *See p107.*

Bar Boulud
Daniel Boulud, one of the top French chefs in the US, opened his first overseas branch in Knightsbridge in summer 2010. It's as slick as you'd expect a New York-run operation in Knightsbridge to be. *See p91.*

Caravan
Some ex-Caprice Holdings folk have set up this all-day café, bar and coffee roastery. As they say in the Antipodes: 'ripper'. *See p42.*

Dean Street Townhouse
Richard Caring's Soho House Group have turned a Soho townhouse into one of the area's see-and-be-seen spots, and also created an appealing retro British menu. *See p57.*

Dishoom
An interesting interpretation of a Bombay-style café, in Covent Garden. It's much smarter than the originals, and all the better for it. *See p133.*

Galvin La Chapelle
The Galvin brothers continue to produce high-calibre, smart, French-accented restaurants, this time in a high-ceilinged former church hall beside Old Spitalfields Market. *See p97.*

Gauthier Soho
Chef Alexis Gauthier has decamped from Roussillon restaurant in Pimlico to take over the Soho townhouse that used to be Lindsay House. The food has wowed the critics, though the atmosphere is a bit hushed and reverential. *See p93.*

Hix
Mark Hix's flagship restaurant in Soho (*see p58*), which celebrates seasonal British food. The basement bar, Mark's Bar (*see p14*), is also a hot ticket.

Koffmann's
Pierre Koffmann returns to the stove, in the Berkeley hotel in Knightsbridge where he once held three Michelin stars. *See p127.*

Koya
Think you know Japanese noodle bars? Think again. Koya is a full-blown udon specialist, where the noodles are stretched the traditional way using the feet. Even our colleagues from *Time Out Tokyo* were impressed. *See p171.*

The Luxe
MasterChef presenter John Torode's restaurant and brasserie in Old Spitalfields Market. The ground-floor café is a hit, the first-floor restaurant somewhat less so. *See p215.*

Looking east

A combination of low rents, perceived 'cool' factor and possibly even the cash injection in the run-up to the London 2012 Olympics Games and Paralympic Games have all been contributing factors in the rise of east London's fortunes. For cafés and innovative dining ventures, east London is now the most dynamic area of the capital – especially when compared to the relatively moribund west or north (come on Chelsea! And what about you, Hampstead?). There are now a score of excellent neighbourhood cafés, such as Hackney Pearl or Towpath (for both, *see p50*). It's true they're low-rent locations, but for the many artists and creative types who have been moving steadily eastwards out of Shoreditch and Clerkenwell in recent years, they have become the hubs of their communities.

And not all the new developments in east London have been cheap: chef Nuno Mendes chose Bethnal Green as the location for his innovative restaurant Viajante (*see p226*), where guests typically pay around £75 per head for interesting, experimental cooking – it's been a huge hit, and is booked weeks in advance.

The caffeine revolution

A related trend has been the spectacular growth of independent coffee bars over the last year. Just like the first London gastropubs during the 1980s and '90s, coffee bars are cheap to set up, and require relatively little in the way of kitchens or expensive equipment.

Some, such as Prufrock Coffee (in Shoreditch) and Tapped & Packed (in Fitzrovia – for both, *see p13*), take coffee geekery to new levels. One pop-up coffee shop, Penny University (now closed),

Manson
Chef Gemma Tulley's creative cooking in a casual Fulham bistro produces the likes of jerusalem artichoke cheesecake with peanut butter. *See p211*.

Mennula
A smart Italian restaurant on the Fitzrovia site that was once Passione. *See p150*.

Old Brewery
Alastair Hook's Meantime Brewery bagged a prime site inside the Old Royal Naval College in Greenwich to build this microbrewery, pub, daytime café and evening restaurant serving British food and great beers. *See p59*.

Orange Public House & Hotel
The former Orange Brewery, revamped by new owners who also run the Thomas Cubitt in Belgravia, is now an upmarket restaurant posing as a gastropub. Very nice it is too. *See p102*.

Paramount
Open to the public at last (it was a members' club from 2008-10), this fine dining restaurant at the top of Centre Point now offers cooking to match the great views. *See p201*.

Pizza East
Shoreditch House took over the former warehouse that once housed the T Bar and turned it into a cool, urban, New York-inspired pizzeria. *See p161*.

Polpo
A Venetian-style bacaro (wine bar), serving small plates to an appreciative Soho crowd. The owners quickly followed up with Polpetto – a mini version above the French House on Dean Street. *See p155*.

Santa Maria
Simple but excellent pizzeria in Ealing – currently London's best. *See p161*.

Towpath
Food writer Lori De Mori and her talented team run this charming waterside café on the Regent's Canal in De Beauvoir Town, N1. There's outdoor seating on a moored pontoon. *See p50*.

Trullo
This splendid Italian neighbourhood restaurant in Highbury, with dishes – and interior – in the modern Italian mould, was a hit as soon as it opened. *See p163*.

Viajante
Chef Nuno Mendes' impressive new restaurant in the former town hall in Bethnal Green is a suitable showcase for his very creative and experimental cooking. *See p226*.

Zucca
Bermondsey is the unlikely setting for this slick, modernist Italian restaurant serving remarkably good food at very reasonable prices. *See p159*.

was the creation of coffee guru James Hoffman, and served only filter coffees – no espresso, and no milk either. It's no coincidence that many of the proprietors are young, male, and three years ago might have been devoting their attention to two turntables and a microphone instead.

An unusually high proportion of these places are Antipodean-run, as New Zealand and Australia's urban centres excel at good coffee shops. We created a category for Best New Cup Of Coffee in the 2010 Time Out Eating & Drinking Awards in recognition of the highly original and fastidious work being done by this new generation of coffee baristas. Researching this fast-changing scene, and trying out the best of the coffee bars, has caused our reviewers many sleepless nights. For the best of them, see www.bit.ly/coffeebars.

Blogging and Twitter

One of the key trends of the last year has been the continued rise of food blogging and Twitter (the two are closely related, as food bloggers tend to be active tweeters). Try to follow every London restaurant-related tweet and you'll quickly burn out. There are now dozens of London food bloggers worth following, and many hundreds more who make the occasional interesting post. Rather than undermining or replacing previously existing media – the high-profile national critics, the established restaurant guides – they provide additional voices and tips for enthusiasts. Select bloggers and Twitter channels can be a very useful source of news and entertaining gossip if you have a special area of interest – for example coffee, Chinese food or cakes.

If you're not already using Twitter, do give it a try. If you don't know where to start, you could do worse than follow the tweets posted by Time Out London's food and drink editors at www.twitter.

Hix. See p10.

com/timeouteatdrink (in August 2010, we had more than 8,000 followers, and growing). Time Out has featured some of the best London food blogs, but it's in the nature of these things that they change quickly – good bloggers lose interest, and new ones appear, in a matter of weeks. Part of the fun of the blogosphere is discovering new blogs and good tweeters for yourself.

Going underground

So-called 'underground' restaurants have continued to thrive in London. The capital has always had them – charging strangers to attend a dinner party in someone's home is nothing new – but there are now dozens that vary in approach from the professional and very expensive (such as the Loft Project, http://theloftproject.co.uk) to the quirky and great value (such as the Hidden Tea Room, www.hiddentearoom.com), through to the shambolic, erratic and disappointing. A few of these amateur caterers now run their enterprises as a full-time profession, but most do it as a bit of fun in addition to their main occupation.

Usually, diners find out about them by word of mouth, but because the media coverage has been so intense they are also easy to find online (for example, at www.bit.ly/undergroundeats). Booking is usually done online, you pay cash, and don't ask too many questions about drinks licensing or health and safety regulations. If you decide to try one, do not expect restaurant-standard food, or restaurant-standard service – even though you may be paying restaurant prices. Go instead in a spirit of trying out a different sort of dining experience, and a slightly offbeat way of meeting new people.

Pop-ups

When is a pop-up not a pop-up? When it's there for too long, we suppose. The last year saw pop-up bar/restaurants on the scale of the hugely impressive Double Club (the sensation of 2009, a Congolese and western restaurant, bar and cultural event put together by a team including Mourad Mazouz of Momo and Sketch), though we were also treated to delights such as the aforementioned Penny University coffee shop for just a couple of months, and celebrated chef Pierre Koffmann's pop-up restaurant on the rooftop of Selfridges. (Following the success of the pop-up, Koffmann has come out of retirement to open a new restaurant – Koffmann's, *see p127* – inside the Berkeley hotel.)

But perhaps one of the most unlikely pop-ups is the bar on the tenth floor of a multistorey car park in Peckham, called Frank's Café & Campari Bar. Frank's had its second outing in summer

Cha Cha Moon

查查月亮

Chinese noodle bar
中食面馆

Cha Cha Moon is a Chinese noodle bar that goes beyond noodle pop culture and in to the soul of regional Chinese cooking. It delves further across Asia to give you both authentic and classic dishes as well as regional dishes.

'Yau famously spent months perfecting the broths for the soups on the largely noodle-based menu, and it has paid off... The use of authentic ingredients makes the restaurant more interesting than many other purveyors of noodles in London...Very good value for money!'

Time Out

15 - 21 Ganton Street, London W1F 9BN
020 7297 9800 www.chachamoon.com

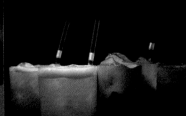

Bistrot Bruno Loubet

2010 and, judging by its enormous success, it seems likely it will return in summer 2011. We certainly hope so.

Celebrity chefs

There's life in the celeb chef restaurant yet. No, not the Jamies and Gordons of this world, but restaurants where the famous chef actually cooks on the premises. Bruno Loubet made a spectacular return to London in spring 2010, after several years off the London scene while he was working in Australia. Bistrot Bruno Loubet (*see p88*), in Clerkenwell's Zetter hotel, met with great critical acclaim. Loubet's modern French food has evolved over the decade since he was last one of London's best chefs; at the same

time, the man himself has relaxed. The result is a restaurant with exceptional food that's laid-back and extremely good value – currently one of London's best.

Another London chef who's continued to make waves, though he's seldom behind the stoves in his own restaurants these days, is Mark Hix. With a career that currently spans cookery writing as well as running British restaurants, he's also the darling of the Brit Art scene, as demonstrated by the artworks (Emin, Hirst, Noble & Webster) displayed in his flagship Soho restaurant, Hix (*see p58*). Mark Hix's recipes – in this case, cooked by Kevin Gratton, formerly of Scott's – celebrate British ingredients and seasonality. The restaurant has had great acclaim from the professional critics (many of whom know Mark Hix personally), but has had a more mixed reception elsewhere. We continue to be wowed by both the restaurant and the excellent cocktail bar (Mark's Bar) in its basement.

Not all our celebrity chefs are quite so home-grown. New York's Daniel Boulud – one of the most lauded chefs in the US – opened his first overseas branch in Knightsbridge in May 2010, called Bar Boulud. It's arguably a cookie-cutter copy of Bar Boulud in New York, but it's still startling to see the difference between the slickness of a Big Apple fine dining establishment and those of our own big operators. Bar Boulud was very well received, not least because the price-to-value ratio is exceptional. And it really does serve the best burgers in London.

So, with the benefit of hindsight, it wasn't a bad year at all.

Goodbye

We bid farewell to those restaurants that have shut in the past year.

Bloom's
A Golders Green institution, eclipsed by a new wave of Jewish and kosher eating places.

Boxwood Café
Ramsay Holdings' brasserie in the Berkeley hotel is now Pierre Koffmann's new place.

Deep
Scandinavian sustainable seafood restaurant that couldn't sustain itself.

Eat & Two Veg
Vegetarian fast food that was concept-driven, but didn't amount to a hill of beans.

Konstam at the Prince Albert
Eat-local British restaurant that lost its appeal.

Parsian
Good Iranian restaurant in Willesden that failed to attract enough local custom.

Passione
Chef Gennaro Contaldo's passion has clearly been diverted elsewhere.

Potemkin
Failed to strike a revolution in Russian dining.

Quality Chop House
The 'progressive working-class caterer' could not progress any further.

St Alban
Corbin and King's Mediterranean restaurant, now gone for a long lunch.

Snazz Sichuan
Once hot and numbing, but now stone cold.

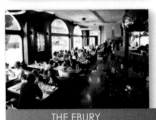

Time Out's 21st annual
Eating & Drinking
Awards 2010

Time Out has an unrivalled reputation for promoting the best of London's eating and drinking places – something of which we are very proud. It is not just those with the grandest credentials that we champion, either, but the little places that are, in their own field, worthy of note. This is the ethos behind our broad coverage of London's gastronomic delights – from weekly reviews in *Time Out* magazine to our numerous guides. And this is why our annual Eating & Drinking Awards take in not only London's restaurant élite, but also representatives from neighbourhood restaurants, gastropubs and cafés, as independently selected by a panel of Time Out judges.

The award categories, which vary each year, reflect the diverse needs and tastes of London's diners and drinkers; for example, the Best New Cup of Coffee award illustrates the capital's recent enthusiasm for espresso bars. With a fresh crop of reviews appearing each week in *Time Out* magazine (and on our website, www.timeout.com/restaurants), the list of potential candidates can seem dauntingly long. The judges revisit every shortlisted venue as normal paying punters (we never accept PR invitations or freebies), so that a final decision can be reached.

SPONSOR'S AWARD

For the results of the award for Best Spanish Food & Drink, presented in association with Wines from Spain, *see p229*.

And the winners are... in alphabetical order

BEST NEW BAR
Winner
Bar Pepito

Runners-up
Purl
Mark's Bar
Southampton Arms
For all, see p14.

BEST NEW CAFÉ
Winner
Hackney Pearl *See p50.*

Runners-up
Bond & Brook *See p44.*
Lanka *See p50.*
Towpath *See p50.*

BEST NEW CHEAP EATS
Winner
Gilak (Middle Eastern) *See p198.*

Runners-up
Koya (Japanese) *See p171.*
Mamuska! (East European) *See p77.*
Santa Maria (Italian) *See p161.*

BEST NEW CUP OF COFFEE
Winner
Espresso Room

Runners-up
Kaffeine
Prufrock Coffee
Tapped & Packed
For all, see right.

BEST NEW DESIGN
Winner
Old Brewery (British) *See p59.*

Runners-up
Dishoom (Indian) *See p133.*
The Luxe (Modern European) *See p215.*
Zucca (Italian) *See p159.*

BEST NEW GASTROPUB
Winner
Princess of Shoreditch *See p111.*

Runners-up
Antelope *See p107.*
Draft House *See p107.*
Orange Public House & Hotel *See p102.*

BEST NEW LOCAL RESTAURANT
Winner
Angels & Gypsies (Spanish) *See p235.*

Runners-up
Caravan (Brasseries) *See p42.*
Old Brewery (British) *See p59.*
Trullo (Italian) *See p163.*

BEST NEW RESTAURANT
Winner
Hix (British) *See p58.*

Runners-up
Bar Boulud (French) *See p91.*
Bistrot Bruno Loubet (French) *See p88.*
Zucca (Italian) *See p159.*

This year's judges:
Jessica Cargill Thompson
Simon Coppock
Alexi Duggins
Richard Ehrlich
Euan Ferguson
Sarah Guy
Charmaine Mok
Cath Phillips

Best new cup of coffee
WINNER

Espresso Room
31-35 Great Ormond Street, WC1N 3HZ (07932 137380, www.theespressoroom.com). Russell Square tube. **Open** *7.30am-5pm Mon-Fri.*
Espresso enthusiasts will find no better place to indulge in their preferred poison than Ben Townsend's dedicated coffee bar. It's a tiny broom cupboard of a shop, with two L-shaped benches for perching, and standing room for a handful of people. The small team of baristas are highly trained, and Townsend is almost always present to call the shots. A single espresso (using Square Mile's summer blend) was nicely balanced, with high notes of caramel and cherry. The milky coffees are a joy, with thick velvety milk; a macchiato is spot-on if you don't want to lose too much of the espresso's clarity. For those who prefer extra sweetness, a toffee-like Costa Rican brown sugar is available.
Map 4 L4.

RUNNERS-UP
Kaffeine
66 Great Titchfield Street, W1W 7QJ (7580 6755, www.kaffeine.co.uk). Oxford Circus tube. **Open** *7.30am-6pm Mon-Fri; 9am-6pm Sat.*
This is the kind of coffee shop that has reminded many an Aussie of home, thanks to the cheerful, personable service from owner Peter Dore-Smith and his team of baristas. A Square Mile summer-blend espresso was luxuriously syrupy, almost saline, and thick on the tongue with hints of buttery caramel. A flat white was a cup of milky fruitiness, the espresso mellowing out into a flavour of chocolate mousse with raspberry (with just a bit of tartness).
Map 9 J5.

Prufrock Coffee
140 Shoreditch High Street, E1 6JE (7033 0500, http://prufrockcoffee.com). Shoreditch High Street rail. **Open** *10.30am-6pm Mon-Fri; 11am-5pm Sat; 11am-4pm Sun.*
No coffee connoisseur could bypass Prufrock. What's the big fuss? It's mainly because the shiny Victoria Arduino espresso machine has been routinely operated by top coffee names, from 2009 Swedish Barista Champion Mattias Björklund to Gwylim Davies, the UK's first World Barista Champion. They rarely get things wrong (though the flavours were oddly off-kilter in a recent Square Mile summer espresso). Better was a flat white, with its toasty brown bread and caramelised sugar profiles.
Map 6 R4.

Tapped & Packed
26 Rathbone Place, W1T 1JD (7580 2163, www.tappedand packed.co.uk). Tottenham Court Road tube. **Open** *8am-7pm Mon-Fri; 9am-7pm Sat.*
T&P offers filtered brews as well as espresso-based drinks. Three main coffee roaster brands are used (Square Mile, Climpson & Sons, Union Hand Roasters), between them offering a handful of different single-origin beans and coffee blends. For filter coffee, pour-over and cafetière options are available, plus two more specialist methods: siphon and Aeropress. An Aeropress brew of a stunning Tegu AA from Kenya was sweet and tea-like; quite acidic and plummy, with a very fruity character.
Map 17 B2.

AWARDS 2010

Best new bar

Bar Pepito

Varnishers Yard, Regents Quarter, N1 9FD (7841 7331, www.camino.uk.com/pepito). King's Cross tube/rail.
Open/food served 6pm-midnight Tue-Fri; 7pm-midnight Sat. **Dishes** £2-£15.50. **Credit** AmEx, MC, V.
You could throw a feather from one end to the other of this tiny offshoot of the raucously successful Camino (*see p229*), but a drink and a nibble here will transport you to a different world. The all-Spanish staff take enormous pride in their sherry bar, and with good reason: the selection encompasses every style of these often neglected wines and every one on the list is a cracker. Customers perch on high stools at the tiny tables and waiters come to offer whatever guidance is needed. If you don't know your way around sherry, place yourself in their hands. Tasters are offered to the uncertain. The tapas are jaw-droppingly good too, with olives, cured pork and cheeses all five-star stuff. Tortas de barros, a creamy sheep's milk cheese from Estremadura, is served with tomato jam to fabulous effect. Sitting in Bar Pepito is like being in Spain, yet the grimy hubbub of Kings Cross is a 30-second walk away. Many of the customers when we visited were Spanish: follow their lead.
Available for hire. Disabled: toilet. Tables outdoors (14, courtyard). **Map 4 L3**.

RUNNERS-UP

Mark's Bar

Hix, 66-70 Brewer Street, W1F 9UP (7292 3518, www.hixsoho.co.uk). Piccadilly Circus tube. **Open/meals served** noon-12.30am Mon-Sat; 11am-11pm Sun. **Main courses** £14.75-£32.50. **Set meal** (4.30-6.30pm Mon-Fri, noon-6.30pm Sat, noon-10pm Sun) £15.50 2 courses, £19.50 3 courses. **Credit** AmEx, DC, MC, V.

Much about this bar is reminiscent of Manhattan – low lighting, smoky mirrors, cool but comfortable furnishings – but British chef Mark Hix has stamped his personality on the place with an apothecary-style shelf of own-made infusions, ambitious bar snacks and a bar billiards table. Cocktail supremo Nick Strangeway has helped produce a long list of cocktail curiosities, including a group of historic drinks with detailed provenance, and another of 'Hix specials'. We had to wait too long for our drinks, but they were worth waiting for. The martini service is exquisite: drink and garnish in a tiny glass with the remainder in a jug relaxing on ice in a mini bucket. Of the historical curiosities, the Celebration (rum, grapefruit, redcurrant syrup and gin) was perfectly balanced and beautifully served in a metal goblet. A gimlet (gin and lime cordial) was textbook stuff, and a bar snack of Blytheburgh pork crackling served with apple sauce was rich and scrumptious. Couldn't be better; full Marks to Hix. *See also p58. Babies and children admitted until 5pm. Booking advisable lunch. Disabled: toilet.* **Map 17 A4**.

Purl

50 Blandford Street, W1U 7HX (7935 0835, www.purl-london.com). Bond Street tube. **Open** 5-11.30pm Mon-Thur; 5pm-midnight Fri, Sat. **Credit** AmEx, MC, V.
A loveable place that aims to recreate the atmosphere of a New York speakeasy, Purl's decor is simple but endearingly eclectic. The bar occupies the basement of a Georgian house and features low vaulted ceilings and lots of individual seating areas. The list of original cocktail creations is grounded in a confident mastery of classicism. Silver fizz, a variant on the gorgeous Ramos gin fizz, using gin, lemon, sugar syrup, egg white and fizzy water, is made with precise two-stage shaking to guarantee the right texture; this is as good a cocktail as you'll find anywhere. A martini was less satisfactory – well made, but the room-temperature gin stirred in ice warmed too quickly in the glass. We worry slightly about the basement's humidity, counteracted by dehumidifiers on a summer evening, but the owners say no one has complained, and you shouldn't regard it as a reason to avoid Purl – it's a wonderful bar.
Available for hire. Booking advisable. **Map 9 G5**.

Southampton Arms

139 Highgate Road, NW5 1LE (07 958 780073, www.thesouthamptonarms.co.uk). Gospel Oak rail.
Open/snacks served noon-midnight daily.
Credit MC, V.
The idea behind this terrific place is audaciously simple: take a grim old boozer and strip it back to bare floors, dark paint, a few old photos and a working fireplace. 'Ale/Cider/Meat' announces the sign on the side of the building, and that's what you get: a changing roster of ales and ciders, all from independent British producers, plus a dozen or so spirits. Old-fashioned bar snacks include fantastic pork pies and sausage rolls, and there are joints of roast pork for slicing on to baps. Prices are reasonable, and the staff know their business. If you want advice on what to drink, you'll get it with enthusiasm (and perhaps a free taste if you're uncertain). The line-up of casks changes regularly, but Borough Hill cider is a regular, as are ales from Brodies, Redemption and Williams Brothers. Drinking here is a bit like dropping in on an old friend who lives in a slightly shabby but utterly comfortable country cottage – it's a brilliant idea, perfectly executed.
Babies and children admitted. Entertainment: bands 8pm Wed, 6pm Sun. Tables outdoors (10, garden).

GRAFTON HOUSE

A much favoured haunt of the Clapham locals, Grafton House Restaurant, Bar and Garden is now in its 5th year!

The Restaurant
Serving robust seasonal dishes using expertly sourced British ingredients from the finest producers.

We believe all our meat, free range chicken and fresh fish should be cooked simply on the grill. Our dishes are served with the optional addition of a carefully prepared sauce which brings out the intense flavours of the food. Keeping it simple means keeping it local, so we use only the finest home grown produce from the farmers and fish mongers of Great Britain.

The Bar
HAPPY HOUR...As well as serving fantastic cocktails, the bar is now running happy hour every Tuesday - Friday from 5.30pm - 8pm (10pm Friday), offering fantastic deals on everything from wine and bottled beer to cocktails!

The Garden
The beautiful new beer garden is now open every day from midday to 10pm and is available for alfresco drinking and dining! And when the sun shines there is a live band in the Garden every Sunday from 1pm until 6pm!

Exclusive areas for bookings. No fee or minimum spend.

LARGE PLASMA TV'S & 7FT PROJECTOR FOR ALL MAJOR SPORTING EVENTS!

DJ'S EVERY FRIDAY & SATURDAY TILL LATE!

13 Old Town, Clapham, SW4   •   020 7498 5559   •   www.graftonhouseuk.com

Time Out's Hot 50

The editors of **London's Best Restaurants** have picked 50 places, entirely subjectively, that we believe offer some of London's most interesting eating experiences. We're not saying these venues have the best food and drink in the capital, but we believe each adds something life-enhancing to our city. Here they are, in alphabetical order. Each review is marked with a `HOT 50` symbol in the relevant chapter of the guide.

Amaya
Indian p135.
Sparkling and sophisticated modern Indian grill.

Baltic
East European p76.
From blinis to bozbash, Baltic makes East European food cool.

Barrafina
Spanish p230.
The Hart brothers take inspiration from Barcelona tapas bar Cal Pep and run with it.

Barshu
Chinese p67.
The fiery flavours of Sichuanese cooking, served in style.

Bentley's Oyster Bar & Grill
Fish p80.
Take a seat at the art nouveau bar for freshly shucked oysters and London's best fish pie.

Bistrot Bruno Loubet
French p88.
The Zetter hotel's dining room is reborn under Bruno Loubet.

Bistrotheque
French p95.
Bistro food, modish bar and camp cabaret make an original combination at this east London hotspot.

Buen Ayre
The Americas p40.
Argentinian parrillada (steak grill) with everything from ribeyes to sweetbreads.

Busaba Eathai
Thai p239.
It may be under new ownership, but this rapidly expanding Thai chain still attracts queues.

Le Café Anglais
Modern European p208.
Rowley Leigh's buzzy Bayswater brasserie.

Cah Chi
Korean p183.
Head to Raynes Park or Earlsfield for a taste of home-style Korean cooking.

Caravan
Brasseries & Cafés p42.
A restaurant, bar and coffee roastery where beans are ethically sourced and expertly blended to suit the season.

Club Gascon
French p89.
Inventive cuisine inspired by the ingredients of south-west France and daintily presented for sharing.

Cow
Gastropubs p105.
Tom Conran's lively Notting Hill pub has long been a favourite for fruits de mer.

Czechoslovak Restaurant
East European p78.
The city's only Czech restaurant and bar is a piece of living history, offering dumplings, pancakes and potatoes.

Eyre Brothers
Global p120.
Restaurant and tapas bar serving the best of the Iberian peninsula.

Fish Club
Fish p83.
Coley, mullet and cuttlefish are some of the unexpected delights at this modern chippie.

La Fromagerie
Brasseries & Cafés p44.
The cheese will please at this charming deli-café, but so will all the other goodies on sale.

Le Gavroche
Hotels & Haute Cuisine p129.
A landmark restaurant with a famously good-value set lunch – so everyone can enjoy the Roux dynasty's take on French cuisine.

Hakkasan
Chinese p64.
Alan Yau may have sold up, but this remains a hot destination for Chinese cooking and cocktails.

Harwood Arms
Gastropubs p105.
British country produce stars at this Fulham pub with dining room.

Hawksmoor
The Americas p33.
Will Beckett and Huw Gott's hip Spitalfields steakhouse and cocktail bar will soon take the stage in Covent Garden.

Hibiscus
Hotels & Haute Cuisine p129.
From Lyon via Ludlow, Claude Bosi's flair has found an appreciative London audience.

Hix Soho
British p58.
Another addition to Mark Hix's growing empire: a British restaurant with delightful downstairs bar.

Locanda Locatelli
Italian p152.
Smooth decor and fine Italian food make for a seductive evening.

Lola Rojo
Spanish p232.
Bringing a slice of Spain's *nueva cocina* to south-west London.

Mandalay
Global p187.
Sample first-rate Burmese fare at this otherwise basic caff.

Masa
Global p120.
The Middle East meets the Indian subcontinent in an unsung corner of Harrow.

Momo
North African p129.
Eat to the beat at Mourad Mazouz's evocative Moroccan restaurant, bar and tearoom.

Moro
Spanish p228.
Dishes from Extremadura to the Near East, at this enduringly popular Exmouth Market stalwart.

Nahm
Thai p239.
A regal dining room of golden hues, home to David Thompson's unsurpassed Royal Thai cuisine.

Ottolenghi
Brasseries & Cafés p51.
Glamorous café by day, exquisite fusion restaurant by night.

Petersham Nurseries Café
Modern European p217.
A delightfully bucolic setting for Skye Gyngell's seasonally inspired meals.

Princess Victoria
Gastropubs p103.
Brilliant conversion of a Victorian gin palace to pub and restaurant.

The Providores & Tapa Room
Pan-Asian & Fusion p223.
World-beating fusion fare served all day, from banana and pecan french toast to grilled scallops with crab and quinoa dumplings.

Rasa Samudra
Indian p135.
A rare opportunity to sample the authentic and surprisingly fiery fish cookery of Kerala.

The River Café
Italian p157.
The wood-fired oven takes centre stage in this world-famous, yet relaxed, Hammersmith classic.

Roka
Japanese p167.
Big windows and memorable cooking: Roka is still Fitzrovia's place to see and be seen.

St John
British p54.
Fergus Henderson's uncompromising approach to food, and especially meat, has inspired a new generation of chefs both here and abroad.

Sakonis
Indian p148.
The original Indian vegetarian chat (snack) house, serving South Indian and Gujarati dishes.

Sketch
Hotels & Haute Cuisine p130.
Pierre Gagnaire's astonishing food isn't the only talking point at this stylish celebration of art and luxury.

Song Que
Vietnamese p259.
Iconic Vietnamese canteen on Shoreditch's 'pho mile'.

Sushi-Hiro
Japanese p172.
East meets west (London) at this restaurant for sushi purists.

Sweetings
Fish p79.
Old-world bonhomie and classic British fish dishes since 1889.

Tiroler Hut
Eating & Entertainment p35.
Tongue-in-cheek party place decorated in Tyrol ski lodge style, complete with accordion music and cowbell shows.

Towpath
Brasseries & Cafés p50.
Quirky waterside café in N1.

Les Trois Garçons
French p95.
Home to hippo heads, stuffed bulldogs and a collection of vintage handbags, as well as some terrific French cuisine.

Vinoteca
Wine Bars p263.
A model wine bar with well-priced, well-rendered cooking, and all wines available to take home at retail price.

Wapping Food
Modern European p215.
Victorian pumping station museum/art-gallery serving inventive modern cooking and an Australian wine list.

The Wolseley
Brasseries & Cafés p46.
Corbin and King have made this former car showroom one of London's most exciting destinations, day or night.

THE BLUES KITCHEN

LONDON'S BEST BLUES BAR
111-113 CAMDEN HIGH ST, NW1 7JN

Where to...

Got the hunger, the people, the occasion, but not the venue? These suggestions will help you find the perfect spot to eat, drink and be merry.

GO FOR BREAKFAST
Breakfast is offered every day unless stated otherwise. *See also* **Brasseries & Cafés**.

Albion British p62
Ambassador (Mon-Fri) Modern European p202
Bistrot Bruno Loubet French p88
Botanist Modern European p211
Canteen British p62
Caravan Brasseries & Cafés p42
Cecconi's Italian p152
Cinnamon Club (Mon-Fri) Indian p141
The Diner The Americas p35
Dishoom Indian p133
Dorchester Grill Room British p62
Engineer Gastropubs p111
Fifteen (Trattoria) Italian p160
Fifth Floor (Café, Mon-Sat) Modern European p204
Garufa The Americas p40
Goring Hotel British p53
The Landau Hotels & Haute Cuisine p126
Lutyens French p87
The Luxe Modern European p215
The Modern Pantry (Mon-Fri) Pan-Asian & Fusion p221
Nicole's (Mon-Sat) Modern European p206
Orange Public House & Hotel Gastropubs p102
The Providores & Tapa Room Pan-Asian & Fusion p223
Roast (Mon-Sat) British p61
Sakonis (Sat, Sun) Indian p148
Simpson's-in-the-Strand (Mon-Fri) British p53
Smiths of Smithfield Modern European p202
Sotheby's Café (Mon-Fri) Modern European p206
The Terrace (Mon-Fri) Modern European p203
Tom's Kitchen Brasseries & Cafés p49
York & Albany Modern European p216

EAT/DRINK BY THE WATERSIDE
See also the Southbank Centre branches of Giraffe, Strada and Wagamama.

Blueprint Café Modern European p214
Gaucho (Tower Bridge and Richmond branches) The Americas p37
Narrow Gastropubs p110
Royal China (Docklands branch) Chinese p71
Skylon Modern European p214 (Blueprint Café)

ENJOY THE VIEW
Blueprint Café Modern European p214
Le Coq d'Argent French p97 (Almeida)
Galvin at Windows French p97 (Galvin Café a Vin)
Oxo Tower Restaurant, Bar & Brasserie Modern European p204 (Fifth Floor)
Inn The Park British p45
Paramount Modern European p201
Plateau Modern European p214 (Blueprint Café)
Roast British p61
Rhodes Twenty Four British p52
Skylon Modern European p214 (Blueprint Café)
Tate Modern Café Brasseries & Cafés p169
Smiths of Smithfield (Top Floor) Modern European p202

SHARE DISHES
Angels & Gypsies Spanish p235
Barrica Spanish p228
Bocca di Lupo Italian p154
Caravan Brasseries & Cafés p42
Club Gascon French p89

Dehesa Spanish p230
Dinings Japanese p168
Ibérica Food & Culture Spanish p229
Lalibela African & Caribbean p27
Norfolk Arms Gastropubs p100
Ottolenghi Brasseries & Cafés p51
La Petite Maison French p92
Tayyab's Indian p147
Terroirs Wine Bars p266
Tom's Kitchen Brasseries & Cafés p49

TAKE THE KIDS
See also p86 **Best family chains**.

Ambassador Modern European p202
Blue Elephant Thai p244
The Depot Brasseries & Cafés p47
Engineer Gastropubs p111
Harrison's Brasseries & Cafés p49
Masala Zone Indian p147
Rousillon French p87

PEOPLE-WATCH
Le Café Anglais Modern European p208
Eyre Brothers Global p120
Hix British p58
The Ivy Modern European p203
Mr Chow Chinese p64
Quo Vadis British p58
Scott's Fish p80
Sketch Hotels & Haute Cuisine p130
Tate Modern Café Brasseries & Cafés p169
The Wolseley Brasseries & Cafés p46
Zuma Japanese p167

TRY UNUSUAL DISHES
See also **Global**.

Adulis African & Caribbean p26
Asadal Korean p181
Baozi Inn Chinese p69
Champor-Champor Pan-Asian & Fusion p225
Esarn Kheaw Thai p243
Faanoos Middle Eastern p197
Hélène Darroze at the Connaught Hotels & Haute Cuisine p129
Hereford Road British p58
Hibiscus Hotels & Haute Cuisine p129

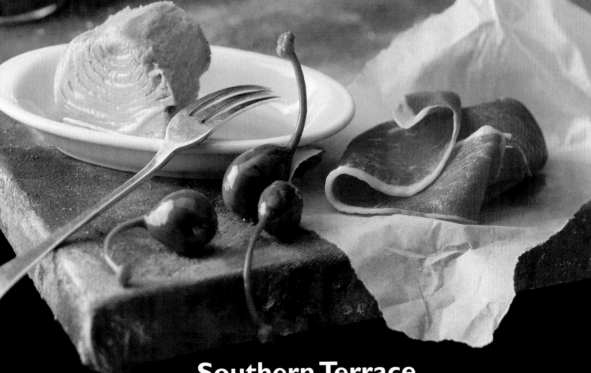

Hunan Chinese p63
Lola Rojo Spanish p232
Nahm Thai p239
The Providores & Tapa Room
 Pan-Asian & Fusion p223
Saf Vegetarian p256
Saké No Hana Japanese p171
Song Que Vietnamese p259
Tbilisi East European p78
Texture Hotels & Haute Cuisine p128
Umu Japanese p170

DO BRUNCH
See also **Brasseries & Cafés**.

Ambassador (Sat, Sun)
 Modern European p202
Bistrot Bruno Loubet (Sat, Sun)
 French p88
Christopher's (Sat, Sun)
 The Americas p45
Joe Allen (Sat, Sun)
 The Americas p45
The Modern Pantry (Sat, Sun)
 Pan-Asian & Fusion p221
Ransome's Dock (Sat, Sun)
 Modern European p212
Sam's Brasserie & Bar
 Modern European p209

DINE ALFRESCO
Clerkenwell Kitchen Brasseries
 & Cafés p42
Clissold Arms Gastropubs p116
Duke of Sussex Gastropubs p102
Ealing Park Tavern Gastropubs p102
Engineer Gastropubs p111
Geales Fish p81
Greek Affair Greek p121
Inn The Park British p45
Lemonia Greek p124
Narrow Gastropubs p110
El Parador Spanish p237
Petersham Nurseries Café
 Modern European p217
The River Café Italian p157
Royal China (Docklands branch)
 Chinese p71
Scott's Fish p80

The Terrace Modern European p203
Towpath Brasseries & Cafés p50
La Trouvaille French p93

TAKE A DATE
Almeida French p97
Amaya Indian p135
Andrew Edmunds Modern
 European p207
Angelus French p93
L'Anima Italian p149
Assaggi Italian p157
L'Autre Pied Modern European p204
The Bingham Hotels & Haute
 Cuisine p132
Bistrotheque French p95
Bob Bob Ricard
 Brasseries & Cafés p46
Le Café Anglais
 Modern European p208
Eyre Brothers Global p120
Hakkasan Chinese p64
Lamberts Modern European p212
Locanda Locatelli Italian p152
Magdalen British p61
Maze Hotels & Haute Cuisine p130
Pasha North African p218
Roka Japanese p167
Rosemary Lane French p88
St Pancras Grand Brasseries
 & Cafés p43
Saké No Hana Japanese p171
Sardo Italian p150
J Sheekey Fish p79
Theo Randall at the Intercontinental
 Italian p154
Les Trois Garçons French p95
Upstairs Modern European p212
Wapping Food Modern European
 p215

EAT AT THE BAR
Anchor & Hope Gastropubs p108
Arbutus Modern European p207
Barrafina Spanish p230
Bentley's Oyster Bar & Grill Fish p80
Bocca di Lupo Italian p154
Le Caprice Modern European p207
Dehesa Spanish p230
Eyre Brothers Global p120
Maze Hotels & Haute Cuisine p130
Moro Spanish p228
Roka Japanese p167
J Sheekey Fish p79
Tapas Brindisa Spanish p235
Tom's Kitchen Brasseries
 & Cafés p49
Wright Brothers Oyster
 & Porter House Fish p85

GRAB A MEAL BEFORE A SHOW
Almeida French p97
Anchor & Hope Gastropubs p108
Axis Modern European p203

Botanist Modern European p211
Canteen (South Bank branch)
 British p62
Gaucho Piccadilly The Americas p37
Noura Middle Eastern p193
Ottolenghi Brasseries & Cafés p51
Veeraswamy Indian p136

EAT LATE
Floridita The Americas p37
Gilgamesh Pan-Asian & Fusion p226
Joe Allen The Americas p45
Mangal II Turkish p249
The Wolseley Brasseries
 & Cafés p46

LOVE THE LOOK
Amaya Indian p135
L'Anima Italian p149
L'Autre Pied Modern European p204
L'Atelier de Joël Robuchon
 Modern European p203
Baltic East European p76
Benares Indian p136
Bob Bob Ricard Brasseries
 & Cafés p46
Comptoir Libanais
 Middle Eastern p199
China Tang Chinese p66
Dinings Japanese p168
Fifth Floor Modern European p204
Hakkasan Chinese p64
The Landau Hotels & Haute
 Cuisine p126
The Luxe Modern European p215
Pearl Bar & Restaurant
 Hotels & Haute Cuisine p127
Pearl Liang Chinese p67
Petersham Nurseries Café
 Modern European p217
St Pancras Grand Brasseries
 & Cafés p43
Saké No Hana Japanese p171
Sketch Hotels & Haute Cuisine p130
Les Trois Garçons French p95
Wapping Food Modern
 European p215
Yauatcha Chinese p68
Zuma Japanese p167

Restaurants

African & Caribbean

As London's Afro-Caribbean population has diversified, so too have its Caribbean restaurants, which can no longer all be thrust into the 'cheap, cheery and laid-back' pigeonhole. Thus, there's **Mango Room** with its hip crowd and slick cocktails; **Island Fusion**, where Jamaican cooking comes with a Mod Euro influence; and **Cottons**, which updates Caribbean cuisine in a setting that verges on the straitlaced.

In contrast, the capital's African restaurants are perhaps at an earlier stage in the assimilation process. For a start, they represent the cuisines of an entire continent (though we've separated off the Maghrebi restaurants of North Africa, starting on p218, and the South African game specialist Chakalaka, which can be found on p119 in the Global chapter). The broadly similar cooking styles of Eritrea and Ethiopia are widely available, though you can sample Somali dishes at **The Village** and Nigerian specialities at **805 Bar Restaurant**. Many proprietors are keen to combat ignorance about their homeland's culture among the wider community. At **Mosob**, for instance, you're likely to receive a lesson in the geography and architecture of Eritrea, along with wonderful spicy stews, from the friendly owner.

AFRICAN

West

Hammersmith

The Village
95 Fulham Palace Road, W6 8JA (8741 7453).
Hammersmith tube. **Meals served** 11.30am-11.30pm daily. **Main courses** £7-£8. **Set lunch** £5. **Credit** AmEx, MC, V. Somali

The Village was a neat but almost empty basement space with intrusive R&B until our two waitresses spun into action. One turned down the volume, while the other took our drinks order and swiftly returned with two tall glasses of fresh mango shake and a fruit cocktail smoothie. Somali food is a Horn of Africa delicacy that's rare on London's restaurant circuit, and the contemporary halal menu here makes a good introduction to the cuisine. Two excellent main dishes are the malay gaduud (crispy salmon steak served with spinach, mash potato and a fruit salsa) and the daqay ari lyo bariis (marinated tender lamb fillet with spiced rice and salad). Plates and portions are huge,

yet the cooking exhibits a subtle use of herbs and spices. It's fair to say that Somali diners are happy to eat late, so by 10pm there was a steady stream of families and couples stopping by for full meals, coffee or the gorgeous shakes and smoothies. Service was efficient and friendly, and once the urban bass line was eclipsed by strains of Somali folk music, the vibe seemed authentically north-east African and a million miles from the busy Fulham Palace Road.
Available for hire. Babies and children admitted. Takeaway service. **Map 20 C5**.

Westbourne Park

Mosob
339 Harrow Road, W9 3RB (7266 2012, www.mosob. co.uk). Westbourne Park tube. **Meals served** 6pm-midnight Mon-Fri; 3pm-midnight Sat, Sun. **Main courses** £6.50-£9.95. **Set meal** £12.50 per person (minimum 4), £14 per person (minimum 2). **Credit** AmEx, MC, V. Eritrean

Such is the welcome at this family-run favourite, you're likely to depart feeling you've made new friends. You might even vow to visit Asmara, Eritrea's capital, after the owner has shown you his well-thumbed book of the city's modernist architecture.

Tradition holds sway on the menu, with a list of various spicy stews served on stainless steel plates atop spongy injera. Perhaps start with mini sambusas: three crisp little samosas packed with spicy meat, fish or veg; order awaze dips (thick yoghurt and hot pepper) as accompaniments. Next, pick your injera topping. We can vouch for the mixed vegetable bebe'ainetu: two dahl-like lentil dishes (one red, one yellow, both appetising), spinach, and a carrot, cabbage and green bean mix. The sourness of the injera also made a good foil for the rich awaze qulwa (beef fried with onions, chillies and pepper in a tomato-based sauce). Mosob is a congenial little hangout with dark wooden flooring, well-worn tables, maroon walls, a rough-hewn wooden bar and various attractive artefacts dotted around. Eritrean music plays, takeaway customers drop by, and the traditional coffee ceremony (incense and all) is a pleasing way to round off an evening.
Babies and children welcome: high chairs. Booking advisable. Separate room for parties, seats 22. Takeaway service.
Map 1 A4.

South

Brixton

Asmara
386 Coldharbour Lane, SW9 8LF (7737 4144). Brixton tube/rail. **Dinner served** 5.30pm-midnight daily. **Main courses** £6.50-£9. **Set meal** £28 (2 people) vegetarian, £30 (2 people) meat. **Credit** MC, V. Eritrean
More often than not it's those leaving or going to the nearby Ritzy Cinema who make up the distinctly mixed customer base at Asmara. The pinewood theme throughout the restaurant is broken up by a few north-east African artefacts, woven tablecloths, and sofas dand basket-weave tables in the window area. Much of the home-style Eritrean cuisine is served on platters lined with injera, but if you find this sourdough pancake-like bread too filling (or sour) choose rice or cracked wheat as an accompaniment. Spicy kulwa (tender lamb cubes with fresh tomatoes) and derho alicha (mildly spiced chicken stew) make good choices, particularly when eaten traditionally by tearing off pieces of injera as you go. Portions are reasonably large. At the end of the meal, it's enjoyable to kick back with traditional coffee, which involves a ritual of presenting freshly roasted dark beans to every table, for diners to appreciate the aroma. Otherwise, there's ice-cream, or yoghurt and honey for dessert. Staff are quietly efficient, friendly and generally keep out of sight.
Babies and children welcome: high chairs. Booking advisable. Separate room for parties, seats 35. Takeaway service. Vegan dishes. Vegetarian menu. **Map 22 E2**.

Kennington

Adulis
44-46 Brixton Road, SW9 6BT (7587 0055, www.adulis. co.uk). Oval tube. **Meals served** 5pm-midnight Mon-Thur; 1pm-midnight Fri, Sun; noon-midnight Sat. **Main courses** £8.45-£10.95. **Credit** MC, V. Eritrean
A Brixton Road landmark, Adulis has evolved significantly over its 15-year existence. It's a dual-fronted venue, having expanded some years ago into the premises next door. Local Eritreans have made the restaurant a focal point for their community, yet there's generally an all-nations range of diners

Mosob

on any given evening. Live events involving music or the spoken word take place in the basement, while main dishes are served in the ground-floor dining room, at dark wood tables surrounded by craftwork, wall hangings and the wafting aroma of incense. From the extensive menu, we went straight for the tibsi (lamb cubes fried in purified ghee butter with onions, rosemary and green chilli), which came with a crisp side salad and generous rolls of injera bread. Equally good was the ghemberi (fresh prawns fried with mixed herbs and served with rice). The traditional coffee – presented with frankincense and popcorn – packs a powerful punch, and will keep you alert for hours. Undeniably friendly, Adulis is the kind of place where regulars are greeted with hugs or slaps on the back by the otherwise impassive owner.

Babies and children welcome: high chairs. Booking advisable weekends. Separate room for parties, seats 20. Takeaway service. **Map 16 M13.**

South East

Peckham

805 Bar Restaurant

805 Old Kent Road, SE15 1NX (7639 0808, www.805 restaurant.com). Elephant & Castle tube/rail then 53 bus. **Meals served** 2pm-midnight daily. **Main courses** £7-£15. **Set meal** £9-£15. **Credit** MC, V. Nigerian
A decade after its inception, 805 continues to thrive. The surroundings – with traffic on the southbound carriageway of the A2 raging outside – may not be the loveliest, and the venue's exterior may be rather nondescript, but inside you'll find London's premier Nigerian restaurant. It's an airy, well-kempt

place with seating for 150, white walls displaying vibrant African art, and afrobeat on the sound system. Wealthy Nigerian families gather here, along with many other fans of the cuisine, to sample a menu that lists many classic dishes of the region. The selection allows you to be as hardcore as you like, perhaps starting timidly with corn on the cob, or boldly ordering nkwobi (spiced cow's foot) or santana (marinated chicken gizzards). The aptly named beermate (spiced beef) comes in medium or large portions. Main courses include jollof rice with various meat or fish accompaniments, egusi stews, grills (tilapia, say, with chilli sauce, salad and fried plantain) and side dishes such as moyin moyin (steamed bean pudding). Expect plates to be piled high. Staff are friendly and informative, but service can be tardy.

Babies and children welcome: high chairs. Disabled: toilet. Separate room for parties, seats 55. Tables outdoors (6, pavement). Takeaway service.

North

Kentish Town

Queen of Sheba

12 Fortess Road, NW5 2EU (7284 3947, www.thequeen ofsheba.co.uk). Kentish Town tube/rail. **Meals served** 5.30-11pm daily. **Main courses** £5-£10.50. **Set meal** £28 (2-3 people). **Credit** AmEx, MC, V. Ethiopian
This cosy corner spot has many loyal British and European customers, a tribute to the ready warmth of the welcome. Ethiopian cuisine is famous for its use of meat, but in keeping with the religious tradition of fasting two days a week, vegetarians also get a varied choice of main courses, based on

AFRICAN & CARIBBEAN

roasted chickpeas, fosolia beans, split peas and lentils. Meat lovers can revel in beef (raw or cooked), lamb and chicken. If you can't decide, try one of the suggested menus for two or three people to share. Portions are modest, so you might easily fit in two stews with injera (included) and a couple of side dishes or starters (the spicy house salad, say, or crisp fried sambossa pastry filled with veg or marinated meat). The fieriest dishes are marked as such; as our friendly waiter explained, the 'hot' yebeg wot was 'not as hot as vindaloo', but this spicy lamb stew certainly caused a sweat. Chicken with spinach (doro and gomen) was more subtle, with hints of ginger, garlic and jalapeño. The house white wine – only a tenner – is reliably good value. Our one disappointment was a damp, rather flabby platter of injera.

Available for hire. Babies and children welcome: high chairs. Booking advisable Fri, Sat. Takeaway service. Vegan dishes. Vegetarian menu. **Map 26 B4**.

Tufnell Park

Lalibela
137 Fortess Road, NW5 2HR (7284 0600). Tufnell Park tube or 134 bus. **Dinner served** 6pm-midnight daily. **Main courses** £8.50-£10.95. **Credit** MC, V. Ethiopian
A fond favourite with locals and expats for more than 15 years, Lalibela is a cosy spot decked out in a riot of carved wood, fabrics and trinkets. Through its windows you get broad views of leafy balconies across the street. The service could be more professional, but is mostly sweet and charming. The huge menu offers all the classics – doro wot (chicken stew with hard-boiled eggs), yebeg wot (lamb with berbere) and kitfo (seasoned chopped raw beef). While much is spicy, there are dishes such as chicken stew with cream, green pepper and spring onion in which the only fire is the tealight under the serving bowl keeping it warm. Vegetarians have an excellent choice too, and vegetable side dishes such as okra in spicy tomato sauce are tempting add-ons to the meaty fare. First comes the correctly sour injera bread, served both flat on the plate and rolled into tight cylinders for dipping in the stews that are spooned into the centre. The wine list is cursory, and the Ethiopian lager indistinctive, but it's the post-prandial coffee ceremony for which this cuisine is famous. Don't miss it.
Babies and children welcome: high chairs. Booking advisable. Takeaway service. Vegetarian menu. **Map 26 B3**.

CARIBBEAN

Central
Clerkenwell & Farringdon

Cottons
70 Exmouth Market, EC1R 4QP (7833 3332, www.cottons-restaurant.co.uk). Farringdon tube/rail or bus 19, 38, 341. **Lunch served** noon-4pm Mon-Fri. **Dinner served** 5.30-11pm Mon-Thur; 6.30-11pm Fri, Sat. **Meals served** noon-11pm Sun. **Main courses** £12.50-£14.50. **Credit** MC, V.
With its crisp white tablecloths and black-shirted waiters shuffling quietly between tables, Cottons is a far cry from the rambunctious West Indian eateries peppering the streets of Brixton. It's certainly friendly, and the list of rum cocktails is second to none, but there's something stilted about the densely

Menu

AFRICAN

Accra or **akara**: bean fritters.
Aloco: fried plantain with hot tomato sauce.
Asaro: yam and sweet potato porridge.
Ayeb or **iab**: fresh yoghurt cheese made from strained yoghurt.
Berbere: an Ethiopian spice mix made with many hot and aromatic spices.
Cassava, **manioc** or **yuca**: a family of coarse roots that are boiled and pounded to make bread and various other farinaceous dishes. There are bitter and sweet varieties (the bitter variety is poisonous until cooked).
Egusi: ground melon seeds, added to stews and soups as a thickening agent.
Froi: fish and shrimp aubergine stew.
Fufu: a stiff pudding of maize or cassava (qv) flour, or pounded yam (qv).
Gari: a solid, heavy pudding made from ground fermented cassava (qv), served with thick soups.
Ground rice: a kind of stiff rice pudding served to accompany soup.
Injera, **enjera** or **enjerra**: a soft, spongy Ethiopian and Eritrean flatbread made with teff/tef (a grain originally from Ethiopia), wheat, barley, oats or cornmeal. Fermented with yeast, it should have a distinct sour tang.
Jollof rice: like a hot, spicy risotto, with tomatoes, onions and (usually) chicken.
Kelewele or **do-do**: fried plantain.
Kenkey: a starchy pudding that's prepared by pounding dried maize and water into a paste, then steaming inside plantain leaves. Usually eaten with meat, fish or vegetable stews.
Moi-moi, **moin-moin** or **moyin moyin**: steamed beancake, served with meat or fish.
Ogbono: a large seed similar to egusi (qv). Although it doesn't thicken as much, it is used in a similar way.
Pepper soup: a light, peppery soup made with either fish or meat.
Shito: a dark red-hot pepper paste from Ghana, made from dried shrimps blended with onions and tomatoes.
Suya: a spicy Nigerian meat kebab.
Tuo or **tuwo**: a stiff rice pudding, sometimes served as rice balls to accompany soup.
Ugba: Nigerian soy beans; also called oil beans.
Waakye: a dish of rice and black-eyed beans mixed with meat or chicken in gravy.
Waatse: rice and black-eyed beans cooked together.
Wot or **we'ts**: a thick, dark sauce made from slowly cooked onions, garlic, butter and spices – an essential component in the aromatic stews of East Africa. Doro wot, a stew containing chicken and hard-boiled eggs, is a particularly common dish.

Menu

CARIBBEAN

Ackee: a red-skinned fruit with yellow flesh that looks and tastes like scrambled eggs when cooked; traditionally served in a Jamaican dish of salt cod, onion and peppers.

Bammy or **bammie**: pancake-shaped, deep-fried cassava (qv) bread, often served with fried fish.

Breadfruit: this football-sized fruit has sweet creamy flesh that's a cross between sweet potato and chestnut. Eaten as a vegetable.

Bush tea: herbal tea made from cerese (a Jamaican vine plant), mint or fennel.

Callaloo: the spinach-like leaves of either taro or malanga, often used as a base for a thick soup flavoured with pork or crab meat.

Coo-coo: a polenta-like cake of cornmeal and okra.

Cow foot: a stew made from the hoof of the cow, boiled with vegetables. The cartilage gives the stew a gummy or gelatinous texture.

Curried goat: usually lamb in London; the meat is marinated and slow-cooked until tender.

Dasheen: a root vegetable with a texture similar to yam (qv).

Escoveitched (or **escovitch**) **fish**: fish fried or grilled, then pickled in a tangy sauce with onions, sweet peppers and vinegar; similar to escabèche.

Festival: deep-fried, slightly sweet dumpling often served with fried fish.

Foo-foo: a Barbadian dish of pounded plantains, seasoned, rolled into balls and served hot.

Jerk: chicken or pork marinated in chilli spices, slowly roasted or barbecued.

Patty or **pattie**: a savoury pastry snack, made with turmeric-coloured shortcrust pastry, usually filled with beef, saltfish or vegetables.

Peas or **beans**: black-eyed beans, black beans, green peas and red kidney beans.

Pepperpot: traditionally a stew of meat and cassereep, a juice obtained from cassava (qv).

Phoulorie: a Trinidadian snack of fried doughballs often eaten with a sweet tamarind sauce.

Plantain or **plantin**: a savoury variety of banana that is cooked like potato.

Rice and peas: rice cooked with kidney or gungo beans, pepper seasoning and coconut milk.

Saltfish: salt cod, classically mixed with ackee (qv) or callaloo (qv).

Sorrel: not the herb, but a type of hibiscus with a sour-sweet flavour.

Soursop: a dark green, slightly spiny fruit; the pulp, blended with milk and sugar, is a refreshing drink.

Yam: a large tuber, with a yellow or white flesh and slightly nutty flavour.

packed seating in the dining room. Tables are set with wine glasses and fan-arrangement napkins; the walls hold a curious mix of prints (from art deco champagne posters to photos of Muhammad Ali). Combine all this with a faintly cheesy electric piano player, and the effect on our last visit was of a rum shack crossed with an upmarket hotel lobby. In fairness, the kitchen does its best to justify the ambience (and relatively high prices) with its modern take on Caribbean dishes. When this works – as in a piquant starter of jerk duck salad with wine and ginger dressing, or another of spiced salmon fillet with rosemary cassava cake and avocado and pineapple salsa – such niggles fade. When it doesn't (a recent goat curry was mostly bone), it's hard not to wish the balance was more in favour of the rum shack and less the hotel lobby.

Available for hire. Babies and children welcome: high chairs. Entertainment: DJs 9.30pm-2am Fri, Sat. Separate room for parties, seats 65. Tables outdoors (5, patio). Takeaway service. **Map 5 N4**.
For branch see index.

Soho

Jerk City
189 Wardour Street, W1F 8ZD (7287 2878). Tottenham Court Road tube. **Meals served** noon-10.30pm Mon-Wed; noon-11pm Thur-Sat; noon-8pm Sun. **Main courses** £6-£8.50. **Credit** MC, V.

Jerk City brings a burst of Caribbean sunshine to the West End, making it an ideal pit-stop when dreary London days produce cravings for saltfish dumplings, rice and peas, or jerk chicken (not the strongest dish here, but still a popular option for those wanting a taste of home). It's a warm little place where the friendly staff serve authentic island food to a mix of enthusiastic Soho diners. Pine tables, Afro-Caribbean art and the alluring smell of spices produce a cosy atmosphere – perhaps a little too cosy when the place gets busy. Yet despite the chaos, we reckon the best time to visit is during the lunchtime rush, as sometimes the food can taste a little dry after the peak run, and dishes often run out. In colder weather, hearty home-style dishes, such as oxtail stew with butter beans or curried mutton, hit the spot both in terms of flavour and proportion – though some West Indians might tut at the interpretation of the latter dish. There are desserts too: cakes that hint at the tropics, with banana or coconut versions tempting many a dieter.

Babies and children welcome: high chairs; nappy-changing facilities. Takeaway service. **Map 17 B3**.

Savannah Jerk
187 Wardour Street, W1F 8ZB (7437 7770). Tottenham Court Road tube. **Meals served** 11am-11pm Mon-Sat; noon-8pm Sun. **Main courses** £7-£9. **Credit** AmEx, MC, V.

We challenge you to find a restaurant in central London where you can fill up on better Caribbean food for the princely sum of around £25 for two people. What's more, Savannah Jerk is no dive, with its spacious, smart interiors and excellent rum-stocked bar. The Caribbean chefs believe that people deserve a substantial feed at lunchtime, and the portion sizes reflect this generosity. Slow-cooked, tender curried mutton is a dark, flavoursome dish with a punch; don't miss it, particularly on a chilly evening. The jerk sauce on a chicken-wing starter was a superb example of the classic Caribbean condiment: fiery and fruity all at once. We recommend ginger beer instead of wine if you order the jerk chicken, as the ginger and bubbles highlight the scotch bonnets, allspice and ginger in the sauce. *Takeaway service.* **Map 17 B3**.

South East
Crystal Palace

Island Fusion

57B Westow Hill, SE19 1TS (8761 5544, www.island fusion.co.uk). Gypsy Hill or Crystal Palace rail. **Dinner served** 5-11pm Mon-Sat; 4-10pm Sun. **Main courses** £9.50-£17.50. **Credit** MC, V.

Word of mouth has spread fast during Island Fusion's two years of operation. The food, in keeping with the 'Fusion' element of the name, reflects Modern European as well as Caribbean influences. Much thought has gone into the dishes, which go far beyond familiar 'yard food' staples. Apart from the notable exception of Barbados duck, Jamaican cookery dominates, with choices such as Trench Town jerk chicken breast and Portland jerk pork prominently displayed on the menu. Ackee and saltfish spring rolls are the only concession to the national dish, and even the jerk options are subtly spiced and married with rice or sweet potato mash, plantain or chilli garlic potatoes. Fleet-footed waitresses ensure that meals reach each table swiftly – even for larger parties. The subterranean restaurant area is a decent spot for intimate dining, furnished in floor-to-ceiling bamboo and lit, in the evening, by hanging lanterns. Even the painted backdrop of a sunset scene seems subtle in the relatively small space.

Babies and children welcome (until 7pm): high chairs. Booking advisable. Takeaway service; delivery service (over £12 within 3-mile radius).

Cottons. See p27.

North
Camden Town & Chalk Farm

Mango Room

10-12 Kentish Town Road, NW1 8NH (7482 5065, www.mangoroom.co.uk). Camden Town tube. **Meals served** noon-11pm daily. **Main courses** £10-£13. **Credit** AmEx, MC, V.

It may be more formal than neighbouring eateries on this insalubrious stretch of Camden, but the Mango Room has a relaxed vibe that helps it slot into the area. The restaurant is spread across three units: a bar, a middle room well suited to groups, and a spacious dining room displaying pleasing modern art evoking the tropics. Brightly coloured walls and bare brick provide a quirky, upbeat feel, but the owners have sensibly avoided holiday-island clichés, and the hip clientele appreciates this. Food leans to the elegant end of the Caribbean spectrum. It can be terrific, but the kitchen occasionally lets itself down – on our latest visit, because of no roti, no breadfruit and two very disappointing desserts. Dishes range from classics (ackee and saltfish, jerk chicken, curry goat) to more considered fare such as grilled sea bass with curried coconut and sweet pepper sauce, accompanied by tomato stuffed with ackee and green pepper. Fabulously tender lamb rump arrived with red wine and thyme sauce and a mash of sweet and white potatoes. There's a reasonable array of wines by glass and bottle (South African, Portuguese), but cocktails are the best choice; the appealing list includes a lovely non-alcoholic fruit punch with grenadine and pineapple, ensuring everyone feels welcome to the party.

Babies and children welcome: high chairs. Booking advisable weekends. Separate room for parties, seats 20. Takeaway service. Vegan dishes. **Map 27 D2**.

AFRICAN & CARIBBEAN

The Americas

NORTH AMERICAN

What is it about North American restaurants and the propensity to replicate? So many of the supposedly US restaurants that reach our shores owe more to boardroom templates than down-home cooking. Perhaps they are authentically reproducing the virulent capitalism of the homeland, yet few manage to recreate successfully those big Stateside flavours. Thankfully, there are exceptions. Despite now numbering five branches across London, **Bodean's** remains our favourite place for a Kansas-style barbecue, burnt ends and all. And top steakhouse **Hawksmoor** (itself about to spawn, in Covent Garden) shows to what heights a restaurant can soar when superb produce is sourced with due dedication. Sometimes, though, it's the rollicking diner vibe that's the attraction – with a side order of cheese and a strong line in cocktails. **Dollar Grills & Martinis** fits the bill for a fun night out, though **Lucky 7** also manages to inject a measure of character into the diner mould.

Central

Clerkenwell & Farringdon

Dollar Grills & Martinis

2 Exmouth Market, EC1R 4PX (7278 0077, www.dollar grillsandmartinis.com). Farringdon tube/rail or 19, 38 bus. Bar **Open** 6pm-1am Tue, Wed; 6pm-2am Thur; 6pm-3am Fri, Sat. **Main courses** £5.
Restaurant **Lunch served** noon-5pm daily. **Dinner served** 5-11pm Mon-Thur; 5-11.30pm Fri, Sat; 5-10pm Sun. **Main courses** £9.95-£19.95.
Both **Credit** AmEx, MC, V.
The decor isn't quite as gaudy as the Las Vegas Strip, but neon-lit Dollar Grills & Martinis certainly grabs the attention from its prime corner spot on Exmouth Market. The cosy ground-floor restaurant serves burgers, steaks, seafood and nachos, while the basement lounge offers a full house of martinis, champagne cocktails, sours, daiquiris and more. Burgers (8oz regular, 9oz for 'million dollar' burgers dressed with the likes of mango salsa, jalapeño chillies, buffalo mozzarella and guacamole) are made from chopped (not minced) Scottish steak, and come with a highly respectable side salad as well as crunchy house fries. Only the ribeye steaks are from US grain-fed cattle; rump, sirloin and fillet come from Argentina and the wagyu from Chile – these are shown off altogether on the 21oz tasting board (£58.95 for two). Two-for-one cocktail deals (Sunday to Thursday) are good value at £8.95, though the five concoctions offered are on the fruitily feminine side. There's a £5 lunch deal too, that lets you choose between a hot dog, burger, steak, and chicken salad, plus other options. Even though waiters might try to sell extra side dishes that you don't need, we like this place: it's fun.
Babies and children admitted. Booking advisable weekends. Entertainment: DJs 8pm Fri, Sat. Tables outdoors (10, pavement). Takeaway service. **Map 5 N4.**

Fitzrovia

Eagle Bar Diner

3-5 Rathbone Place, W1T 1HJ (7637 1418, www.eagle bardiner.com). Tottenham Court Road tube. **Open** noon-11pm Mon-Wed; noon-1am Thur, Fri; 10.30am-1am Sat; 11am-6pm Sun. **Main courses** £5.95-£14.50. **Credit** AmEx, MC, V.

Steak your claim

London's steakhouses have come a long way since the days when the chains dominated, and overcooked rump from who-knows-where jostled with gammon and pineapple rings on the laminated menu. Provenance is now stressed, and animal feeds are often listed in elaborate detail.

Butcher & Grill

39-41 Parkgate Road, SW11 4NP (7924 3999, www.thebutcherandgrill.com). Clapham Junction rail or 19, 49, 170, 319, 345 bus. **Breakfast served** 8.30am-noon daily. **Lunch served** noon-3.30pm Mon-Sat; noon-4pm Sun. **Dinner served** 6-11pm Mon-Sat.
Beef and lamb from East Sussex, free-range pork from southern England and barn-reared, RSPCA-endorsed chickens appear both on the butcher's counter and on the menu in the capacious bar-restaurants at B&Gs brace of operations in Battersea and Wimbledon. Steaks range from onglets to T-bones, and wine matching is a highlight.
Map 21 C1.
For branch see index.

High Timber

8 High Timber Street, EC4V 3PA (7248 1777, www.hightimber.com). Mansion House tube. **Lunch served** noon-3pm, **dinner served** 6.30-10pm Mon-Fri.
Gaze across the river at the Globe Theatre as you tuck into Lake District beef (matured for a minimum of 28 days) at this classy one-year-old. Sauces include black perigord truffle butter, and Mod Euro starters and desserts complete the pretty picture.
Map 11 O7.

Maze Grill

10-13 Grosvenor Square, W1K 6JP (7495 2211, www.gordonramsay.com/mazegrill). Bond Street tube. **Breakfast served** 6.45am-10.30am, **lunch served** noon-3pm, **dinner served** 5.30-10.30pm daily.
A Gordon Ramsay evocation of a New York-style steakhouse where the meat ranges from Hereford grass-fed (aged 25 days) to wagyu '9th grade' gold style. Get a table looking over Grosvenor Square, rather than at the nondescript hotel-chain interior. There's a good-value set lunch (£18 2 courses, £21 3 courses).
Map 9 G6.

Palm

1 Pont Street, SW1X 9EJ (7201 0710, www.the palm.com/london). Knightsbridge or Sloane Square tube. **Dinner served** 6-11pm Mon-Fri. **Meals served** noon-11pm Sat; noon-10pm Sun.
Offering an upscale take on a Stateside steakhouse, this London outpost of a venerable US chain knocks out aged USDA prime New York sirloins, along with equally pricey seafood. An evocation of 1920s high society is the aim.
Map 15 G10.

Popeseye Steak House

108 Blythe Road, W14 0HD (7610 4578, www.popeseye.com). Kensington (Olympia) tube/rail. **Dinner served** 7-10.30pm Mon-Sat.
Grass-fed Aberdeen Angus from the Highlands is hung for a minimum of 28 days and served as fillet, sirloin or popeseye (rump). The menu holds little besides chips and salad, but the wine list is full of beefy reds. There's a branch in Putney.
Map 20 C3.
For branch see index.

Le Relais de Venise l'entrecôte

120 Marylebone Lane, W1U 2QG (7486 0878, www.relaisdevenise.com). Bond Street tube. **Lunch served** noon-2.30pm Mon-Thur; noon-2.45pm Fri; 12.30-3.30pm Sat, Sun. **Dinner served** 6-10.45pm Mon-Fri; 6.30-10.45pm Sat; 6.30-10.30pm Sun.
An oh-so-French paean to steak frites – the only main course offered, served with a moreish 'secret sauce' – Le Relais attracts throngs to its woody, brasserie-like restaurants in Marylebone and near the Barbican. Start with salad, end with one of a handful of puds, and choose how you want your meat: it's easy.
Map 9 G5.
For branch see index.

High Timber

THE AMERICAS

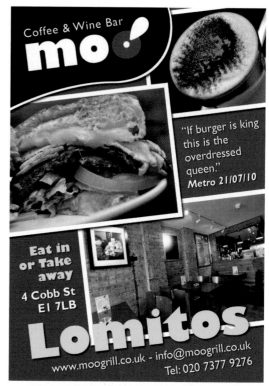

Local office workers fly down to this popular spot to grab reasonably priced meals in an upbeat setting. In contrast to diner clichés, the Eagle's brown and green decor could be described as 'New York bar meets The Jetsons', with curvy chairs and high-backed banquettes. All the flavours of American diner cuisine are here – maple syrup, blueberries, key lime, monterey jack, bacon, beef and barbecue. Breakfast is served all day. Beefburgers and shakes are the strongest suit, but the menu also takes in the likes of duck and grapefruit salad, and a meze plate. Kids have plenty of choice (4oz burger, hot dog, pasta, or herb-coated chicken with barbecue sauce). At night the place morphs into a noisy West End drinking hole and party venue, with DJs and a stupendous choice of cocktails. The peanut butter martini has become a signature, though there's also an extensive range of classics made with premium spirits, and tempting twists such as the Eagle iced tea (raspberry vodka, blood orange, passionfruit, vanilla and lemonade). Service is affable if not slick. The concept seems set for expansion, and the Eagle has already landed at Newcastle International Airport.
Babies and children welcome: children's menu. Booking advisable weekends. Disabled: toilet. Entertainment: DJs 7.30pm Thur-Sat. Takeaway service. **Map 17 B2.**

Soho

Bodean's
10 Poland Street, W1F 8PZ (7287 7575, www.bodeans bbq.com). Oxford Circus or Piccadilly Circus tube. **Lunch served** noon-3pm, **dinner served** 5.30-11pm Mon-Fri. **Meals served** noon-11pm Sat; noon-10.30pm Sun. **Main courses** £8-£16. **Credit** AmEx, MC, V.
Over in Kansas, they take their barbecues seriously. The owner of Bodean's came from the smoke-pit capital of the USA to show London how it's done, and seven years and five branches on, we can still say this is the best barbecue in the city. The Soho branch is our favourite for its street-level 'deli': a more casual arrangement where you walk in, order at the counter and tuck into a pared-down menu that omits some of the more superfluous choices – you don't go to Bodean's for enchiladas. It's all about the ribs, the pulled pork, the half chickens and the 'burnt ends' of beef brisket, smoked and slow-grilled to uncommon tenderness and served with the (inevitably) secret sweet and piquant sauce. Vegetarians should keep walking – there's nothing to see here. A bonus is that the formerly dreary choice of beer has been updated; in addition to Coors Light and Sol, you can now find the likes of Sierra Nevada's ales, although they're not available in all branches.
Available for hire. Babies and children welcome: children's menu; high-chairs; nappy-changing facilities. Tables outdoors (10, pavement). Takeaway service. **Map 17 A3.** **For branches see index.**

West

Westbourne Park

Lucky 7
127 Westbourne Park Road, W2 5QL (7727 6771, www.lucky7london.co.uk). Royal Oak or Westbourne Park tube. **Meals served** noon-10.30pm Mon; 10am-10.30pm Tue-Thur; 9am-11pm Fri, Sat; 9am-10.30pm Sun. **Main courses** £4.50-£12.95. **Credit** MC, V.

Bodean's

Americans don't do small, so Tom Conran's teeny diner – just six green booths in front of an open kitchen – has to aim for an authentic neighbourhood vibe. Still, don't come expecting a chirpy uniformed waitress à la Doris from *Groundhog Day*; the cooler-than-thou staff are insouciant at times. The day starts with 'cwoffee', bowls of Lucky Charms and Captain Crunch, breakfast burritos, pancakes, and fry-ups featuring hash browns. Later there are burgers, plus a choice of 'chiles', cobb and caesar salads, beer-battered onion rings, BLTs, crab cake sandwiches and the turkey dee lite (ground turkey white meat with bacon, cheese and avocado). The beer list, while not supersized, puts the emphasis on quality with Sierra Nevada, Anchor Steam beer and the esteemed Doggy Style pale ale. On the wagon? Here's your chance to try a root-beer float, a cream soda, or even venture an extra-thick shake with Oreos and peanut butter. Prices reflect the challenging rents in this corner of town, so look elsewhere to find London's best-value fast food. Nevertheless, Lucky 7 is a welcome and characterful, alternative to the cookie-cutter burger chains.
Babies and children welcome: children's menu. Bookings not accepted. Separate room for parties, seats 35. Takeaway service. **Map 7 A5.**

East

Spitalfields

Hawksmoor `HOT 50`
157 Commercial Street, E1 6BJ (7247 7392, www.the hawksmoor.com). Liverpool Street tube/rail or Shoreditch High Street rail. **Lunch served** noon-3.30pm Mon-Fri.

Brunch served 11am-4pm Sat, Sun. **Dinner served** 6-10.30pm Mon-Sat. **Main courses** £15-£30. **Credit** AmEx, MC, V.

This Spitalfields steakhouse has wooed much of London since opening in 2006; word-of-blog has only served to create an even bigger buzz around the restaurant and its food. A case of the emperor's new clothes? We think not. Hawksmoor's USP is in supplying excellent produce cooked well, focusing on top-quality beef from renowned London butcher Ginger Pig. There's a serious attitude to beef provenance and an impressive list of breeds; Longhorn is always available, but guest breeds range from Herefords to Lincoln Reds. The savvy staff do a terrific job of explaining the differences. Steaks are seared on Josper charcoal grills to crusty-outside, tender-inside perfection. The menu doesn't stop at the bovine, with Tamworth pork ribs, crab and samphire salad, and lobsters all making an appearance. The luxe burger, studded with nuggets of bone marrow, might seem to be gilding the lily, but it's certainly pretty good. For dessert, chocolate fudge sundaes and strawberry trifle are dependable options. Hawksmoor's looks aren't a forte (it occupies a mundane, low-ceilinged room behind a drab frontage), but owners Will Beckett and Huw Gott have long had dreams of expansion, and a new Covent Garden branch opened in 2010.

Babies and children welcome: high chairs. Booking advisable. Separate room for parties, seats 16. **Map 6 R5**.
For branch see index.

North

Camden Town & Chalk Farm

The Diner

2 Jamestown Road, NW1 7BY (7485 5223, www.good lifediner.com). Camden Town tube. **Meals served** 10am-11pm Mon-Thur; 10am-11.30pm Fri; 9am-11.30pm Sat; 9am-11pm Sun. **Main courses** £5-£8.50. **Credit** AmEx, MC, V.

The sizeable queue of international customers waiting for tables at this jumping joint is well looked after by the flock of delightful, straight-haired bambis who work here. Management stops short of making staff wear peaked caps and roller skates, but otherwise the Diner determinedly checks most of the Americana boxes, from the lettering on the windows to the free filter coffee refills. It's a popular choice for families who enjoy sitting in the red leather booths. The cooking could be better – even taking into account that this is what many consider to be junk food. Philly cheese steak sandwich is good enough, but a lurid chilli cheese dog was a lightweight, lacking even token salad – and you have to wonder why the Diner puts its name to the signature fries, which are simply sprinkled with coarse cajun spice mix. Still, the corn dogs are devilishly moist, the burgers good-looking, and the drinks list fun (Sleeman's Honey Brown is on draught and served authentically chilled). For dessert, be sure to share the blueberry and peanut butter sundae – so wrong, yet so right. By contrast, the New York cheesecake wasn't even as good as the vanilla ice-cream accompanying it.

Babies and children welcome: high chairs; nappy-changing facilities. Booking advisable. Disabled: toilet. Tables outdoors (13, terrace; 8, pavement). Takeaway service. **Map 27 C2**.
For branches see index.

Side orders

Want some unusual entertainment with your meal? Try one of the following.

Dans Le Noir?

30-31 Clerkenwell Green, EC1R 0DU (7253 1100, www.danslenoir.com/london). Farringdon tube/rail. **Dinner served** (fixed sittings) 6.45pm, 7.15pm Mon-Wed; 6.45pm, 7.15pm, 9.15pm, 9.45pm Thur-Sat. A novel experience, where you eat in complete darkness, letting you focus on your sense of taste and smell. The set dinner costs £39 for two courses, £44 for three. **Map 5 N4**.

Lucky Voice

52 Poland Street, W1F 7LR (7439 3660, www.luckyvoice.co.uk). Oxford Circus tube. **Open/food served** 5.30pm-1am Mon-Thur; 3pm-1am Fri, Sat; 3-10.30pm Sun. An extensive drinks menu should help to loosen your vocal chords in one of the Japanese-style private karaoke booths (£5-£11.50/hr per person, over-21s only). Food is pizzas and snacks. There's a branch in Islington. **Map 17 A3**. **For branch see index**.

Sarastro

126 Drury Lane, WC2B 5QG (7836 0101, www.sarastro-restaurant.com). Covent Garden or Holborn tube. **Meals served** noon-11pm Mon-Thur; noon-11.30pm Fri, Sat; noon-10.30pm Sun. Mediterranean-Turkish cuisine served in lavish operatic surroundings. Expect live opera performances on Monday and Sunday, and a swing and Motown vocalist on Wednesday or Thursday. **Map 18 F3**.

Tiroler Hut

27 Westbourne Grove, W2 4UA (7727 3981, www.tirolerhut.co.uk). Bayswater or Queensway tube. **Open** 6.30pm-1am Tue-Sun. **Dinner served** 6.30pm-12.30am Tue-Sun. Regular cowbell performances and singalongs are all to be expected at this Austrian restaurant, decked out like an Alpine ski-chalet. **Map 7 B6**.

Troubadour

263-267 Old Brompton Road, SW5 9JA (7370 1434, www.troubadour.co.uk). West Brompton tube/rail. *Café* **Open** 9am-midnight, **meals served** 9am-11pm daily. *Wine bar/shop* **Open** noon-10pm daily. *Club* **Open** 8pm-midnight Mon-Wed, Sun; 8pm-2am Thur-Sat. **Meals served** 8-11pm daily. A bohemian London legend; Bob Dylan (among others) played here in the '60s. Bands perform most nights in the cellar, and other entertainment includes poetry readings and open-mic nights. **Map 13 B11**.

LATIN AMERICAN

The food of two countries dominates London's Latin American restaurant scene: Mexico and Argentina. That said, most of the 'Mexican' establishments offer an anglicised version of Tex-Mex cooking. An alternative is **Green & Red**, which provides a repertoire that, for once, is more Mex (in fact, Jaliscan) than Tex. Also noteworthy are Notting Hill's **Taqueria** and Euston's **Mestizo**. Argentinian cuisine, on the other hand, is in rude health here. Steak tends to run the show, but given the quality, that's understandable. **Buen Ayre** still stands out from the herd, with a beefy Argentinian wine list to support its huge parrilla-grilled steaks, but honourable mention should also go to **Garufa** for its varied vegetarian dishes. Food from elsewhere in the continent is best represented at **Sabor**, where dishes range from Colombian street-food snacks to Brazilian seafood stews.

The draw of Latin American establishments is often more to do with high jinks than high falutin' gastronomy. Thus **Floridita** capitalises on the popularity of Cuban music (and mojitos), attracting a lively crowd who come for a party rather than a feed.

Central

Covent Garden

Cantina Laredo

10 Upper St Martin's Lane, WC2H 9FB (7420 0630, www.cantinalaredo.com). Covent Garden or Leicester Square tube. **Meals served** noon-11.30pm Mon-Thur; noon-midnight Fri, Sat; noon-10.30pm Sun. **Main courses** £8.95-£26.95. **Credit** AmEx, MC, V. Mexican
Bookings aren't taken at Cantina Laredo and, although it was busy on our visit (mainly with tourists), we were seated straight away. Right from the start, the US-style drilled service seemed overly chummy, cheesy and scripted – but couldn't be faulted for efficiency or attentiveness. A ceviche of seafood ('bought fresh daily', as every customer is informed) contained scallops, prawns and fish along with avocado, pepper and coriander, and was spry and explosively bright. Another starter, of chilli con queso served with (unlimited) tortilla chips, was molten, moreish and complex. To test the chain's claim to specialise in seafood, we tried a pescado del dia: sea bass with coriander and citrus beurre blanc. It was perfectly cooked, and the sauce ('made from scratch every day, as all sauces are,' we were told) was light and zesty. The other main dish, chicken enchiladas de mole, was a disappointment, covered in a sickly,

almost unpleasant version of that complicated sauce (mole) made from dried peppers. Desserts are authentically sweet – custard flan, strawberry buñuelos (doughnut-style fried batter) – and some come on a 'sizzling' skillet. For the money, we're after a bit more excitement and a sense of discovery from this super-slick concept.

Available for hire. Babies and children welcome: children's menu; high chairs; nappy-changing facilities. Disabled: toilet. Separate room for parties, seats 20. Tables outdoors (9, pavement). Takeaway service. Vegetarian menu. **Map 18 D4**.

Wahaca
66 Chandos Place, WC2N 4HG (7240 1883, www. wahaca.co.uk). Covent Garden or Leicester Square tube. **Meals served** noon-11pm Mon-Sat; noon-10.30pm Sun. **Main courses** £3.25-£9.95. **Credit** AmEx, MC, V.
Mexican
Eating street food in Mexico is a laid-back, chatty, cheap, wholesome experience. Going to Wahaca – which sells itself as a street-food purveyor – is the opposite. Most evenings, queues form up the stairs, and office workers drink cocktails while preparing noisily for a packaged experience. By not taking reservations, Wahaca aims to generate excitement. Does it deliver? Only partially, we reckon. The classic quesadillas, burritos and platos fuertes (mains, including a slow-roasted pork pibil and enchiladas) are fair value. Two can share four to five items, drink a bottle of acceptable wine, and have change from £40. But the real test is the food, and the cooking rarely rises above the complexity of a burrito bar. The meat in some of our dishes was dry; fillings are sometimes mean-spirited too. As snacks, the antojitos are OK, but there's little to savour. The vibe of the big room is 'eat fast, go home'. Owner Thomasina Miers drew her inspiration from Oaxaca's amazing Casa Oaxaca restaurant; unfortunately, London has nothing similar. Wahaca Covent Garden was followed by branches in Canary Wharf and Westfield Shopping Centre – which says a lot. This is pretentious chain food and if it's almost worth the money, it's not worth the bother.
Babies and children welcome: high chairs; nappy-changing facilities. Bookings not accepted. Disabled: toilet.
Map 18 D5.
For branches see index.

Fitzrovia

Mestizo
103 Hampstead Road, NW1 3EL (7387 4064, www.mestizomx.com). Warren Street tube or Euston tube/rail. **Meals served** noon-11pm Mon-Sat. **Lunch served** noon-4pm, **dinner served** 5-10pm Sun. **Main courses** £9.80-£24. **Credit** AmEx, MC, V. Mexican
There's something winningly authentic about Mestizo. Its drab location, just north of Euston Road, could be a working-class neighbourhood of Lima or Laredo. The Mexican owners (who also run a branch in Madrid) have created a warm, welcoming interior with crimson walls, smart tablecloths, a vibrantly coloured Aztec calendar, and a TV showing idealised images of Mexico. The food is honest and filling. Authentic Mexican mains such as crêpes filled with huitlacoche (a fungus that grows on maize), and the classic meat dishes – arrachera and tampiqueña – use quality produce and aren't so fiery you can't taste the vegetables, beans and guacamole. Tasty tamales and tacos are also offered; try the nopal cactus taco: a delicious,

unusually textured vegetable. The kitchen also makes its own mole poblano sauce (from prunes, nuts, chillies and bitter chocolate). All main courses come with a pot of black beans and crumbled cheese. The prawns in the ceviche seemed crisp and fresh, but the tangy lemon-based sauce doesn't need the extras of tomato and avocado. With good, earthy cooking, low prices (£5.40 for a sizeable tamal) and 120 tequilas, Mestizo has much in its favour.
Available for hire. Babies and children welcome: high chairs. Booking advisable weekend. Disabled: toilet. Separate room for parties, seats 80. Takeaway service. **Map 3 J3**.

Piccadilly

Gaucho Piccadilly
25 Swallow Street, W1B 4QR (7734 4040, www.gaucho restaurants.co.uk). Piccadilly Circus tube. **Meals served** noon-10.30pm Mon, Sun; noon-11pm Tue-Sat. **Main courses** £12.25-£37. **Credit** AmEx, MC, V. Argentinian
It's part of an Israeli-owned restaurant chain, and is staffed by an international bunch of fashionistas, but what Gaucho lacks in authenticity, it makes up for in quality. From the Paraguayan-style cheesy breads to the dulce de leche pancakes, via the succulent empanadas, meat and fish dishes, the food is impeccably sourced and carefully prepared. The main event is the beef; before the meal, a waiter comes over with the five main steak cuts and explains how they're best served and accompanied. If you want the meatiest meat, choose ribeye, though the fillet is heavenly for those frightened of fat. Service is attentive and can verge on the invasive, especially at the Piccadilly and Richmond outposts – have a polite word and the waiters will back off. The truly impressive wine list is pricey, but the house malbec is usually excellent. The newest branch is in Smithfield, bringing meat to London's carnopolis, as it were, and there's an O2 outlet where show-goers can hire a private suite. Even more lavish, the Hampstead branch has a private dining room (and a lovely outside space), and you can hire your own sommelier and grill chef – for a hefty sum.
Babies and children welcome: high chairs. Booking advisable Thur-Sat. Separate rooms for parties, seating 14-16. Takeaway service. **Map 17 A5**.
For branches see index.

Soho

Floridita
100 Wardour Street, W1F 0TN (7314 4000, www.floriditalondon.com). Tottenham Court Road tube. *Bar* **Open** 5.30pm-2am Tue, Wed; 5.30pm-3am Thur-Sat. *Restaurant* **Dinner served** 5.30pm-midnight Tue, Wed; 5.30pm-1am Thur-Sat. **Main courses** £13.50-£35. **Admission** (after 9pm Fri, Sat) £10. *Both* **Credit** AmEx, MC, V. Cuban
We're guessing that it's the location and concept that keep this Cuban bar-restaurant so packed; based on our recent visits, it's not the food. The Cuban theme is a loose one. Yes, a Cuban salsa band takes the stage most nights from 9pm, but the decor is a nod to Miami kitsch, and the menu wanders around the Americas: from Mexican quesadillas to hamburgers to Brazilian steak. Our meal started off in fine form with a ceviche that was fresh and not overpowering citrusy, but things then went downhill. A medium-rare picanha steak was stringy and chewy, while the suckling pig was a huge slab of pork whose flavour was only slightly rescued by the accompanying

Brazilian black bean, bacon and chorizo feijoada stew. On the plus side, service was attentive, friendly and honest; our waiter informed us that 'we don't really do Cuban food… but some of the dishes have a flavour of Cuba'. So, if you're yearning for genuine Cuban cooking, try the ropa vieja at Sabor, and come here with a gang of pals for mojitos and music.

Booking advisable. Disabled: toilet. Dress: smart casual. Entertainment: musicians, DJ 9pm Tue-Thur; 10pm Fri, Sat. Separate rooms for parties, seating 52-72. **Map 17 B3**.

West

Bayswater

Taqueria

139-143 Westbourne Grove, W11 2RS (7229 4734, www.taqueria.co.uk). Notting Hill Gate tube. **Meals served** noon-11pm Mon-Thur, Sun; noon-11.30pm Fri; noon-10.30pm Sat. **Main courses** £5.50-£8.50. **Set lunch** (noon-4.30pm Mon-Fri) £6 1 course. **Credit** MC, V.
Mexican
Taqueria is sometimes guilty of inconsistency, but this bright, disarming eaterie (it's intentionally more café/cantina than restaurant) remains one of London's best venues for authentic Mexican food. It also has the UK's only corn tortilla-making machine. High-quality ingredients feature strongly, from refried beans, crumbled cheese and salsa, to beer-battered pollack with avocado mash, cabbage, salsa and chipotle mayonnaise. The eggs, chicken and pork are free-range, the milk and cream organic, the scallops Marine Stewardship Council-certified – but prices are keen for the area. Tacos such as cochinita pibil (slow-cooked achiote- and citrus-marinated pork) with habanero-pickled onions, or alambres (chargrilled skirt steak with peppers and melted cheese), are great for nights of serious tequila sipping; the drinks list runs to 23 types of the Mexican spirit, plus beers, margaritas and wine. Daytimes are family-friendly; under-fives can enjoy cheese or chicken quesadillas, or a combo plate that includes rice, plantain and avocado, and licuados (milkshakes) of mango, guava or chocolate. Tuesday is tamale day. Owned by the Cool Chile Company (a familiar sight at markets, including Borough), Taqueria has a small selection of Mexican groceries for sale near the entrance.
Babies and children welcome: high chairs. Bookings not accepted Fri-Sun. **Map 7 A6**.

South

Battersea

Santa Maria del Sur

129 Queenstown Road, SW8 3RH (7622 2088, www.santamariadelsur.co.uk). Queenstown Road rail. **Lunch served** noon-3pm Sat, Sun. **Dinner served** 6-10pm daily. **Main courses** £12-£19. **Credit** MC, V. Argentinian
Following a recent successful appearance on Gordon Ramsay's *The F Word* (they made it to the semi-final), Alberto Abbate and his Argentinian team were booked solidly at weekends for several months. It has calmed down a bit now and, fortunately, the quality and authenticity remain the same. A slick front-of-house operation and smooth new tango sounds disguise a classic parrilla (charcoal grill) in the kitchen. Thick steaks

Get a Brazilian

Do you crave a meat-fest with a South American slant and unlimited helpings? If so, canter down to one of London's rodizios. These Brazilian all-you-can-eat venues come with waiters who serve food straight on to your plate at your table, and continue serving until you say stop. The word 'rodizio' refers to the style of service, rather than the cuisine, so in Brazil you'll find these restaurants providing all sorts of food, from pasta to pizza to sushi. Outside South America, they tend to be churrascarias – grill houses – that focus on meat. There are a fair few such establishments in London, but bear in mind that here, as in Rio, waiters often try to fill up guests with chicken, ham, linguiça (a large, cured pork sausage) and bread before bringing out the better, more expensive cuts of meat that everyone is waiting for: sirloin, fillet steak and picanha (rump cap). And yes, the whole thing is a vegetarian's worst nightmare – though there's always a free salad bar. These are our favourite rodizios.

Amber Grill Rodizio

47 Station Road, NW10 4UP (8963 1588, www.ambergrill.co.uk). Willesden Junction tube/rail. **Lunch served** noon-6pm, **dinner served** 6-11pm Mon-Fri. **Meals served** noon-11pm Sat, Sun.

Rodizio Preto

72 Wilton Road, SW1V 1DE (7233 8668, www.rodiziopreto.co.uk). Victoria tube/rail. **Lunch served** noon-3pm, **dinner served** 6-11pm Mon-Fri. **Meals served** noon-11pm Sat; noon-9.30pm Sun. **Map 15 J10**.

Rodizio Rico

111 Westbourne Grove, W2 4UW (7792 4035, www.rodiziorico.com). Bayswater tube. **Dinner served** 6pm-midnight Mon-Fri. **Meals served** noon-midnight Sat, Sun.
Map 7 B6.
For branches see index.

Sabor Brasileiro

639 Harrow Road, NW10 5NU (8969 1149). Kensal Green tube/rail. **Meals served** noon-7pm daily.

sourced from the pampas are charred alongside spicy chorizo sausages, black pudding from Spain, discs of provolone cheese and, if they're available, sweetbreads. Ask a question about any plate and you'll get a warm, enthusiastic explanation that will make you want to cross the ocean for a holiday in BA. Keep to the classics – meat empanadas, mid-priced malbec, steak and salad – and you can't go wrong. There are parrilladas (mini grills) stacked with carnal stuff meant for sharing, but don't order unless you're ravenous. The best desserts are the don pedro (ice-cream in whisky) and dulce de leche cheesecake. An extensive wine list invites customers to try sparkling whites, malamados (dessert wines) and aguardientes from Mendoza. *Babies and children welcome: high chairs. Booking advisable weekends.*

THE AMERICAS

South East

Bermondsey

Constancia

52 Tanner Street, SE1 3PH (7234 0676, www.constancia. co.uk). Bermondsey tube or London Bridge tube/rail. **Dinner served** 6-10.30pm Tue-Sat. **Meals served** 1.30-9.30pm Sun. **Main courses** £8.50-£22.50. **Set meal** £19, £23.50 per person (minimum 2). **Credit** MC, V. Argentinian

Created from the shell of a Bermondsey pub, Constancia is one of London's more refined Argentinian restaurants. The menu features such staples as meat empanadas (made by the owner's aunt), peppery chorizo sausages and lean, perfumed steaks, but also strays from the homeland with some style; the acorn-fed Iberian pork shoulder loin is delicious and comes with salsa criolla, a sharper variant of the classic chimichurri condiment – it can be ordered as a starter (5oz) or a main (8oz). The 11oz ribeye is the tastiest of the big steaks, and is best eaten simply with sides of chips and tomato, onion and leaf salad. Even vegetarians have a few decent choices, including a spinach, cheese and onion empanada, grilled aubergines, and a spinach, mushroom and parmesan salad. Cheesecakes are the best desserts: the fruits of the forest option is the most flavoursome; the dulce de leche is great, though perhaps too sweet and gooey for some palates. The all-Hispanic staff provide a friendly, warm welcome. With City workers increasingly crossing the river to try a proper slab of beef, Constancia could have a lucrative future. Booking is essential on Fridays and Saturdays, and the restaurant is constantly busy.
Babies and children admitted. Booking essential dinner Fri, Sat. Disabled: toilet. **Map 12 R9**.

Blackheath

Buenos Aires Café

17 Royal Parade, SE3 0TL (8318 5333, www.buenos airesltd.com). Blackheath rail. **Lunch served** noon-3pm Mon-Fri; noon-4pm Sat, Sun. **Dinner served** 6-10.30pm daily. **Main courses** £8.50-£26. **Credit** MC, V. Argentinian

Forget the 'café' tag, the Buenos Aires is a relatively smart restaurant, with framed photos of Maradona and Che Guevara adorning the walls. On our lunchtime midweek visit the place was quiet, but this gave us ample opportunity to enjoy spectacular views across Blackheath through the huge windows. Staff could have been a little more pleased to see us, however, and a little less abrupt. Argentinian cuisine owes a great deal to the country's large Italian immigrant population. The menu here reflects this by featuring much of what you might find in an Italian deli, pizzeria or pasta joint – plus, of course, beef. A starter of grilled marinated artichokes and good olives got the meal off to a decent start. A main course of butternut squash ravioli was delicious and perfectly cooked (bucking the trend for vegetarian options being an afterthought in meat-centric restaurants), though a side dish of spinach was unexciting. Nevertheless, Argentinian restaurants tend to be graded on the quality of their beef, and in our experience this kitchen certainly passes the test; a 400g sirloin steak was enormous, juicy and flavourful. We just hope the staff cheer up.
Babies and children welcome: booster seats. Booking advisable; essential Fri, Sat. Tables outdoors (4, pavement). **For branch see index.**

East

Shoreditch

Green & Red

51 Bethnal Green Road, E1 6LA (7749 9670, www.greenred.co.uk). Shoreditch High Street rail. *Bar* **Open** 6.30pm-midnight Thur; 5.30pm-1am Fri, Sat. *Restaurant* **Dinner served** 6-11pm daily. **Dishes** £6-£8. *Both* **Credit** AmEx, MC, V. Mexican

Bridging the gap between good-time party food and authentic Mexican, Green & Red specialises in the cuisine of the state of Jalisco. The look is East End cool – a tacky Virgen de Guadalupe here, a scuffed leather sofa there, and a bar populated by locals quietly sipping Sol after work. Service is friendly and laid-back. On each table you'll find a useful guide to ingredients entitled 'WTF am I eating', which runs through everything from totopos (corn chips) to habanero chillies. A starter of octopus ceviche was delicately spiced and refreshing; the chorizo with potato and onions had plenty of rich flavours; but a chilli con carne was forgettable. Main courses are designed to be eaten messily with small corn tortillas. The carne asada (steak with chipotle salsa) was tender, with spot-on spicing in the salsa. Chicken with chilli, cumin and the epazote herb had succulent meat, but needed more kick. The only let down was the pork belly: extremely fatty and too guilty a pleasure. Given the Shoreditch location, the basement bar and the vast number of tequilas and cocktails offered, Green & Red makes an ideal start to a night out.
Available for hire. Babies and children welcome: high chairs. Disabled: toilet. Takeaway service. **Map 6 S4**.

Gaucho Piccadilly. See p37.

North East

Hackney

Buen Ayre HOT 50

50 Broadway Market, E8 4QJ (7275 9900, www.buen ayre.co.uk). London Fields rail or 26, 48, 55, 106, 236 bus. **Lunch served** noon-3.30pm Thur-Sun. **Dinner served** 6-10.30pm daily. **Main courses** £7.50-£22. **Credit** MC, V.
Argentinian
Unless they're happy eating just-melted provolone cheese and portobello mushrooms, vegetarians should steer clear of this big-and-beefy Argentinian grill restaurant. The massive parrilla (charcoal grill) forms the centrepiece of the wooden-floored, plainly decorated dining room, so don't wear your dry-clean-only rags; the smell of divine chargrilled meat will pervade all fabrics and cling for days. A buzzing atmosphere – aided by the tendency of parties at the slightly cramped, rough-hewn wooden tables to share massive chunks of meat – is also helped along by an extensive Argentinian wine list (try one of the hefty malbecs, such as 2007 La Colonia, Bodegas Norton, with your meat) and the beat-the-clock two-hour dining limit. Starters are limited, for good reason. Save your stomach for the parrilladas (for a minimum of two hungry eaters), which entitle you to a belt-busting amount of grilled beef along with all the extras: black pudding, sausages, mushrooms and so on. For those with heroic appetites, there are plenty of desserts. The focus is on rich, sweet concoctions, including dulce de leche, pancakes, and caramelised bread pudding.
Babies and children welcome: high chairs. Booking advisable. Disabled: toilet. Tables outdoors (5, garden).

Buenos Aires Café. See p39.

North

Highbury

Garufa

104 Highbury Park, N5 2XE (7226 0070, www.garufa. co.uk). Arsenal tube. **Meals served** 10am-10.30pm daily. **Main courses** £12-£34. **Set lunch** £9.80-£12.50 1 course incl glass of wine, beer or soft drink. **Credit** MC, V.
Argentinian
More homely than sister-restaurant Santa Maria del Sur, Garufa is a homage to Argentina. Sepia images of Buenos Aires hang on bare-brick walls, and table lamps in red glass create a romantic, nostalgic atmosphere. Staff play quiet old tangos to complete the experience. Steaks, sourced from a handful of importers, are sublime. Have fillet if you like buttery lean meat, or dive into a huge ribeye if you prefer the extra taste that escapes from marbled flesh. The menu also contains several vegetarian dishes, including carefully grilled aubergine with tomato sauce and provolone cheese. On our visit, a single fish special was available: salmon with roquefort, which, surprisingly, works, as the creaminess of the cheese complements the succulent pink fish. The best desserts are the pancakes and crème caramels, though you might want to spend time exploring the impressive, all-Argentinian wine list before finishing. Garufa has recently introduced lunch specials; at £12.50, the Gardel, which includes a pint of beer or glass of wine, a milanesa de cuadril (breaded rump steak) with salad or chips, or ribeye with chips or salad, is great value. There's also a breakfast with rump steak that costs under a tenner.
Babies and children welcome: children's menu (until 5pm); high chairs; nappy-changing facilities. Booking advisable.

Islington

Sabor

108 Essex Road, N1 8LX (7226 5551, www.sabor.co.uk). Angel tube or Essex Road rail or 38, 73 bus. **Dinner served** 6-10pm Tue, Wed; 6-11pm Thur, Fri. **Meals served** noon-11pm Sat, Sun. **Main courses** £11.50-£19.50. **Set lunch** £15 2 courses, £17.50 3 courses. **Credit** MC, V. Pan-South American
You'll find restaurants like Sabor in the cooler parts of Mexico City or São Paulo; the space is bright and airy without a pan pipe in sight, and the menu is packed with enticement. On our last visit, the waitress – a chirpy, tattooed Brazilian – had to return three times before we'd decided what to order. The focus is on modern pan-Latin American cuisine, from Colombian street-food staples to Cuban classics. A starter of patacones (fried plantain) came with beetroot and pineapple, shredded chicken breast and perfect guacamole. Even this, however, was put in the shade by the monkfish ceviche: supremely fresh-tasting fish, carefully marinated in lime and garnished with just the right amount of onion and chilli. To follow, moqueca (seafood stew from Brazil's north-eastern state of Bahia) was rich, filling and generous with its swordfish, prawns, squid and mussels. Pastel de acelga (filo pastry filled with feta and spinach) was moist, flavourful and, like all the other dishes, well presented. The drinks list takes in Old and New World wines and a variety of cocktails (including delicious, if pricey, non-alcoholic versions). Sabor's top-quality, good-value food explains why, even midweek, the place gets full.
Babies and children welcome: high chairs. Booking advisable.
Map 5 P1.

THE AMERICAS

Brasseries & Cafés

Antipodean immigration has injected a great sense of vitality to many areas of the restaurant trade, but none more apparent than the café sector. Australians and New Zealanders have a seemingly innate talent for producing breakfast, coffee drinks and cake. To illustrate, look no further than this year's Best New Café award winner, **Hackney Pearl**, run by Australian James Morgan, or, indeed, last year's winner, **Lantana**. We also like the ground-floor café-bar at the **Luxe** (*see p215*) in Spitalfields – owned by Aussie boy John Torode – and Exmouth Market brasserie **Caravan**, where New Zealander Miles Kirby, former chef at the perennially popular **Providores & Tapa Room** (*see p223*), controls the kitchen. However, prize for the year's quirkiest opening must go to American Lori de Mori, whose **Towpath** café brings authentic Tuscan cooking, grilled cheese sandwiches and treacle tart to passers-by on the Regent's Canal in Dalston. As our critics report, **Tom's Kitchen** in Chelsea and the highly original **La Fromagerie** in Marylebone prove Brits can hold their own in this category, but the real winners amid all this competition are Londoners.

Central

Belgravia

Chelsea Brasserie

7-12 Sloane Square, SW1W 8EG (7881 5999, www.chelsea-brasserie.co.uk). Sloane Square tube. **Lunch served** 11.30am-3.30pm Mon-Sat. **Brunch served** 11am-4pm Sun. **Dinner served** 6-10.30pm Mon-Sat. **Main courses** £13-£21.50. **Set dinner** (6-7.30pm) £19.75 2 courses. **Credit** MC, V. Prices are higher here than the brasserie norm, but then this polished establishment is no run-of-the-mill local. Service is impeccable, and the decor, while not cutting-edge, acts as a handsome backdrop to the well-heeled tourists and SW1 locals who make up the clientele. Continental and english breakfasts are served, so there are cold meats and cheeses available as well as porridge. Later in the day, starters run from a plate of Dorset crab and Forman's London-cured smoked salmon, via pigeon breast tartelette with celeriac purée and red wine and cherry sauce, to sashimi of yellowfin tuna with wasabi, ginger and lime. The cooking is good – sometimes very good, as in a main of pan-fried calf's liver with caramelised shallots, smoked bacon and sage jus, with creamy mash – though roast beef salad with frisée, radish, cold potato and horseradish cream was a bit workaday. Finish with excellent coffee and a pudding such as tarte tatin with crème fraîche, or summer berry compote with panna cotta. As befits a proper brasserie, the bar can provide anything from fresh juices to a bloody mary. *Babies and children welcome: children's menu; high chairs. Booking essential. Disabled: lift; toilet. Dress: smart casual. Separate room for parties, seats 14. Tables outdoors (4, pavement).* **Map 15 G10**.

City

Café Below

St Mary-le-Bow, Cheapside, EC2V 6AU (7329 0789, www.cafebelow.co.uk). St Paul's tube or Bank tube/DLR. **Breakfast served** 7.30-11am, **lunch served** 11.30am-3pm, **snacks served** 2.30-5.30pm, **dinner served** 5.30-9pm Mon-Fri. **Main courses** £6.20-£12.50. **Credit** MC, V. Long-established vegetarian cafeteria the Place Below has renamed itself and, even more radically, added meat to the menu and started opening for dinner. We heartily approve – the crypt premises are lovely, but best suited to the evening (or winter), and our meat dishes were top-notch. Thyme-marinated bavette with rocket, horseradish cream and roast new potatoes had two sizeable chunks of moist, tender beef; we mopped the plate clean. Equally enjoyable was a chorizo burger with sweet potato wedges and roast garlic aïoli. Own-made rosemary focaccia impressed us too, as did the smoky baba ganoush, and chocolate

Caravan

and chestnut cake with stem ginger ice-cream. Portions are generous (the Spanish plate of serrano ham, chorizo, roast peppers, gordal olives, habas fritas and focaccia defeated us) and prices fair (the bavette was £12.50). Complaints were few: slightly dry brown bread with a smoked salmon starter, and the (otherwise delightful) waitress spray-cleaning a nearby table while we ate. A short wine list is supplemented by beer, cider and perry. Cakes and sandwiches are served all day, or pop in for a bacon butty at breakfast. A smashing local restaurant, and a wonderful contrast to neighbouring expense-account eateries. *Available for hire. Babies and children welcome: high chairs. Tables outdoors (20, churchyard). Takeaway service. Vegan dishes.* **Map 11 P6**.

Clerkenwell & Farringdon

Caravan `HOT 50`

2010 RUNNER-UP BEST NEW LOCAL RESTAURANT
11-13 Exmouth Market, EC1R 4QD (7833 8115, www. caravanonexmouth.co.uk). Farringdon tube/rail. **Meals served** 8am-10.30pm Mon-Fri; 10am-10.30pm Sat; 10am-4pm Sun. **Main courses** £4.50-£15. **Credit** AmEx, MC, V. Caravan has slotted into the Exmouth Market dining scene with consummate ease. On a midweek summer's evening, tables inside and out were packed and the small bar area was jammed.

The casual vibe and industrial-funky design – rough wooden tables, white pipework, an enamel jug filled with yellow daisies, light fittings made from old-fashioned cow-milking bottles – are part of the appeal, but it's the food that is the main draw. There are some large dishes but most people choose the small plates, and share. Expect a parade of unusual, international tastes (chef is New Zealander Miles Kirby, late of the Providores). Peanut butter and blue cheese wontons exploded on the tongue; squid 'pancake', drizzled with mayo and Japanese brown sauce, was soft and yielding; salt beef fritters with green beans packed a meaty punch. Puds are just as inventive: take the custardy orangewater blancmange with intense raspberry sorbet and crunchy pistachios. There's also weekend brunch (banana caramel porridge, fry-ups, cornbread french toast with bacon), and a fairly priced drinks list that includes excellent coffee (roasted daily on the premises), cocktails, juices and wine. Young staff zip busily between tables, but are never too rushed to smile. *Babies and children welcome: high chairs. Booking advisable. Tables outdoors (7, pavement). Takeaway service.* **Map 5 N4**.

Clerkenwell Kitchen

27-31 Clerkenwell Close, EC1R 0AT (7101 9959, www.the clerkenwellkitchen.co.uk). Angel tube or Farringdon tube/rail. **Meals served** 8am-5pm Mon-Fri. **Main courses** £4.50-£14. **Credit** MC, V.

You wouldn't guess from first impressions that this stylish outfit is a standard bearer for supporting sustainable food production, fairtrade, and traditional farming methods, yet it won our Best Sustainable Restaurant award in 2008 against high-profile competition. The kitchen, run by émigrés from River Cottage and La Fromagerie, has a clear formula that works a treat. Every day, the chefs cook six lunch dishes and two puds, served in the spacious café. They also bake cakes and prepare sandwiches, tarts and soups to take away. There'll be a few vegetarian choices (bruschetta with slow-roasted courgette and goat's curd, perhaps), a proper meat-and-potatoes dish (pork chop with watercress, charlotte potatoes and caper dressing), a main-course salad (lamb, runner beans and red onions with salsa verde) and something using seafood such as mackerel, sardines, crab or squid. Expect seasonal fruit for dessert (gooseberry fool in July), alongside a reliable brownie with cream. The drinks list is brief but excellent, featuring best-of-Blighty stuff like Union coffee, Meantime beers, Chegworth Valley juices and Chapel Down wines. Service is friendly and relaxed yet professional – the right tone for an eaterie that's part of an office development. At the back is a lovely alfresco courtyard, perfect for summer lunches.
Babies and children welcome: high chairs. Disabled: toilet. Tables outdoors (8, courtyard). Takeaway service.
Map 5 N4.

Fitzrovia

Lantana
13 Charlotte Place, W1T 1SN (7637 3347, www.lantana cafe.co.uk). Goode Street tube. **Meals served** 8am-3pm Mon-Wed; 8am-3pm, 5-9pm Thur, Fri; 9am-3pm Sat, Sun. **Main courses** £4.50-£10.50. **Credit** MC, V.
Since winning Time Out's award for Best New Café 2009, Lantana has confidently expanded into the premises next door, easing the flow of takeaway customers in its cramped dining area. We hope it improves things as this is a popular spot – whether for coffee and cake (Friand, Hummingbird), a cooked breakfast, or gourmet sandwiches and savouries – and when it's busy, it's difficult to move around. Staff are friendly but often don't help matters. There's a natural reluctance to turn punters away, yet on our latest visit a staff member enjoyed a break at one table while customers were being asked to move so more people could be squeezed in. It's also a little confusing to what extent there is table service (someone at the next table was told to go and pour his own water when he asked for a glass of tap). We had a long wait for food and, when it finally arrived, it wasn't hot enough. But we appreciated the doorstop slices of delicious french toast and well-sourced bacon. The combination didn't quite work with the accompanying pears in red wine, let alone the lime- and pistachio-flavoured mascarpone, but if you stick to simple dishes and the strong Square Mile coffee you're likely to come away satisfied.
Babies and children admitted. Tables outdoors (2, pavement). Takeaway service. **Map 17 B1**.

King's Cross

St Pancras Grand
Upper Concourse, St Pancras International, Euston Road, NW1 2QP (7870 9900, www.searcys.co.uk/stpancrasgrand). King's Cross tube/rail. **Meals served** 7am-10.30pm Mon-Sat; 8am-9.30pm Sun. **Main courses** £9.50-£19. **Set meal** £19 2 courses, £25 3 courses. **Credit** AmEx, MC, V.

We've had mixed experiences at this sumptuously designed restaurant in the St Pancras Eurostar terminal. It's a handy spot, whether you're about to take the train, work locally or simply want to see the magnificent building. Food and drink are supplied throughout the day, from cooked breakfasts to afternoon teas and cocktails before dinner. Martin Brudnizki's art deco-style decor doffs its cap to the golden age of travel. The menu's British theme is unreservedly welcome, as is the campaigning oyster selection that shows the French a thing or two. However, like the champagne bar opposite, the place is run by Searcy's and (like the champagne bar) the food pricing is discouragingly overconfident. Service has wowed us in the past, but this time it was indifferent, making the meal too long and leaving us feeling unwanted. Rustic dishes such as ham hock with colcannon and parsley sauce, or cumberland sausages with mash and red onion gravy seem safer choices

Clerkenwell Kitchen

than restaurant fare such as chicken leg with spring greens, tarragon, tomato and red wine sauce. For dessert, steamed ginger pudding tasted no better than a supermarket version, though the accompanying ginger ice-cream was first-rate. *Available for hire. Babies and children welcome: children's menu; high chair. Booking advisable dinner and weekends. Disabled: toilet. Entertainment: jazz 6.30-10.30pm Sun. Separate room for parties, seats 14.* **Map 4 L3**.

Marylebone

La Fromagerie `HOT 50`
2-6 Moxon Street, W1U 4EW (7935 0341, www.la fromagerie.co.uk). Baker Street or Bond Street tube. **Open** 8am-7.30pm Mon-Fri; 9am-7pm Sat; 10am-6pm Sun. **Main courses** £6-£15. **Minimum** (12.30-2.30pm) £10. **Credit** AmEx, MC, V.
It began in a Highbury garage, with Patricia Michelson selling cheeses she'd brought back from holiday to friends and neighbours. Now, in fashionable Marylebone, were it not for the seductive refrigerated room at one end, you could eat here happily and barely think about cheese. A stunning selection of speciality fruit and veg greets customers on arrival, then there are artisan breads, a table of cakes and other sweet things, and rows of gourmet bottles and packages. Deli-style meat options on the all-day 'tasting café' menu range from baked ham with maple glaze to goose rillettes, foie gras and truffle terrine, jambon persillé, and snails in garlic butter. From 12.30pm the kitchen produces a few seasonal dishes such as a Frenchified beef pie with mashed potato, salad of ratte potatoes with trompette and girolle mushrooms, and Mexican-inspired poached chicken with black rice and guacamole. Breakfasts include own-made baked beans on Poilâne toast, even bacon

sandwiches. Ingredients are first-rate, but consequent pricing isn't so easy to swallow (own-made cereals with posh French yoghurts, £4.95-£5.25), and there's a minimum charge of £10 zat lunch. Nevertheless, this is a great spot of true originality. *Available for hire (evenings). Babies and children admitted. Takeaway service.* **Map 3 G3**.
For branch see index.

Mayfair

Bond & Brook
2010 RUNNER-UP BEST NEW CAFÉ
2nd floor, Fenwick, 63 New Bond Street, W1S 1RQ (7629 0273, www.fenwick.co.uk). Bond Street tube. **Breakfast served** 10am-noon Mon-Sat. **Meals served** noon-6.30pm Mon-Wed, Fri, Sat; noon-8pm Thur. **Tea served** 3-6.30pm Mon-Wed, Fri, Sat; 3-8pm Thur. **Main courses** £10.50-£24. **Set tea** £17.50. **Credit** AmEx, MC, V.
It's very hard to find fault with this polished all-day eaterie, operated by events caterer Rhubarb in upmarket department store Fenwick. It claims to be a restaurant, but evidence points towards a much more casual offering – breakfast, brunch, light lunch dishes, and a superb afternoon tea with an arrangement of beautiful cakes. Although the menu is aimed at fatigued and fashionable shoppers looking for something that won't require too much belt-loosening, food is elegant and flavour-packed: dainty crab cakes with beans, rosemary-speared roasted quail or linguine alle vongole, for example. The space is eye-catching; shelves of design books and mirrored walls are inspired by the rails of couture on the shop floor, and a curvy pewter bar tailor-made for champagne flutes takes centre stage. Service is as smooth as you'd expect in such an elegant setting. Fenwick has

BRASSERIES & CAFÉS

long been a destination for the fashion-hungry, but Bond & Brook elevates it to a destination for the plain hungry as well. *Available for hire. Babies and children welcome: high chairs; nappy-changing facilities. Disabled: toilet.* **Map 9 H6.**

Truc Vert

42 North Audley Street, W1K 6ZR (7491 9988, www.trucvert.co.uk). Bond Street tube. **Meals served** 7.30am-10pm Mon-Fri; 9am-10pm Sat; 9am-3pm Sun. **Main courses** £14.95-£17.50. **Credit** AmEx, MC, V. Named after a beach in south-west France, Truc Vert's sparsely decorated deli-restaurant looks rather underdressed for Mayfair. Shelves of jams and cereal, crates of wine, and chunky wooden furniture lend it a rustic, farmhouse atmosphere. Cheery, knowledgeable staff give a warm welcome and coo over children. There's even a small monthly market here on Saturdays, and jazz on Friday evenings. Sadly, the prices are far from provincial – expect a fillet steak price tag for a toulouse sausage. The daily changing menu attracts a French expat crowd ranging from businessmen to bourgeois-bohemians. Charcuterie and shellfish dominate the starters, with dishes including that creamy coastal favourite, lobster bisque, and spicy North African merguez sausages. Mains comprise expensive varieties of meat and fish; on our last visit we enjoyed perfectly pink wild boar steaks with lentils, and delicate halibut with a well-balanced feta risotto. Profiteroles arrived with a chocolate sauce that had separated out, making us regret not sticking to the own-made ice-creams and sorbets. *Available for hire. Babies and children welcome: high chairs; nappy-changing facilities. Booking advisable. Entertainment: jazz 7-10pm Fri. Tables outdoors (12, pavement). Takeaway service. Vegetarian menu.* **Map 9 G6.**

Capital eats

It can be hard to find a decent meal in London's tourist hotspots, but there are some old favourites (and relative newcomers) that are worth a visit.

Christopher's

18 Wellington Street, WC2E 7DD (7240 4222, www.christophersgrill.com). Covent Garden tube. *Bar* **Open/snacks served** noon-midnight Mon-Fri; 11.30am-1am Sat; 11.30am-10.30pm Sun. *Restaurant* **Lunch served** noon-3pm Mon-Fri. **Brunch served** 11.30am-3.30pm Sat, Sun. **Dinner served** 5-11.30pm Mon-Sat; 5-10.30pm Sun. A handsome, grown-up American brasserie in the heart of Covent Garden. The food can be variable, but the ground-floor bar is a prime spot for cocktails. **Map 18 F4.**

Elena's L'Étoile

30 Charlotte Street, W1T 2NG (7636 7189, www.elenasletoile.co.uk). Goodge Street or Tottenham Court Road tube. **Lunch served** noon-2.30pm Mon-Fri. **Dinner served** 6-10.30pm Mon-Sat. The classic dishes (calf's liver, roast lamb, crème brûlée) are the best at this legendary French restaurant, furnished with red velvet chairs and celebrity photos, and within striking distance of the British Museum. **Map 17 B1.**

Inn The Park

St James's Park, SW1A 2BJ (7451 9999, www.innthepark.com). St James's Park tube. **Breakfast served** 8-11am Mon-Fri; 9-11am Sat, Sun. **Lunch served** noon-3pm Mon-Fri; noon-4pm Sat, Sun. **Tea served** 3-5pm Mon-Fri; 4-5pm Sat, Sun. **Dinner served** 6-9pm daily. Come summer, the terrace tables are the best spot for bucolic gazing while grazing at this Oliver Peyton venture. Wood pigeon salad, sea trout with samphire, and lemon posset are typical of the seasonal British menu. **Map 10 K8.**

Joe Allen

13 Exeter Street, WC2E 7DT (7836 0651, www.joe allen.co.uk). Covent Garden tube. **Breakfast served** 8-11.30am Mon-Fri. **Brunch served** 11.30am-4pm Sat, Sun. **Meals served** noon-12.30am Mon-Fri; 11.30am-12.30am Sat; 11.30am-11.30pm Sun. The luvvies' favourite, this New York-style brasserie offers comfort cooking and swift service against a backdrop of theatrical memorabilia. **Map 18 E4.**

Kettners

29 Romilly Street, W1D 5HP (7734 6112, www.kettners.com). Leicester Square or Piccadilly Circus tube. **Meals served** noon-11pm Mon-Thur; noon-11.30pm Fri, Sat; noon-9.30pm Sun. Established by Auguste Kettner in 1867, long part of Pizza Express and now a French/European brasserie. Food is hit and miss, but the decor is lovely. **Map 17 C4.**

Mon Plaisir

21 Monmouth Street, WC2H 9DD (7836 7243, www.monplaisir.co.uk). Covent Garden tube. **Meals served** noon-11.15pm Mon-Fri. **Lunch served** noon-2.15pm, **dinner served** 5.45-11.15pm Sat. The French restaurant of Hollywood cliché brought to colourful life, complete with accented staff and soupe à l'oignon. **Map 18 D3.**

Restaurant at St Paul's

St Paul's Cathedral, St Paul's Churchyard, EC4M 8AD (7248 2469, www.restaurantatstpauls.co.uk). St Paul's tube. *Café* **Open/meals served** 9am-5pm Mon-Sat; 10am-4pm Sun. *Restaurant* **Lunch served** noon-3pm, **tea served** 3-4.30pm daily. Seasonality and provenance are the focus of the British menu at this calm, beautifully designed restaurant in the crypt. Excellent afternoon tea too. **Map 11 O6.**

BRASSERIES & CAFÉS

Piccadilly

The Wolseley [HOT 50]

160 Piccadilly, W1J 9EB (7499 6996, www.thewolseley.
com). Green Park tube. **Breakfast served** 7-11.30am
Mon-Fri; 8-11.30am Sat, Sun. **Lunch served** noon-3pm
Mon-Fri; noon-3.30pm Sat, Sun. **Tea served** 3-6.30pm
Mon-Fri; 3.30-5.30pm Sat; 3.30-6.30pm Sun. **Dinner
served** 5.30pm-midnight Mon-Sat; 5.30-11pm Sun.
All-day menu served 11.30am-midnight daily. **Main
courses** £6.75-£28.75. **Set tea** £9.75-£21. **Cover** £2.
Credit AmEx, DC, MC, V.
On a good day, the Wolseley makes you feel as glamorous as
the celeb and media regulars you'll probably spot here. On a
bad day – peak hour during a particularly bustling lunch,
perhaps – you could be perched on small tables near the front
door and made to feel inadequate for not ordering a sufficiently
sumptuous meal. At first, the idea was that customers could
pop into the café for cake and coffee, yet this has become
impractical as demand for the main dining room has grown.
Still, better eating in the café, or the fun bar opposite, than in
the foyer. Some great chefs have passed through the Wolseley's
kitchens (Chris Galvin, Claire Clark), but the cooking
generally punches below its weight. Reliable dishes include the omelette
arnold bennett, ice-cream coupes and no-brainers like a dozen
Islay rock oysters or the fruits de mer. Plats du jour are suitably
diverse: faschierter braten (a traditional Austrian dish of
minced meat, potatoes and onions) on Wednesday; chicken,
ham and leek pie on Thursday; seven-hour lamb on Saturday.
The attitude of staff ranges from charming to authentic French
brasserie-style (brusque, indifferent), but let's face it, you're not
here for the service.
*Babies and children welcome: high chairs; nappy-changing
facilities. Booking advisable. Disabled: toilet.* **Map 9 J7.**

Soho

Bob Bob Ricard

1 Upper James Street, W1F 9DF (3145 1000, www.bob
bobricard.com). Piccadilly Circus tube. **Meals served**
noon-11.30pm Mon-Fri; 11am-11.30pm Sat; 11am-10.30pm
Sun. **Main courses** £12-£40. **Credit** AmEx, DC, MC, V.
In more ways than one, this nearly new brasserie is from a
different age. Its astounding design (which won it a Time Out
award in 2009) provides a surreal, vividly coloured, Ivy-esque
take on the 1930s, with the capacious dining room and bar
flaunting mirrored ceilings, mosaic flooring, walls with myriad
swans flying into the blue, and turquoise booth seating. Staff
look like managers from a Willy Wonka factory, with their
smart pink waistcoats or turquoise dresses. There's a new
Russian slant to the menu, so before standard brasserie mains
of Cornish crab cake or chateaubriand, you could start with
jellied ox tongue or zakuski snacks and vodka. Beef tea soup
involved a teapot of stock being poured over boiled quail's egg,
morsels of steak, and pasta; in flavour it was strikingly similar
to Bovril. Better was chicory, pear and cured ham salad with
cubes of olive-oil jelly and almonds. For mains, we took the
Slavic route with juicy meat pelmeni dumplings served with
vinegar and sour cream. All well and good, but with vegetables
and bread charged extra, our light meal for two cost more than
£60 without wine. A different age indeed – the pre-crunch era
of conspicuous consumption.
*Booking advisable. Disabled: toilet. Separate room for
parties, seats 10.* **Map 17 A4.**

Princi

135 Wardour Street, W1F 0UT (7478 8888,
www.princi.co.uk). Leicester Square or Tottenham Court
Road tube. **Meals served** 7am-midnight Mon-Sat;
9am-11pm Sun. **Main courses** £5-£8.50. **Credit** AmEx,
MC, V.
Since opening a couple of years ago, Princi has become the
principal hangout for Italians-who-lunch, Soho's media pack
and the occasional student opting for something nicer than a
supermarket baguette. Long black granite counters filled with
comestibles stretch across the length of the room, starting with
sweets by the door and ending with hot savouries and drinks
at the back. It's all very tempting, but the ordering system is
still a bit of a shambles, with no real queue to join, different
sections for different foods, and harried staff. Try, if you can,
to visit off-peak; then, you're able to sit down quietly on any of
the stools at (otherwise packed) communal tables and enjoy big
rectangular slices of pizza, or platefuls of fresh, Italian-style
salads and pastas made like nonna's own. Come winter, there
are hot dishes such as osso buco too, or you could take home a
giant Princi-made panettone for the Christmas holidays. A slice
of Milan in the heart of Soho.
*Babies and children admitted. Bookings not accepted.
Disabled: toilet. Takeaway service; delivery service
(over £100 within 3-mile radius).* **Map 17 B4.**

West

Chiswick

High Road Brasserie

162-166 Chiswick High Road, W4 1PR (8742 7474,
www.highroadhouse.co.uk). Turnham Green tube.
Breakfast served 7am-noon Mon-Fri; 9am-noon
Sat, Sun. **Meals served** noon-11pm Mon-Thur; noon-
midnight Fri. **Brunch served** noon-4pm Sat, Sun.
Meals served 4pm-10.30pm Sat; 4pm-10pm Sun.
Main courses £10-£22. **Set lunch** £12.50 2 courses,
£15 3 courses. **Credit** AmEx, MC, V.
Part of the Soho House group, this stylish place epitomises
Chiswick cool. The wide pavement permits a large outdoor
space, while inside feels just like a Parisian brasserie, with
striking touches such as the quilt-like floor of Victorian tiles.
Breakfast is served from 7am (9am weekends), there are
separate brunch and lunch menus, and a diverse all-day/dinner
menu. You can also have a drink or snack at any time, even
afternoon tea. The place buzzes most of the day with a mix of
locals, tourists and shoppers of all ages, although couples and
suits predominate in the evening. The staff are pleasant,
unobtrusive and full of sound advice; the kitchen is flexible
(happy to add bacon to breakfast pancakes). During our
summer's evening visit, the dining room was largely empty and
blessedly cool. Scallops were plump and cooked just right, their
crushed pea and bacon accompaniment perfectly judged. A
carpaccio of beef with rocket and parmesan was also
everything it should have been, if over-chilled. To follow, whole
sea bass with braised fennel was memorable, and calf's liver
(a little stringy in places) with bacon and polenta was full-
flavoured, with a rich anise-tinged jus.
*Babies and children welcome: crayons; high chairs;
nappy-changing facilities. Booking advisable dinner
and weekends. Disabled: toilet. Tables outdoors
(8, pavement).*

Ladbroke Grove

Electric Brasserie
191 Portobello Road, W11 2ED (7908 9696, www.the-electric.co.uk). Ladbroke Grove tube. **Meals served** 8am-11pm Mon-Fri; 8am-5pm, 6-11pm Sat; 8am-5pm, 6-10pm Sun. **Main courses** £10-£28. **Set lunch** (noon-7pm Mon-Fri) £13 2 courses, £16 3 courses. **Credit** AmEx, MC, V.
It's hard not to get caught up in the buzz surrounding this sparkling Portobello Road stalwart attached to the Electric Cinema. The venue has a flair for making even long-suffering mums feel like A-listers for the evening. In fair weather, the front terrace fills with media types cutting deals over ice buckets; tables in the front room are subject to the clatter of the open kitchen. At the rear is the dining room proper, an intimate wooden space lined with red leather banquette seating and chunky wooden tables, and lent an art deco feel by the central chandelier and globe lamps reflected in the big mirrors. A straightforward card menu offers tapas-style small plates

The Wolseley

alongside conventional starters; our special of chicken liver pâté was velvet smooth and served with buttery toasted brioche (and plenty of it, though we were told to shout if we wanted more). Mains are also superb – from roasted cod fillet, served crispy skin up on a bed of braised peas and bacon, to a perfectly pink duck breast with gooseberry relish. Only a tin bucket of slightly burnt chips missed the mark. Service is exemplary, from the front of house to the back.
Babies and children welcome: booster seats; children's menu; crayons; high chairs; nappy-changing facilities. Booking advisable Thur-Sun. Disabled: toilet. Tables outdoors (6, terrace). Vegetarian menu. **Map 19 B3**.

Westbourne Grove

Daylesford Organic
208-210 Westbourne Grove, W11 2RH (7313 8050, www.daylesfordorganic.com). Ladbroke Grove or Notting Hill Gate tube. **Open** 8.30am-7pm Mon-Sat; 10am-4pm Sun. **Main courses** £9.95-£13.95. **Credit** AmEx, MC, V.
A hip and sophisticated Notting Hill crowd turns up in droves to this farm shop-cum-brasserie. Their chic outfits fit perfectly with the understated decor: whitewashed boarding, stripped wood, and woven baskets overflowing with organic produce. This, the newest Daylesford branch, is spead over three floors, with a raw bar in the basement, a bustling café on the ground floor, and a larder of fabulous produce from the home farm in Gloucestershire upstairs. It was the café that we chose for weekend brunch. The menu is limited, but has enough to tempt: buttery pastries, a nursery food staple such as shepherd's pie, eggs royale with perfect, oozing yolks, and salads for the health-conscious. A raw summer vegetable salad was lifted by fresh mint and a kick of chilli. The food tends to be a little uninspired and the service can be terrible, but the ingredients are the finest. If you lived nearby, you'd be here often too.
Babies and children welcome: crayons; high chairs; nappy-changing facilities. Booking advisable dinner. Disabled: toilet. Tables outdoors (6, pavement). Takeaway service. Vegetarian menu. **Map 7 A6**.
For branch see index.

South West
Barnes

The Depot
Tideway Yard, 125 Mortlake High Street, SW14 8SN (8878 9462, www.depotbrasserie.co.uk). Barnes, Barnes Bridge or Mortlake rail, or 209 bus. **Brunch served** 9.30am-11.45pm Sat. **Lunch served** noon-3pm Mon-Fri; 12.30-3.30pm Sat; noon-4pm Sun. **Dinner served** 6-11pm Mon-Sat; 6-10.30pm Sun. **Main courses** £9.95-£15. **Set meal** (noon-3pm Mon-Fri) £12.50 2 courses, £15.50 3 courses. **Credit** AmEx, DC, MC, V.
A mainstay of the Barnes/Mortlake dining scene, the Depot is a welcoming spot that caters well for a quick drink, casual supper or family celebration. You can dine outdoors in the front courtyard, but the prime seats (especially at sunset) are inside overlooking the Thames. Polished wood floors and furniture (plus a few smart banquettes), mellow lighting and flamboyant paintings fill the long narrow space; there's a bar at one end, but most people are here to eat. Sensibly so. The seasonal menu aims to please all-comers, with the likes of rock oysters or foie

gras for the hedonists, chargrilled côte de boeuf, chips and béarnaise for the classicists, and slow-roast pork belly with steamed chinese greens and shiitake broth for those wanting a touch of eastern promise. We've experienced the occasional blip in the more experimental dishes, but the cooking is usually reliably good. Desserts are a highlight; eton mess is always a hit, and we like the poshed-up comfort puddings (sticky toffee and date pudding with banana ice-cream, say). Keen pricing, a wide-ranging wine list and special promotions ensure a loyal local following; after nearly 25 years in business, the Depot knows its audience.

Available for hire. Babies and children welcome: children's menu; crayons; high chairs; nappy-changing facilities. Booking advisable. Tables outdoors (11, courtyard).

Orange Pekoe

3 White Hart Lane, SW13 0PX (8876 6070, www. orangepekoeteas.com). Barnes Bridge rail or 209 bus.
Meals served 7.30am-5.30pm Mon-Fri; 9am-5.30pm Sat, Sun. **Main courses** £4.50-£8. **Credit** AmEx, MC, V.
Winner of our Best Tea Room award in 2008, Orange Pekoe has certainly won hearts in Barnes. Arrive early at lunchtime or you'll have to fight the local blonde lovelies for a seat in the small interior or at one of the wobbly metal tables next to the roundabout. Wooden tables, white brick walls, flamboyant wallpaper, and pretty tea cups on cherub plinths provide a charming setting; a skylight and mirror at one end help magnify the cosy space. Shelves of black canisters in the front room bear witness to the seriousness with which tea is taken here; around 50 loose leaf teas and 20 herbal infusions are available, from the café's own breakfast blend to high-grade Japanese green tea gyokuro asahi, costing £26 for 100g. You can try any tea for £3.60 a pot. The coffee drinks are good too. Food includes scrumptious cakes and scones, cheese or pâté platters and classy sandwiches, as well as some hot snacky dishes (soup, superior cheese on toast, eggs florentine). Friendly young staff cope well with the stream of customers, whether toddlers or octogenarians.
Babies and children welcome: crayons; high chairs; nappy-changing facilities. Tables outdoors (5, pavement). Takeaway service.

Chelsea

Gallery Mess

Saatchi Gallery, Duke of York's HQ, King's Road, SW3 4LY (7730 8135, www.saatchi-gallery.co.uk). Sloane Square tube. **Breakfast served** 10-11.30am daily.
Meals served 11.30am-9.30pm Mon-Sat; 11.30am-7pm Sun. **Main courses** £9.50-£17. **Set tea** (2.30-6pm) £12.
Credit AmEx, MC, V.
It's no surprise that the brasserie at the Saatchi Gallery is full of modern art (all for sale), but even if you couldn't care less about the visuals, the food makes a visit worthwhile. In fine weather, the most covetable tables are outside overlooking Duke of York Square; you don't get forgotten out there as staff are an attentive bunch. Indoors, there's a sense of space thanks to the high ceilings. The menu runs from breakfast to late supper and includes an afternoon tea option, with sandwiches, scones and cakes. From 11.30am onwards, you can order dishes such as English asparagus with poached egg, hollandaise and prosciutto; a sharing plate of Spanish charcuterie served with honey, olives and bread; tortellini with goat's cheese, red pepper and a smoked tomato sauce; or a burger with all the trimmings.

Gallery Mess

This last dish is hard to resist – the chips are good and the juicy burger tastes as close to homemade as you'll find in London. The drinks list also has something for everyone, and includes a set of classic cocktails, from a martini to a caipirinha. Go on a Saturday and you can browse the farmers' market. *Babies and children welcome: high chairs; nappy-changing facilities. Booking advisable lunch and dinner. Disabled: toilet. Separate room for parties, seats 30. Tables outdoors until 5.30pm (30, terrace).* **Map 14 F11**.

Tom's Kitchen

27 Cale Street, SW3 3QP (7349 0202, www.toms kitchen.co.uk). Sloane Square or South Kensington tube. **Breakfast served** 8-11am, **lunch served** noon-3pm Mon-Fri. **Brunch served** 10am-4pm Sat, Sun. **Dinner served** 6-11pm daily. **Main courses** £14.50-£29.50. **Credit** AmEx, MC, V.

Tom Aikens' new joint venture with Compass Catering at Somerset House (replacing the Admiralty restaurant) was about to open as we went to press, but you only have to spend five minutes in the Chelsea Green original to wish there were more like it. The semi-communal dining room includes places at the long marble bar, where solo diners can watch the chefs in action. Wear a pink striped shirt and Prince Harry haircut to feel most at home, though staff are friendly to all. Breakfast is our favourite time to visit: the pancakes and waffles are superb, the ingredients for the full english sourced carefully, the coffee just-so. At other times Tom's Kitchen usually hits the mark: Devon crab salad needed more crab to match the fennel and orange accompaniments, but an open steak sandwich was both perfect and pretty. Comfort-food dishes are thrilling: cod and salmon fish pie sings with fresh herbs. Our copper saucepan of baked alaska (one of a few dishes for sharing) was theatrically flamed at table: a shame the meringue was too burnt, but a good idea to use panettone and quality vanilla ice-cream. Wines start at a steep £20.50 a bottle, though there's reasonable choice under £25. *Babies and children welcome: high chairs; nappy-changing facilities. Booking advisable dinner and weekends. Disabled: toilet. Separate rooms for parties, seating 22 and 40.* **Map 14 E11**.

South

Balham

Harrison's

15-19 Bedford Hill, SW12 9EX (8675 6900, www. harrisonsbalham.co.uk). Balham tube/rail. **Lunch served** noon-4pm Mon-Fri. **Dinner served** 6-10.30pm Mon-Sat; 6-10pm Sun. **Breakfast served** 9am-noon, **brunch served** 12.15-4pm Sat, Sun. **Reduced menu served** 2-6pm Mon-Fri; 4-6pm Sat, Sun. **Main courses** £9.50-£17.50. **Set lunch** (Mon-Sat) £13 2 courses, £15 3 courses; (Sun) £16 3 courses. **Set dinner** £14 2 courses, £17 3 courses. **Credit** AmEx, MC, V.

There's an undeniable air of slickness to Harrison's, with its black and white tiled floors, zinc bar and funky lighting. The place is owned by Sam Harrison (a protégé of Rick Stein), who also runs Sam's Brasserie & Bar in Chiswick; the two restaurants share a laid-back, friendly vibe, and both have professional service. The menu isn't what you could call challenging, however, focusing on crowd-pleasing dishes that

aren't likely to furrow the brow. A starter of chilli and garlic grilled squid, including tender tentacle tendrils and rocket, looked attractive but the portion seemed a bit meagre for £7.50. A nicely seared salmon burger with wasabi mayo was a fine example of the 'classics with a twist' genre in which Harrison's specialises – even if the bun was a touch bland. We couldn't fault the ultra-light gnocchi, although the accompanying grilled vegetables were uninspiring. The varied wine list includes an admirable selection by the glass and 50cl carafe. Monday evening is BYO night, with no corkage charge. *Babies and children welcome: children's menu; crayons; high chairs; nappy-changing facilities. Booking advisable Fri-Sun. Disabled: toilet. Separate rooms for parties, seating 24 and 40. Tables outdoors (4, terrace).*

South East

Bankside

The Table

83 Southwark Street, SE1 0HX (7401 2760, www.the tablecafe.com). Southwark tube or London Bridge tube/rail. **Meals served** 7.30am-5pm Mon-Fri. **Dinner served** 6-10.30pm Thur, Fri. **Brunch served** 8.30am-4pm Sat, Sun. **Main courses** £5-£25. **Credit** AmEx, MC, V.

The Table café, a former winner of our Best Cheap Eats award, has always had a restaurant sensibility, but this year it began opening for dinner on Thursday and Friday. The evening menu offers a soup, a few salads, burgers (as per the lunch menu), and mains such as chargrilled mackerel with baby clams and capers, or broad bean, mint and artichoke risotto. The prime draw, however, is a studious choice of steaks (all Welsh black beef), served with hand-cut potato wedges. Sides, if you need them, might be grilled san marzano tomatoes or fresh peas in the pod. Sources (Billingsgate fish, Hoel y Bryn Farm's organic chicken, Carroll's heritage potatoes, Valrhona chocolate) are promoted with pride, and cooked in the open-plan kitchen, which lends a bit of theatre to the Zen-like simplicity of the dining room. Weekday breakfasts and lunches nourish the local office trade; there's a daily-changing salad buffet sold by weight, plus a choice of tarts, pasta (baby courgette and lemon verbena penne, beef lasagne, for example) and the likes of roast chicken with preserved lemon and mint-flavoured couscous. *Babies and children welcome: high chairs. Disabled: toilet. Tables outdoors (8, terrace). Takeaway service.* **Map 11 O8**.

Blackheath

Chapters All Day Dining

43-45 Montpelier Vale, SE3 0TJ (8333 2666, www. chaptersrestaurants.com). Blackheath rail. **Breakfast served** 8-11.30am Mon-Fri; 8am-noon Sat; 9am-noon Sun. **Lunch served** noon-3pm Mon-Sat; 11am-4pm Sun. **Tea served** 3-6pm Mon-Sat; 4-6pm Sun. **Dinner served** 6-11pm Mon-Sat; 6-9pm Sun. **Main courses** £8.95-£23.95. **Credit** AmEx, MC, V.

True to its name, you can come to Chapters for breakfast, brunch, lunch, afternoon tea, cocktails (at the brushed steel bar), a snack, or a full three courses. Given all that coming and going, there's a bustling feel, with families welcomed, and pavement tables looking out over the wide expanse of Blackheath. Chapters is sister to highly regarded Chapter One in Bromley,

and although not of the same lofty standard, produces some extremely pleasing flavours, not least the tender belly pork (with chewy crackling), beautifully seasoned and accompanied by apple and prune chutney and syrupy cider sauce. The star turn is the Josper oven whose charcoal embers give the steaks, chops and burgers an authentic barbecue taste – though you'd be advised to order on the rare side as the extreme heat can cook too quickly. In contrast to the cold efficiency of the online booking system, service is delightfully friendly. Sadly, texture was lacking throughout our meal. Although dishes such as the Josper-smoked aubergine with buffalo mozzarella tasted great, all its constituent parts were squishy, and the white chocolate cheesecake forfeited its crunch by being immersed in the (delicious) juices of a strawberry and basil salad.
Babies and children welcome: children's menu; high chairs; nappy-changing facilities. Booking essential dinner and weekends. Disabled: lift; toilet. Tables outdoors (4, pavement).

Crystal Palace

Joanna's
56 Westow Hill, SE19 1RX (8670 4052, www.joannas. uk.com). Crystal Palace or Gipsy Hill rail. **Breakfast served** 10am-noon daily. **Meals served** noon-11pm Mon-Sat; noon-10.30pm Sun. **Main courses** £9.95-£25.95. **Set meal** (lunch Mon-Sat, dinner Mon-Thur) £8.95 1 course, £12.95 2 courses, £16.95 3 courses. **Credit** AmEx, MC, V.
Opened in 1978 as a burger bar and piano joint, Joanna's has matured into a relaxed, colonial-style dining room with comfortable leather chairs, linen-clad tables and whirring ceiling fans. It's hard to believe that the maître d's reception booth, the well-stocked dark wood bar, and the wood/glass screens haven't been here since the Belle Epoque. Food also leans towards the traditional – roast beef and yorkshire, lobster, crispy haddock goujons with minted pea purée, a fluffy cottage pie, caesar salad – and there's a fine selection of steaks and proper burgers. Classics from other cultures appear too, such as king prawn tempura with soy, chilli and coriander. A warm chorizo and pan-fried new potato salad demonstrated that the kitchen knows how to poach an egg, which bodes well for the brunch menu. Desserts are old school: squidgy chocolate brownie sundae, a subtly spiced caramelised apple pancake with vanilla ice-cream. Happy, chattering south Londoners create a bustling atmosphere, and the friendly staff welcome children. The best tables are by the windows, with views as far as the City. For long business lunches or clandestine trysts, nab the private booth tucked at the back, .
Babies and children welcome until 6pm: booster seats; children's menu; high chairs. Booking advisable; essential weekends. Tables outdoors (3, pavement).

North East
Dalston

Towpath `HOT 50`
2010 RUNNER-UP BEST NEW CAFÉ
Regent's Canal towpath, between Whitmore Bridge and Kingsland Road Bridge, N1 5SB (no phone). Haggerston rail. **Open** 8am-dusk Tue-Fri; 9am-dusk Sat; 10am-dusk Sun. **Main courses** £3-£6.50. **No credit cards**.

The joggers, cyclists and narrowboats that patrol the Dalston stretch of the Regent's Canal were thrown off course for a while in early 2010, when Towpath first appeared on the bank of the waterway. Surely this tiny café, with its gourmet Florentine coffee, precise Italian food and summer-garden furniture covered in rustic flour sacks had no place amid the housing estates and decaying warehouses of waterside Hackney. It was opened without the faintest whisper of publicity by food writer Lori De Mori and her husband, photographer Jason Lowe, but word soon spread and on sunny days, hordes of hungry visitors hover around hoping for a seat. An ingenious response to overcrowding is a moored pontoon, equipped with more tables. The appeal is obvious; Towpath is a whimsical one-off and as idyllic as it's possible to be so close to the Kingsland Road. It is also committed to serving simple, seasonal food from a chalked-up menu (granola or porridge with quince at breakfast, pork rillettes with piccalilli, or roast lamb with anchovy and chard later). It feels like a real labour of love: wilfully small-scale – there's no takeaway, even for coffee – and unaffectedly personal.
Babies and children admitted. Bookings not accepted. Tables outdoors (7, towpath).

Hackney Wick

Hackney Pearl
2010 WINNER BEST NEW CAFÉ
11 Prince Edward Road, E9 5LX (8510 3605, www. thehackneypearl.com). Hackney Wick rail. **Open** 10am-11pm, **lunch served** 10am-4pm, **dinner served** 6-10pm Tue-Sun. **Main courses** £9.50-£14.50. **Credit** MC, V.
At the vibrant heart of the artists' enclave of Hackney Wick, Hackney Pearl is a café-bar that's very sure of itself and perfectly fits the brief for a friendly neighbourhood hangout. With its community-focused informality, the place feels like a reaction to 'regeneration projects' promised by developers. The owners have made something special out of not very much. Two former shop units are enlivened by a set-up that seems salvaged from a rather groovy thrift shop: colourful rugs, Formica tables, and old dressers. The compact menu lists simple but imaginative food: a bright Turkish-style meze plate with superb bread, or sweetcorn fritters with chilli jam and crème fraîche, for instance. Evenings are occasionally given over to guest chefs from London restaurants such as St John. You're also treated to well-sourced drinks (Square Mile coffee, Meantime beer, bloody marys, an extensive wine list) and an atmosphere so relaxed it's almost horizontal. The venue has become at one with the Wick through involvement with artists' studios and events such as the Hackney Wicked festival. It may be out of the way for most, but a visit here is a heartening experience whether you arrive from Fish Island or Eel Pie Island.
Available for hire. Babies and children welcome: high-chairs; nappy-changing facilities. Booking advisable. Disabled: toilet. Tables outdoors (7, terrace). Takeaway service.

North
Camden Town & Chalk Farm

Lanka
2010 RUNNER-UP BEST NEW CAFÉ
71 Regent's Park Road, NW1 8UY (7483 2544, www. lanka-uk.com). Chalk Farm tube. **Open** 9am-7pm Mon-Fri; 8am-7pm Sat, Sun. **Credit** MC, V.

Harrison's. See p49.

There's one huge, unimpeachable reason for visiting this prim and proper Primrose Hill café, and it's not the refined decor, the plum location on Regent's Park Road or the gourmet teas and coffees, commendable as they all are. The glass counter display, the first thing to grab the attention upon entering this slender room, holds the answer. Chef Masayuki Hara's cakes, pastries, tarts, confections, macaroons and desserts – delectable sweetmeats that would delight the finest Parisian pâtissier – are here finessed further with Japanese micro-engineering. These delicate creations are a grown-up riposte to the toy-box cupcakes currently rotting the teeth of the fashionable across London. Eastern flavours such as green tea, sesame and ponzu are used with traditional fruits, nuts, glazes and mousses. Teas are all imported from Sri Lanka, and include rare loose-leaf blends (many available boxed), fruit infusions and iced tea cocktails. With such exceptional afters to be had, it's perhaps not surprising that savouries don't always measure up, and you might need to spend big to leave Lanka stuffed. But it would be a strong-willed visitor indeed who managed a trip here without sampling a superlative cake.
Babies and children welcome. Tables outdoors (2, pavement). Takeaway service. **Map 27 A2**.

Islington

Ottolenghi HOT 50
287 Upper Street, N1 2TZ (7288 1454, www. ottolenghi.co.uk). Angel tube or Highbury & Islington tube/rail. **Meals served** 8am-10pm Mon-Wed; 8am-10.30pm Thur-Sat; 9am-7pm Sun. **Main courses** £8-£10. **Credit** AmEx, MC, V.
Most Ottolenghi outlets (there are four in London at the time of writing) are small traiteur/takeaway set-ups, but the Islington branch has tables to seat around 50, and a kitchen producing food from breakfast until late. The still-cool, mostly white interior (there's the odd coloured Panton chair at the communal Corian table) is the epitome of sleek, all the better to put the focus on the colourful dishes. Mornings feature toasters on the table to DIY, a cornucopia of breads, muffins and pastries at front, and hot delights such as brioche french toast with yoghurt and compote, and buffalo mozzarella tortilla with red pepper salsa. At lunch the emphasis is on the inventive Mediterranean-inspired salads displayed so appetisingly on the counter. Then there's dinner, for which you must book, or risk never trying. Dishes are generously meze-sized and designed for sharing; in a good meal for two you would enjoy six to eight and even with that number to play with, whittling down the choices isn't easy. Delicate deep-fried courgette flowers with herby ricotta stuffing and a drizzle of date syrup encapsulates seasonality, skill and flair, while baby squid, lightly crusted with spices, and served with faro and saffron-scented yoghurt typifies the originality that have made owner Yotam Ottolenghi's cookbooks such hits.
Babies and children welcome: high chairs. Booking advisable dinner; not accepted lunch. Tables outdoors (2, pavement). Takeaway service. **Map 5 O1**.
For branches see index.

North West

Queen's Park

Hugo's
21-25 Lonsdale Road, NW6 6RA (7372 1232). Queen's Park tube/rail. **Meals served** 9.30am-11pm daily. **Main courses** £11.50-£15.80. **Credit** MC, V.
Tucked down a row of pretty, commercial mews buildings, off Salusbury Road with its chichi independent cafés and shops, Hugo's feels like a neighbourhood secret. The locals seem to like it and come for the all-day brunch menu and unfussy alternatives. Deep-red walls and simple wooden furniture suggest a warmth that isn't always matched by the somewhat diffident staff. The atmosphere is laid-back, sometimes too much so; our weekday lunch of eggs florentine and burger and chips took well over 30 minutes to arrive. None of the other diners seemed surprised by the wait; perhaps they're regulars. When it came, the eggs florentine was perfectly put together: soft egg perched on tasty spinach and an English muffin, with creamy hollandaise on top. The burger and chips were disappointing, though; both lacked flavour, and the chips weren't crisp enough. When we asked to see a dessert menu, we were told the chefs hadn't had time to make any because they were preparing for a charity event in the evening. OK, we were offered strawberries and ice-cream, and perhaps it seems churlish to complain under the circumstances, but for us, this confirmed the impression that Hugo's could try harder.
Available for hire. Babies and children welcome: crayons; high chairs; nappy-changing facilities. Booking advisable weekends. Entertainment: musicians 8pm Thur, Sun. Tables outdoors (7, pavement). Takeaway service. **Map 1 A1**.

British

The British food renaissance continues, with new restaurants opening in the past year including **Hix** (winner of our Best New Restaurant award 2010), **Dean Street Townhouse**, the **Old Brewery** and **Palmers** – all notable, but refreshingly different in attitude, pricing and type. It's also worth underlining what quality there is on offer: a good few of London's Britpack number among the best places to eat in any cuisine: big-hitters include **Rhodes Twenty Four**, **St John**, **Launceston Place**, **Albermarle** and **Corrigan's Mayfair**. Easier on the pocket, but also playing their part in reinvigorating the native cuisine are the likes of **Hereford Road**, **Rochelle Canteen** and **Great Queen Street** – and you won't need a jacket in any of them.

We have to report two losses amid this expansion: Farringdon's handsome **Quality Chop House**, originally opened in the late 19th century, and relaunched in the early 1980s. It's to be hoped that it will reopen in some form. **Konstam**, the eat-local champion in King's Cross, was another one to go under.

If meat is particularly dear to your heart (and stomach), also take a look at London's classic British restaurants (*see opposite*) and best steakhouses (*see p31*), many of them with a Brit flavour.

Central

City

Rhodes Twenty Four
24th floor, Tower 42, Old Broad Street, EC2N 1HQ (7877 7703, www.rhodes24.co.uk). Bank tube/DLR or Liverpool Street tube/rail. **Lunch served** noon-2.15pm, **dinner served** 6-8.30pm Mon-Fri. **Main courses** £18.50-£29.80. **Credit** AmEx, DC, MC, V.
Food and views at Rhodes Twenty Four, perched high above the City, are consistently amazing. By contrast, the decor is almost offensively bland. No matter, concentrate on the plate or the skyline instead. Starters range from cauliflower soup with a lightly spiced seared scallop, to oxtail cottage pie with red wine gravy. We loved the warm ticklemore goat's cheese and ramson (wild garlic) tartlet: very creamy but cut with a delicious tang. Star main was Blythburgh pork loin with braised, smoked bacon potatoes, caramelised apples and pork gravy: all cooked just-so, the flavours ideally matched, and with the bonus of a sliver of perfect crackling. Almost as sublime was a fractionally undercooked pan-fried black sea bream, with a foam-topped English tomato and basil risotto and a crisp fennel salad. A varied selection of (six) tip-top cheeses makes a fine finish, or there are the likes of warm date pudding with toffee sauce and sticky toffee ice-cream. Petits fours are equally lovely. Such excellence doesn't come cheap – three courses cost around £50, and the hefty wine list will add substantially to the bill. Staff are well drilled yet very approachable, which gives the bar and dining room a relaxed air, despite the inevitable preponderance of suits. Similarly assured food is offered in more flamboyant surroundings at Rhodes W1 in the Cumberland hotel next to Marble Arch, where there's both a brasserie and a restaurant.
Available for hire. Babies and children welcome: high chair. Booking essential, 2-4 wks in advance. Disabled: lift; toilet. Dress: smart casual. **Map 12 Q6.**
For branch (Rhodes W1) see index.

Clerkenwell & Farringdon

Medcalf
38-40 Exmouth Market, EC1R 4QE (7833 3533, www. medcalfbar.co.uk). Farringdon tube/rail or 19, 38, 341 bus. **Lunch served** noon-3pm Mon-Fri; noon-4pm Sat, Sun. **Dinner served** 6-10pm Mon-Thur; 5.30-10.30pm Fri; 5.30-10pm Sat. **Main courses** £8.50-£14.50. **Credit** MC, V.

British classics

The following restaurants have either been around for a 100 years or more (Rules was established in 1798), or just feel as though they have. All offer a 'best of British' experience, with game, roasts and fine wines to the fore; none of them is exactly a bargain. Dress smartly.

Boisdale of Belgravia

13-15 Eccleston Street, SW1W 9LX (7730 6922, www.boisdale.co.uk). Victoria tube/rail.
Bar **Open** noon-1am Mon-Fri; 6pm-1am Sat.
Restaurant **Lunch served** noon-2.30pm Mon-Fri.
Dinner served 6-11.15pm Mon-Sat.
All things Scottish (as well as cigars and evening jazz) are celebrated at this tartan-clad Belgravia restaurant and bar. Hebridean crab, Ayrshire bacon, Aberdeenshire beef and, of course, haggis all make an appearance on a menu that also features salads and pasta dishes while majoring in meat, fish and game. The list of whiskies is a long one.
Map 15 H10.
For branch (Boisdale of Bishopsgate) see index.

Goring Hotel

Beeston Place, Grosvenor Gardens, SW1W 0JW (7396 9000, www.goringhotel.co.uk). Victoria tube/rail. **Breakfast served** 7-10am Mon-Fri; 7-10.30am Sat; 7.30-10.30am Sun. **Lunch served** 12.30-2.30pm Mon-Fri, Sun. **Dinner served** 6-10pm daily.
The dining room at this family-run hotel has moved with the times, and these days sports a Linley-furnished interior and Swarovski chandeliers. Classic dishes have been lightly revamped too – the Goring fish cake comes with pea shoots and clam chowder – but the glory of the cheese trolley remains.
Map 15 H9.

Boisdale

Goring Hotel

Rules

35 Maiden Lane, WC2E 7LB (7836 5314, www.rules.co.uk). Covent Garden tube. **Meals served** noon-11.30pm Mon-Sat; noon-10.30pm Sun.
Proud of its position as London's oldest restaurant, Rules does well not to have become a complete tourist trap. The atmospheric premises, punctilious waiters and classic dishes (Morecambe Bay potted shrimps, raspberry syllabub trifle) are matched by a wine list to reckon with.
Map 18 E5.

Simpson's-in-the-Strand

100 Strand, WC2R 0EW (7836 9112, www.simpsonsinthestrand.co.uk). Embankment tube or Charing Cross tube/rail. **Breakfast served** 7.15-10.30am Mon-Fri. **Lunch served** 12.15-2.45pm Mon-Sat; 12.15-3pm Sun. **Dinner served** 5.45-10.45pm Mon-Sat; (Grand Divan) 6-9pm Sun.
The glory days of Simpson's may be behind it and the Grand Divan dining room showing signs of age, but the traditional dishes (lobster soup, steak and kidney pudding, treacle sponge), plus the roast beef on its silver-domed trolley, still pull in the diners.
Map 18 E5.

Wiltons

55 Jermyn Street, SW1Y 6LX (7629 9955, www.wiltons.co.uk). Green Park or Piccadilly Circus tube. **Lunch served** noon-2.30pm, **dinner served** 6-10.30pm Mon-Fri.
A glimpse of a more privileged way of life comes at a price at this discreet St James's stalwart, recently enlivened by the arrival of Andrew Turner as head chef. Diners are cosseted by motherly waitresses, and served the likes of beef consommé followed by game (grouse, venison, woodcock) or a tip-top mixed grill. Single gents tend to perch at the oyster bar.
Map 17 B5.

BRITISH

Dean Street Townhouse. See p57.

These two knocked together rooms, with a bar and a small patio, all furnished in a pleasing, slightly beaten-up way, give no hint of the sterling nature of the kitchen here. The look of the place, and the vast choice of drinks (from sherry to draught cider, with plenty of wine and bottled beer in between), lead you to expect a good night out rather than a fine feed. Lunch is laid-back, and there's space in which to admire the current art exhibition; evenings are more hectic, but either way, it's always worth ordering some food. Typical starters might be duck heart and lardons on toast, or broccoli and stilton soup

with garlic croûtons, followed by pan-fried plaice with leeks, fennel and brown shrimp butter, or guinea fowl with chargrilled treviso and broad beans. Big, meaty dishes – such as lamb rump with fondant potato, roast shallot and runner beans – are flavour-packed winners. Traditional puddings complete the menu: bakewell tart with clotted cream, or baked vanilla cheesecake with cherry compote, for example. Around for a few years now, Medcalf is well on its way to becoming an Exmouth Market stalwart.

Babies and children welcome: high chairs. Booking advisable dinner. Disabled: toilet. Separate room for parties, seats 18. Tables outdoors (7, pavement; 5, garden). **Map 5 N4**.

St John

26 St John Street, EC1M 4AY (7251 0848, www.stjohn restaurant.com). Barbican tube or Farringdon tube/rail. **Lunch served** noon-3pm Mon-Fri; 1-3pm Sun. **Dinner served** 6-11pm Mon-Sat. **Main courses** £13.50-£22.50. **Credit** AmEx, DC, MC, V.

St John opened in 1994 and in the intervening years has managed to become world famous without losing its mojo. Fergus Henderson's ideals – central to which is 'nose to tail' eating – remain vital to the enterprise, and the place (a white-painted ex-smokehouse) still looks much the same. The spacious ground-floor bar serves the likes of mighty cheese sandwiches, grilled whitebait and melt-in-the-mouth eccles cakes. The full menu, available in the first-floor restaurant, changes with every sitting, and is always devotedly seasonal. In early summer, starters of peas in the pod, berkswell cheese with broad beans, and brown crab meat on toast are typical; follow these with smoked eel, potato and sorrel, or ox heart with beetroot and horseradish. Spotted dick and custard is welcome throughout the year; we're also very fond of the sorbet-with-a-glass-of-vodka combos. Staff are professional but not starchy, the atmosphere is relaxed, and prices are slightly under what other well-fêted restaurants would charge. Bottles from the largely French wine list can be bought to take home, as can the bread and some baked goods. These are produced at St John Bread & Wine in Spitalfields, which has the same ethos and decor in one big room, but is more brasserie-like, with a slew of dishes costing around £7 (cured lamb and green tomatoes, say). The big news for 2010 is that the St John Hotel, restaurant and bar is opening in autumn in the old Manzi's building off Leicester Square.

Babies and children welcome: high chairs. Booking advisable dinner and weekends. Disabled: toilet (bar). Separate room for parties, seats 18. **Map 5 O5**.
For branches (St John Bread & Wine, St John Hotel) see index.

Gloucester Road

Launceston Place

1A Launceston Place, W8 5RL (7937 6912, www.dandd london.com). Gloucester Road tube. **Lunch served** noon-2.30pm Tue-Sat; noon-3pm Sun. **Dinner served** 6-10.30pm Mon-Sat; 6.30-9.30pm Sun. **Set lunch** £20 3 courses; (Sun) £26 3 courses. **Set dinner** £45 3 courses, £58 tasting menu. **Credit** AmEx, MC, V.

The set lunch here is among London's best-value deals. Head chef Tristan Welch is clearly a magician. Portions are generous, there's no skimping on ingredients, and you get many extras: in our case, a dreamy fresh yoghurt amuse bouche, followed later by Pimm's jelly with a bracing lime granita; every table

BRITISH

also sports ultra-posh crisps. Food quality is amazing: duck egg on toast with Somerset truffles was a near-divine medley; beef (meat and marrow) with beetroot risotto and wild garlic sauce was wildly rich and moreish; even tomato soup with basil cappuccino had a beautiful combination of flavours. The best main course – despite heavy competition – was Denham Castle lamb with prettily piped pommes purée. Cornish mackerel with cucumber and pickled onions had the looks, but couldn't beat the lamb for taste, while pork crubeens (fried patties) with onions, capers and mustard was wickedly good, yet slightly too much for a hot day. Perfectly summery was a super-light, dark chocolate and raspberry mousse, but most memorable was the pan-sized tarte tatin (for two) with clotted cream: a heavenly, heavily caramelised apple-fest. Service is professional, but comes with a smile. The warren of dark interlinked rooms won't be to everyone's taste, but they add cosiness to what is quite a 'haute' experience. Big spenders can try the tasting menu, and delve into the serious wine list.
Available for hire. Babies and children welcome: high chairs. Booking advisable. Disabled: toilet. Separate room for parties, seats 10. **Map 7 C9.**

Holborn

Great Queen Street
32 Great Queen Street, WC2B 5AA (7242 0622). Covent Garden or Holborn tube.
Bar **Open** 5-11.30pm Tue-Sat.
Restaurant **Lunch served** noon-2.30pm Mon-Sat; noon-3pm Sun. **Dinner served** 6-10.30pm Mon-Sat.
Main courses £10.80-£22.
Both **Credit** MC, V.
A back-to-basics Brit restaurant, all rough-hewn tables and minimal decoration, where the draw is the food. Great Queen Street's very seasonal menu changes often. Though the kitchen is known for its big, meaty dishes, the likes of baked egg and peppers; chilled beetroot and yoghurt soup; or cured sea trout and pickled cucumber also please. Scottish onglet, roast Tamworth with gooseberry sauce, or pig and game terrine satisfy hearty appetites. At dinner there are usually sharing dishes to be had, such as chicken pie (for two) or seven-hour lamb shoulder with dauphinoise potatoes (for four or five). Puddings, such as apricot and almond tart or chocolate fritters, always include a very good own-made ice-cream or sorbet. We like the regularly changing aperitif too; a summer's lunch might feature elderflower and prosecco fizz. Staff are young and efficient, but don't stand on ceremony – the atmosphere is relaxed and the room can get noisy. Sister to the Anchor & Hope gastropub in Waterloo, GQS has the great advantage over its sibling that you can book a table.
Babies and children admitted. Booking advisable. Disabled: toilet. Tables outdoors (4, pavement). **Map 18 E3.**

Mayfair

Albemarle
Brown's Hotel, 33-34 Albemarle Street, W1S 4BP (7493 6020, www.thealbemarlerestaurant.com). Green Park tube.
Lunch served noon-3pm Mon-Sat; 12.30-3pm Sun.
Dinner served 6-10.30pm Mon-Sat; 7-10.30pm Sun.
Main courses £14.50-£32.50. **Set meal** £25 2 courses, £30 3 courses. **Credit** AmEx, DC, MC, V.
The modern art-strewn dining room at Brown's Hotel is so much more enticing than most hotel restaurants. A blend of period and modern furnishings, comfortable chairs and charming staff makes for a relaxed and enjoyable meal – even before you get to the excitement of the menu. Seasonal British ingredients are used throughout. Start, perhaps, with gull's eggs with celery salt and mayonnaise, or Cornish lambs' sweetbreads with wild boar bacon and ramsons (wild garlic)/ Next, Newlyn monkfish curry, Kingairloch red deer fillet with neeps and haggis, or chargrilled Kentish lamb cutlets with bubble and squeak. Finish with Worcester rhubarb and bramely apple crumble (for two) or ginger parkin. There are also savouries, cheeses and a lunchtime carving trolley bearing a different beast every day (Sunday sees roast rib of Hereford beef with yorkshire pudding). Vegetarians get their own menu, and there's a great-value set meal (which on Sunday includes the roast). The wine list and level of service are all you'd expect from an establishment owned by Rocco Forte, but it's executive chef Lee Streeton's kitchen that makes the place.
Babies and children welcome: children's menu; crayons; high chairs. Booking advisable. Disabled: toilet (hotel). Separate rooms for parties, seating 2-70. Vegetarian menu. **Map 9 J7.**

Corrigan's Mayfair
28 Upper Grosvenor Street, W1K 7EH (7499 9943, www.corrigansmayfair.com). Marble Arch tube. **Lunch served** noon-3pm Mon-Fri; noon-4pm Sun. **Dinner served** 6-10.30pm Mon-Sat; 6-9.30pm Sun. **Main courses** £9-£26. **Set lunch** (Mon-Fri) £27 3 courses incl carafe of wine. **Set meal** (Sun) £27 3 courses.
Credit AmEx, MC, V.
For high-end dining with a friendly smile, it's hard to beat Richard Corrigan's restaurant. Given this, Corrigan's appeals as much to those spending their own money as it does to the expense-account crowd. There's a chef's table for the ultimate show-off treat. The premises are Mayfair-luxe, with super-white linen, comfortable bucket chairs and well-spaced tables. The simple dish descriptions don't do justice to the works of art that appear on the plate, or indeed the flavours involved. Start with beef shin consommé and horseradish dumplings, fillet of mackerel and rhubarb compote, or leek, potato and sheep's cheese torte. Then move on to john dory with red wine and razor clam, saddle of wild rabbit with girolles and asparagus, or Elwy Valley lamb with broad beans and confit bacon. Sides include goose-fat chips. Finish with rice pudding, toasted nuts and hot caramel, crème caramel or Thai mango with chilli and lime. The 300-strong wine list proudly showcases many small producers; most diners will be happy to rely on the helpful sommelier to walk them though it. The weekday set lunch is a snip for cooking of this quality.
Babies and children welcome: high chairs. Booking essential. Disabled: toilet. Separate rooms for parties, seating 8-30. **Map 9 G7.**

Dorchester Grill Room
The Dorchester, 53 Park Lane, W1K 1QA (7629 8888, www.thedorchester.com). Hyde Park Corner tube.
Breakfast served 7-10.30am Mon-Fri; 8-11am Sat, Sun.
Lunch served noon-2.30pm Mon-Fri; 12.30-3.30pm Sat, Sun. **Dinner served** 6.30-11pm Mon-Fri; 6-11pm Sat; 7-10.30pm Sun. **Main courses** £19-£46. **Set lunch** (Mon-Sat) £21.50 2 courses, £25.50 3 courses. **Set dinner** (6.30-7.30pm) £25.50 2 courses, £29.50 3 courses. **Set meal** £60-£80 tasting menu (£85.50-£115.50 incl wine).
Credit AmEx, DC, MC, V.

BRITISH

More fun than a hotel dining room has any right to be, the Grill Room is decorated with crazy Scots warrior murals and tartan a-go-go, and staffed by a professional yet unstarchy crew. The dress code is relaxed – possibly a little too relaxed for those who don't want to see American leisurewear while fine dining. The set lunch and dinner menus are such good value that we rarely stray; those wishing to experience the full carte can expect hefty prices and the same excellent cooking from the kitchen of head chef Brian Hughson. Grills range from dover sole with spinach and fondant potatoes to fillet of Angus beef with wild garlic barley risotto, bacon, onion and mushroom. Spring onion and lime ravioli with samphire, broad beans and fennel is a less meaty option. Starters might be seared Orkney scallops with sardine pie and cauliflower purée, or wild English rabbit and brawn terrine with parsley purée and piccalilli sauce. Finish in style with excellent coffee and petits fours.
Babies and children welcome (Sat, Sun): high chairs. Booking advisable; essential weekends. Disabled: toilet. Dress: smart casual. **Map 9 G7**.

Soho

Dean Street Townhouse

69-71 Dean Street, W1D 4QJ (7434 1775, www.dean streettownhouse.com). Piccadilly Circus or Tottenham Court Road tube. **Breakfast served** 7.30-11.30am, **tea served** 3-6pm daily. **Meals served** 11.30am-11.30pm Mon-Sat; 11.30am-10.30pm Sun. **Main courses** £15-£24. **Set meal** (5-7.30pm) £17 2 courses, £21 3 courses. **Credit** AmEx, MC, V.

Dean Street Townhouse is a fine hotel with a neighbouring dining room and bar that look sultry, even a little burlesque, under permanently low lights. The food is old-fashioned British and includes a superb mince and tatties – piquant, properly browned, full-flavoured, wonderful in texture, and tasting of… childhood. Yes, the Soho House group, still one of the coolest hospitality outfits in our city, has decided that the future is sherry trifle or treacle sponge with custard. Despite dishes such as grilled squid with spiced chickpeas, or Cornish

Hix. See p58.

brill with ceps, much of the menu is deeply retro. It's also unusually well done, with such precision in the cooking and marvellous flavours that it would make any 1970s dinner-party host proud. Salt beef was near gelatinous in texture, yet an explosion of flavour; the brussels sprouts were young, tender, lightly cooked and nutty in taste. Try Dean Street for high tea, if it takes your fancy: sardines on toast, fish fingers and chips, and macaroni cheese are among the many temptations. Dining by the bar is busy, cramped and loud, so get a seat in the quieter dining room if you can.

Babies and children welcome: high chairs; nappy-changing facilities. Booking essential. Disabled: toilet. Separate room for parties, seats 12. Tables outdoors (7, terrace). **Map 17 B3**.

Hix HOT 50

2010 WINNER BEST NEW RESTAURANT
2010 RUNNER-UP BEST NEW BAR
66-70 Brewer Street, W1F 9UP (7292 3518, www.hix soho.co.uk). Piccadilly Circus tube. **Lunch served** noon-5.30pm daily. **Dinner served** 5.30-11.30pm Mon-Sat; 5.30-10.30pm Sun. **Main courses** £14.75-£35.50. **Set meal** (4.30-6.30pm, 10.30-11.30pm Mon-Sat; noon-10.30pm Sun) £15.50 2 courses, £19.50 3 courses. **Credit** AmEx, MC, V.
Although both Hix (Soho) and Hix Oyster & Chop House (Smithfield) are recognisably siblings, the newer Brewer Street joint is altogether more slick. The dimly lit basement bar, Mark's, is a homage to New York – albeit with a bar billiards table – from the tin ceiling tiles to the professionally mixed cocktails (try a lovely, lip-pursing Forbidden Sour). The ground-floor dining room is more modern and pared down, but boasts crazy mobiles by YBAs Damien Hirst and Sarah Lucas. Prices are centre-of-town high: a starter of whipped broad beans with goat's curd and broad bean flowers (fried in scrumpy) cost £10.25. However, as with all the starters we tried – 'heaven and earth' (a mousse-like black pudding), prawn cocktail, and salt beef salad – it was delightful. Next, from a set of mains including hangar steak with beets, watercress and horseradish, fish fingers with chips and mushy peas, and Blythburgh pork chop with wild fennel and Mendip snails, only the chop disappointed – it was just too dry. Puddings range from traditional (ice-creams and summer pudding) to unusual (sea buckthorn berry posset). All were top-notch. The wine list is similarly assured. Service throughout is friendly yet professional. All in all, much though we like the more meat-obsessed, male-heavy Hix Oyster & Chop House, this Soho operation has snatched pole position. The latest addition to the stable is a restaurant and champagne bar in Selfridges.
Available for hire. Babies and children welcome: high chairs; nappy-changing facilities. Booking advisable. Disabled: toilet. Separate room for parties, seats 10. **Map 17 A4**.
For branches (Hix at Selfridges, Hix Oyster & Chop House) see index.

Quo Vadis

26-29 Dean Street, W1D 3LL (7437 9585, www.quo vadissoho.co.uk). Leicester Square, Piccadilly Circus or Tottenham Court Road tube. **Lunch served** noon-2.30pm, **dinner served** 5.30-10.30pm Mon-Sat. **Main courses** £12.50-£27. **Set meal** (noon-2.30pm, 5.30-6.30pm) £17.50 2 courses, £19.50 3 courses. **Cover** £2. **Credit** AmEx, MC, V.
A Soho classic that's aged gracefully, partly thanks to current owners Sam and Eddie Hart, partly because Quo Vadis has always been beautiful. Light shines through stained-glass windows on white linen, gleaming glassware and mirrors; modern art adds interest. Tables can seem cramped when it's busy, but lunches are calmer and staff have more time for diners. Our primary beef is with the food; not every dish is as special as prices suggest. The set lunch is reasonable value, but add the cover charge, vegetables (around a fiver), a glass of wine and service and it's hard to escape for under £35. And although pistou, followed by lamb rump with vegetables, then bitter chocolate mousse topped with salted caramel, was fine, only the main course was memorable. From the carte – broadly British, with continental flourishes – a starter of beetroot and st tola (an Irish goat's cheese) tart and a main of john dory with peas and baby gem looked and tasted good, but so they should at £7.50 and £21.50 respectively. Triple-cooked chips are worth ordering, yet overall the meal failed to match the setting. Upstairs you'll find a members' club and private dining rooms.
Booking advisable. Babies and children admitted. Separate rooms for parties, seating 12 and 24. Tables outdoors (6, terrace). **Map 17 B3**.

West

Bayswater

Hereford Road

3 Hereford Road, W2 4AB (7727 1144, www.hereford road.org). Bayswater tube. **Lunch served** noon-3pm Mon-Fri; noon-3.30pm Sat; noon-4pm Sun. **Dinner served**

Quo Vadis

BRITISH

Old Brewery

6-10.30pm Mon-Sat; 6-10pm Sun. **Main courses** 9.50-£14.50. **Set lunch** (Mon-Fri) £13 2 courses, £15.50 3 courses. **Credit** AmEx, MC, V.

Opened in autumn 2007, Hereford Road has – quite rightly – become a must-visit destination, particularly for fans of the St John diaspora. Chef Tom Pemberton used to run the kitchen at St John Bread & Wine, and it shows in the best possible way. Duck livers with green beans and tarragon, or beetroot, sorrel and cow's curd could be followed by roast wood pigeon with broad beans and bacon, or grilled mackerel with roast tomatoes and crème fraîche; puddings include the likes of rhubarb eton mess or rum and raisin ice-cream. It's all good honest stuff cooked well and without fuss. The short yet intriguing wine list includes options by the glass and carafe. The building is a nicely designed refit of what was a butcher's shop; the restaurant is a long rectangle, but never dark thanks to a huge circular skylight and some white tiled walls. Cheerful, efficient staff add to the positive experience of dining here. The lunch deals are very generous indeed given the all-round quality. *Babies and children welcome: high chairs. Booking advisable. Disabled: toilet. Tables outdoors (3, pavement).* **Map 7 B6**.

South East

East Dulwich

Franklins

157 Lordship Lane, SE22 8HX (8299 9598, www. franklinsrestaurant.com). East Dulwich rail. **Meals served** 11am-10.30pm Mon-Fri; 10am-10.30pm Sat; noon-10pm Sun. **Main courses** £11-£18. **Set lunch** (noon-5pm Mon-Fri Jan-Nov) £13.50 2 courses, £16.50 3 courses. **Credit** AmEx, MC, V.

British food is taken seriously at this restaurant/bar, both the provenance and the miles it has to travel – so vegetables come from Kent, oysters from Mersea Island, mutton from an organic farm in Berkshire. The end result is commendable, though prices are rather high for a local restaurant (a starter of brandade and toast costs £8, and calf's liver with spinach and bacon is £15.50). Thank heavens for the set lunch: three courses from the main menu and no skimping. The front bar (stripped wood and leather sofas) retains its pub-like charm, while the small back-room restaurant is a simple brick-walled space with a view into the kitchen. Dishes are at the robust end of Brit dining. There's always something like rolled spleen with red onions, parsley, radish and cornichons (a starter) on the menu, plus more populist options, such as whole rainbow trout with cucumber, fennel and dill, or fillet of beef with horseradish. To finish, choose from puds (chocolate pot, bread and butter pudding), cheeses or savouries. Franklins also runs a farm shop at no.155, where dishes are available to take away. *Available for hire. Babies and children welcome: high chairs; nappy-changing facilities. Booking advisable. Disabled: toilet. Separate room for parties, seats 34. Tables outdoors (4, pavement).* **Map 23 C4**.

Greenwich

Old Brewery

2010 WINNER BEST NEW DESIGN
2010 RUNNER-UP BEST NEW LOCAL RESTAURANT
Pepys Building, Old Royal Naval College, SE10 9LW (3327 1280, www.oldbrewerygreenwich.com). Cutty Sark DLR.

BRITISH

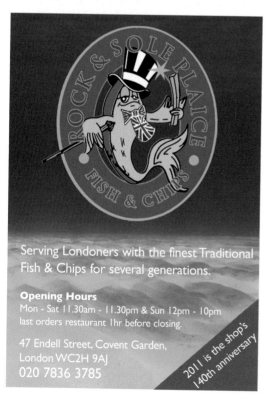

Café **Meals served** 10am-5pm daily. **Main courses**
£6-£16.50.
Bar **Open** noon-11pm daily. **Lunch served** noon-5pm,
dinner served 6-10.30pm daily. **Main courses**
£6-£16.50.
Restaurant **Dinner served** 6-10.30pm daily.
Main courses £10.50-£17.50.
All **Credit** MC, V.
Set off the street in the handsome, historic Pepys building, just
behind the *Cutty Sark*, the Old Brewery is an ambitous venture.
By day it's a café for the Discover Greenwich tourist attraction
next door; by night it's a restaurant. There's a small bar, with
tables outside in a large walled courtyard – a lovely spot in
which to test the 50-strong beer list that includes the artisan
ales of the Meantime Brewery (the company behind this
operation) plus a global array of bottled varieties. Inside is a
vast, high-ceilinged space, its maroon and dark orange walls
decorated with an abstract bottle pattern and a history of
British brewing, with oversized aluminium light shades and a
wave-like artwork of bottles. Meantime's gleaming copper
brewing barrels dominate one end. Creating an intimate
atmosphere in such a cavernous venue is tricky, though the
personable young staff are friendly, and red-clothed booths
along one side offer privacy. The short menu highlights
provenance (Herdwick mutton, Cornish cockles, Kilravock pork
belly) and seasonality, with matching beers suggested for each
dish. Tasty (but lukewarm) Dorset scallops worked with the
additions of squash purée and a subtle cumin dressing; less so
curried cauliflower soup with an onion bhaji floating in it. Best
was a main of pearlescent steamed hake (a huge chunk) in a
light vegetable broth, with samphire and mussels: simple but
delicious. Clued-up locals should head here pronto; it's too good
to leave to the tourists.
Babies and children welcome: high chairs; nappy-changing
facilities. Booking advisable. Disabled: toilet. Tables outdoors
(20, garden). Takeaway service.

London Bridge & Borough

Magdalen
152 Tooley Street, SE1 2TU (7403 1342, www.magdalen
restaurant.co.uk). London Bridge tube/rail. **Lunch served**
noon-2.30pm Mon-Fri. **Dinner served** 6.30-10pm Mon-Sat.
Main courses £13.50-£20. **Set lunch** £15.50 2 courses,
£18.50 3 courses. **Credit** AmEx, MC, V.
On a corner of a fairly traffic-heavy thoroughfare, Magdalen
is easy to miss. Inside, it's unfussy yet comfortable, with a small
bar, dark plum walls and smart white linen – neither trendy
nor overly traditional. What makes the place worth discovering
is the food, which has originality, flair and personality. Kidneys,
liver, pig's head and rarer cuts of British meat are prominent,
and there's an opulent full-on character to the cooking, but
delicacy too. The kitchen's care for details should be a lesson
to not-quite-there restaurants. The frequently changing menu
makes a good read: preserved rabbit with red onion and
chickpeas turned out to be a refreshing summer salad; and
Hereford snails on toast with bone marrow and cress had a nice
punch of garlic. Most outstanding were the mains: beautifully
tender rack of veal; and a fabulously flavour-rich fish stew of
hake, plaice, clams and aïoli. To finish, a fragrant and very
cleverly executed peach jelly with pistachio ice-cream made a
perfect, delicate counterpoint. Service is welcoming and
attentive, the wine list pricey but high quality. Magdalen's
lunch menu, offering a choice from the main menu, is a gift.

Babies and children admitted. Booking advisable.
Disabled: toilet. Separate rooms for parties, seating 8-35.
Map 12 Q8.

Roast
The Floral Hall, Borough Market, Stoney Street,
SE1 1TL (7940 1300, www.roast-restaurant.com).
London Bridge tube/rail. **Breakfast served** 7-11am
Mon-Fri; 8-11.30am Sat. **Lunch served** noon-3pm Mon,
Tue; noon-4pm Wed-Sat; 11.30am-6pm Sun. **Dinner**
served 5.30-11pm Mon-Fri; 6-11pm Sat. **Main courses**
£14.50-£24.50. **Set lunch** (Sun) £22 2 courses, £26
3 courses. **Credit** AmEx, MC, V.
Roast is one hard-working establishment. Set above Borough
Market and offering expansive views of the retail action below,
it's busy from breakfast (tattie scone with smoked streaky
bacon, field mushrooms and fried egg, for instance) through
to classy bar bites (who could resist the fish fingers with
tartare sauce or cocktail chipolatas in worcestershire sauce?).
At lunch and dinner, the choice can feel overwhelming: not
only whether to have Wye Valley asparagus with minted
butter sauce or potted salt beef with gherkins and Hoxton rye
bread, followed by slow-roast Wicks Manor pork belly with
mash and bramley apple sauce, or beetroot pan haggerty with
pea shoots and poached egg – but also which of the ten-plus
side dishes to order. After this, there are the likes of toffee
apple sundae or gooseberry queen of puddings, or a selection
of English cheeses. On the plus side, quality rarely seems to
suffer, despite the many options. The drinks list is similarly
wide-ranging, with a strong suit in teas, rums, whiskies and
cocktails. Roast is equally popular for business or pleasure,
and deservedly so.
Available for hire. Babies and children welcome: children's
menu; high chairs. Booking advisable. Disabled: lift; toilet.
Dress: smart casual. **Map 11 P8**.

East

Bethnal Green

Palmers
238 Roman Road, E2 0RY (8980 5590, www.palmers
restaurant.net). Bethnal Green tube/rail or 8 bus. **Lunch**
served noon-3pm, **dinner served** 6-10.30pm Mon-Sat.
Meals served noon-9pm Sun. **Main courses** £9.50-
£16.50. **Credit** AmEx, MC, V.
Dining options on the Roman Road generally start and finish
with fried chicken, so Palmers is an eye-opener. Take a glance
at the menu: lobster and crab ravioli with parmesan crisp;
roasted cod with 'textures' of jerusalem artichoke – not your
usual East End nosh. Dishes are served in a rather bland beige
interior that's enlivened by almost biologically close-up prints
of various foodstuffs. The concise, keenly priced menu
changes regularly. Pork and rabbit rillettes were buttery,
perfectly seasoned and served with a pleasantly sharp and
fruity apricot relish. Another starter, scallops with slow-
cooked pork belly and Madeira sauce, came with a strip of
perfect crackling and a generous three bivalves; the very
friendly owner told us he visits Billingsgate several times a
week to pick up his seafood. Further evidence of his
excursions came in a stew of prawns, mussels, white fish and
new potatoes in a rich broth of tomato and dill. We also
enjoyed a comforting ribeye steak with huge hand-cut chips.

The small bar and visible kitchen reveal the intimate scale of the venture; dad runs the floor, with his sons behind the stove. A neighbourhood restaurant that's worth a journey.
Available for hire. Babies and children admitted. Booking advisable weekends. Disabled: toilet. Takeaway service.

Shoreditch

Albion

2-4 Boundary Street, E2 7DD (7729 1051, www.albion caff.co.uk). Shoreditch High Street rail. **Meals served** 8am-midnight daily. **Main courses** £8-£10. **Credit** AmEx, MC, V.

Albion is an inviting, light-filled space with big windows and pavement seating under awnings. At one end is a deli selling British produce: tins of fudge, fresh veg, baked goods. Colour is provided by red leather and wood banquettes, otherwise it's a muted palette. Brown sauce and tomato ketchup bottles sit atop white wipe-down tables, but the classy cutlery, pressed white napkins, quirky enamelware (water jugs, coffee pots) and expensive lights (Brit classic Bestlite) underline that this is no caff. The informality extends to the menu which is nicely unfussy. Reservations are only taken for large groups, so there's often a queue. Sunday brunch – a tasty but slightly skimpy kipper, an excellent full english, an enjoyable bloody mary and some superb coffee – was judged worth the wait. The all-day menu covers most bases, at reasonable prices: from a neat ham omelette or piled-high sausage and mash, to the likes of a cream tea or a late-night kedgeree. Check out the pork crackling and apple sauce appetiser: £2.25 for a mighty slice. Diners contain a sprinkling of the Shoreditch fashion crowd, but everyone is made welcome and there vibe is friendly. Young staff whisk about, mostly to good effect.
Babies and children welcome: high chairs; nappy-changing facilities. Bookings not accepted for fewer than 7 people. Disabled: toilet. Tables outdoors (10, pavement). Takeaway service. **Map 6 R4**.

Rochelle Canteen

Rochelle School, Arnold Circus, E2 7ES (7729 5677, www.arnoldandhenderson.com). Shoreditch High Street rail. **Breakfast served** 9-11am, **lunch served** noon-3pm Mon-Fri. **Main courses** £8.50-£15. **Unlicensed**. **Corkage** £5. **Credit** MC, V.

It's clear that Margot Henderson (of Arnold & Henderson, the team behind Rochelle Canteen) shares a food philosophy with her husband Fergus (founder of St John). The daily-changing lunch menu – it's not open for dinner – is brief and pithy. You could start with asparagus soup, rabbit brawn and cornichons, or peas, broad beans and rocket, before ordering roast chicken, pearl barley and aïoli, or halibut, fennel and green sauce, or lentils, beetroot and goat's curd (a St John classic). Puds might be chocolate pot or poached rhubarb and elderflower ice-cream. Whatever your options on the day, dishes will invariably be delicious, seasonal and excellent value. We like the easy-going atmosphere. Although many diners are regulars (the place started life providing lunches for the surrounding artists' studios based at the Rochelle School premises), everyone is made welcome. The small room is a plain, light-filled space; converted from an old bike shed, it has big windows and is divided into a dining area in one half, with the kitchen in the other. The view – over what was the school playground – is of a lawn. High walls keep out the realities of an E2 postcode; you'll need to ring a bell to gain entry to this arty sanctum.

Available for hire, evenings only. Babies and children welcome: high chairs; nappy-changing facilities. Booking advisable Thur, Fri. Tables outdoors (12, courtyard). **Map 6 S4**.

Spitalfields

Canteen

2 Crispin Place, off Brushfield Street, E1 6DW (0845 686 1122, www.canteen.co.uk). Liverpool Street tube/rail. **Meals served** 8am-11pm Mon-Fri; 9am-11pm Sat; 9am-10pm Sun. **Main courses** £8-£14.50. **Credit** AmEx, MC, V.

A lot of thought has gone into the design of this small chain, from the typeface on the menus to the handsome British-made furniture (the website goes into enjoyable detail about the designers involved in everything from the lighting to the coat hooks). The four branches aren't identical, but overall the result is uncluttered and quietly stylish. The menu runs from breakfast and all-day snacks (hot buttered arbroath smokie, roast tomatoes on toast) to mains (daily pies and roasts, plus the likes of lamb, potato and leek stew), taking in salads (beets, goat's curd, pea shoots and pumpkin seeds) and cakes (chocolate and beetroot cake is a must-try) along the way. Not every dish works – treacle tart with jersey cream tasted good, but had an oddly spongy texture – but on the whole prices are so reasonable that would be churlish to complain. An extensive drinks list includes British ales, ciders and perries, plus cocktails and own-made lemonade. The willing young staff add to the welcoming atmosphere. A safe bet without being bland.
Babies and children welcome: high chairs. Bookings not accepted lunch Sat, Sun. Disabled: toilet. Tables outdoors (10, plaza). Takeaway service. **Map 12 R5**.
For branches see index.

North

Camden Town & Chalk Farm

Market

43 Parkway, NW1 7PN (7267 9700, www.market restaurant.co.uk). Camden Town tube. **Lunch served** noon-2.30pm, **dinner served** 6-10.30pm Mon-Sat. **Meals served** 1-3.30pm Sun. **Main courses** £9-£14. **Set lunch** (Mon-Fri) £10 2 courses. **Credit** AmEx, DC, MC, V.

A very useful place to know, Market is an honest-to-goodness neighbourhood restaurant in an area lacking such places. An unassuming frontage hides an equally low-key dining room, with bare brick walls and zinc-topped tables. The short, regularly changing menu is broadly British with the occasional European flourish (gazpacho, say, or gnocchi with peas, broad beans and ragstone cheese). Start with a zingy salad (chicory, stilton, beetroot and walnut) or the more robust mix of salt beef with green beans, mustard and soft egg, before moving on to chicken and ham pie or whole grilled plaice with hollandaise and some of the marvellous chips. Desserts are nicely balanced between comfort puddings (steamed jam sponge) and the likes of grilled figs with pistachio ice-cream, or there's always cheese with oatcakes and chutney. The weekday set lunch is a steal. There's a roast on Sundays, a useful range of drinks and a welcoming attitude – all in all, well worth a visit.
Babies and children welcome: high chairs. Booking advisable. Separate room for parties, seats 12. Tables outdoors (2, pavement). **Map 27 C2**.

BRITISH

Chinese

The barriers are being broken down. In the past we complained that some of the most enticing dishes in London's traditional Cantonese restaurants only appeared on the Chinese-script menu. Restaurant owners believed that westerners would balk at flavour pairings such as salted fish and minced pork, or such textural treats as ducks' tongues or sea cucumber. Two changes have transformed perceptions. First, enlightened restaurateurs such as Alan Yau (creator of **Hakkasan** and **Yauatcha**) realised that Londoners were among the world's most adventurous diners, with a keen appetite for new flavours. Second, at around the same time as Yau was making Chinese food fashionable, new restaurants from the other major gastronomic regions of China started to flourish, by serving authentic, sometimes fiery dishes. **Barshu** was one of the first of the Sichuan contingent, and continues to prosper. Dalston's **Shanghai** offers dishes from Taiwan and Shanghai among its specials, and **North China** has a menu devoted to the cooking of Beijing and its vicinity. Top Cantonese restaurants have responded to these developments with daring innovations, and at **Royal China Club** you can now savour the likes of sea cucumber sautéed with foie gras.

Central

Belgravia

Hunan
51 Pimlico Road, SW1W 8NE (7730 5712, www.hunan london.com). Sloane Square tube. **Lunch served** 12.30-2pm, **dinner served** 6.30-11pm Mon-Sat. **Set meal** £39.80-£150 per person (minimum 2). **Credit** AmEx, DC, MC, V.
The past five years have seen a blossoming of authentic regional Chinese restaurants in London – but the Taiwanese family who own Hunan have been serving fare purportedly inspired by Chairman Mao's home province for far longer than that. First-time visitors are in for a treat at this menu-free establishment, where allergies and dietary requirements are noted before the kitchen creates a steady stream of little dishes (reminiscent of a tasting menu) for each table to share. The formula is the same every night, but standards are high and flavours enjoyable, if muted to suit the Pimlico business crowd. Meals start with a wonderfully light soup of chicken or crab, served in pork broth accented with ginger in a bamboo cup. Later, you'll be served roast duck – of Chinatown standard. The

quality of ingredients (meat in particular) and lightness of touch are a far cry from the fiery peasant fare typically served in central China. Diners are unlikely to leave disappointed, especially if they've sampled a fine bottle from the giant wine list; ask for Michael's help in pairing these classy vintages with the food. The dining room is elegant enough, if cramped. *Babies and children admitted. Booking essential. Vegetarian menu.* **Map 15 G11**.

Chinatown

Haozhan
8 Gerrard Street, W1D 5PJ (7434 3838, www.haozhan. co.uk). Leicester Square tube. **Meals served** noon-11.30pm Mon-Thur; noon-midnight Fri, Sat; noon-10.30pm Sun. **Main courses** £6-£38. **Set lunch** (Mon-Fri) £8 2 courses, £10 3 courses. **Credit** AmEx, MC, V.
When Haozhan opened a few years ago, it brought a touch of smartness to Chinatown's main thoroughfare. The black wood interior, the primary colour accents, and the more-fashionable-than-usual café-style tables and chairs heralded a new sophistication. Sadly, we've often been disappointed by the fusion-style dishes that emerge from the kitchen. Coffee ribs are a popular and tasty choice, but the wasabi-flavoured deep-

fried prawns are served with rather too much mayonnaise. And when does fusion become a generic mishmash? The menu is peppered with Thai curries and Malaysian flavours, leaving little that is authentically Chinese – despite the restaurant's name and location. Haozhan's Sichuanese vegetables supposedly take their influence from the fiery western Chinese province, though we found them drab and bland. In contrast, a clay pot of Taiwanese sanpei (chicken thighs braised in their own liquid with peppers and sweet basil) was light and flavourful. Nevertheless, it was difficult for us to be entirely comfortable eating in a purportedly Chinese restaurant that puts lobster with cheese and ham on its menu – with no apparent irony.
Babies and children welcome: high chairs. Booking advisable Wed-Sat. **Map 17 C4**.

Imperial China

White Bear Yard, 25A Lisle Street, WC2H 7BA (7734 3388, www.imperial-china.co.uk). Leicester Square or Piccadilly Circus tube. **Meals served** noon-11.30pm Mon-Sat; 11.30am-10.30pm Sun. **Dim sum served** noon-5pm daily. **Main courses** £5.90-£26.50. **Dim sum** £2.30-£3.60. **Set meal** £18-£33.50 per person (minimum 2). **Minimum** £10. **Credit** AmEx, MC, V.
An oasis of serenity in the Chinatown maelstrom, Imperial China is reached down a Lisle Street alley that opens into a little courtyard complete with wooden footbridge and bijou fishpond. Inside, you'll find a good-looking room decorated in subdued dark wood and cream hues, with linen-clothed tables and low lighting; there's extensive seating on upper floors too. The à la carte menu of Cantonese dishes is most notable for its seafood choice, with lobster, crab, abalone and sea bass jockeying for position. To accompany such a high-roller's banquet, the drinks list contains a clutch of fine wines, as well as champagnes, cocktails and sakés. Otherwise, the main-course choice consists of a mundane array of competently rendered stir-fries, with few esoteric ingredients or labour-intensive cooking techniques. More interesting (and inexpensive) is the lunchtime dim sum selection – which attracts Chinese families at the weekends, when things tend to get hectic. As well as all the usual snacks, you'll encounter such enticements as curry chicken pie, steamed beef and pineapple dumplings in 'butterfly shape', and steamed glutinous rice with meat wrapped in yam. Staff might be forgetful on occasion, but are usually hospitable.
Babies and children admitted. Booking advisable. Disabled: toilet. Separate rooms for parties, seating 10-70. Tables outdoors (5, courtyard). **Map 17 C4**.

Joy King Lau

3 Leicester Street, WC2H 7BL (7437 1132, www.joyking lau.com). Leicester Square or Piccadilly Circus tube. **Meals served** noon-11.30pm Mon-Sat; 11.30am-10.30pm Sun. **Dim sum served** noon-5pm Mon-Sat; 11am-5pm Sun. **Main courses** £6.80-£20. **Dim sum** £2.20-£4.80. **Set meal** £10-£35 per person (minimum 2). **Credit** AmEx, MC, V.
Long frequented by London's Chinese diners, Joy King Lau typifies Chinatown restaurants of the old school. Instead of any design flimflam, you get four rather cramped floors of closely packed tables behind an unpretentious frontage just off Lisle Street. A divergent bunch of dim sum devotees is attracted: young and old, tourists and Londoners, Chinese and others. Those in the know arrive early for the lunchtime snacks,

sampling reliably rendered classics such as yam croquette, prawn cheung fun or chiu chow fun gwor. Steamed dumplings can lack a little delicacy as the afternoon progresses, but useful alternatives such as curried whelks or spicy tripe are on hand. Fill up with the likes of salted fish and meat with rice, or delve into the equally extensive menu of noodle or congee dishes (fried pulled noodle with shredded meat and preserved vegetables, perhaps). The gargantuan menu of main dishes gets fewer takers, but incorporates ample marine life (lobster, crab, or abalone with fish lips, for example) among its 260 mostly stir-fried choices.
Babies and children welcome: high chairs. Booking advisable weekends. Takeaway service. **Map 17 C5**.

Fitzrovia

Hakkasan HOT 50

8 Hanway Place, W1T 1HD (7927 7000, www.hakkasan. com). Tottenham Court Road tube.
Bar **Open** noon-12.30am Mon-Wed; noon-1.30am Thur-Sat; noon-midnight Sun.
Restaurant **Lunch/dim sum served** noon-3pm Mon-Fri; noon-4pm Sat, Sun. **Dinner served** 6-11pm Mon-Wed, Sun; 6pm-midnight Thur-Sat. **Main courses** £9.50-£58. **Dim sum** £3-£20.
Both **Credit** AmEx, MC, V.
In a year when Brit cuisine, beautiful brasseries and Modern European openings have stolen the spotlight, Hakkasan is getting dangerously close to becoming stuck in the past. The setting is still gloriously recherché, a capacious basement den of sultry oriental opulence, but in more austere times it can seem slightly over-the-top. Not that the monied customers mind. They come for an elevated version of the Chinese food they know – delicate dim sum, exquisitely handcrafted and steamed, fried or braised to perfection – or for high-end dishes where the lightest fried rice might appear alongside succulent fish roasted with champagne. Even the takeaway favourite, sweetcorn soup, is given an extra luxe factor by way of sweet strands of swimmer crab. The menu reads enticingly throughout, combining traditional ingredients with modern interpretations and techniques. For atmosphere, Hakkasan is second to none; low lighting and dark-coloured walls, tables and chairs create the illusion of your neighbours fading into the darkness, while the buzz keeps the room alive. Service can be attentive and aloof in equal measure, as we've found on several visits. The excellent adjoining bar is worth a visit in its own right for its superb cocktails, globe-trotting wine list and high-quality snacks; it gets extremely busy, though.
Available for hire. Babies and children admitted. Booking essential, 6 weeks in advance. Disabled: lift; toilet. Entertainment: DJs 9pm daily. **Map 17 C2**.

Knightsbridge

Mr Chow

151 Knightsbridge, SW1X 7PA (7589 7347, www. mrchow.com). Knightsbridge tube. **Lunch served** 12.30-3pm Tue-Sun. **Dinner served** 7pm-midnight daily. **Main courses** £12.50-£25. **Set lunch** £23. **Set dinner** £38. **Credit** AmEx, DC, MC, V.
This Knightsbridge stalwart opened on St Valentine's Day in 1968, so Mr Chow's relationship with discerning Londoners is obviously time-tested. Perhaps it was the dapper, European decor – thick linen, polished silverware, marble floors – that

Barshu. See p67.

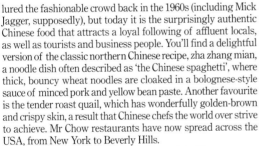

lured the fashionable crowd back in the 1960s (including Mick Jagger, supposedly), but today it is the surprisingly authentic Chinese food that attracts a loyal following of affluent locals, as well as tourists and business people. You'll find a delightful version of the classic northern Chinese recipe, zha zhang mian, a noodle dish often described as 'the Chinese spaghetti', where thick, bouncy wheat noodles are cloaked in a bolognese-style sauce of minced pork and yellow bean paste. Another favourite is the tender roast quail, which has wonderfully golden-brown and crispy skin, a result that Chinese chefs the world over strive to achieve. Mr Chow restaurants have now spread across the USA, from New York to Beverly Hills.
Babies and children admitted. Booking advisable; essential dinner. Separate rooms for parties, seating 20-75. **Map 8 F9**.

Marylebone

Phoenix Palace
5 Glentworth Street, NW1 5PG (7486 3515, www.phoenix palace.uk.com). Baker Street tube. **Meals served** noon-11.30pm Mon-Sat; 11am-10.30pm Sun. **Dim sum served** noon-5pm Mon-Sat; 11am-5pm Sun. **Main courses** £6.50-£25. **Dim sum** £2-£3.80. **Set meal** £20-£48 per person (minimum 2). **Credit** AmEx, MC, V.
Popular with politicians and embassy staff from the surrounding area, Phoenix Palace can seem like a step back in time, with its gaudy lanterns, faux antiques, gilded fans and good-luck lions. Happily, the food strikes a more authentic and fresh note than the decor, consisting of an extensive range of dishes that will entice the most conservative British diners to the most adventurous Chinese. Lobster, abalone and crab

feature prominently, often ordered as a centrepiece to a banquet. Braised mashed prawn in tofu, pepper and aubergine was typical of the soft and sweet Cantonese food served here: the flavours distinct and true, the dish soothing. In contrast, pan-fried scallops with black pepper and asparagus was short on both flavour and scallops: a distinctly under-generous portion considering the £14.80 price tag. On the waiter's recommendation, we plumped for steamed turbot with shredded pork and loganberry, which again seemed not very good value, though it was perfectly cooked and had a pleasing contrast of flavours. The dim sum menu is a standard list, but nevertheless keeps many lunchtime guests returning regularly.
Babies and children welcome: high chairs. Booking advisable. Separate rooms for parties, seating 12-30. Takeaway service; delivery service (over £10 within 1-mile radius). **Map 2 F4**.

Royal China Club
40-42 Baker Street, NW8 6ER (7486 3898, www.royal chinagroup.co.uk). Baker Street or Marble Arch tube. **Meals/dim sum served** noon-4.45pm Mon-Thur; noon-11.30pm Fri, Sat; noon-10.30pm Sun. **Main courses** £9-£50. **Dim sum** £3-£7.50. **Credit** AmEx, MC, V.
The glossy thoroughbred of the Royal China stable, RCC inhabits a swish room with lacquer wall panels the colour of hoisin sauce, and back-lit wooden slates that give a golden glow to proceedings. The place certainly draws a crowd. Service was efficient during a recent meal, although the waitresses seemed to have forgotten how to smile. We've always been impressed by the dim sum here, but this time decided to discover how the carte matched up. The kitchen specialises in unusual seafood and has a creative streak. Thus, white 'sea cucumber' is sautéed with foie gras, the echinoderm providing an enjoyable texture

(soft and supple, like a clam) with the liver adding a new meaty dimension. Stir-fried veal with black pepper and garlic was amazingly tender, and we were also astounded by the sweetness of the steamed luffa gourd topped with garlic. Our final choice, braised fish maw with pumpkin slices, was made special by a distinctive fish sauce. The selection of 40 teas is worth exploring. The extensive wine list is pricey; so too is the food, but this is classy cooking of rare refinement.
Babies and children admitted. Booking advisable Sat, Sun. Separate room for parties, seats 24. Takeaway service. **Map 9 G5**.

Mayfair

China Tang

The Dorchester, 53 Park Lane, W1K 1QA (7629 9988, www.thedorchester.com). Hyde Park Corner tube. **Meals/dim sum served** 11.30am-11.45pm daily. **Main courses** £12-£48. **Dim sum** £4-£5. **Set lunch** £15. **Credit** AmEx, DC, MC, V.

The self-proclaimed 'inherently British' Dorchester hotel is the unlikely location for one of the capital's finest Chinese restaurants. David Tang, founder of the stylish China Clubs in Beijing, Hong Kong and Singapore (as well as chic lifestyle emporium Shanghai Tang), brings colonial and art deco glamour, plus a substantial measure of oriental elegance, to the room, which has hosted celebrities from Kate Moss to, er, Prince Andrew. China Tang would get full marks for decor alone, but the food lives up to its starry surroundings. The perfectly executed cooking is primarily Cantonese, though regional specialities such as Sichuan mapo tofu and Hakka-style pork belly with preserved vegetables add extra intrigue. You can splash out on abalone (costing upwards of £50) or

show off with your appreciation of fried bird's nest (around £30), but even humble dishes such as roasted pigeon (a hawker-stall classic) wow the palate. As you might expect, there are plenty of impressive wines and spirits on the monumental drinks list, all as enthusiastically priced as the food.
Babies and children welcome: high chairs. Booking advisable. Disabled: lift; toilet. Separate rooms for parties, seating 18-50. **Map 9 G7**.

Princess Garden

8-10 North Audley Street, W1K 6ZD (7493 3223, www.princessgardenofmayfair.com). Bond Street tube. **Lunch served** noon-4pm Mon-Fri; noon-4.30pm Sat, Sun. **Dinner served** 6.30-11pm Mon-Sat; 6.30-10.30pm Sun. **Dim sum served** noon-4pm daily. **Main courses** £7.50-£12. **Dim sum** £2.30-£3.80. **Set lunch** £12 per person (minimum 2). **Set dinner** £30-£85 per person (minimum 2). **Credit** AmEx, DC, MC, V.

Feng shui-ed to the hilt, this rather stark establishment is a great hunk of Hong Kong in Mayfair, with stone lions guarding the entrance, a bar area reminiscent of a first-class airport lounge, marble floors, Chinese artworks and occasional flashes of auspicious red. It's an excellent destination for classic Cantonese dim sum, as well as peking duck, seafood, specialities from northern China and modern creations. Luxuries abound: lobster, abalone, dover sole – even veal. Here is your opportunity to try the slippery delight that is sea cucumber, braised and served with shrimp caviar, or abalone. Less adventurous eaters will also find plenty to interest them: beef in black bean sauce, sweet and sour fish, lemon chicken and crispy fried seaweed – all produced to a higher standard than your local takeaway. There's plenty of choice for vegetarians too. Staff are very polite, and eager to assist with

menu queries. For special occasions, check out the private rooms, cosier than the elegant main dining room but still stylish. *Babies and children welcome: high chairs. Booking advisable. Separate rooms for parties, seating 6-50. Takeaway service.* **Map 9 G6**.

Paddington

Pearl Liang

8 Sheldon Square, W2 6EZ (7289 7000, www.pearlliang. co.uk). Paddington tube/rail. **Meals served** noon-11pm daily. **Main courses** £6.80-£28. **Set meal** £25 per person (minimum 2); £38-£68 per person (minimum 4). **Credit** AmEx, MC, V.

Pearl Liang is tucked in the lower part of a modern steel-and-glass development, a short walk west of Paddington station. Inside, the room is smartly dressed in pink. The details are stylish, from the mural of a plum branch, to low chairs covered in mauve fabric. Although the restaurant isn't easy to find, this hasn't stopped young hipsters packing out the place at lunchtime. The kitchen's reputation is built around its dim sum. At first sight, the carte appears to be mainstream Cantonese, but it strays farther afield with the likes of sashimi lobster and pad thai. We started with an unusual prawn dumpling, stirred into life by a touch of wasabi. Dim sum from the steamer strengthened our optimism, with inventive morsels of prawn, pea shoot and canopy-leaf dumpling, as well as almost translucent cheung fun filled with monk's vegetables. We happily wolfed a pan-fried turnip cake, trying to ignore two grouchy waitresses who dampened the mood.
Babies and children welcome: high chairs. Booking advisable. Disabled: toilet. Separate room for parties, seats 40. Takeaway service. **Map 8 D5**.

Soho

Barshu [HOT 50]

28 Frith Street, W1D 5LF (7287 6688, www.bar-shu.co.uk). Leicester Square or Tottenham Court Road tube. **Meals served** noon-11pm Mon-Thur, Sun; noon-11.30pm Fri, Sat. **Main courses** £8.90-£28.90. **Credit** AmEx, MC, V.

Since opening in 2006, Barshu has done much to popularise Sichuan cuisine in London. Its owners now run two other restaurants nearby, Ba Shan and Baozi Inn, prompting fears that its culinary skills have been diluted. We had quibbles on our latest visit, but these had more to do with high prices and glum service (with staff plonking plates on the table). The cooking continues to thrill, although it wasn't faultless. A dive into the large menu with its helpful illustrations reveals a number of 'blood and guts' dishes that might not be an ideal choice for a first date. Our meal got off to a promising start with crunchy ribbons of jellyfish brought to life by a dark vinegar sauce and sesame oil. Next, the strong flavours of slow-cooked dong po pork knuckle in chilli oil gave our taste buds an invigorating whack. Seasoning in some dishes can miss the mark; fish fragrant aubergine was a little too sweet, while cheng du dry-braised sea bass with preserved mustard greens was fearlessly authentic yet overly salty. Still, Barshu remains an exceedingly charming venue, its decor modelled on that of an old Beijing teahouse, complete with elaborate wood carvings and tasselled lanterns.
Available for hire. Babies and children welcome: high chairs. Booking advisable. Disabled: toilet. Separate room for parties, seats 24. **Map 17 C3**.

Dim sum

Char siu bao: fluffy steamed bun stuffed with barbecued pork in a sweet-savoury sauce.

Char siu puff pastry or **roast pork puff**: triangular puff-pastry snack, filled with barbecued pork, scattered with sesame seeds and oven-baked.

Cheung fun: slithery sheets of steamed rice pasta wrapped around fresh prawns, barbecued pork, deep-fried dough sticks, or other fillings, splashed with a sweet soy-based sauce.

Chiu chow fun gwor: soft steamed dumpling with a wheat-starch wrapper, filled with pork, vegetables and peanuts.

Chive dumpling: steamed prawn meat and chinese chives in a translucent wrapper.

Har gau: steamed minced prawn dumpling with a translucent wheat-starch wrapper.

Nor mai gai or **steamed glutinous rice in lotus leaf**: lotus-leaf parcel enclosing moist sticky rice with chicken, mushrooms, salty duck-egg yolks and other bits and pieces, infused with the herby fragrance of the leaf.

Paper-wrapped prawns: tissue-thin rice paper enclosing prawn meat, sometimes scattered with sesame seeds, deep-fried.

Sago cream with yam: cool, sweet soup of coconut milk with sago pearls and morsels of taro.

Scallop dumpling: delicate steamed dumpling filled with scallop (sometimes prawn) and vegetables.

Shark's fin dumpling: small steamed dumpling with a wheaten wrapper pinched into a frilly cockscomb shape on top, stuffed with a mix of pork, prawn and slippery strands of shark's fin.

Siu loon bao or **xiao long bao**: Shanghai-style round dumpling with a whirled pattern on top and a juicy minced pork and soup filling.

Siu mai: little dumpling with an open top, a wheat-flour wrapper and a minced pork filling. Traditionally topped with crab coral, although minced carrot and other substitutes are common.

Taro croquette or **yam croquette**: egg-shaped, deep-fried dumpling with a frizzy, melt-in-your-mouth outer layer of mashed taro, and a savoury minced pork filling.

Turnip paste: a heavy slab of creamy paste made from glutinous rice flour and white oriental radishes, studded with wind-dried pork, sausage and dried shrimps and fried to a golden brown.

CHINESE

Yauatcha

*15 Broadwick Street, W1F 0DL (7494 8888, www.
yauatcha.com). Leicester Square, Piccadilly Circus or
Tottenham Court Road tube.* **Dim sum served** noon-
11.45pm Mon-Sat; noon-10.30pm Sun. **Dim sum** £3-£12.
Set meal (3-6pm Mon-Fri) £28.88 2 people. **Credit**
AmEx, MC, V.

Gone are the displays of whimsical pastries, though the
trademark, bizarrely coloured macaroons remain. Otherwise,
it's business as usual at this stalwart of modern Chinese dining.
All-day dim sum might be more common in London now, but
Yauatcha was one of the first to champion the idea. As at sister
restaurant, Hakkasan, the dim sum have a touch of refinement
that seems to please the hip young clientele. We prefer the
quieter ground-floor room with its streams of natural light, but
for a clubbier vibe, the basement is supreme – a vision of neon
blues and light-sucking blacks. Service veers from friendly to
haughty, but remains efficient at all times. Premium ingredients
often crop up in dim sum snacks, such as scallops or king crab
in the porky siu mai, or wagyu beef in the cheung fun.
Generally, though, the menu remains true to the roots of
Cantonese cookery. A great tea list (though more guidance
would be helpful), commendable cocktails and prime wines
make Yauatcha a top choice if you're looking to impress.
*Babies and children admitted. Booking advisable. Disabled:
lift; toilet.* **Map 17 B3**.

West

Acton

North China

*305 Uxbridge Road, W3 9QU (8992 9183, www.north
china.co.uk). Acton Town tube or 207 bus.* **Lunch served**
noon-2.30pm daily. **Dinner served** 6-11pm Mon-Fri,

Sun; 6-11.30pm Fri, Sat. **Main courses** £5.50-£12.80.
Set meal £14.50-£22.50 per person (minimum 2).
Credit AmEx, MC, V.

Too often, suburban Chinese restaurants are showy, expensive
and inauthentic; North China is none of these. Behind an
attractive, curved-glass façade set back from Uxbridge Road,
it's a seemly, compact place with peach-coloured walls and a
tinkly piano soundtrack. Even midweek, smart-casual (non-
Chinese) locals come here. The cuisine of Beijing and its
environs is the forte (including proper peking duck), though you
need to ask for the specials menu. From this, the mix of three
cold starters is recommended: smoked fish (sweet, meaty fillets);
brawn-like jelly of pork; chilli-flecked glass-noodle salad with
shredded chicken – a pleasurable balance of flavours and
textures. Northern China is the region of wheat and lamb, so
instead of rice, choose sweet and doughy silver-thread rolls
(steamed or with a crisp coating), and shredded pork with own-
made noodles (appetisingly coated in sesame oil, though ours
were just overcooked). Lamb casserole (from the main menu)
was salty yet rich and tender; spring onion pancakes were crisp
and creamy. The meal seemed rather oily, though this was
mainly down to our selection of dishes. Although staff were
happy and willing, the kitchen ran slow at times. Nevertheless,
pricing is moderate and the food fascinating.
*Babies and children welcome: high chairs. Booking
advisable; essential dinner Fri, Sat. Separate room for
parties, seats 36. Takeaway service; delivery service
(over £20 within 2-mile radius). Vegetarian menu.*

Bayswater

Gold Mine

102 Queensway, W2 3RR (7792 8331). Bayswater tube.
Meals served noon-11.15pm daily. **Main courses**
£6.80-£20. **Set meal** £15-£20 per person (minimum 2).
Credit MC, V.

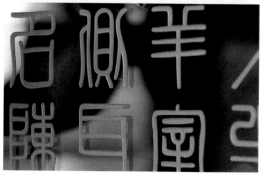

Pearl Liang. See p67.

Chinatown on the cheap

For oriental dining in the West End, Chinatown has been the wallet-friendly option since its inception some 60 years ago – though this southern section of Soho, centred on pedestrianised Gerrard Street, hasn't always been up to par in terms of quality. The strong hold that Cantonese restaurants have had on the area is finally relaxing, with more establishments offering regional cuisines.

Baozi Inn was one of the first to shake things up with its bold northern Chinese food (and dumplings); its owners quickly followed their success by opening **Ba Shan** (just beyond Chinatown's borders, in Soho). **Leong's Legends** is another fairly recent arrival, devoted to the still under-represented Taiwanese style of cooking; it offers Londoners a taste of delectable soup-filled pork dumplings (xiao long bao – arguably invented in Shanghai, but quickly popularised by the Taiwanese), gooey oyster omelettes and pork belly buns. Buoyed by its achievements, the same team opened a second branch, the rather unimaginatively named Leong's Legends Continues, nearby on Lisle Street. And over on Ganton Street, Alan Yau's budget noodle bar **Cha Cha Moon** woos diners with big bowls of regional Chinese and South-East Asian noodle dishes.

Despite the increased competition, Chinatown's Cantonese contingent still charges on unstoppably. **Four Seasons**, Bayswater's famed purveyor of roast duck, confidently set up stall in the middle of Gerrard Street in 2009, and continues to offer stunning roast meats at low prices; the nightly queues and consequent speedy table-turning don't seem to deter aficionados of all things fowl. **Canton** is also reliable for inexpensive barbecued duck and pork, as well as hotpots, noodle dishes, stir-fries and soups. **Wong Kei**, still one of the best-known eateries in the area, has had a minor refurbishment and remains a renowned spot for one-plate meals, soothing noodles and a side helping of people-watching. Likewise, **HK Diner**, **Café de Hong Kong** and **Café TPT** continue to be the haunts of London's Chinese students, thanks to their winning formula of big portions of rice and noodle dishes (roast meats are a highlight at all three), low prices and ubiquitous bubble tea drinks – cheesy Cantonese and Mandarin pop music notwithstanding.

Baozi Inn
25 Newport Court, WC2H 7JS (7287 6877). Leicester Square tube. **Meals served** 11.30am-10pm daily.
Map 17 C4.

Ba Shan
24 Romilly Street, W1D 5AH (7287 3266). Leicester Square tube. **Meals served** noon-11pm Mon-Thur, Sun; noon-11.30pm Fri, Sat.
Map 17 C4.

Café de Hong Kong
47-49 Charing Cross Road, WC2H 0AN (7534 9898). Leicester Square or Tottenham Court Road tube. **Meals served** 11am-11pm Mon-Sat; 11am-10.30pm Sun.
Map 17 C4.

Café TPT
21 Wardour Street, W1D 6PN (7734 7980). Leicester Square, Piccadilly Circus or Tottenham Court Road tube. **Meals served** noon-1am daily.
Map 17 B5.

Cha Cha Moon
15-21 Ganton Street, W1F 9BN (7297 9800, www.chachamoon.com). Oxford Circus or Piccadilly Circus tube. **Meals served** 11.30am-11pm Mon-Thur; 11.30am-11.30pm Fri, Sat; 11.30am-10.30pm Sun.
Map 17 A4.

Canton
11 Newport Place, WC2H 7JR (7437 6220). Leicester Square, Piccadilly Circus or Tottenham Court Road tube. **Meals served** noon-11.30pm Mon-Thur, Sun; noon-12.30am Fri, Sat.
Map 17 C4.

Four Seasons
12 Gerrard Street, W1D 5PR (7494 0870). Leicester Square, Piccadilly Circus or Tottenham Court Road tube. **Meals served** noon-1am Mon-Sat; 11am-1am Sun.
Map 17 C4.

HK Diner
22 Wardour Street, W1D 6QQ (7434 9544). Leicester Square, Piccadilly Circus or Tottenham Court Road tube. **Meals served** 11am-4am daily.
Map 17 C4.

Leong's Legends
4 Macclesfield Street, W1D 6AX (7287 0288). Leicester Square, Piccadilly Circus or Tottenham Court Road tube. **Meals served** noon-11pm, **dim sum served** noon-5pm daily.
Map 17 C4.
For branch see index.

Wong Kei
41-43 Wardour Street, W1D 6PY (7437 8408). Leicester Square, Piccadilly Circus or Tottenham Court Road tube. tube. **Meals served** noon-11.30pm Mon-Sat; noon-10.30pm Sun.
Map 17 B4.

CHINESE

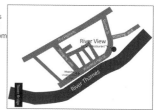

An enthusiastic crowd populates Gold Mine even on midweek evenings. Chinese diners tend to predominate in parties of various sizes – from couples to large groups seated at round tables. The long narrow premises can just about cope; white walls, mirrors and paintings of Chinese water scenes help to lighten proceedings. Service can vary too (from the gleeful to the abrupt, in our experience), but is usually swift. Though a relative newcomer to west London's Chinese enclave, the restaurant already has a reputation for roast meats – and it's well deserved judging from our best dish, a luscious, gorgeously fatty 'roast duck Cantonese style' with moist flesh and memorable gravy. Satisfactory too were the crunchy-fresh gai lan (chinese broccoli) in garlic sauce, and the 'chef's special soup', featuring all manner of ingredients (meat, seafood, beancurd sheets) in flavourful stock. In comparison, the mixed seafood with green bean vermicelli and satay sauce (one of a number of enticing hotpots) disappointed; though the prawns were plump and taut, the sliced scallops and squid curls seemed overcooked and the flavour one-paced. Next time, we'll try the braised chicken with pig's liver and chinese sausage, or perhaps ducks' feet with sea cucumber and fish lips.
Babies and children welcome: high chairs. Booking advisable. Takeaway service. **Map 7 C6**.

Magic Wok
100 Queensway, W2 3RR (7792 9767). Bayswater or Queensway tube. **Meals served** noon-11pm daily. **Main courses** £6.50-£18. **Set meal** £12.50 per person (minimum 2); £25 per person (minimum 4). **Credit** AmEx, MC, V.
Over many years, Magic Wok has never failed to conjure up a decent meal for us. True, its menu scarcely seems to have changed in nearly two decades, and execution of dishes can sometimes lack sparkle, but the restaurant deserves credit for being among the first to offer a broad spectrum of real Cantonese food to those unfamiliar with Chinese script. From the start its entire specials menu was translated into English, and this is where to look for enticements; the full menu includes scores of the usual stir-fries. Hotpots are generally fail-safe (a sumptuous stewed belly pork with preserved vegetables or lamb belly with red dates and dried beancurd skin), but the roast meats have their admirers too, and we also relish the deep-fried oysters (crisp coating, voluptuous interior). The restaurant might look mundane, with its narrow frontage opening out to a larger windowless rear section containing the occasional round banqueting table, but kind staff and pleasingly modest pricing create a cheery vibe.
Babies and children admitted. Booking advisable dinner. Separate room for parties, seats 30. Takeaway service. Vegetarian menu. **Map 7 C6**.

Mandarin Kitchen
14-16 Queensway, W2 3RX (7727 9012). Bayswater or Queensway tube. **Meals served** noon-11.30pm daily. **Main courses** £5.90-£28. **Set meal** £10.90 per person (minimum 2); £20 per person (minimum 4). **Credit** AmEx, MC, V.
Seemingly untouched by any of the newfound trendiness of Chinese cooking in London, Mandarin Kitchen relies on an established reputation for seafood to fill its cavernous premises. The restaurant has been a landmark on Queensway for well over a quarter of a century, and its design – somewhere between a 1970s wine bar and Baker Street underground station (Circle Line) – scarcely seems to have

changed in that time. Still, the banquettes are comfy, and Chinese business people continue to lunch at the large round tables, perhaps choosing the renowned lobster with noodles (which is usually expertly cooked). Tourists feature strongly in the evenings. Service can be abrupt, but over the years, we've found that the staff mellow towards diners ordering proper Cantonese food: the likes of oysters with ginger and spring onions, XO jellyfish with smoked chicken and arctic clam wrap (an appetisingly crunchy starter), or steamed aubergine stuffed with minced prawns. Too much cornflour in the sauces has been a problem in the past.
Babies and children welcome: booster seats. Booking advisable dinner. Takeaway service. **Map 7 C7**.

Royal China
13 Queensway, W2 4QJ (7221 2535, www.royalchina group.co.uk). Bayswater or Queensway tube. **Meals served** noon-11pm Mon-Thur; noon-11.30pm Fri, Sat; 11am-10pm Sun. **Dim sum served** noon-4.45pm Mon-Sat; 11am-4.45pm Sun. **Main courses** £7.50-£50. **Dim sum** £2.30-£5. **Set meal** £30-£38 per person (minimum 2). **Credit** AmEx, MC, V.
More than a decade before non-Chinese Londoners woke to the joys of dim sum, Royal China did much to raise the standard of the lunchtime snacks in the capital. For years, its Bayswater branch had few equals, dumpling-wise, and although competition is now much fiercer, this smart, capacious restaurant – decorated in the group's trademark gold and shiny black lacquer – continues to be a major player. The kitchen doesn't shy away from cross-cultural innovation (witness the minced fish paste with wasabi sauce on the specials menu), though the standard dim sum list also includes plenty to set the pulse racing. We love the steamed satay cuttlefish, and the black sesame paste dumplings in peanut crumbs (a positively sexy dessert first made famous here). The lengthy menu of main dishes also attracts a diverse crowd in the evenings, from local Chinese to passing tourists. The 'chef's favourites' menu (steamed cod with dried yellow bean sauce, for example) is worth investigating and hotpots (chicken with abalone, say) have their fans too. Staff are almost invariably efficient and generally helpful. The other Royal China outlets, in Marylebone, Fulham and Docklands, usually offer a similar high quality of food and service.
Babies and children admitted. Booking advisable (not accepted lunch Sat, Sun). Separate rooms for parties, seating 20-40. Takeaway service. Vegetarian menu. **Map 7 C7**.
For branches see index.

Kensington

Min Jiang
10th floor, Royal Garden Hotel, 2-4 Kensington High Street, W8 4PT (7361 1988, www.minjiang.co.uk). High Street Kensington tube. **Lunch/dim sum served** noon-3pm, **dinner served** 6-10.30pm daily. **Main courses** £10-£48. **Dim sum** £3.60-£5.20. **Set lunch** (Mon-Fri) £19.80. **Set dinner** £48-£68 per person (minimum 2). **Credit** AmEx, MC, V.
Located on the tenth floor of the Royal Garden Hotel, Min Jiang boasts fabulous views over Kensington Gardens and beyond – though the impressive vista is only possible during daylight hours. Much money has been spent here, so the interior is swish, with lattice screens and faux Ming pottery. The service

CHINESE

Royal China. See p71.

typical of such places, with an abundance of gilded accents to the furnishings, bright cut-glass chandeliers, lively diners, and a soundtrack of dire 1980s instrumentals in the toilets. The restaurant and its cheerful staff try to be all things to all people – which is a mistake. It's best to stick to the traditional Cantonese food on the menu, as we've found that the Sichuan- and Beijing-style dishes tend to be lacklustre. Dragon Castle opened to great acclaim a few years ago (proper Chinese food isn't the norm in this part of town), and although it might seem a little tired these days, the Cantonese fare, and particularly the dim sum, can still be first rate. With the latter, timing is everything, and the kitchen generally gets it right, serving perfectly steamed siu mai and har gau, along with more exotic offerings such as tripe and tiny spare ribs. Deep-fried soft-shell crabs with salt and pepper are a perennial favourite.
Babies and children welcome: high chairs. Booking advisable Fri, Sat. Disabled: toilet. Separate room for parties, seats 60. Takeaway service. Vegetarian menu.

East

Docklands

Yi-Ban
London Regatta Centre, Dockside Road, E16 2QT (7473 6699, www.yi-ban.co.uk). Royal Albert DLR. **Meals served** noon-11pm Mon-Sat; 11am-10.30pm Sun. **Dim sum served** noon-5pm daily. **Main courses** £4-£30. **Dim sum** £2.20-£4. **Set meal** £18-£32 per person (minimum 2). **Credit** AmEx, MC, V.
Yi-Ban is one of the few places in London where the food is as good as the view. Granted, the vista is not a wrap-around panorama over the London skyline, nor does it offer sparkling Thames-side views at sunset, but the restaurant's position overlooking London City Airport has its own particular brand of charm. The long, spacious room takes cues from hotel dining areas and Chinese wedding banquets; gold lamé in particular makes an amusing appearance. The staff are a charming bunch, serving with style and efficiency. Many diners – often exiles from the nearby ExCeL exhibition centre – dig happily into crispy duck pancakes and sweet-and-sour pork. Our advice is to bypass these and go for the more interesting dishes, such as west lake soup, an aromatic beef broth with egg white and coriander. Or you might want to give Cantonese-style crispy roast pork belly a try. By day, the dim sum menu is a delight, deviating from the usual choices towards dishes such as braised turnips with beef giblets, as well as listing a soothing range of congee bowls (lean pork with preserved egg is a classic).
Babies and children welcome: booster seats; high chairs. Booking advisable. Disabled: toilet. Entertainment: jazz 8pm Fri, Sat. Takeaway service. Vegetarian menu.

North East

Dalston

Shanghai
41 Kingsland High Street, E8 2JS (7254 2878). Dalston Kingsland rail or 38, 67, 76, 149 bus. **Meals served** noon-11pm, **dim sum served** noon-5pm daily. **Main courses** £5.50-£7.80. **Dim sum** £2.10-£4.50. **Set meal** £15.80-£19 per person (minimum 2). **Credit** MC, V.

has improved recently, and on our latest visit we found the staff considerate and friendly. This is a good place to sample authentic beijing duck; order the dish and you'll get a chance to admire the carving skills of the chef at your table – a sure-fire hit with first-timers. From the inventive dim sum list we enjoyed steamed pumpkin dumpling with mixed seafood, and delicate crispy prawn and asparagus roll. The standard of food on the carte can vary, and some prices are on the high side. However, fine ingredients as well as minimal MSG are big pluses. Two dishes in particular were exemplary: a peppery pan-fried ribeye beef with almonds, served with a yakiniku sauce (more usually associated with Japanese grilled meat dishes); and Shanghai-style tofu with mixed seafood. Mango cream with sago and pomelo ensured a happy ending.
Babies and children welcome: high chairs; nappy-changing facilities. Booking advisable; essential Fri-Sun. Disabled: lift; toilet. Separate room for parties, seats 20. **Map 7 B8**.

South East

Elephant & Castle

Dragon Castle
100 Walworth Road, SE17 1JL (7277 3388). Elephant & Castle tube/rail. **Meals served** noon-11.30pm Mon-Sat; 11.30am-10.30pm Sun. **Main courses** £5.50-£25. **Set meals** £15.80-£34.80 per person (minimum 2). **Credit** AmEx, MC, V.
This gaudy banqueting hall, set amid the tower blocks of the Walworth Road, would be quite at home in a second- or third-tier mainland Chinese city. The feel of the capacious venue is

This former pie and mash shop is a curious hybrid that fits right into Dalston's eclectic high street. Its previous incarnation is apparent from the decor – wooden booths, marble-topped bar and tiled walls – but the menu is staunchly oriental. As bold as its vibrant red signage, Shanghai's repertoire of dishes makes a welcome change from the Cantonese hegemony that generally holds sway in London. Regional Chinese highlights include several ingredients popular in Hakka cookery (sweet preserved vegetables, for instance) and combinations favoured by the Shanghainese (diced vegetables mixed into rice; oversized, juicy meatballs known colloquially as 'lion heads'), as well as Taiwanese 'three cup' chicken (where the bird is cooked with a mixture of soy sauce, rice wine and sesame oil). There's a decent choice of wine for consideration too, though most diners stick with Tsingtao beer or pots of tea. Crowds also flock here for the dim sum, though in our experience the quality has been variable. With such an unfocused menu, it can be difficult to extract the truly competent dishes from the mere crowd-pleasers. If in doubt ask the staff, who are more helpful than most.

Babies and children welcome: high chairs. Booking advisable. Disabled: toilet. Separate rooms for parties, both seating 45. Takeaway service. **Map 25 B5**.

North

Camden Town & Chalk Farm

Yum Cha Silks & Spice
27-28 Chalk Farm Road, NW1 8AG (7482 2228, www.yumchasilksandspice.co.uk). Chalk Farm tube.

Min Jiang. See p71.

Meals/dim sum served noon-11pm Mon-Thur; noon-midnight Fri, Sat; noon-10.30pm Sun. **Main courses** £6.95-£10.95. **Dim sum** £2.40-£4.50. **Credit** AmEx, MC, V. There's something of a split personality to the kitchen of this café-bar and takeaway opposite Camden's Stables Market. On one hand it offers all-day dim sum, cooked to a pretty high standard; on the other there's an à la carte menu containing undemanding pan-Asian fare such as crispy aromatic duck, laksa, chow mein and nasi goreng. A lively crowd attends even early in the week, some clearly tempted by a 50% discount offer on the evening dim sum menu. This is a shorter list than that provided at lunchtime, so go during traditional yum cha hours for the likes of dried shrimp and mushroom cheung fun, shredded black fungus with chillies and vinegar, egg tarts, and sweet soup of grapefruit, peach and sago. Dish presentation is not the finest, but there was no denying the fresh, true flavours of sesame pastry roll with prawn and squid, and golden crisp-fried parcels filled with prawns, bamboo shoots and coriander. Our only quibble was with the minced chicken siu mai, which was rubbery and overcooked. Some items took a while to appear from the kitchen, but waiting staff are enthusiastic and friendly. Both the tea list and cocktail selection are better than average too.

Babies and children welcome: high chairs. Booking advisable weekends. Disabled: toilet. Separate rooms for parties, seating 5-40. Tables outdoors (7, pavement). Takeaway service; delivery service (over £15 within 3-mile radius). **Map 27 C1**.

Outer London

Ilford, Essex

Mandarin Palace
559-561 Cranbrook Road, Ilford, Essex IG2 6JZ (8550 7661). Gants Hill tube. **Lunch served** noon-4pm, **dinner served** 6.30-11.30pm Mon-Sat. **Meals served** noon-11.30pm Sun. **Dim sum served** noon-4pm Mon-Sat; noon-5pm Sun. **Main courses** £15-£22. **Dim sum** £2.30-£3.80. **Set meal** £22.50 per person (minimum 2); £27.50 per person (minimum 4). **Credit** AmEx, MC, V.
A high-quality Chinese restaurant that's situated on top of an underground station in Ilford is not something you might expect, but Mandarin Palace is certainly worth a journey. Inside, the room is decorated in an extravagant fashion with lanterns, green roof tiles and faux jade screens; it's also packed with enough antiques to fill an emporium. On a lunchtime visit, our initial contact with the staff wasn't promising, and their brusque manner only dissipated when the owner appeared. We tucked into dim sum, kicking off with a translucent prawn and chive dumpling, followed by textbook steamed pork buns. Cheung fun, first steamed, then fried and topped with sesame seeds, was raised to another level by a piquant XO sauce. From the specials list, braised beancurd stuffed with shredded prawns was equally enjoyable. The delectable meal ended with a pungent durian puff pastry. Mandarin Palace's evening menu is ambitious, listing the likes of shark's fin, fish maw and hotpots. Locals are lucky to have such a good-value venue serving proper Chinese food.

Babies and children welcome: high chairs. Separate room for parties, seats 50. Takeaway service; delivery service (over £20 within 2-mile radius).
For branch see index.

East European

Students of London's eccentric byways will find rich pickings here. Although relatively few in number, the capital's east European restaurants cover a spectrum of habitats and styles. You want quirky? Try the gorgeously old-fashioned **Czechoslovak Restaurant**, with its post-war fittings, dumpling-heavy menu and exquisite seemliness. Or does trendy take your fancy? Head for **Baltic**, where a menu of updated eastern European classics is served in one of the most stylish bar-restaurants in town. Old-school character? The **Gay Hussar** takes some beating, with its wood-panelled walls full of caricatures of diners-past (many of them famous politicians), and its Hungarian food served with practised formality.

Newer restaurants reflect the diversity of eastern European migrants to this country since the fall of the Berlin Wall and the expansion of the European Union. Georgia is particularly well represented in London, with eateries ranging from established local **Tbilisi** to elegant newcomer **Tamada**. Poland too has several restaurants devoted to its cooking; our current favourite is **Tatra**. The biggest news for this year is that the South Ken institution **Daquise** has been taken over by an upmarket Polish restaurant group; initial impressions are mixed, but the food remains true to its roots.

Central

Soho

Gay Hussar
2 Greek Street, W1D 4NB (7437 0973, www.gayhussar. co.uk). Tottenham Court Road tube. **Lunch served** 12.15-2.30pm, **dinner served** 5.30-10.45pm Mon-Sat. **Main courses** £9.75-£16.95. **Set lunch** £18.50 2 courses, £21 3 courses. **Credit** AmEx, DC, MC, V. Hungarian
In the course of over half a century, the Hussar has become famous for its political shenanigans and its Hungarian food (a cuisine unique in eastern Europe for its liberal use of spicing). Throughout, the restaurant has attracted hordes of tourists and parliamentarians – more of the former lately. However, on our most recent visit, the kitchen seemed to be resting on its laurels. The cosy room, its walls covered in caricatures of politicians, and the personable, long-serving staff remain, but the food seemed at best homemade and tasty, at worst on the wrong side of retro. The renowned cherry soup was uneventful, as was the crispy duck (saved only by fluffy potatoes coated in dripping). The strudel with poppy seeds was fragrant, yet the accompaniments revealed an apparent laziness in the kitchen, with a blob of whipped cream that tasted as if it had come from a can and a wafer that also seemed mass-produced. Much better was a fish terrine, which produced nostalgic smiles with its tangy beetroot and horseradish sauce, and a delicate cucumber salad. A main course of tender venison goulash with crimson paprika and pearls of egg pasta tarhonya, also reminded us of the restaurant's past glories.
Babies and children welcome: high chairs. Booking essential dinner. Separate rooms for parties, seating 12 and 24.
Map 17 C3.

South Kensington

Gessler Daquise
20 Thurloe Street, SW7 2LT (7589 6117, http://gessler london.com). South Kensington tube. **Meals served** noon-11pm daily. **Main courses** £6-£14.50. **Set lunch** (noon-3.30pm Mon-Fri) £9.50 2 courses. **Credit** MC, V. Polish
After decades of service, where big portions of homely Polish cooking were dispensed with great charm, Daquise has changed. This cherished former café was recently bought by Warsaw restaurant group Gessler. Some days after the

re-opening, we found the results poignantly mixed. The interior is now a luminous space of stripped wooden floors, glass and 'old-money' furnishings. We loved the menu (where wild game and river fish now feature), but were bemused by the service, which seemed to border on the absurdly inefficient. A troop of nervous waiters was led by an obliging but forgetful maître d'. Mistakes and awkwardness ensued. Even the simplest dishes were served silver-style, which looked plain poncey. Happily, the food reminded us of the old Daquise. Barszcz and chlodnik soups were intense and refreshing; a delicate pâté of pike-perch contrasted well with the dried fruit in it; and dumplings, stuffed unusually with beef and venison, were melt-in-the-mouth, if under-seasoned. We enjoyed the (slightly burnt) pancakes with cream cheese and cranberries. The drinks list is scanty, and could do with more wines by the glass, and vodka. The new Daquise needs time and care, but we hope it flourishes.
Babies and children admitted. Booking advisable.
Separate room for parties, seats 25. **Map 14 D10**.

West

Bayswater

Antony's
54 Porchester Road, W2 6ET (7243 8743). Royal Oak tube.
Dinner served 6pm-midnight Mon-Sat. **Main courses** £4-£25. **Credit** MC, V. Polish
Antony's Polish owner has an eye for style. The room of crisp, white tablecloths, dark furniture and artfully presented dishes – modestly sized, served in posh bowls – prepares diners for exceptional Polish cooking. Alas, apart from a beautiful, sweet borscht with fresh dill and delicate tortellini, our food was disappointing. The pierogi dumplings had a striking similarity to shop-bought versions and contained a hard-to-identify potato and cheese filling; a Polish sausage was salty and little better than what you might find in a corner-shop, although it arrived with a decent mustard and sour cream sauce; pork knuckle with apple sauce was too dry, had no recognisable hint of apple, and was accompanied by flabby chips, oily courgettes and carrots sprinkled with soggy sesame seeds. The homely goodness encountered on previous visits was only discernible in some crisp potato pancakes that were slightly over-seasoned but tasty. Antony's offers a curious retro pan-European menu (carbonara and lasagne included), yet though it desires to project a cosmopolitan image, it seems instead outdated. We hope the kitchen will regain its earlier flair for producing good Polish nosh with a light touch. The airy atmosphere and relaxed, if slightly restrained, service certainly deserve it.
Available for hire. Babies and children welcome: high chairs. Booking advisable weekends. Separate room for parties, seats 30. **Map 7 C5**.

Hammersmith

Knaypa
268 King Street, W6 0SP (8563 2887, www.theknaypa. co.uk). Hammersmith tube. **Lunch served** noon-3pm, **dinner served** 6-10.30pm Mon-Thur. **Meals served** noon-10.30pm Fri, Sat; noon-9.30pm Sun. **Main courses** £6.99-£16.49. **Credit** AmEx, MC, V. Polish
Knaypa is rather different from London's more homely Polish restaurants, set apart by its striking rococo-style decor of black wallpaper and curved furniture, and its infectious atmosphere

(helped by charming service and long candlelit tables for big parties). The food too – although consisting of hearty Polish classics – is a notch lighter and more beautifully presented. A chilled soup of beetroot and cucumber, doused in dill, conjured up Polish summer meadows; the vegetarian cabbage wraps of wild mushrooms and rice were light and full of early September forest aromas. A more substantial beef goulash, poured over potato pancakes that had been architecturally stacked up, was full of rich flavours and crisp textures. And even though our starter of herring tasted as if it had come from a pack, it was saved by a zingy apple and onion sauce. Don't shy away from the complimentary smalec, served with chewy rye bread; this little pot of pork dripping, packed with garlic, will scare away any chills, especially if taken with shorts of Wyborowa vodka. 'If only it were 20°C colder,' we mused, walking out into the summer night.
Available for hire. Babies and children welcome: high chairs. Booking advisable weekends. Separate room for parties, seats 38. Tables outdoors (2, pavement). Vegetarian menu.
Map 20 A4.

Kensington

Mimino
197C Kensington High Street, W8 6BA (7937 1551, www.mimino.co.uk). Kensington High Street tube. **Dinner served** 6-11pm Mon-Thur; 6pm-midnight Fri, Sat. **Main courses** £10-£15. **Credit** MC, V. Georgian
Mimino gets its name from an old Soviet-Georgian comedy film, full of modest jokes and warm banter. The plush, windowless interior of this Georgian restaurant is more suitable for a hushed dinner à deux than for raucous celebrations. Service can be indifferent, but the food is enticing, consisting of Georgian classics (many of them vegetarian) served in copious quantities. A chilled stew of aubergines and peppers with well-mingled flavours; tart leek and walnut balls; and an appetising, albeit too peppery, lobio (red bean paste) – are all part of the good-value meze for two. Main courses tend to be hefty, but lightly spiced. Try khinkali (order in advance); these onion-shaped steamed dumplings filled with minced meat look heavy,

Tbilisi. See p78.

but they burst with juices. Accompany them with adjika, a hot pepper paste. Or better still, get a bowl of kharcho, a thick broth of sharp tomatoes and beef, together with some cheesy khachapuri flatbread. To drink, choose Tarhun, a feverishly green lemonade reminiscent of the good old Soviet days, or for more sophistication, select from the impressive list of wines: perhaps oaky Mukuzani or dry Bagrationi champagne. *Available for hire. Babies and children welcome: high chairs. Booking advisable weekends. Takeaway service.* **Map 7 A9**.

Shepherd's Bush

Tatra

24 Goldhawk Road, W12 8DH (8749 8193). Goldhawk Road tube. **Lunch served** noon-4pm, **dinner served** 6-11pm Mon-Fri. **Meals served** noon-11pm Sat; noon-10pm Sun. **Main courses** £8.50-£13.50. **Set lunch** £10.50 2 courses, £13.50 3 courses. **Credit** AmEx, MC, V. Polish

Buckwheat risotto might sound rather worthy and ascetic, but Tatra's indulgent kasza with wild mushrooms and cream is a revelation. Lush, nutty but redolent with herbs, this reinvented Polish classic was both comforting and playful. The dish, and the rest of this thoughtful, eclectic menu, is the brainchild of a young Polish chef who clearly liked playing with his food as a child. The results aren't always successful – witness an unnerving combination of spicy mackerel with prunes and pine nuts (called peanuts here) – but they inspire you to explore the menu. We were pleased with the golabki (paper-thin cabbage leaves encasing minced meat, with a bright tomato sauce) and the very tasty fried dumplings. We also enjoyed the (slightly heavy) crème brûlée with drunken cherries and a sensational blackcurrant vodka, almost jam-like in consistency.

Tatra has gained confidence since our last visit and gathered regulars. In appearance it resembles a gastropub, with mauve colours and exposed brickwork; leather chairs lend extra class. Added attractions include a menu that changes every few weeks, many more flavoured vodkas and sweet service. *Available for hire. Babies and children welcome: high chairs. Booking advisable weekends. Disabled: toilet. Tables outdoors (1, pavement).* **Map 20 B2**.

South

Waterloo

Baltic HOT 50

74 Blackfriars Road, SE1 8HA (7928 1111, www.baltic restaurant.co.uk). Southwark tube. **Lunch served** noon-3pm, **dinner served** 5.30-11.15pm Mon-Sat. **Meals served** noon-10.30pm Sun. **Main courses** £10.50-£17. **Set meal** £14.50 2 courses, £17.50 3 courses. **Credit** AmEx, MC, V. East European

The architect-led interior of this pioneering restaurant and bar remains as fresh and bracing as a dip in the Baltic Sea. Unusually, jazz is as much a speciality as the chlodnik, but it certainly adds to the cool of this enduring hotspot. Owner Jan Woroniecki first introduced his vision of east European cuisine to London in 1989 at Kensington favourite Wódka – a former dairy that remains a casually genteel place to enjoy blinis, goulash and golabki, or grilled halloumi and watermelon salad. Baltic is flashier and more ambitious, with an enlivening buzz even at quiet sittings. Both restaurants seek to put a stylish spin on Polish, Russian and Hungarian classics, but the pan-east European brief means there are more Mediterranean

Menu

Dishes followed by (Cz) indicate a Czech dish; (G) Georgian; (H) Hungarian; (P) Polish; (R) Russian. Others have no particular affiliation.

Bigos (P): classic hunter's stew made with sauerkraut, various meats and sausage, mushrooms and juniper.
Borscht: beetroot soup. There are many varieties: Ukrainian borscht is thick with vegetables; the Polish version (barszcz) is clear. There are also white and green types. Often garnished with sour cream, boiled egg or mini dumplings.
Caviar: fish roe. Most highly prized is that of the sturgeon (beluga, oscietra and sevruga, in descending order of expense), though keta or salmon caviar is underrated.
Chlodnik (P): cold beetroot soup, bright pink in colour, served with sour cream.
Galabki, **golabki** or **golubtsy**: cabbage parcels, usually stuffed with rice or kasha (qv) and sometimes meat.
Golonka (P): pork knuckle, often cooked in beer.
Goulash or **gulasz (H)**: rich beef soup.
Kasha or **kasza**: buckwheat, delicious roasted: fluffy, with a nutty flavour.
Kaszanka (P): type of blood sausage that's made with buckwheat.
Khachapuri (G): flatbread; sometimes called Georgian pizza.
Kielbasa (P): sausage. Poland has dozens of widely differing styles.

Knedliky (Cz): bread dumplings.
Kolduny (P): small meat-filled dumplings (scaled-down pierogi, qv) often served in beetroot soup.
Koulebiaka, **kulebiak** or **coulebiac (R)**: type of pie made with layered salmon or sturgeon, with eggs, dill, rice and mushrooms.
Krupnik (P): barley soup, and the name of a honey vodka (because of the golden colour of barley).
Latke: grated potato pancakes, fried.
Makowiec or **makietki (P)**: poppy seed cake.
Mizeria (P): cucumber salad; very thinly sliced and dressed with sour cream.
Nalesniki (P): cream cheese pancakes.
Paczki (P): doughnuts, often filled with plum jam.
Pierogi (P): ravioli-style dumplings. Typical fillings are sauerkraut and mushroom, curd cheese or fruit (cherries, apples).
Pirogi (large) or **pirozhki** (small) **(R)**: filled pies made with yeasty dough.
Placki (P): potato pancakes.
Shashlik: Caucasian spit-roasted meat.
Uszka or **ushka**: small ear-shaped dumplings served in soup.
Zakuski (R) or **zakaski (P)**: starters, traditionally covering a whole table. The many dishes can include pickles, marinated vegetables and fish, herring, smoked eel, aspic, mushrooms, radishes with butter, salads and caviar.
Zrazy (P): beef rolls stuffed with bacon, pickled cucumber and mustard.
Zurek (P): sour rye soup.

flavours (aubergine, fennel, peppers, tomato) than you might expect. Devilled lambs' kidneys is a favourite on Baltic's keenly priced set lunch/pre-theatre menus, yet the kitchen sensibly recognises it has to cater to locals and office workers, not just gastronauts; those who find even chicken kiev too adventurous can be satisfied with Aberdeen Angus sirloin, salad and chips, and a chocolate fondant. The wine list mixes bottles from Hungary and Slovenia with French, Spanish and South African varieties, while cocktails use own-flavoured vodkas and superior brands such as Wyborowa as a launch-pad for intriguing fruit and vegetable concoctions (try the beetroot martini). Something for everyone, then.
Babies and children admitted: high chairs. Disabled: toilet. Separate room for parties, seats 30. Tables outdoors (4, terrace). **Map 11 N8**.
For branch (Wódka) see index.

South East
Elephant & Castle

Mamuska!
2010 RUNNER-UP BEST NEW CHEAP EATS
First floor, Elephant & Castle Shopping Centre, SE1 6TE (07 986 352 810, www.mamuska.net). Elephant & Castle tube/rail. **Meals served** 7.30am-11pm Mon-Sat; 9am-11pm Sun. **Main courses** £5. **No credit cards**. Polish

Among the Elephant & Castle Shopping Centre's collection of money-transfer centres, passport photo booths and stalls hawking gaudy jewellery, lies a take on the bar mleczny – the Polish milk bar, an iconic type of Communist subsidised canteen. Part-owned by a Canadian, this is a westernised style of 'milk bar', with an open-plan kitchen and a menu that keeps Brit sensitivities in mind. As you might expect from the location, the place has a rudimentary feel, with the large-windowed shop unit reminiscent of a bus terminal caff. Service is from the counter, the walls are of black- and white-painted breeze blocks, the collection of mismatched furniture ranges from varnished dining room tables to little pock-marked square desks, and menus are laminated. But unlike its neighbours, Mamuska! has charm. 'Your mother will hate us!' claims a humour-packed menu, presumably geared to a clientele based around students tucking into vast portions of slippery pierogi, and Polish couples sipping big bottles of Zywiec beer or 50ml vodka shots (available from the freezer, chilled or at room temperature) as they enjoy a range of hearty stews, and tenderised, breaded meats. Portions are gigantic, mainly served with dill-scattered boiled potatoes. Though cooking can be basic, a sweet, tangy beetroot soup served in a laboratory-style beaker was impressive. Don't order your starters and main courses at the same time, or your table might be swamped with enough food to sink a battleship.
Available for hire. Babies and children welcome: children's menu; high chairs. Booking advisable. Takeaway service; delivery service (over £20 within 3-mile radius).

North

Camden Town & Chalk Farm

Trojka

101 Regents Park Road, NW1 8UR (7483 3765, www. troykarestaurant.co.uk). Chalk Farm tube. **Meals served** 9am-10.30pm daily. **Main courses** £8-£14.95. **Set lunch** (Mon-Fri) £7.95-£11.95 2 courses. **Licensed. Corkage** £5 wine, £15 spirits. **Credit** MC, V. Russian

Trojka has something of a dual personality. On the one hand it's a cosy all-day café, serving fry-ups and cappuccinos; on the other, it's an evocative Russian tea room, lined with old brass urns, heavy gilt-framed paintings and nearly 60 Russian dolls. Flip to the Russian side of the laminated menu and you'll find a choice of around 20 zakuski, plus caviar and fish roe at various prices. Mains are undeniably hearty with strong, true flavours; there's no missing the mushrooms, buckwheat and salmon in the homely coulebiac. Gypsy latke pairs classic beef goulash with moist potato pancakes and smetana (sour cream sauce). For warmer weather, there are new potatoes served with smoked trout or marinated herring, and butter bean ratatouille with latke and kasha, but most of the food will see you through winter in Siberia. Service was sweet yet inexplicably slow during an off-peak visit. The drinks list lacks oomph too, though our summery Russian lager was enjoyable, and frozen vodkas are available. To finish, don't miss the freshly cooked, beautifully lacy crêpes filled with cream cheese and sultanas – far more satisfying than Trojka's ho-hum baked cheesecake. *Babies and children welcome: high chairs. Booking advisable dinner Fri, Sat. Entertainment: Russian folk music 8-10.30pm Fri, Sat. Tables outdoors (4, pavement). Takeaway service.* **Map 27 A1**.

Highbury

Tbilisi

91 Holloway Road, N7 8LT (7607 2536). Highbury & Islington tube/rail. **Dinner served** 6.30-11pm daily. **Main courses** £8.75-£10.95. **Credit** AmEx, MC, V. Georgian

You'll get a worthwhile introduction to Georgia's exuberant cuisine at evening-only Tbilisi. OK, you might need a love of cornflour when sampling some dishes, and a sense of humour when deciphering the oddly spelled menu, but the food is generously portioned and modestly priced. The interior looks proud yet hospitable, with a striking black and red colour scheme, lacquered surfaces and expensive bottles of Georgian wine on display. Georgian classics with a few eastern European twists grace the menu. An ample meze included ispanakhi (intensely lemony, if a touch stringy, spinach and walnut dip), a warm aubergine stew, and khachapuri bread with salty 'Turkish' cheese. The 'distinctive Georgian' chicken soup was made with good stock, much dill and thickened with cornflour. Best were the succulent bean bread containing abundant black pepper, and a chicken stew with walnut paste – reminiscent of a good chicken korma, alas accompanied by a nursery-like porridge of rice and cornflour. A grape juice jelly would have made a refreshing foil to the preceding substantial courses, were it not for too much cornflour (yet again). Nevertheless, Tbilisi is a proper local, with Georgians popping in for a bite, unobtrusive service and heart-gladdening food. *Available for hire. Babies and children admitted. Booking advisable Fri, Sat. Separate room for parties, seats 40. Takeaway service.*

North West

St John's Wood

Tamada

122 Boundary Road, NW8 0RH (7372 2882, www.tamada. co.uk). Kilburn Park or St John's Wood tube, or Kilburn High Road rail. **Lunch served** noon-3pm Sat, Sun. **Dinner served** 6-11pm Tue-Sun. **Main courses** £9-£18. **Credit** MC, V. Georgian

'Chic' is not a word commonly used to describe London's east European restaurants – which often decorate themselves in nouveau riche sparkles or folkloric homeliness. Tamada is an exception, with its muted colour scheme, antique silverware and eloquently written menu. Even on a weekday, the place was filled with quiet parties, seduced by the enchanting service, exquisite food and high-quality Georgian wines. The menu is succinct, and includes a separate section for Georgian breads. It sticks to tradition, yet the quality of execution is higher than the norm. We relished a dish of mellow steamed spinach and walnut balls, a potent beef and rice kharcho soup, and superb khinkali (so juicy were these gigantic dumplings filled with minced meat that their delicate moulds seemed like edible soup holders). More unusual were a bubbling pot of pork offal, and pickled vegetables containing curiously delicious flower buds of the bladdernut shrub. Syrupy black Georgian coffee, served with a morsel of layered walnut cake, was good enough on its own to ensure we will return here; likewise the lush Mukuzani wine and the chacha (Georgian grape 'vodka'). *Babies and children welcome: high chair. Booking advisable Fri, Sat. Tables outdoors (2, pavement). Takeaway service.* **Map 1 C1**.

West Hampstead

Czechoslovak Restaurant   `HOT 50`

74 West End Lane, NW6 2LX (7372 1193, www.czecho slovak-restaurant.co.uk). West Hampstead tube. **Dinner served** 5-10pm Tue-Fri. **Meals served** noon-10pm Sat, Sun. **Main courses** £4-£12. **No credit cards.** Czech

In premises more akin to a plush Eastbourne guesthouse, this cherished purveyor of eastern European ballast has been open for more than 60 years. The venue's primary purpose is as a social club for Czech and Slovak émigrés, so it includes a bar (cream walls, blue flooring, pine panelling) with Pilsner Urquell on tap and a flatscreen TV tuned to Czech soaps or football. For an undiluted retro treat, however, head to the restaurant, where swirly carpets, an ornate mantelpiece, glittering chandeliers and flowing net curtains transport you to the era of chandlewick bedspreads. The menu offers ample opportunity to top up your calories, perhaps by starting with fried bread with garlic and cheese, or fried goose liver. Brawn or roll-mops seem lightweights in comparison. To follow, we recommend the roast beef in vegetable and cream sauce with sliced knedliky dumplings, but the enormous choice also includes deep-fried potato pancake with bacon, various schnitzels, barbecued or braised meats, and pan-fried trout. Astonishingly, there's even a vegetarian section, though breaded quorn schnitzel or fried cauliflower aren't the healthiest options. Bring a meal to a heart-stopping conclusion with apricot dumpling topped with cinnamon, sugar, butter and whipped cream. *Babies and children welcome: high chairs. Booking advisable weekends. Disabled: toilet. Separate room for parties, seats 25. Vegetarian menu.* **Map 28 A3**.

Fish

London's fish restaurants are a curious mix of ancient and modern. Some of the capital's oldest dining establishments specialise in marine life – the staunchly traditional likes of **Sweetings**, which has been trading from the same City premises since 1889, and **Bentley's Oyster Bar & Grill**, whose ancestry can be traced back to World War I. Two of the most famous old-timers add a large measure of glamour to this upper-crust British template: **J Sheekey** and **Scott's** (both now owned by Caprice Holdings) have benefited from the popularity of high-protein, low-fat fish among the calorie-conscious beau monde. Among the newer breed of fish restaurants, **Applebee's Café** uses sparklingly fresh specimens from its fishmonger's business to create Mediterranean-style dishes. To find out which stocks of fish and seafood are certified as sustainable, consult the Marine Stewardship Council's website (www.msc.org).

Central

City

Sweetings `HOT 50`
39 Queen Victoria Street, EC4N 4SA (7248 3062).
Mansion House tube. **Lunch served** 11.30am-3pm Mon-Fri. **Main courses** £12-£27.50. **Credit** AmEx, MC, V.
As much a City institution as the Old Lady of Threadneedle Street, Sweetings has been providing unfussy fishy lunches from the same corner site since 1889. Arrive early or late otherwise you'll invariably have to wait in the bar (no bookings are taken), along with the predominantly suited clientele, for a seat at the shared wooden tables in the back room (surrounded by old cartoons, photos and cricketing memorabilia) or on a high stool in the front. The long-serving, white-jacketed staff are an affable, no-nonsense lot – much like the food – and are well used to being trapped behind their counter, doling out cutlery and topping up wine glasses, for the entire lunchtime. Fish and chips, smoked eel, potted shrimps and market-fresh fish (offered grilled, steamed or fried, on or off the bone) is typical of the traditional, simply cooked fare; there are also specials such as lobster salad. A public school background isn't essential to appreciate Sweetings' eccentricities, though a liking for steamed syrup pudding and spotted dick will help. Don't expect to linger with a coffee at the end of your meal; it's not served in order to speed up customer turnover.

Available for hire (dinner only). Babies and children admitted. Bookings not accepted. Takeaway service.
Map 11 P6.

Leicester Square

J Sheekey
28-32 St Martin's Court, WC2N 4AL (7240 2565, www. j-sheekey.co.uk). Leicester Square tube. **Lunch served** noon-3pm Mon-Sat; noon-3.30pm Sun. **Dinner served** 5.30pm-midnight Mon-Sat; 6-11pm Sun. **Main courses** £13.50-£39.50. **Set lunch** (Sat, Sun) £25.50 3 courses. **Credit** AmEx, DC, MC, V.
Sheekey's is the consummate theatreland restaurant. Its walls are lined with acting greats, as often are its tables (along with those who aspire to be), and the buzz is as thrilling as an opening night. Many diners opt for the fondly remembered salmon fish cake or spectacular fruits de mer. Nevertheless, it's worth casting your net wider: perhaps a starter of pickled arctic herring with potato salad and dill sauce, followed by a fillet of organic salmon with Suffolk bacon and razor clams. Don't forget to check the weekly specials for the likes of grilled turbot with béarnaise for two, or a lobster salad featuring new-season potatoes and asparagus. British cheeses, welsh rarebit and herring roes on toast provide appealing savoury alternatives to the lengthy list of puds. Staff don't always perform at their best, at times giving the impression they're too cool for school, but on the whole Sheekey's is a slick show and

Scott's

FISH

still one of the hottest tickets in town. Enjoy it for a fraction of the price at weekend lunchtimes when the mood is relaxed and friendly and a £25.50 set menu takes centre stage.
Babies and children welcome: colouring books; high chairs. Booking essential. Disabled: toilet. Vegan dishes. Vegetarian menu. **Map 18 D5**.

Mayfair

Scott's

20 Mount Street, W1K 2HE (7495 7309, www.scotts-restaurant.com). Bond Street or Green Park tube. **Meals served** noon-10.30pm Mon-Sat; noon-10pm Sun. **Main courses** £15-£39.50. **Cover** £2. **Credit** AmEx, DC, MC, V.
The menus of Scott's and J Sheekey aren't identical, and the decors are vastly different, but there's an undeniable sense of formula to these Caprice Holdings operations. Scott's is the flashier, wealthier younger sibling – a hedge-fund manager to Sheekey's theatrical sophisticate – but the moment the corporate bread basket lands on the table you know you're visiting a blood brother. Scott's pricing may suggest a desire to keep out hoi polloi, yet it attracts a diverse crowd, particularly at weekends when family groups sit alongside sports-casual celebs, couples of all ages, and friends who've come up west for posh fish and chips. Tables are laid around a large central bar and a space-age-style crustacea altar laden with oysters, caviar and other goodies. Such seafood and a clutch of asparagus dishes could make the list of starters redundant, but there's a further dozen or so offered, including a lovely heritage vegetable salad with goat's cheese to keep many a waist-watching WAG happy. The cooking is mostly accurate – we enjoyed wonderfully tender razor clams sautéed with seashore vegetables and cured ham, and moist, herb-roasted monkfish – though rhubarb and custard trifle easily outclassed a bland chocolate tart for dessert.
Babies and children welcome: high chairs. Booking essential. Disabled: toilet. Separate room for parties, seats 40. Tables outdoors (7, pavement). Vegan dishes. Vegetarian menu. **Map 9 G7**.

Piccadilly

Bentley's Oyster Bar & Grill `HOT 50`
11-15 Swallow Street, W1B 4DG (7734 4756, www. bentleysoysterbarandgrill.co.uk). Piccadilly Circus tube.
Oyster Bar **Meals served** noon-midnight Mon-Sat; noon-10pm Sun. **Main courses** £8.75-£36.
Restaurant **Lunch served** noon-3pm Mon-Fri. **Dinner served** 6-11pm Mon-Sat. **Main courses** £18.95-£38.
Both **Credit** AmEx, MC, V.
The classy alfresco terrace has made Bentley's an even more attractive dining destination and, as long as the weather's in agreement, we'd choose this or the ground-floor oyster bar over the upstairs grill restaurant any day. Add in the private dining rooms, and the operation – which first opened in 1916 – extends over three floors of this Victorian building. The decor of the oyster bar has an Arts and Crafts flavour, with red leather and marble surfaces; its retro vibe adds to the fun of supping here, whether alone, in pairs or a group of four (tables are small). Our only complaint is with the service: not from the dextrous chaps shucking oysters at the bar, but the length of time cooked dishes take to arrive from the kitchen and the over-relaxed attitude of those staff working what few tables there are. Don't ignore the bread basket: the soda bread is superb (as

it should be, given owner Richard Corrigan's Irish heritage). First-timers and the unconfident should opt for the reliable fish pie accompanied by bottles of green Tabasco sauce. Adventurous foodies will revel in the likes of mackerel and oyster tartare, or squid stuffed with chorizo and feta. Cheese figures large on the dessert list, but who could turn down wild damson and blackberry trifle paired with a glass of Sauternes? *Booking advisable. Disabled: toilet. Dress: smart casual; no shorts. Separate rooms for parties, seating 14 and 60.* **Map 17 A5**.

West

Notting Hill

Geales

2 Farmer Street, W8 7SN (7727 7528, www.geales.com). Notting Hill Gate tube. **Lunch served** noon-2.30pm Tue-Fri. **Dinner served** 6-10.30pm Mon-Fri. **Meals served** noon-10.30pm Sat; noon-9.30pm Sun. **Main courses** £8-£29.50. **Set lunch** (noon-2.30pm Tue-Fri) £9.95 2 courses. **Credit** AmEx, MC, V.

In tandem with Notting Hill's gentrification, this former chippy (established in 1939 on what is still a fetching little backstreet) has leapt up the social ladder since the '90s. Glance at Geales' effortlessly sleek diners and you may think that prawns and lemon aïoli, followed by lobster linguini with garlic and tomatoes, or perhaps a seafood platter, would be mainstays of the menu. Yet though these dishes are on the list, and there's a champagne and oyster bar to boot, British seaside classics more than hold their own: the likes of battered cod, chips and mushy peas (at £19.85, including 'discretionary' 12.5% service, mind), followed by apple and blackberry crumble or jam roly poly. Vegetarians aren't forgotten (there are salads and a wild mushroom tart) and neither are meat-eaters (with various grilled steaks), but fish is the thing – witness the vintage photos of fisher-folk decorating the battleship-grey walls on both ground floor and first. Standards are generally high. *Babies and children admitted. Booking advisable Fri, Sat. Separate room for parties, seats 12. Tables outdoors (10, pavement).* **Map 7 A7**. **For branch see index.**

South East

London Bridge & Borough

Applebee's Café

5 Stoney Street, SE1 9AA (7407 5777, www.applebees fish.com). London Bridge tube/rail. **Lunch served** noon-3.30pm Tue-Thur; 11.30am-4pm Fri; 11.30am-4.30pm Sat. **Dinner served** 6-10pm Tue-Thur, Sat; 6-10.30pm Fri. **Main courses** £11.50-£23. **Set lunch** £14.50-£17.50 2 courses. **Credit** MC, V.

This Borough Market favourite prides itself on its unpretentiousness. It has chequered orange, white and blue tiles, banquettes down one side, and seats along the bar from where customers – some conducting business meetings, some socialising – can watch the day's catch being prepared. Applebee's is looking a little scuffed at the edges, but the food remains memorable for all the right reasons. Come in the daytime, and you can also buy fish from the shop at the front

Wright Brothers. See p85.

FISH

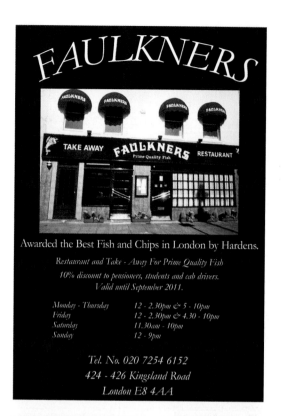

Best fish & chips

No fish chapter would be complete without our favourite purveyors of fine white flesh in crisp, light batter, with golden chips on the side.

Brady's

513 Old York Road, SW18 1TF (8877 9599, www.bradysfish.co.uk). Wandsworth Town rail or 28, 44 bus. **Lunch served** 12.30-2.30pm Fri, Sat. **Dinner served** 6.30-10pm Tue-Thur, Sat; 6.30-10.30pm Fri. Brady's was a pioneer of upmarket fish and chips – witness excellent grilled fish options that complement the traditionally fried. Quality produce, simply cooked. **Map 21 A4**.

Fish Central

149-155 Central Street, EC1V 8AP (7253 4970, www.fishcentral.co.uk). Old Street tube/rail or 55 bus. **Lunch served** 11.30am-2.30pm Mon-Sat. **Dinner served** 5-10.30pm Mon-Thur; 5-11pm Fri, Sat. As smartly attired as the City workers among its clientele, Fish Central enhances the traditional options with some adventurous daily specials and wine or tap beers. **Map 5 P3**.

Fish Club HOT 50

189 St John's Hill, SW11 1TH (7978 7115, www.thefishclub.com). Clapham Junction rail. **Meals served** 5-10pm Mon; noon-10pm Tue-Sun. The classiest chippy in London, Fish Club has an in-floor water feature, clued-up staff and great fish, with sustainable (coley instead of cod) and unusual (pan-fried cuttlefish) varieties on offer. **Map 21 B4**. **For branch see index**.

Fish House

126-128 Lauriston Road, E9 7LH (8533 3327). Mile End tube then 277 bus. **Meals served** noon-10pm Mon-Fri (full menu from 6pm); 11am-10pm Sat, Sun. Another upmarket option, Victoria Park's Fish House offers variety but not consistency: you might win with scallops, but lose with overcooked chips. The eton mess rarely falters.

Fisher's

19 Fulham High Street, SW6 3JH (7610 9808, www.fishersfishandchips.com). Putney Bridge tube. **Lunch served** noon-3pm, **dinner served** 5.30-11.30pm Mon-Fri. **Meals served** noon-11.30pm Sat; 1-11pm Sun. Fisher's is all about huge portions of old-fashioned fish and chips, with own-made tartare sauce and excellent mushy peas. Fish is also available steamed or breaded.

Nautilus

27-29 Fortune Green Road, NW6 1DT (7435 2532). West Hampstead tube/rail then 328 bus.

Lunch served 11.30am-2.30pm, **dinner served** 4.30-10pm Mon-Sat. Unsophisticated decor, but immaculately fried fish in big portions – with beer and wine to wash it down. **Map 28 A1**.

Olley's

65-69 Norwood Road, SE24 9AA (8671 8259, www.olleys.info). Herne Hill rail or 3, 68, 196 bus. **Lunch served** noon-3pm, **dinner served** 5-10.30pm Tue-Sun. Fried, grilled or served in tomato and herb sauce, this Herne Hill favourite dishes up everything from hake to mahi mahi, some sophisticated booze and a fine Brockwell Park view. **Map 23 A5**.

Sea Shell

49-51 Lisson Grove, NW1 6UH (7224 9000, www.seashellrestaurant.co.uk). Marylebone tube/rail. **Lunch served** noon-2.30pm, **dinner served** 5-10.30pm Mon-Fri. **Meals served** noon-10.30pm Sat. Reopening in summer 2010 after a spruce-up (including a new aquarium), the vast Sea Shell continues to produce fried and grilled fish, plus fancy-dan options such as scallops, to be scoffed with a slurp of draught beer or wine. **Map 2 F4**.

Two Brothers Fish Restaurant

297-303 Regent's Park Road, N3 1DP (8346 0469, www.twobrothers.co.uk). Finchley Central tube. **Lunch served** noon-2.30pm, **dinner served** 5.30-10.15pm Tue-Sat. The smart-casual setting (banquettes, no less) is perfect for fine arbroath smokies and fried halibut.

FISH

Geales. See p81.

to take home. The main menu changes little, but there's always a specials board. Plump sweet scallops came with soy sauce and spring onions. Italian fish soup had a good fishy flavour, but lacked seasoning. Fish and chips were excellent, and seafood gnocchi tasty and satisfying. The kitchen's pastry chef has a light touch: witness a gorgeous mango and passionfruit cheesecake. Rhubarb crème brûlée was light and fruity, although it arrived, disconcertingly, in a billowing linen napkin sprinkled with cocoa powder. The Wanstead branch of Applebee's was taken over by new management early in 2010. On our visit some time afterwards it was having an identity crisis: badly cooked Morrocan specials served alongside flaccid fish and chips – don't be confused by the name and logo.
Available for hire. Babies and children admitted. Booking advisable. Disabled: toilet. Tables outdoors (4, pavement). Takeaway service. **Map 11 P8**.

Wright Brothers Oyster & Porter House
11 Stoney Street, SE1 9AD (7403 9554, www.wrightbros. eu.com). London Bridge tube/rail. **Lunch served** noon-3pm Mon-Fri; noon-4pm Sat. **Dinner served** 6-10pm Mon-Sat. **Main courses** £7.30-£25.50. **Credit** AmEx, MC, V.
Wright Brothers is very much an eat-and-run sort of place, with all seating at high-backed stools, and efficient waitresses operating at speed despite the cramped conditions. But the fast turnover suits busy office workers, and the quality of the seafood means diners are prepared to perch. The menu is written on blackboards above the bar, and always lists several oyster combinations. This time we tried oysters Japanese-style, with wasabi, ginger and soy – pretty as a picture and punchily flavoured. Next, grilled plaice with brown butter and new potatoes was a fine piece of fish, cooked just so; sea trout with cucumber, brown shrimps and more new potatoes also lit up the taste buds. Tomato and shallot side salad made a refreshing counterpoint. A limited choice of afters (crème brûlée, cheese plate) is offered, alongside excellent coffee. Sunday brunch brings the likes of smoked haddock kedgeree, and scrambled eggs with Hederman's organic smoked salmon. The wine list has plenty of choice, with riesling prominent on our visit. There's a cosy atmosphere in winter; in summer, grab a table near the open entrance, looking on to Borough Market. A branch in Soho is planned.
Booking advisable. Disabled: toilet. Tables outdoors (4, pavement). **Map 11 P8**.

North East
South Woodford

Ark Fish Restaurant
142 Hermon Hill, E18 1QH (8989 5345, www.arkfish restaurant.com). South Woodford tube. **Lunch served** noon-2.15pm Tue-Sat. **Dinner served** 5.30-9.45pm Tue-Thur; 5.30-10.15pm Fri, Sat. **Meals served** noon-8.45pm Sun. **Main courses** £7.50-£24.25. **Credit** MC, V.
Whelks, winkles, cockles and fresh peeled prawns… it sounds like the start of a nursery rhyme. You can't get more East End than this. South Woodford's Ark is a family-run business that has a long history sourcing fish at Billingsgate. Waiting staff and fellow diners are straight-talking cockneys with a fantastic line in poetic and comic self-expression; Mike Leigh could lift whole scenes from here. We ordered some whelks: 'Good luck,' said our waitress with a sarcastic eyebrow raise. And fresh as

they were, we couldn't finish the sizeable gastropods. 'Like rubber, aren't they?' our waitress deadpanned when she saw our pile of uneaten snails; 'some people love 'em, though'. For mains, a wide choice of fish comes fried, steamed or grilled, with chips, mash or boiled potatoes. We ordered fried plaice and chips and a steamed whole lemon sole with boiled potatoes and mushy peas. Both fish and accompanying vegetables were cooked to perfection. Ark sticks to traditional fish dishes with no twists and hardly any adornments. When your raw ingredients are this good, why mess abaaaaat?
Babies and children welcome: children's menu; high chairs. Bookings not accepted.

North
Finsbury Park

Chez Liline
101 Stroud Green Road, N4 3PX (7263 6550). Finsbury Park tube/rail. **Lunch served** noon-3pm, **dinner served** 6.30-11pm Tue-Sun. **Main courses** £12.75-£22.75. **Set lunch** £10 2 courses. **Set dinner** £12.50 2 courses. **Credit** MC, V.
Finsbury Park's smartest restaurant is nevertheless a homely affair with colourful beach-themed art adding a splash of modernity. Chez Liline specialises in Mauritian seafood dishes, the prime ingredients of which are slapping-fresh and benefit from expert timing on the stove. On our visit, specials celebrated a surfeit of lobster, with several options offering half the crustacean with a sizeable piece of fish (red snapper, say) and a variety of sauces reflecting Mauritian cuisine's French, Chinese and Indian influences. Prawns doused in tomato, chilli and aromatic thyme sauce were just the right side of translucent and beautifully tender. Sautéed sweet potatoes and fluffy basmati rice were better side dishes than the coleslaw-style vegetable pickle that came with the prawns. The hand-scrawled wine list we were given on a clipboard had no reds at all, but the bargain-priced house white – a chardonnay from the Veneto – went down a treat. To finish, crème brûlée had a good vanilla flavour and crunchy top; crêpes suzette lacked buttery richness. Service was as slow and deliberate as an old steam liner: perfectly pleasant, but two hours for two courses in an uncrowded restaurant made everything seem plodding.
Available for hire. Babies and children welcome: high chairs. Booking advisable. Tables outdoors (2, pavement).

Bentley's. See p80.

Best family chains

All the following chains cater admirably for families, with children's menus, high chairs, nappy-changing facilities and decent prices. Youngsters also tend to love the noodle dishes at **Wagamama** and the conveyor-belt fun of **Yo! Sushi** (for both, *see p225*).

Byron

222 Kensington High Street, W8 7RG (7361 1717, www.byronhamburgers.com). High Street Kensington tube. **Meals served** noon-11pm Mon-Thur; noon-11.30pm Fri; 11am-11.30pm Sat; 11am-10.30pm Sun. At Byron (motto: 'proper hamburgers') the unfussy, 6oz classic burger costs just £6.25. Rapid expansion means there are now ten outlets, from Covent Garden to Canary Wharf. **Map 7 A9**.
For branches see index.

Giraffe

Riverside Level 1, Royal Festival Hall, Belvedere Road, SE1 8XX (7928 2004, www.giraffe.net). Embankment tube or Waterloo tube/rail. **Meals served** 8am-10.45pm Mon-Fri; 9am-10.45pm Sat; 9am-10.15pm Sun.
Giraffe's cheery orange colour scheme, soundtrack of world music, and international flavours (burgers, burritos, pasta, sushi rice salad) is a hit with all ages.
Map 10 M8.
For branches see index.

Gourmet Burger Kitchen

Upper Southern Terrace, Westfield Shopping Centre, W12 7GB (8749 1246, www.gbk.co.uk). Wood Lane tube. **Meals served** noon-11pm Mon-Fri; 11am-11pm Sat; 11am-10pm Sun.
Jamaican, Mexican and Thai burgers join the ever-popular Kiwiburger at this well-established New Zealand-inspired chain. Chicken, lamb and buffalo appear too, alongside multiple veggie options.
Map 20 C1.
For branches see index.

Nando's

57-59 Goodge Street, W1T 1TH (7637 0708, www.nandos.co.uk). Tottenham Court Road tube. **Meals served** 11.30am-11pm Mon-Thur; 11.30am-11.30pm Fri, Sat; 11.30am-10.30pm Sun.
Grilled chicken with spicy peri-peri sauce is the mainstay at this budget Portuguese-inspired chain. Fast food, yes, but in a good way.
Map 17 A1.
For branches see index.

Islington

The Fish Shop

360-362 St John Street, EC1V 4NR (7837 1199, www.thefishshop.net). Angel tube or 19, 38, 341 bus. **Lunch served** noon-3pm, **dinner served** 5.30-11pm Tue-Sat. **Main courses** £10.50-£17. **Set meal** (5.30-7pm Tue-Sat) £16 2 courses. **Credit** AmEx, MC, V.
Come during daylight hours to enjoy the Fish Shop's expanse of plate-glass windows. Inside is a cleverly designed, three-level conversion with decor as crisp as the skin on a pan-fried fillet of bream. The semi-open kitchen balances flavours – often Mediterranean – with confidence; witness the crab and avocado cocktail with basil dressing. Our mussels were sandy and slightly overcooked, but pleasingly sweet and swimming in such delicious wine broth it seemed truculent to complain. Similarly fresh was roast gurnard, its backbone neatly removed and replaced with fennel, accompanied by rocket and purple potatoes to strike a pose with the bright orange skin of the fish. Desserts are good; let yourself be wowed by the rich and crunchy crème brûlée topped with white peach and fresh basil sorbet. A wine list starting at £17 is hardly kind for a neighbourhood restaurant, even in Islington, but there's an agreeable list of beers, mostly from Pitfield Brewery, which used to be based nearby. Service was spot-on during our latest visit; the well-to-do, grown-up crowd tying lunch or dinner to a performance at Sadler's Wells expects nothing less.
Available for hire. Babies and children welcome: high chairs. Booking advisable dinner Fri, Sat. Disabled: toilet. Tables outdoors (7, terrace). **Map 5 O3**.

Outer London

Croydon, Surrey

Fish & Grill

48-50 South End, Croydon, Surrey CR0 1DP (8774 4060, www.fishandgrill.co.uk). South Croydon rail or 119, 466 bus. **Meals served** noon-10.30pm daily. **Main courses** £10.95-£44. **Set lunch** £11.95 2 courses, £14.95 3 courses. **Credit** AmEx, MC, V.
Chef-proprietor Malcolm John runs a trio of French neighbourhood restaurants; this is his foray into the world of British fish and chips. Pretty posh fish and chips, mind – the chips presented in a little tin pot, the fish (served whole on the bone) ranging from Cornish lemon sole to grilled lobster, with no batter in sight. Cod appears only in the form of cod cheeks steamed in banana leaves, with basmati rice; pleasant enough but too timidly spiced to generate much excitement. Four plump sardines with a zingy broad bean and caper dressing was tastier, though we could have done with more chips. There's also a selection of meaty mains (T-bone, veal escalope, chateaubriand) for the fish-phobic. The themed wine list ('fresh and lively', 'rich and structured') starts at a winning £12.50 a bottle. Bare dark wood tables and paper menus lend a casual air, but the split-level setting is otherwise smart and masculine, in shades of green and brown, with exposed brickwork and high-backed banquettes. Open french doors provided a cooling breeze for a throng of local customers that included dating couples, a girly gaggle and an ebullient family gathering.
Available for hire. Babies and children welcome: children's menu; high chairs. Booking advisable Fri, Sat. Disabled: toilet. Tables outdoors (3, pavement).

French

It has been a year of excitement for lovers of French cuisine. The Galvin brothers of **Galvin at Windows** and **Galvin Bistrot de Luxe** fame joined the clutch of high-calibre restaurateurs opening in Spitalfields, but instead of the old market, they've chosen a Grade II-listed Victorian church hall, St Botolph's, to house **Galvin La Chapelle** and **Galvin Café a Vin**. Meanwhile, Alexis Gauthier, of highly esteemed Pimlico fine-diner **Roussillon**, launched **Gauthier Soho** in a Romilly Street townhouse that was once the site of Richard Corrigan's Lindsay House. New York heavyweight Daniel Boulud has debuted in the capital with **Bar Boulud**, a luxe brasserie in the basement of the Mandarin Oriental Hyde Park hotel; just over the road at the Berkeley is where chef-of-chefs Pierre Koffmann finally decided to come out of retirement with **Koffman's** (*see p126*). In Farringdon, the trendy Zetter hotel (now infamous thanks to Hazel Blears and the House of Commons expenses scandal) upgraded its dining options with the help of Bordeaux-born Bruno Loubet. Loubet was a much-talked-about chef in London during the 1990s, and critics and customers have warmly welcomed his return from a lengthy spell working in Australia to open **Bistrot Bruno Loubet**.

Central

Belgravia

Roussillon
16 St Barnabas Street, SW1W 8PE (7730 5550, www.roussillon.co.uk). Sloane Square tube. **Lunch served** noon-2.30pm Mon-Fri. **Dinner served** 6.30-10.30pm Mon-Sat. **Set lunch** £35 3 courses incl half bottle of wine. **Set dinner** £60 3 courses. **Set meal** £65-£78 tasting menu. **Credit** AmEx, MC, V.
Roussillon's decor and ambience are conservative to the point of staidness; it's a pleasant and comfortable room but about as stylish as school uniform, whose navy and maroon colours the furnishings mimic. Things are livelier on the plate, with subversive touches enlivening traditional haute cusine mores. The good-value set lunch includes wine and a cavalcade of amuse-bouche. Baby artichokes on a smear of olive with confit garlic tomatoes were exquisite (Roussillon has a reputation for revering vegetables, and even a menu devoted to them). Mains of poached and roasted skate wing with saffron potatoes and samphire, and lamb with kidney were controlled to deliver maximum flavour. Throughout, the palate was teased into

alertness by surprising tastes and textures: a non-oily pine nut sauce, scattered flowers, aniseed notes with strawberries, and the crackle of Space Dust in the chocolate case of a raspberry mousse. The wine list focuses on the south-west of France, but for the set lunch went to the Loire for a Touraine sauvignon and to Alsace for a pinot noir, which worked well. We have no complaints about the food or value, but the combined effect of a half-full room, slightly disengaged service and ageing decor leaves something to be desired in terms of the overall experience. *Booking essential dinner and Fri-Sun.* **Map 15 G11**.

City

Lutyens
85 Fleet Street, EC4Y 1AE (7583 8385, www.lutyens-restaurant.co.uk). City Thameslink or Blackfriars rail, or 4, 11, 15, 23, 26 bus.
Bar **Open** noon-midnight , **breakfast served** 7.30-10.30am, **meals served** noon-9pm Mon-Fri. **Main courses** £12.50-£18. **Set lunch** £17.50 2 courses.
Restaurant **Lunch served** noon-3.30pm, **dinner served** 5.30-10pm Mon-Fri. **Main courses** £12.50-£33. **Set meal** (5.30-10pm) £39.50 3 courses incl half bottle of wine.
Both **Credit** AmEx, MC, V.

Sir Terence Conran's latest restaurant venture occupies Fleet Street's venerable Reuters/AP building, designed by Edwin Lutyens in the 1930s. It's an iconic spot, next door to St Bride's Church, opposite the gorgeous, art deco, ex-Daily Express building and down the road from Goldman Sachs. Lutyens is a typical Conran operation, with a buzzy bar in stylish, masculine tones of white, maroon and dark wood, and a separate, more formal dining room. Service is warm and polished; the maître d' greeted the stream of mainly male diners with practised first-name bonhomie. In the restaurant you can feast on the likes of lobster mousse or steak tartare, followed by Landaise chicken, braised lamb or dover sole;

Lutyens. See p87.

crustacea looms large too, of course. Eating in the bar is a simpler affair (though oysters and a petit plateau de fruits de mer are also available here). The set lunch was a mixed blessing, yielding creamy, tangy mackerel pâté and a juicy beef burger with crispy chips, but also crab hash that was more like a fish cake, squishily textured and with a distinctly odd-tasting basil mayo. A problem with the kitchen's gas supply resulted in a half-hour wait for our mains, but the staff couldn't have been more apologetic, offering complimentary glasses of champagne (and knocking a chunk off the bill).
Babies and children welcome: high chairs. Booking advisable. Disabled: lift; toilet. Separate rooms for parties, seating 6-20. **Map 11 N6.**

Rosemary Lane

61 Royal Mint Street, E1 8LG (7481 2602, www. rosemarylane.btinternet.co.uk). Tower Hill tube or Fenchurch Street rail or Tower Gateway DLR. **Lunch served** noon-2.30pm Mon-Fri. **Dinner served** 5.30-10pm Mon-Fri; 6-10pm Sat. **Meals served** by appointment Sun. **Main courses** £13-£19. **Set meal** £15 2 courses, £18 3 courses. **Set dinner** (Sat) £32 tasting menu. **Credit** AmEx, MC, V.
A converted pub on an East End thoroughfare provides an unassuming home to some of London's best French food. Trappings of the old boozer remain, including wood-panelled walls and a bar, though the addition of closely spaced tables and banquette seating has produced a brasserie feel. Rosemary Lane's proximity to the City attracts clued-up professionals, but reasonable prices and friendly service also draw in locals. Although the menu is short, the food is exceptional: characterised by seasonal ingredients in winning flavour combinations. It's so good, you'll want to close your eyes while eating. Parma ham, rocket and fig salad came with a spiced orange and dijon dressing, while silky chicken liver pâté was paired with lemon-pickled red onion. Entremets of own-made sorbets prepare the palate for the next hit of flavours. On our visit, gnocchi was the sole vegetarian main, yet the plump russet dumplings didn't disappoint, served with zingy lemon beurre blanc, colourful courgette ribbons, broad beans and herbs. For a sojourn away from European flavours, we sampled ginger-glazed poussin with lime dressing – spot-on too. End on a high with the heart-stopping caramel-centred chocolate fondant with valencia orange ice-cream.
Available for hire. Babies and children admitted. Booking advisable lunch. Dress: smart casual. **Map 12 S7.**

Clerkenwell & Farringdon

Bistrot Bruno Loubet   HOT 50
2010 RUNNER-UP BEST NEW RESTAURANT
St John's Square, 86-88 Clerkenwell Road, EC1M 5RJ (7324 4455, www.thezetter.com/en/restaurant). Farringdon tube/rail. **Breakfast served** 7-10.30am Mon-Fri; 7.30-11am Sat, Sun. **Lunch served** noon-2.30pm Mon-Fri. **Brunch served** noon-3pm Sat, Sun. **Dinner served** 6-10.30pm Mon-Sat; 6-10pm Sun. **Main courses** £15-£18.50. **Credit** AmEx, MC, V.
Bruno Loubet has completely reinvigorated the restaurant at the Zetter hotel. The short menu now reads like a dream. Beetroot ravioli, fried breadcrumbs and sage with rocket salad was a set of prettily arranged little parcels bursting with sweet flavour; soused mackerel, watercress salad and buckwheat bread with prawn butter was a robust but balanced plateful.

To follow, quail and pistachio dodine with spinach and egg yolk raviolo had a wonderful flavour and confirmed the skill at work; braised beef indochine with mango and herb salad featured rich, meltingly tender meat perfectly offset by the tangy salad. Proof the kitchen is mortal came in a dessert of fig 'carpaccio' with pistachio crumble and lemon and olive oil ice-cream – the flavours underwhelmed and the elements didn't gel. The room is fairly plain, with dashes of quirky decor (including a waiters' station made from refashioned furniture, and various retro lamps). At the front is a bar, and there's a dining room with a kitchen view at the back; huge windows look over St John's Square. Tables are squeezed into this slightly awkward space, but there's a buzz of happy diners regardless. A restaurant with a real – and rare – wow factor. *Babies and children welcome: high chairs. Booking essential. Disabled: toilet. Separate rooms for parties, seating 40-50. Tables outdoors (9, terrace).* **Map 5 O4**.

Club Gascon HOT 50
57 West Smithfield, EC1A 9DS (7796 0600, www.club gascon.com). Barbican tube or Farringdon tube/rail. **Lunch served** noon-2pm Mon-Fri. **Dinner served** 7-10pm Mon-Thur; 7-10.30pm Fri, Sat. **Dishes** £12-£26. **Set lunch** £22-£28 3 courses. **Set meal** £55 5 courses (£85 incl wine). **Credit** AmEx, MC, V.
The only membership this club requires is the ability to pay for the food and wine, but if you're looking for a true gustatory experience in plush surrounds, Pascal Aussignac and Vincent Labeyrie's Smithfield flagship is where to head. At lunchtime you'll hear big deals being discussed, but the decor and dish presentation (pretty, modestly sized portions for sharing) are romantic enough for a date. Food traditional to – and inspired by – the south-west of France is the kitchen's raison d'être. Hence, duck magret carpaccio may come with wasabi and crunchy peas, or sturgeon bordelaise with sweet onions and samphire. Carefully conceived vegetable dishes (aligot with girolles and truffle vinaigrette, say, or courgette flower primavera with seaweed tartare) and several delectable ways with seafood make Club Gascon a viable choice for those who eschew meat. The seasonal tasting menu (for the whole table) offers five dishes plus amuses for £55; add £30 per person for matching wines.

The adjacent Cellar Gascon wine bar has classy bar food of a type unrivalled in the capital – not just in the quality of ingredients, but in the way they're assembled: think seared beef fillet with blackcurrant and violet mustard, or confit rabbit with anchovies and garlic. Check the web for deals such as half-price on bottles of wine and champagne costing over £50 on Mondays and Tuesdays. On the other side of the market, Le Comptoir Gascon offers more rustic cooking (pork belly with parsnip purée and mushrooms, London's best chips), plus own-baked breads and pâtisserie to take home, in casual yet stylish surrounds. The company also runs Le Cercle near Sloane Square, a discreet if rather Sloaney basement dining room with food and wine every bit as good as the Smithfield mothership. *Available for hire. Booking essential.* **Map 11 O5**. **For branches (Cellar Gascon, Le Cercle, Le Comptoir Gascon) see index**.

Eastside Inn
40 St John Street, EC1M 4AY (7490 9230, www.esilondon. com). Farringdon tube/rail. **Lunch served** noon-2.30pm, **snacks served** 2.30-7pm, **dinner served** 7-10pm Tue-Sat. **Main courses** £13-£20. **Credit** AmEx, MC, V.
Bjorn van der Horst's idiosyncratic restaurant and bar turns out stellar food in slightly odd surroundings. The decor is hotel lobby-luxe, but the warmth of the staff and the quality of cooking – produced from a very open kitchen in the dining

Bistrot Bruno Loubet

room – won us over. There's a generosity of spirit here, exemplified by the motto 'our home is your home' on the menu, the greeting by the man himself, and the extras, from amuse-bouche to petits fours. Prices are anything but greedy. Wine by the glass starts at £3.25 – unheard of at this level, especially when accompanied by the lightest cheese puffs – and hors d'oeuvres at £3.50. These are only slightly smaller than starters: own-cured gravadlax and soft cheese with garlic and herbs went down a treat, but a starter of spider crab salad with Jersey Royals, samphire and herbs stole the show. Coq au vin (Wednesday's plat du jour) and stuffed courgettes mentonnaise (with spinach, chard, parmesan and pine nuts) were good, but shaded by that day's special, Saudi prawn with fennel – a tasty whopper of a crustacean. Even a zingy raspberry sorbet was surpassed by pudding: apricot soufflé with thyme and almond sorbet. This is inventive, delicious cooking that deserves a wider audience.

Babies and children admitted. Booking advisable. Separate room for parties, seats 14. **Map 5 O5**.

Covent Garden

Clos Maggiore

33 King Street, WC2E 8JD (7379 9696, www.clos maggiore.com). Covent Garden or Leicester Square tube. **Lunch served** noon-2.30pm daily. **Dinner served** 5-11pm Mon-Sat; 5-10pm Sun. **Main courses** £15.50-£21.50. **Set lunch** (Mon-Fri) £19.50 3 courses or 2 courses incl half bottle of wine; (Sat, Sun) £24.50 2 courses incl half bottle of wine. **Set dinner** (Fri, Sat) £19.50 2 courses. **Set meal** £55 tasting menu. **Credit** AmEx, MC, V.

Just off Covent Garden's bustling piazza, Clos Maggiore transports you to a picturesque corner of Provence. An elegant boxwood-lined dining room leads to an intimate indoor courtyard filled with fake blossoms and fairy lights. The idyllic decor makes the restaurant a magnet for couples, especially after dark when there are candles and a flickering log fire. A sophisticated provençal-inspired menu highlights the provenance of produce, and the carefully sourced ingredients shine through in the dishes. We took advantage of the exceptionally low-priced set lunch menu, which includes luxuries such as Devon crab (this came topped with citrusy marjoram and crunchy celeriac roulade). A fillet of Cornish sea bream came with smoky chorizo-infused durum wheat; and a dish of succulent roasted Landes coquelet was nicely balanced with pulses coated in basil pesto. Desserts are equally memorable, our favourite being prized provençal gariguette strawberries served with basil sorbet and warm mini madeleines. The framed awards on the walls are for the wine, and hidden away is one of London's most extensive cellars with over 2,000 bins; there's a wide price range of bottles, and a sommelier on hand for guidance.

Babies and children welcome: high chairs. Booking advisable; essential weekends, 3 wks in advance for conservatory. Separate room for parties, seats 23. Tables outdoors (6, conservatory). Vegetarian menu. **Map 18 D4**.

Fitzrovia

Villandry

170 Great Portland Street, W1W 5QB (7631 3131, www.villandry.com). Great Portland Street tube. *Bar* **Open** 8am-11pm Mon-Fri; 9am-11pm Sat. **Breakfast served** 8-11.30am, **meals served** noon-10pm Mon-Sat.

Main courses £11.50-£22.50. *Restaurant* **Lunch served** noon-3pm Mon-Sat; 11.30am-4pm Sun. **Dinner served** 6-10.30pm Mon-Sat. **Main courses** £12.50-£22.50. *Both* **Credit** AmEx, MC, V.

Villandry is not what it once was. Not a charming deli-bistro on Marylebone High Street (its 1990s incarnation). Not a flashy food hall on Great Portland Street. Even in recent years, every time we visit something seems to have been reworked – the takeaway area (once a florist's) has been replaced by a baby shop – but there's no denying the exuberance of the place. Turn up on spec to the rear restaurant at lunchtime and staff may not be able to squeeze you in. Proximity to the BBC notwithstanding, famous faces love to breakfast and lunch here, with tables in the charcuterie area especially prized. The menu has an appealing list of ten-or-so starters, mains and puds, plus a plat du jour (coq au vin bordelaise, steak haché) and a fistful of oyster and shellfish options. Yet the cooking rarely wows (for example, seared black bream with sautéed potatoes, roast vine tomatoes and olives was no better than you might knock out at home) and you tend to leave feeling everything's too pricey. Still, something's going right; there's now a branch of Villandry in Bicester, as well as the more casual Villandry Kitchen outlets in Holborn and Chiswick.

Available for hire. Babies and children welcome: children's menu; high chairs. Booking advisable. Tables outdoors (13, pavement). Takeaway service. **Map 3 H5**. **For branches (Villandry Kitchen) see index**.

Knightsbridge

Bar Boulud

2010 RUNNER-UP BEST NEW RESTAURANT
Mandarin Oriental Hyde Park, 66 Knightsbridge, SW1X 7LA (7201 3899, www.barboulud.com/bar bouludlondon.html). Knightsbridge tube. **Lunch served** noon-2.30pm, **dinner served** 5.30-10.30pm daily. **Main courses** £12.50-£23. **Set meal** (lunch, 5.30-7pm) £20 3 courses. **Credit** AmEx, MC, V.

French-born, US-based star chef Daniel Boulud has brought the best of both worlds to the Mandarin Oriental with this 'branch' of one of his New York enterprises. The basement setting has low-key decor with nods to classic brasserie styling. Leisurewear, small children and boisterous groups are happily embraced, resulting in a buzzing restaurant where everyone feels at home. The menu contains a few American dishes (a small yankee burger with exquisite french fries), but is mainly French. Much inspiration comes around Lyon (where Boulud was born). Charcuterie takes centre stage, with an array of terrines, pâtés, hams and sausages, accompanied by delightfully tangy 'hors d'oeuvre' such as carrots with coriander or celery-apple remoulade. Lapin de la garrigue (provençal pulled rabbit with carrot, courgette and herbs), a hefty slice of jewelled jelly, was a highlight. Mains run from croque monsieur to coq au vin and steak frites, plus specials such as wild halibut with ratatouille and tapenade. The latter was surprisingly bland, with only the tapenade adding oomph. To finish, there are cheeses divided by type ('stinky', 'old and hard') and classic puddings; coupe de fruits exotiques was a superior concoction, made magical by a coconut and passionfruit sorbet. Staff are charm itself, whether serving a bottle from the serious wine list, or conjuring up a fresh fruit juice. Prices for this first-class performance are most reasonable, making Bar Boulud a very welcome import.

Babies and children welcome: high chairs. Booking advisable. Disabled: toilet. Dress: smart casual. Separate rooms for parties, seating 16. **Map 8 F9.**

Racine

239 Brompton Road, SW3 2EP (7584 4477, www.racine-restaurant.com). Knightsbridge or South Kensington tube, or 14, 74 bus. **Lunch served** noon-3pm Mon-Fri; noon-3.30pm Sat, Sun. **Dinner served** 6-10.30pm Mon-Sat; 6-10pm Sun. **Main courses** £12.50-£20.75. **Set meal** (lunch, 6-7.30pm Mon-Fri) £15 2 courses, £17.50 3 courses; (lunch, 6-7.30pm Sat, Sun) £17.50 2 courses, £19.50 3 courses. **Credit** AmEx, MC, V.

The concept of 'bistro de luxe' was launched in London when Racine opened its doors in 2002, and despite the increased competition over the years, the restaurant continues to do well. Nevertheless, its interior, never the most colourful, cloaked in dark brown with mirror-lined walls, could now do with sprucing up a little. On our arrival, the courteous staff made sure we were relaxed before bringing the menu. The cooking, under the vigilant eye of Henry Harris, is comforting, and prices are moderate for the location. A Sunday roast has been introduced during the past year. Our meal started with a hot foie gras served with quince, which arrived with a brioche beignet. The results were predictable, yet enjoyable. This is a good venue to sample classic Lyonnaise cooking, and our tête de veau (calf's head) with a ravigote sauce was terrific. For a more luxurious option, you'll not go too wrong with a juicy grilled veal chop paired with roquefort butter. Desserts do not change much, but it's hard to resist the delicious crème caramel. *Available for hire. Babies and children admitted: high chairs. Booking essential. Separate room for parties, seats 18.* **Map 14 E10.**

Bar Boulud. See p91.

Mayfair

La Petite Maison

54 Brooks Mews, W1K 4EG (7495 4774, www.lpmlondon.co.uk). Bond Street tube. **Lunch served** noon-2.30pm Mon-Fri; 12.30-2.45pm Sat; 12.30-3.30pm Sun. **Dinner served** 6-10.30pm Mon-Sat; 6.30-9pm Sun. **Main courses** £13.50-£35. **Credit** AmEx, MC, V.

La Petite Maison first opened in Nice in 1988, pre-empting by five years the World Health Organisation's promotion of the Mediterranean diet as the best choice for cardiovascular well-being. The restaurant became renowned as a celebrity hangout and, while the Mediterranean diet was passé when this branch opened in London, that did nothing to hamper its success. Set behind Claridge's, LPM London hums with a sophisticated, suntanned Euro crowd. Its atmosphere and carefully styled interior (olive oil, tomatoes and lemons substitute as flowers for table decorations) are as bright and breezy as a summer's afternoon on a yacht. The cooking from Raphael Duntoye's kitchen is superb – the menu is crammed with simple yet luxurious dishes – but the trump card is the sharing concept. So many contemporary restaurants have tapas-style menus that are more mismatch than mix-and-match; here, everything works together because it comes from the same cuisine. Lots of salads and seafood (broad beans with pecorino, sardines with grapes, tomatoes and capers) keep the WAGs happy, while the likes of macaroni cheese with summer truffles and whole roast leg of milk-fed Pyrenéean lamb with couscous stick to the ribs of their partners. Prices are high, but c'est la vie. La Petite Maison is reliably good fun. *Babies and children admitted: high chairs. Booking advisable. Tables outdoors (10, terrace).* **Map 9 H6.**

FRENCH

Soho

Gauthier Soho

21 Romilly Street, W1D 5AF (7494 3111, www.gauthier soho.co.uk). Leicester Square or Piccadilly Circus tube. **Lunch served** noon-2.30pm Mon-Fri. **Dinner served** 5.30-10pm Mon-Fri; 5.30-10.30pm Sat. **Set lunch** £18 2 courses, £25 3 courses. **Set dinner** (5.30-7pm, 9.30-10.30pm) £18 2 courses (£26 incl half bottle of wine), £25 3 courses (£35 incl half bottle of wine); (7-9.30pm) £35 3 courses, £45 4 courses, £55 5 courses. **Set meal** £68 tasting menu (£110 incl wine). **Credit** AmEx, MC, V.
Alexis Gauthier, former chef-proprietor at Roussillon, has taken over what was the Lindsay House, a narrow, four-storey Georgian building of small rooms. Blandly decorated in white and grey, Gauthier Soho is a temple of gastronomy where diners sit hushed while black-suited staff mill around. The wine list is long, expensive and French-focused, with much from the south-west. By contrast, the food menus (a tasting menu, three- to five-course menus, lunch or pre-theatre deals) seem almost terse. Expect plenty of unbidden inter-course titillation – lovely chickpea beignets, pre-desserts, scented marshmallows, petits fours – luxury ingredients in small portions, and brilliant sauces. Scallops were pan-seared on one side, served with a brown butter sauce of warm, nutty richness, cut with the sharpness of sherry vinegar. The chicken jus served over some lovage and ricotta-stuffed ravioli, and the beef jus served over medium-rare beef were sublime. Given such a classically inspired, gifted kitchen, we couldn't resist trying the wobbly duck egg soufflé, served in the shell with crostini-like 'soldiers' and a dip of egg yolk-rich chocolate 'curd'. Service wasn't nearly as polished as the silver cloches covering the dishes arriving from the basement.
Available for hire. Babies and children welcome: high chairs. Booking advisable. Separate rooms for parties, seating 4-16. **Map 17 C4**.

La Trouvaille

12A Newburgh Street, W1F 7RR (7287 8488, www. latrouvaille.co.uk). Oxford Circus tube. **Lunch served** noon-3pm Mon-Fri. **Dinner served** 6-11pm Tue-Sat. **Set lunch** £17.50 2 courses, £21.50 3 courses. **Set dinner** £29.50 2 courses, £35 3 courses. **Credit** AmEx, MC, V.
A hidden gem set back from Carnaby Street, La Trouvaille's ground-floor bar has creaky floorboards, brown paper placemats and candles flickering on barrels. By contrast, the upstairs dining room is all starched table linen, monochrome decor and eclectic mirrors. Black-clad waiters bustle about, attending the clientele – tanned, wealthy Londoners and French gourmets. The nouvelle cuisine served here generally offers both style and substance. Smoked salmon rolls stuffed with meaty crab and nerve-tinglingly fresh herbs sparkled against a butternut squash and coconut purée. Another starter, black olive 'panna cotta', divided opinion; it was either subtle or bland, but improved once spread on the own-made bread frequently offered by waiters. A sea bass main course was cooked to moist perfection, but the standout dish was tender rack of lamb served with silky gravy and intense, herby, oven-dried tomatoes. An unexpected 20-minute wait for dessert heightened expectations, yet though commendably gooey, the moelleux's high cocoa content earmarked it strictly for chocoholics. Although not flawless, service was professional and enthusiastic. The cheerful sommelier was summoned to answer a question about the wholly biodynamic wine list; minor slip-ups caused the other waiters to be even friendlier. *Babies and children admitted. Booking advisable. Tables outdoors (8, pavement).* **Map 17 A3**.

West

Bayswater

Angelus

4 Bathhurst Street, W2 2SD (7402 0083, www.angelus restaurant.co.uk). Lancaster Gate tube. **Meals served** 11am-11pm Mon-Sat; 11am-10pm Sun. **Main courses** £18-£33. **Set lunch** £38 3 courses incl half bottle of wine. **Credit** AmEx, MC, V.
Despite appearing to date from the 1970s – the decade the art nouveau decor and especially the back boudoir sitting room of this former pub recalls – Angelus arrived this century. The cooking is bright and contemporary, but *le paradox français* thrives in the combination of dairy produce appearing at every opportunity (check out the magnificent cheeseboard and the creamy, parmesan-enriched and hence un-Italian seafood risotto) and in the hefty, pricey wine list. House champagne is notably toasty; Gospel Green cider a worthy idiosyncrasy. Truffle and white bean soup with an archipelago of truffle oil and generous slice of truffle was comfort at its most luxurious. We enjoyed the assiette d'agneau de Cornouaille, not just for the French vowels in 'Cornwall' and the poitrine, rognon, noisette and farce (breast, kidney, rounded steak and flavoursome faggot), but for the vivid, minutely diced seasonal vegetables with puy lentils. Everything is served by entertainingly accented, dedicated and knowledgeable French staff. Other attractions: a ravishing, intense chocolate fondant with caramelised kumquats and pistachio ice-cream; and tables outside on the pleasant street. Angelus is a slice of Paris to cherish, but unfortunately and inevitably, not at bistro prices. *Babies and children admitted. Booking advisable. Disabled: lift; toilet. Separate room for parties, seats 22. Tables outdoors (5, terrace).* **Map 8 D6**.

Holland Park

The Belvedere

Holland House, off Abbotsbury Road, in Holland Park, W8 6LU (7602 1238, www.belvedererestaurant.co.uk). Holland Park tube. **Lunch served** noon-2.15pm Mon-Sat; noon-2pm, 2.30-4.30pm Sun. **Dinner served** 6-10pm Mon-Sat. **Main courses** £12-£22. **Set meal** (lunch, 6-7pm Mon-Fri) £15.95 2 courses, £19.95 3 courses; (lunch Sat, Sun) £24.95 3 courses. **Credit** AmEx, MC, V.
On a Sunday afternoon, an air of mannered calm prevails in the Belvedere's lofty dining room – once the elegant summer ballroom of Holland House. A piano tinkles in the background, black-aproned waiters glide between tables with unruffled dignity, and french doors open on to the park's manicured formal lawns. Artful contemporary touches (the dramatic Damien Hirst butterfly painting, say) add a playful edge to the interior's muted gold chinoiserie and graceful cream drapes, while the art deco mirrors reflect an equally polished clientele: linen-clad locals, off-duty bankers and impeccably elegant octogenarians. The menu steers towards uncontroversial, well-executed classics, from goat's cheese tart with red onion marmalade to duck confit with puy lentils, superior fish and

chips or handsomely apportioned Sunday roasts. A shame, though, that our sea bass was slightly overcooked, and served with a barely there (albeit artistic) dribble of salsa verde. Quietly charming waiters dispensed professional service and spot-on recommendations – a starter of french toast with a perfect poached egg, wild mushrooms and rich, yellow hollandaise was, just as promised, 'quite delicious'. The dessert menu rounds things off nicely, running from rhubarb crumble to a splendid variant on tarte tatin, involving caramelised bananas and luscious, vanilla-flecked ice-cream.
Available for hire. Babies and children welcome: high chairs. Booking essential. Separate room for parties, seats 20. Tables outdoors (8, terrace).

South West

Wandsworth

Chez Bruce

2 Bellevue Road, SW17 7EG (8672 0114, www.chez bruce.co.uk). Wandsworth Common rail. **Lunch served** noon-2pm Mon-Fri; noon-3pm Sat, Sun. **Dinner served** 6.30-10pm Mon-Thur; 6.30-10.30pm Fri, Sat; 7-9pm Sun. **Set lunch** (Mon-Fri) £25.50 3 courses; (Sat, Sun) £32.50 3 courses. **Set dinner** £42.50 3 courses. **Credit** AmEx, DC, MC, V.

Chez Bruce has been wowing south Londoners and food lovers from further afield since 1995 and, as we went to press, was closed for another refurbishment that includes moving the kitchen and expanding the dining area into the old post office next door. Chef and co-owner Bruce Poole has always sought to offer fine dining in a relaxed environment, so don't expect any bells and whistles in the new interior. What you can expect is first-rate French food with frequent forays into Spain and Italy and occasionally further east. The tempting menu pitches the likes of rare-grilled salmon with sauce vierge, brown shrimps, pea shoots and basil, against fresh tagliatelle with girolles, gazpacho with bocconcini, and spiced mackerel with yoghurt dressing, chickpea salad and aubergine purée – and that's just for starters. Côte de boeuf with chips and béarnaise for two has long been a menu favourite, or you might choose the pig-themed blanquette featuring cheek, roast fillet, boudin blanc and choucroute. Cheeses demand a £5 supplement over the very good desserts, but are offered with a rare sense of celebration. The wine list stretches to 36 pages and is rightly esteemed (it includes Swiss and Canadian varieties); a connoisseur's selection of bottled beers is also offered. Service is the acme of friendly professionalism.

A model restaurant, you might say, and so it has become: the business partnership of Poole and Nigel Platts-Martin also owns Chiswick's La Trompette and Kew's the Glasshouse. In our recent experience, cooking at the latter is similar to, and every bit as good as, its older brother Bruce. La Trompette, whose simple, grown-up interior attracts a local, middle-aged crowd, hasn't quite hit those heights; it's slightly more geared to the cooking of south and south-west France, yet not averse to incorporating the likes of chicory foam and lemongrass jelly in desserts. Its wine list has won many awards.
Babies and children welcome (lunch): high chairs. Booking essential. Disabled: toilet. Separate room for parties, seats 16.
For branches (The Glasshouse, La Trompette) see index.

South

Clapham

Trinity

4 The Polygon, SW4 0JG (7622 1199, www.trinity restaurant.co.uk). Clapham Common tube. **Lunch served** 12.30-2.30pm Tue-Sat; noon-4.30pm Sun. **Dinner served** 6.30-10.30pm Mon-Sat. **Main courses** £17-£28. **Set lunch** (Tue-Sat) £20 2 courses; (Tue-Sun), £25 3 courses. **Set meal** £20 3 courses. **Cover** £1.50 lunch, £2 dinner. **Credit** AmEx, MC, V.

The dining room here has a low-key elegance completely in tune with the sophisticated food emerging from Adam Byatt's kitchen. Things can get pricey, which makes the set menus a good deal, especially as they feature dishes from the carte. A cover charge always irritates, but at least it includes beautiful bread rolls, served warm, with a sphere of very yellow butter. These set the standard for a thoroughly excellent meal, from a starter of finger-licking-good battered sand eels with zingy aïoli (a special) to a wonderfully vivid dessert of summer berry gazpacho, with little jellies, sorbet and plenty of fruit. Mains of pork (great crackling) with a hot potato 'soup' served in an onion, and salmon with nicely crisped skin, accompanied by peas à la français, pea shoots and braised baby gem lettuce also met with approval. A delightfully unctuous welsh rarebit with pickled onions and a smear of mustard, served on a wooden platter, was worth ordering too. Service is correct, but comes with a smile. Trinity is very much a local (a toddler was tucking into her food with gusto on our visit), yet very serious about what it does, and should be congratulated for pulling off a tricky balancing act with flair.
Babies and children welcome: high chairs. Booking essential. Disabled: toilet. **Map 22 A1**.

Waterloo

RSJ

33 Coin Street, SE1 9NR (7928 4554, www.rsj.uk.com). Waterloo tube/rail. **Lunch served** noon-2.30pm Mon-Fri. **Dinner served** 5.30-11pm Mon-Sat. **Main courses** £12-£19. **Set meal** £16.95 2 courses, £18.95 3 courses. **Credit** AmEx, DC, MC, V.

You can easily pass this unassuming corner restaurant without noticing it. A shame, because not only is it one of the few non-chain eateries convenient to the South Bank, but it offers decent food at a very good price, including a notable three-course menu for just under £19. Also, the wine list demonstrates a keen and up-to-date knowledge of its speciality, the Loire, an undervalued and generally under-represented region with a lot of variety and interest to offer. There are plenty of choices by the glass, chosen to match the food and showcase wines at their optimum drinking age. The simple upstairs space, with its dove-grey walls and changing art, has a little less character than the wine list, but of such stuff are classics made, as RSJ's 30 years in business proves. The menu – French and Mediterranean-inflected, but with British ingredients and influence – is similarly inoffensively pleasant, and pretty well rendered. Hits on our last visit were a subtly flavoured if wobbly crab tian, deliquescent juniper-smoked salmon and halibut with spring salad. The middle-aged clientele and pleasant service contributed to the unchallenging atmosphere.
Babies and children admitted. Booking advisable. Separate rooms for parties, seating 25-40. **Map 11 N8**.

FRENCH

Gauthier Soho. See p93.

East
Bethnal Green

Bistrotheque `HOT 50`
*23-27 Wadeson Street, E2 9DR (8983 7900,
www.bistrotheque.com). Bethnal Green tube/rail
or Cambridge Heath rail, or 55 bus.*
Bar **Open** 6pm-midnight Tue-Sat; 6-11pm Sun.
Restaurant **Brunch served** 11am-4pm Sat, Sun. **Dinner
served** 6.30-10.30pm Mon-Thur, Sun; 6.30-11pm Fri, Sat.
Main courses £12-£22. **Set dinner** (6.30-7.30pm
Mon-Thur) £17.50 3 courses; (6.30-7.15pm Fri, Sat) £30
3 courses.
Both **Credit** AmEx, MC, V.
An east London pioneer only a few years ago, this bar-
restaurant-cabaret complex in an ex-factory building has now
become part of the furniture in E2. In the first-floor restaurant,
the whitewashed industrial look is softened by flowers,
gleaming glassware and a piano. Service can be hit or miss, but
is generally friendly. The menu is similarly variable, but there
are enough sure-fire dishes to excuse a few misses. Stalwart
starters such as steak tartare or salt and chilli squid are
enlivened by the likes of confit tomato and samphire terrine

with basil purée. Fish and chips with pea purée and tartare
sauce is a menu staple, with good reason; seasonal changes
might bring roast courgette, pea and pecorino risotto or grilled
lamb rump with samphire, asparagus and salsa verde.
Puddings run from crème brûlée and chocolate espresso pot to
honey and thyme roasted peaches with mascarpone cheese.
Popular weekend brunches feature pancakes with bacon and
maple syrup, cheeseburger with pancetta and caramelised
onions, eggs benedict and croque monsieur. Cocktails are a
speciality; try them here or in the cosy Napoleon bar on the
ground floor.
*Babies and children admitted: high chairs. Booking
advisable. Disabled: toilet. Entertainment: cabaret (check
website or phone for details); pianist noon-4pm Sun.
Separate rooms for parties, seating 50-80.*

Shoreditch

Boundary
*2-4 Boundary Street, entrance at 9 Redchurch Street,
E2 7DD (7729 1051, www.theboundary.co.uk). Shoreditch
High Street rail.* **Lunch served** noon-3pm Tue-Fri;
noon-4pm Sun. **Dinner served** 6.30-10.30pm Mon-Sat.
Main courses £9.25-£23.50. **Set lunch** £19.50 2 courses,
£24.50 3 courses. **Credit** AmEx, MC, V.
The Anglo-French menu here is very recognisably a Terence
Conran production – the sizeable fruits de mer section is the
first clue – with no concession made to tightened budgets.
Expense-account diners can tuck in to the likes of steak tartare,
Cornish crab or a feast from the charcuterie trolley (sliced
meats, terrines, pâtés and rillettes), followed by braised trotter
with sweetbreads and morels, bouillabaisse or that day's roast
(on Sundays both leg of lamb and rib of beef are available). If
you can resist the splendid cheese chariot, you might have room
for sweet treats such as tarte tatin or rhubarb soufflé (perhaps
accompanied by one of six dessert wines by the glass), or
savouries such as devils on horseback. The restaurant is in a
basement, but there's plenty of light and lots to catch the eye:
not only the many artworks, but also the view of the open
kitchen along one side. Service is pretty formal, and the
atmosphere in general more straitlaced than the Shoreditch
norm. Try British brasserie the Albion (*see p62*) or the seasonal
Rooftop restaurant for more casual dining options within the
Boundary hotel.
*Available for hire. Babies and children welcome: high chairs;
nappy-changing facilities. Booking advisable dinner.
Disabled: lift; toilet.* **Map 6 R4**.

Les Trois Garçons `HOT 50`
*1 Club Row, E1 6JX (7613 1924, www.lestroisgarcons.com).
Shoreditch High Street rail.* **Dinner served** 6-10.30pm
Mon-Thur; 6-11pm Fri, Sat. **Set dinner** £39.50 2 courses,
£45.50 3 courses, £72 tasting menu (£100 incl wine).
Credit AmEx, DC, MC, V.
Housed in an East End pub conversion like no other, Les Trois
Garçons displays baroque chandeliers, hanging vintage
handbags and bejewelled stuffed animals. It's like stumbling
into the mind of taxidermal artist Polly Morgan. Stay calm –
a traditional maître d' and suited staff are here to assure you
that fine dining can sit alongside surreal surroundings.
Although the restaurant is renowned for its accessorised
interior and celebrity sightings, the kitchen's classical French
cuisine has kept culinary pulses racing for more than ten years.
The novel-length dish descriptions flaunt technique, such as

FRENCH

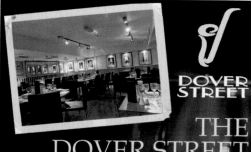

LTG's foie gras cooked au torchon (in a tea towel). Said foie gras had been cured in heavenly Sauternes and arrived with a sweet pear and raisin chutney and slivers of toasted brioche. Pressed Herdwick lamb shoulder was equally impressive, its richness offset by a piquant caper and herb sauce. A shared chateaubriand is a popular main, as is the Gressingham duck leg and breast duo. We were wowed by jumbo seared scallops served in celery and lemongrass butter foam, crowned with curry-cured roe and cauliflower brandade. The wine list deserves praise too, as does the friendly, knowledgeable service.
Available for hire. Booking advisable. Children over 12yrs admitted. Separate room for parties, seats 10.
Map 6 S4.

Spitalfields

Galvin Café a Vin

35 Spital Square, entrance on Bishops Square, E1 6DY (7299 0404, www.galvinrestaurants.com). Liverpool Street tube/rail or Shoreditch High Street rail. **Breakfast served** 8-11.30am, **lunch served** noon-3pm, **dinner served** 6-10.30pm daily. **Main courses** £15-£17.50. **Set meal** (lunch, 6-7pm) £14.95 2 courses. **Credit** AmEx, MC, V.
The Galvin brothers' empire now includes (in order of opening) Galvin Bistrot de Luxe (a benchmark for bistros, in Marylebone); Galvin at Windows (haute cuisine, with views from the 28th floor of the Park Lane Hilton); and Galvin La Chapelle (the beautiful refashioning of St Botolph's Hall). Galvin Café a Vin sits next to the last of these, in a slightly confusing arrangement that includes terraces at front and back, a bar area and quite a small dining space. It can't match La Chapelle for decor or dish dazzle, but it's handsome enough, and prices are considerably kinder on the wallet. Charcuterie maison with celeriac remoulade and cornichons was a generous, well-balanced platter (and only £7.50); crab salad with cucumber, avocado and bottarga was also good, if (bizarrely, given the ingredients) a tad bland. Calf's liver with red chicory, speck, figs and balsamic packed more of a punch; the liver was first rate and cooked just-so. Sea trout with samphire was also well flavoured, with a real blast of the sea. Chocolate and hazelnut pot de crème, plus a fine macchiato, rounded off the meal nicely. As the name suggests (it opened as Café de Luxe, but has since been renamed Café a Vin) there's an emphasis on wine, with plenty by the glass and 'pot' as well as by the bottle. A useful, grown-up spot.
Babies and children welcome: high chairs. Booking advisable. Disabled: toilet. Tables outdoors (15, pavement).
Map 12 R5.
For branches (Galvin at Windows, Galvin Bistrot de Luxe, Galvin La Chapelle) see index.

North

Camden Town & Chalk Farm

L'Absinthe

40 Chalcot Road, NW1 8LS (7483 4848, http:// labsinthe.co.uk). Chalk Farm tube. **Lunch served** noon-2.30pm Mon-Fri; noon-4pm Sat, Sun. **Dinner served** 6-10.30pm Tue-Sat; 6-9.30pm Sun. **Main courses** £8.95-£15.95. **Set lunch** (Tue-Fri) £9.50 2 courses; (Sun) £14.95 2 courses. **Credit** AmEx, MC, V.

A blackboard outside – 'Everything expensive, nothing good' – is the first sign that this cosy local bistro and wine retailer doesn't take itself too seriously. Inside, cheerful green and white walls are painted with the names of famous dishes in the French canon, and the menu shows owner and staff posing for the camera with berets, baguettes and curly moustaches. Waiters are relaxed enough to let children bored with the Asterix and Tintin books draw on the specials board, and the bonhomie is contagious. Cooking tends to the straightforward: starters of Chalk Farm-made smoked salmon, gazpacho, and ham hock terrine, say, followed by hearty meats with a starch and salad. There's no fussing with poncey presentation. A succulent man-sized pork chop came with a finger-licking prune sauce and perfectly creamy pommes purée (or mash, as the menu called it). A special of steak haché was cooked to the French definition of 'medium', topped with chunky sauce vierge and accompanied by good own-made chips. The house crème brûlée, flavoured with absinthe, is a winner, so too the approachable wine list that for premium wines settles for a flat £10 mark-up over the shop price. There should be more places like this.
Babies and children welcome: high chairs. Booking advisable. Tables outdoors (5, pavement). **Map 27 B2**.

Islington

Almeida

30 Almeida Street, N1 1AD (7354 4777, www.dandd london.com). Angel tube or Highbury & Islington tube/rail. **Lunch served** noon-2.30pm Tue-Sat. **Dinner served** 5.30-10.30pm Mon-Sat. **Meals served** noon-3.30pm Sun. **Main courses** £9.50-£15.50. **Set dinner** £27.50 2 courses, £32.50 3 courses. **Set meal** (5.30-6.30pm daily; 9.30-10.30pm Mon-Sat) £15.95 2 courses, £18.95 3 courses. **Credit** AmEx, MC, V.
Almeida trundles along like the trolleys of fermier cheese and own-made charcuterie that made the restaurant so refreshing when it opened in 2001. Head chef Alan Jones uses British ingredients (Scottish langoustines, Maldon rock oysters, Severn & Wye smoked salmon, Denham Estate lamb) to produce refined French cuisine with modern accents, including a stated emphasis on steaming and poaching to create lighter dishes. Keenly priced set menus are the bedrock of any establishment opposite a theatre, and the menu du jour doesn't disappoint. Start, maybe, with chilled English lettuce soup or a terrine of ham hock and foie gras with piccalilli; follow with confit guinea fowl, or sea trout with crushed peas and shellfish velouté. Our eye was taken with the carte's terrine of foie gras with spiced cherries and walnut salad, and slow-braised suckling pig with sauce aux épices. The wide-ranging dessert list is a highlight too. Wines are less francophile than you might expect, with Chilean sauvignon blanc and Portuguese Quinta do Crasto reserva among the list of sommelier's suggestions (bottles can also be purchased for home consumption).
   Almeida is unusual in the D&D London group (formerly Conran Restaurants) for being a local establishment, but it's not D&D's only French restaurant. Almost opposite one another in the City are rooftop Le Coq d'Argent and, on the mezzanine of the Royal Exchange, Sauterelle. The former is the choice for stunning skyline views, but although its kitchen is accomplished, Sauterelle just nudges it for cooking, and has a cheaper set menu – just £22.50 for a meal that might take in ox cheek and ham hock kromeski (croquette) with beetroot and watercress, followed by warm salad of lamb breast and

sweetbread with ratte potatoes and caper herb sauce, and a finale of banana and walnut cake with peanut brittle, caramelised bananas and peanut butter ice-cream.

Babies and children welcome: children's menu; high chairs; nappy-changing facilities. Booking advisable. Disabled: toilet. Separate rooms for parties, seating 10 and 20. Tables outdoors (8, pavement). **Map 5 O1.**

For branches (Le Coq d'Argent, Sauterelle) see index.

Morgan M

489 Liverpool Road, N7 8NS (7609 3560, www. morganm.com). Highbury & Islington tube/rail. **Lunch served** noon-1.30pm Wed-Fri, Sun. **Dinner served** 7-8.45pm Tue-Sat. **Set lunch** (Wed-Fri) £23.50 2 courses, £27.50 3 courses, £39-£45 tasting menu. **Set dinner** £39 3 courses, £43-£48 tasting menu. **Credit** MC, V.
From the smell of an uncovered cheeseboard and the complex, classical menu, to the old world wine list and thickly accented staff – Morgan M is unreservedly French. The restaurant consists of an intimate dining room with immaculately dressed, well-spaced tables and smart decor (including chef-patron Morgan Meunier's own paintings). Ensure you arrive hungry, as dinner is either three courses from the carte or a five-course tasting menu, both featuring amuse-bouche and entremets. We chose the tasting menu, which is only marginally more expensive, though we passed on wine pairings. A cucumber gazpacho with mint sorbet primed the taste buds nicely for an almost overpowering salad of aubergine caviar, confit tomatoes and french beans, with basil pesto, whole roasted garlic and red pepper sorbet. A simpler dish of steamed gnocchi in asparagus cream with summer truffles and girolles was altogether more balanced. Desserts hit the high notes; a raspberry soufflé was served with light pistachio custard poured inside, while a pastry-perfect rhubarb confit tarte came with divine, sweet white wine ice-cream. Monsieur M spoke to each table during the evening, and laughed off the suggestion that he'd just got a new ice-cream maker.
Babies and children admitted (lunch, Sun). Booking essential weekends. Dress: smart casual. Separate room for parties, seats 12. Vegetarian menu.

North West

St John's Wood

L'Aventure

3 Blenheim Terrace, NW8 0EH (7624 6232). St John's Wood tube or 139, 189 bus. **Lunch served** 12.30-2.30pm Mon-Fri. **Dinner served** 7-11pm Mon-Sat. **Set lunch** £16.50 2 courses, £19.50 3 courses. **Set dinner** £29.50 2 courses, £37.50 3 courses. **Credit** AmEx, MC, V.
You might not notice this pocket of France hidden behind luxuriant greenery in a gracious Georgian terrace. Step inside and you leave London's hubbub for the calm reassurance of blinding-white starched linen, sparkling glassware, tapestry-hung walls, hand-written menus in French and properly polite Gallic waiters, who immediately offer to help with the menu's spidery mysteries. L'Aventure exemplifies the dictum that a restaurant experience is as much about atmosphere as the food. The cooking here, however, is by no means secondary. A starter tarte aux légumes with tapenade was exquisite: the pastry crisp and heavenly, the slices of tomato and courgette

marinated in basil. Softly flaking turbot on a bed of tender spinach (thankfully seasoned with only a little salt), with an unusual sweet-and-sour lemon marmalade, was faultless. So too was a tastiest-ever carré d'agneau with à point boulangère potatoes and an aubergine purée. More points were scored by the offer of a quartet of perfectly affinés cheeses without incurring a supplement on the set lunch, and by kitchen staff packing thé à la menthe glasses almost to the brim with leaves. Who needs Eurostar?
Babies and children admitted. Booking advisable dinner. Tables outdoors (6, terrace). **Map 1 C2.**

Outer London

Croydon, Surrey

Le Cassoulet

18 Selsdon Road, Croydon, Surrey CR2 6PA (8633 1818, www.lecassoulet.co.uk). South Croydon rail. **Lunch served** noon-3pm Mon-Sat; noon-4pm Sun. **Dinner served** 6-10.30pm Mon-Thur, Sun; 6-11pm Fri, Sat. **Set lunch** (Mon-Sat) £16.50 3 courses; (Sun) £19.50 3 courses. **Set dinner** £27.50 3 courses. **Credit** AmEx, MC, V.
Chef-patron Malcolm John is on a mission to improve the dining landscape of suburban south London. He's already sorted out South Croydon, with upmarket fish restaurant Fish & Grill (*see*

Boundary. See p95.

p86) and swanky French bistro Le Cassoulet, winner of our Best Local Restaurant award in 2008. The latter offers reliably good, traditional French cooking, with a focus on the south-west, so you'll find the likes of steak tartare, escargots, lamb navarin and, of course, the rich pork, duck and bean stew that is cassoulet. The Sunday set lunch is a particular bargain – with at least six options per course – and deservedly popular. Linen-draped tables, banquette seating, floral wallpaper and rich colours (red, gold, claret) provide a sophisticated backdrop that suits both business lunches and family celebrations.

John's newest venture, Brasserie Vacherin, is an attempt to sprinkle the same stardust over dismal Sutton High Street. It's less formal but still classy-looking, with white tiled walls, dark wood furniture and red banquettes, stylish lighting and a striking sketch-mural on one wall. The all-day menu runs from croque monsieur and croissants for breakfast through to oysters, steaks, whole grilled lemon sole and classic French desserts. The drinks list includes eaux de vie, cocktails, Breton cider and democractically priced wines by the glass, carafe and bottle. The template for all these, and John's first restaurant, is Le Vacherin in Chiswick. It has a slightly more urban feel, but the cooking is recognisably from the same family. It's prix fixe throughout, with dinner only during the week and a Sunday lunch that's just as cheap as in Croydon.

Babies and children welcome: high chairs; nappy-changing facilities. Disabled: toilet.
For branches (Brasserie Vacherin, Le Vacherin) see index.

Richmond, Surrey

Chez Lindsay
11 Hill Rise, Richmond, Surrey TW10 6UQ (8948 7473, www.chezlindsay.co.uk). Richmond tube/rail. Crêperie & Restaurant **Meals served** noon-10.45pm Mon-Sat; noon-10pm Sun.
Crêperie **Main courses** £6.50-£10.75.
Restaurant **Main courses** £9.25-£18.75. **Set lunch** (noon-7pm Mon-Sat) £9.75 2 courses, £11.75 3 courses. **Set dinner** (after 7pm) £19.50 2 courses, £22.50 3 courses.
Both **Credit** MC, V.
A homely celebration of Breton cuisine, this independent bistro and Richmond institution specialises in foaming jugs of cider, plump seafood and buckwheat pancakes, to be eaten at farmhouse-style wooden tables in the sunny dining room. The discreetly attentive waiters swapped our wine glasses for traditional bolées (small bowls) when we ordered the easy-drinking Russet cider, and proved patient as we deliberated over the menu. Fish soup was exceptionally smooth, with studied depth of flavour and a sensibly muted accompanying rouille. From the list of fresh fish, brochettes and steak frites, we chose a 'super complète' galette whose crisp edges (folded inwards to frame a perfectly cooked egg) had the authentic toasted flavour of (organic) buckwheat flour. We recognised the feuilleté of scallops, puff pastry and creamy leeks from our last visit; fortunately, the set menu and specials change daily. After our well-priced mains, the mark-up on desserts raised eyebrows. An extra charge to flambée the crêpes would have doubled their price to nearly £10; instead, we sampled three scoops of punchy calvados ice-cream. It is possible to eat more modestly priced meals at Chez Lindsay, as the prix fixe menus attest.
Babies and children welcome: high chairs. Booking advisable. Separate room for parties, seats 36.

Trinity. See p94

Twickenham, Middlesex

Brula
43 Crown Road, Twickenham, Middx TW1 3EJ (8892 0602, www.brula.co.uk). St Margaret's rail. **Lunch served** noon-3pm daily. **Dinner served** 6-10.30pm Mon-Sat.
Main courses £10 lunch; £16-£18 dinner. **Set lunch** £12.50 2 courses; £16.75 3 courses. **Credit** AmEx, MC, V.
Rubbing shoulders with lifestyle boutiques and posh delis, Brula plays host to happy families in their Sunday best. The small but airy dining room, flooded with light from stained-glass windows, is decorated with ornate mirrors and portraits in various styles. The (daily changing) menu is a coalition of British-sourced seasonal ingredients and classic French recipes, all impeccably presented. The summery flavours in a crab starter – shredded fennel and crunchy pickled cucumber – hit the palate with full force, while a Madeira-infused jelly gave extra oomph to an already refined chicken liver parfait. Ribeye steak, though slightly tough, came with sweet stewed shallots and fresh vegetables; a ramekin of 'hachis parmentier' (French-style cottage pie) proved an unnecessary but irresistibly savoury bonus. Succulent, crisp-skinned chicken, sticky prune and potato cake and peppery braised fennel were all faultless, although the sum of the dish proved less than its parts. Dessert was a lip-smacking combination of elderflower fool and poached strawberries. Sadly, delays between courses prevented lunch from being truly outstanding. Perhaps the kitchen employs fewer staff than were on hand front-of-house. However, five waiters for 12 tables made for countless promptly replenished water jugs, which is never a bad thing.
Babies and children admitted. Booking advisable. Separate rooms for parties, seating 8, 10 and 24. Tables outdoors (1, pavement).

FRENCH

Gastropubs

Now that gastropubs have been with us for around 20 years, they're no longer the bright new thing, and instead are the focus of many a complaint. So let's pause and remember how dire pub food tended to be in the past, and what a revelation it was to be offered good cooking at a reasonable price at a time when there was little available in the mid-price range in London. Today, we can pick and choose from a range of styles of gastropub – back then, we were grateful to find anywhere that cooked real food rather than simply microwaved frozen meals. This year's newcomers are not numerous (hallelujah, some might say), but they do offer a snapshot of the market as it stands: posh Pimlico public house and hotel the **Orange**; Tooting's **Antelope**, a cosy Victorian pub reinvigorated with a daily-changing menu; artisan beer specialist the **Draft House**; and the **Princess of Shoreditch**, which has been given a makeover by new owners.

One positive effect of the gastropub movement is the emergence of gourmet boozers – proper pubs with a connoisseur's choice of beers and ciders, and bar snacks produced to a high standard. Such places are best exemplified this year by the miniature **Southampton Arms** in Gospel Oak, finalist in the 2010 Time Out Best New Bar award (*see p14*). It serves real ales and ciders from small independent British producers, and hot meat in baps.

Central

Bloomsbury

Norfolk Arms

28 Leigh Street, WC1H 9EP (7388 3937, www.norfolk arms.co.uk). Euston tube/rail. **Open** 11am-11pm Mon-Sat; noon-10.30pm Sun. **Lunch served** noon-3pm, **dinner served** 6-10.15pm Mon-Sat. **Meals served** noon-10.15pm Sun. **Main courses** £9.50-£14.50. **Tapas** £2-£12. **Credit** AmEx, MC, V.

Behind a resplendent green-tiled frontage and window boxes of cheery red geraniums, this handsome Victorian hostelry has quietly reinvented itself as a fine little tapas operation. Hefty shoulders of jamón hang in the window, and diners far outnumber drinkers. Even if you drop by for a quiet half of Sagres, it's hard not to succumb to the easy-going charms of the tapas menu. It's a fairly priced and endearingly eclectic list; while classics such as boquerones, marinated octopus, and serrano ham and manchego pinchos might feature, so too could chicken liver pâté on toast with rhubarb and apple chutney, or stuffed vine leaves, or smooth, smoky baba ganoush and pitta bread. Purists may not approve, but it all makes for perfect pub grazing fare. The other side of the daily-changing paper menu lists more substantial, pleasingly seasonal starters and mains – in summer, the likes of pea and mint risotto cake filled with goat's cheese, say, or Welsh lamb and apricot skewers with tabouleh and mint-infused yoghurt. On balmy evenings, the pavement tables are in high demand, looking out on a scruffy but unexpectedly peaceful King's Cross backstreet; in winter, the cosy, dimly lit interior comes into its own.

Babies and children admitted: high chairs. Booking advisable. Separate rooms for parties, seating 10 and 20. Tables outdoors (9, pavement). **Map 4 L3.**

Clerkenwell & Farringdon

Coach & Horses

26-28 Ray Street, EC1R 3DJ (7278 8990, www.thecoach andhorses.com). Farringdon tube/rail. **Open** noon-11pm Mon-Fri; 6-11pm Sat; noon-5pm Sun. **Lunch served** noon-3pm Mon-Fri, Sun. **Dinner served** 6-10pm Mon-Sat. **Main courses** £12.50-£15. **Credit** AmEx, MC, V.

A sensitively updated Victorian pub, with lots of wood and etched glass, where staff are just as happy to serve a pint and a (deluxe) scotch egg as a full meal. There are plenty of drinking options, and the wine list is way better than average; somehow we always end up ordering one of the rosés (there are three available by the glass). Food-wise, choose between a cheese plate or charcuterie board or a snack/starter such as herring roe on toast. Or make it three courses with the addition of roast Elwy Valley lamb rump with lentils, asparagus and salsa verde, followed by pear clafoutis with vanilla cream. And whatever you have, order bread too – it's excellent. Sunday sees a roast added to the mix. Food isn't always perfect, but most dishes are good and prices are ungreedy. The most atmospheric room is the main bar, though there is also another dining room, a small beer garden and a few tables out front. Staff know their stuff and there's a welcoming air to the place. Most importantly, though, the Coach still feels like a local, despite the superiority of its kitchen.
Available for hire. Babies and children welcome: high chairs. Booking advisable. Separate room for parties, seats 30. Tables outdoors (9, garden, 2, pavement). **Map 5 N4.**

Eagle
159 Farringdon Road, EC1R 3AL (7837 1353). Farringdon tube/rail. **Open** noon-11pm Mon-Sat; noon-5pm Sun. **Lunch served** 12.30-3pm Mon-Fri; 12.30-3.30pm Sat, Sun. **Dinner served** 6.30-10.30pm Mon-Sat. **Main courses** £5-£17. **Credit** MC, V.
Wowing Farringdon's office workers and an increasingly wider audience since 1991, Michael Belben's gastropub is refreshingly unlike many of the fine-dining pub restaurants it has inspired. The grill kitchen is squashed behind the bar, where you place your order; tables in the small, resolutely unfancy room may be nabbed by drinkers rather than diners (be aware you may be asked to share). Having said that, most people (and there are many) come to eat from the daily changing menu: maybe the signature bife ana steak sandwich, piquant napoli sausages with tomatoey beans, crab linguine or the Sunday roast. Portions tend to be hefty, which is just as well as dessert is given short shrift. Beers, including Eagle IPA (of course) are sourced from esteemed brewer Charles Wells. The house red is a jolly Spanish garnacha; alternatively, you could opt for a classic cocktail. Service is very much in the traditional pub mould (we've had complaints), so don't come if you want a waiter to drape a napkin into your lap. Still, despite its fame, the Eagle remains one of the best-value pub dining experiences in the capital.
Babies and children admitted. Bookings not accepted. Tables outdoors (4, pavement). **Map 5 N4.**

Peasant
240 St John Street, EC1V 4PH (7336 7726, www. thepeasant.co.uk). Angel tube or Farringdon tube/rail. Bar **Open** noon-11pm Mon-Sat; noon-10.30pm Sun. **Meals served** noon-10.45pm Mon-Sat; noon-9.30pm Sun. **Main courses** £8.50-£14.
Restaurant **Brunch served** noon-3pm Sun. **Dinner served** 6-11pm Tue-Sat. **Main courses** £9.50-£16. *Both* **Credit** AmEx, MC, V.
A very handsome old boozer where you can eat on the ground floor amid the drinkers, or in the calm of the first-floor dining room. There's plenty to admire in both spaces, with retro posters, circus memorabilia and original fittings throughout. On balance we prefer the bar food (welsh rarebit with grilled

tomatoes; Peasant burger with cheese, bacon, chilli relish, salad and fries) – it's far less fussy than the menu upstairs. On our most recent visit, the atmosphere in the restaurant was subdued; staff were efficient, but looked like they'd rather be somewhere else, and the food did little to lift the mood. Generally, there were too many ideas on one plate. A main of pan-fried red mullet with squid kedgeree, cullen skink and parsley was fine, but pork belly with spring roll, chorizo, roast potato, spring cabbage, parsnips and crackling was a spring roll too far. Puddings are more focused: a trio of three delicious ice-creams, say, or rhubarb and elderflower trifle with toasted almonds. The varied drinks list includes several guest ales. For a more straightforward meal, try Sunday lunch, when brunch dishes (marmalade-glazed ham, egg and chips) are served alongside roasts.
Babies and children welcome until 9pm: high chairs. Booking advisable. Tables outdoors (5, garden terrace; 5, pavement). **Map 5 O4.**

Marylebone

Queen's Head & Artichoke
30-32 Albany Street, NW1 4EA (7916 6206, www.theartichoke.net). Great Portland Street or Regent's Park tube. **Open** 11am-11pm Mon-Sat; noon-10.30pm Sun. **Tapas served** noon-10.15pm Mon-Sat; 12.30-10.15pm Sun. **Lunch served** noon-3.30pm Mon-Fri; noon-4pm Sat. **Dinner served** 6-10.15pm Mon-Sat. **Meals served** 12.30-10.15pm Sun. **Tapas** £1.50-£11. **Main courses** £9.50-£15. **Credit** AmEx, MC, V.
Euston Road has not proved to be a psychological barrier to this off-Regent's Park pub and many Fitzrovian office workers stroll here at midday for grown-up lunches. The evocative dark-wood Victorian bar room is cheerfully bright thanks to tall windows and a white ceiling; furniture is gastropub central-issue, but here looks appropriate rather than clichéd. On the

Norfolk Arms

first floor is a more intimate dining room with a cosy fireplace, while the small outdoor smoking section plays plush and louche. Evenings get quite raucous downstairs, so book for the dining room if you want to chat. The menu is similarly multiple-personality, with a sizeable à la carte heavy on seafood and Mediterranean flavours, and a list of more than 40 tapas costing from £1.50 for a free-range soft-boiled egg with paprika, to £11 for selection boards of British cheeses, Spanish charcuterie, or smoked fish. We have fond memories of freshest plump mackerel served with chickpea salad, and the organic 28-day-hung Black Mountain ribeye with sauce au poivre. The international wine list is kindly priced, offering more than 15 bottles under £20. Draught beers include Adnams Best and Marston's Pedigree.

Babies and children admitted. Separate room for parties, seats 55. Tables outdoors (6, garden; 8, pavement). **Map 3 H4.**

Pimlico

Orange Public House & Hotel
2010 RUNNER-UP BEST NEW GASTROPUB
37-39 Pimlico Road, SW1W 8NE (7881 9844, www.theorange.co.uk). Sloane Square tube. **Open** 8am-11.30pm Mon-Thur; 8am-midnight Fri, Sat; 8am-10.30pm Sun. **Breakfast served** 8am-11am daily. **Meals served** noon-10.30pm Mon-Sat; noon-9.30pm Sun. **Main courses** £12.50-£16.50. **Credit** AmEx, MC, V.
An elegant, airy conversion of a former brewery, the Orange is 'rustic' in *Country Living* mode. Stripped wood, textured paint and potted orange trees provide a perfect fit for the posh locale. The 'pub' part of the equation – a single ground-floor room – is a bit too civilised, but the 'gastro' aspect – a dining room beside the bar (no bookings taken) and first-floor restaurant – is fully justified. Creamily rich chicken liver parfait arrived in a little French kilner jar, open but with the pâté sealed off by a layer of port jelly, served with pickled walnuts and toast. Scallops were slightly browned and perfectly juicy, in a gentle lemon and garlic butter. Crispy, salt-crusted sea bream came with a minty pea sauce, squeaky beans and peas, and little herb dumplings. Only the wood-fired pizza was unbalanced: slightly too salty, its big hits of pancetta, gorgonzola and roast garlic overwhelmed the asparagus. Tempting puds include blood orange and champagne jelly with caramel ice-cream. Cocktails run from the safe (bloody mary) to the outlandish (basil martini), the southern European wines are sensibly priced and the few cask ales include a solid, hoppy Harveys. Staff are smiley, helpful and relaxed.
Babies and children welcome: high chairs; nappy-changing facilities. Booking advisable (restaurant). Disabled: toilet. Separate rooms for parties, seating up to 75. Tables outdoors (5, pavement). **Map 15 G11.**

West

Chiswick

Duke of Sussex
75 South Parade, W4 5LF (8742 8801). Chiswick Park tube. **Open** noon-11pm Mon-Thur; noon-midnight Fri, Sat; noon-11pm Sun. **Food served** noon-10.30pm Mon-Sat; noon-9.30pm Sun. **Main courses** £7.50-£16.50. **Credit** MC, V.

The Duke of Sussex has the makings of something special – a grand refurbished dining room with period features aplenty; a sprawling landscaped beer garden; an impressive range of beers, ales and wine; and a massive menu that, on first glance, sounds too good to be true. Unfortunately, it is. The theme, out of kilter with the Victorian surroundings, is Catalan. There are nearly 50 items on the menu, ranging from tapas-style starters to a chewy steak and chips (not cheap at £16). Classic dishes were weak imitations of the real thing: a wedge of tortilla flabby and tasting of the fridge, a gazpacho lacking in flavour and depth. Steaming hot Catalan rice, meatballs and prawns in rich tomato sauce, followed (eventually) by crema catalana were fine, if not especially memorable. What did make an impression was the service, or lack of it. The whole experience took close to three hours, with flustered waiters practically flinging the dishes at us by the end. Strip back the menu and spruce up the service and the Duke could be amazing. As it is, the place seems average at best.
Babies and children welcome: high chairs. Booking advisable dinner. Disabled: toilet. Separate room for parties, seats 64. Tables outdoors (37, back garden; 3, front garden).

Ealing

Ealing Park Tavern
222 South Ealing Road, W5 4RL (8758 1879, www.ealingparktavern.com). South Ealing tube. **Open** 11am-11.30pm Mon-Sat; noon-10.30pm Sun. **Lunch served** noon-3pm Mon-Sat; noon-3.45pm Sun. **Dinner served** 6-10pm Mon-Sat; 6-9pm Sun. **Main courses** £9.50-£19.50. **Credit** AmEx, MC, V.
The Ealing Park Tavern has long held a fine reputation for food, and the change of ownership two years ago has, if anything, cranked it up a level. Chef Jane Collins, formerly at the Belvedere, oversees a pristine open-plan kitchen that bakes its own bread, churns its own ices, and cures and smokes meats and fish on site. Presentation is elegant and pretty, yet portion sizes rarely disappoint (though we could have done with more of our seared lamb loin, confit shoulder and black pudding boulangère). A blackboard lists sizes of available lobsters – why not order a large one to share, chargrilled to smoky perfection and accompanied by samphire, jersey royals and chilli-lime dressing? There's no playground in the garden, but the Tavern remains a good place for families as staff know what children like to eat, and when. All this is not to suggest the pub side of the operation has been forgotten; the huge wood-panelled bar is cosy and as inviting as the ale selection (Cornish Knocker, Hog's Back Bitter, Harveys Best and Twickenham Crane Sundancer on our visit). A persuasive reason to move to South Ealing.
Babies and children welcome until 8pm: high chairs. Tables outdoors (20, garden).

Hammersmith

Carpenter's Arms
91 Black Lion Lane, W6 9BG (8741 8386). Stamford Brook tube. **Open** 11am-11pm Mon-Sat; noon-10pm Sun. **Lunch served** noon-2.30pm Mon-Fri; 12.30-3.30pm Sat; 12.30-5pm Sun. **Dinner served** 6.30-10pm Mon-Fri; 7-10pm Sat; 7-9pm Sun. **Main courses** £10.50-£17. **Credit** AmEx, DC, MC, V.
We've enjoyed good food at the Carpenter's in the past, but on a recent visit the scuffed shabbiness of the interior seemed to

Orange Public House & Hotel

extend both to the physical menus and some dishes. The pub still appears brightly welcoming on approach, set in a rather genteel location just off King Street. On a warm summer's evening, the spacious back yard was clearly popular with local residents. Wooden garden furniture was supplemented somewhat incongruously with rickety little tables from an empty bar/restaurant area, but helpful, friendly staff and clever lighting succeeded in creating a homely feel. There's a nod to seasonality, reasonable choice and some nice touches to the food: lightly sautéed cherries made a pleasing adjunct to pigeon breast; tender ribeye was properly chargrilled; asparagus was painstakingly peeled (perhaps unnecessarily, given its thinness). But bread (charged extra) was dull and dry; a pot of salad had wilted from the heat of the serving plate; sauce reductions were fierce and undistinguished. Apricots in a lemony frangipane were clearly fresh, but a mite too tart and firm for the filling. Wine (a good, if youthful selection) is the drink of choice. Pricing indicates an ambition that, from this showing, is unfulfilled.
Babies and children admitted: high chairs. Booking advisable. Tables outdoors (8, garden). **Map 20 A4**.

Shepherd's Bush

Anglesea Arms
35 Wingate Road, W6 0UR (8749 1291). Goldhawk Road or Ravenscourt Park tube. **Open** 11am-11pm Mon-Sat; noon-10.30pm Sun. **Lunch served** 12.30-2.45pm Mon-Fri; 12.30-3pm Sat; 12.30-3.30pm Sun. **Dinner served** 7-10.30pm Mon-Sat; 6.30-9.30pm Sun. **Main courses** £12-£17.50. **Credit** MC, V.
Look up 'gastropub' in the dictionary and a definition of the always-satisfying Anglesea Arms should spring off the page. This well-loved corner pub does the desired good food, drink and atmosphere thing in buckets. And don't the lucky Brackenbury locals know it? The place is pretty much constantly packed. Whether you're local or not, the pub exudes warmth, helped by the twinkly Irish landlady who keeps tables ticking over without making you feel rushed. At the front is the bar, ideal for sprawling afternoons, where the well-heeled punters are likely to be found lingering over pints of prawns, plates of fresh oysters and the Sunday papers. The small sky-lit back room is dedicated to dining, with the open kitchen turning out top-notch British dishes from a short but tempting menu. A main of braised beef fell meltingly apart with the touch of a fork, but it was the starters that shone particularly brightly. A pig's head terrine was flavourful, coarse and crumbly in the right way, while a salad with ripped mozzarella, asparagus and courgette-flower fritters was simple, stylish and just-so. Much like the place itself.
Babies and children admitted. Tables outdoors (9, pavement). **Map 20 A3**.

Princess Victoria HOT 50
217 Uxbridge Road, W12 9DH (8749 5886, www.princessvictoria.co.uk). Shepherd's Bush tube. **Open** 11.30am-midnight Mon-Sat; 11.30am-11pm Sun. **Lunch served** noon-3pm Mon-Sat; noon-4.30pm Sun. **Dinner served** 6.30-10.30pm Mon-Sat; 6.30-9.30pm Sun. **Main courses** £10.50-£16.50. **Set lunch** (Mon-Fri) £12.50 2 courses; £15 3 courses. **Credit** MC, V.
Long live the Princess – it's truly the people's pub, catering for all. The gastro and the pub parts of the operation are taken equally seriously, with high ambitions in both the kitchen and

PARADISE
BY WAY OF KENSAL GREEN

behind the bar. Pub snacks and à la carte meals are produced with aplomb; whether you want just a quiet pint with the papers or a serious vintage with dinner, you're likely to get satisfaction. A horseshoe-shaped bar dispenses a reassuring range of ales on draught, while a 300-plus wine list offers plenty of choice and great value for money. Distinct areas for dining and elbow-bending fit remarkably well into this former gin palace, beautifully restored to its former glory in shades of grey-blue, with opulent design touches. Potted crab is one of the best dishes: sweet and light, and served with lacy melba toasts. Steak and (triple-cooked) chips makes a satisfying follow-up. Desserts range from sticky toffee pudding to cherry clafoutis. Don't be offended when your friendly waiter asks if you'd like still or sparkling: he's referring to the choice of free tap waters.
Babies and children welcome: high chairs. Booking advisable. Separate room for parties, seats 60. Tables outdoors (10, garden). **Map 20 A2**.

Westbourne Park

Cow HOT 50

89 Westbourne Park Road, W2 5QH (7221 0021, www. thecowlondon.co.uk). Royal Oak or Westbourne Park tube. **Open** noon-11pm Mon-Sat; noon-10.30pm Sun. **Lunch served** noon-3.30pm daily. **Dinner served** 6-10.30pm Mon-Sat; 6-10pm Sun. **Main courses** £12-£15. **Set lunch** (Sun) £24 2 courses, £26 3 courses. **Credit** MC, V.
Tom Conran's popular gastropub features 'domestic and foreign cooking… oysters and Guinness'. Sounds like the bases are all covered, then, for the diverse punters who fill the (white linen-topped) tables on the first floor, and pack the more down-to-earth street-level bar (which is decked out in retro furniture). Despite the pub's name, the menu is all about the fruits of the sea rather than the bovine. Rich, gutsy fish stew comes in a generous portion packed with meaty white fish, salmon and mussels – a cut above what you might find at many pricier establishments. The seafood platters too are a fisherman's dream. Pasta makes a rather incongruous appearance, but it's better to head straight for the mains, which feature the likes of smoked eel with creamy mash, and (one of few nods to the venue's namesake) a ribeye steak with dauphinoise potatoes. The French-leaning wine list offers plenty of seafood-friendly bottles, though there's also a pretty good range of draught lagers, bitters and bottled beers, with the efficient bar staff pulling a great pint.
Available for hire. Babies and children admitted restaurant only. Tables outdoors (2, pavement). **Map 7 A5**.

South West

Barnes

Brown Dog

28 Cross Street, SW13 0AP (8392 2200, www.thebrown dog.co.uk). Barnes Bridge rail. **Open** noon-11pm daily. **Lunch served** noon-3pm Mon-Fri; noon-4pm Sat, Sun. **Dinner served** 7-10pm Mon-Sat; 6-9pm Sun. **Main courses** £10-£18. **Credit** AmEx, MC, V.
Jamie Prudhom, co-founder of the Pig's Ear (*see right*), joined with property developer Alan Lempriere and financial expert Hilary Fairhurst to make over this little pub among the ex-railway workers' cottages – now rather chichi, of course – in

Barnes. As if the name and setting weren't cute enough, there's a pub dog called Willow, who oversees a bar mixing cool designer lighting with old-world pub features. Menus put prime ingredients – Dorset crab, Black Face lamb, 28-day-aged steak – at the centre of modish dishes with plenty of Mediterranean accents (borlotti beans, garlic confit and salsa verde with the lamb; parma ham and panzanella salad with fillet of red mullet). Starters range from Maldon oysters and pints of prawns to the likes of ham hock terrine with piccalilli and sourdough bread, and deep-fried courgette flowers stuffed with lemon and thyme-flavoured ricotta. Choose puds carefully as the list is crammed with temptations.
More recently, the same team took over the Duke of Wellington in Marylebone; both pubs were finalists for our Best New Gastropub award a couple of years ago. The Duke's upstairs dining room is a cramped setting for the rather serious cooking – better, we think, to kick back in the ground-floor bar, which serves the same menu, or enjoy a drink streetside. There's a fine choice of real ales and ciders, as well as an impressive wine selection.
Available for hire. Babies and children welcome: high chairs. Booking advisable. Tables outdoors (12, garden).
For branch (Duke of Wellington) see index.

Chelsea

Pig's Ear

35 Old Church Street, SW3 5BS (7352 2908, www.thepigsear.info). Sloane Square tube.
Pub **Open** noon-11pm Mon-Sat; noon-10.30pm Sun. **Lunch served** 12.30-3pm, **dinner served** 7-10pm Mon-Fri. **Meals served** noon-11pm Sat; noon-10.30pm Sun.
Restaurant **Lunch served** noon-4pm Sun. **Dinner served** 7-10pm Tue-Sat.
Both **Main courses** £13-£15.50. **Credit** AmEx, MC, V.
Behind the picture-postcard old-fashioned frontage is a surprisingly light-filled modern gastropub with green tongue-and-groove woodwork, regulation second-hand furniture and a huge vase of sunflowers. Staff struggle at times to cope with the popularity – the spot is well marked on the gastro tourist circuit, which brings in a diverse crowd in addition to locals of all ages and clever shoppers who have clocked that this corner of residential Chelsea is an easy walk from the King's Road. The zinc-covered bar on the ground floor features Pig's Ear (not brewed on site, but a strong, IPA-tasting beer from Gloucestershire) and the likes of Deuchars IPA, plus popular tap beers and bloody marys. The mainly French wine list starts at £16 a bottle. Upstairs, near the kitchen, the Blue Room restaurant serves complex, rather high-end dishes, such as wild mallard with savoy cabbage, miso-glazed turnips and sour cherries, and plaice with jerusalem artichoke nage, squid and bok choy – but also a classy steak and chips, and jazzed-up macaroni cheese with trompettes des morts. Downstairs, the cramped rear dining area has a bohemian edge, and while casual still proffers more sophistication than many a bar menu.
Available for hire. Babies and children welcome: high chairs. Booking advisable (dining room). **Map 14 E12**.

Fulham

Harwood Arms HOT 50

Corner of Walham Grove and Farm Lane, SW6 1QP (7386 1847, www.harwoodarms.com). Fulham Broadway tube. **Open** 5.30-11pm Mon; noon-11pm Tue-Thur;

noon-midnight Fri, Sat; noon-11pm Sun. **Lunch served**
noon-3pm Tue-Sat; 12.30-4pm Sun. **Dinner served** 6.30-
9.30pm Mon-Sat; 7-9pm Sun. **Main courses** £14-£16.
Credit AmEx, MC, V.

Snagging a table has become far more difficult since a Michelin
star was awarded to this terrific gastropub – a source of
frustration, surely, for the locals who saw it as a neighbourhood
watering hole that happened to serve brilliant food. How
spoiled they are, with the bar stocked with an excellent range
of real ales on draught, an affordable wine list and a menu
conscious of both provenance and seasonality. Co-owner Mike
Robinson (of the Pot Kiln in Berkshire) shoots all the venison
used in dishes such as a platter of roe deer starters (scotch egg,
rissole, tartare, smoked ham), and grilled fallow deer chops.
The posh-country feel is created via rustic design details:
hessian napkins, linen bags in place of a bread basket, slabs
of wood for presentation. Snails with stout-braised oxtail and
bone marrow has become a signature dish, alongside the
superlative venison scotch eggs, though we've also enjoyed
wood pigeon – gamey and pink – served with pigeon tea (a spin
on beef tea), and grilled juicy roe deer with horseradish and
beetroot purée. Desserts include comforting, bramley apple
doughnuts, served warm with whipped cream, or own-made
bourbon biscuits with coffee ice-cream. Service is smart-
shirted, laid-back and friendly. Robinson has also opened a
cookery school in Berkshire, specialising in game and wild
food. The pub is also co-owned by chef Brett Graham, who
runs esteemed French restaurant the Ledbury in Notting Hill.
Available for hire. Babies and children welcome:
children's menu; high chairs. Booking advisable dinner.
Map 13 A12.

Putney

Spencer Arms

237 Lower Richmond Road, SW15 1HJ (8788 0640,
www.thespencerarms.co.uk). Putney Bridge tube or 22,
265, 485 bus. **Open** 11am-midnight Mon-Sat; 11am-
11pm Sun. **Lunch served** noon-3pm Mon-Sat. **Dinner
served** 6-10pm Mon-Sat. **Meals served** noon-9pm Sun.
Main courses £8.95-£17.95. **Credit** AmEx, MC, V.

The Spencer Arms is one of those fine, easy-going
neighbourhood pubs that has sprung up around London in
recent years. There's a TV in one corner and a broad sweep of
bar glittering with bottles and pumps, but this being
Putney/Barnes borders (with Putney Heath spread out
appealingly beyond a cluster of pavement tables), the signs are
to 'the loos' and the flowers in the vases are fresh and dainty.
A muted, costume-drama paint job lends a wholesome
atmosphere, no doubt helped by the fact that the place is rarely
rammed with baying punters. The chefs at work behind their
hatch take the cooking well beyond the commonplace. In the
past, we've tested their ambition and have never been
disappointed with the likes of crab linguine with chilli and
garlic, and sardines with salsa verde. But visit on a Sunday and
you can tuck into exquisite roasts (Suffolk lamb, Norfolk
chicken, Yorkshire pudding plus mounded extras, for about
£15), or spot-on burgers for a tenner. There's no attitude to the
Spencer – although we'd like it if they put as much thought
into their beers as they do their weighty wine list – and they
deserve local support.
Babies and children welcome until 9pm: high chairs;
nappy-changing facilities. Disabled: toilet. Tables outdoors
(11, pavement).

Antelope

Wimbledon

Earl Spencer

*260-262 Merton Road, SW18 5JL (8870 9244, www.
theearlspencer.co.uk). Southfields tube.* **Open** 11am-11pm
Mon-Thur; 11am-midnight Fri, Sat; noon-10.30pm Sun.
Lunch served 12.30-2.30pm Mon-Sat; 12.30-3pm Sun.
Dinner served 7-10pm Mon-Sat; 7-9.30pm Sun. **Main
courses** £8.50-£14. **Credit** AmEx, MC, V.
The credentials that distinguished the Earl Spencer as a
gastropub pioneer are still here: the short menu chalked on a
board, the scrubbed wooden tables, the large central bar offering
good ales (Sharp's Doom Bar, Hook Norton Best), and the
friendly, laid-back staff. The own-made breads and upmarket
bar snacks (pistachios, olives, and Normandy oysters, if you
please) also remain. Maybe it's just that other gastropubs have
caught up, but the menu seems less adventurous than we
remember it. That said, the flavours and combinations mostly
succeed. A salt-beef sandwich, served with a big dill pickle and
mustard, hit the spot, as did a herby warm potato salad. Tender
chargrilled asparagus was a seasonal treat in early summer, yet
the accompanying soft-boiled egg was tepid. A big, steaming
bowl of mussels, fragrant with Thai green-chilli flavours, had
been laced with coconut – though fresh herbs, chillies or lime
wedges would have perked things up more. The Earl continues
to be a popular local pitstop (the seats in the front garden are
at a premium come summer) and wine lovers are well looked
after with a list containing some off-the-beaten-track bottles.
*Babies and children welcome: high chairs. Bookings
not accepted Sun. Separate room for parties, seats 70.
Tables outdoors (10, patio).*

South

Balham

Avalon

*16 Balham Hill, SW12 9EB (8675 8613, www.theavalon
london.co.uk). Clapham South tube.* **Open** noon-11pm
Mon-Wed; noon-midnight Thur; noon-1am Fri, Sat;
noon-10.30pm Sun. **Lunch served** noon-3.30pm Mon-
Fri; noon-4pm Sat. **Dinner served** 6-10.30pm Mon-Sat.
Meals served noon-9pm Sun. **Main courses** £9-£14.95.
Credit AmEx, MC, V.
This huge old pub caters well for the smart set who live at the
posher, Clapham South end of Balham. There's an awning-
covered terrace facing the road for smokers; a small side
garden; a much bigger landscaped garden at the back
(complete with barbecue station); a vast bar serving proper ales
such as Timothy Taylor Landlord or Sambrook's Wandle; and
a high-ceilinged dining room with a steam-punk look that
would fit well into an HG Wells-inspired movie. The menu has
been streamlined to focus on the more obvious classics, such
as steak and chips, grilled plaice, butternut squash risotto and
sticky toffee pudding. A 'garden menu' served outdoors in the
summer might include a piping-hot skewer of lamb souvlaki
served on pitta bread, with a Greek-style salad and bowl of
tzatziki; a bap filled with shoulder of Middle White pork; or
immense, colourful salads.
*Babies and children welcome: children's menu; crayons;
high chairs; nappy-changing facilities. Booking advisable.
Disabled: toilet. Separate room for parties, seats 20. Tables
outdoors (22, garden; 10, pavement; 10 courtyard).*

Battersea

Draft House

2010 RUNNER-UP BEST NEW GASTROPUB
*94 Northcote Road, SW11 6QW (7924 1814, www.
drafthouse.co.uk). Clapham Junction rail.* **Open** noon-
11pm Mon-Fri; 10am-11pm Sat; 10am-10.30pm Sun.
Meals served noon-10pm Mon-Sat; 10am-9pm Sun.
Main courses £8.75-£39. **Credit** AmEx, MC, V.
The open kitchen in the middle of this superb, unstuffy venue
– more a beer-café than a pub – was overloaded: we were told
'the grill was full' when we sat down in the small rear dining
room, featuring bright green school chairs around little tables,
and wall covered in record sleeves and French Riviera liquor
ads. The delay gave us time to admire the 60-strong beer menu,
served by the third-of-a-pint for easier exploration of the fine
mix of local cask ales, American microbrews, Belgian
monastery beers and sundry other oddities. Starters were
pleasingly presented on a shared platter with rocket, relishes
and a pot of ace nibbles that included delicious baby olives.
Three crunchy ox-tongue fritters (more like croquettes) were
full of flavour, but the boquerones came as plain as they'd be
on a deli counter, their gremolata accompaniment lacking zing.
The mains were also rather mixed. A juicy 28-day-aged house
steak (£10.75, rather than £39 to share a T-bone) was cooked
a little less than rare, the chips could have been fluffier and the
béarnaise was short of tarragon, while a chunk of grilled hake,
although properly crispy with moist flaky flesh, came with
bland butterbeans and underpowered salsa verde.
*Booking advisable. Babies and children admitted.
Disabled: toilet. Tables outdoors (7, terrace).* **Map 21 C5**.
For branches see index.

Tooting

Antelope

2010 RUNNER-UP BEST NEW GASTROPUB
*76 Mitcham Road, SW17 9NG (8672 3888, www.antic-
ltd.com/antelope). Tooting Broadway tube.* **Open** 4pm-
midnight Mon-Thur; noon-midnight Fri, Sat; noon-10.30pm
Sun. **Brunch served** 11am-4pm Sat. **Tapas served**
6-10pm Mon; 4-6.30pm Tue-Fri; 11am-4pm, 6.30-10.30pm
Sat; noon-5pm Sun. **Dinner served** 6.30-9.30pm Tue-Fri;
6.30-10.30pm Sat. **Meals served** noon-5pm Sun. **Main
courses** £6.95-£13. **Tapas** £3-£6.50. **Set meal** (Sun)
£14 2 courses. **Credit** MC, V.
The bounciness of our chipper waiter made us feel right at
home in a cavernous space that used to be a Jack Beard's
boozer. Spread through three large rooms and a decent-sized
patio, the Antelope resembles a colonial public school for
hipsters, with trophies (antelope horns, darts cups, a stuffed
fox on a piano), shelved books and even a school mugshot from
Twickenham Grammar. We picked and mixed from bar snacks
(a big, stubby sausage roll is irresistible beer fodder at £1) and
the user-friendly Saturday brunch menu. Suiting the come-one,
come-all ethos, portions were generous. A massive main of
sliced serrano ham, topped by a pair of slightly oversalted but
perfectly glutinous fried eggs, crisp, peppery watercress and a
few big curls of manchego could have crushed two hangovers.
A large wedge of garlicky frittata was too light on stilton,
however, and gloopy sweetcorn fritters needed more red chilli
heat and less sweetened cucumber. Add broad selections of
beer and wine (a large glass that is charmingly served as a
small glass with accompanying carafe) and this becomes the

kind of place you pop into for a quick brunch and stumble home at closing time, big sloppy smile on your face.
Available for hire. Babies and children welcome: high chairs. Booking advisable. Separate room for parties, seats 120. Tables outdoors (20, garden).

Waterloo

Anchor & Hope
36 The Cut, SE1 8LP (7928 9898). Southwark tube or Waterloo tube/rail. **Open** 5-11pm Mon; noon-11pm Tue-Sat; 12.30-5pm Sun. **Lunch served** noon-2.30pm Tue-Sat; 2pm sitting Sun. **Dinner served** 6-10.30pm Mon-Sat. **Main courses** £11.80-£22. **Credit** MC, V.
This monument to all things meaty, seasonal and British put Waterloo on the gastronomic map, and it continues to offer a lively dining experience. The Anchor & Hope specialises in large cuts of beef, lamb or something more gamey for all to share. Its simple tables and chairs are always packed with keen diners; the many wooden surfaces make for a very noisy restaurant. A pared-down menu offers starters such as whitebait or seasonal vegetables, often with a French sauce, generally followed by a meaty main. Roast rib of beef with chips and béarnaise is a winner. The kitchen is dictatorial on how meat is cooked – listen to the chef and you won't be disappointed. A boisterous after-work crowd is drawn here each night, and as no reservations are taken in the evening, you're guaranteed a wait (sometimes for more than an hour) at the bar. Nevertheless, an interesting wine list, and the feeling you're in line for something good, usually make the intervening time pleasant. If only you could hear what your friends were saying.
Babies and children welcome: high chairs. Bookings not accepted Mon-Sat; advisable Sun. Tables outdoors (5, pavement). **Map 11 N8**.

South East

Dulwich

Rosendale
65 Rosendale Road, SE21 8EZ (8670 0812, www.therosendale.co.uk). West Dulwich rail.
Bar **Open** noon-11pm Mon-Thue, Sun; noon-midnight Fri, Sat. **Meals served** noon-10pm daily. **Main courses** £9.50-£16.
Restaurant **Lunch served** noon-3pm Sat; noon-4pm Sun. **Dinner served** 7-10pm Mon-Sat. **Main courses** £13.30-£19.20.
Both **Credit** MC, V.
The Rosendale is a light and airy, modern pub with lively decor. Swathes of yellow patterned wallpaper and vibrant artwork add warmth to a large space. The bar area at the front offers a choice of burgers, salads, fish and chips, and other pub favourites. Walk up a couple of stairs and you're in the restaurant, not markedly different in appearance, but with a menu that's a little more sophisticated. Choose from such dishes as truffle-laced risotto, venison ragoût-stuffed gnocchi, or Cornish plaice with chickpea purée. On Sunday, tuck into a roast featuring great-quality meat and all the trimmings, then follow with one of the tempting desserts. Apple crumble with vanilla ice-cream arrived looking suspiciously smart for a traditional pudding, but it tasted as good as we'd hoped.

Reassuringly, the menu changes according to availability of produce. Staff are friendly and eager to please. This is a popular spot for families, offering a children's menu, high chairs and plenty of room between tables to park a buggy (or for little ones to stretch their legs).
Babies and children welcome: children's menu; high chairs; nappy-changing facilities. Disabled: toilet. Separate rooms for parties, seating 25-100. Tables outdoors (40, garden).

East Dulwich

Herne
2 Forest Hill Road, SE22 0RR (8299 9521, www.the herne.net). East Dulwich or Peckham rail or 12, 197 bus. **Open** noon-1am Mon-Thue, Sun; noon-2am Fri, Sat. **Lunch served** noon-2.30pm Mon-Fri; noon-3.30pm Sat; noon-4pm Sun. **Dinner served** 6.30-9.45pm Mon-Sat. **Main courses** £8.50-£15. **Credit** MC, V.
There are many reasons to visit the Herne: the well-kept ales; the decent wine list; the wood panelling; the cosy nooks; the open fire; the sunny garden with climbing frame; the relaxed, family atmosphere; the regular events, from quizzes to petting zoos… but while the menu isn't bad, it's not the chief draw. Ingredients are of a high quality: organic, free-range and seasonal. And they're treated with respect. Yet dishes can be underwhelming. Starters show the most thought (smoked duck and pomegranate salad or saffron-cured sea bass, perhaps), but mains (Galloway rump steak and hand-cut chips; pan-fried bream with lemon and anchovy potatoes) lack exciting twists. Desserts sounded tempting but were executed with a heavy hand – shortcake overpowered by maple syrup, banoffi tartlet buried under chantilly and chocolate. There's a healthy children's menu (the Herne takes child-friendliness almost to the point of making kids compulsory), but no distinction is made between toddlers and pre-teens, with everything served on plastic (to the humiliation of older children). Service can be chaotic, and although prices are cheaper than at sister gastropub, the Palmerston, the food isn't in the same league. A fantastic pub with a mediocre restaurant.
Babies and children welcome: children's menu; high chairs; nappy-changing facilities. Separate room for parties, seats 60. Tables outdoors (25, garden).

Palmerston
91 Lordship Lane, SE22 8EP (8693 1629, www.the palmerston.net). East Dulwich rail or 185, 176, P13 bus. **Open** noon-11pm Mon-Thur; noon-midnight Fri, Sat; noon-10.30pm Sun. **Lunch served** noon-2.30pm Mon-Fri; noon-3pm Sun, Sun. **Dinner served** 7-10pm Mon-Sat; 7-9.30pm Sun. **Main courses** £11-£16. **Set lunch** (Mon-Fri) £11.50 2 courses, £15 3 courses. **Credit** MC, V.
One of East Dulwich's smarter pubs, the Palmerston has dark-wood panelling, a mosaic floor, crisp table settings and a slick menu. The à la carte is quite pricey, but the kitchen clearly pays attention to both provenance and seasonality; the quality of ingredients makes a meal worth the extra outlay. The weekday set lunch offers good value, and starters of cod goujons and rare roast beef with balsamic onions were both well presented and well executed. Mains sounded equally tempting, but while pork chops with pea purée lived up to expectations, tagliatelle with girolles needed a little something to liven it up. The wine list is extensive and offers a wide selection by the glass. Located on the busy corner of North Cross Road and Lordship Lane,

Princess of Shoreditch. See p111.

the pub is in a prime location for people-watching; tables on the pavement outside are perfect for this. If you like posh food but want to dress down, the Palmerston is where to head. For good pub grub, you may want to try the Bishop further down Lordship Lane.

Babies and children welcome: high chairs; nappy-changing facilities. Booking advisable dinner and weekends. Tables outdoors (6, pavement). **Map 23 C4**.

Rotherhithe

Compass

346-352 Rotherhithe Street, SE16 5EF (7232 2240, www.thecompasslondon.com). Rotherhithe rail or 381 bus. **Open** 5.30-11pm Mon-Thur; 5.30pm-midnight Fri; 10am-midnight Sat; noon-10.30pm Sun. **Dinner served** 6-10pm Mon-Sat. **Meals served** 10am-2pm Sat; noon-5pm Sun. **Main courses** £10-£15. **Credit** MC, V.

The former Deal Porter/Three Compasses has been turned into a friendly little gastropub by the people behind the Fellow in King's Cross. It isn't quite riverside – the Thames view is monopolised by flash flats – but there is a deck facing the pleasant residential street. Inside, you'll find tasteful duck-egg walls, old furniture, a working fireplace and inviting lighting. Gastro favourites pork terrine and cornichons (here containing chunks of black pudding) and potted shrimps (de-potted before arrival at table) were intensely flavoured and confident. A main course of sea bass with lemon butter and wilted spring greens was a generous fillet, seared perfectly and matched with (very salty) capers. Another main of roast chicken (breast and leg)

came with a garlicky leek and potato gratin – again, simple skilful cooking, let down only by over-processed salsa verde. Dessert was a well-kept cheese plate (oxford isis, cashel blue, mull of kintyre cheddar) with sharp tomato chutney and oatcakes. On our visit, real ales were limited to Marston's, Hobgoblin and Brakspear: disappointing when Meantime, Fuller's and Wandle ales are brewed nearby. Nonetheless, the Compass is an impressive addition to the area.

Babies and children admitted. Disabled: toilet. Separate room for parties, seats 12. Tables outdoors (10, garden).

East

Docklands

Gun

27 Coldharbour, E14 9NS (7515 5222, www.thegun docklands.com). Canary Wharf tube. **Open** 11am-midnight Mon-Fri; 11.30am-midnight Sat; 11.30am-11pm Sun. **Brunch served** 11.30am-1pm Sun. **Lunch served** noon-3pm Mon-Fri; noon-4pm Sat, Sun. **Dinner served** 6-10.30pm Mon-Sat; 6.30-9.30pm Sun. **Main courses** £11.50-£23. **Credit** AmEx, MC, V.

It's common for quality to slide as a restaurant chain gets bigger, but this doesn't seem to have happened in the case of Tom and Ed Martin's ETM Group. Their latest opening, the Cadogan Arms on the King's Road, was a finalist in our Best New Gastropub award in 2009. Having started just a decade ago, the brothers' company now has eight properties, from quality boozer the Hat & Tun on Hatton Wall to classy Sloane Square restaurant the Botanist (see p211) – but it's the gastropubs we'll concern ourselves with here. The Gun (2005 Gastropub award winner) remains a favourite: for its watery views, its sophisticated informality and the fact that, on balance, it's still the best place to eat in Docklands. Sink into one of the deep sofas for pub grub such as homemade fish finger sandwiches, sausage rolls or the pint o' prawns that seemed chosen from the start to underline that ETM wanted to keep the 'pub' in their gastropubs. The dinner menu, enjoyed in the bright front bar's dining area, or perhaps next to the mural of Admiral Nelson and his cronies, features the likes of Dexter beef carpaccio with anchovy dressing; shoulder of Norfolk lamb cooked for 12 hours with pearl barley, broad beans and wild garlic broth; British cheeses with chutney, oatcakes and grapes; and poached peach with peach sorbet and candied hazelnuts. The wine list favours France but doesn't forget the New World, or England and Greece. The beers are proper – Adnams Bitter is a regular (as is Aspall's cider), and there's a monthly seasonal ale.

The story is similar throughout the group. We like the versatility of the White Swan: a slim, cosy, wood-panelled bar on the ground floor and swanky City dining room upstairs. The Well is a proper local for Clerkenwell residents and City University types, with quiz nights and weekend brunches adding to the bonhomie. The beautifully decorated Empress of India blurs the gastropub boundaries and offers Victoria Park families more of a brasserie experience, with breakfast, afternoon tea, smoothies and freshly squeezed juices, and a good children's menu. Even here, though, you'll find a pint o' prawns: the flavour of the accompanying mayonnaise may change, but as a signature dish it seems to have held the Martin brothers in good stead.

Available for hire. Babies and children welcome: high chairs. Booking advisable. Disabled: toilet. Separate rooms for parties, seating 14 and 22. Tables outdoors (11, terrace). **Map 24 C2.**
For branches (Cadogan Arms, Empress of India, Prince Arthur, Well, White Swan Pub & Dining Room) see index.

Limehouse

Narrow
44 Narrow Street, E14 8DQ (7592 7950, www.gordon ramsay.com/thenarrow). Limehouse DLR. **Open** 11.30am-11pm Mon-Fri; noon-11.30pm Sat; noon-10.30pm Sun. **Lunch served** 11.30am-3pm Mon-Fri; noon-4pm Sat, Sun. **Dinner served** 6-11pm Mon-Fri; 5.30-11pm Sat; 5.30-10.30pm Sun. **Main courses** £10-£17. **Set menu** (6-10pm Mon-Thur; 6-7pm Fri, Sat; 6-9pm Sun) £18 2 courses, £22 3 courses. **Credit** AmEx, MC, V.
The departure of Mark Sargeant and closure of the Devonshire in Chiswick suggest a loss of momentum in the Gordon Ramsay gastropub division, though we've heard of good experiences by those who've cooked from the spin-off book. What sets the Narrow apart from its siblings and competitors is the stunning waterside location and sizeable terrace. These make the venue a worthy destination whoever is running the kitchen. The fact that the food is reasonably good just adds to the popularity. Early supper and set lunch menus offer three tempting courses for £22; bar snacks start at £2 for pickled whelks. Dishes that stray from pub standards are still classily rustic – braised pork cheeks with pearl barley and smoked bacon risotto, say, or roast Lancashire quail with broad beans and charlotte potatoes. The list of puds is lovely, with plenty

of chocolate and seasonal fruits. Drinkers needn't worry either; from the outset, the Ramsay pub team has taken pride in its beer selection. Real ales include the rarely seen Adnams Oyster and Greene King St Edmunds; other names on the list include Meantime, St Peter's and Innis & Gunn.

Babies and children welcome: high chairs. Booking essential. Disabled: toilet. Separate room for parties, seats 16. Tables outdoors (36, riverside terrace).
For branch (Warrington) see index.

Shoreditch

Princess of Shoreditch
2010 WINNER BEST NEW GASTROPUB
76-78 Paul Street, EC2A 4NE (7729 9270, www.the princessofshoreditch.com). Old Street tube/rail. **Open** noon-11pm Mon-Sat; noon-10pm Sun. **Lunch served** noon-3pm Mon-Fri; noon-4pm Sat. **Dinner served** 6.30-10pm Mon-Sat. **Meals served** noon-8pm Sun. **Main courses** £10.50-£16.50. **Set lunch** £14 2 courses, £18 3 courses. **Credit** AmEx, MC, V.
The former Princess has been rechristened the Princess of Shoreditch, thanks to new owners and a refurb (that hasn't monkeyed about with the historic decor – the place was built in 1742). A laid-back weekend lunch in the ground-floor bar mixed Shoreditch hipsters with a three-generation family group and some gals out for a boisterous gossip. A spiral staircase leads up to separate restaurant, more formal in looks but with the same menu. A couple of the dishes were inspired: candied lemon gave a starter of crab timbale with wood sorrel dressing a real summery kick, nicely reined in by salty capers; lemon tart was a triumph of texture and balance, with rich cream topped by crispy sugar, and an edge from summer berry compote and more candied lemon. With others, we had quibbles: a £9.95 slice of three cheese tart with rich quince sauce was accompanied by dull iceberg and cherry toms, and a mixed roast (perfect for the indecisive – beef, chicken and pork on one plate) was undermined by too much rosemary, and loose-textured belly pork that cried out for some crunchy crackling. Nonetheless, this is indeed a princess among gastropubs, where you're as comfortable quaffing (local cask ales, a respectable list of wines by the glass, bottle and carafe, bloody marys) as scoffing.
Available for hire. Booking advisable; no bookings downstairs bar. Children admitted until 7pm. **Map 6 Q4.**

North

Archway

St John's
91 Junction Road, N19 5QU (7272 1587, www.stjohns tavern.com). Archway tube. **Open** 5-11pm Mon-Thur; noon-11pm Fri, Sat; noon-10.30pm Sun. **Lunch served** noon-3.30pm Fri; noon-4pm Sat, Sun. **Dinner served** 6.30-11pm Mon-Sat; 6.30-9.30pm Sun. **Main courses** £11.25-£18.50. **Credit** AmEx, MC, V.
Where lesser establishments might have common-or-garden crisps behind the bar, this long-standing gastropub has a resplendent stack of own-made – and improbably enormous – pork scratchings. You'll also discover a list of superior bar snacks that runs from individual rock oysters to wonderfully crunchy, paprika-spiked patatas bravas. More substantial food

is served in the adjoining dining room: a murkily lit, unexpectedly cavernous space that combines peculiar portraits, grand chandeliers and green paintwork to charming effect. Above the fireplace, the daily-changing menu is scrawled on an immense blackboard, mixing crowd-pleasing classics (terrines, ribeye steaks and poshed-up fish and chips) with one or two more daring dishes –pig's head soldiers with caper and parsley purée, perhaps. Despite the odd oversight (a bream fillet was violently over-salted on our last visit, and a crumble slightly sparse of topping), St John's exudes an easy, likeable charm, which is aided by a fine array of lesser-known French and Spanish wines, dispensed by the glass, carafe or bottle.
Babies and children welcome: high chairs. Booking essential weekends. Tables outdoors (6, patio). **Map 26 B1.**

Camden Town & Chalk Farm

Engineer
65 Gloucester Avenue, NW1 8JH (7722 0950, www.the-engineer.com). Chalk Farm tube or 31, 168 bus. **Open** 9am-11pm Mon-Sat; 9am-10.30pm Sun. **Breakfast served** 9-11.30am Mon-Fri; 9am-noon Sat, Sun. **Lunch served** noon-3pm Mon-Fri; 12.30-4pm Sat, Sun. **Dinner served** 6.30-11pm Mon-Sat; 6.30-9.30pm Sun. **Main courses** £12.50-£19.50. **Credit** MC, V.
The engineer was Isambard Kingdom Brunel, and the pub named after him is one of the early adopters of the gastropub style. Dining is spread over two floors, with bold floral wallpapers in each room. In summer, those in the know request tables in the sizeable courtyard garden. Despite its culinary credentials, this local favourite is unafraid to host quiz nights or show the Grand National on TV. The menu carries a torch for the days of fusion cuisine, mixing miso-marinated sea bass and pak choi with mashed potato, and setting them alongside such gastropub standards as sirloin steak with béarnaise, and half pints of prawns. Prices are quite high, but this is a prime spot in Primrose Hill, and the ingredients are top-notch. Sardines escabeche is a bold idea successfully executed, so too an inventive vegetarian main of goat's cheese and almond cheesecake. Still, we're puzzled why the kitchen offers 'baker fries' (lightly roasted potato wedges), but deep-fries the fish cakes. The drinks list pleases all, with St Peter's Organic among the tempting draught beers; high-quality spirits, stylish cocktails and a helpfully annotated wine list are alternatives. Staff are as sunny as the garden in July.
Babies and children welcome (restaurant): children's menu; crayons; high chairs; nappy-changing facilities. Booking advisable. Disabled: toilet. Separate rooms for parties seating 20 and 32. Tables outdoors (15, garden).
Map 27 B2.

Crouch End

Queens Pub & Dining Room
26 Broadway Parade, N8 9DE (8340 2031, www.the queenscrouchend.co.uk). Finsbury Park tube/rail then W7 bus, or Crouch Hill rail. **Open** noon-11.30pm Mon-Wed, Sun; noon-midnight Thur-Sat. **Meals served** noon-10pm Mon-Sat; noon-9pm Sun. **Main courses** £5-£16.50. **Credit** AmEx, MC, V.
The refurbishment of this ornate Victorian pub raised the gastro game in Crouch End, and the pretty stained-glass, dark wood panelling and cream floral plasterwork continues to look spick and span, maintained by friendly staff. Tables laid with

wine and water glasses, and yellow roses in bud vases lend a smart edge to the dining room, distinguishing it from the equally good-looking bar. It's a large place, and to encourage steady custom there are draws such as 'fast and fresh' lunch dishes (a choice of three for just a fiver). Breaded plaice with hand-cut chips and tartare sauce was generous and well executed, and less than half the price of the beer-battered haddock on the regular menu. Apart from being given the wrong ice-cream with our sticky toffee pudding, we had no complaints, and enjoyed watching chefs going about their business in the small open kitchen. Thirst-quenching drinks include Crabbies alcoholic ginger beer, and watermelon daquiri, while wine appreciation extends to an annual summer rosé festival. Among the hand-pumped ales are Adnams Gunhill (a dark, ruby beer), Wells Bombardier and Sharp's Doom Bar. The coffee is good too. The Queens is part of the Food & Fuel group; not all its members are gastropubs, but we recommend the Roebuck in Chiswick (stylish, yet good for families) and Chelsea stalwart Lots Road Pub & Dining Room.
Babies and children admitted. Disabled: toilet. Separate room for parties, seats 50. Tables outdoors (12, garden).
For branches (Lots Road Pub & Dining Room, Roebuck) see index.

Villiers Terrace

120 Park Road, N8 8JP (8245 6827, www.villiers terrace.com). Finsbury Park tube/rail then W7 bus, or Hornsey rail. **Open** noon-11pm Mon, Tue; noon-midnight Wed; noon-1am Thur-Sat; noon-11pm Sun. **Meals served** noon-10.30pm daily. **Main courses** £11-£16.50. **Set menu** (noon-3pm, 6-7pm Mon-Fri) £10 2 courses, £13 3 courses. **Credit** MC, V.
The owners call this a 'pub and dining room', but if you're after a no-nonsense menu and traditional decor, head for the Queen's down the road. With a name like Villiers Terrace, what should we expect? A designer bar built from wooden logs, ornate sofas, chandeliers and bold floral wallpapers give a feminine vibe. Cocktails are taken seriously – there's a list of over 30 concoctions containing first-rate spirits and liqueurs – but beer drinkers might feel underwhelmed. The courtyard garden attracts a convivial crowd even on weekdays; there's also a wooden decked street terrace. Slow arrival of dishes from the kitchen sometimes lets down the friendly and adept serving team – and while the food is satisfying, it's not always so stellar to be worth the wait. Ginger cake with toffee sauce was a flabby, half-hearted effort, yet a large porcelain bowl of rhubarb and apple crumble was little short of divine. Clean-tasting vongole linguine is a favourite main with those nabbing the £10 set lunch. Evenings see a sophisticated yet unfussy range of dishes incorporating the likes of smoked sprats, ox cheek, snails and chorizo.
Babies and children welcome: children's menu; high chairs; nappy-changing facilities. Booking advisable dinner Wed-Sun. Separate room for parties, seats 50. Tables outdoors (20, garden; 10, terrace).

East Finchley

Bald-Faced Stag

69 High Road, N2 8AB (8442 1201, www.thebaldfaced stagn2.co.uk). East Finchley tube. **Open** noon-11pm Mon-Wed, Sun; noon-11.30pm Thur; noon-midnight Fri, Sat. **Lunch served** noon-3.30pm Mon-Fri; noon-4.30pm Sat. **Dinner served** 6-10.30pm Mon-Sat. **Meals served** noon-9.30pm Sun. **Main courses** £10-£16.50. **Credit** MC, V.
You may be surprised how many members of the Realpubs group you recognise: the Kilburn-based company has steadily bought up 13 well-positioned, mostly Victorian boozers in north and west London, and gastroed them, installing shiny open kitchens, pretty chandeliers and nostalgic black and white photos of the local area. So far, so depressing, you may think,

Charles Lamb. See p114.

Adult-friendly chains

As a rule, we prefer independent restaurants, but some chains do provide grown-up meals of good quality. For rib-sticking, finger-lickin' barbecue, try **Bodeans** (*see p33*).

Carluccio's Caffè

2A Garrick Street, WC2E 9BH (7836 0990, www.carluccios.com). Covent Garden tube. **Meals served** 8am-11.30pm Mon-Fri; 9am-11.30pm Sat; 9am-10.30pm Sun.
With branches dotted all over town, spick and span in their trademark blue and white livery, Carluccio's manages to keep standards high. Service is usually cheerful, the atmosphere casual without becoming sloppy, ingredients good quality and the Italian dishes always full of flavour.
Map 18 D4.
For branches see index.

Côte

124-126 Wardour Street, W1F 0TY (7287 9280, www.cote-restaurants.co.uk). Oxford Circus, Piccadilly Circus or Tottenham Court Road tube. **Meals served** 8am-11pm Mon-Wed; 8am-midnight Thur, Fri; 9am-midnight Sat; 9am-10.30pm Sun.
Outposts of this French bistro chain (from the people behind Strada) are smart, even a little moody, beneath their rakish striped awnings. The food is a solid round-up of fairly priced, predictable French classics (moules, steak-frites).
Map 17 B3.
For branches see index.

FishWorks

13-19 The Square, Richmond, Surrey TW9 1EA (8948 5965, www.fishworks.co.uk). Richmond tube/rail. **Lunch served** noon-3pm, **dinner served** 6-10.30pm Mon-Fri. **Meals served** noon-10.30pm Sat, Sun.
This neat formula (combining fishmonger's shop and seafood café) has slimmed down to just three branches in Richmond, Marylebone and Piccadilly. The food runs from crab cakes to less ubiquitous options (Devon ray with black butter and capers, say). Prices are a little above the chain restaurant norm.
For branches see index.

Grand Union

53-79 Highgate Road, NW5 1TL (7485 1837, www.gugroup.co.uk). Kentish Town tube/rail. **Meals served** noon-3pm, 5-9pm Mon-Sat; 1-8pm Sun.
A stylish option for lovers of burgers. We're impressed by the chips – fluffy and crisp in the right proportions – less so by the weedy french fries.
Map 26 A4.
For branches see index.

Jamie's Italian

19-23 High Street, Kingston, Surrey KT1 1LL (8912 0110, www.jamiesitalian.com). Kingston rail. **Meals served** noon-11pm Mon-Sat; noon-10.30pm Sun.

Carluccio's Caffè

If you fancy a bit of Mr O's relaxed, rustic Italian cooking, note that there's no booking except for groups at any of his four London branches (the others are in Canary Wharf, Covent Garden and the Westfield Shopping Centre). Expect quality ingredients in tried-and-tested combinations. Fun and energetic.
For branches see index.

The Real Greek

6 Horner Square, Old Spitalfields Market, E1 6EW (7375 1364, www.therealgreek.com). Liverpool Street tube/rail. **Meals served** noon-11pm Mon-Sat; noon-8pm Sun.
The Real Greek delivers reliable hot and cold meze, with appealing additions including summery watermelon, mint and feta salad and more substantial skewers and grills. Rural touches soften the sleekness of the decor in many branches.
Map 12 R5.
For branches see index.

GASTROPUBS

but in most cases they have also substantially improved the range of beers, underlining that drinkers are as welcome as diners. Take the Oxford in Kentish Town, where an outdoor blackboard highlights to passing traffic the weekly-changing selection of real ales – the likes of Hooky Bitter, St Austell Tribute, Sambrooks Wandle or Deuchars IPA. The Old Dairy in Stroud Green has even more on offer, and lays out toys and a playmat each Tuesday afternoon so that new mums can meet and chat over a plate of pasta and a glass of rosé. East Finchley's spacious Bald-Faced Stag offers BYO Mondays in the dining room, dinner jazz once a month, and a regular film quiz in conjunction with the nearby Phoenix cinema. Weekend breakfasts are served at the Queen Adelaide on the Shepherd's Bush/Acton border, which locals welcome as an unpretentious alternative to the esteemed Princess Victoria (see p103).

Menus vary from pub to pub, but expect niceties such as Spanish charcuterie, 28-day dry-aged beef steaks, Suffolk chicken, West Devon lamb, beer-battered fish, a caesar or nicoise salad, eton mess and sticky toffee pudding. The fish is from sustainable sources and meat traceable to the farm of origin – in all, the sort of standardisation we don't mind. Among Realpubs' more recent acquisitions are the high-profile Prince Bonaparte in Notting Hill and the Mitre in Holland Park – they aim to amass 30 outlets during the next four years.
Babies and children admitted (until 7pm). Disabled: toilet. Separate room for parties, capacity 25. Tables outdoors (10, garden; 10, patio).
For branches (Old Dairy, Oxford, Queen Adelaide) see index.

Islington

Charles Lamb
16 Elia Street, N1 8DE (7837 5040, www.thecharles lambpub.com). Angel tube. **Open** 4-11pm Mon, Tue; noon-11pm Wed-Sat; noon-10.30pm Sun. **Lunch served** noon-3pm Wed-Fri; noon-4pm Sat; noon-6pm Sun. **Dinner served** 6-9.30pm Mon-Sat. **Main courses** £8-£12. **Credit** AmEx, MC, V.
'Eat seasonally here' says a sticker in the corner of the Charles Lamb's blackboard menu. It underlines something you'd probably guess from a list including wild garlic and robiola risotto, jerusalem artichoke soup and an inventive asparagus tagine. Dishes at this bijou, green-toned freehouse change daily. Come for a drink before dinner and you may well see the board being wiped down ready for the next menu, and kitchen staff prepping veg in the small dining room. On the bar, a chicken holds sausage rolls for snacking (also made in-house); if you're lucky there'll still be some pea and goat cheese pâté or onion and parmesan tart along with the usual pork scratchings, olives and wasabi peas. The choice of draught beers has always been excellent, but recently there has been a switch to an all-UK line-up, including Fuller's Honeydew and a Charles Lamb lager produced by Meantime. House wines, including a summery rosé, come from the Languedoc; discerning bargain hunters may find bin end specials chalked on the board. Peak times can easily turn to pique times, such is the pub's popularity, and bookings aren't taken, so early arrival for dinner is essential.

Horseshoe. See p116.

GASTROPUBS

Babies and children admitted. Bookings not accepted. Tables outdoors (4, pavement). **Map 5 O2.**

Compass

58 Penton Street, N1 9PZ (7837 3891, www.thecompass n1.co.uk). Angel tube. **Open** 5-11pm Mon, Tue; noon-11pm Wed, Thur; noon-midnight Fri, Sat; noon-10.30pm Sun. **Lunch served** noon-2.45pm Thur-Sat. **Dinner served** 5-9.45pm Mon-Sat. **Meals served** noon-7.45pm Sun. **Main courses** £12-£16. **Credit** MC, V.

This corner building was once a so-so bar called the Salmon & Compass. Half the name lives on in its current incarnation as a gastropub – but it's twice the venue it was. Food is imaginative and generally very good, created by two T-shirted chefs in an open kitchen. We started with a wonderful puréed-pea tart (its pastry moist and buttery) and a novel if slightly less successful dish of 'mackerel fish fingers': a trio of mackerel fillets caked in a flavour-drowning layer of batter. A main of parmesan-encrusted calf's liver from the specials board was terrific, the intensity of the meat offset by delicious mashed potato with truffle oil. Good bavette steak – purpley rare, as requested – came in a brandy sauce with roast potatoes. We didn't have room for either cheesecake or trifle (from the daily changing menu). The Portuguese-focused wine list offers choices by the bottle, the glass and (brilliantly) the 500ml carafe. On our visit, two ale-drinkers at the counter roared jokes at each other and were gently ushered from the wood-panelled interior to benches outside. This is a sit-down venue now, with a kitchen that deserves some ceremony.

Babies and children welcome: high chairs. Booking advisable. Disabled: toilet. Separate room for parties, seats 40. Tables outdoors (9, pavement). **Map 5 N2.**

Marquess Tavern

32 Canonbury Street, N1 2TB (7354 2975, www.the marquesstavern.co.uk). Highbury & Islington tube/rail or Essex Road rail. **Open** 5-11pm Mon-Thur; 4pm-midnight Fri; noon-midnight Sat; noon-10.30pm Sun. **Lunch served** noon-5pm Sat, Sun. **Dinner served** 6-10pm Mon-Sat; 6-8.30pm Sun. **Main courses** £12-£17. **Credit** AmEx, MC, V.

A former winner of Time Out's Gastropub of the Year award and several other prizes, the Marquess Tavern has survived a change of ownership with nary a stumble. The blackboard of beef fore-rib sizes and prices is still here, so too the engaging beer list and the sky-lit rear dining room with its stark white walls and chandelier (out front is a pubbier bar with a few popular roadside tables). Seasonality is a high priority in the kitchen, best exemplified on our visit by a starter of samphire omelette with green salad. Mains for sharing might include a seafood platter with garlic and parsley butter plus radish and potato salad, or herb-crusted rack of Herdwick lamb. We opted for tender, sweet, slow-roast west Devon lamb saddle with 'summer' bubble and squeak and redcurrant jelly. Proper golden-brown chips accompanied the 28-days-hung Angus ribeye, served rarer than requested but given a delightful kick by green peppercorn sauce. Desserts are delectable, if not numerous: black forest trifle with fresh cherries, and gooseberry crème accompanied by a doughy but delicious raspberry blondie, perfectly balanced rich indulgence with zingy fruit flavours. Staff were charming, though not hard pressed on this occasion.

Babies and children welcome until 7pm. Separate room for parties, seats 14. Tables outdoors (6, patio).

Kentish Town

Bull & Last

168 Highgate Road, NW5 1QS (7267 3641, www.thebull andlast.co.uk). Kentish Town tube/rail then 214, C2 bus, or Gospel Oak rail then C11 bus. **Open** noon-11pm Mon-Thur; noon-midnight Fri, Sat; noon-10.30pm Sun. **Lunch served** noon-3pm Mon-Fri; 12.30-3.30pm Sat; 12.30-3.45pm Sun. **Dinner served** 6.30-10pm Mon-Sat; 7-9pm Sun. **Main courses** £12-£18.95. **Credit** MC, V.

Ideal for a post-prandial stroll on Parliament Hill Fields, this 2009 finalist for Time Out's Best New Gastropub award is at times victim of its own success. Take a recent lunch: 90 minutes to deliver a two-course meal, the kitchen clogged by a large table's orders. Problem is: there's often a large party here. The cooking is pretty special, after all – a menu of well-reared ingredients combined in ways that hark to the past yet seem thoroughly modern. Lamb ploughman's comes with an anchovy beignet and bleu d'auvergne cheese; a flaky-topped pie is made with ox cheek accompanied by roast bone marrow. With tables of limited dimensions, the tendency to serve various components of each dish on separate boards or bowls quickly palls (and the cider moules with frites, plus finger bowl, are so good at least one person will want them). You'll find around six bottles under £20 on the wine list, plus bin end deals, but the Bull & Last is serious about its ales, including Black Sheep bitter, Doom Bar and Mad Goose. The superb own-made ice-creams (almond, spiced orange, and walnut and golden sultana are among the many flavours) are available to take away.

Babies and children welcome: high chairs; nappy-changing facilities. Booking advisable. Separate room for parties, seats 70. Tables outdoors (5, pavement).

For branch (Prince of Wales) see index.

Junction Tavern

101 Fortess Road, NW5 1AG (7485 9400, www. junctiontavern.co.uk). Tufnell Park tube or Kentish Town tube/rail. **Open** noon-11pm Mon-Sat; noon-10.30pm Sun. **Lunch served** noon-3pm Mon-Fri; noon-4pm Sat, Sun. **Dinner served** 6.30-10.30pm Mon-Sat; 6.30-9.30pm Sun. **Main courses** £10.50-£15. **Set lunch** (Sun) £15 2 courses. **Credit** MC, V.

Regular visits prove the Junction Tavern to be a reliable source of good (sometimes outstanding) food at extremely reasonable prices. The result? Large crowds even on midweek nights, in the high-ceilinged dining room (with view of the kitchen), the sofa-lined bar and the rear conservatory. In fine weather a garden also comes into play. The menu is sensibly brief: around eight choices per course, changing daily. Star starters include assembled salads – where well-judged vegetable accompaniments embellish a main ingredient of fish, fowl or meat – and a daily soup (though these are occasionally bland). Main-course fish, braised meats and grilled ribeye steak with fat chips are consistently good; the vegetarian dish may be less dependable, as in a poorly cooked risotto. Puddings are rich, sometimes embarrassingly decadent, and always well executed. Service can suffer when under pressure, but usually delivers efficiently, with a smile. Drinks are just right: a short, food-friendly, fairly priced wine list and great real ales properly kept. On Sunday there's a very fine roast. You'd have to work hard to spend £50 a head at dinner here, so it's easy to see why so many locals regard the JT as a second home.

Babies and children admitted until 7pm. Booking advisable weekends. Tables outdoors (20, garden). **Map 26 B4.**

Muswell Hill

Clissold Arms

105 Fortis Green, N2 9HR (8444 4224, www.clissold arms.co.uk). East Finchley tube. **Open** noon-11pm Mon-Thur; noon-midnight Fri, Sat; noon-10.30pm Sun. **Lunch served** noon-4.30pm, **dinner served** 6-10pm Mon-Sat. **Meals served** noon-9pm Sun. **Main courses** £11-£18.50. **Credit** MC, V.

Once the scene of the Kinks' first gig (or more correctly, of the Ray Davies Quartet), today the Clissold Arms attracts stylish families and local celebrities of a certain age with its gleaming wood dining area, open-plan kitchen, dark leather sofas and pleasing outdoor tables. The welcome from the well-trained bar staff is usually very warm. They'll happily guide drinkers through the beers (Landlord and Harveys among them), and will also knock out decent cocktails. We've had mixed experiences dining here, but find it hard to fault the Sunday roasts, whether we choose the sirloin of beef, Middle White loin of pork or rump of Welsh lamb. The dinner menu is occasionally unrestrained, with some dishes containing too many ideas (twice-baked vacherin soufflé with rhubarb and honey truffle dressing, say, or spiced feta samosas with lentil dahl, spinach and confit tomatoes), but seekers of simple comfort cooking can delve into the likes of lamb shoulder shepherd's pie, or sausages and finger-licking onion gravy served on a huge mound of mash. The dark chocolate brownie with vanilla ice-cream is terrific and big enough to share. *Available for hire. Babies and children welcome: children's menu; high chairs; nappy-changing facilities. Booking essential dinner Thur-Sat, lunch Sun. Disabled: toilet. Tables outdoors (15, terrace; 25, garden).*

North West

Hampstead

Horseshoe

28 Heath Street, NW3 6TE (7431 7206). Hampstead tube. **Open** 10am-11pm Mon-Thur; 10am-midnight Fri, Sat; 10am-10.30pm Sun. **Lunch served** noon-3.30pm Mon-Sat; noon-4.30pm Sun. **Dinner served** 6-10pm Mon-Thur; 6.30-11pm Fri, Sat; 6.30-9.30pm Sun. **Main courses** £8-£15. **Set lunch** £7 1 course incl glass of wine. **Credit** AmEx, MC, V.

Although we've had mixed experiences at this chic gastropub over the years, two recent visits have seen the kitchen cooking with flair. The weekday lunch menu offers light meals, hearty gastropub favourites and more sophisticated choices, plus a special deal such as Red Poll beef burger with chips and a glass of house wine or OJ for £7. Vegetarians might opt for broccoli and pine nut wellington. We were won over by a dish of crisp-skinned pollock with samphire and nuggets of crayfish, all doused with buttery lemon pan juices. It's worth forgoing the (not bad) wine list to explore the beers. The pub brews its own ales downstairs, and there's also a great choice of bottled options, including Coopers and Little Creatures from Australia, and Belgian raspberry beer Bacchus. Finish with decent coffee or a slice of moist, rich almond torte studded with dark fudgey prunes and topped with clotted cream. Service can be too laid-back, not least because staff seem to enjoy each other's company, but if you're happy to chill, the Horseshoe makes a relaxing afternoon destination.

Babies and children welcome: high chairs. Booking advisable. Tables outdoors (2, pavement). **Map 28 B2**.

Wells

30 Well Walk, NW3 1BX (7794 3785, www.thewells hampstead.co.uk). Hampstead tube. **Open** noon-11pm Mon-Sat; noon-10.30pm Sun. **Lunch served** noon-3pm Mon-Fri; noon-4pm Sat, Sun. **Dinner served** 6-10pm Mon-Fri; 7-10pm Sat, Sun. **Main courses** £9.95-£18.95. **Credit** MC, V.

A short, if steep, walk from Hampstead Heath, the Wells is a pretty Georgian building with two floors for dining. There are Bugaboos parked at the roadside tables, but this doesn't deter the tie-less business crowd. The ground-floor bar with charcoal coloured walls and black tiling is smartly relaxed and offers the same menu as the more formal upstairs dining rooms (a good choice for a romantic evening). Menu combinations tend to be classic British and European, with a strong seasonal slant. Silky-smooth, tangy gazpacho castellano, made with apple and cumin in addition to the usual tomatoes and peppers, comes well matched with a slab of brown olive bread and croûtons. Freshest king scallops were boldly underdone at centre, and exceptionally succulent alongside pea purée, crunchy bacon and rich meat jus. There's the occasional duff note – minted anglaise lent a creamy toothpaste quality to poached peaches with chocolate sauce – but the intelligence and accuracy of the cooking readily compensates. Wines start at £14 a bottle, the list majoring on French and Italian varieties. Many gastropubs provide a friendly welcome – what impressed here was the warmth of the farewell: another reason why we'll be back. *Babies and children welcome: children's menu; colouring books; high chairs. Disabled: toilet. Separate room for parties, seats 12. Tables outdoors (8, patio).* **Map 28 C2**.

Kilburn

Salusbury

50-52 Salusbury Road, NW6 6NN (7328 3286). Queens Park tube/rail. **Open** 5-11pm Mon; noon-11pm Tue-Thur; noon-midnight Fri, Sat; noon-10.30pm Sun. **Lunch served** 12.30-3.30pm Tue-Sun. **Dinner served** 7-10.15pm Mon-Sat; 7-10pm Sun. **Main courses** £11.80-£16.40. **Credit** MC, V.

Pavement tables packed with a hip young crowd give an indication of this superior gastropub's popularity as a bar. The attraction isn't surprising, when bar snacks include the likes of squid in lemon, and chicken liver crostino with Marsala – tempting dishes that also feature on the menu in the intimate restaurant area. This narrow, pretty space is undiminished by its generic decor of distressed leather upholstery and stripped wooden tables. Fortunately, the food is more adventurous, with spring minestrone, seafood linguine and veal chop milanese suggesting a strong Italian influence. The linguine proved to be robust, packed with seafood and coated in a dense sauce that was rather too rich for a summer pasta dish. A starter salad of shaved white asparagus, black radish and celeriac with pecorino, pomegranate and truffle oil was conversely a little too delicate, the flavours indistinguishable from each other and the whole drenched in oil. Simple squid in lemon, however, was everything it should be: a light batter coating moist, tender squid whose fresh flavour sang. Sadly, few summery desserts were offered, but a pistachio semifreddo and grappa made a perfect end to a meal that reminded us why we love gastropubs. *Available for hire. Babies and children welcome until 7pm: high chairs. Tables outdoors (6, pavement).*

Global

What on earth can't you eat in London? In this chapter we assemble restaurants from rarely represented cuisines from across the world. Many of them are one-offs: the consistently enjoyable **Mandalay**, for instance, is London's only Burmese restaurant, and **Madsen** offers a Danish take on Scandinavian food that's also unique in the capital. Fancy eating some Afghani food? Head for Harrow, where **Masa** continues to serve a varied and well-executed choice of dishes from that country, to expats as well as gastronomic adventurers. Other establishments create curious blends of cookery styles; the **Eyre Brothers** restaurant in Shoreditch offers dishes from the Iberian peninsula, but the proprietors have added a few influences from Mozambique to their Spanish-Portuguese repertoire. In a similar vein, **Numidie** has conjured up a menu of French-Algerian cooking for the folk of Gipsy Hill. Go forth and celebrate London's joyous ethnic diversity – there's no place on earth that can compete.

Central

Edgware Road

Mandalay HOT 50
444 Edgware Road, W2 1EG (7258 3696, www.mandalay way.com). Edgware Road tube. **Lunch served** noon-2.30pm, **dinner served** 6-10.30pm Mon-Sat. **Main courses** £4.40-£7.90. **Set lunch** £3.90 1 course, £5.90 3 courses. **Credit** AmEx, MC, V. Burmese
It's heartening that, despite all the accolades, Mandalay has remained inexpensive and largely unchanged over the past 15 years. This is still London's only Burmese restaurant, and as such draws foodies in search of novelty, as well as crowds of clued-up locals and student types (some of whom are of Burmese origin). The unpretentious and modestly sized interior – red-tiled floor, basic furniture, pictures of Burma – hides behind a drab frontage. It is often full by 7.30pm, but the Ally family cope admirably, and are keen to explain the food of their homeland. The country has borders with a trio of gastronomic superstars (China, India, Thailand) and its cuisine shows influences from all three, as well as featuring distinctive dishes. Mandalay's menu is suitably wide-ranging, so you might start a meal with leafy green fritters, a bottle gourd soup, a shrimp and lettuce salad, or four chicken samosas. Next could follow a Burmese-style omelette curry (from the diverting choice of vegetarian dishes), lamb in tamarind, or lemongrass king prawns, with noodles, rice or a nan as accompaniment. Order a portion of pungent dried-prawn balachaung if you fancy something as a garnish. From the limited drinks list, mango or lychee juice will provide thirst-quenching foils to the spicier dishes; otherwise there are some half a dozen wines and Singaporean Tiger beer (but, sadly, no Myanmar lager). *Available for hire weekdays. Babies and children admitted. Booking essential dinner. Takeaway service.* **Map 2 D4**.

South Kensington

Madsen
20 Old Brompton Road, SW7 3DL (7225 2772, www. madsenrestaurant.com). South Kensington tube. **Open** noon-10pm Mon, Sun; noon-11pm Tue-Thur; noon-midnight Fri, Sat. **Lunch served** noon-4pm Mon-Sat; noon-3.30pm Sun. **Dinner served** 6-9.30pm Mon, Sun; 6-10pm Tue-Thur; 6-11pm Fri, Sat. **Main courses** £11.50-£17.50. **Set lunch** £9.50 smushi; £14.95 vegetarian; £14.50 2 courses, £18.95 3 courses. **Set dinner** £24.95 2 courses, £29.50 3 courses. **Credit** MC, V. Danish
The cool, modern interior at this Scandinavian restaurant is softened by fresh flowers on every table, splashes of red (the colour of the menus and a long banquette down one wall) and the warm welcome. Diners here tend to be affluent locals,

usually rather older than the bright young staff. At lunch there's a choice of smushi (mini versions of Danish open sandwiches, served on good rye bread), of which roast beef with remoulade topped with crispy onions, pickled cucumber and horseradish was much tastier than a bland 'hamburgerryg' (smoked pork loin with tomato, potato and mayonnaise). There's also an excellent herring platter (it comes with three versions: onion, juniper and Madeira-marinated) and various main dishes (which also appear on the dinner menu), such as haddock fish cakes or pork meatballs with potato salad, with side dishes such as beetroot in horseradish cream with lettuce. A vegetarian version of pytt-i-panna (fried cubes of potato, celeriac, celery, red peppers and onions, topped with a fried egg) was nice enough, if a little oily. Drinks include more than a dozen cocktails and some Danish beers, alongside a short European wine list. Charmingly, instead of patio heaters there are cosy red blankets supplied for anyone who wants to dine on the little front terrace.

Available for hire. Babies and children welcome: children's menu; crayons; high chairs; nappy-changing facilities. Booking advisable evenings. Separate room for parties, seats 14. Tables outdoors (4, terrace). Takeaway service. **Map 14 D10.**

South West

Putney

Chakalaka
136 Upper Richmond Road, SW15 2SP (8789 5696, www.chakalakarestaurant.co.uk). East Putney tube or Putney rail. **Dinner served** 6-10.45pm Mon-Fri. **Meals served** noon-10.45pm Sat, Sun. **Main courses** £9.95-£17.95. **Set meal** (dinner Mon-Fri; lunch Sat; lunch & dinner Sun) £16 2 courses. **Credit** AmEx, MC, V.
South African
On our last visit, it was hard to gauge the extent to which Chakalaka owed its custom to the World Cup, which was then in full swing. Whatever the particulars on this occasion, the South African stalwart is certainly popular. Locals have even learned to accept the garish zebra-print exterior. Inside, the decor is no subtler in its evocation of the homeland; the earthy orange walls are hung with signed rugby shirts, Zulu shields and, in case you hadn't quite got the point, a giant 3D relief map of South Africa. As for the food, animal lovers should look elsewhere. The zebra skin lining the bar is fair warning of a menu big on kudu, ostrich and springbok meat – all imported from Namibia. Service can be overly informal, and we've had hit-and-miss meals here. A recent starter of boerewors sausage (served with the tomato salsa from which the restaurant derives its name) lacked the requisite peppery punch, while another of kudu carpaccio was elegantly presented yet similarly short on flavour. Mains were better, from a homely bobotie (spiced lamb casserole with an egg topping) to an elaborate springbok filo parcel topped with camembert and cranberry sauce. Steak challenges and all-you-can-eat rib deals are run for determined carnivores. To drink, there's an exclusively South African wine list, plus Castle Lager and Savanna cider (from South Africa) and Windhoek lager (from Namibia).
Babies and children welcome: high chairs; nappy-changing facilities. Booking advisable. Separate room for parties, seats 60.
For branches see index.

South East
Crystal Palace

Mediterranea
21 Westow Street, SE19 3RY (8771 7327, www. mediterranealondon.com). Crystal Palace or Gipsy Hill rail. **Lunch served** noon-2.30pm, **dinner served** 6-10pm Tue-Fri. **Meals served** noon-11pm Sat; noon-10pm Sun. **Main courses** £9.90-£14.90. **Credit** AmEx, MC, V. Mediterranean
A modest glass-fronted restaurant with bright turquoise walls, Mediterranea feels rather like a cheery no-frills beach café. As you'd expect from the name, the kitchen serves Mediterranean sunshine food, but there's a particular focus on dishes from Sardinia. It's a little surprising to find cooking of such high quality given the unassuming decor, although prices aren't quite as low as the setting might suggest. Be sure to order the carasau bread (a kind of rosemary-flavoured flatbread that's baked in an Italian stone oven): the secret behind the fine selection of pizzas. Starters include own-cured salmon, greek salad, grilled calamares and scallops florentine (which are slathered in a rich cheese sauce with spinach). Pastas, also made in-house, feature heavily: the likes of artichoke and mushroom tortelloni, crab tagliatelle and tomato ravioli. We liked the tomato-based fish stew strewn with doughy balls of fregola (tiny pasta spheres). The rest of the menu consists mainly of Italian bistro dishes such as grilled swordfish and halibut, or roast lamb with Mediterranean vegetables. Desserts include tiramisu, orange crème brûlée and rhubarb crumble tart. There's a sound selection of wines too. Stick around and chat to the super-friendly staff.
Babies and children welcome: high chairs. Booking advisable weekends.

Gipsy Hill

Numidie
48 Westow Hill, SE19 1RX (8766 6166, www.numidie.co.uk). Gipsy Hill rail. **Dinner served** 6-10.30pm Tue-Sat. **Meals served** noon-10.30pm Sun. **Main courses** £9.50-£15. **Set meal** (Tue-Thur) £12.50 2 courses, £14 3 courses; (Fri-Sun) £13.50 2 courses, £15 3 courses. **Credit** MC, V. Algerian
In good company on restaurant-packed Westow Hill, this green-fronted French-Algerian bistro is a safe choice. The venue looks and feels cool, with its massive mirrors, vintage fittings, colourful walls and shabby-chic mismatched crockery. The nicely priced set menus includes such choices as Algerian fish soup, grilled anchovies, falafel or merguez sausages. We liked the melange of flavours in the merguez dish – a smear of tapenade here and a splodge of harissa there nod to both France and North Africa. The wines look both ways too, with a Moroccan rosé among a mainly French list. Couscous is ubiquitous: sometimes with a mixture of kebab meat, at other times with lamb shank or chicken tagine. You'll also encounter undeniably French favourites such as steak and chips. We particularly enjoyed a crisp fish börek with a pot of heady aïoli. Save space for desserts, which feature the likes of cognac crème brûlée, chocolate tart, and pear with pistachios and yoghurt (a lush choice). It's easy to see why Numidie has kept busy for more than a decade.
Babies and children welcome: high chairs; nappy-changing facilities. Booking advisable; essential Fri, Sat. Vegetarian menu.

GLOBAL

East
Shoreditch

Eyre Brothers `HOT 50`

70 Leonard Street, EC2A 4QX (7613 5346, www.eyre brothers.co.uk). Old Street tube/rail. **Lunch served** noon-2.45pm Mon-Fri. **Dinner served** 6.30-10.45pm Mon-Fri; 7-11pm Sat. **Main courses** £15-£27.50. **Credit** AmEx, DC, MC, V. Mediterranean

Not only is the menu here unique – a sophisticated take on Iberian peninsula food – but the place has a distinctive character. The long, dark room is stylish, the soundtrack gratifyingly eclectic (Dr John meets Horace Silver); it appeals both to the City and Shoreditch. Punchy starters included silky caldo verde (cabbage and chouriço soup), Viscaya anchovies with green beans, olives, potatoes and soft-boiled egg (a meal in itself), and sea-fresh razor clams with jamón serrano, broad beans and fino sherry broth. Equally impressive were mains of bacalhau gomes de sá (salt-cod baked with potatoes, onion and red pepper with soft-boiled egg and olives), and medium-rare grilled fillet of marinated Ibérico pork. In comparison, Murcia paella was bland, despite being packed with globe artichoke, peas and various beans, and topped with pea shoots and almond and garlic 'picada' (a sort of pesto). Vanilla cheesecake with passionfruit sauce was good but too sweet – we needed the kick of impeccable cortado coffee. Prices aren't cheap, so thank heavens for the tapas bar (serving until 8.30pm); the alluring sherry and wine list can be sampled in both areas. *Available for hire. Babies and children admitted. Booking advisable Thur-Sat. Disabled: toilet.* **Map 6 Q4.**

Outer London
Harrow, Middlesex

Masa `HOT 50`

24-26 Headstone Drive, Harrow, Middx, HA3 5QH (8861 6213). Harrow & Wealdstone tube/rail. **Meals served** 12.30-11pm daily. **Main courses** £4.50-£12. **Set meal** £19.95 (2 people); £30 (2-3 people); £49.95 (4-5 people). **Unlicensed**. **Corkage** no charge. **Credit** MC, V. Afghan

On a down-at-heel precinct, Masa is a well-attired Afghani restaurant that transcends its surroundings. Inside, you'll find a spacious dining room with maroon and cream walls, an open kitchen, shiny floor tiles, heavy wooden furniture, a sparkling chandelier and a flatscreen TV. Local residents, some of them hailing from Afghanistan, dine here. The menu makes an alluring read, encompassing Middle Eastern cuisine (especially kebabs) and North Indian and Pakistani-style food (karahi curries, for instance), as well as a few distinctively Afghani dishes: ashak (pasta stuffed with leeks) and ash afghani (macaroni and vegetables with meatballs) among them. Prices are low, making this a great spot for sampling the likes of mantoo (chewy pasta parcels packed to bursting with minced lamb, then topped with yoghurty quroot sauce). We've also enjoyed the kebabs (well seared and juicy), the moreish flatbread and the light-as-a-whisper challow rice (spiced with cardamom and cumin). Dogh, a yoghurt drink with cucumber and dried mint, makes a refreshing accompaniment, or you can bring your own alcohol. Staff are quiet and kind. *Babies and children welcome: high chairs. Disabled: toilet. Takeaway service; delivery service (over £12, 3-mile radius).*

Masa

Greek

London's long-established Hellenic community still has its stronghold around Camden Town, which is where many of these restaurants are based, though you'll now find representatives as far apart as Bayswater (**Aphrodite Taverna**, one of our favourites) and South Woodford (**George's Fish & Souvlaki Bar**). Most of these establishments are run by Greek-Cypriots, and reflect the cooking of that island, where Middle Eastern influences such as an emphasis on meze dishes are apparent. As a contrast, try Notting Hill's **Greek Affair**, which specialises in the stew-based cuisine of the Greek mainland.

Although attempts have been made to provide upmarket settings for Greek food, and to update the traditional recipes, the more homespun tavernas have proved to be the longest stayers. Venues that double as chip shops (such as **George's** and **Vrisaki**) are a notable sub-genre, as are those that seek to recreate a holiday atmosphere for tourists returning from the Greek islands. Primrose Hill's **Lemonia** is certainly among London's most popular Greek restaurants and also one of its best.

West

Bayswater

Aphrodite Taverna
15 Hereford Road, W2 4AB (7229 2206, www.aphrodite restaurant.co.uk). Bayswater, Notting Hill Gate or Queensway tube. **Meals served** noon-midnight Mon-Sat. **Main courses** £9.50-£23.50. **Set mezédes** £18 vegetarian, £21 meat, £29.50 fish per person (minimum 2). **Cover** £1. **Credit** AmEx, MC, V.
Taverna by name, taverna by nature – the interior of this cosy, chintzy establishment is stuffed with Greek-Cypriot trappings. The dark wooden bar is topped with a huge bottle of Metaxa, and the dining area is charmingly cluttered with an assortment of mini bouzoukis (Greek mandolins), gourds, plaster Parthenons and Greek pottery. Tables are adorned with oil-burning lamps, and diners are watched over by large paintings of Greek-Cypriots in traditional costume. Nationalistic pride even runs to the proud displaying of a *Daily Mail* article on the health benefits of a Greek diet where 'meat intake is low'. Cheerfully ignoring such findings, Aphrodite offers a menu featuring a substantial range of grills, steak and meaty stews. A delicious plate of stifádo arrived crammed with huge chunks

of tender beef in a rich tomato sauce. When the restaurant is busy, service can be distracted, but at quieter times there's a nicely personal touch, with the chef often emerging to thank diners for coming. Anyone defeated by the size of the portions might also be interrogated by the owner, as she makes sure the cooking's up to scratch. An atmospheric treat.
Available for hire. Babies and children welcome: high chairs. Booking advisable dinner. Tables outdoors (12, terrace). Takeaway service. Vegetarian menu. **Map 7 B6.**

Notting Hill

Greek Affair
1 Hillgate Street, W8 7SP (7792 5226, www.greekaffair. co.uk). Notting Hill Gate tube. **Lunch served** noon-3pm Tue-Sun. **Dinner served** 6-11pm daily. **Main courses** £8.50-£10.50. **Credit** MC, V.
A menu based on food from the Greek mainland and islands makes this multi-floored restaurant a rarity in London's Greek-Cypriot-dominated Hellenic culinary scene. The long list offers seldom-seen dishes such as yiouvetsi (lamb baked in tomato sauce with orzo pasta) and hirino katsarolas (pork casserole in tomato sauce). Rather than the customary basket of pitta, a starter of mixed dips came with crusty white bread, and a portion of very tender calamares was served in a rich, oily

tomato sauce instead of the typical deep-fried batter. Desserts are a highlight: a moist, fragrant karidopita (walnut syrup cake) featured a dark syrup of intense caramel flavours, and the vanilla ice-cream was boosted with a hefty sprinkling of cinnamon. The grey-painted wooden interior has a modern, contemporary feel, but our sunny Saturday evening visit saw it curiously empty. We were ushered past an expanse of empty tables to a seat on the slightly shabby roof terrace, joining a smattering of families and couples among the faded quarry tiling, rosemary bushes and bamboo fencing. Greek Affair can lack in atmosphere, then, but there's no faulting the food. *Babies and children welcome: high chairs. Booking advisable. Tables outdoors (10, roof garden). Takeaway service. Vegetarian menu.* **Map 19 C5**.

North East
South Woodford

George's Fish & Souvlaki Bar
164 George Lane, E18 1AY (8989 3970, www.georges fishbar.co.uk). South Woodford tube. **Lunch served** noon-2.30pm Mon-Thur; noon-3pm Fri, Sat. **Dinner served** 5-10.30pm Mon-Sat. **Meals served** 1-9pm Sun. **Main courses** £11-£13.50. **Set lunch** £7.50-£9.50 2 courses. **Set mezédes** £22.50. **Credit** MC, V.
Groups of regulars trade running jokes with the staff at this chip shop-cum-neighbourhood restaurant. Step past the tiles and takeaway prices at the front, and you'll find a dining area sporting pleasing touches of interior design. A big space-enhancing mirror greets diners entering the low-lit, dark wooden restaurant area, where miniature pink and clear glass chandeliers hang above a series of cosy booths. The menu features a seafood selection from 'Demetri's Fish Bar' (available battered, fried in matzo meal or grilled), and huge helpings of chunky chips come with several main courses – but the selection of Cypriot home cooking is George's forte. A starter of gently grilled pastourma sausage was impressively succulent; lamb souvláki was pungent with charcoal flavour; and keftédes (meatballs) had a pleasing kick of parsley. Service tends towards the bubbly and chatty, although during busier periods it can border on the inattentive. An after-dinner drinks list including Greek coffee and Cypriot-style tea (served with cloves and cinnamon) is a pleasant way to end a meal. *Available for hire. Babies and children welcome: children's menu; high chairs. Booking advisable Thur-Sun. Tables outdoors (8, patio). Takeaway service.*

North
Camden Town & Chalk Farm

Daphne
83 Bayham Street, NW1 0AG (7267 7322). Camden Town or Mornington Crescent tube. **Lunch served** noon-2.30pm, **dinner served** 6-11.30pm Mon-Sat. **Main courses**

Lemonia. See p124.

£9-£14.50. **Set lunch** £7.75 2 courses, £9.25 3 courses. **Set mezédes** £16.50 meat or vegetarian, £20.50 fish per person (minimum 2). **Credit** MC, V.

There's a lovely, convivial vibe to this family-run Greek-Cypriot restaurant. Split over three floors, the interior ranges from the floral-patterned booths and monochrome photos of Cypriot village life that decorate the ground floor to the metal baskets of red flowers which line the small roof terrace, via the authentically Mediterranean feel of the uneven whitewashed walls and tiled floors on the first floor. It's the service that is the real treat at Daphne, though. Diners are greeted with warm familiarity, and on our most recent visit the restaurant's matron wandered around engaging customers in conversation about her grandchildren, cracking jokes and offering genial advice about a menu that is peppered with Greek phrases. As well as a specials board offering a long list of fish, the familiar Greek-Cypriot repertoire is pepped up with a variety of more homely dishes, among them skordalia (garlic mashed potatoes), avgolémono soup (egg and lemon) and pourgoúri (cracked wheat pilaf). The cooking can be a bit variable (our sea bream was slightly under-grilled), but a starter of three mini koubes (deep-fried wheat parcels stuffed with minced lamb) was light and crisp, with a subtle yet delicious aroma of cinnamon. On a sunny day, the roof terrace is an ideal destination if you're looking for a relaxed, atmospheric meal.

Available for hire. Babies and children welcome: high chairs. Booking advisable. Tables outdoors (17, roof terrace; 2, veranda). Takeaway service. Vegetarian menu. **Map 27 D2**.

Menu

Dishes followed by (G) indicate a specifically Greek dish; those marked (GC) indicate a Greek-Cypriot speciality; those without an initial have no particular regional affiliation. Spellings on menus often vary.

Afélia (GC): pork cubes stewed in wine, coriander and other herbs.

Avgolémono (G): a sauce made of lemon, egg yolks and chicken stock. Also a soup made with rice, chicken stock, lemon and whole eggs.

Dolmádes (G) or **koupépia (GC)**: young vine leaves stuffed with rice, spices and (usually) minced meat.

Fasólia plakí or **pilakí**: white beans in a tomato, oregano, bay, parsley and garlic sauce.

Garídes: prawns (usually king prawns in the UK), fried or grilled.

Gígantes or **gígandes**: white butter beans baked in tomato sauce; pronounced 'yígandes'.

Halloumi (GC) or **hallúmi**: a cheese that is traditionally made from sheep or goat's milk, but increasingly from cow's milk. Best served fried or grilled.

Horiátiki: Greek 'peasant' salad made from tomato, cucumber, onion, feta and sometimes green pepper, dressed with ladolémono (a mixture of oil and lemon).

Hórta: salad of cooked wild greens.

Houmous, **hoúmmous** or **húmmus** (GC): a dip of puréed chickpeas, sesame seed paste, lemon juice and garlic, garnished with paprika. Originally an Arabic dish.

Htipití or **khtipití**: tangy purée of matured cheeses, flavoured with red peppers.

Kalamári, **kalamarákia** or **calamares**: small squid, usually sliced into rings, with the pieces battered and fried.

Kataïfi or **katayfi**: syrup-soaked 'shredded-wheat' rolls.

Keftédes or **keftedákia (G)**: herby meatballs made with minced pork or lamb (rarely beef), egg, breadcrumbs and possibly grated potato.

Kléftiko (GC): slow-roasted lamb (often shoulder), served on the bone and flavoured with oregano and other herbs.

Kopanistí (G): a cheese dip with a tanginess traditionally coming from natural fermentation, but often boosted with chilli.

Koukiá: broad beans.

Loukánika or **lukánika**: spicy coarse-ground sausages, usually pork and heavily herbed.

Loukoumédes: tiny, spongy dough fritters, dipped in honey. ▶

▶ **Loukoúmi** or **lukúmi**: 'turkish delight' made using syrup, rosewater and pectin, and often studded with nuts.

Loúntza (GC): smoked pork loin.

Marídes: picarel, often mistranslated as (or substituted by) 'whitebait' – small fish best coated in flour and flash-fried.

Melitzanosaláta: grilled aubergine purée.

Meze (the plural is **mezédes**, pronounced 'mezédhes'): a selection of either hot or cold appetisers and main dishes.

Moussaká(s) (G): a baked dish of mince (usually lamb), aubergine and potato slices, topped with béchamel sauce.

Papoutsáki: aubergine 'shoes', slices stuffed with mince, topped with sauce, usually béchamel-like.

Pourgoúri or **bourgoúri (GC)**: a pilaf of cracked wheat, often prepared with stock, onions, crumbled vermicelli and spices.

Saganáki (G): fried cheese, usually kefalotyri; also refers to anything (mussels, spinach) served in a cheese-based red sauce.

Sheftaliá (GC): little pig-gut skins stuffed with minced pork and lamb, onion, parsley, breadcrumbs and spices, then grilled.

Soutzoukákia or **soutzoúki (G)**: baked meat rissoles, which are often topped with a tomato-based sauce.

Soúvla: large cuts of lamb or pork, slow-roasted on a rotary spit.

Souvláki: chunks of meat quick-grilled on a skewer (known in London takeaways as kebab or shish kebab).

Spanakópitta: small turnovers stuffed with spinach, dill and often feta or some other crumbly tart cheese.

Stifádo: a rich meat stew (often made using beef or rabbit) with onions, red wine, tomatoes, cinnamon and bay.

Taboúlleh: generic Middle Eastern starter of pourgoúri (qv), chopped parsley, cucumber chunks, tomatoes and spring onions.

Taramá, properly **taramosaláta**: fish roe pâté, originally made of dried, salted grey mullet roe, but now more often smoked cod roe, plus olive oil, lemon juice and breadcrumbs.

Tavás (GC): lamb, onion, tomato and cumin, cooked in earthenware casseroles.

Tsakistés (GC): split green olives marinated in lemon, garlic, coriander seeds and other optional flavourings.

Tyrópitta (G): similar to spanakópitta (qv) but usually without spinach and with more feta.

Tzatzíki, **dzadzíki (G)** or **talatoúra (GC)**: a dip of shredded cucumber, yoghurt, garlic, lemon juice and mint.

Lemonia

89 Regent's Park Road, NW1 8UY (7586 7454). *Chalk Farm tube.* **Lunch served** noon-3pm Mon-Fri; noon-3.30pm Sun. **Dinner served** 6-11.30pm Mon-Sat. **Main courses** £10.50-£15. **Set lunch** (Mon-Fri) £9 2 courses, £10.50 3 courses. **Set mezédes** £18.50 per person (minimum 2). **Credit** MC, V.

Booking in advance is essential if you want to enjoy a meal at this ultra-popular restaurant. On a Saturday evening, queues can stretch out of the door as the scent of chargrilled meats wafting down the road tempts the hungry hordes of Primrose Hill. Inside, Lemonia is such a vast operation that even if you do have a reservation, getting from door to table can prove a little tricky. Don't worry: the food will be worth the hassle. Although the ceilings are high – particularly in the plant-strewn, botanical garden-like conservatory – the noise from diners is buzzy rather than overpowering. The friendly, attentive staff have a ready sense of humour, but the incredible speed with which dishes fly from the kitchen borders on the hurried. Less than five minutes after we placed our order, a big, squidgy slice of saganáki and a couple of the crispest, lightly browned spanakópitta were sitting on our table. Mains arrived even faster, with a meltingly soft kléftiko the meal's highlight. If you linger, you'll be brought portion after portion of complimentary icing sugar-dusted cubes of rosy loukoúmi, but make sure to leave room for dessert: perhaps galaktoboureko (custard-filled filo with rich clove scenting) or baklava containing chunky chopped pistachios.

Babies and children admitted. Booking essential. Separate room for parties, seats 40. Tables outdoors (6, pavement).
Map 27 A1.
For branch (Limani) see index.

Wood Green

Vrisaki

73 Myddleton Road, N22 8LZ (8889 8760). Bounds Green or Wood Green tube. **Lunch served** noon-4pm, **dinner served** 6-11.30pm Mon-Sat. **Meals served** noon-9pm Sun. **Main courses** £10-£18. **Set mezédes** £19 per person (minimum 2). **Credit** AmEx, MC, V.

Vrisaki's metal deep-fat fryers and chiller cabinets packed with raw meat skewers might suggest you've walked into a chip shop or kebab house, but head through to the back and you'll find one of the perennially popular eating destinations for the Greek-Cypriot community of Wood Green. A concise menu offers a range of chargrilled kebabs and fish, alongside stews such as kléftiko and stifádo, but the restaurant's main draw is the staggering quantity of food served when you order its three-course set meze menu. Large Greek families sit among the fake red and green plants that trail from the ceiling, as elderly waiters clad in leather waistcoats ferry plate after plate to their tables. The selection of dips, herbed pulse salads and seafood medleys that make up the first course alone consists of no fewer than 16 dishes. By the time the smoky pork kebabs, aromatic sheftaliá and fried quails' wings of the final course arrive, most diners have long since begun to plead for a takeaway box. In our experience, there's an emphasis on quantity over quality here, with few dishes impressing, but the jovial waiting staff and fellow customers' animated Hellenic chatter produce a lively community feel.

Available for hire. Babies and children welcome: high chairs. Booking advisable: essential weekends. Takeaway service.

Hotels & Haute Cuisine

It's been a year of change for London's fine dining scene. First, Eric Chavot left the Capital, where he had been head chef for a decade. Gordon Ramsay Holdings saw the departure of both Mark Sargeant and the much-acclaimed Jason Atherton, as well as the closure of Boxwood Café. And after a comparatively short stint, Andrew Turner moved on from the Landau at the Langham Hotel, which he had launched to such acclaim late in 2007.

But it's not all about goodbyes: Gordon Ramsay's **Pétrus** restaurant has resurfaced a knife's throw from its former home, the Berkeley, and Pierre Koffmann has made a warmly welcomed return with the opening of **Koffmann's** in the same hotel. The whole industry is keen to see what Heston Blumenthal will be doing when he arrives at the Mandarin Oriental Hyde Park in autumn 2010, but **Bar Boulud** (*see p91*) at the same hotel is already providing him with stiff competition. Of all the restaurants to experience chef departures in the past year or so, our reviewers found the **Capital** was the only place to really land on its feet, with the arrival of Frenchman Jérôme Ponchelle. Our other favourites this year include **Hélène Darroze at the Connaught**, **Hibiscus** and seafood specialist **One-O-One**.

Central

Belgravia

Pétrus
1 Kinnerton Street, SW1X 8EA (7592 1609, www.gordonramsay.com/petrus). Knightsbridge tube.
Lunch served noon-2pm , **dinner served** 6.30-10pm Mon-Sat. **Set lunch** £25 3 courses. **Set dinner** £55 3 courses. **Set meal** £65 tasting menu. **Credit** AmEx, MC, V.
When Gordon Ramsay opened this Mayfair fine-diner in April 2010, media coverage focused on the kitchen soap opera behind its inception. A restaurant of the same name was run by Ramsay and his protégé Marcus Wareing in the Berkeley hotel. After a friendship-finishing fallout, the pair went their separate ways and the original Pétrus became Marcus Wareing at the Berkeley (*see p127*). This resurrection (just a short walk from its former home) sticks to the tried-and-tested Ramsay template that has won him plaudits for years: Michelin-friendly, Frenchified food in classic combinations, served impeccably by personable staff (led by the effortlessly polished Jean-Philippe Susilovic). The set lunch (good value at £35 for three courses, when all the customary freebies are factored in) doesn't provide many surprises – typical dishes might pair cauliflower with scallops, pork belly with black pudding, lobster with Spanish ham – but it does offer faultless attention to detail and superlative ingredients. Everything is dished up in a luxurious, inoffensive dining room built around a striking circular cellar that houses the red part of the biblical wine list. Not a destination for culinary adventurers, then, but extremely hard to fault for delivery.
Available for hire. Babies and children admitted. Booking essential. Disabled: toilet. Dress: smart casual. Vegetarian menu. **Map 9 G9.**

Bonds

Threadneedles, 5 Threadneedle Street, EC2R 8AY (7657 8088, www.theetoncollection.com). Bank tube/DLR. **Lunch served** noon-2.30pm, **dinner served** 6-10pm Mon-Fri. **Main courses** £12.95-£24.95. **Set lunch** £17.50 3 courses. **Set dinner** £19.50 3 courses. **Credit** AmEx, DC, MC, V.

The Threadneedles hotel was lucky to land head chef Barry Tonks, acclaimed veteran of a succession of Michelin-starred establishments. The restaurant here is a spacious hall where ambitious and sometimes experimental cooking is offered at high, yet not exorbitant, prices. Tonks' menu is modishly replete with breed names, sources and cooking methods (the cod is poached at 48°C, he informs us), but it comprises fairly straightforward Modern European cooking, with nods in the direction of France, Italy and Spain. Spain also features heavily in the bar, which is where we ate from a small, multicultural tapas menu. Don't expect much in atmosphere – the bar is for casual dining and drinking – but the food is special. Apart from disappointing duck spring rolls, everything was wonderful, especially a stew of chorizo and chickpeas, and mushrooms cooked with garlic and chilli: the true taste of Spain in both dishes. Also memorable were the deep-fried prawns with a pomegranate and yoghurt relish, and heavenly chips. The wine list has shockingly kind prices for a City hotel; you might expect the selection to exclude anyone who can't afford a Lamborghini, but it starts below £20 and has good quality throughout. We wish more restaurants at this level made such an effort.

Available for hire. Booking advisable. Disabled: lift; toilet. Dress: smart casual. Separate rooms for parties, seating 8, 14 and 16. **Map 12 Q6.**

Fitzrovia

The Landau

The Langham, 1C Portland Place, W1B 1JA (7965 0165, www.thelandau.com). Oxford Circus tube. **Breakfast served** 7-10.30am Mon-Fri; 7am-noon Sat, Sun. **Lunch served** 12.30-2.30pm Mon-Fri. **Dinner served** 5.30-11pm Mon-Sat. **Main courses** £19-£30. **Set lunch** £21.50 2 courses, £28.50 3 courses. **Set meal** £75 tasting menu (£135 incl wine). **Credit** AmEx, DC, MC, V.

Sumptuously grand, the Landau's dining room is resplendent in wood panelling and antique brass chandeliers, with pastel-shaded upholstery and pink roses on tables. Oval-shaped windows give views of All Souls Church and Broadcasting House. Expect big budget expenditure for choices from the carte; set menus provide more affordable options matched with reasonably priced wines. New head chef Elisha Carter (who replaced Andrew Turner in 2009, and works with new executive chef Graham Chatham) draws upon British-sourced ingredients for a menu inspired by home-grown and pan-European culinary styles. Crimson-hued beetroot gazpacho was notable for its vinegary after-kick, making a tangy contrast to the creaminess of a goat's cheese garnish. The main courses weren't as distinctive. A perfectly cooked lemon sole fillet, cloaked in creamy sauce, was closer to nursery food than a fine-dining experience, the addition of tart grapes clashing with wilted spinach. Seared Cornish lamb fillet, encased in crisp filo-like pastry, was rather overcooked, and its accompaniments – crisp bacon bits, meaty jus, buttery mashed potatoes – were overly rich. Desserts, although decent, were let down by experimental flourishes. Layered chocolate mousse cake, sitting pretty on a base of crushed hazelnut praline, would have been fine as it was, not needing an overpowering layer of sweet mango jelly. We've had exceptional meals here in the past, but this one failed to meet expectations.

Babies and children welcome: children's menu; high chairs. Booking advisable; essential weekends. Disabled: toilet. Dress: smart casual. Separate room for parties, seats 16. **Map 9 H5.**

Pied à Terre

34 Charlotte Street, W1T 2NH (7636 1178, www.pied-a-terre.co.uk). Goodge Street or Tottenham Court Road tube. **Lunch served** 12.30-2.30pm Mon-Fri. **Dinner served** 6-10.45pm Mon-Sat. **Set lunch** £23.50 2 courses. **Set dinner** £70 3 courses. **Set meal** £90 tasting menu (£158 incl wine). **Credit** AmEx, MC, V.

Lunching Fitzrovians who pack the cafés and restaurants of Charlotte Street could walk past Pied à Terre daily and not suspect that some of the most exciting cooking in London was being eaten behind the unassuming frontage. Invite them into the dining room and they may not suspect it either – the awkward layout and lifeless decor don't fire the imagination. But as soon as the food arrives, you know there's something special going on in the kitchen. On our last visit, Aussie head chef Shane Osborn sent out, among other delights, skate wings with watercress flowers and courgette and horseradish soup, and monkfish with salt-crust carrots and orange and cardamom foam. It was a memorable meal that astonished with every forkful. Plates here are compositions of colour, balance and delicate flavours, using many unusual floras (ice plant or

Pétrus. See p125.

Tasmanian pepper berries, for example). Sommelier Mathieu Germond is a real asset, guiding the hesitant through the two-tome wine list and describing to us with infectious enthusiasm the improvised garden on the roof that provides much of the restaurant's herbs and edible blooms. Service can be slow and somewhat arrogant, but Pied à Terre is a gastronome's fantasy that's fully deserving of its excellent reputation.

Babies and children admitted. Booking advisable; essential weekends. Dress: smart casual. Separate room for parties, seats 12. Vegetarian menu. **Map 17 B1.**

Holborn

Pearl Bar & Restaurant

Chancery Court Hotel, 252 High Holborn, WC1V 7EN (7829 7000, www.pearl-restaurant.com). Holborn tube. *Bar* **Open** 11am-11pm Mon-Fri; 6-11pm Sat. *Restaurant* **Lunch served** noon-2.30pm Mon-Fri. **Dinner served** 6-10pm Mon-Sat. **Set lunch** £26 2 courses, £29 3 courses, **Set dinner** £58 3 courses. **Set meal** £70 tasting menu (£120 incl wine). *Both* **Credit** AmEx, DC, MC, V.

Head chef Jun Tanaka has a CV that reads like a Michelin inspector's tick list. Stints at Le Gavroche, Chez Nico and the Square ensured he knew his way round a kitchen by the time he took over this restaurant in the swanky Renaissance Chancery Court hotel in 2004. The name Pearl is appropriate. An elegant, pillared room has been modernised with gentle oyster tones and judiciously flattering illumination, including some clever table lighting that will have you scanning the ceiling for spotlights in vain. It's one of the most graceful dining rooms in the city, but the real star is the food. Tanaka's dishes are masterpieces of texture, colour and contrast, combining immaculately cooked seasonal ingredients in dainty mouthfuls, trickles, sprigs and cubes arranged with the skill of an artist. One memorable recent plateful had three chunks of Cornish lemon sole scattered with delicate purple sprouting broccoli, almonds, ricotta cavatelli and smoked anchovy vinaigrette. This is far from simple cooking, although it never seems overdone or confusing. A meal here is certainly not cheap, yet by our reckoning it's easily worth every penny.

Babies and children welcome restaurant: high chairs. Booking advisable. Disabled: toilet. Entertainment: pianist 7.30pm Wed-Sat. **Map 18 F2.**

Knightsbridge

The Capital

22-24 Basil Street, SW3 1AT (7591 1202, www.capital hotel.co.uk). Knightsbridge tube. **Lunch served** noon-2.30pm, **dinner served** 6.30-10.30pm daily. **Set lunch** £29.50 2 courses, £35 3 courses. **Set meal** £70 tasting menu (£119 incl wine). **Credit** AmEx, DC, MC, V.

This tiny (28 covers) hotel dining room acquired a new chef in 2009. Jérôme Ponchelle cooked at the Connaught under the eminent traditionalist Michel Bourdin, and it shows. The carte looks like haute-cuisine comfort food; tournedos rossini and lobster thermidor both appeared when we were here. A retrograde sop for the Knightsbridge affluentsia? Don't believe it. The Capital is sensational, even for those who can't move beyond the bargain set lunch. Ponchelle's cooking eschews fireworks in favour of simple ideas impeccably executed. Two star dishes were silky fennel and cucumber soup served with three spicy grilled prawns; and lamb steak (cut from the leg)

grilled to split-second perfection and served with a buttery, sweet-potato purée that made us see the humble tuber in a new light. A single flaw crept in to a vegetarian main of quinoa couscous (too crunchy) with sublime roasted vegetables. Desserts were unimpeachable. Everyone but us ordered à la carte, yet the staff treated us paupers with the utmost cordiality and sweetness. That's what we call class. The serious complaint is an old one: the dreamy wine list offers scant choice under £40 – though there is a good selection by the glass.

Booking essential. Dress: smart casual. Separate rooms for parties, seating 10, 14 and 24. **Map 8 F9.**

Koffmann's

The Berkeley, Wilton Place, SW1X 7RL (7107 8844, www.the-berkeley.co.uk/koffmanns.aspx). Hyde Park Corner or Knightsbridge tube. **Lunch served** noon-2.30pm Mon-Fri; noon-3.30pm Sat, Sun. **Dinner served** 6-10.30pm daily. **Main courses** £19-£34. **Set lunch** (Mon-Sat) £18 2 courses, £22.50 3 courses; (Sun) £26 3 courses. **Credit** AmEx, MC, V.

Pierre Koffmann's 2009 pop-up restaurant on Selfridges rooftop had the blogging and tweeting communities salivating in adulation of the masterchef returned, even though most had been nowhere near La Tante Claire at the Berkeley, let alone its former incarnation on Royal Hospital Road. Cue almost inevitable disappointment when he opened a restaurant (a) without the juggernaut of London Restaurant Week and (b) in a basement. On the site of the Boxwood Café (a Gordon Ramsay outfit that in 2009 was performing better than ever), Koffmann's launch is also notable for bringing closure to the sweary one's involvement with the Berkeley, Marcus Wareing having taken over the former Pétrus site in 2008. The new decor includes photos by esteemed food photographer Jean Cazals, and dark vases of sunflowers to contrast with cream and olive tones. Dishes such as charentais melon with bayonne ham, sole meunière, and rib of beef with béarnaise sauce aim to be heartily simple, but the old Tante Claire signatures (scallops with squid ink, pig's trotter stuffed with sweetbreads and morels, pistachio soufflé) remain nigh-on faultless. We loved the snails and girolles in a creamy, truffle-scented parsley-garlic sauce served with mash. Vegetarian options (heritage tomatoes with goat's cheese and basil sorbet, say) and value-priced set lunch menus help make the food accessible to a wide audience, and the wine list starts at £19 a bottle.

Babies and children welcome: high chairs. Booking essential. Disabled: toilet (hotel). Dress: smart casual. Separate room for parties, seats 12. **Map 9 G9.**

Marcus Wareing at the Berkeley

The Berkeley, Wilton Place, SW1X 7RL (7235 1200, www.the-berkeley.co.uk). Hyde Park Corner or Knightsbridge tube. **Lunch served** noon-2.30pm Mon-Fri. **Dinner served** 6-10.45pm Mon-Sat. **Set lunch** £38 3 courses. **Set dinner** £75 3 courses. **Set meal** £95 tasting menu (£155-£200 incl wine). **Credit** AmEx, DC, MC, V.

Wareing's declared aim is to 'make this London's finest restaurant' – always a subjective call, and to assess progress fairly would cost a king's ransom via the seasonal 'menu prestige' and sommelier-selected wines. However, the set lunch menu should give a reasonable snapshot; on the latest showing, the ambitious chef still has a few steps to go. The cosseting reach of the dining space (designed by David Collins) is pitch-perfect, from plush claret furnishings and opulent napery to the silver gleam of silently gliding trolleys. A battalion of efficient staff whisks away plates and crumbs with eagle-eyed efficiency. Set lunch, with just two choices for first and main courses, offers less complexity than the carte and suggests robust rusticity (the ever-popular slab of belly pork), but the overriding notes are of finesse, delicacy and restraint in seasoning. Lacy folds of fennel bulb proved a perfect foil for soft slivers of seared tuna; mustard mousse melted elusively over a rosette of buttery, crunchy cabbage leaf. Sturdier elements can seem misplaced: a powerful sardine vinaigrette did the tuna few favours, despite the neat 'blue fish' conceit. The extras that cut across the cartes, whether soothing (sweet onion velouté with cool nutmeg foam) or palate-wakening (a startling lime granita and cucumber-mint jelly), were a joy. Iced tap water and classy wines by the glass rounded off a memorable experience.

Babies and children welcome: high chairs. Booking essential. Dress: smart; jacket preferred. Separate rooms for parties, seating 8 and 16. Vegetarian menu. **Map 9 G9.**

One-O-One

101 William Street, SW1X 7RN (7290 7101, www. oneoonerestaurant.com). Knightsbridge tube. **Lunch served** noon-2.30pm Mon-Fri; 12.30-2.30pm Sat, Sun. **Dinner served** 7-10.30pm daily. **Main courses** £24-£37. **Set lunch** £19 3 dishes-£35 6 dishes. **Set dinner** £42 3 courses, £72 6 courses. **Credit** AmEx, DC, MC, V.

On a hot day, One-O-One's breezy and serene dining room, coupled with its gracious service team, can transport you to the Côte d'Azur. The design is contemporary, with polished wood panelling adding lustre. As you might expect, the carte is expensive; nevertheless, the lunchtime 'petits plats' (tasting plates) – from £19 for three plates to £35 for six – is something of a bargain. Our selection from these produced a profusion of intricate dishes. Under the guiding hand of Pascal Proyart, renowned for his flair with fish, the food never loses sight of its purpose. The bar was set high by a Norwegian red king crab arriving with smoked salmon, 'onzen' quail egg and cucumber vichyssoise, rounded off by a sensational yuzu sorbet. There's a smouldering talent in the kitchen, and unusual flavours can appear in inspired combinations. Take as example a main course of waxy roasted halibut accompanied by cuttlefish tagliatelle, cassoulet compote and a wild garlic beurre blanc. Meat is equally special; roasted spring lamb with asparagus and parmesan gnocchi was memorable. We ended with ravishing poached strawberries and rhubarb with lychee fromage frais ice-cream. The wine list contains some fabulous bottles, but most cost above £40.

Available for hire. Babies and children welcome: high chairs. Booking advisable Thur-Sun. Disabled: toilet. Dress: smart casual. Separate room for parties, seats 10. **Map 8 F9.**

Marylebone

Texture

34 Portman Street, W1H 7BY (7224 0028, www.texture-restaurant.co.uk). Marble Arch tube.
Bar **Open/snacks served** noon-midnight Tue-Sat.
Restaurant **Lunch served** noon-2.30pm, **dinner served** 6.30-11pm Tue-Sat. **Main courses** £19.50-£27.50.
Set lunch £18.50 2 courses, £22 3 courses. **Set meal** £59 tasting menu (£80-£100 incl wine), £45-£52.50 vegetarian tasting menu.
Both **Credit** AmEx, MC, V.

Honey-coloured seating and blond wood flooring contrasts well with the high plasterwork ceilings and white panelled walls of this elegantly relaxed restaurant. Chef and co-owner Agnar Sverrisson's Icelandic heritage is gently reflected in menus (and some strident landscape paintings) without descending to gimmickry. The cold-climate grain barley makes frequent appearances – served in a meze-style dip appetiser, with roast chicken and jus, in spring vegetable 'risotto', or with mussels, prawns and shellfish broth as an accompaniment to Cornish skate. There's Icelandic cod, of course, cooked fresh, or cured and whipped into brandade, and often paired with Spanish flavours such as chorizo and gazpacho. More unusual is the cod skin dried to a crisp wafer for dipping, but the revelation is skyr, a zingy, yogurt-like cheese delicious served icy-cold with various textures of gariguette strawberries. Nor will you want to miss the Valrhona white chocolate mousse with ice-cream, dill and cucumber. There's a choice of vegetarian tasting menus and a Scandinavian-inspired fish tasting menu. The set lunch is good value, though we'd prefer more generosity in the range of dishes than just two options per course. Co-owner Xavier Rousset's international wine list favours France, but includes curiosities such as Luxembourg riesling, and an unusually decent choice of Madeira and sweet wines.

Available for hire. Babies and children admitted. Disabled: toilet. Separate room for parties, seats 16. Vegetarian menu. **Map 9 G6.**

Mayfair

Alain Ducasse at the Dorchester

The Dorchester, 53 Park Lane, W1K 1QA (7629 8866, www.alainducasse-dorchester.com). Hyde Park Corner tube. **Lunch served** noon-2pm Tue-Fri. **Dinner served** 6.30-10pm Tue-Sat. **Set lunch** £39.50 2 courses, £45 3 courses (both incl 2 glasses of wine, mineral water, coffee). **Set dinner** £75 3 courses, £95 4 courses. **Set meal** £115 tasting menu (£210 incl wine). **Credit** AmEx, DC, MC, V.

This contemporary dining room is luminous and serene, with shades of gold and green. We sat in the front room where overhead illumination came in the form of silver leaves: a nod to nearby Hyde Park. Table spacing is sumptuous, and the range of cutlery and crockery adds further to the sophisticated allure. The signature dish of slow-cooked vegetables in a specially designed pot turned out, disappointingly, to be a plain vegetable stew. But poached wild sea bass was magnificent in its simplicity, the gossamer flesh perfectly matched with a gratinated razor clam, and some calamares stirred into life by a shellfish jus imbued with parsley. The meagre choice of four cheeses is more befitting a bistro than a restaurant of this standing. Nevertheless, it's impossible not to be seduced by the set pieces – starting with outstanding breads (such as bacon fougasse), through to perfect madeleines and dark chocolates, and a final act of brilliantly made mignardises. Desserts offered the most pleasure. A white chocolate ganache infused with rose syrup was served with fresh raspberries and a raspberry coulis; rum baba, which came with a choice of five types of the liquor, knocked our socks off. The staff's relaxed manner and enthusiasm quickly developed into an affinity with the diners. The wine list, which contains numerous prestige French labels, shows no mercy and really only gets going above £50.

Booking advisable. Children admitted. Disabled: toilet (in hotel). Dress: smart. Separate rooms for parties, seating 8-24. **Map 9 G7.**

Le Gavroche `HOT 50`

43 Upper Brook Street, W1K 7QR (7408 0881, www. le-gavroche.co.uk). Marble Arch tube. **Lunch served** noon-2pm Mon-Fri. **Dinner served** 6.30-11pm Mon-Sat. **Main courses** £27-£60. **Set lunch** £48.90 3 courses incl half bottle of wine, mineral water, coffee, petits fours. **Set dinner** £96.40 tasting menu (£152.60 incl wine). **Credit** AmEx, DC, MC, V.

Real culinary dynasty stuff, this. Emily Roux, daughter of Michel Roux Jr, has been training as a chef in France. Will she one day take over the restaurant her grandfather and great-uncle opened in 1967? When her father became Le Gavroche's chef de cuisine in 1991, his aim was to keep some classic dishes but lighten and modernise. So today the kitchen offers hot escalope of foie gras with a cinnamon-scented duck pastilla, alongside simple roast Pyrennean milk-fed lamb with flageolet beans and thyme-scented jus, and the old-school soufflé suissesse (cheese soufflé cooked on double cream) that has been on the menu since Charlie Chaplin, Ava Gardner and Robert Redford attended the launch party. Precision-trained front-of-house staff add plenty of theatre to food presentation, but Michel Jr's modern creations stand well back from the cutting edge. The classics charm because of their comparative rarity, and dishes for two to share – duck pot au feu or roast suckling pig, say – add to the romance of a visit. Gavroche has never been cheap, but the justly famed set lunch is good value. A menu exceptionnel comprises eight seasonal dishes with matching wines. Of course, the encyclopaedic wine list comes with expert guidance; there's a discerning choice of beers too. The conservative decor (red in the bar, bottle green in the basement dining room) may be reminiscent of an outdated country house hotel, but paintings by Miró, Chagall and Picasso subtly underline that this place is the real deal.
Available for hire. Babies and children admitted. Booking essential. Dress: jacket; smart jeans accepted; no trainers. **Map 9 G7.**

Greenhouse

27A Hay's Mews, W1J 5NY (7499 3331, www. greenhouserestaurant.co.uk). Green Park tube. **Lunch served** noon-2.30pm Mon-Fri. **Dinner served** 6.45-11pm Mon-Sat. **Set lunch** £25 2 courses, £29 3 courses. **Set meal** £70 3 courses, £85 tasting menu. **Credit** AmEx, DC, MC, V.

The name of this quietly fabulous restaurant makes sense the minute you step off the cobbled mews in which it hides, and slip past the bubbling fountains in its serene garden. Once you're inside, the discreet decor and glimpses of greenery through the windows have an immediately peaceful effect. This, along with service you could set your watch by (largely administered by consummately unobtrusive French chaps), allows diners to concentrate on what really matters – the sensational food. Since the Marc group took over in 2003, the Greenhouse has been producing modern French dishes that boldly look further afield for inspiration; under Lyon-born executive chef, Antonin Bonnet, it remains one of the most reliably remarkable places to eat in London. Typical dishes might pair foie gras with medlar and saké, or slow-cooked beef with seaweed sabayon. There's an £85 tasting menu for those who want to splash out, but the £29 three-course set lunch is a realistic alternative, and thoughtful touches such as playful amuse bouche and petits fours (whether you have coffee or not) render the meal more alluring still. The creative wine list, at more than 100 pages, makes joyous reading for oenophiles.

Babies and children admitted. Booking essential. Dress: smart casual. Separate room for parties, seats 10. Vegetarian menu. **Map 9 H7.**

Hélène Darroze at the Connaught

The Connaught, Carlos Place, W1K 2AL (3147 7200, www.the-connaught.co.uk). Bond Street tube. **Lunch served** noon-2.30pm Tue-Fri. **Dinner served** 6.30-10.15pm Tue-Sat. **Brunch served** 11am-3pm Sat. **Set lunch** £35 3 courses. **Set dinner** £75 3 courses, £85 7 courses. **Set brunch** £38 3 courses, £43 incl glass of champagne. **Credit** AmEx, MC, V.

Feminine touches seem to pervade every aspect of the dining experience here, from the cheering gold and deep comfort of India Mahdavi's furnishings, via Hélène Darroze's extremely pretty, delicately textured and subtly seasoned dishes, to the friendliness of the waiting staff. There's no absence of precision or sharp attention to detail in any respect. A palate-teaser of grey-green olive 'cake' and phial of deep gold carrot velouté spiced with Darroze's signature espelette pepper consciously echoes the colours and warmth of the dining room. Scallop ceviche with aubergine and lemon 'caviars', was, by contrast, an exercise in the yin-yang balance of coolness and piquancy, soft slither and almost challenging crunch: its colours muted save for a scattering of purple flower petals. Pigeon from Racan was soft and plump as the seared foie gras that partnered it; everything was red-brown hued, including the spicy chocolate sauce that ingeniously melded meats, beetroot and cherries. Venezuelan chocolate cream with vanilla and tonka-bean ice in a fragile wisp of dark chocolate shell, and a final flourish of the grated bean, proved a firecracker of textures and flavours. The set lunch with wine option (a generous two glasses) is a fairly priced dip into culinary brilliance. The staff will even send you home with a perfectly achieved canelé pastry in an olive-grey gift box to prolong the smile of contentment.
Babies and children welcome: high chairs. Booking essential. Disabled: toilet (in hotel). Dress: smart; no jeans or trainers. **Map 9 H7.**

Hibiscus `HOT 50`

29 Maddox Street, W1S 2PA (7629 2999, www.hibiscus restaurant.co.uk). Oxford Circus tube. **Lunch served** noon-2.30pm Tue-Fri. **Dinner served** 6.30-10pm Tue-Fri; 6-10pm Sat. **Set lunch** £29.50 3 courses, £80 6 courses. **Set dinner** £75 3 courses, £95 tasting menu. **Credit** AmEx, MC, V.

Furnished in subtle, pale oak panelling, with an eye-catching floral centrepiece, the dining room at Claude and Claire Bosi's Hibiscus is as subdued as the cooking is adventurous. Service is smooth, the team well acquainted with the menu and happy to offer recommendations. A first course of deliciously squishy poached pheasant egg, matched with crisp-skinned juicy pork belly, delivered a rich and robust contrast to an astringent salad of dandelion leaves tossed in a mustard dressing. Clever flavour combinations were also evident in a chilled pea and creamy coconut-milk soup, poured around a scoop of roasted pistachio nuts, mixed with diced peaches and raw podded peas – an outstanding summery celebration. Main courses were also a triumph. Slow-simmered veal cheek, notable for its tenderness and topping of buttery tomato chutney, worked well with roasted garlic purée, spiked with lemon. It's not all about full-on flavours, though; we loved the subtle nuances of a just-cooked fillet of Cornish mullet, moistened with a refreshingly tangy tarragon-infused sauce. Puddings provided a fitting

HOTELS & HAUTE CUISINE

finale. Yoghurt cheesecake mixture, dolloped over fragrant melon cubes and topped with caramelised breadcrumbs, won our gold star for its light fruity flavour. Having made the move from their famed restaurant in Ludlow, the Bosis have every reason to be proud of their achievement here.

Babies and children welcome: high chairs. Booking essential. Disabled: toilet. Separate room for parties, seats 18. Vegetarian menu. **Map 9 J6.**

Maze

13-15 Grosvenor Square, W1K 6JP (7107 0000, www. gordonramsay.com). Bond Street tube. **Lunch served** noon-2.30pm, **dinner served** 6-10.30pm daily. **Main courses** £15-£29.50. **Set lunch** £28.50 4 courses, £35.50 5 courses, £42.50 6 courses. **Credit** AmEx, DC, MC, V.

Once a beacon in the Gordon Ramsay group, Maze has witnessed the departure of Jason Atherton, followed by its recently appointed executive chef, James Durrant. Despite such changes, service remains reassuringly smooth, knowledgeable and friendly. The glamorous bar provides a classy line in cocktails for the monied customers. It's a spacious venue, furnished in shades of coffee and cream, and fronted by large windows looking on to leafy Grosvenor Square. Maze has earned its culinary spurs for serving sophisticated, European-style morsels, some containing pan-Asian ingredients – though, on our visit, the set menu consisted of Modern British choices. Chilled lobster cream was notable for its full-flavoured shellfish stock mellowed with cream. Poured around a mound of flaked crayfish, the soup unleashed surprise hits of lovely lemony avocado purée. Two-hour cooked duck egg wasn't as triumphant; we weren't convinced by the mushroom purée base, which detracted from the smoky character of juicy mussels and tender asparagus spears. A parade of indulgent dishes followed; our favourite was a meltingly tender morsel of boneless rabbit, served with fresh-tasting minted risotto studded with broad beans. Most desserts didn't make the grade, except for an outstanding creamy rice pudding, streaked with warm orange-and-thyme marmalade and molten chocolate.

Babies and children admitted. Booking essential. Dress: smart casual; no trainers. Separate rooms for parties, seating 15 and 36. **Map 9 G6.**

Sketch `HOT 50`

9 Conduit Street, W1S 2XZ (7659 4500, www.sketch.uk.com). Oxford Circus tube.
Lecture Room & Library **Lunch served** noon-2.30pm Tue-Fri. **Dinner served** 7-10.30pm Tue-Sat. **Main courses** £28-£55. **Set lunch** £30 2 courses, £35 3 courses. **Set meal** £70-£95 tasting menu.
Parlour@Sketch **Meals served** 8.30am-9pm Mon-Fri; 10am-9pm Sat. **Main courses** £9-£17.
The Gallery **Dinner served** 7-10pm Mon-Sat. **Main courses** £19-£35.
All **Credit** AmEx, MC, V.

For a place with a velvet rope and staff guarding entry to its upper echelons, Sketch is remarkably relaxed and friendly, pretentious and unpretentious at the same time. Sure, it helps if money's no object when dining in the top-floor Lecture Room & Library, but Pierre Gagnaire's inventive cuisine is not just available in expensive tasting menus. The delightful, tongue-in-cheek Parlour café-bar, with its inventive sandwiches and main courses (from classic mac-n-cheese to a fresh take on steak tartare, served with egg mollet), is more affordable, though still premium-priced. And there's the Gallery, an arty,

music-pumping brasserie with videos playing on the upper walls. Its 'pared down gastronomy' brief is exemplified in dishes such as beetroot salad with raspberry sorbet, gingerbread and shavings of raw vegetables. Main courses cost from £11 (green pea risotto with rocket coulis) to £35 (duck foie gras mousse with spelt, braised duck, baby leek, summer truffles and lettuce) – and the bread basket is another £5. The see-and-be-seen crowd tends not to be as eccentric as the space, but the buzz is energising. The same can hardly be said of the Lecture Room, where the service is warm and the decor sumptuous, but the complex cooking demands a level of appreciation that becomes exhausting. It's all about showcasing what Gagnaire can do with ingredients, so foie gras is teased into chantilly-style cream, baked potato is made into ice-cream to serve with roast beef in peppered butter, and it's not unusual for dishes to comprise 20 key flavours. The food is certainly astounding, but you have to be in the mood for it.

Available for hire. Babies and children welcome: high chairs. Booking advisable. Bookings not accepted Parlour. Dress: smart casual. Separate rooms for parties, seating 12 upwards. **Map 9 J6.**

The Square

6-10 Bruton Street, W1J 6PU (7495 7100, www.square restaurant.com). Bond Street or Green Park tube. **Lunch served** noon-2.15pm Mon-Fri. **Dinner served** 6.30-10pm Mon-Fri; 6.30-10.30pm Sat; 6.30-9.30pm Sun. **Set lunch** £30 2 courses, £35 3 courses. **Set dinner** £75 3 courses. **Set meal** £100 tasting menu (£155 incl wine). **Credit** AmEx, MC, V.

Consistently rated among London's best fine-dining experiences, the Square is furnished with polished parquet flooring and decorated with abstract art. Tables sport new sets of designer show plates. Our lunch here was characterised by accurate seasoning and finely balanced flavours. Excellent breads were followed by a velvety bite-size boudin blanc atop apple and lentil vinaigrette, with a dollop of cream of chicken liver adding a final luscious touch. Liver was again admirably employed in a dish of roasted wood pigeon (served rare) where duck foie gras provided a silky dimension, and crunch was supplied by a warm salad of french beans with a pesto of summer truffles and blackberries. Fish is a highlight; a john dory fillet came with cannellini beans and a creamy fondue of ovoli mushrooms. Cheeses are kept in prime condition, a reblochon being especially notable. The finale – poached peach with raspberry ripple ice-cream – was a corker. There's good drinking too, with France, and especially Burgundy, taking pride of place on the bewitching wine list.

The team behind the Square, Nigel Platts-Martin and Philip Howard, launched the Ledbury in Notting Hill in 2005 with Australian protégé Brett Graham at the helm; Graham has subsequently matched the Square for Michelin stars (two) and co-owns Fulham gastropub Harwood Arms (*see p105*), which has another. The Ledbury is no mere outpost: in fact, we've often found it outshining its Mayfair sibling. Expect generous yet indulgent dishes such as sika deer loin baked in hay with beetroot, bone marrow and malt, plus an exceptional wine list. The interior is comfortable and, despite the residential area, attracts convivial foodies even on weekday lunchtimes.

Available for hire. Babies and children admitted. Booking advisable. Disabled: toilet. Dress: smart; smart jeans accepted; no trainers. Separate room for parties, seats 18. **Map 9 H7.**
For branch (The Ledbury) see index.

Koffmann's. See p127.

Piccadilly

The Ritz

150 Piccadilly, W1J 9BR (7493 8181, www.theritz hotel.co.uk). Green Park tube. Bar **Open** 11.30am-midnight Mon-Sat; noon-10.30pm Sun. *Restaurant* **Breakfast served** 7-10am Mon-Sat; 8-10am Sun. **Lunch served** 12.30-2.30pm daily. **Tea served** (reserved sittings) 11.30am, 1.30pm, 3.30pm, 5.30pm, 7.30pm daily. **Dinner served** 5.30-10.30pm Mon-Sat; 7-10pm Sun. **Main courses** £25-£40. **Set lunch** £39 3 courses. **Set tea** £38. **Set dinner** £48 4 courses; (Mon-Thur, Sun) £65 4 courses; (Fri, Sat) £95 4 courses. **Credit** AmEx, MC, V.

The magnificence of the spacious Ritz dining room, inspired by the Palace of Versailles and serenaded during evenings by first-class musicians, tends to highlight rather than obscure what we feel is an under-achieving restaurant kitchen. It prides itself on using 'best of British' produce while choosing Bresse chicken and Alsace bacon for its summer dinner menu, but, more importantly, there are better ways to spend the sort of money required to eat à la carte here: starters begin at £17, main courses at £32 and desserts at an outrageous £15. Daily set lunch and dinner menus are more accessibly priced, but the accompanying wine recommendations, at £12-£19 a glass, are just annoying. You'd think this (and the strict dress code) would keep out the hoi polloi, but no: the restaurant attracts a diverse demographic, from old money to young sarf Londoners on a birthday spree. To its credit, the restaurant confidently offers Ritz classic dishes alongside modern creations, so there is something for everybody. Roast pigeon with walnut gnocchi and raisin purée, and turbot with fennel, grapefruit and crayfish typify the contemporary thinking. When it comes to dessert, you'd be foolish to ignore the excellent soufflés (apricot, perhaps, served with roast almond ice-cream) or crêpes suzettes (for two) traditionally cooked tableside by the maitre d'hotel. *Babies and children welcome: children's menu; high chairs. Booking advisable restaurant; essential afternoon tea. Dress: jacket and tie; no jeans or trainers. Entertainment: dinner dance Fri, Sat (restaurant); pianist daily. Separate rooms for parties, seating 16-60. Tables outdoors (8, terrace).* **Map 9 J7**.

South Kensington

Tom Aikens

43 Elystan Street, SW3 3NT (7584 2003, www.tom aikens.co.uk). South Kensington tube. **Lunch served** noon-2.30pm Mon-Fri. **Dinner served** 6.45-10.45pm Mon-Sat. **Set lunch** £39 3 courses, £49 tasting menu. **Set meal** £65 3 courses, £80 tasting menu. **Credit** AmEx, MC, V.

It's hard to remember that Tom Aikens is still only in his early thirties; the chef seems to have been through so many highs (and a few lows) in such a short time. Dining in his flagship restaurant is nothing as frenetic, and we were well looked after by a polite team. The monochromatic room is handsome, with black leather chairs and pretty white orchids and roses. Tables are arranged with privacy in mind. Regrettably, lunch at £39 is no longer the bargain it once was. At dinner, the choice is between the carte, which also features classic dishes from the chef, and the tasting menu. We were immediately seduced by a selection of ten breads, followed by six stunning canapés (most memorable: a brandade with velouté of red pepper, and a pea mousse with ibérico ham). Then, a master class in simplicity: poached lobster tail with English asparagus, asparagus mousse and chervil salad. For main course, Rhug Estate loin of lamb, marinated in ewe's cheese, was amazingly tender but restrained in flavour. This was paired with a hillock of finely shaved parmesan covering aligot potato, along with a slice of salty ewe's cheese and dried green olives. We were puzzled by the addition of an anchovy fritto, but a beignet of parmesan came from the top drawer. Vanilla panna cotta – topped with a slice of salted black summer truffle, and subtly enhanced by black pepper – was sexed up by white chocolate, and truffle ice-cream, but entirely covered in too much truffle-oil foam. To finish, don't leave without trying the brilliant petits fours. Wines are rooted mainly in France, and expensive, although two dozen are served by the glass.

Booking essential. Children admitted. Disabled: toilet. Dress: smart. Separate room for parties, seats 10. **Map 14 E11.**

South West

Chelsea

Aubergine

11 Park Walk, SW10 0AJ (7352 3449, www.aubergine restaurant.co.uk). Bus 14, 345, 414. **Lunch served** noon-2.15pm Mon-Fri. **Dinner served** 7-11pm Mon-Sat. **Main courses** £16.50-£22.50. **Set lunch** £18.50 2 courses, £25 3 courses (£34 incl half bottle of wine). **Set meal** £85 tasting menu (£135 incl wine). **Credit** AmEx, DC, MC, V.
Christophe Renou took over Aubergine's kitchen in 2009, arriving with an impressive CV including a stint at L'Auberge du Vieux Puits in southern France. The carte now offers greater flexibility, and prices have been lowered. The three-course lunch menu is fair value, especially if you include a half bottle of decent wine for only an extra £9. On our visit, Renou and many of his kitchen staff had decamped to a private function, but the reserve team didn't miss a beat. Amuse bouche consisted of salad niçoise on a silver spoon, and a buttery tartlet of black pudding topped with apple gelée. Two plump, juicy scallops arrived with diced tomatoes made special by a delicate dressing with a hint of balsamic and fresh basil. Then followed a ballotine of Label Anglais chicken, its skin perfectly crisp, with tomato concasse and a divine rosemary-scented jus. We couldn't resist the cheeseboard, with seven varieties in fine fettle including a salty, pungent livarot and a ripe, soft reblochon. Pear tart, wasn't as memorable, although the accompanying dark chocolate ice-cream was superb. You can drink handsomely here from a wine list that doesn't stray much beyond France, and although prestige labels no longer dominate, prices are still high. Aubergine remains a highly appealing place for a meal, with personable service, aubergine-coloured carpets, distressed yellow walls and low ceilings.
Available for hire. Booking advisable; essential weekends. Children admitted. Dress: smart casual. **Map 14 D12.**

Gordon Ramsay

68 Royal Hospital Road, SW3 4HP (7352 4441, www.gordonramsay.com). Sloane Square tube. **Lunch served** noon-2.15pm, **dinner served** 6.30-10.15pm Mon-Fri.. **Set lunch** £45 3 courses. **Set meal** £90 3 courses, £120 tasting menu. **Credit** AmEx, DC, MC, V.
'Is this a special occasion?' That's the first thing staff ask when you take your seat in this diminutive, elegantly understated dining room, and it's the introduction to truly astonishing service: not merely efficient and polished, but warm, funny and personal. Staff were relaxed, confident, proud – and with justification. Whatever troubles may afflict other vessels of the Ramsay fleet, the flagship sails on serenely. Six dishes from the set lunch produced five show-stoppers, with attendant accessories (bread, amuse bouche, petits fours) uniformly flawless. Head chef Clare Smyth steers a slightly more Italianate course than her boss. Star dishes: salt cod brandade with Noir de Bigorre ham, poached quail's egg and grilled pepper; porchetta (really a ballotine) containing both pancetta and lardo di colonnata; a main course that's called saltimbocca, but uses a thick, finger-shaped veal fillet rather than the traditional flattened escalope (the fillet is seasoned with the requisite sage and aromatics, then rolled in prosciutto, crumbed and fried to crispness); and both desserts, a banana parfait with salted caramel ice-cream (amazing) and 'minestrone' of summer fruits served with a heavenly jasmine and vanilla syrup. Only one dish, a main of confit salmon, failed to excite. The wine list is a marvel, but why can't there be a few more bottles under £40? Even with that shortcoming, the answer to the opening question is yes. Every visit here is a special occasion, because Gordon Ramsay is an extraordinary restaurant.
Available for hire. Booking essential. Children admitted. Dress: smart; jacket preferred; smart jeans accepted; no trainers. **Map 14 F12.**
For branch (Gordon Ramsay at Claridge's) see index.

Outer London

Richmond, Surrey

The Bingham

61-63 Petersham Road, Richmond, Surrey TW10 6UT (8940 0902, www.thebingham.co.uk). Richmond tube/rail. **Breakfast served** 7-10am Mon-Fri; 8-10am Sat, Sun. **Lunch served** noon-2.15pm Mon-Sat; 12.30-4pm Sun. **Dinner served** 7-10pm Mon-Sat. **Set lunch** £19.50 2 courses, £23 3 courses. **Set meal** £45 3 courses, £65 tasting menu (£105 incl wine). **Credit** AmEx, DC, MC, V.
Tables on a heated terrace, overlooking the Thames at the foot of Richmond Hill, are just one of the Bingham's many attractions. Part of a boutique hotel, the restaurant occupies two smallish connected dining rooms that share a view through french windows. The interior is dauntingly opulent-chic: all pale dusty-gold tones and heavy curtains, with gilt-topped chandeliers and recessed spots to highlight the hand-painted wallpapers. Chef Shay Cooper adds novel yet surprisingly appropriate flavours to seasonal food. An economical way to sample his creations is to order the set lunch. A chilled pea soup with Scottish girolles, parmesan royale (a crisp cockscomb lattice) and herb oil would have resulted in plate-licking in a less august establishment. A main course of firm but very tender organic sea trout was topped with a razor-clam shell filled with the chopped clam, celeriac, pistachios and bacon, all with an almost subliminal hint of vanilla, amply demonstrating Cooper's wizardry. Lemon tart with yoghurt sorbet rather let the meal down, the sorbet lacking flavour and the tart's base fork-defyingly hard. A drinks list full of intriguing wines, many by the glass, together with informed, impeccable and friendly service, round off the pleasures of this waterside gem.
Babies and children welcome: high chairs; nappy-changing facilities. Booking advisable Thur-Sun. Disabled: toilet. Separate room for parties, seats 90. Tables outdoors (8, balcony).

Indian

Londoners should give thanks to their deity of choice for the breadth of high-quality Indian restaurants within their city. The scope is stunning: from basic Sri Lankan caffs such as **Apollo Banana Leaf** in Tooting, to top-flight West End establishments where some of the capital's most talented chefs are given free rein (the likes of Vivek Singh at **Cinnamon Club**, Karunesh Khanna at **Amaya**, and Anirudh Arora at **Moti Mahal**, among others). The capital boasts prime exponents of Pakistani, Sri Lankan and Bangladeshi cookery, as well as restaurants specialisng in regional cuisines from the modern state of India. Vegetarians are well served (try the South Indian food at **Sagar** or the Gujarati specialities at **Ram's**), but so too are piscivores (**Rasa Samudra**) and inveterate meat-eaters (head for the mutton curries and tandooried flesh of Punjabi specialists such as **Lahore Kebab House** or the **New Asian Tandoori Centre**). New arrival **Dishoom** introduces the distinctive flavours and look of the Persian-run 'Irani' cafés of Victorian Bombay. Cast your envious eyes to our city, out-of-towners, and weep.

Central
Covent Garden

Dishoom
2010 RUNNER-UP BEST NEW DESIGN
12 Upper St Martin's Lane, WC2H 9FB (7420 9320, www.dishoom.com). Covent Garden or Leicester Square tube. **Meals served** 8am-11pm Mon-Fri; 10am-11pm Sat; 10am-10pm Sun. **Main courses** £1.90-£9.20. **Credit** AmEx, MC, V. Pan-Indian
Inspired by Mumbai's 'Irani' cafés (cheap, cosmopolitan eateries set up by Persian immigrants in the 1900s), Dishoom has certainly got the look. Solid oak panels, antique mirrors and ceiling fans say retro grandeur; a web of black cables strung around the room for the pendant lights say contemporary and fun. A fascinating display of old magazine covers, nostalgic adverts and fading photos of Indian families adorns the walls. There's also a cosy basement. Parts of the menu are very familiar, such as a stand-out pau bhaji, the street snack that combines a toasted Portuguese-style bread roll (pão) with a filling of spiced vegetable stew (bhaji). But chocolate fondant, classy cocktails, intriguing lassi flavours and smart bottles of wine indicate a far superior dining experience. Keem pau (pau filled with spicy minced lamb), chilli cheese toast and

a rich, earthy house black dahl were superb. The birianis were less impressive, with dry and overcooked rice. There's much more on the menu, from conventional Indian grills and curries (including excellent mutter paneer) to seldom-seen treats such as gola, a shaved-then-flavoured ice dessert. You can also have breakfast here: on bacon nan rolls with chilli jam and coriander, perhaps, or porridge with dates and bananas.
Babies and children welcome: high chairs. Bookings not accepted. Disabled: toilet. Tables outdoors (25, pavement). Takeaway service. **Map 18 D4**.

Moti Mahal
45 Great Queen Street, WC2B 5AA (7240 9329, www.motimahal-uk.com). Covent Garden or Holborn tube. **Lunch served** noon-3pm Mon-Fri. **Dinner served** 5.30-11pm Mon-Sat. **Main courses** £9-£28. **Set lunch** £15-£20. **Set dinner** £25-£56. **Credit** AmEx, MC, V. Modern Indian
The Covent Garden location and numerous online cut-price meal deals (check the website for details) keep this 'Pearl Palace' busy with better-off tourists and opera-goers. Connoisseurs of Indian fine dining should also take note, because although the à la carte prices are high, chef Anirudh Arora's special menus have more wondrous and exotic marvels than a nawab's feast. The carte and various tasting menus all change regularly, but on our visit the 'Grand Trunk Road' was

Dishoom. See p133.

the theme used to showcase the best of regional dishes from Kabul to Calcutta, Sind to Kerala. From our Jaipur set menu, potato koftas had been stuffed with prunes, and served with saffron yoghurt sauce: surprisingly complex and satisfying. Classic dishes such as achari gosht ('pickling spice' lamb curry) were piquant and beautifully made, while more innovative creations, such as a starter of fritters studded with sago 'pearls', are playful interpretations of classic recipes. Our only caveats are that the service can be a little over-attentive (our water glasses were refilled after every sip), and, more worryingly, it's hard to keep to a budget with more temptations on this ravishing menu than at a nautch girls' jamboree.
Available for hire. Babies and children welcome: high chairs. Booking advisable dinner. Dress: smart casual. Tables outdoors (5, pavement). Vegetarian menu. **Map 18 E3**.

Sitaaray

167 Drury Lane, WC2B 5PG (7269 6422, www. sitaaray.com). Covent Garden or Holborn tube. **Lunch served** noon-3pm, **dinner served** 5.30-11pm Mon-Sat.
Set lunch £14.50 2 courses. **Set dinner** (5.30-7pm) £14.50-£16.50 2 courses, £22.95 buffet. **Credit** MC, V.
Pan-Indian

Sitaaray means 'stars' in Hindi, a reference in this case to the Bollywood stars and movie posters that line the walls. These stretch from the golden age of RK Studio, through the polyester years and chubby 'Hero No.1's' to the present day – flatscreen TVs pipe movie clips on to both levels of the restaurant. Yes, the venue has been themed to its maroon-cushioned hilt with Indian movie kitsch, but the cooking has not been relegated to the back row. Grills are the great strength of the kitchen, and the fixed-price, eat-all-you-can buffet is good value as long as you're not having a vegetarian moment. Expect a dozen or so dishes, many of them kebabs. We particularly enjoy the mint-marinated, chargrilled tiny lamb chops; the shami kebabs (pan-fried ground lamb patties flavoured with coriander, onion and chillies); and the unusual variation on shami kebabs, studded with sweetcorn but tasting of fenugreek.
Babies and children admitted. Booking advisable dinner. Disabled: toilet. Takeaway service. **Map 18 E3**.

Fitzrovia

Rasa Samudra `HOT 50`

5 Charlotte Street, W1T 1RE (7637 0222, www.rasa restaurants.com). Goodge Street tube. **Lunch served** noon-3pm Mon-Sat. **Dinner served** 6-10.30pm Mon-Wed, Sun; 6-10.45pm Thur-Sat. **Main courses** £6.50-£12.95. **Set meal** £22.50 vegetarian, £30 seafood. **Credit** AmEx, MC, V. South Indian

The Rasa mini empire took its first step upmarket by opening this seafood specialist in 1999. Though Das Sreedharan's chain now has 11 branches (including three outside London) – some vegetarian, some not – Samudra remains the West End flagship. Behind the trademark pink façade of a Charlotte Street townhouse, you'll find a succession of slightly cramped rooms on the ground and first floors, attractively decorated with carved Keralite artefacts. Kerala also provides inspiration for the menu, which is divided into the vegetarian dishes made famous at Rasa's original (and bargain-priced) Stoke Newington branch, and seafood creations from coastal towns such as Cochin. The seafood feast is the best and simplest way of sampling the range. This can be tailored to include your favourite dishes from the carte: crab varuthathu, for instance (cooked with ginger, curry leaves, chilli and mustard seeds), or tilapia with fish tamarind, roasted coconut and tomatoes. Begin a meal with Rasa's crispy snacks, served with mouth-watering own-made chutneys, before starters such as meen porichathu (fried, marinated kingfish). The vegetarian feast is equally alluring, with nutty stir-fried thorans (shredded cabbage is recommended) providing textural counterpoints to the curries. Service is sweet, though can be slow.

Babies and children welcome: high chairs. Booking advisable. Separate rooms for parties, seating 12-25. Takeaway service. Vegan dishes. Vegetarian menu. **Map 17 B1**.

For branches (Rasa, Rasa Express, Rasa Maricham, Rasa Mudra, Rasa Travancore, Rasa W1) see index.

Knightsbridge

Amaya `HOT 50`

15 Halkin Arcade, 19 Motcomb Street, SW1X 8JT (7823 1166, www.amaya.biz). Knightsbridge tube. **Lunch served** 12.30-2.15pm Mon-Sat; 12.45-2.45pm Sun. **Dinner served** 6.30-11.30pm Mon-Sat; 6.30-10.30pm Sun. **Main courses** £8.50-£25. **Set lunch** £22-£25. **Set dinner** £38.50 tasting menu. **Credit** AmEx, DC, MC, V. Modern Indian

Shiny black granite, sparkling chandeliers and bold splashes of modern art decorate this classy enterprise from the Masala World group (which also runs Veeraswamy, Chutney Mary and the Masala Zone chain). Head chef Karunesh Khanna blends traditional techniques with fresh flavours on his acclaimed tapas-style menu. Skewer-wielding cooks in the open kitchen turn kebabs over coals and slap rotis into clay ovens – it's unmatched culinary theatre. Even during the week, Amaya is packed with well-heeled diners. On our visit, a tangle of green mango and raw papaya shreds heaped into lettuce cups made a refreshing teaser in an array of light bites. Other notables included juicy, rose-scented chicken pieces, steeped in paprika yoghurt and then lightly smoked to perfection. Dori kebab (pounded lamb seasoned with cardamom, mace and ginger) was shaped on skewers and carefully cooked over glowing coals, its flavour more akin to that of delicious warm pâté than coarsely spiced mince. Meltingly soft watercress, spinach and

fig cakes were another triumph, the peppery taste contrasting with the sweetness of figs. Save space for a biriani if you can; they're lighter than most, and more aromatic. Service is spot-on, the cooking sublime, and the atmosphere very convivial.

Babies and children admitted until 8pm. Booking advisable. Disabled: toilet. Dress: smart casual. Separate room for parties, seats 14. **Map 9 G9**.

Marylebone

Trishna London

15-17 Blandford Street, W1U 3DG (7935 5624, www.trishnalondon.com). Bond Street tube. **Lunch served** noon-2.45pm Mon-Sat; noon-3pm Sun. **Dinner served** 6-10.45pm Mon-Sat; 6.30-10.30pm Sun. **Main courses** £6-£17.50. **Set lunch** £19.50 3 courses plus side dish; £25 3 dishes, 1 side dish and carafe wine. **Credit** AmEx, MC, V. South Indian

One of London's best spicy seafood restaurants, Trishna overcomes the slightly awkward dimensions of two narrow dining areas, with a chic decor of whitewashed walls, wooden tables and a soothing grey-green colour scheme. On summer evenings, the expansive french windows are often opened for alfresco dining – an attraction for Marylebone's cocktail and kebab social set. Best known for its fabulous ways with fish and seafood, the kitchen has produced an Indianised tapas selection, with substantial main dishes on hand to fill any gaps. Morsels of squid, fried in crisp, fennel-scented tempura batter, were sublime, with the squid almost buttery in texture. We

Amaya

INDIAN

were bowled over too by butterflied prawns, steeped in lime juice and red chillies before being cooked in their shells over smoky coal. Only the seafood biriani was disappointing, marred by a heavy fried onion masala and an overtly floral flavour. Meat options, although decent, aren't in the same league as the coastal dishes. If you order just one vegetable dish, make it the slow-cooked aubergines, simmered with jaggery-sweetened tamarind and pounded peanuts: much loved for its chutney-like flavour. Staff are well acquainted with the menu and quick off the mark.

Available for hire. Babies and children welcome: high chairs. Booking advisable evenings. Separate room for parties, seats 12. Tables outdoors (3, patio). Vegetarian menu. **Map 9 G5**.

Mayfair

Benares

12A Berkeley Square House, Berkeley Square, W1J 6BS (7629 8886, www.benaresrestaurant.com). Green Park tube. **Lunch served** noon-2.30pm Mon-Sat; noon-3pm Sun. **Dinner served** 5.30-10.30pm Mon-Sat; 6-10pm Sun. **Main courses** £19.50-£45. **Set meal** (lunch, 5.30-6.30pm) £19 2 courses, £25 3 courses. **Credit** AmEx, DC, MC, V. Modern Indian

This first-floor bar and spacious restaurant is sumptuously stylish, attracting a diverse array of customers from romancing couples to affluent professionals. A refurbishment has increased the number of private dining areas, created for wealthy diners with guests to impress. Not everything has changed, though; the appealing blend of Indian artefacts, modern fittings and neutral colour scheme has been retained.

Veeraswamy

Chef-patron Atul Kochhar is renowned for his modern cooking style, and although some dishes get mixed responses, his current repertoire is outstanding. A set menu salad was stunning; simmered mutton slivers, flash-fried with chilli flecks, were tossed with sliced fennel, crunchy croûtons and leafy greens, and coated in a zingy chilli and lime dressing – a fantastic assembly. Main courses were just as admirable. Sautéed bream fillet, paired with large-grained couscous, was notable for its saucy moat of creamy coconut milk infused with ginger, turmeric and curry leaves. Delectable for its smoky succulence, lime-drenched tandoori chicken, steeped in garlic and ginger yoghurt, was pleasingly balanced by the nuttiness of subtly spiced cauliflower cream. Service is exemplary: poised, attentive, supremely professional. Dining here isn't cheap, but the set lunch and early-bird meals are a bargain and the wine list is highly impressive.

Available for hire. Babies and children welcome: high chairs. Booking advisable. Disabled: toilet. Dress: smart casual. Separate rooms for parties, seating 14, 22 and 30. Takeaway service. **Map 9 H7**.

Tamarind

20-22 Queen Street, W1J 5PR (7629 3561, www.tamarind restaurant.com). Green Park tube. **Lunch served** noon-2.45pm Mon-Fri, Sun. **Dinner served** 5.30-11pm Mon-Sat; 6-10.45pm Sun. **Main courses** £12.95-£24.75. **Set lunch** £16.50 2 courses, £18.50 3 courses. **Set dinner** (5.30-6.45pm, 10.30-11pm) £25 3 courses. **Credit** AmEx, DC, MC, V. Pan-Indian

When Tamarind opened in 1995, with its glamorous Emily Todhunter-designed interior transforming a capacious Mayfair basement, London hadn't seen an Indian restaurant like it. Things have moved on a lot since then, and although chef Alfred Prasad's cooking is still excellent, some of the sheen has worn off both the service and the decor. Prices are also very high, which may lead to unrealistic expectations. However, Tamarind's Michelin star does seem deserved when things go well, for example with dishes such as the lamb chettinad, which shows a masterly touch with spices, faithful to the complex cuisine of the wealthy South Indian traders from whom the dish originates. Others, such as the aloo palak (baby potatoes with spinach and fenugreek leaves, £7.95), simply seem too expensive. The more courtly dishes are certainly worth trying – for instance, the exemplary gosht dum biriani, a lamb biriani cooked in an enclosed pot that seals in the aromas and spice flavours. Tamarind is a good choice for special occasions when you or your guest appreciates first-rate Indian food.

Babies and children welcome: children's menu; high chairs. Booking essential. Takeaway service. Vegan dishes. Vegetarian menu. **Map 9 H7**.

Veeraswamy

Mezzanine Floor, Victory House, 99-101 Regent Street, W1B 4RS (7734 1401, www.veeraswamy.com). Piccadilly Circus tube. **Lunch served** noon-2.30pm Mon-Fri; 12.30-2.45pm Sat, Sun. **Dinner served** 5.30-10.45pm Mon-Sat; 6-10.15pm Sun. **Main courses** £14-£29.50. **Set meal** (lunch, 5.30-6.30pm Mon-Sat) £17.50 2 courses; (lunch Sun) £24. **Set dinner** £42. **Credit** AmEx, DC, MC, V. Pan-Indian

The discreet dark entrance on Swallow Street contains only the greeting point and coat room – you have to take the lift up to Veeraswamy proper. Once the doors glide open, you encounter something of a supernova: shimmering screens, coloured glass lanterns, curvaceous chandeliers and plush fabrics. Tables are

THREE OF THE VERY BEST
INDIAN RESTAURANTS

AMAYA

This award winning, Michelin starred, restaurant presents an unmistakable experience for lunch and dinner in Belgravia.

Halkin Arcade, Motcomb Street Knightsbridge, London SW1

Telephone: 020 7823 1166

CHUTNEY MARY

The rich setting, interesting art and romantic candle lighting are secondary details in London's temple of great Indian food.

535 Kings Road Chelsea, London SW10

Telephone: 020 7351 3113

VEERASWAMY

Divine dishes, lovingly prepared and beautifully served in sumptuous surroundings overlooking Regent Street.

Mezzanine Floor, Victory House 99 Regent Street, London W1

Telephone: 020 7734 1401

For details of our outside catering service, please contact our Head Office on 020 7724 2525 or email us at info@realindianfood.com.

MasalaWorld

scattered with rose petals. Then there are the views: not panoramic, but exquisite glimpses of Regent Street's curving architecture, which make this an ideal spot to take out-of-towners (it's also handy for pre-theatre meals). Current owners Ranjit Mathrani and Namita and Camellia Panjabi have redecorated the place twice since taking over in 1997; second-time-lucky, they have produced an appropriately glamorous reimagining of what is claimed to be London's oldest Indian restaurant. The food is pricey, but exquisite. Spice-crusted roast leg of lamb is a party piece among northern Indian Muslims; this version is head chef Uday's creation, inspired by Lucknowi recipes. Don't miss the pineapple curry, a side dish hailing from Mangalore on the west coast. We've fond memories of the mixed seafood platter too, shared as a starter. Classy cocktails (lychee and rose martini, for instance) and beer are pleasing alternatives to the high-end wine list.

Babies and children admitted until 8pm. Booking advisable weekends. Disabled: lift; toilet. Dress: smart casual. Separate room for parties, seats 24. **Map 17 A5**.

Soho

Imli

167-169 Wardour Street, W1F 8WR (7287 4243, www.imli.co.uk). Oxford Circus or Tottenham Court Road tube. **Meals served** noon-11pm Mon-Sat; noon-10pm Sun. **Tapas** £3.95-£7.95. **Set lunch** £8.50-£9.95 2-3 dishes. **Credit** AmEx, MC, V. Pan-Indian

An offshoot of Tamarind restaurant in Mayfair, this is very much the diffusion range of a creative genius's work. It's a down-to-earth canteen that tries to be stylish yet keep prices moderate, and offer an interesting selection of dishes that avoid the obvious. Imli (the Hindi word for 'tamarind') mostly

succeeds in all these endeavours. The only areas where we've found it lacking are the service – sometimes a bit perfunctory – and the atmosphere – it's definitely an eat-then-leave sort of place, with a vibrant colour scheme, plate-glass windows fronting Wardour Street, and functional furniture. You're encouraged to mix and match small dishes; three dishes supposedly equal a two-course meal. As is so often the case, the traditional recipes surpass the more 'modern' Indian dishes, though the menu changes frequently. Imli very often has special offers and participates in online deals, and these can be worth checking out if you're particularly price-conscious.

Babies and children welcome: children's menu; high chairs. Booking advisable Thur-Sat. Disabled: toilet. Separate room for parties, seats 45. Takeaway service; delivery service (over £20 within half-mile radius). **Map 17 B3**.

Red Fort

77 Dean Street, W1D 3SH (7437 2115, www.redfort.co.uk). Leicester Square or Tottenham Court Road tube. *Bar* **Open** 5pm-1am Tue-Sat. *Restaurant* **Lunch served** noon-2.30pm Mon-Fri. **Dinner served** 5.30-11.30pm daily. **Main courses** £15-£18. **Set lunch** £12 2 courses. **Set meal** (5.30-7pm) £16 2 courses incl tea or coffee. *Both* **Credit** AmEx, MC, V. North Indian

The new-look Red Fort has retained its elegant water feature and token artefacts, but the multicoloured stripy carpet is a jarring affront to Moghul styling. Prices are eye-wateringly high – not that this puts off Soho's media moguls. A more kindly priced set menu is available until 7pm; our problem was to persuade a sulky waiter to share it with us. Thankfully, the cooking outshone the service. King prawns, coated in tempura-like batter, were fried to succulent perfection, betraying lovely

Imli

Menu

PAN-INDIAN

Aloo: potato.

Bhajee: vegetables cooked with spices, usually 'dry' rather than sauced.

Bhajia or **bhaji**: vegetables dipped in chickpea-flour batter and deep-fried; also called pakoras.

Bhatura: deep-fried doughy discs.

Bhindi: okra.

Brinjal: aubergine.

Chana or **channa**: chickpeas.

Chat or **chaat**: various savoury snacks featuring combinations of pooris (qv), diced onion and potato, chickpeas, crumbled samosas and pakoras, chutneys and spices.

Dahi: yoghurt.

Dahl or **dal**: a lentil curry similar to thick lentil soup. Countless regional variations exist.

Dhansak: a Parsi casserole of meat, lentils and vegetables, with a mix of hot and tangy flavours.

Kachori: crisp pastry rounds with spiced mung dahl or pea filling.

Murgh or **murg**: chicken.

Mutter, **muter** or **mattar**: peas.

Paneer or **panir**: Indian cheese, a bit like tofu in texture and taste.

Paratha: a large griddle-fried bread that is sometimes stuffed (with spicy mashed potato or minced lamb, for instance).

Pilau, **pillau** or **pullao**: flavoured rice cooked with meat or vegetables. In most British Indian restaurants, pilau rice is simply rice flavoured and coloured with turmeric or (rarely) saffron.

Poori or **puri**: a disc of deep-fried wholewheat bread; the frying makes it puff up like an air-filled cushion.

Raita: a yoghurt mix, usually with cucumber.

Roti: a round, sometimes unleavened, bread, thicker than a chapati and cooked in a tandoor or griddle.

Saag or **sag**: spinach; also called **palak**.

Thali: literally 'metal plate'. A large plate with rice, bread, metal containers of dahl and vegetable curries, pickles and yoghurt.

Vadai or **wada**: a spicy vegetable or lentil fritter; **dahi wada** are lentil fritters soaked in yoghurt, topped with tamarind and date chutneys.

NORTH INDIAN

Biriani or **biryani**: a royal Moghul version of pilau rice, in which meat or vegetables are cooked together with basmati rice, spices and saffron. It's difficult to find an authentic biriani in London restaurants.

Dopiaza or **do pyaza**: cooked with onions.

Kofta: meatballs or vegetable dumplings.

Korma: braised in yoghurt and/or cream and nuts. Often mild, but rich.

Roghan gosht or **rogan josh**: lamb cooked in spicy sauce, a Kashmiri speciality.

Tandoor: clay oven originating in north-west India, in which food is cooked without oil.

Tikka: meat, fish or paneer cut into cubes, then marinated in spicy yoghurt and baked in a tandoor.

SOUTH INDIAN

Adai: fermented rice and lentil pancakes, with a nuttier flavour than dosais (qv).

Avial: a mixed vegetable curry from Kerala with a coconut and yoghurt sauce.

Dosai or **dosa**: thin, shallow-fried pancake, often sculpted into interesting shapes; the very thin ones are called **paper dosai**. Most dosais are made with fermented rice and lentil batter, but variants include **rava dosai**, made with 'cream of wheat' semolina. **Masala dosais** come with a spicy potato filling. All variations are traditionally served with sambar (qv) and coconut chutney.

Idli: steamed sponges of ground rice and lentil batter. Eaten with sambar (qv) and coconut chutney.

Sambar or **sambhar**: a variation on dahl made with a specific hot blend of spices, plus coconut, tamarind and vegetables – particularly drumsticks (like a longer, woodier version of okra; you strip out the edible interior with your teeth).

Thoran: vegetables stir-fried with mustard seeds, curry leaves, chillies and fresh grated coconut.

Uppama: a popular breakfast dish in which onions, spices and, occasionally, vegetables are cooked with semolina using a risotto-like technique.

Uthappam: a spicy, crisp pancake/pizza made with lentil- and rice-flour batter, usually topped with tomato, onions and chillies.

GUJARATI

Bhakarvadi: pastry spirals stuffed with whole spices.

Bhel poori: a snack originating from street stalls in Mumbai, which contains crisp, deep-fried pooris, puffed rice, sev (qv), chopped onion, tomato, potato and more, plus chutneys (chilli, mint and tamarind).

Ganthia: Gujarati name for crisply fried savoury confections made from chickpea flour.

Kadhi: yoghurt and chickpea flour curry, often cooked with dumplings or vegetables.

Khichadi or **khichdi**: rice and lentils mixed with ghee and spices.

Pani poori: bite-sized pooris that are filled with sprouted beans, chickpeas, potato, onion, chutneys, sev (qv) and a thin, spiced watery sauce.

Sev: deep-fried chickpea-flour vermicelli.

SRI LANKAN

Ambul thiyal: sour fish curry cooked dry with spices.

Hoppers: confusingly, hoppers come in two forms, either as saucer-shaped, rice-flour pancakes (try the sweet and delectable milk hopper) or as string hoppers (qv). Hoppers are also known as **appam**.

Maldives fish: small, dried fish with a very intense flavour; an ingredient used in sambols (qv).

Sambols: strongly flavoured relishes, often served hot; they are usually chilli-hot too.

String hoppers (also called **idiappa**): fine rice-flour noodles formed into flat discs. Usually served steamed (in which case they're ideal partners for kiri hodi, a coconut milk curry with onions and turmeric).

INDIAN

hints of coriander, tempered with lime juice and ginger. Equally satisfying were the smoky chicken drumsticks, rubbed with chillies and garam masala: the flavours exquisitely balanced. Main courses were more homespun. Full-flavoured lamb pieces, simmered in a clinging masala, benefited from a forthright onion-ginger-garlic base, spiked with toasted coriander seeds, peppercorns and green cardamom pods. Our waiter didn't offer coffee despite its inclusion on the menu, and we didn't hang around to ask for a cuppa. The regal style of cooking that put Red Fort on London's gastronomic map is but a shadow of its past glory, and although the food is still decent, we miss the culinary finesse and the professional service. *Babies and children admitted. Booking advisable. Dress: smart casual. Vegan dishes. Vegetarian menu.* **Map 17 B3**.

Westminster

Cinnamon Club
Old Westminster Library, 30-32 Great Smith Street, SW1P 3BU (7222 2555, www.cinnamonclub.com). St James's Park or Westminster tube. **Breakfast served** 7.30-9.30am Mon-Fri. **Lunch served** noon-2.30pm, **dinner served** 7.30-9.30pm Mon-Sat. **Main courses** £11-£29. **Set meal** £19 2 courses, £22 3 courses. **Credit** AmEx, DC, MC, V. Modern Indian
The lofty ceilings, wooden panelling and book-lined gallery of what was once a Victorian library make a suitably grand setting for this fine dining restaurant. Executive chef Vivek Singh's Modern Indian creations are expertly rendered by head chef Hari Nagaraj, melding Indian flavours with the presentation you expect in haute cuisine establishments – right down to details such as canapé-style 'pre-starters'. A 'tasting of Bombay Street food' was a stylised miniaturisation of bhel poori and dhokla (steamed gram flour cake): not just pretty, but tasty too. Influences aren't purely Indian; one item described as 'steamed squid parcel' was the Chinese dim sum called cheung fun. The western-style presentation is most effective in dishes that might otherwise look like standard 'curries', such as a variant on lamb chettinad: smoked sirloin of lamb, cooked medium-rare then carved into pink slivers before being gently placed on a chettinad curry sauce of wonderful complexity. Although prices are high (the aforementioned 'lamb curry' cost £25), there are very few places in the UK offering Indian food at this level of innovation and excellence. To avoid the suited politicians who lunch here, consider visiting for breakfast (British, Anglo-Indian, Indian) or even just popping into the basement bar.
Babies and children welcome: high chairs. Booking essential. Disabled: lift; toilet. Dress: smart casual. Separate rooms for parties, seating 30-60. **Map 16 K9**.
For branch (Cinnamon Kitchen) see index.

West

Hammersmith

Sagar
157 King Street, W6 9JT (8741 8563). Hammersmith tube. **Lunch served** noon-3pm Mon-Fri. **Dinner served** 5.30-10.45pm Mon-Thur. **Meals served** noon-11.30pm Fri, Sat; noon-10.45pm Sun. **Main courses** £4.25-£13. **Thalis** £12.25-£14.95. **Credit** AmEx, MC, V. South Indian vegetarian

Sagar

A short walk from the Lyric Hammersmith, Sagar is a worthwhile option if you're dining late or early in the area. Its prices are modest, service is speedy, and the South Indian dishes are cooked to an exemplary standard. This particular style of cooking hails from Udupi in Karnataka, a coastal town renowned for its large Krishna temple; the town has become a pilgrimage site for Hindus, who observe a vegetarian diet while visiting. We've been consistently impressed by Sagar's dosais, which have the right mix of crisp shell and soft pancake interior that is so hard to get right; and by the piquant sambar that accompanies many dishes – including the spongy steamed rice cakes (idlis) that resemble flying saucers and are traditionally a breakfast and snack dish in Karnataka. The decor at this branch is light and attractive, with blond wood furnishings and striking brass statues. Yet while the kitchen here produces excellent renditions of South Indian classics, we've had more mixed experiences at the other outlets.
Babies and children welcome: high chair. Booking advisable. Takeaway service. Vegan dishes. Vegetarian menu.
Map 20 B4.
For branches see index.

Kensington

Zaika

1 Kensington High Street, W8 5NP (7795 6533, www.zaika-restaurant.co.uk). High Street Kensington tube. **Lunch served** noon-2.45pm Tue-Sun. **Dinner served** 6.30-10.45pm Mon-Sat; 6.30-9.45pm Sun. **Main courses** £15-£19.50. **Set lunch** £20 2 courses incl glass of wine and coffee, £25 3 courses incl glass of wine and coffee. **Set meal** £58 tasting menu. **Credit** AmEx, DC, MC, V. Modern Indian

A former bank, Zaika has a smart clubby atmosphere, the interior notable for its high ceiling, sweeping drapes and stone deities. Dark wood panelling and rich maroon and chocolate-brown colours lend warmth to the bar and expansive dining area. Cooking is elaborate, sometimes too much so, but it's always creative, drawing upon global flavours for inspiration. A first course of griddled potato cake, sandwiched with sweet yoghurt and fried gram-flour batter strands, was rather fussy for our taste. Surrounded by a ring of tamarind dots, it needed more tanginess. A substantial main course of masala duck was given a Modern European spin; the tender sautéed breast, surrounded by a dark, sticky moat of meaty jus, was further enriched by buttery parsnip and celeriac mash, finished with a tangle of deep-fried okra. Imaginative, yes, but there was too much unrelenting richness on one plate. A no-messing lamb biriani brought things back on track; aromatic cardamom and cumin, cut through with ginger, gave us the full flavour, it wasn't helped by overcooked rice. Service is smooth and attentive, and the wine list contains some choice selections. *Available for hire. Babies and children welcome: high chair. Booking advisable; essential weekends. Vegetarian menu.* **Map 7 C8**.

South West

East Sheen

Mango & Silk

199 Upper Richmond Road West, SW14 8QT (8876 6220, www.mangoandsilk.co.uk). Mortlake rail or 33, 337, 493 bus. **Lunch served** noon-3pm Sun (group reservation only Sat). **Dinner served** 6-10pm Tue-Thur, Sun; 6-10.30pm Fri, Sat. **Main courses** £7.95-£10.50. **Set buffet** (Sun) £12.95. **Credit** AmEx, MC, V. Pan-Indian

From the look of it, this venue might initially seem to be just another suburban curry house – albeit a tastefully furnished version, with wooden flooring and a white and beige colour scheme. However, the menu and cooking of chef Udit Sarkhel set Mango & Silk apart. Sarkhel was chef at the Bombay Brasserie during the years when it was London's finest Indian restaurant, and he applies the same care and imagination to dishes for his customers in East Sheen. Regional Indian cooking is a particular strength; the chef's upbringing in Calcutta is evident in Bengali dishes such as the fish curry with coconut and mustard (macher malai curry). There are also favourite dishes from Goa, South India and meaty dishes from the north, for example that Punjabi favourite, butter chicken (murgh makhani). Service has always been solicitous on our visits, and prices are very reasonable too, with most main courses costing under a tenner and most starters under a fiver. If you feel truly inspired by Sarkhel's cooking, purchase a copy of his excellent cookbook *The Calcutta Kitchen* – a modern classic.

Babies and children welcome: booster seats; crayons; nappy-changing facilities. Booking advisable. Disabled: toilet. Tables outdoors (2, decking). Takeaway service.

Chelsea

Chutney Mary

535 King's Road, SW10 0SZ (7351 3113, www.chutney mary.com). Fulham Broadway tube or 11, 22 bus. **Lunch served** 12.30-2.45pm Sat, Sun. **Dinner served** 6.30-11.15pm Mon-Sat; 6.30-10.15pm Sun. **Main courses** £14.50-£26. **Set lunch** £22 3 courses. **Credit** AmEx, DC, MC, V. Pan-Indian

Since 1990 Chutney Mary has comfortably slotted in to the top echelon of London's Indian restaurants. The impetus behind its success has come from sisters Namita and Camellia Panjabi, who steered the kitchen from an initial focus on Anglo-Indian dishes to its current celebration of regional cuisines and Modern Indian innovations. The large, lower-ground dining room is reached via a wide staircase from the reception (admire the Moghul-style mirror-work mural on your way down). A refurbishment a few years back has produced a romantic, split-level space best enjoyed at night when oil lamps and candles reflect off sparkly mosaics. The leafy conservatory is the prime spot for lunch. Menus change regularly, but starters might include lotus root kebab with pomegranate coriander and ginger, or pan-fried duck galouti with blueberry chutney, to be followed by lamb shank shakuti, say, or plantain and fig kofta. Special menus are often available (a 'seafood showcase' featuring halibut in mustard sauce, for instance) and the Anglo-Indian puds (ginger bread and butter pudding with orange chilli sorbet) are not to be missed. The wine list is a corker too, and we've found the service to be consistently excellent. Amaya, Veeraswamy and the Masala Zone chain are part of the same group.

Babies and children under 10yrs welcome until 8pm: booster seats. Booking advisable; essential Thur-Sat. Dress: smart casual. Separate room for parties, seats 24. **Map 13 C13**.

Painted Heron

112 Cheyne Walk, SW10 0DJ (7351 5232, www.the paintedheron.com). Sloane Square tube or 11, 19, 22, 319 bus. **Lunch served** noon-2.30pm Mon-Fri. **Dinner served** 6-10.30pm Mon-Sat; 6-9.30pm Sun. **Main courses** £12-£18. **Set meal** £35 4 courses. **Thalis** £15. **Credit** AmEx, MC, V. Modern Indian

As a curry house for the Cheyne Walk set, Painted Heron succeeds admirably, but this smart-casual restaurant, almost Scandinavian in decor, is also a destination for superbly inventive Modern Indian cooking. Save for an ill-fated branch in Kennington some years ago (more fool Kennington), the team rarely puts a foot wrong, with assured service and exquisite dish presentation adding to the classy vibe. The kitchen joyously embraces seasonal produce; side dishes such as strawberry curry, and the fresh English asparagus and broad bean curry, are must-haves when available. Fish such as wild sea trout and cod come from Hastings boats. Rabbit, squab pigeon, guinea fowl, duck and venison – meats often ignored by Indian restaurants – frequently appear too. The menu contains enough familiar names to reassure the unadventurous, but these dishes often come with a twist, such as lamb roghan gosht with apricots, and chicken korma with puréed chickpeas. Start, perhaps, with soft-shell crabs fried in sesame, chilli and lager batter, or tandoori salmon with samphire and basil.

Mint Leaf Restaurant & Bar
Suffolk Place
Haymarket SW1Y
T: 0207 920 9030
reservations@mintleafrestaurant.com
www.mintleafrestaurant.com

mint leaf

Ideally located, both Mint Leaf restaurants offer the finest Indian cuisine in sumptuous surroundings, along with an extensive range of cocktails.

Mint Leaf are synonymous with fine Indian food complemented by friendly, knowledgeable and attentive service. Presenting a gastronomic experience using the finest fresh produce with authentic Indian flavours, we have weekly lunch, pre & post theatre, full a la carte and bespoke menus for all special occasions.

With striking design and equipped with a fully integrated audio and visual system, Mint Leaf restaurants provide the perfect setting for corporate events or private parties. Both venues offer a range of versatile areas suitable for all occasions, perfect for hosting an exciting array of events, from product launches and premieres through to exclusive drinks parties and more intimate dinners. Our secluded Chef's Table is ideal for gourmets or an innovative corporate experience whilst entertaining clients.

Mint Leaf Lounge & Restaurant
Angel Court
Lothbury
Bank EC2
T: 0207 600 0992
reservations@mintleaflounge.com
www.mintleaflounge.com

mint leaf
lounge

Parking can be difficult, and it's not near a tube, but if your wallet can accommodate the premium prices, this place is well worth adding to your to-do list.
Babies and children admitted. Booking advisable weekends. Separate room for parties, seats 35. Tables outdoors (5, garden). Vegan dishes. Vegetarian menu. **Map 14 D13**.

South

Tooting

Apollo Banana Leaf
190 Tooting High Street, SW17 0SF (8696 1423). Tooting Broadway tube. **Lunch served** noon-3pm, **dinner served** 6-10.30pm Mon-Thur. **Meals served** noon-10.30pm Fri-Sun. **Main courses** £3.50-£6.25. **Unlicensed. Corkage** no charge. **Credit** MC, V. Sri Lankan
Tooting has a reputation for low-cost, excellent Indian cooking, and Apollo Banana Leaf is one of the best places to begin any exploration of the area's many Indian and Sri Lankan establishments. This is a very cheap restaurant indeed – you'll struggle to spend £10 per head – and it's BYO for booze, with no corkage charge. As the staff are all Sri Lankan, it makes sense to try the Sri Lankan specialities. Vegetable string-hopper consists of grain-sized cuts of browned vermicelli stir-fried with mixed veg, chilli and curry leaves: spicy, but searingly hot. Crab masala comprises a slithery hot sauce over the broken shell, which makes using your fingers inevitable. The chilli level of the hottest dishes has been toned down for the many non-Tamil diners, which is no bad thing; order a cooling lassi if you can't take the heat. ABL is as modestly furnished as you might expect of a quiet, low-budget neighbourhood spot.
Babies and children welcome: high chairs. Booking advisable weekends. Takeaway service.

East

Whitechapel

Café Spice Namaste
16 Prescot Street, E1 8AZ (7488 9242, www.cafespice. co.uk). Aldgate East or Tower Hill tube, or Tower Gateway DLR. **Lunch served** noon-3pm Mon-Fri. **Dinner served** 6.15-10.30pm Mon-Fri; 6.30-10.30pm Sat. **Main courses** £12.50-£18.55. **Set meal** £30 4 courses, £40 5 courses, £60 tasting menu. **Credit** AmEx, DC, MC, V. Pan-Indian
Despite diluting its Parsee menu in favour of pan-Indian choices, this restaurant remains a magnet for City suits on expense accounts. Its two dining rooms, once part of a Victorian magistrates court, are furnished with swathes of coloured cloth draped over windows, which lend a faded pantomime feel to the interior. Chef-patron Cyrus Todiwala is credited with bringing several Parsee dishes to London, showcasing flavours drawn from Persia and India. A few stalwarts remain on the menu; check out the dhansak, a hearty lamb curry simmered with puréed lentils and pumpkin. Goan prawn curry scored a hit, with succulent prawns cloaked in a masala of pounded red chilli, sharpened with tamarind and soothed with creamy coconut milk. An absence of the promised dried shrimp and onion salad, and overcooked rice, were two small but significant gripes. The non-Parsee dishes failed to measure up. Our tandoori morsels needed urgent attention –

all items on the mixed meat and salmon platter were harshly spiced and acidic. Disappointing Punjabi-style fried spinach flecked with fried paneer lacked garlicky punch and was too salty. We've had far superior meals here in the past; both the service and the cooking were below par on this occasion.
Babies and children welcome: high chairs. Disabled: toilet. Tables outdoors (8, garden). Takeaway service; delivery service (within 2-mile radius). **Map 12 S7**.

Lahore Kebab House
2 Umberston Street, E1 1PY (7488 2551, www.lahore-kebabhouse.com). Aldgate East or Whitechapel tube. **Meals served** noon-midnight daily. **Main courses** £5.50-£9.50. **Unlicensed. Corkage** no charge. **Credit** MC, V. Pakistani
Lahore Kebab House was opened by a nephew of Mohammed Tayyab, owner of the nearbyPunjabi grill bearing his name. Comparisons between the two establishments are inevitable, and it sometimes feels as if Tayyabs has outgrown its relative in both size and status over the years – although Lahore is far from a second-choice destination. The clinical white design, bright lighting and big TV screens aren't especially endearing, but the free BYO and low prices certainly are, as is the uninhibited food. Every dish loudly displays the 40-odd years of experience that the kitchen has gathered while cooking some of the best Pakistani food in London. There's not much in the way of concession to timid western palates. Almost everything comes with a chilli kick that would startle Scoville himself, from the marinated and delightfully charred chicken-leg starter to the profoundly flavourful sauce that coats the unappetising-sounding but joyous 'dry lamb'. Ignore the standard tikka masalas and jalfrezis and you'll find a few lesser-spotted dishes: nihari is slow-cooked lamb shank served on the bone, and changing specials include paya (sheep's foot) and batera (quail).
Babies and children welcome: high chairs. Disabled: toilet. Takeaway service; delivery service (by taxi).

Needoo Grill
87 New Road, E1 1HH (7247 0648, www.needoogrill. co.uk). Whitechapel tube. **Open** 11.30am-11.30pm daily. **Main courses** £6-£20. **Credit** AmEx, MC, V. Pakistani
Needoo Grill, with its boisterous mix of young families and groups of friends, has the vibe of a community meeting place. Run by a former manager of nearby grillhouse Tayyabs, it offers meaty Pakistani-Punjabi staples but also earthy vegetarian dishes, made with care and consideration. Past the grill near the entrance, the decor of the main seating area is as big and bold as the cooking. Sparkly black granite tiles, red leatherette banquettes and plasma screens contrast with the functional wipe-clean tables, paper napkins and metal water pitchers. Grills are the specialities, so our tandoori lamb chops were a let down. Although bashed with a mallet and steeped in gingery lime juice to aid succulence, they were overcooked. In contrast, homely karahi chicken delivered the goods, with a russet-hued fried onion masala spiked with chilli and toasted cumin – a marvellous match with hot tandoori rotis. A vegetarian dish of crushed potatoes, cooked with tender cauliflower florets, tomatoes, ginger and fresh coriander was comfort cooking at its best. Just as enjoyable was a deliciously nutty and smoky tarka dahl, finished with a tumble of fried onions and warming cumin.
Available for hire. Babies and children welcome: high chairs. Tables outdoors (8, pavement). Takeaway service. Vegetarian menu.

INDIAN

Tayyabs

83 Fieldgate Street, E1 1JU (7247 9543, www.tayyabs. co.uk). Aldgate East or Whitechapel tube. **Meals served** noon-11.30pm daily. **Main courses** £6-£10. **Unlicensed. Corkage** no charge. **Credit** AmEx, MC, V. Pakistani
After years spent hiding in a Whitechapel backstreet, the secret's out about this Pakistani grill and curry house, as testified by the nightly queues. Tayyabs' success is down to its handy position (near enough to the ever-expanding City for suits to descend) and its generous prices (including corkage-free BYO). At its best, a meal brings deep, earthy dahls, fiery Punjabi meat curries, seekh kebabs bursting with herbs and spices, and piles of fluffy bread, straight from the open kitchen – and it all costs less than a tenner a head if you choose wisely. However, it's the preternatural popularity that has seen standards slip slightly in our estimation. A recent refurb opened the cellar of this multi-hued, modernised former Victorian pub, and instead of easing pressure, the extra space seems to have increased the mild chaos inherent in getting seated. We've endured a wait of 40 minutes for a booked table, which is almost enough to put us off the main event: the legendary marinated and grilled lamb chops. Lapses in cooking aren't unknown either: during a busy lunch, we were once served under-marinated tandoori fish and oily curries. For a calmer, more consistent experience, visit off-peak.
Babies and children welcome: high chairs. Booking advisable. Outdoor. Separate room for parties, seats 35. Takeaway service.

North

Camden Town & Chalk Farm

Masala Zone

25 Parkway, NW1 7PG (7267 4422, www.masalazone. com). Camden Town tube. **Lunch served** 12.30-3pm, **dinner served** 5.30-11pm Mon-Fri. **Meals served** 12.30-11pm Sat; 12.30-10.30pm Sun. **Main courses** £6.85-£12.95. **Thalis** £8.35-£9.20. **Credit** MC, V. Pan-Indian
Branches of this smart, clever chain are popping up faster than mustard seeds in a hot pan of ghee. Each outlet is decorated with a different theme – on Parkway it's advertising posters of the 1930s and '40s; at Covent Garden Rajasthani puppets hang from the ceiling; in Soho, Islington and Earl's Court the walls feature striking work by tribal artists. The mood is both vibrant and relaxed – as cheering to singletons having a thali for supper, as it is to family groups and couples. Conceived by the Panjabi sisters of Chutney Mary and Amaya fame, Masala Zone is not expensive, yet even so there's a high rotation of attractive discount offers. The menu takes in street-food snacks (springy, grease-free onion bhaji; dahi poori), wraps, grills, curried noodles, curry and rice plates. There are also two sizes of thali; well-trained, multicultural staff describe the daily veg, dahl and raita on your arrival, and you choose which of the curries you would like included – clove-scented lamb roghan gosht, say, or a tomatoey tilapia masala. To drink, try the cola with mint and spices, or the bright, fruity Portuguese rosé created specially to match the fiery dishes.
Babies and children welcome: children's menu; high chairs. Bookings not accepted for fewer than 10 people. Separate room for parties, seats 30. Takeaway service. **Map 27 C2**. **For branches see index.**

North West

Swiss Cottage

Eriki

4-6 Northways Parade, Finchley Road, NW3 5EN (7722 0606, www.eriki.co.uk). Swiss Cottage tube. **Lunch served** noon-2.30pm Mon-Fri, Sun. **Dinner served** 6-10.30pm daily. **Main courses** £10-£12. **Set lunch** £12.95 2 courses. **Credit** MC, V. Pan-Indian
Bringing brightness to an otherwise nondescript street, Eriki is tastefully turned out in a maroon colour scheme, with chunky wooden furniture and wooden screens. Its homely, pan-Indian menu is expansive and the chefs confident in delivery. Goan dishes share top billing with northern curries, South Indian dosais and Kashmiri masalas. A hearty Punjabi lamb curry, cooked with spinach and peppery mustard leaves, featured chunky pieces of tender lamb, surrounded by shreds of leafy greens slow-cooked with golden-fried onions and plenty of garlic and ginger. Sadly, the accompaniments (stone-cold chapatis, and a minuscule bowl of too-sweet raita) detracted from the raunchy flavours of the curry. We had no complaints, however, about the delectable prawn curry, inspired by the western coastal region of Konkan. The fresh coriander masala was notable for its fruity, green mango tartness, which both contrasted with and complemented the warming heat of curry leaves, nutty-tasting mustard seeds and cracked black peppercorns. We're perplexed as to why Eriki isn't more popular with aficionados of authentic home cooking – perhaps it's the steep prices, or the distracted service, which needs to up its game to match the quality of the cooking.

Needoo Grill. See p145.

Available for hire. Babies and children admitted. Booking advisable. Takeaway service; delivery (6-9.45pm, over £20 within 4-mile radius). Vegetarian menu. **Map 28 B4.**

Outer London
Harrow, Middlesex

Ram's
203 Kenton Road, Harrow, Middx HA3 0HD (8907 2022). Kenton tube/rail. **Lunch served** noon-3pm, **dinner served** 6-11pm daily. **Main courses** £4-£5. **Set meal** £22 (unlimited food and soft drinks). **Thalis** £4.99-£8.99. **Credit** MC, V. Gujarati vegetarian
Gujarati residents in Kenton have done well by this homely café, and come here for quality vegetarian meals bursting with sweet-sour regional flavours. Simply furnished, with wipe-clean tables, the spartan interior is enlivened by framed images of Hindu deities, but it's the cooking that remains the attraction. For a taster of Gujarat's diverse cooking styles, order street-food snacks rather than the more substantial main dishes. Pani poori – wafer-thin pastry globes, to be dunked in minted tamarind water – were outstanding for their black salt and chilli kick. Mumbai's famous beach snack, pau bhaji, also lived up to expectations; this mound of crushed potatoes, enriched with tomato masala and much butter, was accompanied by mini toasted bread rolls – simple but satisfying comfort food. Kadhi (a soupy curry made with whipped yoghurt, thickened with gram flour and seasoned with mustard seeds, curry leaves and tart tamarind) worked well with its tender okra. Save space for own-made kulfi spiced with cardamom and streaks of saffron: it's a delectable, creamy treat. Service is well meaning, but can be slow. Be patient: food this tasty is worth the wait.
Available for hire. Babies and children welcome: high chairs. Booking advisable weekends. Disabled: toilet. Takeaway service.

Southall, Middlesex

Brilliant
72-76 Western Road, Southall, Middx UB2 5DZ (8574 1928, www.brilliantrestaurant.com). Southall rail. **Lunch served** noon-3pm Tue-Fri. **Dinner served** 6-11.30pm Tue-Sun. **Main courses** £4.50-£14. **Credit** AmEx, DC, MC, V. East African Indian
Following a major overhaul a few years back, Brilliant has become one of Southall's prime destinations. Even midweek, an upbeat young crowd is drawn here, including local British Asians and others from further afield. The business has been operating since 1975, opened by the Kenyan Asian Anand family on a site away from the Broadway's bustle. Up to 250 diners can now be accommodated, in glitzy dining rooms on the ground and first floors, complete with flatscreen TV (playing Bollywood hits), a burnished copper bar, wooden flooring and keen, black-clad staff. The menu of classic Punjabi food with a few African-Asian tweaks is generally executed to a very high standard. Couples have plenty to choose from – perhaps starting with tandoori salmon or mogo (cassava) chips, before moving on to karahi gosht or mixed veg curry – but communal group dining is the norm. Entire families come to tuck into a whole butter chicken, then follow it with a 'full bowl' of masaladar lamb, serving five. In the past we've relished the delicately fried fish pakora (especially mouth-watering with

the choice of six chutneys) and the aloo cholay (potatoes and chickpeas boosted by zesty mango powder).
Babies and children welcome: high chairs. Booking advisable weekends. Separate room for parties, seats 120. Takeaway service. Vegetarian menu.

New Asian Tandoori Centre (Roxy)
114-118 The Green, Southall, Middx UB2 4BQ (8574 2597). Southall rail. **Meals served** 8am-11pm Mon-Thur; 8am-midnight Fri-Sun. **Main courses** £5-£8. **Credit** MC, V. Punjabi
This canteen-style café and takeaway may not look much, but its Punjabi cooking outshines that of many upmarket restaurants and prices remain cheerfully cheap. Give the biriani option a miss and plump for the excellent breads, curries and renowned yoghurty snacks. Our current favourite is chickpea curry, crammed with fried onions, ginger and the bite of pounded pomegranate seeds. Papadi chat was a splendid contrast of textures and flavours: crisp-fried pastry discs, topped with squidgy lentil dumplings, sitting under a sheet of yoghurt and streaked with sweet tamarind sauce and fresh mint chutney. Chefs put as much effort into vegetarian dishes as the meat curries and grills. We love the gingery notes in mutter paneer: curried green peas, tossed in a chilli-tomato masala, and finished with mallowy cubed paneer. Omnivores should try the butter chicken (tandoori chicken chunks, dunked in a toasted cumin, coriander and buttery tomato sauce): perfect for mopping up with a hot nan. Local Punjabi families favour this spot over more famed cafés on Southall's main street, the Broadway. The icy lassis are the real deal and make first-rate thirst-quenchers. Service is prompt, a tad brusque, but efficient.
Babies and children welcome: high chairs. Disabled: toilet. Separate room for parties, seats 60. Takeaway service. Vegetarian menu.

Wembley, Middlesex

Sakonis `HOT 50`
129 Ealing Road, Wembley, Middx HA0 4BP (8903 9601, www.sakonis.co.uk). Alperton tube. **Breakfast served** 9-11am Sat, Sun. **Meals served** noon-10pm daily. **Main courses** £2-£7.99. **Set buffet** (breakfast) £3.99; (noon-4pm Mon-Fri, noon-5pm Sat, Sun) £7.99; (6-9.30pm) £10.99. **Credit** MC, V. Gujarati vegetarian
A mainstay of the Ealing Road Indian dining scene, Sakonis attracts hordes of shoppers at the weekend, taking a break from the colourful kerfuffle outside to drop in for a bite. It's a sizeable, utilitarian café with tiled walls, melamine tableware and easy-wipe tables. At the front is a snack counter, a well-liked source of takeaways, while to the rear is a buffet popular with South Asian families. We particularly rate the street food – crisp onion bhajis, crunchy bhel pooris – though the dosais filled with potato masala hit the spot too. The menu lists dozens of vegetarian South Indian and Gujarati dishes (idli chat and khichdi among them), as well as an assortment of Indian-style Chinese food (paneer chilli is a favourite) and a couple of pizzas. Milkshakes and fresh fruit juices are the drinks of choice. The weekend breakfast buffet (£3.99 for a feast including idlis, ganthia, dosais, upma, pooris, potato curry and masala tea; served 9-11am) seems an especially good bargain. It is only available here, not at Sakonis' other branch in Harrow.
Babies and children welcome. Takeaway service. Vegetarian menu.
For branch see index.

Italian

Italian cuisine may no longer be seen as the height of fashion, but with several new Italian restaurants launching in the past 12 months (and just as many the year before), its popularity among Londoners is irrefutable. Fortunately, the emphasis is shifting from the premium-priced, fine-dining establishments of recent years to more casual but still stylish eateries, such as Bermondsey's **Zucca** and Soho's **Polpo**. At the top end, such starry establishments as **Locanda Locatelli**, the **River Café** and **Theo Randall at the Intercontinental** continue their reliably high standards, but in these uneasy economic times it's the mid-priced restaurants that may be of most appeal. If you're looking for great pizza, London still has some excellent independent pizzerias; newcomers this year include family-run **Santa Maria** in Ealing and Soho House-owned **Pizza East** in Shoreditch. **Tenore** in Islington also produces fabulous pizzas, as well as many Sardinian specialities.

Central

Belgravia

Olivo
21 Eccleston Street, SW1W 9LX (7730 2505, www.olivo restaurants.com). Sloane Square tube or Victoria tube/rail. **Lunch served** noon-2.30pm Mon-Fri. **Dinner served** 6-10.30pm daily. **Main courses** £14.50-£19. **Set lunch** £21.25 2 courses, £25 3 courses. **Credit** AmEx, DC, MC, V.
Mauro Sanna's Olivo restaurant group has Italian dining pretty much sewn up in Belgravia with three restaurants and a sophisticated delicatessen. Rather than spread the same concept throughout the capital, he has cleverly created three different types of eaterie within a polpette's throw of each other. The surprise is that they're all Sardinian. Olivo, with its distinctive modern-rustic blue and yellow walls, has been serving the likes of spaghetti all bottarga, chargrilled lamb with fregola, and sebada (cheese fritters with honey) to acclaim since 1990 – when young Giorgio Locatelli was the head chef. Five years later, Sanna opened Oliveto, a casual spot with an emphasis on pizza and pasta, and another eye-catching interior by Sardinian architect Pierluigi Piu. However, it's Olivomare (opened in 2007) that's probably the pick of the bunch: a stunning seafood restaurant serving everything from please-all fritto misto and tuna with rocket and tomatoes, to

specialities such as iced raw sea urchin crostini and baby octopus stew. Around 25 Sardinian wines are offered on the group's wine list, including house red and white at £17.50 a bottle; alternatively, try Sardinian beer Ichnusa, or dry, sherry-like vernaccia aperitif. You can also buy the wines for home consumption at Olivino deli. Staff usually get it right, though occasionally the wait between courses is longer than desirable. *Babies and children admitted. Booking advisable.*
Map 15 H10.
For branch (Oliveto, Olivomare) see index.

City

L'Anima
1 Snowden Street, EC2A 2DQ (7422 7000, www.lanima.co.uk). Liverpool Street tube/rail.
Bar **Open/meals served** 9am-midnight Mon-Fri; 5.30-11pm Sat.
Restaurant **Lunch served** 11.45am-3pm Mon-Fri. **Dinner served** 5.30-11pm Mon-Fri; 5.30-11.30pm Sat.
Both **Main courses** £8.50-£28.50. **Set lunch** £24.50 2 courses, £28.50 3 courses. **Credit** AmEx, DC, MC, V.
An edge-of-City bar-restaurant aimed clearly at expense-account diners, L'Anima has prices that might startle regular punters. The only 'bargain' is the set lunch, where a tomato and mozzarella salad with friselle (Calabrian wholemeal dried bread) might be followed by lemon and chilli poussin with olive

Mennula

notch food and drink and immaculate, modern design proved that L'Anima nearly doubled its size in summer 2010.
Babies and children welcome: high chairs. Booking advisable. Disabled: toilet. Separate rooms for parties, seating 6-14. **Map 6 R5.**

Fitzrovia

Mennula

10 Charlotte Street, W1T 2LT (7636 2833, www.mennula.com). Goodge Street or Tottenham Court Road tube. **Lunch served** noon-3pm Mon-Fri; 12.30-3pm Sun. **Dinner served** 6-11pm Mon-Sat; 6-9.30pm Sun. **Main courses** £15.50-£25. **Set menu** (lunch Mon-Fri, dinner Mon-Sat) £17.50 2 courses, £19.50 3 courses. **Credit** AmEx, MC, V.
This slim, L-shaped site is smarter than London's other Sicilian restaurants, and the food of Sicilian-born chef-patron Santino Busciglio is much more refined and contemporary than that island's home cooking. Manager Angelo Todaro (ex-Zafferano) knows how to run a slick operation, but not all his young staff are perfectly drilled; we waited 30 minutes for our wine. Meanwhile, we relished complimentary appetisers of lightly smoked almonds, lemon-marinated olives and ambrosial arancini. The menu is reassuringly brief; fancy plates prettify the more rustic dishes, such as a glass bowl of grilled squid served in a soup-like sauce of leek, potato and olive oil, given distinctively Italian notes by a scoop of black olive paste and capers. You'll also find 'priest-choker' (strozzapreti) pasta with rabbit, Sicilian cassata and a well-chosen selection from Sicily's resurgent wine producers on the all-Italian list. In contrast to the overly sweet variety popular in the US, Mennula's cannoli resemble the real Sicilian thing: cigar-sized tubes of crisply fried, dark pastry flavoured with coffee, cocoa and Marsala wine, and a plain filling of ewe's milk ricotta, sprinkled with grated chocolate. A restaurant that shows great promise.
Available for hire. Booking advisable dinner. Children admitted. Separate room for parties, seats 14. Tables outdoors (3, pavement). **Map 17 B1.**

Sardo

45 Grafton Way, W1T 5DQ (7387 2521, www.sardo-restaurant.com). Warren Street tube. **Lunch served** noon-3pm Mon-Fri. **Dinner served** 6-11pm Mon-Sat. **Main courses** £8.90-£18. **Credit** AmEx, MC, V.
Sardo is one of the select set of addresses that restaurant critics visit when they're off-duty and have to fork out their own money. This may surprise first-time visitors, for there's nothing fancy-schmancy about the place. The interior is confidently unstyled, and the food and service are similarly straightforward, producing a relaxing, convivial setting that's as suited to a first date as a business lunch. The menu reassures non-foodies with classic Italian fare such as grilled tuna or swordfish steaks with rocket and tomatoes, followed by tiramisu. However, gastronauts can revel in a wide choice of Sardinian specialities, from sun-dried tuna loin, to malloreddus (a bug-like pasta shape, served with tomato and sausage sauce), grilled steak topped with ovinfort (ewe's milk blue cheese) and sebadas (cheese-filled pastry drizzled with honey). Look first, though, to the blackboard of daily specials, which often features delicious seafood. The wine list includes all Italy and France, but it's worth sticking with the lovingly selected Sardinian bottles and taking advice from staff on which to order. Sardo Canale, by the Regent's Canal in Primrose Hill, is

oil mash; or pancetta, broad beans and pecorino by grilled organic salmon and mixed leaf salad. All very acceptable, and beautifully presented, but true excitement lies on the main menu. Witness starters of charcoal scallops with n'duja (spicy spreadable salami) and salsa verde, or wild herbs tortelli with balsamic vinegar; or mains of wood-roasted turbot with cherry tomatoes and clams. There are also grills (veal chop, sea bass) and spit roasts (chicken, leg of lamb). Finish with blueberry soufflé or a cheese option, such as taleggio and fig mustard. A proudly Italian wine list includes bottles from lesser-known regions. The bar, which has the same high ceilings and clean lines that give the restaurant such a calm, spacious air, is ideal for a prosecco and a snack. So popular has this blend of top-

a trendier-looking outfit with leather lounges, silky cushions, open brickwork and an enviable courtyard.
Babies and children admitted. Booking advisable. Separate room for parties, seats 36. Tables outdoors (4, patio).
Map 3 J4.
For branch (Sardo Canale) see index.

Knightsbridge

Zafferano
15 Lowndes Street, SW1X 9EY (7235 5800, www.zafferanorestaurant.com). Knightsbridge tube.
Lunch served noon-2.30pm Mon-Fri; 12.30-3pm Sat, Sun. **Dinner served** 7-11pm Mon-Sat; 7-10.30pm Sun.
Main courses £17-£29.50. **Credit** AmEx, DC, MC, V.
Zafferano goes about its business in a quiet and reserved manner, successfully mastering the tricky art of being both formal and relaxing. Furnishings are comfortable rather than ostentatious, but this suits the many regulars who have continued to dine here over the years. Service, under the perennial watchful eye of Enzo Cassini, is attentive and engaging, although some of the newer faces on the staff aren't yet quite the finished article. Pristine ingredients feature throughout the menu. Start with the superb parmesan cheese and salami with freshly made focaccia, brought to the table on a wooden board; or the heavenly creamy burrata with cherry tomato and basil. Best leave room for a pasta dish as well; new this year is a beautifully rich and earthy lasagne of duck with morel mushrooms that had us licking every last morsel from the plate. Fish is always good too. Soft, sweet, roasted line-caught sea bass comes with a dash of vernaccia wine and green olives. To finish, tiramisu, followed by a little cornetto filled with lemon sorbet, made us sing all the way home.
Babies and children welcome: high chairs. Booking essential. Dress: smart casual. Separate room for parties, seats 20.
Map 15 G9.

Marylebone

Il Baretto
43 Blandford Street, W1U 7HF (7486 7340, www.ilbaretto. co.uk). Baker Street tube. **Lunch served** noon-3pm, **dinner served** 6.30-11pm Mon-Sat. **Main courses** £10-£28. **Credit** AmEx, MC, V.
Don't be fooled by appearances. The name might translate as 'little bar', and the drinking area that greets you on entering this neighbourhood trattoria is certainly compact enough to justify it. But the venue's real draw lies below the collection of small brown leather pouffes, spirits bottles housed in ornate, gold-painted frames, and black, wrought-iron chandeliers. The basement dining area's artfully rough paint job and smart brown leather seating was packed with a crowd of tourists and

Pizza chains

There's much that isn't great about chain restaurants, factory-style preparation and soulless corporate branding being just two problems. But the big four pizza chains do try to concentrate on quality as well as throughput.

ASK
216 Haverstock Hill, NW3 2AE (7433 3896, www.askrestaurants.com). Belsize Park tube.
Meals served noon-11pm Mon-Thur; noon-11.30pm Fri, Sat; noon-10pm Sun.
There are now approaching 120 ASKs around the UK, serving a long list of pastas (including some al forno), pizzas, calzone and a trio of risottos. The estiva is a new addition to the pizza menu: a tomato and mozzarella base that's topped with baby mozzarella, rocket and prosciutto when it's fresh from the oven.
Map 28 B3.
For branches see index.

Pizza Express
187 Kentish Town Road, NW1 8PD (7267 0101, www.pizzaexpress.com). Kentish Town tube/ rail or Kentish Town West rail. **Meals served** 11.30am-11pm Mon-Thur, Sun; 11.30am-11.30pm Fri, Sat.
The granddaddy of the mid-market pizza chain, Pizza Express has survived changes of ownership and regular bouts of menu updating. The usual pizzas and pastas have recently been joined by specials invented by L'Anima's Francesco Mazzei (including the rusichella pizza, with crispy pancetta on marinated roasted tomatoes). Leggera pizzas are lower-cal versions of classic pizzas by dint of having their centres removed and filled with salad. Neat, eh?
Map 27 D1.
For branches see index.

Strada
4 South Grove, N6 6BS (8347 8686, www.strada. co.uk). Highgate tube. **Meals served** 11.30am-11pm Mon-Sat; 11.30am-10.30pm Sun.
A favourite with young couples on a cheapish date, Strada's contemporary-styled restaurants can generate a fair buzz. Food is a notch up from many of the chains, with ingredients such as seared tuna in the salads, and rosemary-marinated chargrilled ribeye among the mains. Pizza toppings feature the likes of speck with gorgonzola, or goat's cheese with roasted artichokes and tomatoes.
For branches see index.

Zizzi
20 Bow Street, WC2E 7AW (7836 6101, www.zizzi. co.uk). Covent Garden tube. **Meals served** noon-11.30pm Mon-Sat; noon-11pm Sun.
Upmarket brethren of ASK, and rival to Strada, Zizzi was first launched in 1999 and now numbers more than 100 UK outlets. As well as classy pastas (Sicilian casareccia with spicy chicken, plum tomatoes and spinach) and salads, you'll find a new line of 'rustica' pizzas with such toppings as tiger prawns, courgettes and mozzarella (on one half), and spicy sausage, tomato sauce and chillies (on the other).
Map 18 E4.
For branches see index.

ITALIAN

after-work City boys enjoying a menu of simple Italian dishes whose appeal lies in the precision of the unfussy cooking. The pasta in our penne with spicy sausage was al dente to the point of springiness; an uncluttered smoked salmon pizza allowed the tubular strands of earthy ricotta to shine; and the stewed cherries surrounding a vanilla panna cotta were stunningly unctuous. Service was charismatically Italian (expect to be greeted by a multitude of 'buona sera's), without being over-attentive or loud. Unfortunately, the same can't be said of the restaurant; the low ceilings can make this a noisy choice during busier periods.
Babies and children welcome: high chairs. Booking essential. Separate room for parties, seats 20. Tables outdoors (2, pavement). **Map 9 G5.**

Locanda Locatelli [HOT 50]

8 Seymour Street, W1H 7JZ (7935 9088, www.locanda locatelli.com). Marble Arch tube. **Lunch served** noon-3pm Mon-Fri; noon-3.30pm Sat, Sun. **Dinner served** 6.45-11pm Mon-Thur; 6.45-11.30pm Fri, Sat; 6.45-10.15pm Sun. **Main courses** £24-£29.50. **Credit** AmEx, MC, V.
That this temple of Italian fine dining, complete with celebrity chef and hotel location, can offer 750ml bottles of good wine at just £12 puts to shame all those restaurants whose wine lists start at £20 and above. Indeed, the only unwelcoming thing about this reliable spot is the occasional sniffy attitude when booking. Locanda Locatelli's sultry interior of beige leather booths, etched glass screens and low lighting stays just the right side of lap-dancing club; even with sun streaming in the windows it's not a convincing decor for lunchtime, though families are encouraged on Sundays when the mood is pleasantly relaxed compared to the evening's sophisticated glamour. The menu is crammed with dishes that have become signatures, and while prices are high, generosity is evident: a bread basket featuring seven or eight varieties; a fluffy mountain of black truffle shavings atop the pillow-soft gnocchi with goat's cheese; the delivery of petits fours without an order for coffee. Roast monkfish (a paragon of the art) with rocket and sweet walnut-caper sauce came with a delightful bonus of delicate samphire, while tomato soup with razor clams and fregola had more of that delicious bread, toasted and streaked with olive oil. The dessert list offers a mix of classics (tiramisu, tart of the day, a huge choice of ices) and molecular-style creations that finish the meal on a gastronomic high.
Babies and children welcome: high chairs. Booking advisable. Disabled: toilet. Dress: smart casual. **Map 9 G6.**

Mayfair

Alloro

19-20 Dover Street, W1S 4LU (7495 4768, www.alloro-restaurant.co.uk). Green Park tube.
Bar **Open** noon-10pm Mon-Fri; 7-10pm Sat. **Lunch served** noon-2.30pm Mon-Fri. **Dinner served** 7-10.30pm Mon-Sat. **Main courses** £12-£16.75.
Restaurant **Lunch served** noon-2.30pm Mon-Fri.
Dinner served 7-10.30pm Mon-Sat. **Set lunch** £29.50 2 courses, £33.50 3 courses. **Set dinner** £29.50 2 courses, £35 3 courses, £39 4 courses.
Both **Credit** AmEx, DC, MC, V.
This elegant veteran continues to impress, raising its game in subtle ways. One particularly welcome addition is a larger choice of wines by the glass, and under £35 a bottle, to the well-chosen, all-Italian list. Yet even without that bonus, this

would have been a memorable meal. The menu offers seven or eight antipasti, primi, secondi and dolci, plus a couple of specials. Rusticity characterised our two specials: a gleaming ball of burrata with roasted vegetables; and strozzapreti (own-made pasta, shaped like rolled ribbons) in a silky, improbably flavourful ragù of beef and wild mushrooms – one of the best we've eaten in London. Another starter, carpaccio of porchetta (roast suckling pig) with a green salad, was simple and stunningly good. Confit rabbit leg with pancetta and heavenly little button onions has been on the menu for ages – for good reason, as it's a perfectly balanced dish. Service, sometimes erratic on earlier visits, was near flawless and unswervingly sweet. Several nearby tables were occupied by Italians, always a pleasing sign. Il Baretto, the adjoining bar, produces excellent cocktails at prices that are low for Mayfair. If Alloro maintains these standards, it should be around forever.
Available for hire. Babies and children admitted. Booking advisable. Separate room for parties, seats 16. **Map 9 J7.**

Bar Trattoria Semplice

22 Woodstock Street, W1C 2AP (7491 8638, www.bar trattoriasemplice.com). Bond Street tube. **Lunch served** noon-3pm Mon-Fri; 12.45-3.45pm Sun. **Dinner served** 6-11pm Mon-Thur; 6-11.30pm Fri; 6.15-9.30pm Sun. **Meals served** 12.30-11.30pm Sat. **Main courses** £11.25-£18.95. **Set lunch** (Mon-Fri) £16.75 2 courses incl glass of wine. **Credit** AmEx, MC, V.
This is the more casual offshoot of fancy Ristorante Semplice; while the ristorante's high-end food presentation is over-fussy, in our experience, this trattoria is too casual by far. On a warm summer night, we could barely get in the for 100 or so Italians at a function who were occupying the pavement and the staff's entire attention. Diners were offered a standard Italian menu of unsurprising starters, a few own-made pastas and half a dozen main courses. Porchetta, which arrived with a pile of long-ago shredded lettuce, was indifferent at best; a tomato and mozzarella salad was poor for the £9.75 it turned out to cost (the waiter had been unable to price the specials for us). Mains were better. A cod special came with only a (good) rocket and tomato salad, but the fish was fresh and perfectly cooked; ravioli was clearly recently made, though its large puddle of butter would not be to everyone's taste. The few waiters swung between rude and solicitous; the party seemed to be their priority. The trattoria's decor is in the show-flat style of stripped wood floor and large lampshades, with much beige and brown; Ristorante Semplice's interior is embellished with waves of gold. Both offer a good selection of regional Italian wines at Mayfair prices.
Available for hire. Babies and children welcome: high chairs. Separate room for parties, seats 25. Tables outdoors (6, terrace). **Map 9 H6.**
For branch (Ristorante Semplice) see index.

Cecconi's

5-5A Burlington Gardens, W1S 3EP (7434 1500, www.cecconis.co.uk). Bond Street tube. **Breakfast served** 7am-noon Mon-Fri; 8am-noon Sat, Sun. **Meals served** noon-11.30pm Mon-Fri. **Brunch served** noon-5pm Sat, Sun. **Dinner served** 5-11.30pm Sat; 5-10.30pm Sun. **Main courses** £12-£28. **Credit** AmEx, MC, V.
If Cecconi's didn't exist, someone would probably have to invent it. This corner of Mayfair is surprisingly free of decent alfresco options, let alone a friendly, glamorous corner spot that segues smoothly from 7am cappuccino and granola, to midday

Fratelli la Bufala

If you have been brought up and taught correctly, the benefits will always shine through. There's no better example of this than Mimo Rimoli, owner of South End Green's popular Fratelli la Bufala. Born in Pozzuoli, Naples (birthplace of Sofia Loren), the Italian was destined to make his mark in the restaurant world. While Mimo was growing into the man he is today, his family restaurant business was continuing to grow.

For 4 consecutive years now the restaurant has been nominated for the Archant Food and Drink Awards and in 2009 won the Italian category for the North of London. Nominations and shortlists have been received from The Evening Standard London Restaurant Awards.

Fratelli la Bufala is a brand that showcases the gastronomic heritage of Naples, using bufalo meat and mozzarella cheese. The bufalo meat is healthy, low in fat and beautifully tender. Whilst the acclaimed Fratelli la Bufala were springing up all over Italy, the rest of the world was taking notice. Mimo decided he would be the first to bring the family business to England.

'Best Italian'
Ham & High

Showing the same passion he has had for art and motorcycles, Mimo threw himself into creating a menu that showcased what Fratelli la Bufala was all about.

Lip-smacking and healthy bufalo fillets have 60% less fat than beef. We also serve sausages, mozzarella and authentic pizzas, all cooked in a traditional rural Italian way, with the emphasis on quality and freshness.

We now have a daily fish special with a list of seasonal fish dishes which are proving to be extremely popular. Choose from fresh sea bass and sea bream baked in the wood oven, king prawns, scallops and seared tuna or halibut steaks. Our fish menu sells quickly so booking is essential at the weekends and evenings. Famous in Italy for its family and group welcome the restaurant is now able to offer children's portions and cater for larger groups and outside functions.

Northwest London has some fantastic restaurants and it is places like Fratelli la Bufala that bring something different.

Best pizza in North London
Time Out

45a South End Road, NW3
www.fratellilabufala.com

020 7435 7814

food&
drink
awards
ARCHANT LONDON

lobster salad, then cocktail-hour crostini and evening lamb shank with artichokes and potatoes. Tables are set around a slightly deco, square central bar, vividly dressed in black and white marble and green leather: a scheme designed by Ilse Crawford when the Soho House group took control in 2005. It still looks the business. As befits a place serving cicchetti (Venetian-style tapas), there's a good choice of wines by the glass and carafe; bottles start at £18.50 for sangiovese and trebbiano from Salento. There are also many cocktails, and Peroni on draught. At £46 for three courses, the set menu (for groups of eight-plus) is no bargain. Better to opt for a plate of pasta – tagliatelle with cime di rapa, gorgonzola and walnuts, say, or veal cannelloni – or simple main courses such as beef tagliata, and roast chicken with truffle mash. Despite the lengthy opening hours, snagging a table for dinner can be a challenge – which only adds to the allure.
Babies and children welcome: high chairs. Booking essential. Disabled: toilet. Dress: smart casual. Tables outdoors (10, terrace). **Map 9 J7**.

Murano

20-22 Queen Street, W1J 5PR (7592 1222, www.gordonramsay.com/murano). Green Park tube. **Lunch served** noon-2.30pm, **dinner served** 6.30-10.15pm. **Set lunch** £25 2 courses. **Set meal** £50 3 courses, £75 tasting menu. **Credit** AmEx, DC, MC, V.
Angela Hartnett MBE is executive chef of this protectorate of the Gordon Ramsay empire. If our meals are fair indication, the marriage of her Italian family roots with Ramsay's haute cuisine is a tense one – some ingredients arrive at the table so primped you can imagine them wishing they'd been cooked at the River Café. The set lunch, carte and tasting menu all proffer some delightfully simple fare (peach and fresh almond salad with basil and broad beans, say, or any of the seasonal risottos), but they are interspersed with dishes such as smoked Gloucestershire pork belly with onion and horseradish purée and lemon curd. The interior's lovely compilation of creamy hues is offset by modern chandeliers, retro carpet and a serious wall of wine chillers behind a carefully lit bar. Like the menu, the wine list isn't pure Italian and has very little under £35 a bottle; however, nearly 30 wines are offered by the glass, costing £6 to £37 – though for just 125ml. Service is of the superb standard normally enjoyed at Ramsay's higher caste venues, but frankly, at these prices, so it should be.
Babies and children welcome: high chairs. Booking essential; Fri, Sat dinner 1 mth ahead. Disabled: toilet. Dress: smart casual. Separate room for parties, seats 12. **Map 9 H8**.

Theo Randall at the Intercontinental

1 Hamilton Place, Park Lane, W1J 7QY (7409 3131, www.theorandall.com). Hyde Park Corner tube. **Lunch served** noon-3pm Mon-Fri. **Dinner served** 5.45-11pm Mon-Sat. **Main courses** £24-£35. **Set meal** (lunch, 5.45-7pm, 9-11pm) £23 2 courses, £27 3 courses. **Credit** AmEx, DC, MC, V.
In recent years, the former executive chef of the River Café has stepped from the shadow of its famous owners and taken some limelight for himself, and for his eponymous restaurant in this swanky hotel opposite Hyde Park. The room has no verdant views, but is cheerful, with bright artwork, grass-themed glass screens, and red and green walls that sensibly don't mimic the Italian flag. We like the spaciousness of room, tables and chairs, though the place can feel lonely and slightly embarrassing

when quiet. It's quite a departure from the River Café – until you see the menu, which is full of simple, produce-led delights. The wood-fired oven plays a key role in the secondi: turbot with capers, parsley, roast peppers and swiss chard; or Marsala-marinated Anjou pigeon on sourdough bruschetta with slow-cooked peas and pancetta. Fresh pasta might come as cappelletti stuffed with slow-cooked veal, taglierini with brown shrimps and artichokes, or ravioli of mixed greens and sheep's milk ricotta. Start with a bellini-style aperitivo of fresh white peach juice, peach liqueur and prosecco; finish with Amalfi lemon tart or strawberry sorbet. The bill might be higher than expected, but the food will have been excellent.
Babies and children welcome: high chairs. Booking advisable. Disabled: lift; toilet. Dress: smart casual. Separate room for parties, seats 28. **Map 9 G8**.

Via Condotti

23 Conduit Street, W1S 2XS (7493 7050, www.via condotti.co.uk). Oxford Circus tube. **Lunch served** noon-3pm Mon-Fri; 12.30-3pm Sat. **Dinner served** 5.45-10.30pm Mon-Sat. **Main courses** £13.50-£19.50. **Set meal** (lunch, 5.45-7pm) £15 2 courses, £18.50-27.50 3 courses. **Credit** AmEx, MC, V.
Named after the swish Roman thoroughfare, Via Condotti provides understated elegance and pared down Italian restaurant food on one of Mayfair's swankiest shopping streets. Prices aren't extortionate for the location and for the quality of classic combinations distinctively presented (buffalo mozzarella with a skinned plum tomato quartered into fleshy 'petals', for example). This metropolitan, rather than rustic, style of Italian cooking depends on the quality of ingredients to stand out; the mozzarella was good, yet not as exceptionally creamily unctuous as it can be. Seafood shone out. Squid, chargrilled to juicy, smoky, caramelised perfection on delicate slices of sweet, earthy beetroot, and a special of sea bream with potatoes, artichoke hearts and olive dressing were both spot-on. But stodgy scialatielli pasta with an unattractive veal and carrot ragù put the kibosh on our appetite for pudding (from a short list that includes an inevitable tiramisu). Service was efficient, but not effusive service (a top-up of tap water would have been appreciated). It seems that in the past year Via Condotti has become a little less like being in Rome and a little more middle of the road.
Babies and children admitted. Booking advisable. Separate rooms for parties, seating 18-35. **Map 9 J6**.

Soho

Bocca di Lupo

12 Archer Street, W1D 7BB (7734 2223, www.bocca dilupo.com). Piccadilly Circus tube. **Lunch served** 12.30-3pm Mon-Sat; noon-4pm Sun. **Dinner served** 5.30-11pm Mon-Sat. **Main courses** £8.50-£22. **Credit** AmEx, MC, V.
Bocca di Lupo, one of the most celebrated Italian restaurants to have opened in London in recent years, has broad appeal. The dining room is smart but cramped, and suffers from terrible acoustics. An open kitchen showcases skill and efficiency, and service is unpretentious. The menu is divided appealingly into little plates of quality raw or cured items, deep-fried vegetables and fish, superb fresh pastas and risottos and soups, before moving on to more substantial grilled and roasted meats and fish. The combinations of sometimes unusual seasonal ingredients are sophisticated, and each dish is given a regional designation, a testament to the chef's

dedication to genuine Italian cuisine. Similarly, the wine list is a celebration of the best Italy has to offer, at reasonable prices. Ordering a tapas-like selection of small and large plates is the way to go here – there are so many delicious things, it would be a shame to restrict your companions to individual dishes. Save room for the tempting array of desserts. The Soho location and a spate of good reviews have contributed to make this a perennially popular restaurant – book well in advance and be prepared for a packed and noisy room.
Babies and children welcome: booster seats. Booking advisable. Disabled: toilet. Separate room for parties, seats 35. **Map 17 B4.**

Polpo

41 Beak Street, W1F 9SB (7734 4479, www.polpo.co.uk). Piccadilly Circus tube. **Lunch served** noon-3pm Mon-Sat; noon-4pm Sun. **Dinner served** 5.30-11pm Mon-Sat. **Dishes** £1-£11. **Credit** AmEx, MC, V.

This charming new bacaro (Venetian-style wine bar) has a fashionably distressed look: white wall tiles, a bronze-coloured tin ceiling, and low-wattage light bulbs that give it a faux patina. Wine – from four good importers – is brought in rustic jugs of 250ml or 500ml, but disingenuously dispensed into tumblers. Chef Tom Oldroyd worked briefly at nearby Bocca di Lupo, an influence that has clearly informed the procession of small, flavour-packed dishes here. Some choices are classically Venetian, such as a cicchetti (Venetian bar snack) of grilled polenta topped with moist salt cod. Others are more creative, such as slivers of cuttlefish, cooked in their black ink in the Venetian way (which can then resemble mud from the Grand Canal) – but embroidered with gremolata, the lemon zest, garlic and parsley make the dish glow. An order of three savoury dishes per person seems about right. Customers are greeted at the door by charming co-owner Russell Norman, who used to handle front-of-house at society favourite, Le Caprice. He sized us up and put us at the back. Minutes later, the first of the 'celebs' arrived, and were placed at one of the good tables.
Babies and children welcome: high chairs. Booking advisable lunch. Bookings not accepted dinner. Separate room for parties, seats 10-25. **Map 17 A4.**

South Kensington

Daphne's

112 Draycott Avenue, SW3 3AE (7589 4257, www. daphnes-restaurant.co.uk). South Kensington tube. **Lunch served** noon-3pm Mon-Fri. **Dinner served** 5.30-11.30pm Mon-Fri. **Meals served** noon-11.30pm Sat; noon-10.30pm Sun. **Main courses** £12.75-£26.50. **Set meal** (until 7pm) £16.50 2 courses, £18.50 3 courses. **Credit** AmEx, DC, MC, V.

The eagle-eyed may recognise the corporate bread basket, and the odd celebrity, but otherwise there's little to indicate that this Brompton Cross charmer is a sister to Scott's, J Sheekey and the Ivy. Creamy-gold mottled paintwork, well-spaced tables, white linens and immaculate yet friendly staff create a wonderfully relaxed vibe in both the front dining room and rear skylit section. A table amid the potted trees in the latter is a

Polpo

real treat on winter days. The menu seems to have been refocused on classic Italian cooking since über-chef Mark Hix left Caprice Holdings. Reliable favourites include meatballs in tomato sauce with roast potatoes, girolle risotto, and linguine alle vongole. There's a good choice of fish dishes on the secondi (lemon sole with brown shrimps and capers, and roast gilt-head bream among them), but also roast lamb and chicken, plus veal, beef and calf's liver. The set meal is less exciting, but substantially cheaper than the carte. The mostly Italian wine list offers several options by the glass or carafe; if you're prepared to pay a bit more than £30 a bottle, the special wines of the month are worth investigating.

Babies and children welcome: high chairs. Booking advisable. Separate room for parties, seats 40. **Map 14 E10.**

Westminster

Quirinale
North Court, 1 Great Peter Street, SW1P 3LL (7222 7080, www.quirinale.co.uk). St James's Park or Westminster tube. **Lunch served** noon-2.30pm Mon-Fri. **Dinner served** 6-10.30pm Mon-Sat. **Main courses** £19.50-£26. **Set meal** (lunch, 6-7.30pm) £19 2 courses, £23 3 courses. **Credit** AmEx, DC, MC, V.

Any good restaurant this close to Westminster is bound to be filled with pinstriped politicians looking for gutsy but gourmet food, fine wine and a discreet basement location to discuss the business of the day. And so it was when we unsuited, unbooted civilians arrived to be greeted by the arched eyebrow of the snooty maître d'. The male-dominated room whiffs of 1980s excess. It's a brightly lit, slightly scuffed space, with starched tablecloths and grinning-through-gritted-teeth service that make it reminiscent of date-restaurants in US sitcoms. Staff forgot to bring bread until halfway through our starter, but never mind – the food and expansive (but expensive) wine list are top-notch. The menu is reassuringly simple, with pasta, pesce and carne staples all present and correct. A generous beef carpaccio starter melted in the mouth, tender pork saltimbocca and a main of bigoli with rich duck ragù ripe for slurping showed finesse. Three cheeses, from one of London's best Italian cheese selections, finished off a fine but very filling meal. Lean times probably won't mean leaner MPs, then.

Available for hire. Babies and children admitted. Booking advisable lunch. **Map 16 L10.**

West

Bayswater

Assaggi
1st floor, 39 Chepstow Place, W2 4TS (7792 5501). Bayswater, Notting Hill Gate or Queensway tube. **Lunch served** 12.30-2.30pm Mon-Fri; 1-2.20pm Sat. **Dinner served** 7.30-11pm Mon-Sat. **Main courses** £18-£24. **Credit** MC, V.

A discreet affair this – the sign unobtrusive, the entrance set at the side of the low-key pub that the restaurant sits atop. Once inside, the modestly proportioned room is bright and lively. Light streams over window-box olive trees through tall Georgian windows; walls are cheerful orange, with simple canvases of blue, grey and black; the only other decoration is a spectacular flower arrangement. Assaggi has been a hit for around 15 years because it serves reliably good food (often

Sardinian) in a reliably fun setting. Prices are high, yet diners tend to leave feeling grateful. The cheapest wine (Nuragus, £22.95) is excellent. A jug of tap water is proffered once you sit down, followed by carta di musica (Sardinian crispbread) lightly smeared with olive oil, and focaccia. Start with deep-fried courgette flowers or calamari, burrata with aubergine, or one of three daily pastas – crab with pappardelle, say. Neatly trimmed veal cutlet is wondrously moist, served with shoestring fries. Fish of the day might be turbot, chargrilled to smoky succulence and served with a dressing of crunchy peppers, tomato, olives and tarragon. To finish, order the first-rate tiramisu and espresso-topped vanilla bavarese.

Available for hire. Babies and children admitted. Booking essential. **Map 7 B6.**

Hammersmith

River Café `HOT 50`
Thames Wharf, Rainville Road, W6 9HA (7386 4200, www.rivercafe.co.uk). Hammersmith tube. **Lunch served** 12.30-5pm daily. **Dinner served** 7-11pm Mon-Sat. **Main courses** £12.50-£40. **Credit** AmEx, DC, MC, V.

The good ship River Café continues on course despite the death this year of co-founder Rose Gray. Inside is all cool, calming blues, white and steel with the occasional splash of bright yellow; outside is a pretty little herb and vegetable garden in which guests can sup during good weather. Desserts – almond and strawberry tart, Valpolicella summer pudding, the infamous chocolate nemesis – are lined up along the counter that separates the dining tables from London's most open of open kitchens. Staff are young, friendly and dressed just a little more fashionably than the core Fulham and Kensington customer base. Start with the vegetable antipasto, thick-sliced buffalo mozzarella, or one of the primi: maybe risotto with courgette and courgette flowers in summer, or mullet, clams and sea kale in winter. At Sunday lunch, exceptionally juicy Middle White pork loin chop featured a subtle fennel rub and sat on plump, bead-like cannellini tossed with new season girolles. Swiss chard with crème fraîche was the accompaniment for wood-roast wild sea bass (thick, moist), but another service might see it partnered with peas sott'olio (preserved in oil) and spinach, or baked in a bag and served with castelluccio lentils and samphire. The wine list is far more kindly priced than the menu, with the basic white wine a good grecanico from Sicily at £17.50 a bottle.

Babies and children welcome: high chairs. Booking essential. Disabled: toilet. Separate room for parties, seats 18. Tables outdoors (15, terrace). **Map 20 C5.**

Kensington

Timo
343 Kensington High Street, W8 6NW (7603 3888, www.timorestaurant.net). High Street Kensington tube. **Lunch served** noon-2.30pm, **dinner served** 7-11pm Mon-Sat. **Main courses** £14.90-£21.95. **Set meal** (lunch Mon-Sat, 7-8pm Mon-Thur) £13.90 2 courses, £17.90 3 courses. **Credit** AmEx, MC, V.

With good-value set lunches and smooth, ingratiating service, Timo is popular with local office workers, yet come evening it also works as a date destination. The pale decor is airily elegant, the tables well spaced and the atmosphere serene. The menu comprises a concentrated selection of classics along with more unusual alternatives, so conchiglie with pancetta, tomato and onion might follow carpaccio served with fennel (as well as the expected rocket and parmesan), or buffalo mozzarella with basil, marinated tomatoes and roast aubergines. The dessert list isn't particularly inspiring (tiramisu, pear and almond tart, ice-cream and sorbet), but there's often an enjoyable selection of Italian cheese, served with own-made walnut bread and attracting a £3 surcharge. There's also a surcharge (£2) if you fancy having a main-sized portion of pasta, which means the tempting ravioloni stuffed with braised guinea fowl and cooked with thyme and beetroot butter rises to £12.90. The wine list runs to well over 100 bottles, but not many of them duck under £30 – and even then not by much. *Available for hire. Babies and children admitted. Booking advisable. Separate room for parties, seats 18.* **Map 13 A9**.

South West

Barnes

Riva

169 Church Road, SW13 9HR (8748 0434). Barnes or Barnes Bridge rail, or 33, 209, 283 bus. **Lunch served** 12.15-2.15pm Mon-Fri, Sun. **Dinner served** 7-10.30pm Mon-Sat; 7-9pm Sun. **Main courses** £13-£24. **Credit** AmEx, MC, V.

Well-heeled Barnes supports not one but three long-running and respected restaurants: Modern European favourite Sonny's, riverside brasserie the Depot and this Italian stalwart. Apparently, the late Elizabeth David was a fan, and it's the favourite haunt of many a restaurant critic. What's all the fuss about? The small single room isn't much of a looker and has barely changed in years; wooden chairs, white tablecloths and a mirrored wall are as fancy as it gets. The menu rarely alters either, offering time-honoured classics and specialities from northern Italy, especially Lombardy (home of owner Andrea Riva). There's also a daily-changing starter, pasta, fish and meat dish. Seafood is notably good (especially the tender grilled baby squid with lightly braised wild fresh herbs); we've also enjoyed roast suckling pig and succulent roast lamb. The dessert list is dominated by sorbets and ice-creams, and the all-Italian wine list is a marvel. Service is efficient, but really only warms once you've established yourself as a regular. In proper Italian tradition, Riva shuts for some weeks in August. *Babies and children welcome: high chairs. Booking essential dinner. Tables outdoors (3, pavement).*

Chelsea

La Famiglia

7 Langton Street, SW10 0JL (7351 0761, www.lafamiglia. co.uk). Sloane Square tube then 11, 22 bus, or 31 bus. **Lunch served** noon-2.45pm, **dinner served** 7-11.30pm daily. **Main courses** £8.50-£26. **Cover** £1.85. **Credit** AmEx, MC, V.

Alvaro Maccioni and daughter Marietta run this unpretentious Chelsea bolt-hole that has been serving Tuscan cooking to internationally renowned celebrities and local families for an impressive 35 years. The interior's trademark blue and white tiles amplify the happy hum; if the sound wasn't mostly of braying and hooraying, you could think yourself in central Italy. The lengthy menu is both comforting and uncompromising, promoting seasonal dishes – deep-fried baby artichokes in summer, polenta with porcini in winter –

and flesh foods such as wild boar, pheasant and tripe that aren't often seen in London's trattorias. Portions are generous too, so a plate of fusilli with broccoli and garlic, say, followed by venison sautéed in vin santo sauce, could leave you too full to make the most of the fabulously retro dessert trolley, which is presented and served in suitably theatrical style by the bustling, white-jacketed waiters. Tables in the rear alfresco dining area are much coveted, though you may be surprised by its humble appearance: Chelsea Flower Show, it ain't. *Babies and children welcome: high chairs. Booking advisable dinner & Sun. Tables outdoors (30, garden).* **Map 13 C13**.

Osteria dell'Arancio

383 King's Road, SW10 0LP (7349 8111, www.osteria dellarancio.co.uk). Fulham Broadway or Sloane Square tube. **Lunch served** noon-3pm Tue-Sun. **Dinner served** 6.30-11pm Mon-Sat. **Main courses** £15-£18. **Credit** AmEx, DC, MC, V.

The decor here is an enjoyably bohemian mix of second-hand kitchen tables, white walls, old crockery, coloured glassware and spiky modern art. Even the tables outside by the road have planters full of flowers. The effect is fresh, friendly and welcoming. The menu is enticing too. Having played with more outlandish variations on the Italian norm a few years back, Osteria dell'Arancio seems to have settled back into its stride producing bold, contemporary versions of mamma's favourites. So the excellently chargrilled squid might come with courgette flowers stuffed with ricotta; the scallops with zesty orange sauce. Full-flavoured main courses cover both meat (perhaps a veal chop with rosemary and olives) and fish (turbot in a tomato and olive sauce). For pudding, our all-time favourite remains a terrific chocolate soufflé with proper vanilla ice-cream – squidgy and insubstantial in all the right places. Wine is taken seriously here, with the extensive range of bottles stored in full view behind glass, along with Enomatic machines that keep oxygen from getting into bottles that have been opened to serve by the glass. *Babies and children admitted: high chairs; nappy-changing facilities. Booking advisable. Disabled: toilet. Separate room for parties, seats 35. Tables outdoors (12, terrace).* **Map 14 D12**.

Putney

Enoteca Turi

28 Putney High Street, SW15 1SQ (8785 4449, www.enotecaturi.com). Putney Bridge tube or Putney rail, or 14, 74, 220, 270 bus. **Lunch served** noon-2.30pm, **dinner served** 7-11pm Mon-Sat. **Main courses** £11.50-£21.50. **Set lunch** £15.50 2 courses, £18.50 3 courses. **Set dinner** (Mon-Thur) £25.50 2 courses, £29.50 3 courses. **Credit** AmEx, DC, MC, V.

The key attraction to this restaurant, set at the river end of Putney High Street, is its extraordinary wine list. Running to a daunting – or thrilling, depending on your expertise with wine – number of pages, the list is carefully numbered for easy cross-referencing with the menu. It also has full tasting notes that are a model of clarity, which makes pairing dish and drink a doddle, even for inexperienced bibbers. If you do get stuck, ask the staff, who are polite, knowledgeable and happy to help. The food, a range of hearty regional specialities, is also accomplished. Rabbit is always a winner, whether stuffed, braised or marinated in garlic and sage, but other highlights might include guinea fowl. There are also fine, traditional

Zucca

versions of fish (perhaps turbot cooked with basil, olives, tomatoes and potatoes) and pasta dishes (spaghetti with a lamb ragù, for instance). Panna cotta, with vanilla specks and its wobble just so, winds things up nicely. The handsome dining room is furnished in warm earth tones, with bare wooden floors and crisp white tablecloths. The welcome is always warm too.
Babies and children welcome: high chairs. Booking advisable. Disabled: toilet. Separate room for parties, seats 18.

South East

Bermondsey

Zucca

2010 RUNNER-UP BEST NEW RESTAURANT
2010 RUNNER-UP BEST NEW DESIGN
184 Bermondsey Street, SE1 3TQ (7378 6809, www.zuccalondon.com). London Bridge tube/rail or Bermondsey tube. **Lunch served** noon-3pm Tue-Sun. **Dinner served** 6.30-10pm Tue-Sat. **Main courses** £8.50-£13.95. **Credit** MC, V.
If only more restaurants had Zucca's approach: good food at great prices, served by interested staff with a genuine regard for diners. Sounds simple, but it's pretty rare. The only complaints we have are that the tables are very close together – a problem when you have a loved-up couple on one side, and two loud geezers on the other – and that a couple of the dishes

were a bit salty. That's it; otherwise the evening was a progression of plus-size, flavour-packed dishes, from starters of moreish zucca fritti (battered pumpkin slices), delicate pea ravioli and punchy vitello tonnato, to a finale of dreamy panna cotta with roast peach. Mains of quail with lentils, speck and salsa verde, and grilled squid with borlotti beans, chilli and samphire were top-notch, though the samphire got rather lost under the chilli heat. A huge mixed salad, slightly overdressed, easily fed two, as did the glorious focaccia. This modern Italian menu is partnered by an all-Italian wine list; staff are happy to help or enlarge upon both. Decor is open-plan, with the kitchen completely exposed to view, and lots of shiny white surfaces with the occasional splash of intense orange – we liked it a lot, though the chairs may prove unforgiving over a whole evening. More new restaurants like this, please.
Babies and children welcome: high chairs; nappy-changing facilities. Booking essential dinner. Disabled: toilet.

Tower Bridge

Tentazioni

2 Mill Street, SE1 2BD (7237 1100, www.tentazioni. co.uk). Bermondsey tube or London Bridge tube/rail. **Lunch served** noon-2.45pm Mon-Fri. **Dinner served** 6.30-10.45pm Mon-Sat. **Main courses** £12.25-£20.50. **Set lunch** £11.95 2 courses incl drink, £15 3 courses incl drink and coffee. **Set dinner** £45.50 tasting menu (£65 incl wine). **Credit** AmEx, MC, V.

For more than a decade, this popular local Italian – it's often fully booked at weekends – has been dishing up classy food from a tricky-to-find location on an alley not far from Tower Bridge. The interior of the ground-floor dining room is romantic in plum and red, with changing art on the walls. Helpful staff create a relaxed atmosphere. The menu shows an admirable sense of adventure; a dish such as risotto with foie gras topped with a leg of confit duck in a rich port sauce may read like pure excess, but it will arrive as a combination of carefully balanced flavours. Unusual ingredients such as sea urchin or 24-carat gold leaf might be deployed in other dishes. Portions tend to the gargantuan, so order cautiously to keep room for the fine puddings. The wine list is chosen with imagination, and contains several options under £25; staff are usually delighted to offer pairing recommendations. There's a tasting menu, handy for those who cannot make up their mind, as well as a lunchtime prix fixe option (albeit less adventurous than the carte). Vegetarians are well catered for, with suitable dishes highlighted on the menu.
Available for hire. Babies and children welcome: high chair. Booking advisable dinner Fri, Sat. Separate room for parties, seats 30. **Map 12 S9**.

East

Shoreditch

Fifteen
15 Westland Place, N1 7LP (3375 1515, www.fifteen.net). Old Street tube/rail.
Trattoria **Breakfast served** 7.30-11am Mon-Sat; 8-11am Sun. **Lunch served** noon-3pm Mon-Sat; noon-3.30pm Sun.
Dinner served 6-10pm Mon-Sat; 6-9.30pm Sun. **Main courses** £14-£21.
Restaurant **Lunch served** noon-3pm daily. **Dinner served** 6.30-9.30pm Mon-Thur, Sun; 6-9.30pm Fri, Sat. **Main courses** £17.50-£23. **Set lunch** (Mon-Fri) £24 2 courses, £28 3 courses, £34 4 courses. **Set dinner** £60 tasting menu (£100 incl wine).
Both **Credit** AmEx, MC, V.
Jamie Oliver's charity operation is still quietly providing chef apprenticeships to directionless young people, despite no longer being the most prominent of its figurehead's numerous enterprises. The London flagship has undergone a facelift. A lick of paint and signature hot pink carpet in the basement dining room brighten the venue, but tinny aluminium chairs in the ground-floor trattoria feel less welcoming than the former studied rustic look. The cuisine, broadly Italian with creative liberties taken, encompasses such combinations as risotto with strawberries and balsamic, or belly pork intensified with the powerful flavours of chard, pistachios and anchovies. There's an emphasis on careful sourcing from quality producers and it's all of a reliable standard: the handmade pasta meltingly tender; sauces kept skilfully simple so individual flavours shine; good cuts of meat in satisfying portions. Desserts seem less well thought-through, however, and usually feature at least one uninspiring loaf cake. Service is in the Jamie O spirit – confident and professional, yet chummy. Evenings are often populated by young, special-occasion diners drinking beer, but we feel Fifteen is better suited to daytime, when the airy, buzzy space provides the perfect place to linger over a feel-good weekend brunch.
Babies and children welcome: high chairs. Booking essential restaurant. Disabled: toilet (trattoria).
Map 6 Q3.

ITALIAN

Best independent pizzerias

Thick base or crisp? Weird and wondrous toppings, or the classics? Choosing the best pizzeria is a subjective task, but distinctiveness and character in the face of rapacious competition from the chains go a long way in our book. Here's our pick.

Il Bordello

81 Wapping High Street, E1W 2YN (7481 9950). Wapping rail. **Lunch served** noon-3pm Mon-Fri. **Dinner served** 6-11pm Mon-Sat. **Meals served** 1-10.30pm Sun.
An enjoyably old-fashioned spot, Il Bordello occupies a corner-site basement, with more tables on the cobbles outside. Its menu is packed with Italian classics, from bresaola to veal chop with sage.
For branch (La Figa) see index.

Franco Manca

4 Market Row, Electric Lane, SW9 8LD (7738 3021, www.francomanca.co.uk). Brixton tube/rail. **Meals served** noon-5pm Mon-Sat.
This former Time Out Cheap Eats award-winner has a mix of communal and individual tables within Brixton's covered market. The menu is concise (just six pizzas) and astonishingly cheap – and the pizzas are divine, with thin, flavourful sourdough bases. Try the chorizo and mozzarella topping. A new branch has opened in Chiswick.
Map 22 E2.
For branch see index.

Fratelli la Bufala

45A South End Road, NW3 2QB (7435 7814, www.fratellilabufala.com). Belsize Park tube or Hampstead Heath rail. **Lunch served** noon-3pm Fri. **Dinner served** 6-11pm Mon-Fri. **Meals served** noon-11pm Sat, Sun.
Although this family-friendly buffalo specialist is part of an international franchise, it's the only London outlet and doesn't have a corporate tang. The split-level interior includes a pianist and (more importantly) a wood-fired oven whence comes the likes of the cornetto di bufala pizza, featuring emmenthal, prosciutto and rocket.
Map 28 C3.

The Gowlett

62 Gowlett Road, SE15 4HY (7635 7048). East Dulwich or Peckham Rye rail, or 12, 37, 40, 63, 176, 185, 484 bus. **Open** noon-midnight Mon-Thur; noon-1am Fri, Sat; noon-11.30am Sun. **Lunch served** 12.30-2.30pm, **dinner served** 6.30-10.30pm Mon-Fri. **Meals served** 12.30-10.30pm Sat; 12.30-9pm Sun.
Decent pizzas in a pub are a rarity, so the Gowlett's huge stone-baked versions (handmade from scratch) are much in demand among Peckham families. Grab a 'Gowlettini' (mozzarella, goat's cheese, pine nuts, rocket, prosciutto, sun-dried tomatoes) with a pint of Adnams ale or a glass of organic wine.
Map 23 C3.

Pizza East

56 Shoreditch High Street, E1 6JJ (7729 1888, www.pizzaeast.com). Shoreditch High Street rail. **Meals served** noon-11pm Mon-Wed, Sun; noon-midnight Thur; noon-1am Fri, Sat.
There's an Italian-American slant to the pizzas at this Soho House-owned newcomer, sited in the capacious Tea Building in Shoreditch. Clam pizza (a New England speciality) comes garnished with cherry tomatoes, garlic and pecorino. The vibe is friendly.
Map 6 R4.

Pizza Metro

64 Battersea Rise, SW11 1EQ (7228 3812, www.pizzametropizza.com). Clapham Junction rail. **Dinner served** 6pm-midnight Mon-Fri. **Meals served** noon-midnight Sat, Sun.
Claphamites swarm to Pizza Metro, drawn by its fabulous rectangular pizzas, served from the wood-fired oven on metre-long metal plinths. You'll find all the classic toppings, along with the 'cicciobomba' (featuring own-made pork sausage, aubergine, napoli salami and buffalo ricotta).
Map 21 C4.
For branch see index.

Rossopomodoro

50-52 Monmouth Street, WC2H 9EP (7240 9095, www.rossopomodoro.co.uk). Covent Garden tube. **Meals served** noon-11.30pm daily.
Imported Neapolitan ingredients and a wood-fired oven guarantee scumptious, crisp-based pizzas at this Covent Garden outpost of an Italian chain; there are also branches in Notting Hill and Fulham.
Map 18 D4.
For branches see index.

Santa Maria

2010 RUNNER-UP BEST NEW CHEAP EATS
15 St Mary's Road, W5 5RA (8579 1462, www.santamariapizzeria.com). South Ealing tube. **Meals served** noon-10.30pm daily.
A bright new star among London's pizzerias, Santa Maria already attracts queues of Italians and locals to its cosy, tiny premises. Its young Neapolitan owners produce superb, great-value pizzas from their wood-burning oven. Downsides are a no-bookings policy and rather brusque service.

Story Deli

Old Truman Brewery, 3 Dray Walk, E1 6QL (7247 3137, www.storydeli.com). Shoreditch High Street rail. **Meals served** noon-10.30pm daily.
In an industrial-chic setting, Story produces some very fine pizzas from its wood-fired oven. Bases are thin and crisp; toppings (chalked up on a board) feature high-quality cheeses and organic herbs; portions are large. Try the chanterelle pizza (ricotta, mushrooms, pine nuts, parmesan) if available.
Map 6 S5.

ITALIAN

Lena

66 Great Eastern Street, EC2A 3JT (7739 5714,
www.lenarestaurant.com). Old Street tube/rail.
Bar **Open** noon-midnight Mon-Sat.
Bar & Restaurant **Lunch served** noon-3pm, **dinner**
served 6-11pm Mon-Sat. **Main courses** £12-£21.
Set meal £9.95 2 courses, £13.95 3 courses. **Credit**
AmEx, MC, V.

Lena's kitchen is capable of excellence, such as a starter of burrata on carasau bread (aka carta da musica, Sardinian crispbread) with roast cherry tomatoes and basil dressing, in which creamily good cheese, plump tomatoes and crispy, salty flatbread were a match made in heaven. Sadly, it was also responsible for a main of baked mackerel with fennel, orange and beetroot salad so bitter we couldn't finish it, and a weirdly bland baby squid starter, allegedly stuffed with parmesan, parsley and garlic, in a tomato sauce. Fair-to-middling were a handful of stuzzichini (roast peppers, marinated anchovies, artichoke hearts), mains of aubergine melanzane and ricotta and spinach ravioli, and a dessert of cannoli with ricotta and black cherries. Caffè affogato was great, but then it's hard to get this simple combo of vanilla ice-cream and espresso wrong. Service was affable and reasonably efficient, and the cocktails are enjoyable, but prices are high (that stuffed squid starter costs £11). The decor is disconcerting too – the basement jazz bar is a study in brown, while the ground-floor restaurant mixes white and grey to a less than satisfactory effect. A confused and confusing experience.
Babies and children welcome: high chairs. Booking advisable.
Entertainment: jazz 9pm Fri, Sat. Tables outdoors
(6, pavement). **Map 6 R4**.

North

Archway

500 Restaurant

782 Holloway Road, N19 3JH (7272 3406, www.500
restaurant.co.uk). Archway tube or Upper Holloway rail.
Lunch served noon-3pm Tue-Sat. **Dinner served**
5.30-10pm Tue-Sun. **Main courses** £9.20-£15.50.
Credit MC, V.

That this small neighbourhood Italian on the northern nub of Holloway Road is named after the Fiat Cinquecento seems appropriate, given the constant growl of traffic beyond its glass front. But once inside 500's serene and tasteful single room (pastel walls, pine panelling, soft lighting), you'll hardly notice the hubbub outside. Manager Mario, charm personified, waited on us himself during a Monday lunchtime, bringing for starters a minty, creamy pea soup and a dish of flavourful smoked swordfish set against tart orange segments. Mains were excellent. Delicate and just-chewy-enough gnocchi came in a zingy pork and tomato ragù. Marsala-tinged veal arrived as thick as a hefty paperback, perfectly pink and moist, served on a bed of spinach. The meat was rich and delicious, and before long we were gnawing on the stripped bone. A bottle of house Salento topped a list of 20 reds and 15 whites, none costing more than £35 a bottle. We chose 'tart of the day' for sweet – a tasty apple version – though the classic desserts of tiramisu and semifreddo are fine versions. Our verdict after the test-run? Brrrm-ing great.
Babies and children admitted. Booking essential dinner.
Map 26 C1.

Trullo

Camden Town & Chalk Farm

Caponata

3-7 Delancey Street, NW1 7NL (7387 5959, www.caponata camden.co.uk). Camden Town tube. **Meals served** 9am-10.30pm Mon-Sat; 10am-10pm Sun. **Main courses** £9-£20. **Set meal** £15 2 courses, £21 3 courses. **Credit** AmEx, MC, V.

This clever conversion adjacent to the Forge music venue is a surprisingly smart addition to the centre of Camden. Versatile too, as indicated by the number of people ordering coffees and wine at the front of the ground-floor osteria, while office workers enjoyed lunch in the spectacular skylit central courtyard. Upstairs is a more intimate, formal dining room. Daily express lunch specials and the two-course set menu are keenly priced, but the carte isn't expensive. Dishes range from familiar penne arrabiata to inventive concoctions such as tea-smoked duck breast with caramelised gooseberries and raspberry dressing. Own-made bread is accompanied by Nocellara olive oil. A starter of red mullet fillet with mozzarella- and anchovy-stuffed courgette flower – rich and generous – is typical of the slightly tricksy dishes on the carte. Risotto was anything but plain with its flavourings of smoked haddock and sorrel. The dessert list also offers several twists on classics (crunchy-topped bitter almond brûlée with apricot ice-cream, balsamic strawberries with saffron granita and vanilla cream). The all-Italian wine list contains 17 varieties by the glass; there are also many cocktails. Tight-trousered service is as smooth and sexy as a purring Lamborghini: not the Camden norm, then.
Babies and children welcome: children's menu (brasserie); crayons; high chairs; nappy-changing facilities. Booking advisable. Disabled: lift; toilet. Separate rooms for parties, seating 30-50. Tables outdoors (5, pavement). Takeaway service. **Map 3 J1**.

La Collina

17 Princess Road, NW1 8JR (7483 0192). Camden Town or Chalk Farm tube. **Lunch served** noon-3pm Sat, Sun. **Dinner served** 6.30-11pm daily. **Main courses** £10-£15. **Credit** AmEx, MC, V.

A pleasant neighbourhood restaurant, La Collina struggles a little with lack of space in both the basement and ground-floor dining rooms (which are joined by a spiral staircase). The ground-floor space, decorated with local art, tends to be calmer. There are also tables in the garden, justly prized in fine weather. Food from the downstairs open kitchen is ambitious. The regularly changing menu offers dishes from across Italy, but with a slight prejudice towards the north. Seafood is always a hit here: we've enjoyed rarities such as gnocchetti neri (little gnocchi made using squid-ink) with mussels, octopus and cuttlefish salad, and mezzelune nere (croissant-shaped black pasta parcels filled with sweet and salty crab), as well as more common dishes such as good grilled squid or spaghetti with prawns and langoustines. The likes of herb risotto, braised rabbit or stuffed savoy cabbage fill out the menu. Puddings are less of a strong suit, although we've enjoyed an appealing grappa-drenched panna cotta. Welcoming staff and a pleasingly familiar atmosphere (don't be surprised to hear a little Dean Martin on the stereo) ensure a good mix of Primrose Hill regulars and more casual custom.
Babies and children welcome: high chairs. Booking advisable. Separate room for parties, seats 16. Tables outdoors (14, garden). **Map 27 B2**.

Highbury

Trullo

2010 RUNNER-UP BEST NEW LOCAL RESTAURANT
300-302 St Paul's Road, N1 2LH (7226 2733, www.trullorestaurant.com). Highbury & Islington tube/rail. **Lunch served** 12.30-2.30pm Sat, Sun. **Dinner served** 7-10.30pm Tue-Sat. **Main courses** £10-£20. **Credit** MC, V.

This Highbury Corner newcomer, the creation of chef Tim Siadatin (formerly of Jamie Oliver's Fifteen) and manager Jordan Frieda (ex-River Café), is simplicity incarnate. Paper-covered tables and café chairs fill the small, slate-grey and white room. The subdued lighting and twinkly tea lights are made for romance – if it wasn't for the lack of elbow room. Get a table near the bar if you want to glimpse the chefs at work in the open kitchen. Simplicity is also the watchword of the short, ever-changing menu. Antipasti of earthy girolle and chorizo salad, and tender grilled squid with piquant salsa rossa provided unfussy, perfectly matched flavours. Soft, delicate whole plaice (on the bone) with borlotti beans and herbs was similarly understated. Pasta is made daily, and there's also a charcoal grill for meat and fish. Afters include the likes of raspberry and almond tart or a trio of Italian cheeses. And prices are a revelation; starters and puds cost £4-£7, mains top out at £14. The all-Italian wine list has only a handful of wines by the glass, so you might as well get a bottle, especially as all have a very reasonable mark-up of £10. The downside? Rave reviews meant that Trullo was booked out within weeks of opening. The chummy, helpful staff did their best to cope with a packed room, but were sometimes overwhelmed.
Babies and children welcome: high chairs. Booking advisable. Separate room for parties, seats 30.

Islington

Metrogusto

13 Theberton Street, N1 0QY (7226 9400). Angel tube. **Lunch served** 11am-4pm Sat, Sun. **Dinner served** 6-10.30pm Tue-Fri; 6-11pm Sat; 6-10pm Sun. **Main courses** £11.50-£18.50. **Set meal** (lunch, 6-9pm) £14.50 2 courses, £18.50 3 courses. **Credit** AmEx, MC, V.

While the tiled floor and dark wooden furniture won't let you forget you're in a modern Italian restaurant, the dangling objets and wall art at this venue just off Upper Street are decidedly out of the ordinary. We're especially enamoured of the large, almost social-realist paintings of a pair of plump shopkeepers and businessmen in oversized shoes offering the viewer a monkey. We're less excited about the food. Earthy combinations such as tagliatelle with wild boar and rosemary ragù sometimes lack the expected punchiness of flavour. Another drawback can be the service, which seems to have been steadily slowing down over the years we've been visiting. Metrogusto advertises itself as a home of 'progressive Italian cooking', which tends to mean little more than a determined twist on traditional dishes. We've enjoyed the seasonal jerusalem artichoke ravioli with foamy broad bean sauce; and the rosemary ice-cream (perhaps served with chocolate fondant) is a reliable triumph. There's also an intriguing and fairly priced Italian wine list. A distinctive local, then, rather than a one-off culinary sensation.
Babies and children welcome: high chairs. Booking advisable. Separate room for parties, seats 38. Tables outdoors (4, pavement). **Map 5 O1**.

ITALIAN

Tenore

14 Barnsbury Road, N1 0HB (7278 6955,
www.tenore-restaurant.co.uk). Angel tube or bus 73.
Lunch served noon-3pm Sat. **Dinner served**
6-10.30pm Mon-Fri; 6-11pm Sat. **Meals served** noon-
10.30pm Sun. **Main courses** £9.55-£19.50. **Credit**
AmEx, MC, V.

Chef Roberto Tonzanu, who worked with Gennaro Contaldo
(Jamie Oliver's mate and mentor) for several years, now has his
own place in this former pub in Barnsbury. Tonzanu and most
of his staff are Sardinian, and ingredients and dishes from that
island feature prominently on the menu. Bottarga – fish roe
cured in brine, then dried – is an ingredient prized for its
intense fish flavour (with slight off-notes), its saltiness and its
waxy texture. Here, generous slivers are combined with
shavings of fennel bulb and celery for a taste that transports
you straight to Sardinia. Fregola is another speciality, an
oversized couscous that betrays Sardinia's close historical links
to north Africa. Tenore's fregola is cooked with a mussel and
clam broth and topped with prawn and langoustine. Pizzas are
stone-baked in a wood-fired oven; they have a good, crisp crust
but are wafer-thin and slightly elastic through the centre. Ours
was topped with high-quality ingredients: avocado, goat's
cheese, tomato and buffalo mozzarella. There's an enticing, all-
Italian wine list too. Service is sweet: a little too sweet, on the
night of our visit, to deal firmly with a drunken intruder.
Available for hire. Babies and children welcome: high
chairs; nappy-changing facilities. Booking advisable.
Disabled: toilet. Separate room for parties, seats 30.
Tables outdoors (4, pavement; 6, garden). Takeaway
service. **Map 5 N2**.

Assaggi. See p157.

North West
St John's Wood

Vineria

1 Blenheim Terrace, NW8 0EH (7328 5014,
www.vineria.it). St John's Wood tube. **Lunch served**
noon-2.30pm Tue-Sun. **Dinner served** 6.30-10.30pm
Tue-Sat; 6.30-10pm Sun. **Main courses** £10-£20.50.
Set lunch (Tue-Fri) £14.50 2 courses, £19.50 3 courses,
£24.50 4 courses. **Credit** AmEx, MC, V.

If this outpost of a Venetian restaurant group is consciously
cool – from the cutlery design to the startlingly lightweight
glasses in which iced tap water is served; from slim leather
chairs in an airy conservatory to the shaded summer terrace –
it achieves it via understatement, not stuffiness. Take the wine
list: the cream of northern Italy, a fair nod to the south, a
sprinkling of Super Tuscans, yet no descriptions, nor intrusive
'suggestions'. A glass of insufficiently chilled rosé was replaced
without comment at no extra charge. Service was charming,
informative on request and child-friendly. The food (classic
Italian, with inventive touches) generally sparkles, though
again via understated attention to detail, and subtle seasoning.
Diced aubergine was meltingly soft, yet its deeply chargrilled
skin provided a dark, crisp foil to baby-soft burrata; griddled
king prawns were carefully centre-peeled, removing potential
distraction from an array of grilled vegetables. Pasta was spot-
on, with cherry tomatoes melded seamlessly into a passata;
beef fillet was cooked precisely as requested. Most remarkably,
every dish arrived at exactly the same moment, but nothing
was off-key. Make that cool with class.
Babies and children welcome: high chairs. Booking advisable.
Tables outdoors (15, terrace). **Map 1 C2**.

Outer London
Twickenham, Middlesex

A Cena

418 Richmond Road, Twickenham, Middx TW1 2EB
(8288 0108, www.acena.co.uk). Richmond tube/rail.
Lunch served noon-2.30pm Tue-Sun. **Dinner served**
7-10.30pm Mon-Sat. **Main courses** £13.75-£21. **Set**
lunch (Sun) £25 3 courses. **Credit** AmEx, MC, V.

While the narrow frontage makes A Cena ('to dinner') easy to
miss, it would be a shame if you did. This is a relaxed place,
and yet chic in bistro style (white napery, wooden bar and
stripped floors, dripping candles). The menu offers well-made
specialities from across Italy, so you can try Tuscan ribollita
soup or the vinegary Sicilian stemperata sauce (made with
capers, celery and onions) that comes with salmon. Braised
rabbit with peas, pancetta, nutmeg, parmesan and new
potatoes is a favourite for lunch, and there's usually a fine range
of roast meats for dinner (Gloucester Old Spot, Welsh lamb,
guinea fowl). If you have room for dessert, try chocolate tartufo
with raspberries and cream, or the fine selection of cheeses,
served with fig jam. We were also intrigued by the 'zabaglione
cake'. The wine list contains some excellent producers; weekly
specials, served by the third-of-a-bottle carafe, are good value.
Though the greeting at the door may not be effusive, service
once you're inside is charming.
Available for hire. Babies and children welcome: booster
seats. Booking advisable.

Japanese

From expensive and formal to cheap and chipper, London's Japanese dining scene now covers a spectrum of options. It hasn't always been the case. 'Expensive and formal' used to go hand in hand, with half a dozen rather staid establishments in the City and Mayfair designed for business people (mostly Japanese expats) to impress their clients. Now, 'expensive and glamorous' is the norm, as the glittering likes of **Zuma** and its sister **Roka**, **Umu**, Alan Yau's **Saké No Hana**, and **Tsunami** follow the trail blazed by **Nobu**. At the other end of the price scale, pit-stop sushi bars such as **Moshi Moshi Sushi**, budget izakaya joint **Aki** and yakitori specialist **Bincho** are ideal for swift inexpensive lunches. London also has its share of cutting-edge Japanese restaurants that absorb influences from outside the Far East. **Dinings** is one of our current favourites, though gastronomic adventures can also be had at **Chisou** and **So Japanese**.

Central

Chancery Lane

Aki
182 Gray's Inn Road, WC1X 8EW (7837 9281, www.aki demae.com). Chancery Lane tube or bus 38, 55. **Lunch served** noon-2.30pm Mon-Fri. **Dinner served** 6-11pm Mon-Fri; 6-10.30pm Sat. **Main courses** £6-£12. **Set lunch** £10. **Set dinner** £20-£25. **Credit** AmEx, MC, V.
From the plastic sushi in the window to the saké-lined bar, Aki feels like a little slice of Japan. For an added touch of authenticity, the walls are lined with slips of paper covered in handwritten Japanese script, containing details of the menu. Staff chat happily to each other while tending to customers in an unhurried yet efficient way. On the menu there are izakaya classics such as chazuke (rice and green tea soup) as well as sushi and noodle dishes. A dish of tempura, although a little greasy, had batter thin enough for the juicy prawn and tender vegetables to show through – as they should. The sweet soy-based sauce in a portion of ginger pork had plenty of zing and came with accurately cooked rice. The prices here are also very reasonable; a filling four-course lunch special comes to less than £20. The food is far from refined, but it's simple, enjoyable and well priced. In fact, this is just the place for a lively after-work meal, a quick lunch or some saké and shochu tasting.
Babies and children admitted. Booking advisable. Takeaway service. **Map 4 M4.**

City

Moshi Moshi Sushi
24 Upper Level, Liverpool Street Station, EC2M 7QH (7247 3227, www.moshimoshi.co.uk). Liverpool Street tube/rail. **Meals served** 11.30am-10pm Mon-Fri. **Dishes** £1.30-£3.70. **Main courses** £8.50-£12.50. **Credit** MC, V.
Liverpool Street station, behind the Marks & Spencer store, overlooking platform one. It's not the most likely location in which passers-by would go searching for a brilliant kaiten-zushi restaurant. And that's probably just how the regulars like it. While other lesser, more prominent conveyor-belt sushi chains have set up squarely in station concourses and along high streets, Moshi Moshi doesn't tend to toot its horn – though it certainly has the justification. Soaring wooden curves ensconce diners who come for the handmade (as opposed to machine-made) nigiri sushi, notable in its use of fish sourced from sustainable stocks (the company is vehemently opposed to the over-fishing of tuna, and removed it from the menu in 1999). Other small dishes are terrific too: chilled silky tofu with a sour-salty ponzu sauce, for instance, or tempura, or indeed the housewife's favourite, oyako don (chicken and egg rice). A meal here is great value, and also allows you to feel virtuous while you munch.
Babies and children admitted. Disabled: toilet. Takeaway service; delivery service (within 4-mile radius). **Map 12 R5.** **For branch see index.**

Saki

Clerkenwell & Farringdon

Saki

4 West Smithfield, EC1A 9JX (7489 7033, www.saki-food.com). Barbican tube or Farringdon tube/rail.
Bar **Open** 6-10.30pm Mon-Wed; 6pm-12.30am Thur-Sat.
Deli **Open** 10am-7pm Mon-Fri.
Restaurant **Lunch served** 11.45am-2.30pm, **dinner served** 6-10.30pm Mon-Sat. **Set lunch** £8.90-£55. **Set dinner** £28.50 3 courses, £45 5 courses, £65 7 courses.
All **Credit** AmEx, MC, V.
In the heart of West Smithfield, Saki contains a bar, shop and restaurant. The centrepiece of the red-walled dining room is a collection of phallic candles surrounded by counter-style seating. Other curiosities include high-tech toilets with heated seats and buttons to push. Many customers are business people, but it's equally possible to have an intimate meal here. The innovative menu holds options to suit most budgets, as well as a huge list of saké. We opted for a cheapish three-course bento meal and a six-course chef's omakase (recommendation). The latter was noticeably more refined than the former, even down to the thickness of the tempura batter, but both were enjoyable. The highlight of the bento set was a sweet, plump scallop from a beautifully fresh sashimi plate. From the chef's selection, a lobster starter with green nori sauce, yam jelly and salmon eggs stood out for its unusual combination of tastes and textures. Not all the experimental dishes were as successful; seared beef tataki was overpowered with vinegared onions, and the modern classic of black cod with miso was greasy and flabby-skinned. Service was friendly and informative throughout, although not always entirely accurate.
Babies and children admitted. Booking advisable.
Disabled: toilet. Separate room for parties, seats 12.
Takeaway service. Vegan dishes. Vegetarian menu.
Map 11 O5.

Covent Garden

Abeno Too

17-18 Great Newport Street, WC2H 7JE (7379 1160, www.abeno.co.uk). Leicester Square tube. **Meals served** noon-11pm Mon-Sat; noon-10.30pm Sun. **Main courses** £9-£24. **Set lunch** £9.80-£19.80. **Credit** MC, V.
Every day is pancake day at this sleek-lined Leicester Square pitstop, which specialises in Kansai-style okonomiyaki from Osaka. The basic batter contains egg, cabbage, ginger and spring onion. You choose the additions desired (there's a long list of suggested combinations) and friendly, knowledgeable staff mix and cook your pancake in front of you on counter-top hotplates, finishing with a flourish of vividly coloured sauces. Pork? Yes. Bacon? Yes. Cheese? Yes. Salmon? Yes. Altogether? Absolutely – that's the London mix. Or maybe you'd prefer simple squid or prawn, or one of the tasty vegetarian combos, such as mushroom and lotus root. Admittedly, okonomiyaki can be a love or hate thing, but there are plenty of other meal options here too, including noodles, katsu curries and teppanyaki. Whenever we've veered from the way of the pancake, the standard of cooking has been impressive. Prices reflect the quality of ingredients (many, particularly the meats, are claimed to be organic), but there are lunchtime deals to be had, and 10% off all prices on takeaways.
Babies and children welcome: high chairs. Bookings not accepted. Disabled: toilet. Takeaway service. **Map 18 C6**.
For branch see index.

Euston

Sushi of Shiori

44 Drummond Street, NW1 2PA (7388 9962, www.sushiofshiori.co.uk). Euston tube/rail. **Lunch served** 11.30am-2.30pm, **dinner served** 5-9.30pm Mon-Sat. **Dishes** £2.70-£9. **Set lunch** £8-£12. **Set meal** £9-£25. **Credit** MC, V.

A simple shopfront on a quiet street better known for vegetarian Indian restaurants hides an austere sushi bar. Look closely, though, and you'll notice many pretty touches: circular glass placemats with a modern cherry-blossom print, beautiful Japanese crockery, and a pot of blooming orchids beside the till. With room for only nine diners (three at the bar), Sushi of Shiori seems slightly resigned to catering for the takeaway crowd. But sit in and you'll be rewarded with fresh, meticulously crafted sushi and exquisitely presented sushi; watching the itamae (sushi chef) at work is fascinating. Nigiri topped with zuwaigani – a long-legged crab from the Bering Sea – was lightly cooked and meaty, yet sweet and succulent, though not as good as the milky scallops. The only drawback was that the rice in both dishes lacked warmth and suppleness. We'll be back for the ball-shaped temari sushi (here called 'canapé' sushi). Also faultless were a sprightly wakame salad with a dressing pepped up with a mix of ponzu and Korean chilli paste, and an intense red miso soup with wakame and yuba (dried tofu skin).

Available for hire. Babies and children admitted. Booking advisable. Takeaway service. Vegetarian menu. **Map 3 J3**.

Fitzrovia

Roka HOT 50

37 Charlotte Street, W1T 1RR (7580 6464, www.roka restaurant.com). Goodge Street or Tottenham Court Road tube. **Lunch served** noon-2.30pm Mon-Fri; 12.30-4pm Sat, Sun. **Dinner served** 5.30-11.30pm Mon-Sat; 5.30-10.30pm Sun. **Main courses** £10.60-£22.60. **Set meal** £50-£75 tasting menu. **Credit** AmEx, DC, MC, V.

The open aspect to Roka, along with its numerous streetside tables, help generate a certain level of excitement at this swish dining establishment. Once inside, the noise levels can be deafening. Like its older sister, Zuma in Knightsbridge, the concept here is the izakaya – an informal place to eat, drink and watch the chefs beavering away on the robata grill. The interior is stylish, with swathes of wood on display including a counter carved from a tree trunk; the exposed ventilation ducts lend the place an industrial edge. We found the service extremely helpful, despite the number of covers. As for menu recommendations, the flame-grilled tofu, artistically presented with a dip of crushed yuzu, is superb. Also lip-smackingly good are the grilled baby pork ribs, which are pre-cooked with citrusy fruits for extra tenderness and flavour. Chawan mushi, a form of Japanese egg custard with mixed fruits, is a refreshing way to end a meal. It's also worth checking out the Shochu Lounge bar (www.shochulounge.com) in the basement: open for some time, yet still so hip that it hurts. There's an impressive array of shochu-based drinks and Japanese-style cocktails; and the full Roka menu is available too.

Babies and children welcome: high chairs. Booking advisable. Disabled: toilet. Tables outdoors (9, terrace). **Map 17 B1**. **For branch see index**.

Soho Japan

52 Wells Street, W1T 3PR (7323 4661, www.sohojapan. co.uk). Oxford Circus tube. **Lunch served** noon-2.30pm Mon-Fri. **Dinner served** 6-10.30pm Mon-Sat. **Main courses** £6.50-£14 lunch; £10-£22 dinner. **Set lunch** £10-£20. **Credit** AmEx, MC, V.

You'd be forgiven for doing a double take. For a start, Soho Japan is in Fitzrovia. What's more, it doesn't initially resemble a Japanese restaurant. When you enter, a map of the Burgundy wine region and a distinctly pub-like interior greet the eye. It's only when the friendly Japanese waitresses (or polite manager) lead you to a table that you take in the robata grill hidden inside, and the number of Japanese customers. The relaxed vibe and home-style cooking are two of the main attractions. Onigiri (rice balls), katsu (breaded and fried items), set meals, big bowls of udon or soba, and even hambagu (Japanese-style burger patty) feature on the menu; sushi and sashimi are competently prepared. Appropriately, given the restaurant's pub heritage, there are Japanese beers (Asahi and Kirin) on draught, with half-pints available. The rest of the drinks list encompasses saké and shochu, interesting fusion cocktails (shiso martini, for example) and a French-leaning wine list. Service can be a bit slow, but then this is not a gobble-and-go type of establishment. Soho Japan tries to please all, and mostly succeeds.

Babies and children admitted. Booking advisable. Tables outdoors (3, pavement). Takeaway service. **Map 17 A2**. **For branch (Crane & Tortoise) see index**.

Knightsbridge

Zuma

5 Raphael Street, SW7 1DL (7584 1010, www.zuma restaurant.com). Knightsbridge tube. **Bar Open** noon-11pm Mon-Fri; 12.30-11pm Sat; 12.30-10.30pm Sun. *Restaurant* **Lunch served** noon-2.30pm Mon-Fri; 12.30-3.15pm Sat, Sun. **Dinner served** 6-11pm Mon-Sat; 6-10.30pm Sun. **Main courses** £14.80-£70. *Both* **Credit** AmEx, DC, MC, V.

It's hard not to admire the Lamborghinis and other flash motors parked outside this renowned playground of the rich. Inside, the action starts at the bar. The energy generated by the wealthy crowd is intoxicating, making it difficult to believe that the economy is in the doldrums. The interior is hardcore: wood and stone going headlong against concrete and steel. Zuma

Sushi of Shiori

may have expanded beyond the confines of this first restaurant, but we haven't found any drop in the quality of output. Staff, neck-deep in work, seldom drop the ball. It's easy to blow your salary here, especially if you're partial to wagyu beef or sea urchin, but some of the less expensive dishes can be just as rewarding. The sashimi is among the freshest in town. Other menu highlights include grilled asparagus with wafu sauce (a soy-based dressing), and perfect, crispy, deep-fried squid. Tempura and spicy beef tenderloin with red chilli and sweet soy have turned up trumps for us too. Desserts stretch away from the East with the likes of green tea and banana cake served with coconut ice-cream.

Babies and children welcome: high chairs. Booking essential. Disabled: toilet. Separate rooms for parties, seating 12 and 14. **Map 8 F9**.

Marylebone

Dinings

22 Harcourt Street, W1H 4HH (7723 0666). Marylebone tube/rail. **Lunch served** noon-2.30pm Mon-Fri. **Dinner served** 6-10.30pm Mon-Sat. **Main courses** £6.50-£22. **Set lunch** £10-£15. **Credit** AmEx, MC, V.

Set in a Georgian townhouse, Dinings is diminutive, with a plain exterior that give no clue to the extraordinary cooking to be experienced within. The menu – blending Japanese cookery with Hispanic techniques and ingredients – sounds like a globetrotting horror, but the results are usually captivating and memorable for all the right reasons. Tataki and the ceviche-like preparations of fish are exceptional; like every dish here, they arrive immaculately presented. There is, however, some repetition of ingredients: plenty of miso, yuzu, ponzu and various salsas. Sea bass drenched in sharp, almost floral, yuzu juice was refreshing; seared yellowtail with creamy mustard miso was a balance of sweetness and richness. The 'tar tar' chips (small, taco-like crisps) filled with crab meat or salmon, scallop or tuna tartare, are playful morsels big on flavour. We recommend ordering from the specials board, where treats such as crispy pork belly with yuzu miso feature. Desserts continue the fusion theme, with black sesame crème brûlée a particular highlight. Service is kind and helpful, and surprisingly not intrusive given the tiny space.

Available for hire. Babies and children admitted. Booking advisable. Takeaway service. Vegetarian menu. **Map 8 F5**.

Tomoe

62 Marylebone Lane, W1U 2PB (7486 2004). www.tomoe-london.co.uk). Bond Street tube. **Lunch served** noon-2.15pm Tue-Sat. **Dinner served** 6-10.30pm Mon-Sat; 5-9pm Sun. **Dishes** £2.50-£12.90. **Set lunch** £7.90-£12.90. **Minimum** (dinner) £15. **Credit** AmEx, MC, V.

Located on a quiet curve of Marylebone Lane, Tomoe has achieved success mainly through word of mouth. Expectations can be low when you enter – laminated placards have been hastily blue-tacked on to the walls; sheets of calligraphy are now slightly curled around the edges. A tiny sushi bar occupies the low-ceilinged, plainly decorated basement. Nevertheless, the food belies such a shrugged-shoulders aesthetic. Grilled razor clams come thick and juicy, pepped up with ponzu, curls of spring onion and cherry tomato quarters. A curious sushi roll named 'caterpillar' is a length of avocado-wrapped maki; 'antennae' are crafted out of cucumber, and two ikura (salmon eggs) become the bug's 'eyes'. Stick to the simple to sate your appetite: a bowl of cubed raw maguro (tuna) and grated

yamaimo (mountain yam) celebrates the 'neba-neba' (slimy texture) so revered in Japanese cookery. Scallop nigiri wowed us with its delicate sweetness. The bouncy, chewy sanuki udon noodles are also worth trying. Drinks include Ebisu lager, both potato and wheat shochu, and expensive sakés. Take note: bookings are necessary most evenings, and at night there's a rather churlish £15 per person minimum charge.

Babies and children welcome: high chairs. Booking advisable dinner. Takeaway service. **Map 9 H6**.

Mayfair

Chisou

4 Princes Street, W1B 2LE (7629 3931, www.chisou.co.uk). Oxford Circus tube. **Lunch served** noon-2.30pm, **dinner served** 6-10.15pm Mon-Sat. **Main courses** £12-£23.50. **Set lunch** £14-£19.50. **Credit** AmEx, MC, V.

Despite its Mayfair location and reputation as one of London's best Japanese restaurants, Chisou eschews the flash of its trendier competitors. The simple, elegant dining room with pale wooden furniture isn't stark enough to be minimalist, and its modest proportions and occasional screen lend a sense of intimacy. Many regulars think the best seats are at the small sushi bar to the rear. From here, charming chefs produce first-rate sushi and sashimi; for the best overview, order the omakase sashimi (chef's choice of the day's best fish and seafood) or chirashi zushi (around ten fishy titbits plus omelette, marinated mushrooms and seaweed on superb sushi rice). Unusually, there's a good choice of cold noodles dishes, from the purity of inaniwa udon (thin white noodles served on a bamboo mat, with light soy sauce dip) to the more robust ten zaru soba (buckwheat noodles with tempura). Chef's specialities, such as ankimo ponzu (fish liver with ponzu sauce, spring onions and spiced daikon in a saké cup) and grilled fish cakes topped with cod's roe mayo, tend to be less successful. Still, staff are warm, but not over chummy, and can confidently guide you through the excellent list of saké and shochu.

Babies and children welcome: high chairs. Booking essential. Separate rooms for parties, seating 12-20. Tables outdoors (2, terrace). Takeaway service. **Map 9 J6**.

Nobu

1st floor, The Metropolitan, 19 Old Park Lane, W1K 1LB (7447 4747, www.noburestaurants.com). Hyde Park Corner tube. **Lunch served** noon-2.15pm Mon-Fri; 12.30-2.30pm Sat, Sun. **Dinner served** 6-10.15pm Mon-Thur; 6-11pm Fri, Sat; 6-9.30pm Sun. **Dishes** £3.50-£32.75. **Set lunch** £32 bento box; £55, £65. **Set dinner** £75, £95. **Credit** AmEx, MC, V.

Located in the Metropolitan hotel, this London outpost of Nobu was the first European branch of the international chain. Booking a table here can be a challenge, as the place receives hundreds of calls from prospective diners every day. Phone lines shut at 5pm, so don't even bother calling in the evening. The receptionists advise booking precisely one calendar month in advance to get one of the better tables or time slots. If you have this sort of discipline and foresight, you'll be rewarded with a room of anodyne beige-ness, filled with a see-and-be-seen crowd of big spenders for whom dropping £100 or more per head on a meal is nothing out of the ordinary. The main attraction is still chef Mark Edwards' cooking, a curious mix of owner Nobu Matsuhisa's Japanese culinary roots and influences that Matsuhisa picked up while living in Peru: raw seafood with Latin ceviches, for example, or signature Nobu

Best art gallery eats

These days, visitors can eat very well in London's major art venues. Some restaurants are now destinations in their own right, such as the Saatchi Gallery's brasserie, **Gallery Mess** (*see p48*). Also of note are a quartet of Modern European venues: the **Blueprint Café** (*see p214*); **Rex Whistler Restaurant at Tate Britain** (*see p207*); **Wapping Food**; and the **Whitechapel Dining Room** (for both, *see p215*). For the best of the rest, read on.

National Café & National Dining Rooms

National Gallery, Trafalgar Square, WC2N 5DN (7747 2525, www.thenationalcafe.com, www. thenationaldiningrooms.co.uk). Charing Cross tube/rail.
Bakery **Meals served** 10am-5.30pm Mon-Thur, Sat, Sun; 10am-8.30pm Fri.
Restaurant **Lunch served** noon-3.15pm daily. **Dinner served** 5-7pm Fri.
Café **Breakfast served** 8-11.30am, **lunch served** noon-5pm, **tea served** 3-5.30pm daily. **Dinner served** 5.30-11pm Mon-Sat. **Meals served** 10am-6pm Sun.
Oliver Peyton's quietly handsome restaurant in the Sainsbury Wing sets the standards for gallery dining, with fine British cooking – at a price. Stick to the good- value set lunch or the cheaper bakery/café area at the back. The brooding good looks of the National Café in the gallery's East Wing are too often overlooked as a calm evening spot, though prices are a couple of quid more than you'd expect. **Map 17 C5**.

Tate Modern Café: Level 2

2nd floor, Tate Modern, Sumner Street, SE1 9TG (7401 5014, www.tate.org.uk). Southwark tube or London Bridge tube/rail. **Meals served** 10am-5.30pm Mon-Thur, Sun; 10am-9.30pm Fri; 10am-7.30pm Sat.
The Tate's café has a varied and quite sophisticated menu, with much emphasis placed on local and seasonal sourcing. It's also surprisingly good for families, thanks to a keenly priced junior menu and plenty of child-friendly deals – including a free kids' main with an adult main from the regular menu. **Map 11 O7**.

The Wallace

Wallace Collection, Hertford House, Manchester Square, W1U 3BN (7563 9505, www.thewallace restaurant.co.uk). Bond Street tube.
Café **Meals served** 10am-4.30pm daily.
Restaurant **Lunch served** noon-3pm Mon-Fri; noon-3.30pm Sat, Sun. **Dinner served** 5-9.30pm Fri, Sat.
Located in a glass-roofed courtyard in the middle of a wonderful townhouse gallery, this is a spacious, gracious-looking French restaurant. Service can be slow, though, and prices are on the high side. **Map 9 G5**.

JAPANESE

Bincho. See p171.

dishes such as black cod with miso. Presentation is exquisite, the drinks list pricey. The branch, Nobu Berkeley, has a similar Japanese-fusion menu but is showier, with a huge ground-floor bar for blowing those bonuses.

Babies and children welcome: high chairs. Booking essential. Disabled: lift; toilet. Separate rooms for parties. **Map 9 H8**. **For branch (Nobu Berkeley) see index**.

Umu

14-16 Bruton Place, W1J 6LX (7499 8881, www.umu restaurant.com). Bond Street or Green Park tube. **Lunch served** noon-2.30pm Mon-Fri. **Dinner served** 6-11pm Mon-Sat. **Main courses** £13-£57. **Set lunch** £21-£95. **Set dinner** £65-£135. **Credit** AmEx, DC, MC, V.

At Umu the experience starts before you even get inside. There's no conventional entrance, instead you place your hand over a sensor that activates a sliding door to reveal the dark and dramatic dining room behind. After you've received a thorough welcome in Japanese, it's time to think about the menu. The Kyoto-style banqueting for which the restaurant is famous starts at £65, so this is no bargain option. Each dish is explained in detail as it arrives, by the efficient but not over-friendly staff. The aubergine in our first course had been imported from Japan, as are many of the ingredients. Deep-fried, simmered in dashi and served with smoky dashi jelly and caviar, the dish had a fine balance of flavours and textures. A whisper of garlic in the seared amberjack that followed added interest, and a red miso soup exhibited an appealing bittersweet edge. However, much of the eight-course meal lacked that wow-factor. Eel and edamame rice was unexciting, and matcha ice-cream with sweet beans made a rather heavy ending. For the slick service and artful cooking, Umu is worth a visit, but given the prices it's probably best to wait for special occasions.

Babies and children admitted. Booking advisable dinner. Dress: smart casual. Separate room for parties, seats 10-12. **Map 9 H7**.

Piccadilly

Yoshino

3 Piccadilly Place, W1J 0DB (7287 6622, www.yoshino.net). Piccadilly Circus tube. **Meals served** noon-9pm Mon-Sat. **Dishes** £2.80-£5.80. **Set meal** £5.80-£19.80 bento box. **Credit** AmEx, MC, V.

For a Japanese restaurant located off Piccadilly, Yoshino offers glimmers of value for the keen diner. The minimalistic sushi bar is a popular lunch spot for bargain hunters, who are attracted by sushi sets for around a tenner. Exquisite slices of sashimi are generous in portion, and the set meal usually comes with a hot dish (say, grilled mackerel), rice, miso soup, pickles, simmered dishes (sweet potato, cabbage) and various small salads. Chirashi sushi is unconventional in its presentation; instead of the usual cuts of fish arranged on a bowl of sushi rice, a neat assembly of sashimi is offered, with seasoned rice and salads in separate lacquered boxes. Desserts are simple but tempting: black sesame panna cotta, tofu ice-cream, or green apple sorbet, for example. Diners seeking a more formal experience can head upstairs to the pristine dining room, but for a quick bite, the ground-floor sushi bar (which also does a brisk trade in takeaways at lunch) is just fine. Staff are generally swift and polite. In all, this is a well-rounded restaurant in the heart of W1.

Babies and children admitted. Booking advisable. Takeaway service. **Map 17 A5**.

Donzoko

St James's

Matsuri

15 Bury Street, SW1Y 6AL (7839 1101, www.matsuri-restaurant.com). Green Park tube. **Lunch served** noon-2.30pm Mon-Sat; noon-3pm Sun. **Dinner served** 6-10.30pm Mon-Sat; 6-10pm Sun. **Dishes** £2.50-£10.50. **Main courses** £6.50-£55. **Set lunch** £15-£17.50 1 course, £18-£22 2 courses, £10-£30 bento box. **Set meal** £48-£160 5 courses. **Credit** AmEx, MC, V.

After a devastating fire in 2009, Matsuri's Holborn outpost remains a ghostly shell. Fans of the restaurant's teppanyaki grills should make their way to this larger St James's branch, where a dramatic basement space (filled with trinkets, such as antique kimonos) is dedicated entirely to the craft. Diners are seated at islands, around double steel grills manned by two teppanyaki chefs at peak times. The theatrics should get both adults and children squeaking with joy – a signature dessert, 'fireball' ice-cream, is produced by flambéeing a large block of vanilla ice-cream (the chefs turn down the lighting for this spectacle). The clanging of steel against steel makes for a jovial atmosphere, but we wish the extractor fans above the hotplates were more efficient; you might well emerge smelling of grease and smoke after dining here. Okonomiyaki, a Japanese street-food favourite, comes as a massive omelette full of bacon, shredded cabbage and soba noodles, topped with bonito fish flakes: fine, but not a patch on the real thing. The

set lunches are good value, especially the generous bento boxes. Sashimi is fresh and sweet too, though the table-top food certainly steals the show.
Available for hire. Babies and children welcome: high chairs. Booking advisable. Disabled: toilet. Takeaway service. **Map 17 J8**.

Saké No Hana

23 St James's Street, SW1A 1HA (7925 8988). Green Park tube. **Lunch served** noon-3pm, **dinner served** 6-11.30pm Mon-Sat. **Main courses** £4-£40. **Set meal** £45-£65. **Credit** AmEx, MC, V.

Saké No Hana – always something of a looker – has been recently remodelled, the bar swapping places with its sushi counterpart. From the dimly lit reception, ascend escalators to a first-floor dining room with huge windows and swathes of cedar wood, much of it suspended from the ceiling. Friendly staff sashay around dressed in black, looking after customers very well. The menu too has been overhauled; now raw fish is available alongside robata dishes, as well as noodles and shabu shabu. The cooking may not be as ground-breaking as originally, but there are still innovative dishes. Some of the most intriguing recipes contain little or no meat; we were blown away by the agedashidofu, which came with three coatings (bonito, seaweed and rice cracker), and deep-fried mashed taro with shiitake mushrooms and rocket. Braised aubergine was also delicious, though we were less convinced by the accompanying scraps of duck meat. Sushi can be ordered singly, and our fatty tuna and eel were faultless. We ended with a boozy sakura saké jelly with mixed berries, which arrived with a separate shot of the rice wine. Noble sakés head the drinks list, augmented by cocktails and wines, but exploration requires a fat wallet.
Available for hire. Babies and children admitted. Booking advisable. Disabled: lift; toilet. **Map 9 J8**.

Soho

Bincho

16 Old Compton Street, W1D 4TL (7287 9111, www.bincho.co.uk). Leicester Square or Tottenham Court Road tube. **Lunch served** noon-3pm, **dinner served** 5-11.30pm Mon-Fri. **Meals served** 12.30-11.30pm Sat; 1.30-10.30pm Sun. **Main courses** £1.50-£2.50. **Set lunch** £6.50-£8.50. **Set dinner** £10-£25. **Credit** AmEx, MC, V.

Booking is essential if you want to get a taste of Bincho. Its handy Soho location draws in those looking for a quick bite at the counter, and others in search of a long saké-swilling session. The venue is suited to both types of punter, and the staff are accommodating. Stylish black and red decor and solid wooden tables mix the best of modern lounge design with rustic Japanese izakayas; the place simply oozes cool. The specialities are yakitori and kushiyaki grills, cooked to smoky perfection over large banks of glowing charcoals (the restaurant's name refers to binchotan, or charcoal) and brushed with tare (a mix of soy sauce, mirin, saké and sugar) or sprinkled with sea salt. Negima (chicken and leek), sori (chicken oysters) and tsukune (juicy minced chicken rolled into balls) are perennial favourites, while small plates, such as refreshing batons of daikon sprinkled with crunchy fish roe, or sticky fried rice with chicken and mushroom, are equally enjoyable and serve to bulk out the meal. Desserts contain some fun flavours (yuzu, green tea and soya milk, for instance), the cocktails are refreshing, and the saké list is diverse and well priced.

Available for hire. Babies and children welcome: high chairs. Booking advisable. Disabled: toilet. Separate room for parties, seats 18. Tables outdoors (2, pavement). Takeaway service. **Map 17 C3**.

Donzoko

15 Kingly Street, W1B 5PS (7734 1974). Oxford Circus or Piccadilly Circus tube. **Lunch served** noon-2.30pm Mon-Fri. **Dinner served** 6-10pm Mon-Sat. **Main courses** £5-£28. **Set lunch** £6.50-£30. **Credit** AmEx, MC, V.

Many people never move beyond Donzoko's set lunches, which are inexpensive (often under £10) and of consistently high quality. The venue's consequent lunchtime popularity is no mean feat in a part of town where Japanese restaurants are common. Set-lunchers would do well to explore further, however, because there are other ways to assemble a good meal here – at little extra cost. Daily specials throw up all sorts of intriguing possibilities, as in a lunch where two specials (deep-fried sprats in spicy vinegar sauce, and boiled tuna with a sweet ginger sauce) provided the centrepiece. The tuna was cooked until it resembled braised beef in both texture and flavour. The cold sprats and their batter were softened to squidginess by an acidic marinade – disconcerting and delicious. Surrounding these were small dishes: outstanding sashimi of raw octopus and heavenly marinated mackerel, and a notable prawn tempura maki. The result: a light, exquisite lunch for £12 a head. Standard dishes such as tempura and teriyakis are reliable, and the speciality skewered dishes are also well-executed. An enormous list of sakés provides all the alcoholic stimulation you need. Service (sometimes delivered with shaky English) tries hard and can be very sweet.
Babies and children admitted. Booking advisable. Takeaway service. **Map 17 A4**.

Koya

2010 RUNNER-UP BEST NEW CHEAP EATS
49 Frith Street, W1D 4SG (7434 4463, www.koya.co.uk). Tottenham Court Road tube. **Lunch served** noon-3pm, **dinner served** 5.30-10.30pm Mon-Sat. **Main courses** £6.50-£11.50. **Credit** MC, V.

Word doesn't seem to have gotten out about this new addition to Soho's low-cost eateries. On a Monday evening, the contemporarily spartan, canteen-ish decor played host to a handful of Asian diners sitting beneath the racks of wooden plaques that double as menus, while a few western couples confusedly pulled rope-like strands of udon noodles out of bowls; these thick white wheat noodles (made with flour imported from Japan and softened water from the Thames) are Koya's speciality. The menu also offers a small selection of rice-based dishes served with miso soup. Curry and prawn tempura, despite the delicate flavour and light batter of the crustacea, was marred by a gloopy sauce overly laden with turmeric; better to stick to the udon. These are served three ways: in big bowls of hot broth, cold with a dip or (cold) pouring sauce, or cold with a bowl of hot broth for dunking. Enoki and oyster mushroom-studded broth came with a hefty portion of chilled gelatinous noodles topped with shredded seaweed and a ball of walnut paste (for adding to the broth) that was so deliciously sweet and chunky it might have been a melted bar of nut toffee. Bonus points for the impressively clued-up staff: even a non-Asian waitress spoke Japanese.
Babies and children welcome: booster seat. Bookings not accepted. Vegan dishes. **Map 17 C3**.

JAPANESE

So Japanese

3-4 Warwick Street, W1B 5LS (7292 0760, www.so restaurant.com). Piccadilly Circus tube. **Lunch served** noon-3pm Mon-Fri. **Dinner served** 5-10.30pm Mon-Thur; 5-11pm Fri. **Meals served** noon-11pm Sat. **Main courses** £12-£30. **Set lunch** £6.95-£16. **Credit** AmEx, MC, V.

Its name sounds like a proclamation of authenticity, but So Japanese is no ordinary sushi bar and restaurant. The interior is attractively done up with natural elements (a long wooden bar with tree-log details), and suggestions of Japanese fine dining (sparkling display cases of premium sakés, beautiful crockery and tableware). It's not until you look at the menu that hints of French gastronomy catch your eye; a daily meat special may feature bavette steak, while chicken teriyaki uses a 'poulet noir from Challans'. You can even get seared foie gras on rice. If you're not into French-Japanese fusion, stick to the traditional sushi and sashimi, which are well prepared and immaculately presented. The appetisers are stunning too; a scallop and daikon salad consisted of three plump, sweetly seared scallops with refreshing ribbons of daikon and a hint of yuzu mayonnaise. The inspiring drinks list has plenty of top sakés, and premium Japanese teas served in heavy teapots. *Available for hire. Babies and children admitted. Separate room for parties, seats 4. Takeaway service.* **Map 17 A5.**

West

Ealing

Sushi-Hiro `HOT 50`

1 Station Parade, Uxbridge Road, W5 3LD (8896 3175). Ealing Common tube. **Lunch served** 11am-1.30pm,

dinner served 4.30-9pm Tue-Sun. **Dishes** 60p-£3.20. **Set meal** £8-£18. **Credit** AmEx, MC, V.

Leafy Ealing may seem like an incongruous place to find one of London's best raw-fish specialists, but this sushi stalwart has stood the test of time. Despite changing hands recently, Sushi-Hiro has retained its low-key (some might say boring) looks and friendly vibe. The place is little more than a central sushi bar with a few small tables in a brightly lit shopfront dining room, but what it may lack in style it makes up for in substance. Diners peruse the menu, write their orders on the provided checklist, order a cold Japanese beer or saké, then sit back and wait for the fresh fish parade to start. Turbot and yellowtail sashimi were in pristine condition, as was nigiri of red clam and spicy-smooth chilli cod roe. A dish of pressed rice topped with lightly vinegared, tiger-skinned mackerel looked as beautiful as it tasted, and maki of shiso and squid, and a natto (fermented soy bean) roll, were equally well rendered. The sushi bar is the best place to get a view of the sushi chefs' deft skills up close; book a seat there if you can. Last orders are at 8pm, so arrive early. *Babies and children welcome: high chairs. Booking advisable Fri, Sat. Takeaway service.*

Hammersmith

Tosa

332 King Street, W6 0RR (8748 0002). Ravenscourt Park or Stamford Brook tube. **Lunch served** 12.30-2.30pm daily. **Dinner served** 6-11pm Mon-Sat; 6-10.30pm Sun. **Main courses** £6-£13. **Set lunch** £10. **Set meal** £28 3 courses. **Credit** AmEx, MC, V.

As a specialist in kushiyaki (grilled skewers), izakaya-style dishes, saké, beer, sushi and sashimi, Tosa is consistently

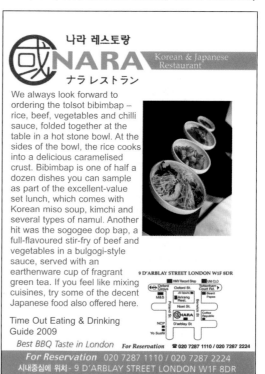

JAPANESE

Menu

Daikon: a long, white radish (aka mooli), often grated or cut into fine strips.

Dashi: the basic stock for Japanese soups and simmered dishes. It's often made from flakes of dried bonito (a type of tuna) and konbu (kelp).

Edamame: fresh soy beans boiled in their pods and sprinkled with salt.

Izakaya: 'a place where there is saké'; an after-work drinking den frequented by Japanese businessmen, usually serving a wide range of reasonably priced food.

Katsu: breaded and deep-fried meat, hence **tonkatsu** (pork katsu) and **katsu curry** (tonkatsu or chicken katsu with mild vegetable curry).

Mirin: a sweetened rice spirit used in many Japanese sauces and dressings.

Miso: a thick paste of fermented soy beans, used in miso soup and dressings. Miso comes in a wide variety of styles, ranging from 'white' to 'red', slightly sweet to very salty and earthy, crunchy or smooth.

Noodles: second only to rice as Japan's favourite staple. Served hot or cold, dry or in soup, and sometimes fried. The most common types are **ramen** (Chinese-style egg noodles), **udon** (thick white wheat-flour noodles), **soba** (buckwheat noodles), and **somen** (thin white wheat-flour noodles).

Nori: sheets of dried seaweed.

Okonomiyaki: the Japanese equivalent of filled pancakes or a Spanish omelette, whereby various ingredients are added to a batter mix and cooked on a hotplate, usually in front of diners.

Ponzu: usually short for ponzu joyu, a mixture of the juice of a Japanese citrus fruit (ponzu) and soy sauce. Used as a dip.

Saké: rice wine, around 15% alcohol. Usually served hot, but may be chilled.

Sashimi: raw sliced fish.

Shabu shabu: a pan of stock is heated at the table and plates of thinly sliced raw beef and vegetables are cooked in it piece by piece. The broth is then portioned out and drunk.

Shiso: perilla or beefsteak plant. A nettle-like leaf of the mint family that is often served with sashimi.

Shochu: Japan's colourless answer to vodka is distilled from raw materials such as wheat, rice and potatoes.

Sushi: raw fish, shellfish or vegetables with rice. There are different formats: **nigiri** (lozenge-shaped), **hosomaki** (thin-rolled), **futomaki** (thick-rolled), **temaki** (hand-rolled), **gunkan maki** (nigiri with a nori wrap), **chirashi** (scattered on top of a bowl of rice), and **uramaki** or **ISO maki** (inside-out rolls).

Tataki: meat or fish quickly seared, then marinated in vinegar, sliced thinly, and seasoned with ginger.

Tea: black tea is fermented, while green tea is heat-treated by steam to prevent the leaves fermenting. **Matcha** is powdered green tea, and has a high caffeine content. **Bancha** is the coarsest grade of green tea, which has been roasted; it contains stems and twigs as well as leaves, and is usually served free with a meal.

Tempura: fish, shellfish or vegetables dipped in a light batter and deep-fried. Served with a dip to which you add finely grated daikon (qv) and fresh ginger.

Teppanyaki: 'grilled on an iron plate. In modern Japanese restaurants, a chef standing at a hotplate (teppan) is surrounded by several diners. Slivers of beef, fish and vegetables are cooked with a dazzling display of knifework and deposited on your plate.

Teriyaki: cooking method by which meat or fish is grilled and served in a sauce made of a thick reduction of Japanese soy sauce, saké (qv), sugar and spice.

Wakame: a type of young seaweed most commonly used in miso soup and kaiso (seaweed) salad.

Yakitori: grilled chicken (breast, wings, liver, gizzard, heart) served on skewers.

Yuzu: a grapefruit-like citrus fruit.

packed with Hammersmith locals and suited Japanese businessmen. The skewers are cooked on a smoky robata grill at the front of the restaurant, where a few diners can get a front-row seat; otherwise, the small wooden tables at the back under a skylight make a cosy perch. The skewers (around two dozen, taking in poultry, pork, seafood, vegetables and offal) are keenly priced and freshly grilled to order. Ox tongue was of a nice thickness, bouncy on the teeth and lightly caramelised; chicken livers had a sweet tare glaze and a creamy texture; tebasaki (chicken wings) were crisp-skinned and juicy. A small plate of excellent salmon carpaccio soused with ponzu and garnished with micro shiso leaves was a triumph. Only own-made takoyaki (octopus dumplings) disappointed; the morsels were lukewarm, tasting as if they had been cooked far in advance and reheated. To drink, order Asahi or Kirin beer, or some reasonably priced saké, and finish with scoops of refreshing green tea and chestnut ice-cream.

Babies and children admitted. Booking advisable. Tables outdoors (3, patio). Takeaway service. **Map 20 A4.**
For branch see index.

South West
Putney

Chosan

292 Upper Richmond Road, SW15 6TH (8788 9626). East Putney tube or Putney rail. **Lunch served** noon-2.30pm daily. **Dinner served** 6.30-10.30pm Mon-Sat; 6.30-10pm Sun. **Main courses** £3.30-£20. **Set lunch** £7.90-£13.90. **Set dinner** £18.90-£20.90; £19.90-£24.90 bento box. **Credit** MC, V.

Lucky Putney: this genuine mom-and-pop eaterie is a wonderful place to have in the neighbourhood. The room is small yet cosy, seating perhaps only two dozen diners at a time. Knick-knacks give the space character, be they framed photographs of Mount Fuji or an assortment of empty saké bottles on the wall. Chosan is the opposite of London's buttoned-up, fine dining Japanese establishments: sounds of cooking emanate from beyond a curtained doorway; the sushi chef chats happily to his audience; and the food conjures up

memories of Japanese homes. Donburis (rice bowls) topped with softly cooked egg and crisp pork cutlets, or with glossy, meaty, grilled eel, are done well and show care in their preparation. The sushi counter is stacked high with wooden boats, on which are presented thick slices of fresh sashimi (check the wooden tablets above the bar for the day's specials). You won't get much sophistication here, but, more importantly, you will get an enjoyable and modestly priced meal.
Babies and children admitted. Separate room for parties, seats 30. Takeaway service.

South

Clapham

Tsunami
5-7 Voltaire Road, SW4 6DQ (7978 1610, www.tsunami restaurant.co.uk). Clapham North tube. **Lunch served** 12.30-4pm Sat, Sun. **Dinner served** 6-10.30pm Mon-Thur; 6-11pm Fri; 5.30-11pm Sat; 6-9.30pm Sun. **Main courses** £7.70-£19.50. **Set lunch** (Sat, Sun) £10.50. **Credit** MC, V.
This cool Clapham institution might be a prime place to see and be seen, but local families (prams and all) have also claimed it as their own. So expect to see dressed-up trendies nibbling on edamame, but also children being spoon-fed creamy nasu goma (aubergine grilled with sesame paste). The hip, dimly lit interior is enhanced by the elegantly presented dishes, from a menu that gathers culinary influences from across the globe; orthodox, Tsunami is not. Still, we wish the chefs would think more carefully about dishes such as scallops with masago (a highly prized fish roe), which was overwhelmed by a heavy, whisky-flambéed sauce. Over the years we've learnt to stick to the sushi and sashimi, which are generally faultless, or to order dishes that are restrained in their flavour combinations. An oyster shooter that comprises classic ingredients – saké, ponzu, quail's egg and chilli-flecked grated daikon (momiji oroshi) – went down a treat, and we like the sound of steamed razor clams with fresh coriander, chilli, chives and vermicelli noodles. The slick, glowing bar offers oriental-inspired cocktails.
Babies and children welcome: high chairs. Booking advisable; essential weekends. Takeaway service.
Map 22 B1.

North

Crouch End

Wow Simply Japanese
18 Crouch End Hill, N8 8AA (8340 4539). Finsbury Park tube/rail then W3, W7 bus, or Crouch Hill rail. **Lunch served** noon-2.30pm Wed-Sat. **Dinner served** 6-10.30pm Mon-Sat; 6-10pm Sun. **Main courses** £7.80-£35. **Set lunch** £5.90-£8.90. **Credit** MC, V.
Located in hip Crouch End, Wow has the kind of appearance and atmosphere you would expect from a trendy Japanese eaterie. The design is clean and the service unhurried and efficient, but the food is inconsistent. As well as the standard offering of sushi, tempura and other Japanese classics, there are more innovative dishes such as poppy-seed crusted tuna sashimi and an interesting list of daily specials. The sea bass maki tempura with balsamic teriyaki sauce, chosen from the

specials board, was surprisingly good; the attractively presented spiral of fish was infused with aromatic shiso and encased in light, crisp tempura batter. Nasu dengaku (grilled aubergine with sweet miso sauce) from the standard menu was well cooked and creamy, although the miso topping could have done with some time under the grill. From the three dessert options (fruit, ice-cream and banana tempura), the green tea ice-cream had a disappointingly crystalline texture and not enough flavour. All in all, Wow doesn't live up to its name, but can provide a passable meal at a reasonable price.
Babies and children welcome: high chairs. Booking advisable. Takeaway service.

Islington

Sa Sa Sushi
422 St John Street, EC1V 4NJ (7837 1155, www.sasa sushi.co.uk). Angel tube. **Lunch served** noon-2.30pm Mon-Sat. **Dinner served** 5.30-10pm Mon-Thur; 5.30-11pm Fri, Sat. **Main courses** £3.50-£18. **Sushi** £1.20-£2.50. **Set dinner** £22.50-£30.50. **Credit** AmEx, MC, V.
Located in a slightly dingy row of shops just past Angel tube station, Sa Sa Sushi is more appealing on the inside than out. The cool, cream interior and friendly service create a relaxed and accessible atmosphere. Customers include families with kids who are cooed over by the staff. Yet while the service is attentive, from cheery welcomes to constant tea top-ups, the food can be hit or miss. Mixed sashimi salad contained a pleasing selection of fresh-tasting fish with an earthy sesame dressing; thin slivers of pink-edged radish and shredded carrot enhanced the dish's appearance. Scallop butter-yaki, on the other hand, was a disaster. The puddle of strong, salty brown sauce in which the shellfish swam added nothing to their overcooked flesh. A tuna maki was also of mixed quality. The fish had a lovely, silky texture and plenty of flavour, but the roll was bursting at the seams with its contents spilling out. Judging by previous visits, and the high quality of the fish that the kitchen uses, this was not Sa Sa Sushi at its best.
Babies and children welcome: high chairs. Booking advisable. Disabled: toilet. Takeaway service; delivery service (over £15 within 2-mile radius). **Map 5 N3.**

North West

Golders Green

Café Japan
626 Finchley Road, NW11 7RR (8455 6854, www.cafe japan.co.uk). Golders Green tube or 13, 82 bus. **Lunch served** noon-2pm Wed-Sun. **Dinner served** 6-10pm Wed-Sat; 6-9.30pm Sun. **Main courses** £8-£9. **Set lunch** £8.50. **Set dinner** £12-£17. **Credit** MC, V.
Café Japan has been around for the best part of two decades. Even now, its sushi chefs have their work cut out for them most nights – as well as preparing sushi and sashimi for a packed house, they often have to deal with a steady stream of punters wanting a takeaway. You might experience a brief delay in getting food when this happens, but the waiting staff do the best they can, and each dish is served with a smile. A tiny salamander broiler in the open sushi bar/kitchen is used to cook deliciously caramelised unagi (eel). Popular orders include grilled yellowtail collar, the meat rich and oily; also outstanding is butterfish sashimi, the flesh creamy and sweet. If you're after

Koya. See p171.

sushi, but can't decide which dish, order omakase (chef's choice). Eating here is not a relaxing experience, as space is limited and Café Japan's popularity means there's a quick turnover of tables. No wonder so many customers prefer to take their food home to enjoy at their own pace.
Babies and children admitted. Booking advisable. Takeaway service.

Hampstead

Jin Kichi
73 Heath Street, NW3 6UG (7794 6158, www.jinkichi. com). Hampstead tube. **Lunch served** 12.30-2pm Sat, Sun. **Dinner served** 6-11pm Tue-Sat; 6-10pm Sun. **Main courses** £4.90-£14.80. **Set lunch** £8.80-£15.90. **Credit** AmEx, MC, V.
This skewer specialist looks and feels slightly out of kilter with the genteel Hampstead street on which it resides. Inside, tables are tightly packed and the din from raucous diners eating and drinking can be disorienting – you could be in a local izakaya in Japan. The smell of the charcoal grill is intoxicating: a sticky, smoky scent indicative of heat, meat and tare (the soy sauce, mirin, saké and sugar mixture used to baste most cooked skewers). The chefs focus on the grill, and you'll do well to order accordingly; the sushi and sashimi on our visits have been fine, but nothing to keep us returning. The menu lists more than a dozen varieties of skewers, encompassing chicken parts, vegetables, pork, duck and offal. Dine like the regulars and order chilled Japanese beer (Asahi Super Dry, Sapporo, Kirin) to go with the food. There's saké too, but most of the better varieties are only sold by the (expensive) bottle.
Babies and children welcome: high chairs. Booking advisable. Takeaway service. **Map 28 B2**.

Willesden

Sushi-Say
33B Walm Lane, NW2 5SH (8459 2971). Willesden Green tube. **Lunch served** noon-3.30pm Sat, Sun. **Dinner served** 6.30-10pm Wed-Fri; 6.30-10.30pm Sat; 6-9.30pm Sun. **Main courses** £7.20-£24.60. **Set dinner** £23.50-£39.50. **Credit** MC, V.
Despite its unassuming exterior and the location on a slightly dingy high street, Sushi-Say is a real gem. This explains why you might find it difficult to get a table here. Even during the week it's worth booking ahead (leave a message as staff won't necessarily answer the phone). In the cream-coloured dining room, bustling with well-to-do north-west Londoners, there are various seating options, from stools at the sushi counter to small tables, and even a traditional tatami room at the back. The lengthy menu is filled with a solid selection of classics, contemporary dishes and set meals, which the attentive staff are happy to explain. A reasonably priced six-course sashimi set contained the fattest slices of raw fish we've ever encountered; they were undoubtedly of a high quality, but slightly overwhelming. Oysters from the specials menu were equally large, with a silky texture, pleasant iodine kick and a well-balanced vinegar sauce as accompaniment. Every dish we tried was well executed; particularly memorable were the garlic chives in miso sauce, and a dessert of sweet, fragrant chunks of sharon fruit.
Babies and children welcome: high chairs. Booking advisable. Separate room for parties, seats 8. Takeaway service. Vegetarian menu.

Jewish

There are two main strands to Jewish cookery, but it's getting increasingly difficult to find one of them in London restaurants. Ashkenazi cuisine has its roots in eastern Europe, so dishes such as dumplings, pickled vegetables and borscht are part of the repertoire. Bloom's was the capital's most renowned exponent of this style of food, but in June 2010 this famous old business, which opened its first restaurant in Whitechapel in 1920, went into liquidation. The other strand to the cuisine, Sephardi cookery, hails from the Mediterranean region and is exemplified by the menus at **Dizengoff** and **Solly's**. Meze-style dishes such as falafel, houmous and tabouleh often feature. Perhaps the capital's most stylish Jewish restaurant is **Bevis Marks**, which has tried to update aspects of the cuisine; here you can have chopped liver with orange marmalade compote, or duck confit with puy lentils and balsamic reduction.

All the restaurants included in this chapter are kosher – that is, they adhere to the strict laws of kashrut. However, some do not serve 'Jewish' food, as such. **Novellino**, for instance, is an Italian trattoria, while **La Fiesta** serves kosher London's best Argentinian steaks.

Central

City

Bevis Marks Restaurant

4 Heneage Lane, EC3A 5DQ (7283 2220, www.bevismarks therestaurant.com). Aldgate tube or Liverpool Street tube/ rail. **Lunch served** noon-2.15pm Mon-Fri. **Dinner served** 5.30-8.30pm Mon-Thur. **Main courses** £14.95-£23.95. **Credit** AmEx, MC, V.

Still the most stylish of London's kosher venues, Bevis Marks is where to go for elegant service and upmarket cooking. Prices are expectedly high (especially for the wines). As you sit at the linen-covered tables on dark wood chairs, you can see into the adjacent 18th-century synagogue with its impressive brass chandeliers. The menu is a fusion of Jewish and Modern European food. Alongside chicken soup, there's chopped liver with orange compote, and Thai-style salt beef with sweet chilli sauce. Main courses include halibut with tomato and caper salsa, a vegetarian pasta dish, and confit duck with puy lentils and balsamic reduction. The ribeye steak with chunky chips is always popular, but we felt that the not-so-moist chargrilled chicken breast on a bed of couscous needed a sauce. A starter of spring vegetable salad could have been more varied and generous. Such lapses are only occasional, but disappointing. Shepherd's pie with fresh peas had a rich, savoury filling and smooth potato topping, but we're not sure it merited a price of £19. Desserts, especially well-flavoured parev ices, are a strong point. Surprisingly, the fruit salad, though pleasantly rose-scented, was lacklustre. Better to end with melt-in-the-mouth apple and blackberry crumble or a chocolate brownie. *Available for hire. Babies and children admitted. Booking advisable lunch. Disabled: toilet. Kosher supervised (Shephardi). Tables outdoors (3, courtyard). Takeaway service; delivery service (over £10).* **Map 12 R6**.

North

Finchley

Olive Restaurant

224 Regent's Park Road, N3 3HP (8343 3188, www.olive kosherrestaurant.co.uk). Finchley Central tube. **Meals served** noon-11pm Mon-Thur, Sun. **Main courses** £10-£18. **Set lunch** (noon-3pm daily) £10.95 3 courses. **Set meal** £18.95-£22.95 3 courses. **Credit** AmEx, MC, V.

A welcome bowl of signature olives arrived while we were looking at the wall hangings and calligraphy that decorate what the menu proudly proclaims is 'Europe's first kosher Persian restaurant'. Olive's £18.95 set meal includes starters of sesame-crusted chicken wings, houmous and shirazi salad (finely chopped cucumber, onion, parsley and tomato, with an olive oil and lime dressing). Mirza ghasemi (an aubergine, garlic, egg and tomato dip) had a good texture and was mildly spiced and seasoned, while falafel came in five generous sized balls flavoured with black mustard seeds: crisp outside, light within. We added noon taftoon flatbread, freshly baked in a clay oven and studded with sesame seeds. To follow, ghaime was very tender stewed lamb in a sun-dried lime and saffron sauce, served with split peas and a generous mountain of rice. Koobideh (fragrant spiced chopped lamb grilled on the skewer), also came with plenty of rice and salad. Service is willing and swift; the staff provided mint leaf tea to make up for the disappointing lack of baklava. You might not be eating haute cuisine at this restaurant, but you will find authentic cooking served in clean and calm surroundings.
Available for hire. Babies and children welcome: children's menu; high chairs. Booking advisable. Disabled: toilet. Kosher supervised (Beth Din). Tables outdoors (3, pavement). Takeaway service.

North West

Golders Green

Dizengoff
118 Golders Green Road, NW11 8HB (8458 7003). Golders Green tube. **Meals served** 11am-midnight Mon-Thur, Sun; 11am-1hr before sabbath Fri; 1hr after sabbath-midnight Sat. **Main courses** £12-£18. **Set lunch** £12.95. **Credit** AmEx, MC, V.
The experienced owner of this Israeli establishment has wisely decided to start offering a sensibly priced lunch menu. Business in this part of Golders Green has been on the decline, and even the set meal hasn't created a lunchtime rush. With few other customers to watch, you might contemplate the views of Tel Aviv on the wall (showing Dizengoff Street as its hub). The main menu includes juicy grills – the lamb is usually tender and flavourful – and fried kibbe (a crisp bulgur shell with savoury meat filling). Rice is Iraqi-style and perfectly cooked. The set lunch offers a few starters including soup. Minestrone was hot and flavourful, and the chicken soup also gained praise. From the spit comes lamb shwarma – a good-sized portion served with fluffy rice and a small salad of rocket, grated carrot and beetroot. Chicken schnitzel was less generous, but tender, with thin chips that could have been crisper. Pleasant staff bring coffee, lemon or mint tea, but it's worth asking them to add a syrupy pastry for afters. Linen tablecloths instead of paper coverings would improve the experience here, but then, times are hard.
Babies and children welcome: children's menu; high chairs. Booking essential weekends. Kosher supervised (Shephardi). Tables outdoors (3, pavement). Takeaway service.

La Fiesta
235 Golders Green Road, NW11 9ES (8458 0444). Brent Cross tube. **Meals served** noon-11pm Mon-Thur, Sun. **Main courses** £8.75-£26.50. **Set lunch** £15.50 3 courses. **Credit** MC, V.

A passer-by would miss this Argentinian steakhouse, hidden as it is behind a standard café. Head for the back, though, and you'll find rustic tables and pictures of gauchos on the walls. The lighting is low, verging on gloomy, but the arrival of complimentary olives, bread and chimichurri sauce brightens the spirits. The menu is for carnivores – with only two fish choices and little for vegetarians – but the meat, grilled over hot coals, is kosher London's best. A starter of empanadas or tomato or roasted pepper soup is tempting, though remember that the sizzling meat is preceded by a large mixed-leaf salad. A small brazier arrives piled high with thick, juicy cuts: half a grilled chicken, brochettes of beef cubes with chorizo, or asado ribs (tougher and marbled with fat). Lamb cutlets are succulent, the entrecôte steaks charred and perfectly cooked inside (order a large one and share, if you like your steak thick and rare).

Olive Restaurant

Chunky chips are crisper than the garlicky sautéed potatoes. Our vegetable brochette was disappointing, with flavourless peppers and onion cooked too fast for tenderness. Desserts, including Argentinian crêpe, are adorned with faux-cream; luckily, you'll probably be too full to be tempted.
Babies and children welcome: children's menu; high chairs. Booking advisable. Kosher supervised (Beth Din). Takeaway service.

Novellino

103 Golders Green Road, NW11 8EN (8458 7273).
Golders Green tube. **Meals served** 8.30am-11.30pm Mon-Thur, Sun; 8.30am-4pm Fri. **Main courses** £9-£18. **Credit** AmEx, MC, V.
Locals flock to this trattoria-style café for its wide choice of fish and dairy dishes. Italian starter specialities include bruschetta, risotto and gnocchi, but, surprisingly, there's also sushi and spring rolls. Aubergine parmigiana was rich and tomatoey, with a fairly thin sauce. Another starter, tuna carpaccio, needed more of its accompanying balsamic reduction. Two fish main courses – grilled salmon and Moroccan sea bass fillet – were both succulent, served with sautéed potatoes and little mushroom pastries. Vegetarians get a wide choice of imaginative and appetising dishes, including fresh soups (bread costs extra), savoury tarts, and watermelon and feta salad. Pasta too comes in many guises. Desserts are well worth exploring; aside from the scrumptious-looking pâtisserie in the cabinet, there's tiramisu, pear tart, passionfruit mousse and 'plenitud' (something deeply chocolatey). Prices are high, though you can expect competent cooking and pleasant service. Novellino could do with redecoration, but this doesn't seem to matter to diners choosing it for lunchtime meetings or those opting for a leisurely evening meal.
Babies and children welcome: children's menu; high chairs. Booking advisable. Disabled: toilet. Kosher supervised (Beth Din). Tables outdoors (5, pavement). Takeaway service.

Solly's

146-150 Golders Green Road, NW11 8HE (8455 2121).
Golders Green tube. **Lunch served** 11.30am-5pm Fri. **Meals served** 11.30am-11pm Mon-Thur, Sun. *Winter* 1hr after sabbath-1am Sat. **Main courses** £10-£16. **Set dinner** £28 3 courses. **No credit cards**.
Standards at one of London's best kosher restaurants seem to be slipping. The takeaway option is tasty as ever, with light, crispy falafel, succulent chicken and lamb shwarma, fresh, herby tabouleh, and aubergine deliciously sautéed in olive oil. But once you sit down, prices shoot up (it's cash only too). The appetiser selection is extensive; unable to decide, we went for the hot and cold starter plates. Although poorly presented, the cigars, spicy sausage, falafel and chicken wings were mouth-watering, complemented by tahini and thick garlic sauce. The cold selection consisted of very small portions of dishes similar to those served with the takeaway meat. Although it's hard to go wrong with kebabs, chips and salad, the lamb wasn't as juicy as we recalled, the salad was mostly cabbage, and the chips didn't taste like own-made. An enormous steak – almost enough for two – came perfectly cooked, medium-rare and pink as we'd ordered, and Iraqi rice with vermicelli is always a treat. The laffa and pitta breads straight from the oven were memorable too. Among the enticing desserts, baklava is always a winner, or you could just enjoy fresh mint tea.
Babies and children welcome: high chairs. Disabled: toilet. Kosher supervised (Beth Din). Takeaway service.

Adam's

Hendon

Adam's

2 Sentinel Square, NW4 2EL (8202 2327). Hendon Central tube. **Meals served** noon-midnight Mon-Thur, Sun. **Lunch served** *Summer* noon-5pm Fri. **Dinner served** *Winter* 10pm-2am Sat. **Main courses** £3.50-£14. **Credit** MC, V.

You have to know it's there if you're going to find it. Tucked away behind Brent Street, Hendon's mini-Israel, is Adam's, a great little café and takeaway. A few tables have been placed outside and there's more space within to enjoy a quick meal or wait to collect food for Shabbat. At lunchtime, try the good-value shwarma: you're offered a choice between chicken, or lamb and turkey. Both are savoury and tasty, not over-spiced and come served in a generous portion with a side order of rice or chips. The chips weren't quite crisp enough, though we were pleased to have a choice of a dozen salads to fill our plates. The best of these are the oily aubergine or spicy salsa, but there's crunchy red or white cabbage, own-made pickles and refreshing Israeli salad too. Hot sandwiches are available dished up in baguettes, pitta or the larger puffy laffa. More substantial meat options include lamb chops, ribeye and beef kebabs. If you're entertaining a crowd over Shabbat, order from the selection of specialities: Iraqi tabeet (slow-cooked stuffed chicken), kibbe in beetroot sauce, or the Moroccan stuffed artichokes with couscous. Adam's can even rustle up the spicy Libyan salmon dish of chraime. A great range of flavours in a small, unpretentious venue.

Available for hire. Babies and children welcome: children's menu; high chairs. Disabled: toilet. Kosher supervised (Beth Din). Tables outdoors (6, pavement). Takeaway service. Vegetarian menu.

Eighty-Six Bistro Bar

86 Brent Street, NW4 2ES (8202 5575). Hendon Central tube. **Lunch served** noon-3pm Sun. **Dinner served** 5.30-11pm Mon-Thur, Sun. **Main courses** £12.95-£26. **Credit** MC, V.

At Sunday lunchtime, the long benches of Eighty-Six Bistro Bar were deserted and its staff seemed unprepared, with many menu items 'not ready yet'. By the evening, however, the place was absolutely bustling. Wall posters provide a hint of French atmosphere, but the prices are a notch higher than the bistro norm. In recompense, starter portions are often large enough for a main course, and the menu lists the likes of foie gras and goose burgers (whether these are available is another question). Chicken liver pâté was a smooth-textured circle of intense flavour, garnished with mixed leaves and a slick of caramel sauce. Hot baked aubergine with tahina was provided in a generous serving, but tasted rather more bland than when it's given the Mediterranean treatment with garlic and tomato. Our main courses were also hit and miss. Grills (lamb or steak) looked appetising, and 'rose roast beef' (intended as a starter) was generous. Expecting pink beef, we were surprised to get a thin, dark steak – it's a shame staff didn't ask how we wanted it cooked. The accompanying grilled peppers and courgette were tasty. Roast duck and plum sauce was disappointing (dry and tasting as if pre-cooked), but a bowl of freshly fried chips was overflowing. Come here with a full wallet, but don't expect the full bistro experience.

Babies and children welcome: high chairs. Booking advisable. Kosher supervised (Federation). Takeaway service.

Menu

Baklava: filo pastry layered with almonds or pistachios and soaked in scented syrup.

Borekas: triangles of filo pastry with savoury fillings like cheese or spinach.

Borscht: a classic beetroot soup served either hot or cold, often with sour cream.

Challah or **cholla**: egg-rich, slightly sweet plaited bread for the Sabbath.

Chicken soup: a clear, golden broth made from chicken and vegetables.

Cholent: a hearty, long-simmered bean, vegetable and (sometimes) meat stew, traditionally served for the sabbath.

Chopped liver: chicken or calf's liver fried with onions, finely chopped and mixed with hard-boiled egg and chicken fat. Served cold, often with extra egg and onions.

Chrane or **chrain**: a pungent sauce made from grated horseradish and beetroot, served with cold fish.

Cigars: rolls of filo pastry with a sweet or savoury filling.

Falafel: spicy, deep-fried balls of ground chickpeas, served with houmous and tahina (sesame paste).

Gefilte fish: white fish minced with onions, made into balls and poached or fried; served cold. The sweetened version is Polish.

Kataifi or **konafa**: shredded filo pastry wrapped around a nut or cheese filling, soaked in syrup.

Kibbe, **kuba**, **kooba**, **kubbeh** or **kobeiba**: oval patties, handmade from a shell of crushed wheat (bulgar) filled with minced meat, pine nuts and spices. Shaping and filling the shells before frying is the skill.

Knaidlach or **kneidlach**: dumplings made from matzo (qv) meal and eggs, poached until they float 'like clouds' in chicken soup.

Kreplach: pockets of noodle dough filled with meat and served in soup, or with sweet fillings and eaten with sour cream.

Laffa: large puffy pitta bread used to enclose falafel or shwarma (qv).

Latkes: grated potato mixed with egg and fried into crisp pancakes.

Lockshen: egg noodles boiled and served in soup. When cold, they can be mixed with egg, sugar and cinnamon and baked into a pudding.

Matzo or **matzah**: flat squares of unleavened bread. When ground into meal, it is used to make a crisp coating for fish or schnitzel.

Parev or **parve**: a term describing food that is neither meat nor dairy.

Rugelach: crescent-shaped biscuits made from a rich, cream cheese pastry, filled with nuts, jam or chocolate. Popular in Israel and the US.

Shwarma: layers of lamb or turkey, cooked on a spit, served with pitta.

Worsht: beef salami, sliced thinly to eat raw, but usually cut in thick pieces and fried when served with eggs or chips.

JEWISH

Korean

Korean cooking has much in common with Japanese, but enthusiastically adds a healthy and fiery dose of chilli to the equation via seasoning sauces such as gochujang, and the national pickle kimchi (fermented cabbage with chilli). In addition, as seen at many of the restaurants in this chapter, Koreans put the barbecue not so much centre stage as centre of the table. Even smart, sophisticated eateries such as **Ran** and **Asadal** feature tabletop barbecues, on which staff gracefully and intuitively cook your chosen meat, poultry, seafood and vegetables in front of you, ready to wrap in soft, buttery lettuce leaves and dip in tangy concoctions. Why isn't this gloriously punchy and nutritious cuisine better known? The signs are that it's getting there, slowly. The Korean restaurant heartlands may be in the West End and New Malden, but the esteemed **Cah Chi** now has a branch in Earlsfield, **Dotori** has been a hit in Finsbury Park, and reliable **Kimchee** is still thrilling locals in Golders Green.

Central

Chinatown

Corean Chilli
*51 Charing Cross Road, WC2H 0NE (7734 6737).
Leicester Square tube.* **Meals served** noon-midnight daily. **Main courses** £6.50-£15. **Set lunch** £5-£6. **Credit** (over £15) MC, V.
There's a plentiful supply of inexpensive yet decent Korean caffs in London, and Chinatown's Corean Chilli has become a popular option for students. Don't expect much from the all-encompassing menu, which places emphasis on filling noodles and rice dishes rather than refined cuisine. You'll find the likes of cheap ramen topped with egg, vegetables or seafood, but also the standard bibimbaps, chigaes and large casseroles. The simple, blocky furniture makes it evident that this is not a place for lingering. Barbecues are also a cut-price version: cooked on portable gas burners rather than on sizzling hotplates set into the table. Kimchi fried rice (part of a lunch deal) came with a fried egg, the creamy yolk offsetting the sharpness of the fermented cabbage (which was a bit too sour for our liking). Fried mandu (dumplings) were deep-fried rather than pan-fried, yet were agreeably grease-free; the accompanying dip was ordinary soy sauce, not the traditional vinegar-tinged version. Soothing yet tangy plum tea is a reliable choice for sharpening the appetite. Corean Chilli may not be a particularly noteworthy destination, but the food is filling and the service commendably warm for a wallet-friendly pitstop.
Babies and children welcome: high chairs. Booking advisable dinner Fri, Sat. Separate room for parties, seats 15. **Map 17 C4.**

Covent Garden

Naru
230 Shaftesbury Avenue, WC2H 8EG (7379 7962, www.narurestaurant.com). Tottenham Court Road tube. **Lunch served** noon-3pm, **dinner served** 5.30-11pm Mon-Sat. **Main courses** £8-£13. **Credit** MC, V.
Unusually, there are no barbecue grills set into the tables at this relative newcomer at the east end of Shaftesbury Avenue – instead, everything is cooked in the kitchen rather than on the tabletop. Dishes are designed to impress; you'll find a refinement in the presentation of each plate that is emphasised by delicate garnishes and beautiful crockery. The room is well thought out too. Rice paper lanterns and Korean calligraphy adorn the walls, while warm wooden furniture accents a homely atmosphere. A traditional tolsot bibimbap arrived as a colourful array of mixed vegetables and glossy egg yolk, with fish roe that burst in the mouth. As with most Korean restaurants, Naru's stews are a strong point. More atypically, there are desserts on the menu, but these do need a little extra

work. A 'well being tiramisu' arrived as a curious tower of crushed red beans, green tea ice-cream and carrot – healthy, yes, but not the most appealing of puddings. The care and good intentions put into the food is reflected in the service. Drinks are limited to the usual array of wines and Korean beers. *Available for hire. Babies and children admitted. Booking advisable Thur, Fri. Tables outdoors (2, pavement). Takeaway service.* **Map 18 D2**.

Fitzrovia

Koba

11 Rathbone Street, W1T 1NA (7580 8825, www.koba-london.com). Goodge Street or Tottenham Court Road tube. **Lunch served** noon-3pm Mon-Sat. **Dinner served** 6-11pm daily. **Main courses** £5.90-£9.50. **Set lunch** £5.90-£11. **Set meal** £25-£35. **Credit** AmEx, MC, V.
Dining at Koba is rarely a disappointment. There's a confidence about the operation, from the sleekness of the design (lots of dark wood and streamlined barbecue extractor fans) to the helpful staff and flawless food. The soondoobu chigae here is surely among London's best – a bubbling cauldron of fiery, deeply flavoured seafood stew textured with soft curdled tofu and a poached egg. Once, we had a dud version that tasted bland and thin, but it was promptly replaced with the real deal and a plate of complimentary cucumber pickles offered as an apology. Yuk hwe (beef tartare) was stellar too, the sweetly flavoured raw beef melding expertly with crunchy, juicy pear slivers. The bigger jeongols (casseroles) are great for sharing, and are usually chock-full of vegetables, marinated meats and slithery noodles. Koba offers some of London's highest quality Korean cooking, at prices that rival lesser set-ups. The lunchtime deals (starting at around £6) are extremely good value and offer an insight into the skills of the kitchen at a fraction of the cost of dinner.
Babies and children welcome: high chairs. Booking advisable. Disabled: toilet. Takeaway service. **Map 17 B1**.

Holborn

Asadal

227 High Holborn, WC1V 7DA (7430 9006, www.asadal. co.uk). Holborn tube. **Lunch served** noon-3pm Mon-Sat. **Dinner served** 6-11pm Mon-Sat; 6-10.30pm Sun. **Main courses** £6-£20. **Set lunch** £8.50-£15.80. **Set dinner** £17.50-£30. **Credit** AmEx, MC, V.
Originally established in the 'Little Korea' of New Malden, Asadal is one of the cuisine's few family-run restaurants to have moved successfully to central London. Its den-like basement room below the entrance to Holborn tube station is a surprisingly elegant space. The dining area is partitioned by screens and fake hedges for privacy; subtle design touches come in the form of dim lighting, smooth wood and ornamental masks. Such attention to detail is extended to the food, which showcases the finer side of Korean cuisine. The extensive menu is annotated with educational dish descriptions and images. Barbecued meats (around 15 choices) are cooked with care and confidence at the table, but fresh lettuce and soy bean paste for wrapping the hot morsels cost extra. There's a limited selection of wines by the glass, so stick to Korean beer (Hite). Asadal is one of the pricier West End Korean restaurants, but the surroundings and excellently prepared food often more than make up for the cost. The lunchtime set meals offer greater choice than usual, and are a smart way to sample the food.

Cah Chi. See p183.

Babies and children welcome: high chairs. Booking advisable. Disabled: toilet. Separate rooms for parties, seating 6 and 12. Takeaway service. **Map 18 E2**.

Leicester Square

Jindalle

6 Panton Street, SW1Y 4DL (7930 8881). Piccadilly Circus tube. **Meals served** noon-11pm daily. **Main courses** £7.90-£17.90. **Set lunch** £4.95-£7.95. **Set dinner** (5-9pm) £8.90. **Credit** AmEx, MC, V.

Leicester Square is a minefield when it comes to finding somewhere to eat. Even the less-trodden path of Panton Street (the quieter road from the southern corner of the square) is riddled with mediocre eateries, which makes Jindalle a welcome sight, and a good pre-theatre option. The room is long and spacious, with the tables set comfortably apart and the obligatory barbecue extractor fans hovering above – which helps alleviate the rather plain brick-and-wood decor. Service can be slightly haphazard (on one occasion we were moved from table to table three times), but once you're settled down with the menu, the fun begins. The list contains one of the most exhaustive selections of Korean barbecued meats (beef, pork, chicken), seafood and vegetables in London – and these are what to choose. To accompany your barbecue, order plenty of Korean beers or soju: the best foils for the heat and grease. Ox tongue with lemon juice was a textural delight, appropriately served with a traditional dip of sesame oil, salt and pepper. Less successful was the bibimbap; it was on the bland side and not hot enough to produce those irresistible crunchy layers of toasted rice at the bottom of the bowl.

Babies and children welcome: high chairs. Booking advisable. **Map 17 C5**.

Mayfair

Kaya

42 Albemarle Street, W1S 4JH (7499 0622, www.kaya restaurant.co.uk). Green Park tube. **Lunch served** noon-3pm, **dinner served** 6-11pm Mon-Sat. **Main courses** £9-£20. **Set lunch** £10-£15. **Credit** AmEx, MC, V.

For the best part of three decades, Kaya has been serving Korean food of regal refinement – appropriate enough, given the restaurant's name refers to an ancient southern Korean kingdom that was known for its exquisite craftsmanship. Diners here leave all thoughts of loud, boisterous barbecue restaurants and slapdash presentation at the (sliding screen) door; they come to enjoy the finer side of this complex cuisine. The experience is polished from start to finish. Waitresses glide gracefully through the restaurant wearing traditional dress (hanbok). Nature-inspired wood and stone furnishings also complement the rarefied atmosphere. The menu embraces classical techniques and high-quality ingredients, and is best expressed through the 'royal dinner' set meal. This eight-course feast includes starters such as naengchae (jelly fish and seafood in mustard sauce), traditional dishes such as kalbi and gu shul pan (a selection of nine appetisers served in a lacquered box), before ending with gwail (fresh fruits) and sikhye (fermented rice punch). Candles and classical music add to the tranquil dining experience. The prices at Kaya are high, but the whole package is well worth the expense.

Babies and children admitted. Booking advisable. Disabled: toilet. Separate rooms for parties, seating 8 and 12. **Map 9 J7**.

Soho

Jin

16 Bateman Street, W1D 3AH (7734 0908). Leicester Square or Tottenham Court Road tube. **Lunch served** noon-3pm, **dinner served** 6-10.30pm Mon-Fri. **Meals served** noon-10.30pm Sat. **Main courses** £8-£15. **Set lunch** £6.50-£10. **Set dinner** £35-£40. **Credit** AmEx, MC, V.

Jin's decor feels slightly dated these days, with an impression of faux opulence given by shades of dark purple, sleek granite tabletops and smart-shirted waiters and waitresses. Most of the clientele – a mix of trendy young Korean professionals and older western patrons drawn in by the smart, inoffensive interiors – ordered the barbecue and appeared to relish it, but we enjoyed sticky stir-fried rice cakes and seafood in a surprisingly fiery chilli sauce. Haemultang (seafood broth) was large but generally weak in flavour: surprising considering the amount of seafood within. It's worth considering the Chinese-Korean specialities too: jajang myun (pork and noodles in black bean sauce) or sweet-and-sour tansuyuk (pork with orange and pineapple pieces). Fresh pear juice is a cooling foil to the chilli-spiked stews and savoury grills, though there's also a good beer and wine list. Staff are welcoming and attentive to diners' needs; we were pleased to overhear a waitress (as she prepared the sizzling barbecue at the neighbouring table) advise that the beef was ready to be eaten if they preferred it medium-rare.

Babies and children admitted. Booking advisable weekends. Separate room for parties, seats 10. Takeaway service. **Map 17 C3**.

Myung Ga

1 Kingly Street, W1B 5PA (7734 8220, www.myungga. co.uk). Oxford Circus or Piccadilly Circus tube. **Lunch served** noon-3pm Mon-Sat. **Dinner served** 5.30-10.30pm Mon-Sat; 4.30-10.30pm Sun. **Main courses** £7.50-£8.90. **Set lunch** £11-£13.50. **Set dinner** £25-£45. **Credit** AmEx, MC, V.

Myung Ga feels like it has been here forever. The exterior looks slightly worn and doesn't give much scope for peeking inside, but reject any initial prejudices and you'll be rewarded with warm service and enjoyable Korean cooking. The dining room is often full of Korean and Japanese customers, both regulars and visitors (this is one of those places that gets mentioned in plenty of foreign guidebooks). The restaurant also boasts a roster of celebrity visitors on its website; everyone has been here, from Hong Kong actress Maggie Cheung to Korean heart-throb Jang Dong-Gun and documentary film-maker Nick Broomfield. The food has a touch of homeliness about it, which makes a meal a comforting experience. Barbecues are a mainstay, naturally, but there are plenty of other tempting dishes, especially from the menu's 'special traditional Korean dishes' section: glistening chapch'ae, aromatic with sesame oil; ojingeo hoe (steamed squid with sour and chilli sauce); or stir-fried kimchi with pork belly. The wide selection of panch'an, including pickled cucumber, seaweed salad and shredded radishes, would do a Korean housewife proud. Pear-flavoured Korean rice beer is on the drinks list.

Babies and children welcome: high chairs. Booking advisable. Separate room for parties, seats 12. **Map 17 A4**.

Nara

9 D'Arblay Street, W1F 8DR (7287 2224). Oxford Circus or Tottenham Court Road tube. **Lunch served**

KOREAN

Corean Chilli. See p180.

noon-3.30pm Mon-Sat. **Dinner served** 5.30-11pm daily. **Main courses** £6.90-£30. **Set lunch** £6.90. **Set dinner** £8.50. **Credit** AmEx, MC, V.

Nara sits on the fence by offering a menu that contains both Japanese and Korean dishes, but we recommend ignoring the former and making your selections among the latter. As with most Soho haunts, the lunch deals lure in plenty of ravenous students and local office workers. At night, the menu is still pretty good value, with keenly priced barbecue dishes and generous portions. Design statements or atmospheric surroundings don't come high on the list of priorities here; blocky and black is the theme, with accents of 1980s purple. There's also cheery Korean pop music in the background. On occasion, the service can also leave something to be desired. Focus on the food to banish these niggles – it's the details that impress, such as the elusive ko sari (bracken, a mountain fern) in the collection of namul side plates, or the freshness of squid in a stir-fried dish with spicy sauce and vegetables. Hotpots for two or three people are often on the menu, making this an ideal place for groups with big appetites.

Babies and children admitted. Takeaway service.
Map 17 B3.

Ran

58-59 Great Marlborough Street, W1F 7JY (7434 1650, www.ranrestaurant.com). Oxford Circus tube. **Lunch served** noon-3pm Mon-Sat. **Dinner served** 6-11pm daily. **Main courses** £5.90-£12. **Set lunch** £7-£18. **Set dinner** £23-£69. **Credit** AmEx, MC, V.

Ran is one of the more upmarket Korean restaurants in town, but it's not stuffy: the friendly service and relaxed atmosphere are delightful. The dining room is a commanding space, with dark charcoal tones, high-backed chairs and intelligent lighting. Most impressive, however, are the silver exhaust fans that suck up every last trace of barbecue smoke from the sizzling hotplates set into the tables. Try the smoky Korean flatbread starter, a spin on traditional p'ajeon but with a fluffier texture that contrasts well with the bouncy chunks of seafood within. Ssam, the term used to describe dishes of meat wrapped in vegetable leaves, is a speciality here; baskets of crisp lettuce leaves are provided with the meat, along with lightly dressed slivers of spring onions, whole cloves of pungent garlic, soy bean paste and dipping sauces for diners to pick and mix at their leisure. In comparison, we've found the soups and stews merely average, a short-rib stew being slightly tame in flavour (though large in portion). Come to Ran for the tableside theatrics and the fun of barbecue and ssam.

Babies and children welcome: high chairs. Booking advisable. Separate rooms for parties, seating 12 and 30. Takeaway service. **Map 17 A3**.

South West

Raynes Park

Cah Chi `HOT 50`

34 Durham Road, SW20 0TW (8947 1081, www.cahchi. com). Raynes Park rail or 57, 131 bus. **Lunch served** noon-3pm, **dinner served** 5-11pm Tue-Fri. **Meals served** noon-10.30pm Sat, Sun. **Main courses** £6-£14. **Set dinner** £18 3 courses. **Corkage** £2. **Credit** MC, V.

When the Cho family opened this first branch of Cah Chi in 1993, they were taking quite a risk. A residential street in suburban Raynes Park isn't in the heart of New Malden's Korean community. Would their customers appreciate the Korean home-style dishes, such as the pigs' ears casseroles, pig's liver dishes and blood pudding? The gamble paid off, however, as Cah Chi (meaning 'together') was quickly sought out by London's Koreans. Nowadays the restaurant is also increasingly popular with non-Korean customers, who relish the warm and homely atmosphere, the excellent cooking, the low prices and the BYO policy. The restaurant's attention to detail is clear; Cah Chi makes its own fermented soy bean pastes, used in dishes such as ga-ji ku-l (grilled aubergine topped with sweet 'miso' paste). The own-made kimchi is a relatively mild version, the Chinese leaf stained red from chilli, and the salty, sour taste of the fermentation dominant. The Earlsfield branch attracts mainly Western customers for its barbecue food, and as a result the menu doesn't list the more unusual dishes that are available here.

Babies and children welcome: high chairs. Booking essential. Separate room for parties, seats 18. Takeaway service.
For branch see index.

KOREAN

Menu

Chilli appears at every opportunity on Korean menus. Other common ingredients include soy sauce (different to both the Chinese and Japanese varieties), sesame oil, sugar, sesame seeds, garlic, ginger and various fermented soy bean pastes. Until the late 1970s eating meat was a luxury in Korea, so the quality of vegetarian dishes is high.

Given the spicy nature and overall flavour of Korean food, drinks such as chilled lager or vodka-like soju/shoju are the best matches. A wonderful non-alcoholic alternative that's always available, although not always listed on the menu, is barley tea (porich'a). Often served free of charge, it has a light dry taste that works perfectly with the food. Korean restaurants don't usually offer desserts (some serve orange or watermelon with the bill).

Spellings on menus vary hugely; we have given the most common.

Bibimbap or **pibimbap**: rice, vegetables and meat with a raw/fried egg dropped on top, often served on a hot stone.
Bindaedok, **bindaedoek** or **pindaetteok**: a mung bean pancake.
Bokum: a stir-fried dish, usually including chilli.
Bulgogi or **pulgogi**: thin slices of beef marinated in pear sap (or a similar sweet dressing) and barbecued at the table; often eaten rolled in a lettuce leaf with shredded spring onion and fermented bean paste.
Chang, **jang** or **denjang**: various fermented soy bean pastes.
Chapch'ae or **chap chee**: mixed vegetables and beef cooked with transparent vermicelli or noodles.
Cheon, **jeon** or **jon**: meaning 'something flat'; this can range from a pancake containing vegetables, meat or seafood, to thinly sliced vegetables, beancurd or other ingredients, in a light batter.
Cheyuk: pork.
Chigae or **jigae**: a hot stew that contains fermented bean paste and chillies.
Gim or **kim**: dried seaweed, toasted and seasoned with salt and sesame oil.
Gu shul pan: a traditional lacquered tray that has nine compartments containing individual appetisers.
Hobak chun or **hobak jun**: sliced marrow in a light egg batter.
Japch'ae or **jap chee**: alternative spellings for chapch'ae (qv).

North
Finsbury Park

Dotori
3 Stroud Green Road, N4 2DQ (7263 3562). Finsbury Park tube/rail. **Lunch served** noon-3pm, **dinner served** 5-11pm Tue-Sun. **Main courses** £6.50-£32. **Set lunch** £6.50-£7 2 courses. **Set meal** £12-£25. **Credit** MC, V.
This Korean-Japanese hybrid is hugely popular with locals, so it's wise to book ahead (many diners were turned away on our visit). It's not somewhere for romance or titillating conversation; the space is diminutive, with tables set in (very) close proximity. The menu contains an equal number of pages dedicated to both Japanese and Korean cuisines, but it's clear that the Korean section takes centre stage. This dominance is also reflected in the decor, with paper lanterns patterned with hangul (Korean script) and traditional laughing wooden Korean masks hanging on the walls. Nevertheless, we were intrigued by the sushi rolls: 'rainbow' maki featured green tea mayonnaise and fresh fish and prawns draped over, rather than rolled into, the rice; a house special featured marinated beef and crunchy gourd pickle. Plenty of diners opt for bibimbap, and ours was competently executed, if not quite hot enough. Soondooboo chigae was fiery, yet came with an overcooked egg. Service can be frustratingly slow, though friendly; our neighbours, a pair of regulars, seemed resigned to the fact and were delighted that, this time, their gyoza 'only took six minutes to arrive'.
Available for hire. Babies and children welcome: nappy-changing facilities. Booking advisable dinner. Takeaway service. Vegetarian menu.

North West
Golders Green

Kimchee
887 Finchley Road, NW11 8RR (8455 1035). Golders Green tube. **Lunch served** noon-3pm Tue-Fri; noon-4pm Sat, Sun. **Dinner served** 6-11pm Tue-Sun. **Main courses** £5.90-£8.50. **Set lunch** £5.90-£6.90. **Credit** MC, V.
It may have the serene decor of a traditional yeogwan (Korean inn), but Saturday evenings see this joint jumping with Korean hipsters and young families. Aim for the left side of the room if you want a leisurely meal; the bench seating to the right can play havoc with a weak back. Staff are practised and sweet, though they do get rushed. Still, their intuitive sharing of tabletop barbecue cooking duties is remarkable, ensuring that even challenging ingredients such as squid remain delightfully tender. Kimchee's sizeable barbecue list takes in duck, chicken, pork and prawns, plus the classic beef cuts. We love the marinated ribeye. On a springtime visit, accompanying veg included mandolin-cut slices of swede and kabocha squash, along with the expected beansprouts and onions. Start perhaps with the puffy, deep-fried chicken pieces, or textbook chapch'ae (stir-fried cellophane noodles with vegetables and beef). Whole wheat noodles brought a distinctively nutty flavour to the huge plates of jajang myun – pork and noodles doused in inky black bean sauce, a South Korean favourite. Unlike some London Korean restaurants, Kimchee charges for glasses of cold barley tea, but 80p isn't much to pay for something so enjoyable.
Babies and children welcome: high chairs. Booking essential Fri-Sun. Takeaway service.

Outer London
New Malden, Surrey

Hankook
Ground floor, Falcon House, 257 Burlington Road, KT3 4NE (8942 1188). Motspur Park rail. **Lunch served** noon-3pm Mon, Tue, Fri. **Dinner served** 6-11pm Mon-Fri. **Meals served** noon-11pm Sat, Sun. **Main courses** £6.50-£50. **Credit** MC, V.

On a weekday lunchtime visit, this elegant restaurant flanked by industrial buildings was devoid of custom. At night, it's a rather different story. That's when legions of New Malden locals (many of them Korean families) and unwinding businessmen come here to indulge in the extensive menu of Korean classics, while ensconced in private rooms separated by sliding paper screens. Comical chilli peppers on the menu denote the properly spicy dishes, such as the life-awakening kalbi (tender beef ribs in a 'cabbage leaf spicy broth'). Quiet, helpful waitresses brought out half a dozen small dishes of panch'an and namul: kimchi, seasoned courgettes, tteok (glutinous rice cakes) in a spicy-sweet sauce, marinated mushrooms, and an unorthodox though delicious potato salad and a pasta salad. The kimchi p'ajeon (pancake), perfectly crisp and golden, filled the length and width of the large, heavy plate on which it was served. Note the tanks of marine life (lobster, fish, crab) at the back of the room and order accordingly – seafood is a house speciality here. Mandu (dumplings) are also made on site, fresh for the evening service. You're unlikely to leave Hankook disappointed.

Babies and children welcome: high chairs. Booking essential dinner Fri, Sat.

Jee Cee Neh
74 Burlington Road, KT3 4NU (8942 0682). New Malden rail. **Lunch served** noon-3pm, **dinner served** 6-11pm daily. **Main courses** £7-£13. **Credit** (over £20) MC, V.

Jee Cee Neh's location on the mostly residential Burlington Road means it is often filled with locals who have walked here from home – families with young children and, more frequently, suited businessmen knocking back soju or Hite beer while tackling mountains of grilled meats and bowls of rice. The room is plainly furnished with wooden tables and chairs, and screens that separate the front half of the restaurant from the back. If you need to catch your waiter's attention, electronic bells have been installed on each table. Time and again we've been impressed by the generosity of the staff and kitchen, which provide smiling and personable service and big portions of top-quality Korean cooking. The casseroles make a good centrepiece to any meal. The large bubbling pots arrive loaded with broths that are richly complex, whether they use the milky, beef-bone base or the jarringly red, kimchi and chilli base. Our kimchi version was simple by description, but included a large hunk of spoon-tender pork belly that fell delightfully into strands, and a half-head of cabbage kimchi, which was dutifully snipped by a waiter into bite-sized portions at the table. A seafood variation included whole octopus along with juicy clams, pieces of crab and flaky morsels of fish. You could dine happily on this alone, with bowls of rice to mop up the soup, but the dumplings, barbecued meats and noodles are usually too tempting to resist.

Available for hire. Babies and children welcome: high chairs. Disabled: toilet. Separate room for parties, seats 20. Takeaway service.

Jjim: fish or meat stewed for a long time in soy sauce, sugar and garlic.
Jeongol or **chungol**: casserole.
Kalbi, **galbi** or **kalbee**: beef spare ribs, marinated and barbecued.
Kimchi, **kim chee** or **kimch'i**: fermented pickled vegetables, usually chinese cabbage, white radishes, cucumber or greens, served in a small bowl with a spicy chilli sauce.
Kkaktugi or **kkakttugi**: pickled radish.
Koch'ujang: a hot, red bean paste.
Kook, **gook**, **kuk** or **guk**: soup. Koreans have an enormous variety of soups, from consommé-like liquid to meaty broths of noodles, dumplings, meat or fish.
Ko sari na mool or **gosari namul**: cooked bracken stalks with sesame seeds.
Mandu kuk or **man doo kook**: clear soup with steamed meat dumplings.
Naengmyun: cold noodle dishes, usually featuring thin, elastic buckwheat noodles.
Namul or **na mool**: vegetable side dishes.
Ojingeo: squid.
P'ajeon or **pa jun**: flour pancake with spring onions and (usually) seafood.
Panch'an: side dishes; they usually include pickled vegetables, but possibly also tofu, fish, seaweed or beans.
Pap, **bap**, **bab** or **pahb**: cooked rice.
Pokkeum or **pokkm**: stir-fry; common types include cheyuk pokkeum (pork), ojingeo pokkeum (squid).
Shinseollo, **shinsonro**, **shinsulro** or **sin sollo**: 'royal casserole'; a meat soup with seaweed, seafood, eggs and vegetables, all of which is cooked at the table.
Soju or **shoju**: a strong Korean vodka, often drunk as an aperitif.
Teoppap or **toppap**: 'on top of rice'; for example, ojingeo teoppap is squid served on rice.
Toenjang: seasoned (usually with chilli) soy bean paste.
Tolsot bibimbap: tolsot (or dolsot) is a sizzling hot stone bowl that makes the bibimbap (qv) a little crunchy on the sides.
Tteokpokki: bars of compressed rice (tteok is a rice cake) fried on a hotplate with veg and sausages, in a chilli sauce.
Twaeji gogi: pork.
T'wigim, **twigim** or **tuigim**: fish, prawns or vegetables dipped in batter and deep-fried until golden brown.
Yach'ae: vegetables.
Yuk hwe, **yukhoe** or **yukhwoe**: shredded raw beef, strips of pear and egg yolk, served chilled.
Yukkaejang: spicy beef soup.

KOREAN

Malaysian, Indonesian & Singaporean

Real melting pot stuff, this. The food of Malaysia, Singapore and Indonesia is an amalgam of cooking styles – Chinese, Indian and Peranakan (Nyonya) as well as Malay and Indonesian – which may be why this corner of the world has so many 'national' dishes. Think satay, laksa, char kway teow (fried flat noodles), nasi lemak, rendang, Hainanese chicken rice, chilli crab and roti prata.

Hawker dishes and street food are important facets of the cuisine and, while prices are not as cheap as dining at Singapore's Tiong Bahru market (minus air fare), several of London's best restaurants in this category are good value, not least **Kiasu** on Queensway, a former winner of our Best Cheap Eats award, and relative newcomer **Rasa Sayang** in Chinatown. If you want to dress up and splash out on food and cocktails, South Kensington's **Awana** is ideal, and may afford a little star-spotting. Otherwise, smart Swiss Cottage eaterie **Singapore Garden** is consistently awarded top marks by our reviewers and the many expats who travel across London to eat there.

Central

Chinatown

New Fook Lam Moon
10 Gerrard Street, W1D 5PW (7734 7615). Leicester Square tube. **Meals served** noon-11.30pm Mon-Sat; noon-10.30pm Sun. **Main courses** £6.90-£11. **Set meal** £11.50-£27 per person (minimum 2). **Credit** MC, V.
Set amid the kerfuffle of Chinatown's main street, New Fook Lam Moon at first glance looks like many Cantonese caffs in the locality – especially given its window display of roast meats. Inside, you'll find a 70-seater restaurant with dining rooms on the ground floor and in the basement. The surprise comes when you peruse the menu, which, along with Cantonese standards, contains some enticing Malaysian dishes. Our waitress was patient and helpful, keen to ensure we didn't miss the Malaysian specialities. Always available is bak kut teh (pork rib soup with aromatic herbs), a common breakfast dish eaten for its reputed medicinal properties. Traditional fried dough sticks are provided for dunking. We decided against the fish head curry, and chilli crab (fresh, sweet crab meat in a rich, thick sambal sauce) and chose a marvellous Malaysian-style steamed turbot, the glistening fish brought to life by a piquant yellow bean and chilli sauce. As a side dish, stir-fried beans in a spicy sauce turned out to be a generous portion of petai pods, string beans, okra and aubergine in a hot and pungent blachan sauce: a veritable monsoon of flavours. Complimentary fresh oranges provided a calming end to proceedings.
Babies and children welcome: high chairs. Booking advisable. Takeaway service. **Map 17 C4.**

Rasa Sayang

5 Macclesfield Street, W1D 6AY (7734 1382). Leicester Square or Piccadilly Circus tube. **Meals served** noon-11pm daily. **Main courses** £6.90-£18.80. **Credit** AmEx, MC, V.
Competition is tough in Soho, but this didn't deter the owners of Noodle Oodle in Oxford Street from opening Rasa Sayang at the end of 2008. Dining takes place on two floors; the snug ground-floor room with its blond wood furniture may be spartan, but it's preferable to the dimly lit basement. The restaurant veers from being almost empty to being rammed with chattering Malaysian families. Prices are geared to a stuttering economy, and service is willing and efficient. The menu encompasses many of the favourite dishes to be found at hawker stalls in the Straits (chilli crabs, Hainanese chicken rice, roti canai) and new dishes are added regularly. Consistency can be a problem. Satay arrived with a watery peanut sauce, and the nasi lemak was dry and lacking in flavour. Far better was char kway teow with prawns, although the wok-fried dishes are sometimes a touch oily. Ondeh-ondeh (glutinous rice balls covered with desiccated coconut, and filled with palm sugar, which oozes out when you bite into them) made a thoroughly enjoyable end to the meal. To drink, try the teh tarik ('stretched tea', milky and frothy), which on a warm day brings you several steps closer to South-east Asia.
Babies and children admitted. Booking advisable. Separate room for parties, seats 30. Takeaway service. **Map 17 C4.**

Clerkenwell & Farringdon

54

54 Farringdon Road, EC1R 3BL (7336 0603, www.54farringdon.com). Farringdon tube/rail. **Lunch served** noon-3pm Thur, Fri. **Dinner served** 6-10.45pm Mon-Sat. **Main courses** £9.50-£15. **Set meal** £14.95 3 courses. **Credit** AmEx, MC, V.
The dining room may not be large, but lattice screens and silks are used to becoming effect, and red floral walls help project an alluring glow. A cool soundtrack also contributes to the relaxed atmosphere, as does the cheerful service. We're pleased that the number of British dishes once offered on the menu has been reduced to a handful. It's also good to see a few surprises, such as pasembur, a salad found on the street stalls of Penang that consists of deep-fried beancurd, prawn fritters and shredded cucumber, nicely capped with a piquant peanut sauce. Far less rewarding was the itik masak kicap, where a tasty dark soya sauce couldn't redeem some chewy duck breast. Instead, if it's available, try the penang laksa; the authentic hot and sour flavours are jazzed up with chopped cucumber, lettuce and tamarind. And to bring a meal to a refreshing hot-and-cold conclusion, order pisang goreng (banana fritters) with lemongrass ice-cream. Visit at lunch for a quiet dining experience; it's much busier come the evening.
Available for hire. Babies and children welcome: high chairs. Booking essential Fri, Sat. Disabled: toilet. Separate room for parties, seats 30. Tables outdoors (2, pavement). **Map 5 N5.**

Sedap

102 Old Street, EC1V 9AY (7490 0200, www.sedap.co.uk). Old Street tube/rail. **Lunch served** 11.30am-3pm Mon-Fri. **Dinner served** 5-11pm daily. **Main courses** £5.70-£7.50. **Set lunch** £5.95-£6.95 2 courses. **Credit** MC, V.
The Yeohs have settled well since moving here from their former outfit, Nyonya in Notting Hill. Two generations of the family run the restaurant, and service is welcoming. Sedap is a spick and span venue, where black furnishings are set against a backdrop of olive green. Nyonya or Peranakan food is a fusion of Chinese and Malay cuisines, and the menu encapsulates this cooking style. Chicken satay came with a sauce that had just the right balance of peanuts and spices. The char kway teow is renowned, but we have mixed feelings about the seafood char mee (yellow noodles in a thick soya sauce) – even though the freshly made blachan (hot shrimp paste) is fabulous. Perhaps the restaurant could buy higher quality ingredients in some instances, but we've nothing but praise for the curry tumis: fleshy pieces of sea bream and okra served in a hot and sour sauce. To finish, don't miss the traditional Nyonya kueh (coconut cakes in a variety of bright colours, including blue). The set lunch menus are a steal.
Available for hire. Babies and children admitted. Booking advisable evenings. Separate room for parties, seats 14. Takeaway service; delivery service (over £10 within 1-mile radius). **Map 5 P4.**

South Kensington

Awana

85 Sloane Avenue, SW3 3DX (7584 8880, www.awana.co.uk). South Kensington tube. **Lunch served** noon-3pm daily. **Dinner served** 6-11pm Mon-Fri, Sun; 6-11.30pm Sat. **Main courses** £12-£25. **Set lunch** £12.50 2 courses, £15 3 courses. **Set dinner** £40-£45 tasting menu. **Credit** AmEx, DC, MC, V.
Awana is one of the most expensive Malaysian restaurants in town, but it does provide diners with upmarket surroundings,

Kiasu. See p189.

including an entire jungle's worth of polished teak and red leather covers. The lofty prices don't seem to deter locals, and business was brisk during our visit. You can eat at the bar, by the satay counter, or in the main dining room. The meandering menu is a little confusing, making it difficult to settle on a final order, and though staff are helpful, they can be forgetful. We've also noticed that some of the more costly dishes on the set-price menus have been removed recently. Nevertheless, this is certainly the place to visit if you enjoy snacks on sticks; you'll be hard pushed to find anywhere in London that serves better chicken or mixed seafood satay. Roti canai started our meal with gusto, followed by a favourite hawker dish of char kway teow, with scallops and prawns (which was laced with a little too much sambal). Awana's version of curry kapitan, a Nyonya classic, features guinea fowl lifted by lemongrass, lime leaves and chilli. We also enjoyed dessert: a spot-on cendol.
Available for hire. Babies and children welcome: high chairs. Booking essential Thur; advisable Fri, Sat. Takeaway service. Vegetarian menu. **Map 14 E10**.

West

Bayswater

Kiasu

48 Queensway, W2 3RY (7727 8810). Bayswater or Queensway tube. **Meals served** noon-11pm daily. **Main courses** £6.90-£8. **Credit** (minimum £10) MC, V.
Kiasu ('afraid of losing') is a Hokkien term used to indicate the competitive spirit of Singaporeans, and it has been cheekily adopted here. The decor's witty inscriptions of various kiasu phrases add to the fun. We always enjoy the buzz here, and the restaurant was packed to the rafters on our latest visit, though the service was unusually lethargic. The menu resembles a greatest hits collection of Straits cooking, with pad thai, Vietnamese pho soup and Filipino adobo stew thrown into the mix for good measure. We kicked back in Straits style and ordered kueh pie tee (playfully pastry cups filled with shredded yam bean, bamboo shoots, pork and prawns), but the pastry wasn't flaky enough. This was followed by a tasty curry mee: a rich coconut curry served with tofu, chicken pieces and unexpectedly paired with Cantonese-style roast pork. On hot days, don't miss the ais kacang (commonly known as 'ABC'), packed with azuki beans, grass jelly and palm seeds topped with a heap of shaved ice – a treat indeed.
Babies and children welcome: high chairs. Booking advisable dinner. Separate room for parties, seats 50. Takeaway service. **Map 7 C6**.

Paddington

Satay House

13 Sale Place, W2 1PX (7723 6763, www.satay-house. co.uk). Edgware Road tube or Paddington tube/rail. **Lunch served** noon-3pm, **dinner served** 6-11pm daily. **Main courses** £5-£18.50. **Set meal** £15.50-£26.50 per person (minimum 2). **Credit** AmEx, MC, V.
The first thing you might ask is, 'Is the satay any good?' Satay House's version comes properly garnished with chewy rice cakes, cucumber and onion, and is slightly sweeter than normal; great, but perhaps not the best in town. Still, Malaysian expats come here for a taste of home, via properly comforting dishes such as beef rendang. This features fork-tender meat

Menu

Blachan, belacan or **blacan**: dried fermented shrimp paste.
Char kway teow or **char kwai teow**: a stir-fry of rice noodles with meat and/or seafood with dark soy sauce and beansprouts. A Hakka Chinese-derived speciality of Singapore.
Gado gado: a salad of blanched vegetables with a peanut-based sauce.
Gula melaka: palm sugar, an important ingredient with a distinctive caramel flavour added to a sago and coconut-milk pudding of the same name.
Hainanese chicken rice: poached chicken served with rice cooked in chicken stock, light chicken broth and a chilli-ginger dipping sauce.
Ikan bilis or **ikan teri**: tiny fish, often fried and made into a dry sambal (qv) with peanuts.
Laksa: a noodle dish with either coconut milk or tamarind as the stock base.
Mee: noodles.
Mee goreng: fried egg noodles with meat, prawns and vegetables.
Nasi ayam: rice cooked in chicken broth, served with roast or steamed chicken and a light soup.
Nasi goreng: fried rice with shrimp paste, garlic, onions, chillies and soy sauce.
Nasi lemak: coconut rice on a plate with a selection of curries and fish dishes topped with ikan bilis (qv).
Nonya or **Nyonya**: the name referring to both the women and the dishes of the Straits Chinese community.
Otak otak: a Nonya (qv) speciality made from eggs, fish and coconut milk.
Pandan leaves: a variety of the screwpine plant; used to add colour and fragrance to both savoury and sweet dishes.
Peranakan: refers to the descendants of Chinese settlers who first came to Malacca (now Melaka), a seaport on the Malaysian west coast, in the 17th century. It is generally applied to those born of Sino-Malay extraction who adopted Malay customs, costume and cuisine, the community being known as 'Straits Chinese'. The cuisine is also known as Nonya.
Rendang: meat cooked in coconut milk.
Roti canai: a South Indian/Malaysian breakfast dish of fried unleavened bread served with a dip of either chicken curry or dal.
Sambal: there are several types of sambal, often made of fiery chilli sauce, onions and coconut oil; it can be served as a side dish or used as a relish.
Satay: there are two types – terkan (minced and moulded to the skewer) and chochok ('shish', more common in London). Beef or chicken are the traditional choices, though prawn is now often available too. Satay is served with a rich spicy sauce made from onions, lemongrass, galangal, and chillies in tamarind sauce; it is sweetened and thickened with ground peanuts.

MALAYSIAN, INDONESIAN & SINGAPOREAN

and a sauce that has been slow-cooked until it's an intense deep brown and almost 'dry'; a gradual chilli burn warms the stomach and the heart. Flavours are mostly big: try murtabak, a popular Malay dish brought to the peninsula by way of India. A crêpe-like roti filled with spiced minced lamb and briefly shallow-fried, it was delicious, if not entirely greaseless. Finish the meal with some cooling desserts, such as street-stall favourite ais kacang – sweet red beans, grass jelly and creamed sweetcorn topped with a refreshing combination of shaved ice mixed with condensed milk. The place is popular; diners filled both the ground floor and the basement, which are simply decorated with an understated elegance (bamboo chairs, oak tables, hibiscus motifs).

Babies and children welcome: high chairs. Booking advisable. Separate room for parties, seats 35. Takeaway service. Vegetarian menu. **Map 8 E5**.

Awana. See p187.

Westbourne Grove

C&R Restaurant
52 Westbourne Grove, W2 5SH (7221 7979). Bayswater tube. **Meals served** noon-11pm Mon, Wed-Fri; noon-11.30pm Sat; noon-10.30pm Sun. **Main courses** £7-£12.50. **Set meal** £16 vegetarian, £19 meat per person (minimum 2). **Credit** AmEx, MC, V.

This bustling restaurant, popular with expats and locals, is smarter than its sister café in Soho. The interior is fresh and modern, with blond wood chairs, grey banquettes and black flooring. Bold red prints help brighten the inoffensive magnolia colour scheme. The kitchen produces a huge array of dishes from cuisines that span China and South-east Asia. Hotpots such as fish head curry are a popular choice. Service is frustratingly variable: some staff are attentive, others glum. The cooking can be hit or miss too. Prawn crackers are worth ordering, as they actually taste of prawns. Gado gado was a let down, arriving with a bland peanut sauce devoid of the usual fragrant spices; residual water at the bottom of the dish (from the beansprouts) was unwelcome. But everything worked with the Penang-style prawn noodle soup: sparkling seafood and chicken in a spicy shrimp broth. Standards dipped again for the finale, a somewhat clumpy gula melaka.

Babies and children welcome: high chairs. Takeaway service. **Map 7 B6**.
For branch (C&R Café) see index.

North West
Swiss Cottage

Singapore Garden
83A Fairfax Road, NW6 4DY (7624 8233, www.singapore garden.co.uk). Swiss Cottage tube. **Lunch served** noon-3pm Mon-Sat; noon-4pm Sun. **Dinner served** 6-11pm Mon-Thur, Sun; 6-11.30pm Fri, Sat. **Main courses** £7.50-£29. **Set meal** £28-£38.50 per person (minimum 2). **Minimum charge** £15 per person. **Credit** AmEx, MC, V.

Plush furnishings, leafy views and ritzy cocktails make this long-established favourite as suitable for dressy evenings out as for a lingering Sunday lunch or lazy weeknight. Locals routinely mistake Singapore Garden for a luxe Chinese takeaway, though the Singaporean and Malaysian section of the menu is well promoted and executed with verve. The additional list of seasonal specials tends to have a familiar ring from visit to visit, but rewards exploration. Among our favourites are squid blachan (tender white squid chunks stir-fried with shrimp paste and glistening sugar snap peas), the oyster omelette (ho jien), and fried sa fun – ribbons of rice noodle served with a sauce of mixed meats, prawns and fish cake. Kueh pie tee (top-hat shaped cups stuffed with vegetables) makes a good starter, and don't forget to order a side of roti canai, wonderfully buttery flatbread served with creamy curry sauce. Wine prices are quite high, but the four house choices are good enough for most occasions. Service from the bevy of elegantly costumed waitresses is warmly professional and practised. You may leave craving a similarly slick local, and Chiswick residents have it: Singapore Garden has a takeaway-and-delivery-only operation on the High Road.

Babies and children admitted. Booking essential. Disabled: toilet. Takeaway service; delivery service (within 1-mile radius). **Map 28 A4**.

Middle Eastern

A few years ago, London's Middle Eastern restaurants went through a luxurious phase, where sumptuous decor was as important as the chefs, food and waiters. Then things took a turn to the trendy with the opening of Marylebone's highly stylised **Comptoir Libanais** and its simpler but still-funky rival **Yalla Yalla** in Soho. This year, Iranian outfit **Anar** in Ladbroke Grove joins the trendsters' ranks, but the other three newcomers have more of a neighbourhood vibe. First is café-restaurant **Zengi** in Spitalfields, named after a 12th-century Turkish dynasty that ruled parts of what is now Syria and northern Iraq. It serves dishes from across that region, and joins long-established **Abu Zaad** (now on the Edgware Road as well as in Shepherd's Bush) as one of the few places to enjoy Syrian food in the capital. Second is **Gilak**, on the Holloway Road, which specialises in the cooking of north Iranian province Gilan, and is therefore a good choice for fish, rice and vegetarian dishes. Iranian, and also traditional, is our third new arrival, **Zeytoon**, which already has gathered a strong following among expats in Cricklewood. The sweet-sour flavours characteristic of Iranian cooking make it notably different from the cuisine of the Lebanon, which forms the bulk of this section, but both are good for sharing.

Central
Edgware Road

Maroush I
21 Edgware Road, W2 2JE (7723 0773, www.maroush. com). Marble Arch tube. **Meals served** noon-2am daily. **Main courses** £12.95-£18. **Credit** AmEx, DC, MC, V. Lebanese

Maroush is a big name on the London Lebanese restaurant scene. With numerous offshoots around town, its formula of traditional food and smart surroundings has certainly proved a success. At this, the original branch, a cosmopolitan crowd containing many Arab residents and visitors heads to the basement to enjoy the all-encompassing meze list, the grills and (this branch's USP) the nightly entertainment. Low lighting engenders a nightclub feel, and musicians, singers and belly dancers take to the floor; it can get pretty lively. High-quality food is an integral aspect of the Maroush brand. Almost every imaginable meze dish is available: from dips (houmous and baba ganoush) to pastries (fatayer and arayes – a baked pastry with lamb) and hot dishes (fuul, sujuk and beid ghanem –

lambs' testicles with lemon and olive oil). More unusual are the 'Maroush specialities': five dishes of raw lamb in various guises, all served with little piles of variously coloured, powdered spices – a rare pleasure for those who have acquired the taste. At most other Maroush outposts, you'll find the same traditional, well-prepared food, but more sedate surroundings. *Available for hire. Babies and children welcome: high chairs. Booking advisable. Entertainment: belly dancers and musicians 9.30pm Tue-Sat. Separate room for parties, seats 25. Takeaway service; delivery service (over £20).* **Map 8 F6.**
For branches (Maroush Gardens, Maroush II, Maroush III, Maroush IV, Maroush V, Randa) see index.

Marylebone

Fairuz
3 Blandford Street, W1U 3DA (7486 8108, www.fairuz. uk.com). Baker Street or Bond Street tube. **Meals served** noon-11.30pm Mon-Sat; noon-11pm Sun. **Main courses** £12.95-£19.95. **Set meze** £19.95. **Set meal** £26.95 3 courses. **Cover** £1.50. **Credit** AmEx, MC, V. Lebanese

Menu

See also the menus in **North African** and **Turkish**.

MEZE

Baba ganoush: Egyptian name for moutabal (qv).

Basturma: smoked beef.

Batata hara: potatoes fried with peppers and chilli.

Fatayer: a soft pastry, filled with cheese, onions, spinach and pine kernels.

Fattoush: fresh vegetable salad containing shards of toasted pitta bread and sumac (qv).

Fuul or **fuul medames**: brown broad beans that are mashed and seasoned with olive oil, lemon juice and garlic.

Kibbeh: highly seasoned mix of minced lamb, cracked wheat and onion, deep-fried in balls. For meze it is often served raw (**kibbeh nayeh**) like steak tartare.

Labneh: cream cheese made from yoghurt.

Moujadara: lentils, rice and caramelised onions mixed together.

Moutabal: a purée of chargrilled aubergines mixed with sesame sauce, garlic and lemon juice.

Muhamara: dip of crushed mixed nuts with red peppers, spices and pomegranate molasses.

Sambousek: small pastries filled with mince, onion and pine kernels.

Sujuk: spicy Lebanese sausages.

Sumac: an astringent and fruity-tasting spice made from dried sumac seeds.

Tabouleh: a salad of chopped parsley, tomatoes, crushed wheat, onions, olive oil and lemon juice.

MAINS

Shawarma: meat (usually lamb) marinated then grilled on a spit and sliced kebab-style.

Shish kebab: cubes of marinated lamb grilled on a skewer, often with tomatoes, onions and sweet peppers.

Shish taouk: like shish kebab, but with chicken rather than lamb.

IRANIAN DISHES

Ash-e reshteh: soup with noodles, spinach, pulses and dried herbs.

Ghorm-e sabzi: lamb with greens, kidney beans and dried limes.

Joojeh or **jujeh**: chicken marinated in saffron, lemon and onion.

Kashk, **qurut** or **quroot**: a salty whey.

Kashk-e bademjan: baked aubergines mixed with herbs and whey.

Khoresht-e fesenjan or **fesenjoon**: chicken cooked in ground walnut and pomegranate sauce.

Kuku-ye sabzi: finely chopped fresh herbs with eggs, baked in the oven.

Masto musir: shallot-flavoured yoghurt.

Mirza ghasemi: crushed baked aubergines, tomatoes, garlic and herbs mixed with egg.

Sabzi: a plate of fresh herb leaves (usually mint and dill) often served with a cube of feta.

A small venue, with rough-hewn whitewashed walls, closely packed rustic tables and an open front with a terrace for summer dining, Fairuz is more Greek taverna than typical Lebanese restaurant. It's a lively and popular place – so popular that staff (somewhat annoyingly) dictate dining times to fit in two sittings a night. We enjoyed the vibe on a recent visit, but the crowded space and slightly frenetic air made things less than relaxing. The food and service had something of a production-line feel. Among an all-vegetarian selection of mezes, there were some big splashes of flavour and texture: a thick, garlic-infused houmous; perfectly grilled, chewy halloumi; citrusy, herby tabouleh; and a crisp fattoush salad (with no sogginess in the grilled pitta squares). But spinach fatayer was burnt, and the spinach inside was a dark, dank green. Fuul was gloriously runny, mellow and delicious, with plenty of good olive oil, but it was lukewarm. Falafel were forgotten and (when finally served) tasted as if they had come from a supermarket, with none of the exterior crunchiness or spiciness we were expecting. In all, this was an enjoyable meal, but we felt Fairuz was resting on its laurels.

Babies and children welcome: high chairs. Booking advisable dinner. Separate room for parties, seats 25. Takeaway service; delivery service (within 5-mile radius). **Map 9 G5.**

Levant

Jason Court, 76 Wigmore Street, W1U 2SJ (7224 1111, www.levant.co.uk). Bond Street tube.
Bar **Open** noon-12.30am Mon-Wed, Sun; noon-2.30am Thur-Sat.
Restaurant **Meals served** 6-11.30pm Mon-Fri; noon-11.30pm Sat, Sun. **Main courses** £12.50-£26. **Set lunch** (noon-5.30pm Sat, Sun) £12.50 2 courses. **Set dinner** (Wed-Sat) £28-£50 3 courses; £50 kharuf feast.
Both **Credit** AmEx, DC, MC, V. Lebanese
Outside, you're in an alley just off Marylebone High Street; inside, a lamp-lit staircase leads down to a heavy wooden door. Open it and you'll find yourself plunged into an oriental fantasy. Levant is all about opulent fabrics, filigreed and tasselled metal lamps, rose petals and belly dancers. The party atmosphere extends from the cushioned seating of the meze bar (with a professional range of cocktails served alongside small dishes) into the main restaurant. The dancers, who perform every evening, are a major part of the deal, and DJs spin Arabic sounds at weekends until 2am. Amid the festivities, the food has not been forgotten. Perhaps surprisingly for a place like this, the kitchen produces classic Lebanese dishes, and to a good standard. There's a strong focus on meze: salads such as tabouleh and fattoush; hot dishes such as falafel (crisply fried outside, fluffy inside) and sujuk; dips including a silky houmous (there's a version with meat too), baba ganoush and nutty muhamara. There's a much smaller selection of meat and fish mains, but groups might enjoy the exotic indulgence of muhammar, a whole, marinated shoulder of lamb served with couscous, figs, apricots, prunes and dates.

Booking advisable. Entertainment: belly dancer 9pm Mon-Wed, Sun; 8.30pm, 11pm Thur-Sat; DJs 10pm-2am Fri, Sat. Separate room for parties, seats 10-14. Takeaway service. **Map 9 G6.**

Mayfair

Al Sultan

51-52 Hertford Street, W1J 7ST (7408 1155). Green Park or Hyde Park Corner tube. **Meals served** noon-11pm daily. **Main courses** £13.50-£20. **Cover** £2. **Minimum** £20. **Credit** AmEx, DC, MC, V. Lebanese

Years ago, all London Lebanese restaurants were like Al Sultan, sporting white tablecloths, black-suited waiters, bright lights, a rather chilly formality and the optional extra of faux-classical pillars. While some have moved on to ambient music, soft lamplight and funky decor, Al Sultan remains firmly ensconced in the old school. We've had mixed experiences here as far as welcome and service are concerned, but the food has usually been right on target. The menu is pretty comprehensive (that's the traditional way), listing 42 mezes and 23 grills at the last count. This means you'll find hardcore dishes here, such as kibbeh nayeh (raw minced lamb blended with crushed wheat and spices) and beid ghanam (lambs' testicles fried with garlic and lemon). Otherwise, we've enjoyed the likes of citrusy fattoush salad with crisp pitta squares, sprinkled with plenty of sumac; fatayer with melt-in-the-mouth pastry and a fresh spinach filling; and perfectly grilled slices of salty halloumi sprinkled with nigella seeds. Grills – we like the kafta halabiyeh, lamb meatballs with onion and parsley – are tender and well cooked, and there's also a dish of the day featuring the likes of kousa (stuffed aubergines and courgettes in tomato sauce).
Available for hire. Babies and children welcome: high chairs. Booking advisable dinner. Tables outdoors (4, pavement). Takeaway service; delivery service (over £35 within 4-mile radius). Vegetarian menu. **Map 9 H8.**

Mohsen. See p196.

St James's

Noura

122 Jermyn Street, SW1Y 4UJ (7839 2020, www.noura.co.uk). Green Park or Piccadilly Circus tube. **Meals served** noon-midnight daily. **Main courses** £14-£22. **Set lunch** £22.50 2 courses. **Set meal** (5-7pm) £16.50 2 courses. **Credit** AmEx, DC, MC, V. Lebanese

The small Noura chain is all about elegance. In the Noura Central branch, as in the others, design is key; a sense of occasion is generated by eclectic, luxurious furnishings that incorporate shimmering fabric hangings and soft lighting. The look provides a backdrop for a carefully chosen roster of popular hot and cold mezes and mains. The kitchen makes no attempt to veer off the tried and tested path of traditional Lebanese cookery. Dips such as houmous (there's a spicy houmous beiruty too) and labneh make a great foil for dishes with bite: the likes of basturma, grilled halloumi and batinjan makdous (pickled baby aubergines with walnuts and olive oil). Warm, mellow fuul joins other classics such as falafel and kibbeh, along with a few hot houmous dishes (including houmous shawarma, with sliced lamb), plus moujadara (lentils and rice with caramelised onions). Salads – citrusy tabouleh and spicy fattoush, for instance – round off the meze selection. As you'd expect, grills dominate the main courses, but there are some baked dishes such as loubieh (green beans) cooked in a stew with lamb and tomatoes. We've never had a duff dish here, and pleasant, professional service adds to the appeal.
Available for hire. Babies and children welcome: high chairs. Disabled: toilet. **Map 10 K7.**
For branches see index.

Soho

Yalla Yalla

1 Green's Court, W1F 0HA (7287 7663, www.yalla-yalla.co.uk). Piccadilly Circus tube. **Meals served** 10am-midnight Mon-Sat; 10am-10pm Sun. **Main courses** £6.50-£10.50. **Set lunch** £5.50 2 courses. **Set meal** £7.50 2 courses. **Credit** MC, V. Lebanese

Bijou, charming and usually crowded, Yalla Yalla is painted white, its walls decorated in photos of old Beirut. Yellow lamps hang over a takeaway counter crammed with delectable-looking treats, and rustic wooden tables and stools complete the appealing picture. Things were uncharacteristically quiet on a recent lunchtime visit, and a power cut meant there was no lighting and no hot dishes. This is an informal spot, but the details are remembered: we were brought a little dish of olives and another of pickled vegetables; and small jugs of olive oil were on each table. The meze dishes were pretty faultless: a small portion of dense, garlicky houmous beautifully served in a swirl with an indentation of olive oil and some chickpeas; crisp fattoush salad, reddened with splashes of citrusy sumac; and spicy little sujuk sausages, served in a tomato-based, herby sauce (the kitchen managed to heat them on the gas). Grills augment the meze menu. Takeaway dishes (which can also be eaten-in) include wraps (shish taouk, falafel, halloumi and more); savoury pastries such as manakeesh bi zaatar (warmed bread with olive oil dusted with zaatar spice); and sweets such as baklava. It's a winning formula.
Babies and children welcome: high chairs. Booking advisable dinner. Tables outdoors (2, pavement). Takeaway service. **Map 17 B4.**

Faanoos. See p197.

West
Bayswater

Al Waha

*75 Westbourne Grove, W2 4UL (7229 0806, www.
alwaharestaurant.com). Bayswater or Queensway tube.*
Meals served noon-11.30pm daily. **Main courses**
£10.50-£13.50. **Set lunch** £12.50. **Set dinner** £21 per
person (minimum 2) 2 courses, £25 per person (minimum 2)
3 courses. **Cover** £1.50. **Minimum** £13.50 (dinner).
Credit MC, V. Lebanese
Set in an intimate space on Westbourne Grove, quietly done
out in whites and browns with framed Arabic calligraphy on
the walls, Al Waha is smart yet not flashy. Staff are efficient
and welcoming in a professional way, while food is classical
Lebanese and consistently top-tier – a fact appreciated by the
mixed clientele of Arabs and westerners. Among the meze
favourites are moujadara, with caramelised onions adding a
sweet flavour to the lentils and rice, and fuul medames, the
fasolia beans turning to a comforting mush, and served with
lashings of good olive oil. Fuul moukala, the version of fuul
made with green fasolia beans, lemon, coriander and olive oil,
makes a zesty contrast, as does crisp, crunchy fattoush.
Fatayers emerge from the kitchen perfectly golden, halloumi is
grilled just so. Grills maintain the same high standards (and
while hardly cheap, at £11-£13 they're less pricey than in some
similar restaurants). We reserve special praise for the kharoof
mahshi, a dish of the day: tender lamb served with delicately
spiced rice with nuts, and a cucumber and yoghurt salad.
*Babies and children welcome until 7pm. Booking advisable;
essential dinner. Tables outdoors (4, patio). Takeaway
service; delivery service (over £20 within 3-mile radius).*
Map 7 B6.

Hammersmith

Mahdi

*217 King Street, W6 9JT (8563 7007, www.mahdi
restaurant.co.uk). Hammersmith or Ravenscourt Park tube.*
Meals served noon-11pm daily. **Main courses** £5-£12.
Set lunch (noon-6pm Mon-Fri) £4.50-£5.90 1 course.
Unlicensed no alcohol allowed. **Credit** MC, V. Iranian
Many Iranian restaurants strive to emulate the informality of
the dinner parties at which so much of their nation's cuisine is
served. Not so with Mahdi, a sprawling space akin to an
oriental food hall, its arching brick walls hung with carpets,
its shelves cluttered with colourful trinkets. A stuffed peacock
keeps watch over a fountain in one corner. Service tends to be
swift and unsmiling, and the tables are crammed so close
together that at peak times it's hard not to feel your
conversation merging with those on either side of you. For all
that, Mahdi remains one of London's most popular Iranian
restaurants thanks to the quality of its cooking and the
diversity of its menu. Don't miss its less commonly found
starters, such as ash-e reshteh, a smoky bean and noodle soup
thickened with whey. Mains are gargantuan (taking home a
doggie bag is standard practice) and cover a range of grilled
chicken and lamb kebabs as well as stews and dishes such as
baghali polo ba mahicheh: rice flavoured with dill and broad
beans, accompanied by a melt-in-the-mouth lamb shank.
Booking advisable. Disabled: toilet. Takeaway service.
Map 20 B4.
For branch see index.

YallaYalla

يلا يلا

Yalla Yalla Beirut Street Food
1 Green's Court, W1F 0HA London

T 020 7287 7663 /
F 020 7287 7663
www.yalla-yalla.co.uk

Yalla Yalla is an excellent choice for workday lunches...Hot dishes include sauteed chicken livers with pomegranate molasses and slow-cooked stew of lamb shoulder with red pepper and butternut squash...To drink there are fresh juices, orange blossom-scented lemonade and mint tea, and also Lebanese wines and beer.

Time Out

Zengi. See p198.

Ladbroke Grove

Anar

*349 Portobello Road, W10 5SA (8960 6555, www.anar
persiankitchen.co.uk). Ladbroke Grove tube.* **Meals served**
noon-11pm Mon-Thur; noon-11.30pm Fri, Sat; noon-10pm
Sun. **Main courses** £7-£25. **Set meze** £8. **Credit** AmEx,
MC, V. Iranian

There's nothing conventional about Anar's approach to
contemporary Persian cuisine. You'll find none of the gaudy
orientalism prevalent at other Iranian restaurants in London,
but rather a bare-brick interior lit by candles, a mix of modern
banquettes and small cubic stools, and tall windows
overlooking the residential end of Portobello Road. There's
even a wine list (but only one bottled beer). Music on our visit
was Arabic, not Iranian, and the downstairs toilet promoted an
Ancienne Ambiance candle called 'Persia' ('as recommended
by *Vogue*'). Will London's stubbornly traditional Iranian set be
swung by such tactics? It seems an idle question, given that
Anar's target audience appears to be experimental Notting Hill
locals, of which there were many on our visit, mispronouncing
starters and struggling to locate main courses not featuring
lamb. Not that the food should trouble even staunch
traditionalists; a starter of ash-e reshteh (bean and noodle soup)
was fine, if served in an unnecessarily dramatic terracotta pot
complete with lid, and zereshk polo ba morgh was a decent
version of a Persian kitchen classic: a mound of saffron rice
with sour barberries, served with a side of braised chicken. A
worthy addition to the area.
*Available for hire. Babies and children admitted. Tables
outdoors (2, pavement). Takeaway service; delivery service
(over £15).* **Map 19 A1**.

Olympia

Mohsen

*152 Warwick Road, W14 8PS (7602 9888). Earl's Court
tube or Kensington (Olympia) tube/rail.* **Meals served**
noon-midnight daily. **Main courses** £12-£15. **Unlicensed**.
Corkage no charge. **No credit cards**. Iranian

It is consistency, not evolution, that has kept this place among
our favourite Iranian restaurants for so long. Some of its
Kensington contemporaries have meddled with their formula
– diluting their all-Iranian staff, employing belly dancers and
catering to hordes of late-night kebab seekers – but Mohsen
has retained the family atmosphere that remains its biggest
draw. Expect little in the way of frills; the plastic laminated
menus and smattering of dog-eared travel posters haven't
changed in years. But neither has the warmth of the welcome
from Mrs Mohsen, who frequently wanders between the
packed tables sharing jokes with regulars, many of them on
first-name terms. Starters such as mirza ghasemi (baked
aubergine dip with eggs and onions) are perfect when paired
with a plate of fresh sabzi greens and a basket of bread hot
from the oven. Kebabs are well seasoned and served in more
manageable portions than at many Persian restaurants. There's
also a daily changing special, favoured by those looking for
more traditional food; the ghorm-e sabzi (lamb stew with
greens and kidney beans) is among London's finest examples
of this popular Iranian dish.
Babies and children admitted. Takeaway service.
Map 13 A10.

Shepherd's Bush

Abu Zaad

*29 Uxbridge Road, W12 8LH (8749 5107, www.abuzaad.
co.uk). Shepherd's Bush Market tube.* **Meals served**
11am-11pm daily. **Main courses** £5-£14. **Unlicensed**
no alcohol allowed. **Credit** AmEx, MC, V. Syrian

Abu Zaad is one of those unspoiled local restaurants that we
hope will never change. Outside, posters offer lunchtime and
takeaway meal deals. The interior is brownish, with carved
wooden walls aiming for a feel of the Middle East. A big
painting of Old Damascus, along with pottery and other
artefacts, puts a distinctive Syrian stamp on the place. The
menu contains a full list of meze dishes (Syrian cooking is
similar to Lebanese), along with meat-and-rice and oven-baked
main courses: the likes of chicken or lamb kabseh (marinated,
grilled meat, served with spiced rice simmered in stock) and

lamb shakrieh (lamb cubes cooked in yoghurt). After a starter of thick, garlicky houmous served with distinctive Syrian flatbread, our frika with chicken was half a bird, pasted with spicy marinade then grilled and served with a dome of flavoured bulgar, pine nuts and peas – simple, honest, good-value food. There are many juices too, including exotic fruits such as pomegranate, and specialities such as lemon juice with mint. Add jovial yet efficient staff and you have all you need for a keenly priced, feel-good meal.

Babies and children welcome: high chairs. Booking advisable weekends. Separate room for parties, seats 30. Takeaway service. **Map 20 B2**.

For branch see index.

Sufi

70 Askew Road, W12 9BJ (8834 4888, www.sufi restaurant.com). Hammersmith tube then 266 bus. **Meals served** noon-11pm daily. **Main courses** £6.50-£13.50. **Credit** MC, V. Iranian

It's a struggle to recall a duff dish, let alone a disappointing meal, at Sufi in the four years since it opened. This is one of a handful of Iranian restaurants in the capital that manage to combine a homely atmosphere with authentic cuisine. As such, it is revered by both locals, who see it as a reliable source of midweek takeaways, and Iranians who travel across town to dine here at weekends. The interior is cosy and eminently unfussy. The sand-coloured walls of the two rooms are decorated with shelves of shisha pipes and paintings of stoic-looking poets and hung with the occasional sitar. A clay oven stands guard. It's the perfect environment in which to sample a range of more unusual Iranian delicacies. Starters include kookoo sabzi (a fragrant herb omelette spiked with barberries) and olives in a northern Iranian-style marinade of pomegranate juice and crushed walnuts. Mains consist of kebabs, stews and plenty of fish options. On our last visit, which coincided with Iranian New Year, we were offered a seasonal, off-the-menu dish of grilled mahi sefid (a Caspian freshwater fish), crisp-skinned and flaky and served with heaps of herbed rice.

Babies and children welcome: children's menu; high chairs. Separate room for parties, seats 40. Takeaway service. **Map 20 A2**.

South West

East Sheen

Faanoos

481 Upper Richmond Road West, SW14 7PU (8878 5738, www.faanoosrestaurant.com). Mortlake rail or 33, 337, 493 bus. **Meals served** noon-11pm daily. **Main courses** £4.95-£8.95. **Credit** MC, V. Iranian

Finding an Iranian restaurant beyond the pull of Kensington's expat community is no mean feat; discovering one south of the river is little short of a miracle. So Faanoos remains a beacon for less conveniently located fans of Persian cooking – appropriate for a restaurant whose name means 'lantern' in Farsi. It's quite a restrained affair, closer aesthetically to a Tehran tea shop than a glamorous pre-Revolutionary dinner party. The small room features mud-coloured walls hung with rugs, and unframed paintings of bearded clerics; it lends itself well to romantic liaisons and hushed political conspiracies by candlelight. We've not always been impressed with starters in

the past – masto musir and salad olivieh have occasionally seemed workmanlike – but the lemon- and saffron-marinated chicken joojeh kebab is something of a masterclass in the art. Saffron-tinted rice comes with or without a handful of sharp red barberries; add a side of torshi (mixed vegetable pickle) and you're looking at a meal that you'd struggle to top in Tehran, let alone north of the Thames. A branch opened in Chiswick in 2010, with a turquoise-tiled brick oven turning out terrific taftoon bread in full view of high-street shoppers.

Babies and children welcome: high chairs. Booking advisable. Dress: smart casual. Tables outdoors (2, pavement). Takeaway service.

For branch see index.

South East

London Bridge & Borough

Hiba

Maya House, 134-138 Borough High Street, SE1 1LB (7357 9633). Borough tube. **Meals served** noon-11pm Mon-Thur; noon-midnight Fri, Sat. **Main courses** £9.75-£13. **Set meal** £45 (minimum 2) 2 courses , £96 (minimum 4) 3 courses incl wine. **Credit** AmEx, MC, V. Lebanese

Gilak. See p198.

Hiba has established itself as an outpost of Lebanese cuisine in the previously uncharted territory of Borough. Its location – nowhere near the usual Lebanese stomping grounds – and its warm retro decor of dark wood jazzed up with splashes of orange and olive, set it apart. Subtle, low lighting adds to an atmosphere of warmth and merriment, and the feel-good vibe carries on late into the evening, with dinner served until midnight at weekends to an appreciative and lively crowd. The food is classic Lebanese cooking and very good too. We've seldom had a duff dish here, from perfect falafel – crisp on the outside, soft and fluffy within – to a houmous beiruty that was dense, luscious and spiced with dashes of chilli. We've also enjoyed bright, fresh bitinjan rahib (aubergine mashed with garlic and tomato), and perfectly grilled slices of halloumi that added bite to a great range of flavours. Grills excel too; farrouj meshwi (garlic chicken) was beautifully tender, with garlicky mayonnaise a perfect accompaniment. Complimentary baklava makes a great finish.

Available for hire. Babies and children welcome until 7pm. Disabled: toilet. Tables outdoors (4, pavement). Takeaway service. **Map 11 P8**.

of Whitechapel. Although the narrow street-level space only has a few seats beside the long open kitchen, there's a hidden basement room with cosy alcoves, colourful cushions and twinkling glass lanterns. The restaurant's name comes from the 12th-century dynasty that ruled over an area that now includes Turkey, Syria and northern Iraq. Middle Eastern staples are done well here; we especially rate the punchy moutabal, spicy lamb kebabs and excellent breads from the wood-fired oven. The menu also contains some interesting variations on the theme. Bahmia is a slow-cooked stew of okra in a tomato and garlic sauce, sometimes made with lamb ribs but here left vegetarian. The friendly Kurdish owner Sam, a retired doctor, is often on hand to talk guests through the menu: hallab kuba (an Iraqi version of kibbeh) is a deep-fried rice shell stuffed with minced lamb, turmeric, parsley and pine nuts; and mousel kuba (from the city of Mosul) is thin slices of cracked wheat filled with minced lamb, raisins and almonds. Try them for the full experience.

Available for hire. Babies and children welcome: high chair. Booking advisable. Tables outdoors (4, pavement). Takeaway service. **Map 12 S5**.

East

Spitalfields

Zengi

44 Commercial Street, E1 6LT (7426 0700). Aldgate East tube. **Meals served** noon-11pm daily. **Main courses** £2.50-£14. **Credit** MC, V. Iraqi

A short stroll from Spitalfields, Zengi stands out among the wipe-clean caffs and fried chicken bars that populate this part

North

Archway

Gilak

2010 WINNER BEST NEW CHEAP EATS
663 Holloway Road, N19 5SE (7272 1692). Archway tube or Upper Holloway rail. **Meals served** noon-11pm daily. **Main courses** £6.99-£14.50. **Set meal** £38 (minimum 4). **Credit** MC, V. Iranian

Cheap as chickpeas

Fuul and falafel, along with koshari (a blend of rice, pasta and lentils mixed in a tomato sauce), are Egyptian street staples and for millions of people form the basis of lunch every day. Falafel goes down a storm in Syria and Lebanon too, along with flatbread dishes, served pizza-style with cheese or minced meat or – perhaps the most delicious – just a drizzle of olive oil and a dusting of zaatar spice. Fruit juices are extremely popular, with juice bars everywhere, immediately identifiable by the string bags of fruit hanging above the counter.

Some London restaurateurs have realised that Middle Eastern street food travels well and has wide appeal: it's fast food, but tasty and healthy. **Ranoush Juice** (part of the Maroush chain) has long provided food and juices to an Arabic clientele on Edgware Road, but it has now been joined by some very different establishments that are taking the tradition in different directions, such as cheap, cheery **Fresco** and design-led **Comptoir Libanais**.

Open until the early hours, Ranoush Juice gets frenetic on summer nights, with customers calling in for shawarma sandwiches, choosing meze dishes from a selection displayed behind a glass counter, and – of course – drinking freshly squeezed juices. Service is brisk, so presentation may not be as artistic as at other members of the Maroush family, but standards are high. There are a few marble-topped tables, though most customers take their treats away with them.

Juices come in bigger glasses and even greater variety at Fresco. Hardcore 'energisers' (containing ingredients such as broccoli and beets) join plain juices, fruit milkshakes and mixed-fruit cocktails in keeping the juicer whirring for most of the day. This unpretentious and cheery café (there's waitress service) and also a takeaway has a range of meze dishes displayed behind the counter. At lunchtimes the place is rammed with a cosmopolitan crowd of locals and workers.

Le Comptoir Libanais is a major departure in the world of Lebanese food. Big on concept and design, with bold, geometric black-and-white floor tiles and vivid murals in Arabic film poster and Arabic advert style, it tends to attract style-conscious Londoners. Ready-made wraps (falafel, say, or kofta) are lined up behind the glass counter, and a good range of meze snacks is available too, along with larger dishes such as tagines, tempting Lebanese-inspired sweets (the likes of honey and pistachio éclairs, as well as more traditional baklava) and a range of fruit cocktails and smoothies. The venue contains a deli too.

Comptoir Libanais
65 Wigmore Street, W1U 1PZ (7935 1110, www.lecomptoir.co.uk). Bond Street tube.
Meals served 8am-8pm daily. Lebanese
Map 8 G6.
For branch see index.

Fresco
25 Westbourne Grove, W2 4UA (7221 2355, www.frescojuices.co.uk). Bayswater or Royal Oak tube. **Meals served** 8am-11pm daily. Lebanese
Map 7 B6.
For branches see index.

Ranoush Juice
43 Edgware Road, W2 2JE (7723 5929, www.maroush.com). Marble Arch tube. **Meals served** 8am-3am daily. Lebanese
Map 8 F6.
For branches (Beirut Express, Maroush Ranoush, Ranoush Juice) see index.

There's an impressively refined atmosphere to this neighbourhood Iranian restaurant. Gentle blue and white lighting strafes the ceiling; soft classical music plays; and the white tablecloths are illuminated by candles, as the majority of the clientele converse happily with the waiting staff in their native tongue. Service is friendly, efficient and knowledgeable enough to provide admirable detail on a menu that specialises in cooking from Iran's Gilan region – where owner Maji Hokami hails from. Starters consist largely of dips and salads. A herb, cheese and walnut sabsi-o-panir salad was packed with sprightly bunches of tarragon, basil, mint and parsley. Main courses are divided into stews and grilled meats, with the lamb kabab torsh a highlight: pink, tender and with a sharp kick to it. Most mains come with rice; a chicken dish of zereshk polo ba morgh was rendered crunchy and sweet by chunks of pistachio and glistening barberries stirred through soft rice topped by a sharp, sour pomegranate sauce. There's also a small selection of Iranian desserts, although the fried saffron, flour and rosewater balls of our honey-soaked zoolbia were a little too chewy really to impress.
Available for hire. Babies and children welcome: high chairs. Booking advisable. Takeaway service. **Map 26 C1**.

Camden Town & Chalk Farm

Tandis
73 Haverstock Hill, NW3 4SL (7586 8079). Chalk Farm tube. **Meals served** noon-11.30pm Mon-Thur, Sun; noon-midnight Fri, Sat. **Main courses** £7.50-£13.90. **Credit** AmEx, MC, V. Iranian
The unusually glitzy decor at Tandis was inherited from the previous tenant, but what's wrong with having a swish local Iranian restaurant? This spot gets many things right, from the thoughtful welcome to the syrup-soaked Persian pastries (zoolbia). It deserves to be busier. The menu is long, yet is based on store-cupboard staples and repeated ingredients. To start, a generous bowl of wild garlic and yoghurt dip was super-creamy, with kashk-e bademjan (aubergine mashed with onions, walnuts, herbs and whey) making an appealing contrast – just right for scooping up with crisp seed-studded flatbread. Mains are similarly plentiful, with various grills and stews of complex tangy flavours (lamb, split pea and dried lime, for example). Vegetarians will love exploring dishes such as spinach stew with plums (stones included). The mounds of accompanying rice are exquisitely loose, displaying a smattering of saffron-

coloured grains on top. Sicilian house wines cost a convivial £12.95 a bottle. Finish with a glass of cubed saffron and bright green pistachio ice-creams. At the front is a sizeable flagstone terrace with black wooden tables and chairs; this was used for shisha-smoking on our visit, but more could be made of it. *Babies and children welcome: high chairs. Booking advisable Fri, Sat. Separate rooms for parties, seating 14-30. Tables outdoors (5, terrace). Takeaway service.*

North West

Cricklewood

Zeytoon

94-96 Cricklewood Broadway, NW2 3EL (8830 7434, www.zeytoon.co.uk). Cricklewood rail. **Meals served** 12.30-11pm daily. **Main courses** £6.95-£11.95. **Set meze** £13.95. **Credit** AmEx, MC, V. Afghan/Iranian
Set against a backdrop of morbid boozers and tawdry takeaways, Zeytoon is a cultural and culinary oasis for Cricklewood's Iranian and Afghan expats. Expect to dine alongside extended families, moon-eyed couples and gaggles of hijab-wearing teenage girls giggling over photos on their mobile phones. Outside, old men set the world to rights over tea and shisha smoke; inside, the walls are sculpted into ornate arches, scrawled with calligraphic Farsi and painted with wistful Middle Eastern women frolicking among deer or dancing around clouds. Elsewhere there are hung tapestries and doorways topped with tasselled rugs, and chunky wooden tables and chairs. Food is top-notch, from traditional Persian starters such as kashk-e bademjan (aubergine dip here topped with crisp fried onions and crumbled walnuts) to authentic Iranian and Afghan mains. Of the former, we sampled fesenjoon (chicken in a rich walnut and pomegranate sauce); of the latter, a helping of hearty kofta chalow (meatballs in a spicy tomato and split-pea sauce) – both came with mountains of saffron rice. Finish with a bowl of Persian bastani ice-cream flavoured with rosewater and studded with pistachio pieces.

Available for hire. Babies and children welcome: high chairs. Booking advisable. Disabled: toilet. Separate room for parties, seats 100. Tables outdoors (6, pavement). Takeaway service.

Outer London

Wembley, Middlesex

Mesopotamia

115 Wembley Park Drive, Wembley, Middx HA9 8HG (8453 5555, www.mesopotamia.ltd.uk). Wembley Park tube. **Dinner served** 5.30pm-midnight Mon-Sat. **Main courses** £8-£15.50. **Set meze** £19.95-£24.95. **Credit** AmEx, DC, MC, V. Iraqi
The contrast is stunning: outside is traffic-clogged Wembley; inside is Middle Eastern romance. Under a ceiling of billowing silk, Mesopotamia's long, dimly lit interior is decorated with an intricately carved dresser, a wall frieze of Babylonian beasts and palms in relief, and dark, metallic light fittings. It's an enchanting spot, helped along by kindly service from the Anglo-Iraqi owners (though proceedings can slow during busy spells). The menu encompasses various meze starters followed by mains of kebabs or stews. Well-priced set meals give a good idea of the range and can be tailored to requirements. The houmous might be over-puréed for some tastes, and our fattoush was an Anglicised version consisting mostly of iceberg lettuce and tomatoes dressed with pomegranate sauce, but the sweet-savoury flavours of the house-special tamar waya laban (puréed dates with walnut, onion and yoghurt) added interest. To follow, fesenjoon featured succulent chicken in a tart pomegranate and walnut sauce, though the best dish was tapsey semak: a steak of the freshest flaky white fish in a spicy tomato and coriander sauce. Special set dinners are served before events at Wembley Stadium.
Available for hire. Babies and children welcome: children's menu; high chairs. Booking advisable. Takeaway service. Vegetarian menu.

Tandis. See p199.

Modern European

Modern European cooking is one of Londoners' favourite cuisines when eating out. It's a contemporary style, yet generally without the complex preparation and overwrought presentation that is the trademark of haute cuisine. Best of all, these restaurants tend to offer something for everybody: try them for business, romantic dates, lunch with friends or family get-togethers. You might have ribeye steak with béarnaise sauce and goose fat chips followed by a good crème brûlée, or enjoy the culinary experimentation of something like an Asia-meets-Italy plate of five-spice monkfish with saffron risotto and crab spring roll – all this, by the way, from the menu of newcomer **Paramount**, which sits atop Centre Point in the heart of the capital. Among our other favourites this year are **Giaconda Dining Room** and another family-run outfit, **Patterson's**. Both are in the West End, but you don't have to travel into town to experience good Modern European cooking: entries here stretch from Barnes to Brixton, Wapping to West Hampstead.

Central

Bloomsbury

Giaconda Dining Room
9 Denmark Street, WC2H 8LS (7240 3334, www.giaconda dining.com). Tottenham Court Road tube. **Lunch served** noon-2.15pm, **dinner served** 6-9.15pm Mon-Fri. **Main courses** £12-£14. **Cover** £1. **Credit** AmEx, MC, V.
A small, indeed rather cramped, room that gives no hint of the talent at work in the little kitchen at the rear. The Giaconda won our Best New Restaurant award in 2009. It is run by Australians Paul (chef) and Tracey (front of house) Merrony, and has the air of a perfect neighbourhood restaurant – that happens to be in the centre of town. The menu changes just enough to add interest, but there's a grill of the day (sirloin steak with green salad always pleases) and a choice of fish specials. Recently tried dishes included an excellent crab bisque (too rich and generous a portion to finish), steak tartare (spot-on) and sautéed veal kidneys with bacon, field mushrooms and potatoes (a sizzling treat). The only misfire was a starter of braised fennel and carrots with feta – nice ingredients, but the dish didn't gel. We should have stuck with old favourite cervelle de canut (soft fresh cheese, herbs, walnut oil, green salad and toast). Puds are fail-safes such as eton mess and crème brûlée, or you could have a chocolate truffle

with good coffee. Service is unfussy yet efficient, and the atmosphere mellow. London needs more restaurants like this. *Babies and children admitted. Booking advisable.* **Map 17 C3**.

Paramount
32nd floor, Centre Point, 101-103 New Oxford Street, WC1A 1DD (7420 2900, www.paramount.uk.net). Tottenham Court Road tube. **Breakfast served** 8-10am Mon-Fri. **Lunch served** noon-3pm Mon-Fri; 10am-3pm Sat. **Dinner served** 6-11pm Mon-Sat. **Main courses** £14.50-£25.50. **Set lunch** £18.50 2 courses, £23.50 3 courses. **Credit** AmEx, MC, V.
In autumn 2008, a private members' club opened on the 32nd floor of the Centre Point building – one month after the recession had begun in earnest. Owners Pierre and Kathleen Condou have now hired an excellent chef, and opened it to the public. The Tom Dixon-designed interior is upstaged by the view, but chef Colin Layfield's menu is surprisingly good. Not cheap, but *quelle finesse*! A twice-baked roquefort soufflé starter arrived on a black slate drizzled with aged balsamic vinegar. Beetroot-stained cured salmon, topped by a little fillet of seared salmon, overlaying a green streak of pea purée, was even prettier. Main courses include a very refined bouillabaisse that incorporates carved, saffron-steeped potatoes, plus all the trimmings. Any molecular gastronaut would be proud of the dessert; a tiny lemon tart served as a plinth for a lozenge of

crème fraîche parfait and a mini scoop of champagne sorbet, the plate decorated with a champagne foam, shreds of pistachio-green sponge and little pearl-shaped raspberry jellies. Service was friendly and the dishes arrived promptly. Breakfast and lunch are particularly appealing if you find the dinner prices too vertiginous. The attached bar is open only to members or diners.
Booking advisable. Disabled: lift; toilet. Dress: smart. Separate room for parties, seats 150. **Map 17 C2**.

Clerkenwell & Farringdon

Ambassador

55 Exmouth Market, EC1R 4QL (7837 0009, www.the ambassadorcafe.co.uk). Farringdon tube/rail or 19, 38, 341 bus. **Breakfast/lunch served** 9am-3pm Mon-Fri. **Brunch served** 10am-4pm Sat, Sun. **Dinner served** 6-11pm Mon-Sat. **Main courses** £9.50-£17. **Set lunch** (noon-3pm Mon-Sat) £10 2 courses, £15 3 courses. **Set dinner** £15 2 courses, £20 3 courses. **Credit** AmEx, MC, V.
The Ambassador deserves a bit more fuss and attention – it doesn't get half the glory that other starrier Exmouth Market places do, nor is it a twentysomething drinking haunt. Instead, this is a great local restaurant, serving unflashy but seasonal dishes, and a tempting weekend brunch (including pancakes with smoked streaky bacon and maple syrup). Typical starters on a summer's day could include burrata with artichoke, peas and mint, or roast sardines with panzanella. Mains might be fennel and lemon risotto with ricotta and chervil, warm salad of duck confit, black pudding and french beans, or roast rump of lamb with borlotti beans, heirloom tomatoes, parsley and garlic. Finish with chocolate pot or watermelon salad with lime. The kitchen is assured and the waiting staff are welcoming. Prices are competitive too – and it's perfectly possible to kick back with a bar snack and a drink (from a fine choice of wine, beer and cocktails) instead of a full meal. The big airy room is comfortable and softly lit, and in warm weather the front windows open out continental-style.
Available for hire. Babies and children welcome: children's menu; crayons; high chairs; toys. Booking advisable. Tables outdoors (10, pavement). **Map 5 N4**.

Smiths of Smithfield

67-77 Charterhouse Street, EC1M 6HJ (7251 7950, www.smithsofsmithfield.co.uk). Barbican tube or Farringdon tube/rail.
Café-bar **Open** 7am-11pm Mon-Fri; 10am-11.30pm Sat; 9.30am-10.30pm Sun. **Meals served** 7am-4.45pm Mon-Fri; 10am-4.45pm Sat; 9.30am-4.45pm Sun. **Main courses** £5.50-£8.50.
Wine Rooms **Dinner served** 6-10.45pm Mon-Sat; 5-9.30pm Sun. **Main courses** £5.50-£20.
Dining Room **Lunch served** noon-2.45pm Mon-Fri. **Dinner served** 6-10.45pm Mon-Sat. **Main courses** £12-£28.
Top Floor **Lunch served** noon-2.45pm Mon-Fri; 12.30-3.45pm Sun. **Dinner served** 6-10.45pm Mon-Sat. **Main courses** £16-£30.
All **Credit** AmEx, DC, MC, V.
Unlike many chefs hosting TV cookery programmes, Australian-born John Torode has earned his culinary stripes in real restaurant kitchens, and he heads this sucessful set-up opposite the meat market. There's something for everyone here: a ground-floor café-bar serving hearty, no-fuss breakfasts and

Paramount. See p201.

MODERN EUROPEAN

mugs of cappuccino (enjoy some solitude or have a meeting); from late afternoon it becomes a noisy bar-boozer with DJs. Next up, the Wine Rooms, which offer 20 wines by the glass, 140 bins and treats such as own-made pork scratchings, potted shrimps, salt beef and meatball sandwiches. On the second floor is a casual restaurant that emphasises chargrilling and Mediterranean flavours, while top of the tree is the rooftop Top Floor restaurant with timber-decked terrace, eye-popping views over the City, and a menu committed to rare-breed and organic British meats. If your wallet can cope (most mains are over £20), this is the perfect spot to take visitors for Sunday brunch or lunch. Start with oysters, or try the Thai-style crab omelette with bisque, and follow with steak and kidney pudding with red cabbage and truffle mash, or venison loin with celeriac, wild garlic and game sauce. Torode himself has described this vast operation as a beast, but it's also a beauty. *Babies and children welcome (restaurant): high chairs. Disabled: toilet. Entertainment (ground floor): DJs 7pm Thur-Sat. Separate rooms for parties, seating 12 and 24. Tables outdoors (4, pavement; 6, terrace).* **Map 11 O5**.

Covent Garden

L'Atelier de Joël Robuchon
13-15 West Street, WC2H 9NE (7010 8600, www.joel-robuchon.com). Leicester Square tube. Bar **Open** noon-12.30am Mon-Sat; noon-10.30pm Sun. *Ground floor* **Lunch served** noon-2.30pm, **dinner served** 5.30-10.30pm daily. **Main courses** £15-£55. **Set meal** (noon-2.30pm, 5.30-6.30pm) £22 2 courses, £27 3 courses. *First floor* **Dinner served** 6.30-11.30pm Mon-Sat. **Main courses** £15-£55. *All* **Credit** AmEx, MC, V.
Before he 'retired', French super-chef Joël Robuchon had a constellation of awards under his belt for his luxurious haute cuisine. This polished operation (down a Covent Garden backstreet that would be called 'quiet' if the Ivy wasn't a couple of doors away) is his stab at an informal restaurant. A very successful stab it is too – there are Ateliers in several cities around the world. There's a concept at work here; the venue includes three separate areas (the bar, the restaurant and L'Atelier itself), and all provide combinations of the same menus, of which there are several. Most people visit for the small tasting dishes: plates of Modern European tapas-style dishes listed simply by their primary ingredient ('le pied de cochon', 'l'oeuf', 'le foie gras') served from a central open kitchen. There is, of course, more traditional table service too. Much of the food is highly inventive and everything is beautifully presented; the unusual delivery belies the flawless technique on display. Decor is bold: all black lacquer and blood red, with a wall of plants providing horticultural contrast. *Available for hire. Babies and children admitted. Booking essential. Disabled: toilet. Dress: smart casual.* **Map 17 C3**.

Axis
One Aldwych, 1 Aldwych, WC2B 4BZ (7300 0300, www.onealdwych.com). Covent Garden or Embankment tube or Charing Cross tube/rail. **Lunch served** noon-2.30pm Mon-Fri. **Dinner served** 5.30-10.30pm Mon-Fri; 5.30-11.30pm Sat. **Main courses** £17-£22. **Set meal** (noon-2.30pm Mon-Fri; 5.30-7pm, 10-10.45pm Mon-Sat) £16.75 2 courses, £19.75 3 courses. **Credit** AmEx, DC, MC, V.

Should you be looking for a mellow, stylish hideaway for quiet conversation in central London, this could be it. Once you've descended the oddly narrow, stone-clad spiral staircase into the drum-shaped hotel basement, not a sound enters from the traffic outside and the ambient sounds are muted. Decor is carefully styled in subtle colours, with a row of metal bamboo poles the only odd note. Service is smooth and very attentive. The kitchen can certainly turn it on when needed: chilled tomato consommé with basil and poached langoustines, from a special summer menu highlighting British tomatoes, was an absolutely exquisite infusion of elusive flavours. From the main menu, welsh rarebit with plum tomato salad was a satisfyingly refined version of an everyday standby. Breast of chicken with tarragon, a rich jus and a variety of fresh veg, on the other hand, was enjoyable though more routine. Seared scallops came with a fennel purée that had an oddly bitter taste. Prices are quite high for both the main menu and wines, but the set lunch and pre- and post-theatre menu is a bargain. *Available for hire. Babies and children welcome: high chairs. Booking advisable. Disabled: toilet. Separate room for parties, seats 18. Vegetarian menu.* **Map 18 F4**.

The Ivy
1 West Street, WC2H 9NQ (7836 4751, www.the-ivy.co.uk). Leicester Square tube. **Lunch served** noon-3pm Mon-Sat; noon-3.30pm Sun. **Dinner served** 5.30pm-midnight Mon-Sat; 5.30-11pm Sun. **Main courses** £9.25-£35. **Cover** £2. **Credit** AmEx, DC, MC, V.
Firmly entrenched in cliché as the place where celebrities go to be photographed entering or emerging (oh, and to eat), the Ivy surprises us every year with just how pleasant it is. Behind the famous chequered and stained glass, staff are impeccably sweet and helpful. On a Saturday lunchtime, we were seated in a leather booth on a far edge: perfect vantage for peering into the wood-panelled room (no celebs: perhaps they were in the private members' club upstairs). From a menu dominated by British classics, we steered around the famously priced shepherd's pie (£17) and intstead chose Cornish lamb with sweetbreads: a delicate portion of both, but big on meaty flavours. Butternut squash risotto was fine, if lacking punch; starters of tuna sashimi in a spicy soy dressing, and a rich, salty, seafood bisque, were both excellent. To drink, we opted for tart and tasty cranberry cocktails over wine from a huge list. Desserts include baked alaska to share and trifle. On the table next to us, the charming head waiter noticed an unfinished portion and struck it from the bill without being asked. Quiet class: so unlike the cliché. *Babies and children welcome: high chairs. Booking essential, 4-6 wks in advance. Separate room for parties, seats 60. Vegan dishes. Vegetarian menu.* **Map 18 D4**.

Holborn

The Terrace
Lincoln's Inn Fields, WC2A 3LJ (7430 1234, www.the terrace.info). Holborn tube. **Breakfast served** 9-11am, **lunch served** noon-3pm, **dinner served** 5.30-8pm Mon-Fri. **Main courses** £10.50-£17.95. **Set lunch** £16.95 2 courses, £18.95 3 courses. **Credit** MC, V.
Sheltered amid greenery in the middle of Lincoln's Inn Fields, the Terrace is an unexpected hideaway, housed in a discreet single-storey building with terrace behind. Inside, decoration is pleasantly low-key; outside, tables and multicoloured chairs are chic and plastic. Food comes with a Caribbean twist, visible

in summery dishes such as jerk chicken caesar salad or lobster and mango salad. A starter of smoked chicken and mozzarella salad came with a ring of lovely green olive oil flecked with spots of balsamic: a perfect, light combination. Grilled halloumi with leaves was another success: a thick, succulent slab of mild golden cheese with a subtle dressing, capers adding bite. To follow, mackerel and squid with green salad was also enjoyable, precisely cooked and with fresh, simple flavours. Linguine with parmesan, however, was quite bland; more cheese in the creamy sauce would have added some punch. Portions aren't large, so we couldn't resist pudding: a luxurious eton mess, with cream, strawberries and chewy chunks of meringue. The Terrace's cheapest white wine, Le Lesc vin de pays du Gers from Gascony (£15.50), is light yet full of flavour, setting the tone well for our meal.

Available for hire. Babies and children welcome: high chairs. Booking advisable. Disabled: toilet. Tables outdoors (15, terrace). **Map 10 M6.**

King's Cross

Acorn House

69 Swinton Street, WC1X 9NT (7812 1842, www.acorn houserestaurant.com). King's Cross tube/rail. **Lunch served** noon-3pm Mon-Fri; noon-4pm Sun. **Dinner served** 6-10pm Mon-Fri; 5.30-10pm Sat. **Main courses** £11-£16. **Credit** AmEx, MC, V.

Acorn House's raison d'être is as a 'social enterprise', minimising energy use, ensuring ingredients aren't air-freighted, purifying water on site, recycling, monitoring meat sources and so on. The first sign that the restaurant is different is its location: an unprepossessing building near King's Cross. Inside, the look is low-key and slightly retro. The long space has an open kitchen at one end and an unused counter at the other, lending it a slightly disconsolate air. Local produce is used where possible, but (somewhat confusingly) the kitchen's Italian slant means that much is imported. A starter of globe artichoke with st maure goat's cheese, mint and other leaves had impeccable ingredients yet was bland; chargrilled mackerel with green tomatoes and frisée featured fresh, well-cooked fish, but again there was nothing imaginative about the flavours or combinations. Sicilian pale aubergine, tomatoes, chilli and mozzarella was pleasant-tasting, though a bit undercooked – and pricey at £12. Pork belly with spring onions and mash was better, the thick, salty crust a good match for the potato.

Available for hire. Babies and children welcome: high chairs, nappy-changing facilities. Booking advisable weekends. Disabled: lift; toilet. Takeaway service. **Map 4 M3.**

Knightsbridge

Fifth Floor

Harvey Nichols, Knightsbridge, SW1X 7RJ (7235 5250, www.harveynichols.com). Knightsbridge tube.
Café **Breakfast served** 8am-noon, **lunch served** noon-3.30pm, **dinner served** 6-10.30pm Mon-Sat. **Brunch served** 11am-5pm Sun. **Tea served** 3-6pm daily. **Main courses** £9.50-£15.
Restaurant **Lunch served** noon-2.45pm Mon-Thur; noon-3.45pm Fri, Sat. **Brunch served** noon-4pm Sun. **Tea served** 2.30-5.30pm Mon-Sat; 3-5pm Sun. **Dinner served** 6-10.45pm Mon-Sat. **Set lunch** £19.50 2 courses, £24.50 3 courses. **Set dinner** £35 2 courses, £40 3 courses.
Both **Credit** AmEx, DC, MC, V.

Back in the day (1992, to be precise) the opening of Harvey Nichols' Fifth Floor restaurant, café and food hall was big news in the retail trade, and marked the debut of Henry Harris (chef-patron of Racine, *see p92*) as a head chef. His cooking garnered great acclaim for a decade, but since his departure the oval-shaped restaurant has had some ups and downs, including a coolly received white-themed redesign that was once again being tempered as we went to press. Swedish-born chef Jonas Karlsson is now in charge of wooing the ladies who lunch here and his menus are more indulgent than you might expect of a department store famous for its body-hugging designer clothes. Foie gras and pork pâté with pistachio, carrot and apricot chutney and toasted rye bread might be followed by veal loin with truffle gnocchi and a fricassee of morels and peas, then strawberry tiramisu with jelly and boudoir biscuits. Still, there are also plenty of salads, fish and shellfish to please the waist-watchers.

While the Fifth Floor concept was one that extended naturally to other branches of the department store, Harvey Nichols has also opened stand-alone restaurants. Oxo Tower Restaurant, Bar & Brasserie launched in 1996 in a firestorm of publicity; Prism to less fuss in the City three years later. Prices in the Oxo Tower Restaurant tend to hurt a little given the standard of cooking; we prefer the friendly brasserie for its great west-side views, buzzy vibe and better perception of value, though both are ideal for special-occasion dinners when the sights and lights of London are as important as the food and wine. Prism is set in a converted bank that pairs original features with modern red furniture to eye-popping effect. Prices aren't bad given its Leadenhall location, and good ingredients (meat comes from the Ginger Pig) are used to persuasive effect. All mains cost under £20, unless you want to splash out on 300g Longhorn steaks dry-aged for 50 days, and desserts are six quid. The two bars take their cocktails seriously; the accompanying food (served all day) extends to chicken caesar, sausage and mash, and fishcakes.

Babies and children welcome: children's menu; high chairs; nappy-changing facilities. Disabled: lift; toilet. Tables outdoors (15, café terrace). **Map 8 F9.**
For branches (Oxo Tower Restaurant, Bar & Brasserie, Prism) see index.

Marylebone

L'Autre Pied

5-7 Blandford Street, W1U 3DB (7486 9696, www.lautrepied.co.uk). Baker Street tube. **Open** noon-2.30pm, 6-10.30pm Mon-Sat; noon-3pm, 6.30-9.30pm Sun. **Main courses** £21.50-£27.95. **Set meal** (noon-2.30pm Mon-Sat, 6-7pm daily) £20.95 3 courses. **Set lunch** (Sun) £26.50 3 courses. **Credit** AmEx, MC, V.

This Pied à Terre offshoot positively purrs with the pleasure and efficiency of a restaurant at the top of its game. There is the feeling of an invested management curating every detail, but only in the background: the overall impression is relaxed and informal, the multiple awards worn lightly. On a summer night, we decided against the cosy interior with its burgundy booths and whimsical hand-painted walls, and sat at the pavement tables next to the delivery hatch (into which a case of live lobsters was slung as we ate). Don't be fooled by the terse, shopping-list style of the menu: the ingredients are confected into dishes with art both technical and visual. Summer truffle risotto used puffed wild rice and truffle juice for taste and texture contrast; steamed and roasted pigeon

sketch

THE GALLERY
ART GALLERY BY DAY,
GASTRO-BRASSERIE BY NIGHT

THE GLADE
EVENING BAR

SKETCH, A MOSAIC OF EXPERIENCE
SERVED FULL OF WARMTH AND A DASH OF INTRIGUE ON THE SIDE

9 CONDUIT STREET, LONDON, W1S 2XG 020 7659 4500

WWW.SKETCH.UK.COM

breasts were set on an anchovy and mozzarella tart and flanked by rounds of aubergine purée in a geometric style. The wine list trawls the world, but we didn't get much further than the first page for our glasses of Mendocino Country zinfandel and Marche verdicchio, which collaborated beautifully with pigeon and snail, respectively. Coffee came with unstinting petits fours, eliminating the need for dessert. Professional but friendly staff served even the outdoor tables expertly.
Babies and children welcome: high chairs. Booking advisable. Separate room for parties, seats 18. Tables outdoors (3, pavement). **Map 9 G5**.

Mayfair

Nicole's
158 New Bond Street, W1S 2UB (7499 8408, www.nicolefarhi.com). Bond Street or Green Park tube. *Bar* **Open** 8am-6pm Mon-Fri; 10am-6pm Sat. **Meals served** 8am-5.30pm Mon-Fri; 10am-5.30pm Sat. **Main courses** £9-£14.95.
Restaurant **Breakfast served** 8am-noon Mon-Sat. **Lunch served** noon-3.30pm Mon-Fri; noon-4pm Sat. **Tea served** 3.30-6pm Mon-Sat. **Main courses** £19-£25. **Cover** (noon-4pm Mon-Sat) £1.
Both **Credit** AmEx, DC, MC, V.
Tucked beneath the streets of Mayfair, Nicole Farhi's glamour-fuelled basement brasserie exudes sophisticated elegance . It's an ideal posh pit-stop, though the lack of natural light and stream of well-dressed tourists are somewhat reminiscent of a business-class airport lounge. The menu is on the pricey side, but service is first-rate; before ordering, you're offered a variety of artisan breads studded with nuts, raisins and herbs. Starters comprise such simple favourites as grilled squid, mezze, and asparagus with serrano ham. We opted for roast quail with peach and pistachio salad, which was fine except for some tasteless, unripe peaches. A main of calf's liver with smoky bacon was pleasant, while pan-fried sea bass with roast artichokes, fennel and black olives had a delicious balance of flavours and textures. The best dish was dessert: a wonderful own-made lemon tart with thin, nutty pastry, a silky, tangy interior and a crunchy brûlée topping. With such excellent pâtisserie, it's no wonder Nicole's afternoon teas are in vogue right now.
Available for hire. Babies and children admitted. Booking advisable. **Map 9 H7**.

Patterson's
4 Mill Street, W1S 2AX (7499 1308, www.pattersons restaurant.co.uk). Bond Street or Oxford Circus tube. **Lunch served** noon-3pm Mon-Fri. **Dinner served** 6-11pm Mon-Fri; 5-11pm Sat. **Main courses** £20. **Set lunch** £23 3 courses, £27 3 courses. **Credit** AmEx, MC, V.
An unassumingly excellent family business in the midst of bling-brand Mayfair is something to treasure. And Patterson's regulars certainly do. The set lunch gives exceptional bang for buck, causing appreciative murmurs from the business-dominated clientele. Generous provision of top-quality protein (hake as a main course, juicy nuggets of rabbit and pigeon in a terrine, lamb that tasted of a life well lived) owes much to chef-owner Raymond Patterson's Scottish origins. So does the lack of pretension, though the skill and style (champagne-glazed turbot; bouchée of veal sweetbreads demidoff on the carte) reveal a classic French background. Scallops from the

Hebrides and lobster from creel boats make this a destination for seafood, as fish tanks for decor suggest. From the father-and son-run kitchen come intense, intriguing but not outlandish flavour matches, such as sweet pear purée with the terrine, and sublime creamed cauliflower with a sea trout starter. There's just enough under £30 on the wine list, plus half bottles. Desserts include ravishing, complex concoctions such as rice and butterscotch crème brûlée with pineapple sorbet and a gingersnap. Neat, petite, knowledgeable staff include Mrs Patterson out front.
Available for hire. Babies and children welcome: high chairs. Booking advisable. Separate room for parties, seats 20. **Map 9 H/J6**.

Sotheby's Café
Sotheby's, 34-35 New Bond Street, W1S 2RT (7293 5077, www.sothebys.com/cafe). Bond Street or Oxford Circus tube. **Breakfast served** 9.30-11.30am, **lunch served** noon-3pm, **tea served** 3-4.45pm Mon-Fri. **Main courses** £14-£17.50. **Set tea** £6.25. **Credit** AmEx, DC, MC, V.
A grand auction has a 24-carat buzz, and seated inside Sotheby's diminutive café – in an alcove off the main lobby – you get a prime view of proceedings. Monied folk glide past carrying catalogues or shimmering handbags. Opposite is a flatscreen TV (showing the auction in progress) and two casually hung pictures: on our visit Franz Holbein and Pieter Brueghel originals, with a guide price for the pair of a cool £5 million. In comparison, the café lunch menu is a steal: a concise but pertinent list of seasonal dishes (just one vegetarian, meat and fish choice for first course and second), plus a side salad and a toasted sandwich (lobster, naturally). Staff are exact, polished and French, flitting between the linen-clothed tables with verve. Gazpacho arrived puréed and just a degree above optimum temperature, but with summery flavours bursting forth. To follow, perfectly seared new-season lamb was as generous a portion as you could hope for, served with Jersey Royals and anchovy aïoli. Breakfast and cream teas have their appointed times, and wine is chosen by Serena Sutcliffe MW. Lavender custard with gooseberries might provide the lunchtime finale. Going, going, gone.
Babies and children admitted. Booking advisable. Disabled: toilet. **Map 9 H6**.

Piccadilly

Criterion
224 Piccadilly, W1J 9HP (7930 0488, www.criterion restaurant.com). Piccadilly Circus tube. **Lunch served** noon-2.30pm, **dinner served** 5.30-11.30pm Mon-Sat. **Main courses** £12.50-£28.50. **Set meal** (lunch, 5.30-7pm, 10-11.30pm) £16.95 2 courses, £19.95 3 courses. **Credit** AmEx, MC, V.
A national treasure, the Criterion has possibly London's most sumptuous dining room: a glittering 1870s Byzantine fantasy with a head start in making any meal memorable. For years, though, no one seems to have known what to do with it: the current Georgian owners have announced big plans, but delivery is another matter. Part of the problem is that the location, once the heart of Empire, is now so tacky. However, it's also close to many theatres, and lately the restaurant has been doing good business with pre- and post-show set menus. Sadly, the set meal we tried deployed fancy names but was ordinary at best. Bresaola with sliced pear and rocket, and pan-

MODERN EUROPEAN

fried sea bream with fennel were both routinely pleasant; but smoked salmon arrived without any detectable flavour of a promised horseradish dressing, and a dry duck-leg confit came with 'pomme purée' that was just hefty mash. Maybe there are fireworks on the carte, but shouldn't set menus give a sampler of what a kitchen can do? Also, lofty wine prices add greatly to the cost of the meal. Some day, someone will make the Criterion special again, but not yet.

Babies and children admitted. Booking advisable. Dress: smart casual. Separate room for parties, seats 70.
Map 17 B5.

Pimlico

Rex Whistler Restaurant at Tate Britain
Tate Britain, Millbank, SW1P 4RG (7887 8825, www.tate.org.uk). Pimlico tube or 87 bus. **Breakfast served** 10-11.30am Sat, Sun. **Lunch served** 11.30am-3pm, **tea served** 3.15-5pm daily. **Main courses** £13.50-£23.95. **Set lunch** £15.95 2 courses, £19.95 3 courses. **Credit** AmEx, DC, MC, V.
The restaurant at Tate Britain does much more than it needs to, for much less that you'd expect. On snacks, drinks and bakery, prices are comparable to those at the cafeteria opposite, but instead of a self-service tray, you get attentive table service, linen-dressed tables and a room that's a gallery in itself: an early Rex Whistler mural tells the story over four walls of 'The Expedition in Pursuit of Rare Meats'. It's a daytime-only restaurant and the food is simple, but seasonal and appealing. Summer lunch might feature poached sea trout with radish and cucumber salad, or guinea fowl with Jersey Royals and a herb reduction; at afternoon tea, a shorter savoury menu is available, typically including a soup, devilled kidneys on toast and a savoury tart. This year's visit encountered a rare snafu: an order given as wild mushroom and chive omelette and dripping-cooked chips arrived as the unusual combination of afternoon tea and chips. On the upside, this allowed us to study the pretty mini cakes and finger sandwiches on their cake stand – good value for £7.25 with tea – but the chips were past their best by the time the omelette arrived, well made but salty. We were compensated with a free drink, and chose one of the exotic smoothies, apricot and guava, from an educated and extensive beverage range; the wine list is among London's best.
Babies and children welcome: high chairs. Booking advisable. Disabled: toilet. Tables outdoors (8, terrace).
Map 16 L11.

St James's

Le Caprice
Arlington House, Arlington Street, SW1A 1RJ (7629 2239, www.caprice-holdings.co.uk). Green Park tube. **Lunch served** noon-3pm Mon-Thur; noon-4pm Fri, Sat. **Dinner served** 5.30pm-midnight Mon-Sat. **Meals served** 11.30am-11pm Sun. **Main courses** £14-£25. **Set dinner** (5.30-6.45pm, after 10.15pm) £15.75 2 courses, £19.75 3 courses. **Cover** £2. **Credit** AmEx, DC, MC, V.
Located on a quiet St James's cul-de-sac, Le Caprice is surprisingly unobtrusive for a renowned glamour magnet. The entrance is marked by a bowler-hatted doorman, a few boxed plants and signage as discreet as blue neon can be. Getting a table is often tough (though we've never had a problem at the weekend). But no matter: on busy nights it's arguably best fun to take one of the chic leather stools at the bar, pristinely laid

with white napkins, silver salt shakers and dark wood pepper grinders. Much more than the chopped steak is delivered 'à l'américaine' – the brunch menu proffers pancakes, bagels, shrimp burger, and chopped salad with smoked chicken, bacon and blue cheese – but you'll also find the likes of pan-fried duck's egg with sautéed foie gras, and slow-roast pork belly with beans and black pudding. Vegetarians and vegans have their own, mostly Italian menu with treats such as girolle and samphire risotto. Wines start at £20 a bottle for Sicilian red and white. There are carafes too, but choice is unfashionably limited; more interesting, if you have the reddies, are the premium US wines. Service is a model of friendly efficiency, so don't worry if you're given a strict timeslot in which to dine.
Babies and children welcome: high chairs. Booking essential, 2 wks in advance. Entertainment: pianist 6.30pm-midnight Mon-Sat, 7-11pm Sun. Vegetarian menu. **Map 9 J8**.

Soho

Andrew Edmunds
46 Lexington Street, W1F 0LW (7437 5708). Leicester Square, Oxford Circus or Piccadilly Circus tube. **Lunch served** 12.30-3pm Mon-Fri; 1-3pm Sat; 1-3.30pm Sun. **Dinner served** 6-10.45pm Mon-Sat; 6-10.30pm Sun. **Main courses** £10-£17. **Credit** MC, V.
Quiet little Lexington Street brings a neighbourhood feel to the centre of Soho, and Andrew Edmunds has been its cherished local for almost 25 years. With a matt-black frontage (next to Edmunds' antique print gallery) and basic wooden furniture, this townhouse restaurant is almost laughably unassuming, and rather cramped. But it's romantic too, whether you're in the bistro-like ground floor or mirror-lined basement. Likewise, the menu – mostly Mediterranean-style dishes scrawled on a sheet – is the antithesis of Mod Euro bluster. Some dishes (precisely cooked cod with decent mash, clams, broad beans, peas and salsa verde, say) are seasonal regulars; others, such as duck breast with rice-noodle salad, dabble in the Orient. Wild mushroom and lentil salad with manchego lacked punch, but the rest of our meal was gratifying: king scallop carpaccio with capers, orange and pea tops (orange juice enhancing beautifully fresh shellfish), followed by warm seafood salad packed with squid, octopus, shrimps and mussels, and lent oomph by chorizo and smoked paprika potatoes. Service is relaxed, friendly and speedy. The constantly changing wine list is a boon (consult the additional list if you're an oenophile). Finish with classic British puds such as eton mess.
Babies and children admitted. Booking essential (not taken more than 1 wk in advance). Tables outdoors (2, pavement).
Map 17 A4.

Arbutus
63-64 Frith Street, W1D 3JW (7734 4545, www.arbutus restaurant.co.uk). Tottenham Court Road tube. **Lunch served** noon-2.30pm Mon-Sat; noon-3pm Sun. **Dinner served** 5-11pm Mon-Thur; 5-11.30pm Fri, Sat; 5.30-10.30pm Sun. **Main courses** £14-£19.95. **Set lunch** £16.95 3 courses. **Set dinner** (5-7pm) £18.95 3 courses. **Credit** AmEx, MC, V.
Chef and co-owner Anthony Demetre is best known for his creative ability to transform thrifty ingredients into fine-dining delights. Unassuming decor and minimalist furnishings in Arbutus' two-roomed dining area give little away – the excellence of the daily changing menu is the big draw. The

Arbutus. See p207.

restaurant attracts Soho media types, food lovers and nearby office groups, which lend it a relaxed, buzzy and sometimes boisterous vibe. Service is faultless. The carte options can be pricey, but the set menus are seriously good value. The food blends British culinary tradition with Modern European cooking styles. A rustic, chunky-textured terrine was sublimely succulent, the meaty, buttery flavours matching divinely with some sweetly acidic fruit chutney. A main of slow-cooked tender lamb, almost gamey in taste, worked well with meltingly soft aubergine slivers and light gnocchi – a marvellous Mediterranean twist. Puds hit the high notes; it's hard to resist the famed 'floating islands' (proper custard, flecked with vanilla, topped with a fluffy poached-in-milk meringue). Wines are well priced, well chosen and available in 250ml carafes.

Sister restaurant Wild Honey in Mayfair offers a similar style of cooking in more intimate, wood-panelled surroundings. Its lunchtime set menu is slightly more expensive than at Arbutus, and it also provides an afternoon tea of sorts (called a 'sweet and savoury menu', served 3-6pm weekdays). In late 2010, Demetre and business partner Will Smith are to open an all-day French brasserie called Les Deux Salons in Covent Garden. *Babies and children admitted: high chairs. Booking advisable.* **Map 17 B3.**
For branch (Wild Honey) see index.

South Kensington

Bibendum
Michelin House, 81 Fulham Road, SW3 6RD (7581 5817, www.bibendum.co.uk). South Kensington tube. **Lunch served** noon-2.30pm Mon-Sat; 12.30-3pm Sun. **Dinner served** 7-11pm Mon-Sat; 7-10.30pm Sun. **Main courses** £17.50-£28.50. **Set lunch** £26.50 2 courses, £29.50 3 courses. **Credit** AmEx, MC, V.
There are many ways to appreciate the art nouveau beauty of the Michelin building. You could start on the covered forecourt, beside the verdant flower stall, with freshly shucked oysters from the crustacea stall or coffee and a smoked chicken and avocado sandwich from the café. The foyer houses the Oyster Bar (and some lovely tilework); it's a casual if noisy setting for more excellent shellfish, light lunches (salad niçoise, smoked salmon, charcuterie to share) and a glass of wine. More serene is Bibendum itself, on the first floor. Light-filled, with crisp white linen, gleaming glassware and comfortable but ugly loose-covered chairs, it's formal but not starchy. The Michelin Man beams down from huge stained-glass windows; well-drilled staff beam at your elbow. Dinner is a pricey business, with starters topping £10 and most mains around £25. Some dishes from the carte are also available at lunch, such as fillet steak au poivre, and roast chicken with tarragon (for two – a signature dish since Simon Hopkinson was chef here). But most people opt for the better-value prix fixe, which offers ample choice and ample portions. Mains of tender, flavourful duck breast, and steamed cod with earthy puy lentils were decent but not outstanding; the salsa verde with the fish was too laden with tarragon. Best was a dessert of intensely fruity blackberry soup with buttermilk sorbet. Expense-accounters will drool over the 800-strong wine list, but there's plenty of choice by the glass, 'pot' and cheaper bottle.
Available for hire. Babies and children welcome: high chairs. Booking advisable. Disabled: lift, toilet. Tables outdoors (8, patio). **Map 14 E10.**
For branch (Bibendum Oyster Bar) see index.

West

Bayswater

Le Café Anglais   `HOT 50`
8 Porchester Gardens, W2 4DB (7221 1415, www. lecafeanglais.co.uk). Bayswater tube. **Lunch served** noon-3.30pm Mon-Fri, Sun. **Brunch served** noon-3.30pm Sat. **Dinner served** 6.30-11pm Mon-Thur; 6.30-11.30pm Fri, Sat; 6.30-10.15pm Sun. **Main courses** £8-£27.50. **Set lunch** (Mon-Fri) £16.50 2 courses, £19.50 3 courses; (Sun) £22 2 courses, £26 3 courses. **Cover** £1.80. **Credit** AmEx, MC, V.

Though it has been open for only a few years, Rowley Leigh's Le Café Anglais feels much more established. The look is of a grand-but-modern brasserie; while eating here feels like a treat, much effort is made (set menus, bridge nights, children's meals) on the neighbourhood restaurant front. The menu is a crowd-pleaser, with enough seasonal changes to keep things fresh (peach and tomato salad, say, or crab risotto or roast leg of lamb with ratatouille). The hors d'oeuvres list is a triumph; order the likes of celeriac remoulade or fennel salami with sweet and sour onion (both are good), but be certain to try parmesan custard with anchovy toast – it instantly became a classic, and deservedly so. Next, you could have grilled sea bass with a choice of dressings, veal cutlet milanese, or something from the rotisserie: chicken with girolles, perhaps, or wood pigeon with braised peas. A big choice of vegetables induces greed; the selection runs from chips or rice pilaf to watercress with vinaigrette or spring greens with garlic. Finally, decide between scoops of ice-cream, cheeses or fresh fruits, or a dessert such as vanilla cheesecake with passionfruit or grilled pineapple with chilli syrup and coconut sorbet. The user-friendly wine list includes some options by the carafe. In short, Le Café Anglais is an excellent restaurant, run with style. As we went to press, a refurbishment was under way and a new, all-day café and oyster bar was about to open at the front of the restaurant, offering plenty of shellfish and seafood, plus sandwiches and light meals.
Available for hire. Babies and children welcome: high chairs. Booking advisable dinner. Disabled: toilet. Separate room for parties, seats 26. **Map 7 C6**.

Chiswick

Sam's Brasserie & Bar
11 Barley Mow Passage, W4 4PH (8987 0555, www.samsbrasserie.co.uk). Chiswick Park or Turnham Green tube. **Open** 9am-midnight Mon-Wed, Sun; 9am-12.30am Thur-Sat. **Food served** 9am-10.30pm Mon-Sat; 9am-10pm Sun. **Main courses** £9.50-£18.50. **Set lunch** (noon-3pm Mon-Fri) £13 2 courses, £16 3 courses. **Credit** AmEx, MC, V.
Sam's (2007 winner of our Best Local Restaurant award) continues to serve the neighbourhood well, its versatility most in evidence during busy weekend brunch. The accommodating bar area is equipped with a giant TV screen, but you're equally welcome to open your laptop or browse the papers. Space is devoted to buggy parking, though serious brunchers can ignore distractions by occupying the two-seater window banquettes. The separate dining area has a relaxed, conversation-friendly atmosphere; views of the open kitchen inspire confidence. Sourcing (not least of seafood) is good and the cooking competent, with some dishes displaying star quality. A plateful of heritage tomatoes seasoned with smoked sea salt was fine, fresh and generous, but no knockout. Best was a chunky fillet of Icelandic cod, which attained that great ideal of crisp, golden skin complementing translucent, pearly flakes of tender flesh, with a perfectly judged saffron aïoli singing in support. Sound bar snacks make a great foil to the interesting beers, but it would be foolish to ignore the enticing wine list, with plenty offered by the glass or carafe. Excellent bread, comforting puds and flexible service round off a cheering experience.
Babies and children welcome: children's menu; high chairs; toys. Booking advisable Thur-Sat. Disabled: toilet.

Kensington

Clarke's
124 Kensington Church Street, W8 4BH (7221 9225, www.sallyclarke.com). Notting Hill Gate tube. **Lunch served** 12.30-2pm Mon-Fri; noon-2pm Sat, Sun. **Dinner served** 6.30-10pm Mon-Sat. **Main courses** £9.50-£22. **Set dinner** £39.50 3 courses. **Credit** AmEx, DC, MC, V.
With views of Kensington Church Street and a charming patio garden, Clarke's is a bright, genteel spot. It's popular with an older crowd, but staff (friendly without being chummy) are good with families and children. After a quarter-century of famously offering a no-choice menu, Sally Clarke felt she had made her point, and some years ago expanded the options. Now there's a three-course set dinner, plus a carte that typically offers three simple yet perfectly cooked dishes per course. Seasonality has always been the watchword, but Clarke's definition of local stretches beyond Surrey, frequently to Italy. A June menu might see Pugliese burrata, san daniele ham and Sicilian figs lining up with Cornish red mullet, Gloucester Old Spot gammon and Woolley Park Farm chicken. Crisp battered courgette flowers came with a roulade of speck ham, goat's cheese, aubergine and asparagus, the plate daubed with basil oil; it was the menu's most complex dish. We followed with pan-roast plaice, Jersey potatoes and intensely creamy dill sauce. The zingy ease of soured cream sorbet with marinated strawberries trounced a well-crafted chocolate soufflé cake with stracciatella (Italian choc chip) ice-cream and espresso syrup.
Available for hire. Babies and children welcome: high chairs. Booking advisable. Separate room for parties, seats 50. **Map 7 B7**.

Notting Hill

Notting Hill Brasserie
92 Kensington Park Road, W11 2PN (7229 4481, www. nottinghillbrasserie.com). Notting Hill Gate tube. **Lunch served** noon-3pm daily. **Dinner served** 6.30-11pm Mon-Sat; 6.30-10.30pm Sun.. **Main courses** £19.50-£25.50. **Set lunch** (Wed-Sat) £17.50 2 courses, £22.50 3 courses; (Sun) £25 2 courses, £30 3 courses. **Credit** AmEx, MC, V.
From the cobbled lane entrance to the grand piano by the bar, there's a sense of old-fashioned opulence about this enduring Notting Hill favourite. It's set in an Edwardian townhouse divided into separate rooms adorned with slightly out-of-place African art. It's all low lighting, clinking champagne glasses and tinkly jazz, and we suspect there have been more than a few marriage proposals here. Thankfully, the food lives up to the surroundings. Head chef Karl Burdock shows great skill and imagination, especially with marine life, transforming tuna niçoise with gazpacho into a work of art, and a crab and prawn cannellone into a long, dumpling-like dream. The fishy theme continued into the mains; lemon sole and halibut were both expertly cooked, and drowning in buttery, velvet sauces; they induced sighs of pleasure all round. Chocolate fondant oozed in all the right ways to round off a near perfect experience. Though the carte is pricey, the set lunches are terrific value. The only let down was a tetchy waiter who took our request for tap water as a personal attack and was frosty for the remainder of the meal.
Babies and children welcome: high chairs; supervised crèche (Sun lunch). Booking advisable. Entertainment: jazz/blues musicians 7pm daily, lunch Sun. Separate rooms for parties, seating 12 and 32. **Map 7 A6**.

South West

Barnes

Sonny's

94 Church Road, SW13 0DQ (8748 0393, www.sonnys. co.uk). Barnes or Barnes Bridge rail, or 33, 209, 283 bus.
Bar **Lunch served** noon-4pm daily. **Brunch served** 10am-noon Sat, Sun.
Restaurant **Lunch served** noon-3pm daily. **Dinner served** 7-10.30pm Mon-Thur; 7-11pm Fri, Sat. **Set dinner** (Mon-Thur) £15.50 2 courses, £18.50 3 courses.
Both **Main courses** £12.50-£17.50. **Set lunch** (Mon-Sat) £13.50 2 courses, £15.50 3 courses; (Sun) £21.50 2 courses, £24.50 3 courses. **Credit** AmEx, MC, V.

Sonny's has been satisfying local appetites since 1986. There's a small upmarket food shop next door and a bar area next to the street, but it's the restaurant at the rear that sees most action. Sage paintwork, white linen, low lighting and a gallery's worth of paintings provide a smart, slightly sombre setting. The cooking seemed rather subdued too. A starter salad of roast beetroot, toasted walnuts and watercress, and a main of double-baked goat's cheese soufflé (from the nicely priced set dinner) were both pleasant enough, but lacked sparkle; the creamed onions surrounding the soufflé were gloopy and served far too hot. The standout dish was a starter of succulent grilled mackerel atop a hillock of houmous and tabouleh, dotted with pomegranate seeds: pretty on the eye, and a fizz of strong flavours on the tongue. Sonny's reputation for desserts is deserved; creamy lemon posset with raspberry sorbet and delicate own-made shortbread sticks was a vivid, summery delight. The wine list is offers plenty of choice by the glass. Staff are well mannered, if a tad too attentive.

Owner Rebecca Mascarenhas's Putney restaurant, the Phoenix, has closed, but Kitchen W8 in Kensington (her venture with Philip Howard of the Square) is worth a visit for its combination of British ingredients with French cooking styles; it also offers fairly priced set menus.
Available for hire. Babies and children welcome: children's menu; high chairs. Booking advisable (restaurant). Separate room for parties, seats 20.

Chelsea

Botanist

7 Sloane Square, SW1W 8EE (7730 0077, www.the botanistonsloanesquare.com). Sloane Square tube.
Breakfast served 8-11.30am Mon-Fri; 9-11.30am Sat, Sun. **Lunch served** noon-3.30pm Mon-Fri; noon-4pm Sat, Sun. **Tea served** 3.30-5.30pm. **Dinner served** 6-10.30pm daily. **Main courses** £14-£19. **Set meal** (lunch, 5.30-6.30pm) £20 2 courses, £25 3 courses. **Credit** AmEx, MC, V.
There's not much in the way of biodiversity in the creatures native to the Botanist. Such a prime patch of Sloane Square was always going to be the habitat of the horse and hound brigade, and this venture from gastropub magnates Ed and Tom Martin leaves no stone unturned in cultivating their approval. The front bar is all cream surfaces and gleaming metal fixtures, with a few stools for those early enough to avoid the hordes. But it's the rear room that steals the show, with large windows flooding the place with light by day, and a mix of artful spot lighting, modern chandeliers and a backlit glass mural of botanical specimens lending the feel of a science fiction ark by night. Food is nothing if not artful: a mackerel

fillet starter came cubed and arranged with studs of lemon confit on a surrealist smear of olive tapenade; a main of chicken breast with mushroom stuffing was cut into thirds and balanced on a bed of spinach and morels. A great deal of thought has gone into presentation and flavour combinations, but portions seem shy given the above-average prices. The wine list is lengthy, and service attentive and knowledgeable.
Babies and children welcome: high chairs. Booking advisable. Disabled: toilet. Tables outdoors (4, pavement).
Map 15 G10.

Fulham

My Dining Room

18 Farm Lane, SW6 1PP (7381 3331, www.mydining room.net). Fulham Broadway tube or 11, 14, 211 bus.
Bar **Open** 11am-midnight Mon-Sat; 11am-11.30pm Sun.
Meals served 11am-11pm Mon-Sat; 11am-10.30pm Sun.
Restaurant **Meals served** noon-10.30pm daily.
Both **Main courses** £9.95-£20. **Set lunch** (Sun) £19.95 4 courses plus aperitif. **Set meal** £15 2 courses. **Credit** AmEx, MC, V.

Though only minutes from Fulham Broadway, little passing traffic means My Dining Room is for those in the know. On a Friday night, this meant the local dating crowd who clearly appreciate the friendly service and halfway house between relaxed pub and fancy restaurant: think gastropub turned chichi. The front bar serves floral syrup cocktails and own-made snacks, but this is really an annex to the main attraction of the rea dining room, adorned with metallic swirling wallpaper and velvet panels. In similar vein to the decor, the chef has ramped up the food from pub grub (crisp fried goat's cheese) to something more distinctive (it came with a beetroot purée and designer leaves). There is certainly a generosity of spirit here: staff brought us a foot-long terrine (for one person) with the bidding to eat as much as we liked. Many dishes are designed to share, such as whole roast chicken or deeply savoury veal and chorizo meatballs served in one dish for the table. Killer puddings include a rose crème brûlée, and perfect chocolate fondant with molten centre.
Babies and children welcome: high chairs. Booking advisable. Disabled: toilet. Tables outdoors (5, pavement; 4, terrace).
Map 13 A13.

Parsons Green

Manson

676 Fulham Road, SW6 5SA (7384 9559, www.manson restaurant.co.uk). Parson's Green tube. **Lunch served** noon-3pm, **dinner served** 6-10.30pm Mon-Fri. **Meals served** 10am-10.30pm Sat, Sun. **Main courses** £12.50-£22.50. **Set lunch** £12.50 2 courses. **Credit** AmEx, MC, V.
The sophistication of Manson's food easily outstrips its casual, bistro-style setting. The last time we ate Gemma Tuley's cooking was at Gordon Ramsay's failed revamp of Foxtrot Oscar. Here, we found the fish and meat cookery flawless. Rump of lamb arrived perfectly pink, yet tender, served on a modish black slate with garnishes evocative of Morocco – some chickpeas, plus a samosa-like pastry with a lamb confit filling. Braised ox cheeks were surrounded by herby green risotto and jus, with flavours that brought to mind the countryside. Many dishes are imaginative, yet firmly grounded in European haute-cuisine traditions. We were too full to try the jerusalem artichoke cheesecake with peanut butter, but

were so impressed by the attention to detail, the perfection of the cooking and the clever combinations of flavours, that we'll be back to try it. The wine list is also decent; locals were quaffing bottles like they were ginger beer. Criticisms? Fraught young waiters ran around with desperate urgency, and we were assailed by the sound of Fulham folk shouting at each other – these people really know how to project.

Babies and children welcome: high chair. Booking advisable. Tables outdoors (4, pavement).

South

Balham

Lamberts

2 Station Parade, Balham High Road, SW12 9AZ (8675 2233, www.lambertsrestaurant.com). Balham tube/rail. **Lunch served** noon-3pm Sat. **Dinner served** 7-10.30pm Mon-Sat. **Meals served** noon-5pm Sun. **Main courses** £14-£18. **Set meal** (Tue-Thur) £20 2 courses, £24 3 courses. **Credit** MC, V.

This strip of road is, frankly, unprepossessing, but Lamberts is one of the best upscale local restaurants in London. The long room is restrained and unflashy, painted a muted yellow, with a velvet banquette taking up most of one side. Well-placed diner-style tables are set off by dainty flowers, and easeful art lines the walls. Staff are smart, smooth and unfussy; a wooden platter of own-made bread with seasoned butter and a bottle of filtered water are slipped on to the table as soon as you're seated. Cooking is inventive and assured. Our starters were vibrant: cold carrot soup with pickled carrots and three bobbing islets of delicious walnut mousse, and exquisite peach and tomato salad with pine nut and sherry dressing. Just as good were mains of fallow deer with puy lentils and roasted violet artichokes, and rare-breed steak with fat chips and a salad of slow-roasted tomatoes. Save room for the exquisite desserts. We enjoyed both our choices: crème fraîche and elderflower tart with a scoop of excellent strawberry sherbet, and a creamy peach parfait with caramelised roast peaches and rapeseed and thyme sable. The extensive drinks list offers a useful range of wines by the glass or carafe, as well as a thoughtful selection of whiskies.

Available for hire. Babies and children welcome: children's menu (weekends); high chairs. Booking advisable; essential weekends.

Battersea

Ransome's Dock

35-37 Parkgate Road, SW11 4NP (7223 1611, www.ransomesdock.co.uk/restaurant). Battersea Park rail or 19, 49, 319, 345 bus. **Brunch served** noon-5pm Sat; noon-3.30pm Sun. **Meals served** noon-11pm Mon-Fri. **Dinner served** 6-11pm Sat. **Main courses** £11.50-£23. **Set lunch** (Sun) £22.50 3 courses. **Set meal** (noon-7.30pm Mon-Fri) £15.50 2 courses. **Credit** AmEx, DC, MC, V.

Opened in 1992, Ransome's Dock has survived (and thrived) by doing its own thing. It's a neighbourhood restaurant, albeit a very good one; the look is faintly staid, with a neat, blue-painted interior and a few tables outside overlooking the dock. The wide-ranging wine list alone is reason for a visit, but the menu is no slouch either. Own-made cheese biscuits with drinks set the tone for a highly civilised evening. A meal of

delightfully savoury salad of chicory, perroche goat's cheese and pear with agresto (spiced walnut, anchovy, parsley and garlic dressing), followed by flavoursome duck breast with pardina lentils, spinach and fresh peas, was slightly overshadowed by two choices from the specials list. Chargrilled squid with romesco sauce was a tender, super-tasty starter, while a large plaice with borlotti beans, girolle mushrooms and tomato vinaigrette had generous proportions and fresh flavours. Puddings run from fruit sorbets to prune and Armagnac soufflé with Armagnac custard; there's also cheese, and coffee with chocolate truffles. Friendly, professional staff go about their business with aplomb, even when confronted with celebrity (Will Young) and rather trying customers (a diner with a voice like a foghorn).

Babies and children welcome: high chairs. Booking advisable. Disabled: toilet. Tables outdoors (10, terrace). **Map 21 C1.**

Tom Ilic

123 Queenstown Road, SW8 3RH (7622 0555, www.tom ilic.com). Battersea Park or Queenstown Road rail. **Lunch served** noon-2.30pm Wed-Sat; noon-3.30pm Sun. **Dinner served** 6-10.30pm Tue-Sat. **Main courses** £11.50-£15.50. **Set lunch** £14.50 2 courses, £16.95 3 courses; (Sun) £16.95 2 courses, £21.50 3 courses. **Set dinner** £16.95 2 courses, £21.50 3 courses. **Credit** AmEx, MC, V.

The workaday decor at Tom Ilic's place in no way prepares diners for the splendid meal that awaits them. The set deals are great value, and even the à la carte is very keenly priced: for example, an impeccable main of roast fillet of Kettyle beef with oxtail raviolo, horseradish soufflé and garlic beans costs £17.95 and could hold its own in any five-star kitchen. Pig is king, though the menu is varied. Devotees should start with braised pig's cheeks and chorizo with garlic mash and pork crackling, and follow with a dégustation of pork with pickled white cabbage and caramelised apple – both are very good. The kitchen knows how to handle fish too: a main of baked sea bass fillet with sautéed girolles and plenty of summer vegetables was flavoursome and beautifully balanced, while salmon three ways (cured, roasted and tartare), with beetroot and orange salad, added interest to the classic smoked salmon starter. Portions don't skimp, but for those who can manage more, there's a cheese board or the likes of dark chocolate fondant with pistachio ice-cream. Service is warm and efficient, even on a busy Friday night. Ignore the surfeit of reddish brown (the paintwork, the tables) and unlovely Queenstown Road, and book a table for one of the best bargains in town.

Babies and children welcome: high chairs. Booking advisable weekends.

Brixton

Upstairs

89B Acre Lane, entrance on Branksome Road, SW2 5TN (7733 8855, www.upstairslondon.com). Clapham Common tube or Brixton tube/rail. **Dinner served** 6.30-10pm Tue-Sat. **Set dinner** £25 2 courses, £30 3 courses, £35 4 courses. **Credit** AmEx, MC, V.

Having pressed the buzzer, diners cannot help but feel privileged on admittance to this secretive restaurant hidden on a side road off Acre Lane. The little first-floor bar has a quirky mix of leather banquettes and retro swivel chairs, where you can relax to chillout music and a cocktail – try the Dublintini (Jameson, lemon juice, almond syrup) – before heading upstairs to the even smaller, tightly packed dining room. The Anglo-

French menu (with a cheese course if desired) is offered at dinner only. Elegantly arranged starters of duck parfait with port dressing, and mackerel with fennel salad were delicious, but as we found with the mains – stone bass with crushed potatoes and baby gem, and bulgar wheat with broad beans and artichokes – portions are small. Raspberry millefeuille was a short slice, just one raspberry wide and two deep, though it tasted delightful. The house wines are very drinkable, and there are several bottles under £25. Smooth service and low-key jazz/crooner music creates an easy-going atmosphere; the speakeasy vibe adds to the contented buzz.
Available for hire. Babies and children admitted. Booking essential. **Map 22 C2.**

Manson. See p211.

South East
Crystal Palace

Exhibition Rooms
69-71 Westow Hill, SE19 1TX (8761 1175, www.the exhibitionrooms.com). Crystal Palace rail. **Lunch served** noon-4pm, **dinner served** 6-10.30pm Mon-Sat. **Meals served** noon-9pm Sun. **Main courses** £9.50-£17. **Set lunch** £10 2 courses, £13 3 courses. **Set dinner** (6-7pm) £12 2 courses, £15 3 courses. **Credit** AmEx, MC, V.
If the Exhibition Rooms is your local, your luck's in. Its name refers to the Great Exhibition of Crystal Palace in 1851 and the decor playfully nods to the event: a greenhouse-like cast-iron gate divides the two main rooms, and a worn wooden door hangs by the bar. The rest is exposed brickwork, khaki walls and stone urns, all softly lit by two chandeliers. The place feels like an upmarket pub, with waiters for bar staff. Downstairs is a lounge bar, busy with leather and zebra-print chairs. The menu emphasises sustainable fish and seasonal produce, so in early summer you might get warm marinated sardines with pickled vegetables and rocket, or asparagus with duck's egg, followed by roasted pollock with razor clams and fine herb risotto, or slow-cooked belly pork with lyonnaise potatoes. It's well-executed French-tinted cooking with plenty of cheffy flourishes. The odd Asian influence is there too, such as a Thai basil salad dressed with Japanese ponzu. The wine and cocktail lists are impressive too. Save space for rhubarb and champagne trifle; it made a rich, luscious end to an immaculate meal.
Babies and children welcome: children's menu; high chairs. Booking advisable; essential weekends. Disabled: toilet. Tables outdoors (9, courtyard).

Greenwich

Inside
19 Greenwich South Street, SE10 8NW (8265 5060, www.insiderestaurant.co.uk). Greenwich rail/DLR. **Lunch served** noon-2.30pm Tue-Fri; noon-3pm Sun. **Dinner served** 6.30-11pm Tue-Sat. **Main courses** £12.95-£18.95. **Set lunch** (Mon-Fri) £11.95 2 courses, £15.95 3 courses; (Sun) £17.95 2 courses, £21.95 3 courses. **Set dinner** (6.30-8pm) £16.95 2 courses, £20.95 3 courses. **Credit** AmEx, MC, V.
Inside claims to be 'the perfect neighbourhood restaurant'; in fact, it's far better than that. Chef Guy Awford and his team create imaginative, precisely balanced and expertly cooked dishes. Ingredients are top quality and, where possible, sourced locally. The menu changes daily. Examples of the complex constructions include: parsnip en croûte with puy lentils, sautéed artichoke, garlic spinach and porcini velouté; and roasted cod, Spanish paprika, white bean and chorizo cassoulet with steamed leeks and tomato coulis. The likes of sweetbreads might also appear, and even the chicken and veg comes inside a brioche. Our steak was so tender it didn't need the steak knife, and was paired with a crisp potato galette. By comparison, desserts sound almost pedestrian, but it's worth trying lemon verbena crème brûlée, or forced rhubarb and apple crumble. Given the quality, the midweek menu is a steal, though on our visit three dishes had supplementary charges. The wine list includes a Rioja from independent producer Bodegas Navajas. The dining room is small and intimate, with a fresh, modern look. The service can be a little too relaxed, but as a whole this place punches well above its weight.

MODERN EUROPEAN

London Bridge & Borough

Delfina

50 Bermondsey Street, SE1 3UD (7357 0244, www.the
delfina.co.uk). London Bridge tube/rail. **Breakfast served**
8-11am, **lunch served** noon-3pm Mon-Fri. **Dinner served**
7-10pm Fri. **Meals served** 11am-5pm Sun. **Main courses**
£9-£16. **Set lunch** £15 2 courses, £19 3 courses. **Credit**
AmEx, DC, MC, V.

A restaurant-café inside a gallery and art centre, Delfina is
instantly relaxing on the eye, with plenty of space and all-white
walls offset by the deep blues of the chairs, water glasses and
the staff's shirts. Abstract paintings line the walls. The food
has a light, bright style to match, and this is one of the growing
band of kitchens that use properly sourced, mostly organic,
quality seasonal ingredients to give dishes a real zing. The
concise main menu and set lunch are both great value. From
the set menu, 'Buccleuch ribeye carpaccio with celeriac
remoulade' revealed a certain use of silly names – it was in fact
British cold roast beef – but the dish made a lovely summer
starter, with a hint of spice. To follow, Middle White pork belly
with fennel and tomato cassoulet had plenty of generous
flavour. Staff are friendly, and the wine list shows the same
welcoming approach, with good labels at prices well below the
norm. Delfina's hours, long limited to weekday lunches and
Friday night, have expanded; the place now opens for breakfast
and on Sundays for brunch and lunch.

Available for hire. Babies and children admitted: high chairs.
Booking advisable. Disabled: toilet. Tables outdoors
(8, pavement). **Map 12 Q9**.

Tower Bridge

Blueprint Café

Design Museum, 28 Shad Thames, SE1 2YD (7378 7031,
www.danddlondon.com). Tower Hill tube, Tower Gateway
DLR, London Bridge tube/rail or 47, 78 bus. **Lunch**
served noon-2.45pm Mon-Sat; noon-3.45pm Sun. **Dinner**
served 6-10.45pm Mon-Sat. **Set meal** £15 2 courses,
£20 3 courses. **Credit** AmEx, DC, MC, V.

If you're looking for a dining room with a view, a quick solution
is to consider those owned by D&D London, the group formerly
known as Conran Restaurants. Their speciality is smart food,
smartly served in smart surrounds: prices reflect the desirable
locations, but standards are generally reliable, and to their
credit, it's often the old Conran involvement that helped make
the locations attractive in the first place. Take Butlers Wharf
next to Tower Bridge for instance – once a no-go area, let alone
a gastronomic destination. Our favourite place here is Blueprint
Café, set above the Design Museum and offering a sensational
City panorama. The appealingly rustic cooking can be patchy,
but is delivered with such bonhomie that one tends to feel
pleased to have come. At street level, Le Pont de la Tour is a
fussier experience designed for business deals by day, romantic
dates by night, and family occasions at the weekend
(traditional Sunday roast is served). The restaurant's adjacent
bar and grill offers more casual environs in which to enjoy
oysters, fruits de mer, burgers or fish cakes. Butlers Wharf
Chop House majors on traditional British dishes – bang on
trend, you may think – but our last few visits have left us
disappointed and the over-confident pricing has always been
tailored to City gents.

For a treat, it's better to head to Skylon in the Royal Festival
Hall, where the occasional culinary or service misfires are

soothed by sensational Embankment views. If it's a special occasion, the pastry chefs can create a bespoke cake. The grill is intended to be more relaxed than the restaurant, but in truth both are pretty spiffy. At Canary Wharf, Plateau offers a similar formula: impressive views and decorative touches; a bar and grill serving heartier, simpler food than the main restaurant; accomplished service and a wine list that's good but no bargain. Orrery, above the Conran Shop on Marylebone High Street, was at one time under chef Chris Galvin and held a Michelin star. That award no longer stands, but we think the cooking at Orrery continues to have the edge over the other restaurants in the group, and its wine list is outstanding.
Available for hire. Babies and children welcome: high chair. Booking advisable dinner. Disabled: lift; toilet (museum). Tables outdoors (4, terrace). **Map 12 S9.**
For branches (The Avenue, Bluebird, Butlers Wharf Chop House, Kensington Place, Orrery, Plateau, Le Pont de la Tour, Skylon) see index.

East

Spitalfields

The Luxe
2010 RUNNER-UP BEST NEW DESIGN
109 Commercial Street, E1 6BG (7101 1751, www.theluxe.co.uk). Liverpool Street tube/rail or Shoreditch High Street rail.
Café-bar **Open** 8am-11.30pm Mon-Sat; 9.30am-10pm Sun. **Meals served** 8.30am-4.30pm Mon-Sat; 9.30am-4.45pm Sun. **Main courses** £7.50-£11.50
Restaurant **Lunch served** noon-3pm Mon-Fri; noon-4pm Sun. **Dinner served** 6-9.30pm Mon-Sat. **Main courses** £13-£15.
Both **Credit** AmEx, MC, V.
Spitalfields' Grade II-listed Old Flower Market building is now Luxe by name, luxe by nature. Owned by *Masterchef* judge John Torode, it's reminiscent of his other venture, Smiths of Smithfield (*see p202*), in that a different eating and drinking experience is offered on each floor. The bustling ground-floor café-bar has a charming terrace at the back, and is a pleasing spot for breakfast (waffles, sausage butties, mushrooms on toast with poached eggs and hollandaise) or a casual lunch (superfood salads, barbecued pulled pork sandwiches, grilled fish). All wines are under £25, then there are juices, smoothies, milkshakes and beers. The basement bar (a music venue) is dark and moody. Centrepiece of the premium-priced first-floor dining room is a show kitchen – with white marble bar cut out and filled with logs – and the cooking. Silk wallpaper painted with birds makes reference to the Huguenot silk weavers and songbird breeders who once occupied the area; floral-patterned china is a nod to the building's original use. It's a stylish, sensitive place to enjoy the likes of Japanese glazed mackerel with pickled cucumber and sesame, followed by Middle White pork chop with soft herb polenta, and strawberry trifle accompanied by shortbread.
Available for hire. Babies and children welcome: high chairs; nappy-changing facilities. Booking advisable restaurant. Bookings not accepted café. Disabled: lift; toilet. Separate rooms for parties, seating 30-120. Tables outdoors (3, pavement). Takeaway service. **Map 12 R5.**

Wapping

Wapping Food `HOT 50`
Wapping Hydraulic Power Station, Wapping Wall, E1W 3ST (7680 2080, www.thewappingproject.com). Wapping tube or Shadwell DLR. **Lunch served** noon-3.30pm Mon-Fri; 1-4pm Sat, Sun. **Brunch served** 10.30am-noon Sat, Sun. **Dinner served** 6.30-11pm Mon-Fri; 7-11pm Sat. **Tapas served** 6.30-11pm Mon-Sat. **Main courses** £11-£22. **Dishes** £3-£6. **Credit** AmEx, MC, V.
Part Victorian pumping station relic, part art gallery, part restaurant, and altogether wacky and wonderful, the Wapping Project is one of those venues to set aside for a special trip, if only to sample the high-quality food. The frequently changing menu is fresh and seasonal, so in summer you might find starters such as razor clams with chorizo and pickled broad beans, then a main of wild sea bass with cucumber, samphire and watercress; or pressed foie gras, gooseberry jelly and toasted almonds followed by baked polenta, wild asparagus, gorgonzola, morels, rocket and pine nuts. The turbine hall surroundings are as industrial as can be; glowing candles provide softness in the evening. The fabulous, all-Australian wine list is carefully constructed, avoiding mass-produced plonk for more interesting bottles. Such sourcing is reflected in the pricing, though the wines by the glass are chosen to match well with most dishes. Much of the food we've tried here has been inspirational and deliciously unpredictable. This extends to the desserts: black pepper ice-cream with strawberries, say, or passionfruit and buttermilk panna cotta.
Babies and children welcome: high chairs. Booking essential Wed-Sun. Disabled: toilet. Entertainment: performances and exhibitions; phone for details. Tables outdoors (20, garden).

Whitechapel

Whitechapel Gallery Dining Room
Whitechapel Gallery, 77-82 Whitechapel High Street, E1 7QX (7522 7888, www.whitechapelgallery.org/dine). Aldgate East tube. **Lunch served** noon-2.30pm Tue-Sat; noon-2.30pm Sun. **Dinner served** 5.30-11pm Wed-Sat. **Main courses** £13.75-£18. **Credit** AmEx, MC, V.
Chef Michael Paul has taken over from Maria Elia in this vibrant art gallery restaurant that opened in 2009. The attractive 1892 façade of the former Whitechapel Library has been preserved, and ceiling-height windows, along with tall mirrors and stylish blond wood chairs, bring much-needed light into the small space. Old library-card drawers lining one wall add a nostalgic touch. Paul makes skilful use of interesting produce such as lemon verbena, wild garlic and Kentish sparkling wine (used in a bellini with strawberries: English, of course). The seasonal menu emphasises provenance and might include rump of Romney Marsh lamb, or Gloucester Old Spot pork terrine with gala apple salad. An attractively arranged plate of courgettes with confit lemon and sorrel was tinged with bitterness, but the accompanying cashel blue soufflé was wonderfully cloud-like. The meal concluded on a high: a multi-layered delight of a dessert containing lavender-dotted shortbread alongside a tumbler of quality strawberries, vanilla-specked custard and delectable swiss roll, topped with a sprinkling of zingy popping candy. Cheerful staff (who deal with problems graciously), and customers who range from East End arty to posh arty, create a pleasant atmosphere.

Babies and children welcome: high chairs; nappy-changing facilities. Booking advisable. Disabled: toilet. Separate room for parties, seats 14. **Map 12 S9**.

North East

Wanstead

Hadley House

27 High Street, E11 2AA (8989 8855). Snaresbrook or Wanstead tube. **Lunch served** noon-2.45pm Tue-Sat; noon-4.45pm Sun. **Dinner served** 6-10pm Tue-Sat. **Main courses** £11-£16. **Set lunch** (Tue-Sat) £15 2 courses; (Sun) £16 2 courses. **Set dinner** (Tue-Thur) £15 2 courses (£20 incl wine). **Credit** MC, V.

Welcoming, unaffected staff, and a handful of pavement tables beneath a tasteful awning set the tone at this inviting venue. The understated room feels spacious, decorated in blond wood and local art. Diners are presented with a long menu that pleasantly compounds indecision. The set dinner is excellent value; nibbles at under £2 are a steal. Two carefully filleted sardines, tails intact, splayed over buttery brioche, started our meal well. A summery main of spaghetti with goat's cheese and asparagus suffered from overcooked pasta, but featured a generous helping of the green spears and finely balanced seasoning. Spicy beef salad was an anglicised version of a South-East Asian staple that lacked zing and heat. It contained super-fresh veg, but in too great a proportion; the beef was tender but could have been rarer, and its leanness came at the expense of flavour. Dessert was a nostalgic treat, marrying strawberries and cream with Kendal mint cake-studded panna cotta, topped with swirls of own-made marshmallow. Perhaps the cooking could show more finesse, but the warm service and fantastic value make Hadley House a local gem.

Available for hire. Babies and children welcome (lunch, Sun): high chairs. Booking advisable. Tables outdoors (7, patio).

North

Camden Town & Chalk Farm

York & Albany

127-129 Parkway, NW1 7PS (7388 3344, www.gordon ramsay.com/yorkandalbany). Camden Town tube. **Breakfast served** 7-10.30am Mon-Fri; 7-11.30am Sat, Sun. **Lunch served** noon-3pm Mon-Sat. **Dinner served** 6-11pm Mon-Sat. **Meals served** noon-8pm Sun. **Main courses** £15-£22. **Set lunch** £18 2 courses, £21 3 courses. **Set meal** (6-7pm Mon-Sat) £21 3 courses; (noon-7pm Sun) £18 2 courses, £21 3 courses. **Credit** AmEx, MC, V.

This edge-of-Camden combo of boutique hotel, bar, restaurant and deli has much going for it, but its membership of the Gordon Ramsay empire is both a draw and its Achilles heel. For a start, service, though friendly, is often slow and inept (particularly in the spacious bar/breakfast room). Then, the main issue: the food isn't as good as expected. And, to finish, prices are almost wildly optimistic. Witness a bar meal of scotch egg with greasy new potato salad for £12, and the need to remind staff to bring the drinks. This may explain why, on a Friday evening, the place was far from busy (though the fact it wasn't rammed made for a pleasurable atmosphere). The serene decor, with high-backed sofas, retro lamps and creamy

Ramsay signature hues, makes a pleasing retreat from Parkway – and a lovely spot to linger over breakfast and papers. The courtyard behind the dining room is a light-filled space for convivial weekend lunches of, say, confit salmon with sweetcorn purée and spring onions, followed by braised pig's cheeks with crushed braeburn apples and salad of elderflower, chicory and raisins. Camden needed somewhere like this, just not quite like this.

Babies and children welcome: high chairs; nappy changing facilities. Booking essential. Disabled: toilet. Separate rooms for parties, seating 24 and 70. Tables outdoors (6, pavement). **Map 3 H1**.

Islington

Frederick's

Camden Passage, N1 8EG (7359 2888, www.fredericks. co.uk). Angel tube. **Lunch served** noon-2.30pm, **dinner served** 5.45-10.30pm Mon-Sat. **Main courses** £12.50-£26. **Set meal** (lunch; dinner Mon, Tue; 5.45-7pm Wed-Sat) £14 2 courses, £17 3 courses. **Credit** MC, V.

There's a palpable sense of occasion at Frederick's, especially if you dine in the large rear conservatory where picture windows overlook a garden. There's also a popular bar at the front. The restaurant has been here for years, but still feels fresh: smart, spacious, with white walls and grey slate floors – a place for pleasure rather than business. Both our starters were winners: luscious, buttery scallops with tiny cubes of pancetta were matched with a small portion of risotto, whose creaminess and dense flavour verged on perfection; and a dome of tuna tartare with avocado, which melded fresh, smooth textures and flavours with a dash of hot wasabi. A main of duck with pak choi and oyster mushrooms was also a success, the oriental twist of the vegetables (with a trace of soy sauce) blending well with rare, juicy, chunky pieces of duck. No such luck with our other main – grouper fillet with an odd taste and texture – but this was immediately and politely replaced. Chocolate pot was another mini flavour bomb, the dark, dense chocolate contrasting with white chocolate ice-cream.

Babies and children welcome: children's menu; high chairs. Booking advisable weekends. Separate rooms for parties, seating 16 and 30. Tables outdoors (12, garden). **Map 5 O2**.

North West

West Hampstead

Green Room

182 Broadhurst Gardens, NW6 3AY (7372 8188, www.thegreenroomnw6.com). West Hampstead tube/rail. **Meals served** 6.30-10.30pm daily. **Main courses** £11-£17. **Set meal** (Mon-Thur, Sun) £15 2 courses, £19.50 3 courses. **Credit** MC, V.

The west end of Broadhurst Gardens hosts one of residential London's little restaurant clusters, and the Green Room is among the most popular venues. It's equally attractive for a celebration or for simply calling by when you're in 'can't cook/ won't cook' mood on a Sunday evening. The Anglo-French owners are especially attentive, and the decor – mixing silver mirror-effect flock wallpaper, bright cushions and quirky modern artwork – is an engaging blend of chic and cosy. The set menu, an excellent bargain, has three frequently changing

MODERN EUROPEAN

Exhibition Rooms. See p213.

options for each course (plus as much own-baked bread as you wish). There's always a soup of the day among the starters (button mushroom and juniper, on our last visit); alternatives might include a prettily presented pâté with sweet apple chutney. Ingredients are well chosen and notably fresh. For mains, the risotto of the day (another menu staple, this time with tomato and mozzarella) was rather more ordinary, yet still satisfying, while chicken fillet with spinach, mash and pepper sauce was simple but enlivened by great-quality meat. Wines are also good value. To splash out a little more, choose from the extensive full menu, which contains some inventive dishes: pan-fried sea bass with lemongrass and rosemary, say.
Babies and children welcome: high chairs. Booking advisable; essential Fri, Sat. Separate room for parties, seats 16. Takeaway service. **Map 28 3A**.

Walnut

280 West End Lane, NW6 1LJ (7794 7772, www.walnut walnut.com). West Hampstead tube/rail. **Dinner served** 6.30-11pm Tue-Sun. **Lunch served** by arrangement. **Main courses** £9.50-£16. **Credit** AmEx, DC, MC, V.
A place that stands out from local-restaurant routine as much as Walnut has to be applauded. Opening hours are a little cranky (no lunch, except for special bookings). From the raised, mezzanine-style open kitchen, chef-owner Aidan Doyle watches over his domain with individual and highly professional attention. The dining space is comfortably mellow, in greens, pinks and, indeed, walnut brown. The menu slogan 'local, seasonal, sustainable' is taken very seriously, with an impressive range of energy-saving practices in the kitchen and expert sourcing of first-rate, wherever-possible British and organic ingredients, deployed in frequently changing menus that are inventive without any pointless gimmickry. Sparkling flavours were a characteristic of a recent meal: standing alone in a superbly fresh crayfish tail salad; beautifully blended with a just-right touch of garlic and a thyme cream sauce in a dish of English asparagus ravioli. Excellent, fresh fish and seafood from sustainable stocks is a speciality, but there's plenty for meat-eaters too – often with intricate yet subtle accompaniments, such as a rich whisky and orange marmalade with duck – and original vegetarian choices. The wine list has been assembled with as much care as the menu.
Available for hire. Babies and children welcome: high chairs; nappy-changing facilities. Booking advisable weekends. Tables outdoors (4, pavement). **Map 28 A2**.

Outer London

Richmond, Surrey

Petersham Nurseries Café   `HOT 50`

Church Lane, off Petersham Road, Richmond, Surrey TW10 7AG (8605 3627, www.petershamnurseries.com). Richmond tube/rail then 30 min walk or 65 bus. **Lunch served** 12.30-3pm Wed-Sun. **Main courses** £19.50-£29.50. **Credit** AmEx, MC, V.
Skye Gyngell's lovely, seasonal food has the perfect backdrop in this slightly otherworldly setting: a glasshouse filled with scented plants and charmingly mismatched bits and pieces – the epitome of rustic chic. The look is slightly spoiled by so many diners being identikit locals (neatly turned-out blondes accompanied by men in chinos), but at these prices, that's who you attract. In other respects, a meal here rarely fails to please. Gazpacho, or Dorset scallops with radicchio and roast red peppers might be followed by wild sea bass with new potatoes, spinach and salmoriglio (a Sicilian relish of garlic, lemon and marjoram), or beef fillet with white beans, datterini tomatoes, chard and salsa verde. Desserts (strawberry sorbet, say, or almond tart with roasted yellow peaches and crème fraîche) always include a cheese: st tola with honey and apricots, perhaps. Wine comes from small estates, with plentiful tasting notes. Willing service is by keen young staff, and there's something of a holiday atmosphere; it's hard to believe this is only ten miles from central London. The impecunious can take solace in the pretty tea room next door; called the Teahouse, it serves soups, sandwiches, cakes and various whole-leaf teas.
Babies and children welcome: high chairs; nappy-changing facilities. Booking essential, 2-4 wks in advance. Disabled: toilet. Tables outdoors (25, garden).

North African

An invigorating dose of glamour was injected into the entire North African restaurant scene in London in 1997 with the opening of **Momo**. And although the phalanx of fashionistas has now moved on to pastures new, a little of the stardust remains. It's easy to see why these venues are so alluring. Harem-like, dimly lit dining rooms have a romantic appeal, and the food offers an enticing variation on Middle Eastern and eastern Mediterranean cuisine, with classic tagine stews and couscous, as well as meze-like appetisers. **Adam's Café** is still one of our favourites, supplying an unusual and great-value menu in gorgeously intimate surroundings. **Sidi Maarouf** is another attractive prospect when you're looking for a Moroccan/Lebanese night out, and **Original Tagines** conjures an elegantly relaxed neighbourhood vibe. But if you're out to impress or to celebrate, Momo continues to be the kingpin.

Central

Edgware Road

Sidi Maarouf
56-58 Edgware Road, W2 2JE (7724 0525, www.maroush. com). Marble Arch tube. **Meals served** noon-12.30pm Mon-Sat; noon-midnight Sun. **Main courses** £14-£18. **Set meal** £30-£35 4 courses. **Credit** AmEx, DC, MC, V.
On a warm summer's evening, Sidi Maarouf's outdoor tables are perfect for enjoying an apple-scented shisha and mint tea. The Mediterranean aromas are juxtaposed with the buzz of the Edgware Road. Inside, dark wooden tables, studded leather seats, opulent brocade drapes and glowing silk lanterns seem Middle Eastern rather than Moroccan – a feeling emphasised by a musician performing Arabic standards. Visit at the weekend if you're keen to shake your stuff with the belly dancer. This is a Moroccan restaurant Lebanese-style. Part of the Maroush chain, there's slightly stiff but not unfriendly service, and good Lebanese wines; Ksara Sunset rosé is great for light summer drinking, or you could savour full-bodied oaky Ksara reds. Well-reduced tagines and silkily light couscous show a strong Moroccan hand in the kitchen. Alternatively, try the kemia (meze-style snacks): rough-cut spicy lamb sausages are robustly flavoursome; briouats (stuffed with eggy minced lamb or lemony chicken spiked with warming ginger) are enjoyably crisp. Zingy fresh fattoush sprinkled with sharp,

citrusy sumac makes a perfect foil for the heavier dishes. In all, an enjoyable restaurant for couples or groups.
Available for hire. Babies and children admitted. Booking advisable. Entertainment: belly dancer 9.30pm, 10.30pm Thur-Sun. Tables outdoors (6, pavement). **Map 8 F6.**

Gloucester Road

Pasha
1 Gloucester Road, SW7 4PP (7589 7969, www.pasha-restaurant.co.uk). Gloucester Road tube. **Meals served** noon-11pm Mon-Wed, Sun; noon-midnight Thur-Sat. **Main courses** £13-£26. **Set meal** £30-£40 per person (minimum 2). **Credit** AmEx, DC, MC, V.
For voluptuous glamour, Pasha's Arabian Nights decor is incomparable. The heavy carved wooden door opens on to a vista of swishing beaded lamps, intricate North African-style tiles, intimate recesses with harem-like wooden trellises, pink and orange silk cushions and hammered brass tables – all scattered with rose petals. But on our most recent visit, something had gone awry. For a start, no tap water was available due to a murmured excuse about plumbing problems. Initially only pricey set 'feast' menus were proffered, the à la carte appearing only when we asked. Beetroot salad had little sign of its promised cinnamon, orange and honey dressing; over-salty but nicely crisp courgette and cheese fritters were short on courgette; our usual favourite, deep-fried baby squid with coconut and chilli dipping sauce, had the texture of

rubber bands. To follow, s'csou darna (couscous with lamb shank, chicken and merguez), often one of London's best, was bland and watery. Even the belly dancers seemed tacky. A delicate Volubilia Gris rosé from Meknes partially saved the evening, but we left disappointed, not even tempted by a tiered stand of pistachio turkish delight and pastries. We've had much better meals here, so hope Pasha returns to form soon. *Available for hire. Babies and children welcome: high chairs. Booking advisable. Separate room for parties, seats 20. Tables outdoors (2, pavement). Takeaway service.* **Map 13 C9**.

Marylebone

Original Tagines

7A Dorset Street, W1U 6QN (7935 1545). Baker Street tube. **Meals served** noon-midnight Mon-Thur, Sat. **Dinner served** 6.30-11pm Fri, Sun. **Main courses** £10.50-£13. **Set lunch** £10.50 2 courses. **Credit** MC, V.
No more than a preserved lemon's throw from Baker Street, Original Tagines has the feel of a neighbourhood local without the usual excess of ethnic paraphernalia. Instead, it's all creamy hues with the occasional bit of gilt, carved wood and coloured glass. A window in the rear wall offers views of the kitchen. The concise wine list incorporates a reasonable choice under £20, including a pleasing Californian blend of chardonnay and pinot grigio that makes an ideal aperitif to accompany the peppery harissa, olives and flatbread brought to the table. Starters include the expected harira, zaalouk and houmous, but also kidneys with mustard sauce. Exceptionally juicy kofta meatballs were well seasoned with fresh herbs and spices and delightfully imbued with the flavour of the charcoal grill. Cigar-shaped cheese briouats featured a sumptuously tangy centre surrounded by delicate pastry and a refreshing chopped salad garnish. For mains, there's a selection of couscous dishes and grills, but it seemed wise to order the house speciality: piping hot tagines of moist, tender meats; from a list of 12, we chose chicken with red pepper, and lamb with apricots. Staff were charming and didn't even try to sell us dessert. A restaurant that deserves to thrive.
Available for hire. Babies and children welcome: high chairs. Booking advisable. Tables outdoors (5, pavement). Takeaway service. **Map 3 G5**.

Mayfair

Momo HOT 50

25 Heddon Street, W1B 4BH (7434 4040, www.momo resto.com). Piccadilly Circus tube. **Lunch served** noon-2.30pm Mon-Sat. **Dinner served** 6.30-11.30pm Mon-Sat; 6.30-11pm Sun. **Main courses** £13-£15. **Set lunch** £15 2 courses, £19 3 courses. **Credit** AmEx, DC, MC, V.
Algerian-born Mourad Mazouz is involved in several London and international restaurants, but it's the fabulously ornate Momo, opened in 1997, that made his reputation. Carved wooden screens, tasselled cushions, brass lanterns and low tables transport diners to Morocco's most fashionable imaginary club, to a soundtrack of Maghrebian beats. Tables are tightly packed, adding to the lively mood; come during the day for a more serene vibe. The alfresco terrace on Heddon Street evokes riad-cool and offers shisha pipes; downstairs is Mô Café (mint tea, wraps, meze, pastries) and Bazaar (books, CDs, furniture), plus the luxurious and recently refurbished Kemia bar (Madonna, Kate Moss, Tracey Emin). The restaurant's menu ranges from North African classics such as

harira and chicken tagine with preserved lemons and olives, to modern creations that aren't as inspired by Moroccan ingredients as you might hope: rump of lamb with jerusalem artichoke purée, wild garlic and rosemary jus, for example. The house couscous may seem expensive at £28, but it's laden with lamb shank, grilled skewers and merguez and ideal for sharing. You could start, perhaps, with chermoula-flavoured baby carrots wrapped in grilled aubergine and topped with rocket pesto, or the inventive briouat of cheese, mint and potatoes served with quince marmalade.
Available for hire. Babies and children admitted. Booking advisable weekends. Disabled: toilet. Tables outdoors (14, terrace). **Map 17 A4**.
For branch (Mô Café) see index.

West

Shepherd's Bush

Adam's Café

77 Askew Road, W12 9AH (8743 0572, www.adams cafe.co.uk). Hammersmith tube then 266 bus. **Breakfast served** 7.30am-2pm Mon-Fri; 8.30am-2pm Sat. **Dinner**

Original Tagines

Momo. See p219.

Menu

North African food has similarities with other cuisines; see the menu boxes in **Middle Eastern** and **Turkish**.

Brik: minced lamb or tuna and a raw egg bound together in paper-thin pastry, then fried.
Briouats, **briouettes** or **briwat**: little envelopes of deep-fried, paper-thin ouarka (qv) pastry; can have a savoury filling of ground meat, rice or cheese, or be served as a sweet, flavoured with almond paste, nuts or honey.
Chermoula: a dry marinade of fragrant herbs and spices.
Chicken kedra: chicken stewed in a stock of onions, lemon juice and spices (ginger, cinnamon), sometimes with raisins and chickpeas.
Couscous: granules of processed durum wheat. The name is also given to a dish where the slow-cooked grains are topped with a meat or vegetable stew; couscous royale usually involves lamb, chicken and merguez (qv).
Harira: thick lamb, lentil and chickpea soup.
Harissa: very hot chilli pepper paste flavoured with garlic and spices.
Maakouda: spicy potato fried in breadcrumbs.
Merguez: spicy, paprika-rich lamb sausages.
Ouarka: filo-like pastry.
Pastilla, **bastilla** or **b'stilla**: an ouarka (qv) envelope with a traditional filling of pigeon, almonds, spices and egg, baked then dusted with cinnamon and powdered sugar. In the UK chicken is often substituted for pigeon.
Tagine or **tajine**: a shallow earthenware dish with a conical lid; it gives its name to a slow-simmered stew of meat (usually lamb or chicken) and vegetables, often cooked with olives, preserved lemon, almonds or prunes.
Zaalouk or **zalouk**: a cold spicy aubergine, tomato and garlic dip.

served 7-11pm Mon-Sat. **Set dinner** £11.50 1 course incl mint tea or coffee, £14.50 2 courses, £16.95 3 courses. **Licensed**. **Corkage** (wine only) £3. **Credit** AmEx, MC, V.
You can feel the warmth emanating from this cosy little spot – and it's not just heat from the candles on each table. Since opening in the early 1990s, Adam's has gathered a devoted local following (young and old, couples and groups). They crowd into a bistro-like dining room with yellowing walls and Moorish tiling, or the similarly attired back room. The venue still does service as a caff during the day, but comes into its own at night when a long, varied menu of North African dishes is served by the amicable Tunisian-English owners, Abdel and Frances Boukara. You'll find all the usual tagines and couscous dishes, served in attractive earthenware, but also more rarely seen specialities, such as starters of mixed seafood pancakes (packed with squid, mussels and shrimps, with a cheese and tomato topping), and 'Fatma fingers', filo rolls with a piquant meat filling. Grills include mullet in spicy chermoula sauce. We can vouch for both the couscous royale (though the merguez was a little small) and the chicken and lemon tagine (the moist breast meat lifted by the tang of preserved lemons). Finish with a French dessert (a lemon tart, perhaps) or a Moroccan-style pancake with honey. The wine list includes a new range of nicely priced Tunisian bottles.
Available for hire. Babies and children admitted. Booking advisable weekends. Separate room for parties, seats 24. Vegetarian menu. **Map 20 A1**.

North

Islington

Maghreb

189 Upper Street, N1 1RQ (7226 2305, www.maghreb restaurant.co.uk). Highbury & Islington tube/rail. **Meals served** 6-11.30pm Mon-Thur; 5-11.30pm Fri-Sun. **Main courses** £9.50-£14.50. **Set dinner** £12.95 2 courses, £15.95 3 courses. **Credit** AmEx, MC, V.
Chef-patron Mohamed Faraji's restaurant feels welcoming even on a quiet night. Warm ochre walls and red silk lanterns spread their rosy glow over the narrow room, and a fine soundtrack of urban rai and more traditional North African music helps enhance the relaxed atmosphere. Faraji's mission to innovate, combining Modern European style with Moroccan staples, can backfire. Starters of marinated squid with capers had a strangely dense, meaty texture; crab börek was a touch stodgy; and coriander-infused zaalouk was served too cold (serving it at room temperature instead would have emphasised the complexity of the spicing). The traditional Moroccan mains tend to score more highly than the fusion-style dishes. A portion of lamb tagine with prunes was enough for two. The meat was extremely tender if slightly overcooked, and the sauce tasty, although it needed reducing further to produce an intense, sweet richness of flavour. Tagines are served with couscous, but Turkish-style bread is on hand to mop up the juices in a more authentic manner. To drink, we usually refrain from the small, expensive cocktails and head straight for the impressive Moroccan wine list instead. This contains several bottles that are rarely found in London, such as the oaky, vanilla-toned red L'Excellence de Bonassia.
Available for hire. Babies and children welcome: high chairs. Booking advisable. Separate rooms for parties, seating 38 and 40. Takeaway service. **Map 5 O1**.

Pan-Asian & Fusion

While 'authenticity' is all well and good when compared to dumbed-down versions of national cuisines, it shouldn't be the last word in judging a restaurant. London diners don't expect British, or indeed most European cooking styles, to become ossified, taking no heed of influence from abroad, so why should the cuisines of Asia be different? The countries of South-East Asia, in particular, have long been centres of international commerce, notably important in the spice trade. Culinary ideas frequently spread across borders, and 19th-century imperialism also poured western ingredients and techniques into the mix. Two of our favourite restaurants reflect this multinational vitality: **L'Etranger**, where French and Japanese cuisines are forged to produce the likes of iced oysters with shallot vinegar, yuzu jelly, cucumber and wasabi granita; and the **Modern Pantry**, whose Kiwi chef has conjured up Vietnamese-style braised pigs' cheeks with pickles, thai basil and deep-fried chilli. Newcomer **Viajante**, the creation of Portuguese chef Nuno Mendes, also impresses with its surprising flavours and haute cuisine presentation.

Central

Clerkenwell & Farringdon

The Modern Pantry
47-48 St John's Square, EC1V 4JJ (7250 0833, www.themodernpantry.co.uk). Farringdon tube/rail.
Café **Breakfast served** 8-11am Mon-Fri. **Brunch served** 9am-4pm Sat; 10am-4pm Sun. **Meals served** noon-11pm Mon-Fri; 5.30-11pm Sat; 5.30-10pm Sun. *Restaurant* **Lunch served** noon-3pm Tue-Fri; 10am-4pm Sun. **Dinner served** 6-11pm Tue-Sat. *Both* **Main courses** £13.50-£22.50. **Set lunch** (Mon-Fri) £18.50 2 courses; (Sun) £18.50 2 courses, £23.50 3 courses. **Credit** AmEx, MC, V.
This highly modish refit of adjoining Georgian buildings includes a café/restaurant and takeaway shop on the ground floor, and slightly more formal dining rooms on the first. It's all very monochrome, with copper ceiling lights, but the effect is anything but cold. Nevertheless, it is Anna Hansen's menu that is the real draw. Her heritage (raised in New Zealand) and her long association with Peter Gordon (of The Providores & Tapa Room) can be seen in the signature dish of sugar-cured New Caledonian prawn omelette with spring onion, coriander and smoked chilli sambal. Not every dish gels, but most do, and we applaud the ambition and invention in the likes of Vietnamese-style braised pigs' cheeks with pickles, thai basil and deep-fried chilli; or tonka bean shortbread with lemon custard, gooseberry compote and prosecco jelly. Breakfasts and brunches are also more interesting than most; alongside porridge and toast are options such as eggs with grilled chorizo, caramelised plantain fritters and slow-roast tomatoes. Wines from the wide-ranging list are available to take away. *Available for hire. Babies and children welcome: high chairs. Booking advisable weekends. Disabled: toilet. Separate room for parties, seats 30. Tables outdoors (9, square). Takeaway service.* **Map 5 O4**.

Fitzrovia

Bam-Bou
1 Percy Street, W1T 1DB (7323 9130, www.bam-bou.co.uk). Goodge Street or Tottenham Court Road tube.
Bar **Open** 5.30pm-1am Mon-Sat.
Restaurant **Lunch served** noon-3pm Mon-Fri. **Dinner served** 5.30-11pm Mon-Sat. **Main courses** £9.50-£14.50. **Set meal** (noon-3pm Mon-Fri; 5.30-7pm Mon-Sat) £14.95 2 courses, £18.95 3 courses.
Both **Credit** AmEx, MC, V.
Despite its prime location bang at the bottom of Charlotte Street, the warm hues of dark wooden fittings and the smiles

Crazy Bear

of the staff give this modestly sized dining room more a neighbourhood feel than a West End vibe. Unfortunately, the Chinese, Thai and Vietnamese menu sounds more interesting in theory than it is in reality. All the dishes we tried on a recent visit were serviceable, but never better than that. Prawn and coriander dumplings were plump and very sticky, yet they fell apart too readily; chicken and galangal rolls tasted just like any other spring roll; mekong fish (very similar to cod) had a delicate crispy batter, but its 'three flavour sauce' was steamrollered by chilli. Although we didn't discover a standout dish or dazzling drink, the good-value set menus are a reason to come here (with the three-course option you still get to choose your dessert from the carte), and Bam-Bou's easy charm makes it a welcome retreat in this part of town.
Babies and children admitted. Booking advisable. Separate rooms for parties, seating 8-20. Tables outdoors (4, terrace). **Map 17 B1.**

Crazy Bear

26-28 Whitfield Street, W1T 2RG (7631 0088, www. crazybeargroup.co.uk). Goodge Street or Tottenham Court Road tube.
Bar **Open/dim sum served** noon-10.45pm Mon-Fri; 6-10.45pm Sat; noon-10pm Sun. **Dim sum** £4-£9.
Restaurant **Meals/dim sum served** noon-10.45pm Mon-Fri; 6-10.45pm Sat; noon-10pm Sun. **Main courses** £12-£32. **Set meal** £39-£47 tasting menu.
Both **Credit** AmEx, MC, V.
Decor at this funky bar-restaurant might be as dark, shiny and overstated as an estate agent's suit, but, thankfully, it shows a bit more class. With a VIP cordon and a doorman to greet you, Crazy Bear works hard to conjure up an exclusive vibe without being in any way elitist. It's part of a business that owns a pub/restaurant/hotel and classy deli in rural Oxfordshire. Judging from the dressed-up crowd of animated regulars drawn here, the desire to have a showy night out is as important as the food itself. If you're happiest quaffing from a wide selection of champagne, cocktails and wine, and

enjoy what the owners describe as Modern Thai dining to the tune of clubby tracks, you'll appreciate the place. The mixed dim sum, fried noodles, and crispy sea bream fillets in hot and sour sauce were all OK: better for sharing than savouring. Couples tend to be seated side by side, presumably for ease of people-watching. In the basement is a stylish hangout bar and access to glitzy washrooms with wall-to-wall mirrored surfaces, best navigated sober.
Babies and children admitted. Booking advisable.
Vegan dishes. Vegetarian menu. **Map 17 B1.**

Gloucester Road

L'Etranger

36 Gloucester Road, SW7 4QT (7584 1118, www. etranger.co.uk). Gloucester Road tube. **Lunch served** noon-3pm Mon-Fri. **Brunch served** noon-3pm Sun. **Dinner served** 6-11pm Mon-Sat; 6-10pm Sun. **Main courses** £16.50-£32.50. **Set meal** (lunch, 6-6.45pm Mon-Fri) £16.50 2 courses, £19.50 3 courses; (6-11pm Mon-Sat, 6-10pm Sun) £59-£109 tasting menu. **Credit** AmEx, MC, V.
From the outside, L'Etranger looks just like the kind of upmarket French restaurant you might expect in Kensington. The tastefully decorated dining room is light and relaxed, the friendly staff well turned out. A glance at the menu soon shows there's something more to the place. Fresh tofu with ginger sits happily alongside pan-fried foie gras on a list that describes itself as French with a Japanese influence. The prices also offer variety, with lunch and early-bird menus from £16.50, tasting menus from £59 and à la carte options somewhere in between. We tried the tasting menu, which got off to a rocky start with tuna tartare that had been too liberally seasoned with soy sauce, wasabi and spring onions. This slip was soon eclipsed, though, as each dish seemed to be better than the last. A thick slab of fillet steak rossini was perfectly cooked and juicy, while the yuzu (Japanese citrus) and tofu ice-cream left us wanting more. The real show-stopper was a caramel and macadamia tart with delicate

pastry, a hint of salt and a tart apple sorbet on the side. Even the waiter got excited when he brought it to our table. *Available for hire. Babies and children welcome: high chairs. Booking advisable. Separate room for parties, seating 20. Vegetarian menu.* **Map 13 C9**.

Marylebone

The Providores & Tapa Room `HOT 50`

109 Marylebone High Street, W1U 4RX (7935 6175, www.theprovidores.co.uk). Baker Street or Bond Street tube. *The Providores* **Lunch served** noon-2.45pm Mon-Fri. **Brunch served** noon-2.45pm Sat, Sun. **Dinner served** 6-10.30pm Mon-Sat; 6-10pm Sun. **Main courses** (lunch) £18-£26. **Set dinner** £29 2 courses, £42 3 courses, £52 4 courses, £60 5 courses. **Cover** (brunch) £1.50. *Tapa Room* **Breakfast/brunch served** 9-11.30am Mon-Fri; 10am-3pm Sat, Sun. **Meals served** noon-10.30pm Mon-Fri; 4-10.30pm Sat; 4-10pm Sun. **Tapas** £2-£14.40. *Both* **Credit** AmEx, MC, V.

There are now just two Providores – Peter Gordon and Michael McGrath – but a great sense of teamwork at this beacon of fusion cooking. A compact first-floor dining room features white walls, long leather banquettes and a small workstation-cum-servery-cum-bar in which one of the black-aproned waiters seems permanently locked. Our main, nay only, complaint is with the air-conditioning, or lack of; in warm weather the close-set tables seem to add to the intense humidity. The dinner menu offers 14 starter-sized savoury dishes of eye-widening imagination. Long lists of ingredients make choosing even harder, but rest assured, this is one place where gooseberry compote really does work with the paprika flavours of chorizo and mojo sauce, and roast chicken. Our meal was perfection, from the signature smoked duck laksa to apple pie with miso caramel. OK, maybe the fish sauce flavours in a dish of roast gilt-head bream with coleslaw were too powerful, but the accompanying crab dumpling alone (there's often some sort of deep-fried ball on the plate) made the dish a treat. The wine list offers an encyclopedic selection of New Zealand's finest; the cocktails are first-rate too. Book well in advance for Sunday brunch and lunch. The no-reservations Tapa Room on the ground floor is one of London's premier spots for breakfast – come later in the day and you may struggle to get a seat, such is its deserved popularity.
Babies and children welcome: high chairs. Booking advisable Providores; bookings not accepted Tapa Room. Disabled: toilet. Tables outdoors (2, pavement). **Map 9 G5**.

West

Ladbroke Grove

E&O

14 Blenheim Crescent, W11 1NN (7229 5454, www.rickerrestaurants.com). Ladbroke Grove or Notting Hill Gate tube. *Bar* **Open** noon-midnight Mon-Sat; 12.30-11pm Sun. **Dim sum served** noon-10.30pm Mon-Sat; 12.30-10pm Sun. **Dim sum** £3.50-£9. *Restaurant* **Lunch served** noon-3pm, **dinner served** 6-11pm Mon-Fri. **Meals served** noon-11pm Sat; 12.30-10.30pm Sun. **Main courses** £10.50-£23. *Both* **Credit** AmEx, DC, MC, V.

Stretching from Hoxton to World's End, Will Ricker's pan-Asian empire may have become formulaic over the years – but what a formula. Each restaurant offers an appealing mix of dim sum, salads, tempura, sushi, curries and proteins such as miso-marinated black cod and Korean-style barbecue chicken. The vibe is sexy enough for a date, yet also appeals to families. Children love the shareability of pan-Asian food, and their parents are supported with a serious bar (destinations in their own right) and even kiddie party-planning services. Cocktails are a big draw; the lengthy list of tropical herb, fruit and floral flavours partnered by good spirits includes intrigues such as the Osaka Cyclone and Mekong Fizz. Alternatively, there's a choice of draught beers, including Asahi, and an international wine selection with 175ml glasses starting at around £4.

Viajante. See p226.

What's not to like? Well, the cooking rarely hits the heights the prices do, but the disarmingly friendly service from hipster staff helps compensate. Then there's the satisfying sense that (at E&O, at least), you've dined and drank among the cool crowd; it's a tribute to Ricker's slick operation that they've kept coming back for so long.

Babies and children welcome: children's menu; crayons; high chairs. Booking essential. Separate room for parties, seats 18. Tables outdoors (5, pavement). **Map 19 B3**. **For branches (Eight Over Eight, Great Eastern Dining Room, XO) see index**.

South

Vauxhall

Chino Latino
Park Plaza Riverbank, 18 Albert Embankment, SE1 7TJ (7769 2500, www.chinolatino.co.uk). Vauxhall tube. **Lunch served** noon-2.30pm Mon-Fri. **Dinner served** 6-10.30pm Mon-Sat; 6-10pm Sun. **Main courses** £14.50-£29. **Set meal** £40 tasting menu. **Credit** AmEx, MC, V.

There are branches of Chino Latino in London, Leeds, Nottingham and Cologne, and once inside the restaurant of the Park Plaza Riverbank hotel, you could be in any of these cities. The modish decor and nightclub lighting are handsome, but don't necessarily match the clientele – a raggle-taggle bunch including families, couples and business people. Staff are lovely: welcoming, prompt and happy to explain the menu to those unfamiliar with pan-Asian cuisine. Sharing is encouraged, though if you order the unagi roll with eel and avocado (one of several sushi rolls), or soft-shell crab tempura

with green chilli aïoli, you may want to keep it to yourself. Also enjoyable was a zingy beef fillet salad with plenty of herbs, marinated tofu (four beautiful cubes, each one different), and three chubby pork and prawn gyoza with water chestnuts and a chilli soy sauce. Less special was a seared yellowfin tuna salad rather lost under a slightly gloopy grain-mustard dressing. The wide range of drinks includes saké, cocktails and various teas. Prices are fair, though be wary if you stray from sharing dishes on to mains such as Chilean sea bass with black bean, Shaoxing wine and choi sum (£24).

Available for hire. Babies and children welcome: high chairs. Booking advisable. Disabled: toilet. **Map 16 L11**.

South East

Herne Hill

Lombok
17 Half Moon Lane, SE24 9JU (7733 7131). Herne Hill rail or 37 bus. **Dinner served** 6-10.30pm Tue-Sun. **Main courses** £6-£8. **Credit** MC, V.

Lombok is still squeezing them in – even during the week. Reasonably priced and consistent, it serves this part of Half Moon Lane well. SE24 might be changing, but not this restaurant. The half-smiling staff are polite and attentive enough for such a buzzy little place. South-East Asian artworks adorn the white wooden panelling, and uniformly folded tablecloths keep things neat. It's good to see a menu covering so much ground – Vietnamese wraps, Burmese yellow curry and Singapore chilli crab are all here – and doing it well. Easy options are the red or green Thai curries, and these are spot-on. But it's worth checking out the other pan-Asian dishes. We

looked to Malaysia with prawns marinated in fiery sambal oelek (a sound choice, though the onions were too crunchy). Tom yam and tom kha do their restorative broth thing pretty well, as does a comforting gingery seaweed and shiitake soup. Cute touches, such as a bush of parsley and a kitsch fresh flower as garnish, brought a smile to the dishes. The food won't wow, but it keeps the locals coming.

Babies and children admitted. Booking essential weekends. Takeaway service. **Map 23 A5**.

London Bridge & Borough

Champor-Champor

62-64 Weston Street, SE1 3QJ (7403 4600, www.champor-champor.com). London Bridge tube/rail. **Lunch served** by appointment. **Dinner served** 6-10pm Mon-Sat. **Set meal** £27.50 2 courses, £31.50 3 courses. **Credit** AmEx, MC, V.
The incense-scented, dimly lit interior glows with candlelight and glitters with chandeliers; the deep-toned walls are hung with a museum's-worth of tribal masks, Asian-inspired artworks and curious objets d'art. The effect is charming, transporting diners from the grey of London to an ornate jewel box of a restaurant in some imagined part of Asia. Malaysian food is merely the starting point for chef Adu Amran Hassan's fusion cooking. Our three-course dinner skilfully blended ingredients from Japan to India. A starter of serunding – a Malaysian speciality of dried, spiced beef (a bit like a dried rendang) – was quite moist and tender, served on firm rice cakes with a mango-chilli salsa. A vegetarian-friendly 'egg tofu' topped with a savoury, garlicky 'crumble' was reminiscent of Japanese chawan mushi, served with a small bowl of cherry tomatoes in a laksa-leaf pesto and a fragrant soup. Steamed green-tea pudding, only vaguely sweet and presented, like all the dishes, on delicate crockery, made a fitting end to a pan-Asian feast. Now in its tenth year, Champor-Champor is a popular spot, so booking is recommended. If you get hooked, consider a Saturday afternoon cookery class.

Available for hire. Babies and children welcome: high chairs. Booking essential. Separate room for parties, seats 8. **Map 12 Q9**.

Best oriental chains

Becoming omnipresent in the wake of Wagamama's success, the oriental canteen diner is now a cherished part of London's budget eats landscape.

Banana Tree Canteen
412-416 St John Street, EC1V 4NJ (7278 7565). Angel tube. **Meals served** noon-11pm Mon-Sat; noon-10.30pm Sun.
This canteen-style mini-chain serves Thai, Malaysian, Indonesian and Vietnamese dishes, as well as good-value set meals where you choose your own main.
Map 5 N3.
For branches (Banana Leaf Canteen, Banana Tree Canteen, Street Hawker) see index.

dim t
56-62 Wilton Road, SW1V 1DE (7834 0507, www.dimt.co.uk). Victoria tube/rail. **Meals served** noon-11pm Mon-Sat; noon-10.30pm Sun.
The name is somewhat misleading: choose from, yes, steamed dumplings and Chinese teas, but also oriental staples such as pad thai and teriyaki salmon.
Map 15 J10.
For branches see index.

Feng Sushi
1 Adelaide Road, NW3 3QE (7483 2929, www.fengsushi.co.uk). Chalk Farm tube. **Dinner served** 5-10.30pm Mon-Thur.
Silla Bjerrum's sushi chain distinguishes itself by offering local and sustainable produce, including tofu from Brick Lane and mackerel from Penzance.
Map 27 B1.
For branches see index.

Itsu
118 Draycott Avenue, SW3 3AE (7590 2400, www.itsu.com). South Kensington tube. **Meals served** noon-11pm Mon-Sat; noon-10pm Sun.
An upmarket kaiten-zushi bar, Itsu has a futuristic feel and good duck crystal rolls and chicken teriyaki. Most of its outlets are takeaway shops, but there are four restaurants too.
Map 14 E10.
For branches see index.

Ping Pong
45 Great Marlborough Street, W1F 7JL (7851 6969, www.pingpongdimsum.com). Oxford Circus tube. **Dim sum served** noon-midnight Mon-Sat; noon-10.30pm Sun.
A snazzy dim sum specialist, Ping Pong turns out industrial quantities of dumplings and fancy drinks from a dozen locations around town.
Map 17 A3.
For branches see index.

Wagamama
1 Ropemaker Street, EC2Y 9AW (7588 2688, www.wagamama.com). Moorgate tube/rail. **Meals served** 11.30am-10pm Mon-Fri.
Wagamama was the first – and is still one of the best – canteen-style pan-Asian diners, zooming out udon and soba noodles, grilled or in broth, for diligent slurping. It's now a worldwide phenomenon, with branches as far afield as the States and Australia.
Map 12 Q5.
For branches see index.

Yo! Sushi
52 Poland Street, W1F 7NQ (7287 0443, www.yosushi.com). Oxford Circus tube. **Meals served** noon-11pm Mon-Sat; noon-10.30pm Sun.
Simon Woodroffe's canny idea back in 1997 was to make conveyer-belt sushi western-friendly and fun. You can get larger hot dishes too.
Map 17 A3.
For branches see index.

East
Bethnal Green

Viajante

Patriot Square, E2 9NF (7871 0461, www.viajante.co.uk).
Bethnal Green tube/rail or Cambridge Heath rail. **Lunch
served** noon-2pm, **dinner served** 7-9.30pm daily.
Set lunch £24-£40 3 courses, £45-£70 6 courses.
Set dinner £60-£90 6 courses, £75-£120 9 courses,
£85-£150 12 courses. **Credit** AmEx, MC, V.
Nuno Mendes first made his mark as chef at Bacchus, an
ambitious Hoxton spot, but the backdrop for his experimental
cooking is now Bethnal Green Old Town Hall, recently
converted into a boutique hotel. The lofty dining room of
Viajante (Portuguese for 'traveller') is unpretentious and
relaxed, its smooth wood and icy blue fabrics complemented
by a rotation of big band tunes and lounge music. The open
kitchen provides ample theatre as Mendes and his handful of
chefs (with their many tweezers) put the finishing touches to
the dishes. The humble, ebullient Mendes serves several dishes
himself, but all the staff are charming and clued-up. Diners are
inundated with a flurry of free titbits (creamy galangal and
lemongrass-scented chicken sandwiched with crisp, rendered
chicken skin, for example) before the first course arrives: in our
case a chessboard of squid tartare with squid ink granita,
sprigs of samphire, curls of pink pickled radish and other little
flavour bombs (toasted pine nuts, lemon pulp, heads of enoki
mushrooms and intense dill oil). The parade of sensations
continues through to mushroom-flavoured chocolate truffles
for petits fours. A meal here doesn't come cheap, but it's a fun
ride worth the price.
Babies and children admitted. Booking essential.
Disabled: toilet.

Gilgamesh

North
Camden Town & Chalk Farm

Gilgamesh

*Stables Market, Chalk Farm Road, NW1 8AH (7482
5757, www.gilgameshbar.com). Chalk Farm tube.*
Bar **Open/snacks served** 6pm-2.30am Mon-Thur;
noon-2.30am Fri-Sun.
Restaurant **Lunch served** noon-3pm, **dinner served**
6pm-midnight daily. **Dim sum** £4-£6. **Main courses**
£10-£24.80. **Set lunch** £12 3 courses. **Set meal** £47.50
3 courses.
Both **Credit** AmEx, MC, V.
For those who want to impress a dining companion, this first-
floor love-letter to Babylonian excess could do the trick. If the
highly decorative carved chairs and inlaid tables don't take
your breath away, perhaps the glass roof will. Waiting staff
glide by, carrying dishes of sashimi above billowing clouds of
dry ice. But the dining area is vast, and as the place gets busier,
the pauses between courses get longer. A special promotion (50%
off a £45 set menu) seemed like great value, but the quality of
the eclectic pan-Asian dishes was mediocre. Smoked trout with
star fruit and mango salad made a fresh, zingy starter, yet the
main course of pan-fried grey mullet was overdone, and a Thai
red curry used heat to compensate for its lack of flavour. Our
meal wasn't helped by the fire alarm going off twice, for quite
long periods. Note that Gilgamesh has one odd feature: its only
bank of windows overlooks the railway line, up close.
Babies and children welcome: high chairs. Booking essential.
Disabled: lift; toilet. Dress: smart casual. Vegetarian menu.
Map 27 C1.

Outer London
Barnet, Hertfordshire

Emchai

78 High Street, Barnet, Herts EN5 5SN (8364 9993).
High Barnet tube. **Lunch served** noon-2.30pm daily.
Dinner served 6-11pm Mon-Thur; 6pm-midnight Fri,
Sat; 5-10pm Sun. **Main courses** £4.20-£7.90. **Set meal**
£15-£18.50 per person (minimum 2). **Credit** AmEx, MC, V.
Friendly Emchai is a favourite with north London families, but
at night has enough style and verve to make it popular with
groups of friends out on the town – of Barnet. Inside, fairy
lights set amid spindly branches are positioned against teal
and white walls, while the dark wood tables are paired with
either woven leather or curvy plastic chairs. The lengthy menu
incorporates Malaysian, Chinese, Japanese and Thai
influences. Dishes are served on pretty Japanese stoneware: a
classy detail that helps make the bill seem all the more
reasonable. Many regulars come for the aromatic crispy duck,
which is mesmerisingly deconstructed at the table, but it's
worth looking at the printed paper list of specials: deep-fried
nuggets of smoked chicken stir-fried with spring onions and
garlic, maybe, alongside steamed breast of chicken with goji
berries from the Chinese herbal medicine school of cuisine. The
fairly priced, fruit-forward zinfandel rosé from California
works well with these big flavours, but you could also opt for
oriental lagers, saké or seasonal squeezed-to-order juices.
Available for hire. Babies and children welcome: high chairs.
Booking advisable weekends. Disabled: toilet. Takeaway.

Spanish & Portuguese

Fifteen years ago the Spanish restaurant scene in London was dominated by a lacklustre grab-bag of tapas bars catering to the after-work drinks crowd. Then in 1997, Sam and Sam Clark, two former River Café chefs, opened fashionable **Moro** to instant acclaim. Things quickly changed, aided by Spanish foods importer **Brindisa** (now with three of its own restaurants), which ensured that quality authentic ingredients were readily available. Today our Spanish chapter includes several of London's most exciting eateries, from the nueva cocina of **Lola Rojo** to stylish tapas joints such as **Barrafina** and **Dehesa**, plus high-end stalwart **Cambio de Tercio**. New this year is Fitzrovia's bijou taverna **Barrica**, glamorous **Aqua Nueva** (which benefits from its Regent Street rooftop location) and evocative **Angels & Gypsies**, which has introduced good Spanish cooking to Camberwell.

Portuguese cuisine has long been in the shadow of its flashier neighbour, but **Portal** offers an inventive updating of this essentially rustic food. Otherwise, venues that successfully recreate the relaxed Lusitanian vibe remain our favourites: the likes of **Lisboa Grill** and **O Fado**.

SPANISH

Central

Bloomsbury

Cigala
54 Lamb's Conduit Street, WC1N 3LW (7405 1717, www.cigala.co.uk). Holborn or Russell Square tube.
Bar **Open/tapas served** 5.30-10.45pm Mon-Sat. **Tapas** £2-£16.
Restaurant **Meals served** noon-10.45pm Mon-Fri; 12.30-10.45pm Sat; 12.30-9.45pm Sun. **Main courses** £11-£18. **Set lunch** (noon-3pm Mon-Fri) £15 2 courses, £18 3 courses.
Both **Credit** AmEx, DC, MC, V.
The Bloomsbury set that gathers at Cigala to sip sherries at pavement tables on the pedestrianised street or dine in the airy,

understated dining room is a mixed one: from suave lunchtime suits to artfully unkempt media types and chattering fashionistas. With its pale walls, clean lines and Scandinavian-looking pale wood, the venue exudes an easy and sophisticated elegance. Prices are quite high, but so is the standard of cooking. Dense own-made bread, teamed with fragrant, grassy olive oil, set the benchmark for our meal, followed by rich, creamy croquetas de pollo, offset with a hint of marjoram. Lamb meatballs were plump and herby, while a garlicky escalivada paired grilled peppers with wonderfully sweet slivers of caramelised red onion. A plate of Spanish cheeses proved disappointingly small, although the membrillo and crunchy own-baked bread (wafer-thin and studded with caraway seeds) made some amends. Desserts, by contrast, were substantial: a nutty, almost liquid-centred slab of tarta de chocolate; and some big, blowsy almond meringues, with a heap of boozy prunes and a generous dollop of cream. Service was initially solicitous, but became absent-minded as the tables filled. The drinks list suits all-comers, running from inventive house cocktails to interesting wines.

Available for hire bar. Babies and children welcome: high chairs. Booking advisable. Tables outdoors (11, pavement). **Map 4 M4.**

Clerkenwell & Farringdon

Moro [HOT 50]

34-36 Exmouth Market, EC1R 4QE (7833 8336, www.moro.co.uk). Farringdon tube/rail or 19, 38, 341 bus.
Bar **Open/tapas served** 12.30-10.30pm Mon-Sat.
Tapas £3.50-£14.50.
Restaurant **Lunch served** 12.30-2.30pm, **dinner served** 7-10.30pm Mon-Sat. **Main courses** £14.50-£20.
Both **Credit** AmEx, DC, MC, V.

Well loved for their rustic take on Spanish and North African dishes, Sam and Samantha Clarke have long since put Moro on the culinary map. In summer, tables spill on to the pavement, but even indoors, there's a convivial vibe. The room is furnished with plain wooden flooring and spartan fittings; a lengthy bar provides a perch for punters to linger over tapas and an impressive selection of sherries. The weekly changing menu is dedicated to robust country cooking. Smoky paprika, saffron and sweet cinnamon are the signature spices, added to cuts of meat that are cooked in a wood-fired oven or over charcoal grills. Service is spot-on: quick off the mark, friendly and supremely efficient. We enjoyed the warming heat from deep bowls of whipped yoghurt and lentil soup, fragrant with toasted cumin and especially good when mopped up with crusty sourdough bread. Wood-roasted chicken with garlicky mash was impressive too, the sticky juices from the bird sweetly infused with Pedro Ximénez sherry: a marvellous match with the mash. Portions are substantial, but save space for puds. We're in love with the ice-creams of rosewater and cardamom, and creamy malaga raisin. Moro's new tapas bar, Morito, opened next door in 2010.

Available for hire. Babies and children welcome: high chairs. Booking essential. Disabled: toilet. Tables outdoors (6, pavement). **Map 5 N4.**
For branch (Morito) see index.

Barrica

Fitzrovia

Barrica

2010 WINNER BEST SPANISH FOOD & DRINK
62 Goodge Street, W1T 4NE (7436 9448, www.barrica.co.uk). Goodge Street or Tottenham Court Road tube. **Meals served** noon-11pm Mon-Sat. **Tapas** £1.75-£13.50. **Credit** AmEx, MC, V.

If you're looking for an authentic Spanish experience, this small, busy restaurant is top of the list. It has the feel of a smart taverna, with chequerboard tiled floor, Spanish posters and maps, a hanging ham and moody lighting, yet the effect is sleek and surprisingly unclichéd. Closely packed, see-and-be-seen tables are positioned around the bar and there's a compact seating area at the back. Warm yellow walls are adorned with blackboards offering tempting daily specials on both food and wine. The concise, all-Spanish wine list is savvily food-friendly, with options ranging from fino sherry to seldom-seen grape varieties such as Godello and some superb Spanish brandies. The excellent food comes in proper tapas-sized portions, not the larger raciones you usually get in England, which means you can order more dishes – and the prices are so reasonable there's no reason not to. Traditional terracotta dishes may be used, but the cooking is rather exciting, offering well-considered twists on classic dishes: pork and oxtail meatballs, veal cheeks in rich sherry sauce, chicory leaves with picos cheese. Dessert is equally rewarding; salted caramel choc ice was a pleasing assault on the taste buds. On our latest visit, service was a little slow at first, but nonetheless attentive. Barrica is perfect for an inexpensive and informal night out in the West End, and a place you'll want to visit regularly.

Babies and children admitted. Booking advisable Wed-Sat. Tables outdoors (2, pavement). **Map 17 A1.**

Fino

2010 RUNNER-UP BEST SPANISH FOOD & DRINK
33 Charlotte Street, entrance on Rathbone Street, W1T 1RR (7813 8010, www.finorestaurant.com). Goodge Street or Tottenham Court Road tube. **Lunch**

SPANISH & PORTUGUESE

served noon-2.30pm Mon-Fri. **Dinner served** 6-10.30pm Mon-Sat. **Tapas** £4-£15.50. **Credit** AmEx, MC, V.

In an area that's packed with great restaurants, the unimposing doorway that leads down to Fino is easily missed. However, the reputation of Sam and Eddie Hart's first restaurant ensures that booking is a must. Arrive early to enjoy a tipple from the impressive cocktail and spirits menu. In the restaurant, a smartly dressed clientele fills tables, banquettes and booths with a lively hum of conversation. Decor is sleek and stylish, with colourful prints adorning the walls. Main courses change twice daily, although you'll find that signature dishes such as pork belly are a fixture. Fino offers a modern take on classic Spanish flavours – morcilla iberica with quail eggs, seared tuna on a piquillo pepper salad. In summer, the courgette flowers stuffed with goat's cheese and drizzled with honey are not to be missed. Desserts are equally tempting: indulgent doughnuts with vanilla ice-cream, creamy leche frita. If you haven't had your fill from the regional wine and sherry list, then finish up in the bar with an 'after-dinner cocktail' such as the vodka-based choco-latte. Service is laid-back; our waitress was exceptionally warm and knowledgeable. For a smart night out, this is place to return to time and again.

Available for hire. Babies and children welcome: high chairs. Booking advisable. Disabled: lift; toilet. **Map 17 B1**.

Ibérica Food & Culture

2010 RUNNER-UP BEST SPANISH FOOD & DRINK
195 Great Portland Street, W1W 5PS (7636 8650, www.ibericalondon.com). Great Portland Street tube. **Meals served** 11.30am-11pm Mon-Sat; noon-4pm Sun. **Tapas** £3.50-£12.50. **Main courses** £7-£19. **Credit** AmEx, MC, V.

A tapas bar, a delicatessen with a walk-in cheese and wine room, books, ceramics and a mini-art gallery – Ibérica Food & Culture has a little of everything, and is a real find for hispanophiles. The bright and airy ground-floor tapas bar offers a broad selection of small plates. Alongside authentic dishes such as Asturian fabada you'll find tapas with plenty of flair, such as steamed mussels with sea urchin vinaigrette, and fried chorizo 'lollypops' with pear alioli. On Sundays a shorter menu focuses on the traditional: croquetas, squid with alioli, cured meats and cheeses. The paellas are fabulous. Our sumptuous version was laden with perfectly cooked squid, prawns, langoustine and mussels in vibrant, full-flavoured rice. Angular white plates and slate platters make for stylish presentation. Floor-to-ceiling windows mean that lunch and early evenings are particularly pleasurable. Tables are positioned all the way around the bar and into the treasure trove of a shop, where there's space for large groups. Customers on our visit included a reassuring Spanish contingent, families and couples; weekdays attract a business crowd.

Available for hire. Babies and children welcome: high chairs; nappy-changing facilities. Booking advisable. Separate room for parties, seats 30. Takeaway service. **Map 3 H5**.

King's Cross

Camino

3 Varnishers Yard, Regents Quarter, N1 9FD (7841 7331, www.camino.uk.com). King's Cross tube/rail.
Bar **Tapas served** noon-4pm, 4.30-11pm Mon-Fri; 4.30-11pm Sat, Sun. **Brunch served** noon-4pm Sat, Sun. **Tapas** £3-£7.75.
Restaurant **Breakfast served** 8-11.30am daily. **Lunch served** noon-3pm Mon-Fri. **Brunch served** noon-4pm

Dinner gong

London is currently blessed with an array of superior Spanish restaurants. Here are the finalists for our 2010 Best Spanish Food & Drink award, showcasing the depth and breadth of Spain's gastronomy.

WINNER
Barrica
This Fitzrovia newcomer offers excellent and inventive tapas (in proper portions) in an authentic taverna setting, plus a commendable all-Spanish wine list. *See left.*

RUNNERS-UP
Cambio de Tercio
Enjoy sophisticated and adventurous haute cuisine at this South Kensington stalwart. The wine list is impressively detailed. *See p232.*

Fino
Sleek, stylish and smart, Charlotte Street's Fino adds a modern twist to classic Spanish dishes. Drinks range from cocktails to regional sherries. *See left.*

Ibérica Food & Culture
On a bright, airy corner site, Iberica serves first-rate tapas, and fabulous paella on Sundays. There's a deli, shop and art gallery too. *See left.*

Barrica

Sat, Sun. **Dinner served** 6.30-11pm Mon-Fri; 7-11pm Sat. **Main courses** £10.50-£23. *Both* **Credit** AmEx, MC, V.

Occupying a converted warehouse complex, from which all grime has been stripped, this exuberant bar-restaurant epitomises the new King's Cross: well groomed, ambitious and much-sanitised. Like its sizeable sharing platters, Camino offers 'un poca de todo': a bit of everything. On a weekday morning, when the breakfast bar dispenses hot churros with thick, bittersweet chocolate, and platefuls of eggs, chistorra sausage, bacon and sautéed potatoes, the place is unexpectedly tranquil. Come the evening, proceedings crank up as office workers neck bottles of Sagres and share salty slivers of jamón ibérico. More unusual offerings intersperse the standard croquetas and calamares (morcilla with baked apples and a Pedro Ximénez reduction, say), and a commitment to food provenance runs beyond PR puff, with suppliers of free-range meat and sustainably fished seafood duly listed. Substantial, predominantly meaty mains such as chargrilled steak or shoulder of ibérico pig are served in the adjoining restaurant, whose quasi-industrial styling (bare brick, iron girders) is softened by muted lighting. Across the courtyard, where drinkers cluster around barrels, the latest addition is Bar Pepito (*see p14*), a tiny sherry bar. Big and brash it may be, but Camino hasn't lost sight of the details.
Available for hire. Babies and children welcome: high chairs; nappy-changing facilities. Booking advisable. Disabled: toilet. Tables outdoors (10, garden; 4, pavement). **Map 4 L3.**

Mayfair

El Pirata

5-6 Down Street, W1J 7AQ (7491 3810, www.elpirata. co.uk). Green Park or Hyde Park Corner tube. **Meals served** noon-11.30pm Mon-Fri. **Dinner served** 6-11.30pm Sat. **Main courses** £13.95-£17.50. **Tapas** £1.90-£10.50. **Set lunch** (noon-3pm) £9.95 2 dishes incl glass of wine. **Set meal** £15.95-£20.50 per person (minimum 2). **Credit** AmEx, MC, V.

In rarefied Mayfair, El Pirata remains refreshingly down to earth. Immune to passing trends, it exudes a stately, old-fashioned charm with flower-filled planters out front, red carnations on the tables and framed, familiar Miró and Picasso prints in the airy ground-floor dining area. Past the mirrored bar and down a spiral staircase, the cellar features white-painted brickwork and tightly packed tables, with a couple of charming alcoves for groups – though the intimate feel appeals to courting couples too. At El Pirata's modish sister restaurant in Westbourne Grove, presided over by an ambitious young Ferran Adrià protégé, an edgy take on tapas prevails: valdéon cheese foam with endive, say, or octopus carpaccio with mandarin caviar. At Mayfair, though, it's all about the classics. Elegantly layered escalivada packed a sweet, flavourful punch, while habas con jamón (pan-fried broad beans dotted with dark, deliciously salty chunks of ham) was comfort food of the highest order. Individual dishes don't always succeed: grilled squid was slightly chewy, and the salsa verde accompanying our almejas (baby clams) proved curiously bland and soupy. Nonetheless, competitive prices, sweetly solicitous service and a wide-ranging, regional wine list help smooth over any blips.
Babies and children admitted. Booking advisable dinner. Separate room for parties, seats 65. Tables outdoors (4, pavement). Takeaway service. **Map 9 H8.**
For branch (El Pirata Detapas) see index.

Soho

Aqua Nueva

5th floor, 240 Regent Street, entrance in Argyll Street, W1B 3BR (7478 0540, www.aqua-london.com). Oxford Circus tube. **Lunch served** noon-3pm Mon-Sat. **Dinner served** 6-10.45pm Mon-Wed; 6-11.15pm Thur-Sat. **Main courses** £16-£26. **Tapas** £5.50-£18. **Set meal** (noon-3pm, 6-7.30pm Mon-Thur; noon-3pm Fri, Sat) £19.40 4 courses incl glass of wine. **Credit** AmEx, MC, V.

Aqua, an upmarket 'concept' from Hong Kong, occupies the top floor of what was Dickins & Jones department store. The entrance has velvet drapes and a doorman, who checks your reservation before dispatching you five floors up by lift, to be sized up again by girl greeters. There are two dining rooms, this one – Aqua Nueva – claiming inspiration from Spanish nueva cocina, and next door a sushi bar and sumibiyaki (charcoal grill) called Aqua Kyoto. There's also a cocktail bar and outdoor terraces. Spacious and attractively lit, Nueva has a fairly conventional tapas bar to one side, but there's a more adventurous menu in the dining room. Oxtail was the best dish: a neat block of meat, marinated then slow-cooked, and simply served with carved vegetables. 'Corn soup with beetroot and monte enebro cheese ravioli' came as a lukewarm sweetcorn purée, its 'ravioli' upright dominoes of raw beetroot with cheese dabbed between them. Our dessert was a car crash: sour yoghurt clashing with delicate apple sorbet, plus ice-cream, cooked apple, dark chocolate and spun sugar. Prices are fair for a smart place with perfectly adequate cooking, but the staff appeared to know virtually nothing about the dishes.
Available for hire. Babies and children admitted. Booking advisable Wed-Sat. Disabled: lift; toilet. Dress: smart casual. Separate room for parties, seats 16. **Map 9 J6.**

Barrafina   HOT 50

54 Frith Street, W1D 4SL (7440 1463, www.barrafina. co.uk). Leicester Square or Tottenham Court Road tube. **Tapas served** noon-3pm, 5-11pm Mon-Sat; 1-3.30pm, 5.30-10.30pm Sun. **Tapas** £1.90-£16.50. **Credit** AmEx, MC, V.

If your idea of tapas is slow, quiet bites with a gentle soundtrack of flamenco, forget Barrafina. From noon to 3pm and during the early evening, this small, cramped eating space – it's not a restaurant so much as a stainless-steel bar with a corridor round it – is rammed with office workers, who like to bring their repressed shouts along with their appetites. Fortunately, the food makes up for this. Get a stool at the bar and watch how the waiter-cooks prepare even the most rudimentary tapas; you're sure to be impressed. Tortillas, cooked in special, high-lipped, super-hot frying pans, are often checked by two or three staff to ensure they're moist and spongy enough, but completely sealed. The ultra-fresh octopus is gently seasoned and enlivened with capers. Seafood dishes come steaming and garlicky, though portions can be small. The high-end jabugo ham, while deliciously sweaty, is expensive: £18 for a plate too meagre to share. Excellent wines from Galicia, Duero and other intriguing regions are available by the glass, making this an ideal but rackety pit-stop.
Babies and children welcome: high chairs. Bookings not accepted. Tables outdoors (4, pavement). **Map 17 C3.**

Dehesa

25 Ganton Street, W1F 9BP (7494 4170, www.dehesa.co.uk). Oxford Circus tube. **Tapas served** noon-11pm Mon-Sat; noon-5pm Sun. **Tapas** £3.50-£7.25. **Credit** AmEx, MC, V.

iberica
food & culture

Tradition and evolution: the ongoing debate in Spanish gastronomy. **Two chefs, two Michelin starred Nacho Manzano and Santiago Guerrero,** bring this debate to London. Our kitchen represents both a modern interpretation of traditional Spanish food and the close relationship we have with our ingredients and their provenance.

We go **direct to source** to bring the best Spanish products **to our kitchen and for our customers to buy in our deli or online.**

The "Los Pedroches" denomination of origin is the third to join our collection of Ibérico Hams. A small, new D.O. in the province of Córdoba, Los Pedroches produces ham with a sweet flavour, intense aroma, purple colour and smooth texture.

"La Catedral de Navarra" has become **a favourite brand amongst chefs and those with the most demanding palates.** The Catedral de Navarra piquillo peppers have a delicate, sweet finish that is achieved only by selecting small, slender, red and ripe "Pimientos del Piquillo" and fire roasting and hand peeling them one by one.

We select and import wines from small boutique wineries. One such is **Pagos de Negredo**, from a new denomination of origin, **Arlanza,** created in 2008 and located between Burgos and Palencia. **Pagos de Negredo** is a sumptuous wine made in the classic way from "tinta del pais" grapes grown on vines originally planted in the 19th century.

Iberica Food & Culture
Restaurant - Delicatessen - Wine Store - Art Gallery
195 Great Portland St. London W1W 5PS
+44(0)2076368650
www.ibericalondon.co.uk

Dehesa is in an area so artificially funky that you fear for its soul. No need. Once you've elbowed your way through the Ganton Street crowds, you'll find a venue that's stylish and pleasant but fully focused on the plate and in the glass. The back of the menu is a paean to the pig, in Spanish and Italian derivations, offering hams on and off the bone, including an entry-level, acorn-fed jamón ibérico. There are a few cheeses, too, mixing the expected (manchego) with the wider-ranging (torta de barros). But we found most pleasure in the tapas menu, which pushes genre expectations with such dishes as prettily presented saffron-cured sea trout with spiced aubergine, quails' eggs and beetroot dressing; and squid with grilled chorizo salad, pickled red onions and guindilla chillies. On the simpler side, a classic tortilla was just the right mix of textures. The wine list is pricey, with only a couple of bottles under £20. But we're arguing range not value: our Mallorcan Macia rosé was knowledgeably selected and worth its £28. The comfortable, brown-hued room is dominated by a couple of long tables that you'll be asked to share – and vacate after two hours, at busy times. Capable, friendly staff generate a congenial enough atmosphere for this not to feel a chore. Alternatively, in good weather you can escape to the pleasant pavement tables.

Salt Yard, arranged over two compact floors in Fitzrovia, is Dehesa's older sister, offering a similar selection of well-considered Spanish/Italian food and wine. It's popular with a sophisticated office crowd.

Babies and children admitted. Booking advisable dinner. Separate room for parties, seats 12. Tables outdoors (8, pavement). **Map 17 A4.**

For branch (Salt Yard) see index.

South Kensington

Cambio de Tercio

2010 RUNNER-UP BEST SPANISH FOOD & DRINK
163 Old Brompton Road, SW5 0LJ (7244 8970, www.cambiodetercio.co.uk). *Gloucester Road or South Kensington tube.* **Lunch served** noon-3pm daily. **Dinner served** 7-11.30pm Mon-Sat; 7-11pm Sun. **Main courses** £13.90-£15.50. **Set meal** £25-£50. **Credit** AmEx, DC, MC, V.
Walk into Cambio de Tercio and you're hit by a profusion of colour: deep pink, bright yellow and rich red cover the walls and ceiling. Complementing this are equally vibrant oil paintings with a bull-fighting theme, as might be expected from a restaurant that takes its name from the sport. Black accents and starched white tablecloths temper the paint palette, to make this a sophisticated and funky eaterie. The menu is Spanish haute cuisine and combines adventurous dishes (gazpacho with cherry ice-cream and lobster) with more traditional fare (calamares with alioli). You can order a selection of tapas (some of which are mini versions of the main courses) or starters and mains. Desserts steer away from the usual Spanish restaurant favourites. Sumptuous torrija (bread pudding) with crema catalana ice-cream appears conservative on a menu that also features gin jelly with tonic water sorbet and lime foam. The wine list is comprehensive, offering a wide selection with plenty of background information; sherries and cavas are also given their due. Efficient service tends discreetly to the needs of a well-heeled clientele. This is an ideal venue for a special occasion and there's a room for private parties.
Available for hire. Babies and children admitted. Booking advisable dinner. Separate room for parties, seats 20. Tables outdoors (3, pavement). **Map 13 C11.**

Tendido Cero

174 Old Brompton Road, SW5 0BA (7370 3685, www.cambiodetercio.co.uk). *Gloucester Road or South Kensington tube.* **Tapas served** noon-3pm, 6.30-11pm daily. **Tapas** £4-£14. **Credit** AmEx, MC, V.
Located opposite its sister restaurant, Cambio de Tercio, Tendido Cero offers a menu of modern, artfully presented tapas, but in a slightly less formal atmosphere (with lower prices to match). The cod confited in olive oil, chorizo in cider and recently introduced mini-mini 'hamburgers' of sardine, tomato, padrón pepper and aïoli all make for tasty hot tapas. Gazpacho, rabbit and manzanilla olive terrine, and cheeses with quince, are fabulous cold snacks. Dishes are small, and almost too beautiful to eat, but you get the spectrum of flavours from across the Iberian peninsula and even the Maghreb; try the inventive salad of dried tuna and clean, crisp Moroccan kumato tomatoes. Diners after a 'meal' should choose the squid in ink served with rice, or lamb and white wine casserole (laced with almonds); they cost the same and are more filling. The tortilla is as good as anywhere in town, but the bellota ham, while exceptional, costs £19.75 a throw. Tendido's vast wine list contains few budget options; best order one of the excellent sherries, then enjoy a slow glass of plummy Altun tempranillo. The atmosphere is lively and friendly, and service seems to have improved since our last visit.
Available for hire. Babies and children admitted. Booking advisable dinner Wed-Sat. Tables outdoors (5, pavement). **Map 13 C11.**

For branch (Tendido Cuatro) see index.

South

Battersea

Lola Rojo `HOT 50`

78 Northcote Road, SW11 6QL (7350 2262, www.lolarojo.net). *Clapham Junction rail.* **Lunch served** noon-3pm, **dinner served** 6-10.30pm Mon-Thur. **Meals served** noon-10.30pm Fri-Sun. **Main courses** £7.50-£11. **Set lunch** (Mon-Fri) £7.50 3 tapas, £8.50 1 tapas & 1 rice; (Sun) £15 5 tapas & 1 rice. **Credit** MC, V.
Husband and wife team Antonio Belles and Cristina García opened this smartly casual neighbourhood restaurant in 2006, following with a more spacious Fulham branch around two years later. The decor at both is distinctive – stone tiled floors, white walls and chairs, bold splashes of red (a wall here, a plate there, a picture of a strawberry over yonder). Despite Lola Rojo's sophisticated sense of style, and its embracing of nueva cocina (new-wave Spanish cooking), prices are remarkably fair. The menus vary slightly at each branch, but favourites from both include little gem with herbs and own-made tuna pickle; chorizo lollipops with quince aïoli; spinach and goat's cheese rice (rice dishes tend to be excellent); and the signature white chocolate soup with thyme toffee and mango ice-cream. Finish with keenly priced Enrique Mendoza moscatel de la marina from Alicante, or explore elixirs such as Galician aguardiente, Pacharán Zoco, and anis del mono dulce. The wine list includes fun tasting notes and is helpfully divided by style to showcase up-and-coming producers, although the sherry selection is surprisingly scanty for a restaurant of this calibre. Battersea's Lola Rojo embraces the buzz of Northcote Road market, selling takeaway tapas.

Babies and children admitted: booster seats. Booking advisable Thur-Sat. Tables outdoors (16, terrace). Takeaway service. **Map 21 C5.**
For branch see index.

Vauxhall

Rebato's
169 South Lambeth Road, SW8 1XW (7735 6388, www.rebatos.com). Stockwell tube.
Tapas bar **Open/tapas served** 5.30-10.45pm Mon-Fri; 7-11pm Sat. **Tapas** £2.95-£7.50. **Set meal** £10 6 tapas per person (minimum 2).
Restaurant **Lunch served** noon-2.30pm Mon-Fri. **Dinner served** 7-10.45pm Mon-Sat. **Main courses** £12.95-£15.95. **Set meal** (Mon-Thur) £10 5 courses (minimum 2).
Both **Credit** AmEx, MC, V.
The loveliest thing about Rebato's is that it never changes. Local off-licences, pubs and caffs have largely been reborn as restaurants serving the Portuguese community, but this little spot remains thoroughly Spanish. The front area, with its old polished wood bar and about 20 covers, is for drinks and tapas, though you can order main courses and specials too. The back is bigger, brighter and old-fashioned, resembling the breakfast room in a grand hotel. A solitary leg of jamón divides the spaces. Sherry bottles line the bar alongside plates and footballs, and the walls are bedecked with bullfighting posters, framed prints and Torres wine mirrors. The food is sublime: from a main of suckling pig with crisp skin (served with apple sauce, steamed spinach and crunchy chips), to garlicky calamares, and scrumptious pimento and provolone cheese fritters. Rebato's lacks certain treats (no oxtail, no high-end jabugo ham), yet what it does it does with flair. The wine list is quite pricey, but a Catalan tempranillo (£18.95) was robust enough to match the food. Apple pie was tasty, with fairly

delicate pastry. Modern touches include air-con and Spanish pop music, but otherwise, Rebato's is a cherished *clásico*. *Available for hire. Babies and children admitted. Booking essential. Takeaway service.* **Map 16 L13.**

Waterloo

Mar i Terra
14 Gambia Street, SE1 0XH (7928 7628, www.mari terra.co.uk). Southwark tube or Waterloo tube/rail.
Tapas served noon-3pm, 6-11pm Mon-Fri; 5-11pm Sat. **Tapas** £3.50-£9. **Credit** AmEx, MC, V.
Tucked down a small street off the Cut, Mar i Terra is an unpretentious restaurant that needs no fanfare to attract a steady stream of diners. In the evening, it doesn't take bookings for parties of less than ten, and on a busy Tuesday night, there was some hesitation as to whether there'd be room for two. The furnishings are inviting, with colourful prints, the ubiquitous long Spanish bar and casual wooden tables and chairs. When you first walk in, the room appears quite small, but there's further seating upstairs and a pleasant walled garden to be enjoyed on sunny days. Service by the predominantly Spanish staff is quick and attentive. The rustic-slanted menu offers a tempting selection of tapas – chorizo cooked in cider, stuffed baby squid, asturian bean stew with morcilla, beef braised in Rioja. Food is consistently good and own-made. Some choice desserts, plus a fine selection of Spanish drinks, make it easy to while away time here in relaxed surroundings. The reasonably priced menu doesn't appear to have changed much over the past few years, but if it ain't broke…
Available for hire. Babies and children welcome: high chairs. Bookings not accepted for fewer than 10 people dinner. Separate room for parties, seats 50. Tables outdoors (15, garden). **Map 11 O8.**
For branch see index.

Angels & Gypsies. See p235.

South East

Camberwell

Angels & Gypsies

2010 WINNER BEST NEW LOCAL RESTAURANT
*29-33 Camberwell Church Street, SE5 8TR (7703 5984,
www.churchstreethotel.com). Denmark Hill rail or 36,
185, 436 bus.* **Lunch served** noon-3pm Tue-Thur; noon-
3.30pm Fri, Sat; noon-4pm Sun. **Dinner served** 6-10pm
Mon-Thur, Sun; 6-10.30pm Fri, Sat. **Tapas** £3.50-£9.50.
Credit AmEx, MC, V.
Amid the takeaways and tatty shops of Camberwell's main
drag is the incongruous sight of the Latin-inspired Church
Street Hotel and this, its attached restaurant. Angels & Gypsies
has been a hit since opening in 2009. Design is low-key but
stylish. Plain dark wood tables and pews are set against
exposed brickwork; striking stained-glass pictures of angels
and gypsies around a campfire adorn the walls; and the central
horseshoe bar is lined with attractive ceramic tiles. The tapas-
style menu includes familiar Spanish dishes (jamón croquetas,
tortilla, padrón peppers) alongside more unusual concoctions
(Devon snails with chilli and passata, for example) and home-
grown ingredients (Neal's Yard cheeses). Apart from a warm
minty salad of broad beans and peas, too heavy on the peas,
our choices were excellent. Pulpo a feira – a traditional Galician
recipe – consisted of meltingly tender octopus drizzled with
olive oil and paprika: simple but superb. Roasted pear draped
with melted ragstone goat's cheese and paper-thin serrano ham
provided an intense mix of flavours and textures. Similar care
has gone into the wine list (almost all Spanish), plus the
selection of sherries and rums. Service – from mainly female,
Spanish staff – was swift, informed and charm personified.
*Available for hire. Babies and children welcome: high chairs.
Booking advisable. Separate room for parties, seats 24.
Takeaway service.* **Map 23 B2**.

Herne Hill

Number 22

*22 Half Moon Lane, SE24 9HU (7095 9922, www.
number-22.com). Herne Hill rail or 3, 37, 68 bus.*
Tapas served 5-11pm Mon-Fri; noon-3pm, 5-10.30pm
Sat; noon-9.30pm Sun. **Tapas** £3-£8.50. **Credit** MC, V.
With its chocolate-cappuccino tones, Number 22 provides an
intimate setting ideal for couples. At the front is a deep cherry-
wood bar with low lighting and a grand homely fireplace. A
narrow corridor (speedily navigated by the keen staff) leads to
a walled courtyard – a more informal backdrop for the summer.
Tapas are a mixture of the familiar and the odd curiosity. On
our last visit, zingy cured sardines stuffed with crab meat and
mango mayonnaise were fabulous; we also relished the saltfish
'cigars' (posh fish fingers, in effect). Narrowing down your
tapas selection isn't easy. Chorizo cooked in cider, meat and
fish croquettes and various ways with serrano ham sit among
more substantial choices such as braised rabbit with olives,
and pork belly with saffron and pear. We found the pork belly
not as meltingly tender as it could have been, and the escalivada
(grilled vegetables) were underdone. These small gripes apart,
the cooking is fine, and there's a varied choice of wines,
cocktails and, later, Spanish cheeses. Sunday is paella day and
worth investigating.
*Available for hire. Babies and children welcome: high chairs.
Tables outdoors (6, patio).* **Map 23 A5**.

London Bridge & Borough

Tapas Brindisa

*18-20 Southwark Street, SE1 1TJ (7357 8880,
www.brindisa.com). London Bridge tube/rail.* **Breakfast
served** 9-11am Fri, Sat. **Lunch served** noon-3pm
Mon-Thur; noon-4pm Fri, Sat. **Dinner served** 5.30-11pm
Mon-Sat. **Tapas** £3.20-£22. **Credit** AmEx, MC, V.
Top-quality ingredients have always been the mainstay at
Brindisa, whose genius lies in assembling them into eminently
tempting tapas: a cup of green pea soup with manchego, say,
or pan-fried fillet steak with caramelised onion and torta de
barros cheese on toast. The set-up is equally simple, with a bar
area at one end dotted with high tables, and a close-packed,
concrete-floored dining room at the other. Both are generally
thronged; no bookings are taken, and the waiting list is
invariably long. Behind the bar is a hatch into the kitchen, from
which chefs in immaculate whites produce a succession of
deceptively simple dishes. The flavours shine through. A
hearty wedge of tortilla, crammed with peppers, potato and
chorizo, was served with a dollop of pungent aïoli, while a dish
of pan-fried squid and green beans was studded with sweet,
slow-roasted garlic cloves. Cheese remains a strength, and the
charcuterie is also superb – though a platter of acorn-fed
ibérican goodies can swell the bill alarmingly. Brindisa's
restaurant operations (the company began in 1988 as Spanish
food importers) have expanded to include South Ken's Casa
Brindisa, which serves paella on Sundays, and Soho's Tierra
Brindisa, whose small open kitchen attempts a few more
culinary somersaults than its siblings.
*Babies and children admitted. Bookings not accepted.
Disabled: toilet. Tables outdoors (4, pavement).* **Map 11 P8**.
**For branches (Casa Brindisa, Tierra Brindisa)
see index**.

East

Docklands

El Faro

*3 Turnberry Quay, Pepper Street, E14 9RD (7987 5511,
www.el-faro.co.uk). Crossharbour DLR.* **Lunch served**
noon-3.30pm, **dinner served** 5-11pm Mon-Sat. **Meals
served** *Summer* 1-10pm Sun. *Winter* noon-3pm Sun.
Main courses £14-£17.50. **Tapas** £3.50-£14.50. **Credit**
AmEx, MC, V.
Tucked behind smart residential blocks, El Faro caters to
Docklands bankers and out-of-towners on expense accounts.
The dining room, with its black leather chairs and dark wood,
is elegant yet lacks ambience; the back terrace, with unbroken
views over the water, is a more agreeable spot on a warm
evening. Professional, polite staff bring dishes promptly, but
it's a pity about the angular plates and off-kilter bowls so
beloved of corporate restaurants. The kitchen knows its stuff;
tender strips of squid coated in well-seasoned fresh
breadcrumbs bore no trace of the oil in which they had been
deep-fried. Our portion of Segovian suckling pig didn't spend
14 hours in the oven in vain. It emerged with crisp, sticky
crackling and was served alongside a tiny pile of blood orange
and grapefruit segments whose flavours stood out thrillingly
against the rich, juicy belly meat. Best choice from the chef's
specials was a mixture of blood sausage (from Burgos) and
caramelised onion, crowned with a quivering poached egg.

Desserts, such as hot chocolate coulant with rhubarb millefeuille, are quite pricey, but a meal here won't break the bank if you stick to the lower end of the extensive wine list. *Babies and children welcome: high chairs. Booking advisable. Disabled: toilet. Separate room for parties, seats 70. Tables outdoors (16, terrace).* **Map 24 B3**.

Shoreditch

Laxeiro
93 Columbia Road, E2 7RG (7729 1147, www.laxeiro. co.uk). Hoxton rail. **Lunch served** noon-3pm, **dinner served** 7-11pm Tue-Sat. **Meals served** 9am-4pm Sun. **Tapas** £3.95-£8.50. **Credit** AmEx, MC, V.
This diminutive eaterie fits right into the Columbia Road scene, providing the flower-buying masses on Sunday with a laid-back, convivial bolt-hole from the crush outside. The yellow-painted dining room is small but inviting, and presided over by a magnificently aloof white moggy. Even outside market hours, the place is fiercely popular. The food, like the decor, is artfully rustic. Portions are racione- rather than tapa-sized, which means two dishes apiece should suffice. The menu focuses on classic flavours and simple execution: patatas aïoli was a textbook combination of crunchy, floury potato and unctuous, garlicky mayonnaise; a Pedro Ximénez sherry reduction provided the perfect foil for tender asparagus spears. Barbecued meat and fish is a speciality. In the past we've been impressed by the precision cooking and careful seasoning. On our last visit, though, the kitchen was on erratic form. Hefty slabs of red snapper were overcooked and underwhelming, while wafer-thin slices of barbecued lamb were terribly salty. A dish of fresh, firm, paprika-sprinkled octopus made some amends, as did a crisp, citrusy Muga Blanco Rioja; the wine list remains a delight, with democratically priced house wines and a focus on smaller regional producers.
Babies and children welcome: high chairs. Booking advisable; not accepted Sun. Tables outdoors (3, pavement). Takeaway service. **Map 6 S3**.

North East
Walthamstow

Orford Saloon
32 Orford Road, E17 9NJ (8503 6542). Walthamstow Central tube/rail. **Tapas served** 6-10.30pm Tue-Fri; noon-3pm, 6-10.30pm Sat; noon-3pm, 6-9.30pm Sun. **Tapas** £3.95-£14.50. **Set meal** £11 per person (minimum 2) paella. **Credit** MC, V.
This laid-back neighbourhood tapas bar is filled with the touchstones of Spanish culture, a portrait of flamenco dancers and some Moorish-style tiled tables among them. The British owners clearly brought a few favourite things from Spain when they opened in 2006, including a selection of noteworthy draught beers and a Malagan chef who produces a mix of well-executed but unrefined familiar dishes and more creative daily specials for dedicated locals. The octopus in the pulpo a la gallega was as tender as boiled-egg white, although almost-overcooked potatoes meant the dish's texture suffered slightly. Tortilla, served in generous wedges, lacked the ooze delivered by the best, but was a self-respecting tapa for £4. We enjoyed the contrasting flavours of the chef's special of trout, almonds, pine nuts and a liberal helping of pata negra ham. However,

the best-judged dish was the simplest: fresh green beans cooked with garlic and yet more shavings of ham had a satisfying crunch and intense flavour. Courteous staff welcomed us warmly, greatly adding to the enjoyment of the meal. Like its best counterparts in Spain, the Orford Saloon has become an irreplaceable haunt for the neighbourhood.
Babies and children welcome: high chairs. Booking advisable. Disabled: toilet.

North
Camden Town & Chalk Farm

El Parador
245 Eversholt Street, NW1 1BA (7387 2789, www.elparadorlondon.com). Mornington Crescent tube. **Tapas served** noon-3pm, 6-11pm Mon-Thur; noon-3pm, 6-11.30pm Fri; 6-11.30pm Sat; 6.30-9.30pm Sun. **Tapas** £4.20-£7.60. **Credit** MC, V.
Set amid a down-at-heel row of shops in the hinterland beyond Mornington Crescent station, El Parador is easy to miss. Inside, the paper tablecloths and dated decor look more shabby than chic. One glance at the menu, though, and it's clear that culinary ambitions exceed the decorative finesse. Unusually, vegetarian dishes are a forte: a dish of roughly puréed broad beans, say, spiked with confit garlic and fresh rosemary and scooped up with hunks of bread; or a summer salad of chargrilled artichoke hearts with knobbly, nutty-tasting ratte potatoes, mint and peas in a light, lemony walnut-oil dressing. Setas del campo (wild mushrooms) consisted of a garlicky tangle of unearthly-looking pan-fried Japanese fungi, subtly infused with tarragon, grain mustard and sesame oil. Meat dishes show the same meticulous attention to detail, with an abundance of fresh herbs and marinades. Fish options are quietly inventive; a plate of pan-fried tuna with smoky, bitter-sweet grilled chicory hearts, capers and lemon was bursting with flavour. Add a decent wine list, and by the time you get to dessert (the baked cheesecake of the day is sublime), you won't give a damn about the decor.
Babies and children admitted. Booking advisable for 3 or more. Separate room for parties, seats 30. Tables outdoors (12, garden). **Map 27 D3**.

PORTUGUESE
Central
Clerkenwell & Farringdon

Portal
88 St John Street, EC1M 4EH (7253 6950, www.portal restaurant.com). Barbican tube or Farringdon tube/rail. **Lunch served** noon-3pm Mon-Fri. **Dinner served** 6-10.15pm Mon-Sat. **Main courses** £12-£22. **Credit** AmEx, MC, V.
'Sleek, smart and polished' could describe both Portal's glistening, glass-encased dining room and its Modern European-slanted Portuguese cooking – such are the standards at this glamour-fuelled corner of Clerkenwell. Suckling pig, lobster and morels are just some of the highlights on the menu. For a more casual dining experience, choose the front wine bar,

which has an alluring list of tapas. A quick succession of pretty blue and white terracotta glazed plates arrived, with dishes achieving varying degrees of success. The morcilla (blood sausage) for two made a promising start to our meal, its crisp outer casing giving way to a soft yielding interior. However, some deep-fried risotto balls missed a trick by not being accompanied by a sauce, and the same could be said of the salt cod cakes, which surprisingly lacked sufficient seasoning. Gooey, tangy azeitão sheep's cheese was top notch: so tasty we wished it had been served Lisbon-style, whole and with a spoon. With a little effort, Portal could make tapas one of its key draws, rather than just a selection of bar snacks to help soak up its extensive wine list. Our overall impression of the place was good, but not outstanding.

Babies and children welcome: high chairs. Booking advisable. Disabled: toilet. Separate room for parties, seats 14. Tables outdoors (5, patio). **Map 5 O4.**

Knightsbridge

O Fado

50 Beauchamp Place, SW3 1NY (7589 3002, http:// ofado.co.uk). Knightsbridge or South Kensington tube. **Lunch served** noon-3pm, **dinner served** 6.30pm-11pm Mon-Sat. **Main courses** £10.95-£20.95. **Set lunch** £10-£15 mixed tapas incl drink & coffee, £14.95 2 courses incl drink & coffee. **Cover** £2.50. **Credit** AmEx, MC, V.
On a bank holiday visit here, decorative guitars on the wall were the closest we got to experiencing the nightly live performance of fado, the Portuguese folk music for which this Knightsbridge institution is famous. Nevertheless, it was easy to imagine how a troubadour could conjure up some old-school charm among the candle-lit tables of the cosy basement restaurant. Our applause was saved for a stand-out dish of pork and clams, surrounded by a sweet, salty broth and finished with a blast of fresh coriander – so tasty that a spoon was requested to scoop up every drop. Squid stuffed with Portuguese sausage and served in a tomato sauce was pleasingly tender, but let down slightly by an ill-matched mound of plain rice. Prices in this part of town are usually top-whack. At O Fado a bottle of house red hovers around the £17 mark and there's a compulsory cover charge for bread and olives. On the bright side, portions are ample: a main course each, with a shared starter of golden quenelles of deep-fried salt cod, left us perfectly satisfied.

Babies and children admitted. Booking advisable; essential dinner weekends. Separate room for parties, seats 35. **Map 14 F9.**

South

Brixton

Lisboa Grill

256A Brixton Hill, SW2 1HF (8671 8311). Brixton tube/rail or 45, 109, 118, 250 bus. **Meals served** 7-10.30pm Mon-Fri; noon-10.30pm Sat, Sun. **Main courses** £7.50-£15. **Cover** £1. **Credit** MC, V.
Formerly the Gallery, the Lisboa Grill has retained the balcony dining area that once gave this lively local its name. Diners are whisked through a small, bustling takeaway to the main restaurant at the back. Here they encounter a scene straight from a Lisbon barrio, with pretty blue tiled walls and all the decorative trappings of a Portuguese tasca (tavern). Mammoth

portions of crisp-skinned piri-piri chicken have been served from this kitchen since the days when the concept of a Portuguese spicy-poultry chain was newly hatched. It's a formula the new management hasn't altered. All the families and young couples on our visit were devouring platters of spicy chicken, piled high with accompanying fries. The rest of the menu contains an extensive list of seafood and grills, plus more than half a dozen varieties of bacalhau. Our 'Lisboa style' steak surrounded in unctuous gravy was a little overcooked, but the chicken was melt-in-the mouth and perfectly spiced (a side helping of fiery sauce allows you to regulate the chilli-heat). A smooth gluggable Ribatejo is the house red and there's Superbock beer on tap.

Babies and children welcome: high chairs. Booking advisable. Takeaway service. **Map 22 D3.**

Vauxhall

Casa Madeira

46A-46C Albert Embankment, SE11 5AW (7820 1117, www.madeiralondon.co.uk). Vauxhall tube/rail. **Meals served** *Coffee shop* 6am-9pm daily. *Restaurant* noon-11pm daily. **Main courses** £6.95-£15.95. **Tapas** £3-£5. **Credit** (over £5) AmEx, MC, V.
Housed in a cavernous railway arch off the Albert Embankment, Casa Madeira shares a kitchen with the more informal café next door. Nevertheless, dishes here are served on pristine tablecloths, signifying the restaurant's intention to be a classy prototype of the ever-expanding Madeira brand. Pasta and burgers are listed on the menu alongside fish and meat grills. An aspirational attitude is reflected in the dish presentation, which in our case included a starter of flaming chouriço being set alight at the table, and a slightly charred skewer of charcoal-grilled fish arriving hanging from a stand, with a gravy boat of garlic butter beneath. Piri-piri chicken was a better choice and had a welcome chilli kick. We also loved the over-generous selection of side dishes, which made ordering dessert impossible. Unflappable, warm service and flat-screens pumping out Portuguese satellite TV prevent Casa Madeira from taking itself too seriously. A long menu of tapas dishes, live music every weekend and a sizeable bar at the front make this an attractive venue for groups.

Babies and children admitted. Booking advisable weekends. Entertainment: musicians 7pm Fri, Sat. Tables outdoors (40, pavement). Takeaway service. **Map 16 L11.**
For branches (Bar Madeira, Café 89, Madeira Café, Pico Bar & Grill) see index.

Portal. See p237.

Thai

London's Thai restaurants include one of the world's best (David Thompson's **Nahm**), and four of the most stylish (the **Busaba Eathai** chain, for which Thompson was, incidentally, the original menu consultant). Yet despite these stars, the capital is not blessed with a profusion of restaurants peddling this popular cuisine – most likely because the number of Thai expatriates here is relatively small. Sure, there are plenty of pubs serving Thai food, and many takeaways and local gaffs offering a dumbed-down version of the cuisine, but when it comes to quality... well, the best are on these few pages. One bright point (literally and figuratively) is the expansion of last year's inexpensive newcomer, **Rosa's**, with its pink, red and bamboo-themed decor, from Brick Lane, E1 to Dean Street, W1. We can also look forward to more branches of Busaba Eathai – another was scheduled to open in Shoreditch as we went to press – but only time will tell if the new owners will be able to maintain the high standards of Alan Yau's creation.

Central

Belgravia

Nahm `HOT 50`
The Halkin, Halkin Street, SW1X 7DJ (7333 1234, www.nahm.como.bz). Hyde Park Corner tube. **Lunch served** noon-2.30pm Mon-Fri. **Dinner served** 7-10.45pm Mon-Sat; 7-9.45pm Sun. **Main courses** £9.50-£19.50. **Set lunch** £20 2 courses, £25 3 courses. **Set dinner** £60 3 courses. **Credit** AmEx, DC, MC, V.

David Thompson's elegant restaurant in the Halkin hotel remains one of the very top places for Thai fine dining in London. The room has an understated wood, bronze and gold palette that contrasts with the highly wrought food. Australian-born Thompson seeks to interpret historic Thai cooking, and has written learned tomes on the subject, yet flashes of inspiration bring the dishes firmly into the modern era. For example, a chicken and banana-flower salad unusually, but successfully, includes samphire and palourdes clams. Presentation, as expected of a restaurant of this calibre and price level, is exquisite: dashes of coconut cream here, tiny sprigs of coriander there. Rice arrives in generous portions – feast style – in large bowls. Ask for wine pairings with your food and you'll be rewarded, but expect to dig deep as the wine list is taken almost as seriously as the food. To cut the price of dining here, it's worth looking out for the occasional bargain meal deals to be found on the web. Service is as helpful and smoothly efficient as you'd hope for in such a plush venue. *Available for hire. Babies and children welcome: high chairs; nappy-changing facilities (hotel). Booking advisable. Disabled: toilet. Dress: smart casual. Separate room for parties, seats 30.* **Map 9 G9**.

Leicester Square

Busaba Eathai `HOT 50`
35 Panton Street, SW1Y 4EA (7930 0088, www.busaba. com). Leicester Square or Piccadilly Circus tube. **Meals served** noon-11pm Mon-Thur; noon-11.30pm Fri, Sat; noon-10pm Sun. **Main courses** £6.20-£10.90. **Credit** AmEx, MC, V.

No longer run by restaurateur Alan Yau (he sold his creation in January 2010 for £21.5 million), Busaba Eathai has new owners – a UK private equity firm – who have stepped up expansion of this fast-growing chain. One of the more recent branches is located in a quiet street just off Leicester Square, and it's a perfect spot for munching before or after the theatre. The classic Busaba dishes are consistently interesting, and well executed at all branches: smoky duck breast with tart tamarind sauce; pandan chicken; sen chan pad thai (with crab meat); green curry fried rice with chargrilled chicken. A few of the newer dishes aren't quite so alluring; a wing-bean salad was

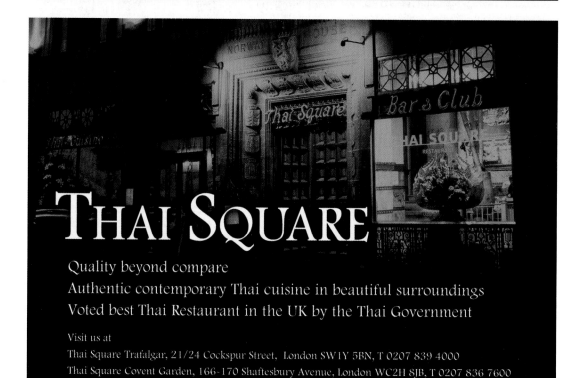

drenched in an overly rich coconut dressing, masking its fresh, pea-like flavour. But Thai-style calamares, all spry and crisp and served with zingy green peppercorns, is a winning dish for many regulars. Staff are graduates from the school of cool, and although service is chummy, they always seem to sit you on the busiest shared table. Drinks range from tropical smoothies and juices (we love the guava collins) to Thai beers and Boylan cherry cola. A dependable, attractive place for excellent modern Thai food on the cheap.

Babies and children admitted. Bookings not accepted. Disabled: toilet. Takeaway service. **Map 17 C5**. **For branches see index.**

Marylebone

Chaopraya Eat-Thai

22 St Christopher's Place, W1U 1NP (7486 0777, www.eatthai.net). Bond Street tube. **Meals served** noon-11pm daily. **Main courses** £10.50-£23.95. **Set lunch** £12.95-£14.95 bento box. **Set dinner** £25-£35 per person (minimum 2-6) 3-4 courses. **Credit** AmEx, MC, V.

These days, Chaopraya seems to have lost some of its sheen. The once opulent-looking room now appears dated, with its cheesy gilded mirrors, red rose wallpaper and painted gold walls. Good Thai food is timeless, however, and on our lunchtime visit the restaurant was healthily populated by nearby workers and regulars stopping off for a blow-out business meal or a simple plate of green chicken curry. Service also seems to lack a little of its former polish, but the staff are still all smiles. You can depend too on the clarity of flavour in many dishes: tom yam koong was sharp with tamarind and lime and had a pleasant chilli kick; green papaya salad was a triumph of sweet-sour-salty tastes; massaman curry wooed us with hints of star anise and earthy sweet potato. Unorthodox profiteroles stuffed with prawn and chicken piqued our interest, but the pastry tasted dry and flat. In keeping with the restaurant's fine-dining aspirations, there's a sizeable wine list to consider, with some interesting choices – a Monsoon Valley red, say, that mixes Thailand's own pokdum grape with shiraz. At lunch, there are good-value set meals, including curious Thai bento-box sets that offer classic dishes in smaller portions.

Available for hire. Babies and children welcome: high chairs. Takeaway service. Vegetarian menu. **Map 9 G6**.

Mayfair

Patara

3&7 Maddox Street, W1S 2QB (7499 6008, www.pataralondon.com). Oxford Circus tube. **Lunch served** noon-2.30pm, **dinner served** 5.30-10.30pm daily. **Main courses** £6.75-£19.95. **Set lunch** £12.50-£15.50 2 courses. **Credit** AmEx, DC, MC, V.

The chic London outposts of this international chain are ideal for a business lunch or a romantic dinner. Patara's menu acknowledges the fashion, among the international monied set, for exotic meats (such as ostrich) and exquisite display. Thai and international flavours are often juxtaposed. Pomelo salad comes with a sweet tamarind dressing sprinkled with coconut flakes; it was good, but might have been better with dried shrimps rather than slices of Scottish smoked salmon, which brought confusion to the dish. A more successful modernisation (or internationalisation) of traditional Thai food was slow-braised beef in coconut reduction, in which the quality of the melt-in-your-mouth meat shone through the rich

Nipa. See p243.

THAI

sauce. Diced lime peel was scattered over the top of the dish, in a fresh echo of the traditional kaffir lime leaves. Many of the meat and fish dishes contain full steaks, rather than the diced morsels more typical in Thailand. The wood-lined dining room of the Oxford Circus branch – furnished with expensive glassware, white linens and a global clientele – could be anywhere. Yes, there's an anonymous demeanour to the place, but the food is distinctive, the service perfect, and the atmosphere elegance itself.

Available for hire. Babies and children admitted. Booking advisable Fri, Sat. Takeaway service. Vegetarian menu.
Map 9 J6.
For branches see index.

West

Bayswater

Nipa
Lancaster London Hotel, Lancaster Terrace, W2 2TY (7262 6737, www.niparestaurant.co.uk). Lancaster Gate tube. Bar **Open** 10am-10pm daily. *Restaurant* **Lunch served** noon-2pm Mon-Fri. **Dinner served** 6.30-10.30pm Mon-Sat. **Main courses** £9.50-£15.50. **Set meal** £29-£34 4 courses. *Both* **Credit** AmEx, DC, MC, V.

Nipa's location – within the Lancaster Hotel, towering over the Lancaster Gate traffic island – is both drawback and asset to this relatively small, exquisite restaurant. A particular atmosphere pervades hotel restaurants, often causing diners to converse in hushed tones. The upside here, though, is a view of the ornate pump-house of the Italian fountains in Kensington Gardens; it could almost be a Bangkok garden palace. Service is effortlessly gracious and the menu intriguing. We plumped for a set dinner beginning with assorted starters, including fish cakes, beef and chicken satays, prawn in beancurd, and deep-fried soft-shell crab. Each plate was decorated with vegetables carved into delicate flowers. The second course was a spicy prawn soup billed as 'very hot' that we'd asked to be moderated. As it was served, the smiling maître d' stood by to ensure it was just right. There followed deep-fried bass with sweet lemony sauce (the skin deliciously caramelised), stir-fried chicken with basil, and wonderful prawn pad thai, plus a generous bowl of perfectly steamed rice. After we'd finished the fresh fruit and coconut ice-cream, and tea, the place filled up and became far from hushed. A memorable, tasty meal.

Babies and children welcome: high chairs; nappy-changing facilities (in hotel). Booking essential Fri, Sat. Disabled: toilet (in hotel). Dress: smart casual. Vegetarian menu.
Map 8 D6.

Shepherd's Bush

Esarn Kheaw
314 Uxbridge Road, W12 7LJ (8743 8930, www.esarn kheaw.com). Shepherd's Bush Market tube or 207, 260, 283 bus. **Lunch served** noon-3pm Mon-Fri. **Dinner served** 6-11pm daily. **Main courses** £7.95-£10.95. **Credit** MC, V.

Little has changed at this family-run restaurant since its inception in the 1990s. The decor is gloriously camp, with melon-green walls, the obligatory portraits of Thai royalty in gilded gold frames, and flamboyant chandeliers hanging from

Menu

Spellings are subject to considerable variation across town. Word divisions vary too: thus, kwaitiew, kwai teo and guey teow are all acceptable spellings for noodles.

Thailand abandoned chopsticks in the 19th century in favour of chunky steel spoons and forks. Using your fingers is usually fine, and essential if you order satay sticks or spare ribs.

STARTERS
Khanom jeep or **ka nom geeb**: dim sum. Little dumplings of minced pork, bamboo shoots and water chestnuts, wrapped in an egg and rice pastry, then steamed.
Khanom pang na koong: prawn sesame toast.
Kratong thong: tiny crispy batter cups ('top hats') filled with mixed vegetables and/or minced meat.
Miang: savoury appetisers with a variety of constituents (mince, ginger, peanuts, roasted coconut, for instance), wrapped in betel leaves.
Popia or **porpia**: spring rolls.
Tod mun pla or **tauk manpla**: small fried fish cakes (should be lightly rubbery in consistency) with virtually no 'fishy' smell or taste.

SOUPS
Poh tak or **tom yam potag**: hot and sour mixed seafood soup.
Tom kha gai or **gai tom kar**: hot and sour chicken soup with coconut milk.
Tom yam or **tom yum**: a hot and sour soup, smelling of lemongrass. **Tom yam koong** is with prawns; **tom yam gai** with chicken; **tom yam hed** with mushrooms.

RICE
Khao, **kow** or **khow**: rice.
Khao nao: sticky rice.
Khao pat: fried rice.
Khao suay: steamed rice.
Pat khai: egg-fried rice.

SALADS
Laab or **larb**: minced and cooked meat incorporating lime juice and other ingredients like ground rice and herbs.
Som tam: a popular cold salad of grated green papaya.
Yam or **yum**: refers to any tossed salad, hot or cold, but it is often hot and sour, flavoured with lemon and chilli.
Yam nua: hot and sour beef salad.
Yam talay: hot and sour seafood salad (served cold). ▶

THAI

the ceiling. The speciality is north-eastern ('Isarn') Thai food, which demonstrates influences from bordering Laos and Cambodia. Representative of the former is a classic dish of larb pla duk (listed as 'spiced catfish north-east style'), a strongly flavoured dish best eaten with sticky rice. Green papaya salad (also 'north-east style') is wetter and more pungent than the fresher som tams in central and southern Thailand, the thick, fermented-fish sauce permeating the salad. The manager was reluctant to let us order chicken 'north-east style', citing the challengingly strong 'anchovy smell' and 'off' flavour of the curry. We persisted – and it paid off. The unusual earthy tones worked well with the mushrooms in the dish, though more of the primary ingredient (chicken) would have been nice. Be firm with the staff if they try to steer you towards pad thai territory; it's worth being adventurous here.

Babies and children welcome: high chairs. Booking advisable. Disabled: toilet. Takeaway service. **Map 20 B1**.

South West

Fulham

The Blue Elephant may be an international chain (with branches throughout Europe and as far afield as Jakarta), but for many it offers a fun introduction to Thai food and culture.

A meal here starts with welcomes from traditionally costumed staff, who lead diners into a room festooned with tropical gardens, walkways and waterfalls. The menu attempts to cater for all, with dishes ranging from the predictable (chicken satay) to the slightly more esoteric (larb gai, a minced chicken salad more typical of north-eastern Thailand and Laos), even including an extensive vegetarian list. Presentation has echoes of royal Thai cuisine (all carved vegetables and impeccable plating), but sometimes style rules over substance, as flavours tend towards the bowdlerised, with timid spicing. Still, diners who come here expecting a memorable experience generally get one – and that includes children, who are welcomed with crayons and, at the popular Sunday brunch service, face painting. A healthy list of alcoholic (mango chilli mohito) and non-alcoholic (vanilla ice tea) cocktails complements the international wine list.

Babies and children welcome: crayons; high chairs; nappy-changing facilities. Booking advisable Sun lunch. Disabled: toilet. Entertainment: face painting Sun lunch. Takeaway service. **Map 13 B13**.

Parsons Green

The comforting scent of lemongrass and a sleeping Buddha statue greet every diner who passes through Sukho's entrance, immediately bestowing a sense of calm and ease. The elegant dining room has one wall of wood panelling in Paul Smith-

THAI

Sukho

esque colours, and mirrors that help to open up the relatively small space. This is a compact yet comfortable restaurant and locals love it. Lunch offers stupendous value, with two courses costing less than £11; there's plenty of choice that doesn't confine diners to predictable Thai classics. The carte, however, offers more intriguing options. Larb gai, a Laos-style minced chicken salad, makes a refreshing start; cooling mint and sweet shallots pepper the dish, with lime and fish sauce (perhaps too much of the latter) creating powerful flavours. Seafood dishes are a highlight of the main courses. Baby squid is stuffed with chopped prawns and chicken, chargrilled, then served with red curry, green peppercorns and shreds of earthy-tasting wild ginger. Desserts too are inspired; try the 'four seasons ice-cream' (coconut ice-cream with palm seeds, jack fruit and caramelised red beans). The polite staff are smartly turned out in jewel-toned silk garments – as refreshingly elegant as the dish presentations.
Babies and children admitted. Booking advisable. Takeaway service. Vegetarian menu.
For branches (Suk Saran, Suksan) see index.

South East

South Norwood

Mantanah
2 Orton Building, Portland Road, SE25 4UD (8771 1148). Norwood Junction rail. **Lunch served** noon-3pm Sat, Sun. **Dinner served** 6-11pm Tue-Sun. **Main courses**

▶ **NOODLES**
Generally speaking, noodles are eaten in greater quantities in the north of Thailand. There are many types of kwaitiew or guey teow noodles. Common ones include sen mee: rice vermicelli; sen yai (river rice noodles): a broad, flat, rice noodle; sen lek: a medium flat noodle, used to make pad thai; ba mee: egg noodles; and woon sen (cellophane noodle): transparent vermicelli made from soy beans or other pulses. These are often prepared as stir-fries.
  Common noodle dishes are:
Khao soi: chicken curry soup with egg noodles; a Burmese/Thai dish, referred to as the national dish of Burma.
Mee krob or mee grob: sweet crispy fried vermicelli.
Pad si-ewe or cee eaw: noodles fried with mixed meat in soy sauce.
Pad thai: stir-fried noodles with shrimps (or chicken and pork), beansprouts and salted turnips, garnished with ground peanuts.

CURRIES
Gaeng, kaeng or gang: the generic name for curry. Yellow curry is the mildest; green curry (gaeng keaw wan or kiew warn) is medium hot and uses green chillies; red curry (gaeng pet) is similar, but uses red chillies.
Jungle curry: often the hottest of the curries, made with red curry paste, bamboo shoots and just about anything else to hand, but no coconut cream.
Massaman or mussaman: also known as Muslim curry, because it originates from the area along the border with Malaysia where many Thais are Muslims. For this reason, pork is never used. It's a rich but mild concoction, with coconut, potato and some peanuts.
Penang, panaeng or panang: a dry, aromatic curry made with 'Penang' curry paste, coconut cream and holy basil.

FISH & SEAFOOD
Hoi: shellfish.
Hor mok talay or haw mog talay: steamed egg mousse with seafood.
Koong, goong or kung: prawns.
Maw: dried fish belly.

THAI

Rosa's (Soho)

£6.95-£13.95. **Set dinner** £18 per person (minimum 2) 3 courses, £25 per person (minimum 2) 4 courses. **Set buffet** (lunch Sun) £7.95. **Credit** AmEx, MC, V.

From the outside, Mantanah looks like a neighbourhood takeaway; in fact, it's a gem of a restaurant, offering strong, contrasting flavours from across Thailand. Within, there is minimal decoration: café furniture, a few faded photographs of the Thai royal family, a tiny garden fishpond. But the menu would put any kind of furnishings in the shade. Do try the regional specialities. Kang tai pla is a hot, pungent, southern Thailand-style curry of tilapia fillet with bamboo shoots, yellow aubergine and green beans in a turmeric-based sauce. Som tam, a salad of shredded green papaya and carrot, accented with dried shrimps, peanuts and tomatoes, is a bold combination of hot, sour and fish flavours from the east. There's also an impressive array of vegetable dishes. We chose morning glory stir-fried in black bean sauce: the ideal sweet and nutty accompaniment. King prawns stir-fried with coriander, pepper, garlic and onions featured plentiful shellfish, perfectly cooked. Take advantage of the friendly service, if you can. The chef often emerges from the kitchen to take your order; put yourself in his hands and you'll get a well-crafted feast for a very reasonable price.

Available for hire. Babies and children admitted. Booking advisable. Takeaway service. Vegetarian menu.

East
Brick Lane

Rosa's

12 Hanbury Street, E1 6QR (7247 1093, www.rosas london.com). Liverpool Street tube/rail or Shoreditch High Street rail. **Meals served** 11am-10.30pm Mon-Thur, Sun; 11am-1pm Fri, Sat. **Main courses** £5.95-£13.50. **Set lunch** £5.50-£11.50 1 course. **Credit** AmEx, MC, V.

With its bright – almost nursery-like – red, pink and wooden interiors, Rosa's epitomises the old cliché of 'cheap and cheerful'. Since opening on the street connecting the riff-raff end of Brick Lane and the chi-chi corner of Spitalfields, this diminutive restaurant has seen further enormous success with its second branch, which opened in Soho in spring 2010. The popularity is partly due to the owners offering the type of chilled out, modernised Thai dining that was first achieved by the Busaba Eathai chain, although Rosa's emphasises the fun and comfort of home-style cooking. The Shoreditch crowd comes here to perch on red stools around mostly communal tables, enjoying plates of curries, stir-fries and wondrous starters such as smoky satay and fiery som tam. The few chargrilled dishes may seem to be a mere afterthought, but there's grill expertise in the kitchen; rack of lamb in a yellow curry had us gnawing at the bones. The menu indicates spice levels – from 'mild use of chillies' to 'damn hot!' – yet some dishes don't quite measure up; a three chilli-rated tom yam soup was merely a bit warm on the Scoville scale (the international measurement of spicy heat). Though Rosa's might not always get things right, it remains an enjoyable feel-good venue providing decent Thai food.

Available for hire. Babies and children admitted. Booking advisable Fri, Sat. Takeaway service. Vegetarian menu.
Map 12 S5.
For branch see index.

Turkish

If you were in any doubt about the integration of Turks in London's melting pot, look no further than mayor Boris Johnson, great-grandson of a Turkish journalist and government minister. BJ's all-time favourite restaurant is his Islington local, **Pasha**, and we agree that it's certainly one of the capital's best Turkish spots. But while London can boast many very decent Turkish grills, we are still lacking an outstanding purveyor of Ottoman cuisine, or indeed anywhere that suggests the need to pull on something smarter than jeans and a T-shirt. We think there's a gap in the market – maybe Boris could pull a few strings? Still, there's much to love about the grill exponents: **19 Numara Bos Cirrik**, **Mangal Ocakbasi**, **Mangal II** and **Petek** are well worth a visit for their smoky kebabs.

Central

Fitzrovia

Özer

5 Langham Place, W1B 3DG (7323 0505, www.sofra.co.uk). Oxford Circus tube.
Bar **Open** noon-11pm daily.
Restaurant **Breakfast** served 8am-noon, **meals served** noon-midnight daily. **Main courses** £8.95-£23.95. **Set meal** (noon-6pm) £12.95; (6pm-midnight) £14.95-£22.
Both **Credit** AmEx, MC, V.
A flagship fine-dining restaurant and bar from Huseyin Özer, the man behind the Sofra chain, Özer works hard to distinguish itself from Turkish eateries majoring in kebabs. The decor, with its wispy fabric drops, white linen tablecloths and mottled red walls, is devoid of ethnic clichés, yet it's this – and Özer's catering to the tourist and office trades that are inevitable around Oxford Circus – that tips the balance unfavourably away from an Ottoman experience. The breakfast menu offers eggs with spicy sausages and feta, yes, but they seem mere tokens alongside the full english, eggs benedict, BLT and porridge. Similarly, main courses include monkfish, venison and prawns in spicy coconut cream sauces, Hakkasan's duck, cress and pine nut salad, and roast beef with yorkshires. Desserts are not, in our experience, special, which is a good excuse to feast from the 45-strong list of hot and cold meze. Twists on the usual houmous and falafel options include vodka-marinated deep-fried squid, broad beans in yoghurt, and a crisp pastry roll of roast duck. The wine list contains four bottles from Turkey: two excellent house wines, plus a pricier chardonnay and merlot. Cocktails from the bar at the front are an alternative.
Available for hire. Babies and children welcome: high chairs. Booking advisable. Disabled: toilet. Tables outdoors (5, pavement). Takeaway service. **Map 9 H5.**
For branches (Sofra) see index.

Marylebone

Ishtar

10-12 Crawford Street, W1U 6AZ (7224 2446, www.ishtarrestaurant.com). Baker Street tube. **Meals served** noon-11pm Mon-Thur, Sun; noon-11.30pm Fri, Sat. **Main courses** £7.95-£15.95. **Set lunch** (noon-6pm) £8.95. **Set meal** £20-£25. **Set meze** £6.50. **Credit** MC, V.
Ishtar's enviable choice of dining areas makes it a reliable option for many occasions. Amid arches in the basement, there are large tables, musicians several nights a week and belly dancing at weekends to get the party going; the ground floor is stylish and modern, more restrained but still capable of generating a buzz; and pavement tables on comparatively quiet Crawford Street are ideal for a relaxing lunch or summer's evening. The international wine list includes two of Anatolia's better-known brands: Cankaya and Yakut at reasonable prices, though cheaper options are available. Deals are offered at lunch and early evening, with a wide variety of dishes (goat's cheese and beetroot salad, iskender, and chicken and walnut salad among them) adding to the sense of value. But while bargain

19 Numara Bos Cirrik I. See p251.

hunters will be satisfied, Ishtar is also elegant enough to take a date. The main menu features suitably refined fare such as kestaneli tavuk (grilled chicken with braised chestnuts, dates, potatoes and carrots in chestnut sauce) and karides tava (prawns with wild mushrooms, spinach, ginger, chilli, garlic and herbs). The choice of rich, creamy puddings and pastries is better than the Turkish norm too. In all, pretty classy.
Babies and children welcome: high chairs. Booking advisable Thur-Sat. Entertainment: musicians Wed-Sat; belly dancer Fri, Sat. Separate room for parties, seats 120. Tables outdoors (6, pavement). Takeaway service. Vegetarian menu. **Map 2 F5**.

Pimlico

Kazan
93-94 Wilton Road, SW1V 1DW (7233 7100, www. kazan-restaurant.com). Victoria tube/rail. **Meals served** noon-10pm Mon-Sat; noon-9.30pm Sun. **Main courses** £11.95-£15.95. **Set meal** (noon-6.30pm) £9.99-£14.95 2 courses. **Credit** MC, V.
Stylish but unpretentious, Kazan is staffed by polite, unobtrusive staff and gets busy at weekday lunchtimes. Tasty Turkish classics are the kitchen's stock-in-trade, most of them from the Anatolian and Aegean regions. Mains such as kuzu pirzola (marinated, chargrilled lamb chops with a lip-stinging garlic mash) and izmir köfte (a meatball, tomato and cumin dish) are abundant and generous in flavour. They're also pricier than in neighbourhood Turkish eateries, but they're a cut above in quality, with tender and smoky spiced meat. The set mezes (containing seven to eight dishes) are generally excellent and good value. The only problem is in fitting such quantities of food on to the rather small tables. The wine list includes Turkish Cankaya white and Yakut red wines, both at £16 a bottle; with Turkey a rising star in the wine world, they're worth trying. If you can manage a dessert, try apricots stuffed with kaymak (clotted cream), or the Ottoman-era dish of su muhallebisi (milk pudding flavoured with rosewater). Kazan has a sister restaurant in the City, but this branch is the original and consequently has a laid-back, smoothly running feel.
Babies and children welcome: high chairs. Booking advisable Fri, Sat. Disabled: toilet. Separate rooms for parties, seating 30 and 50. Tables outdoors (3, pavement). Takeaway service. **Map 15 J11**.
For branch see index.

South
Waterloo

Tas
33 The Cut, SE1 8LF (7928 2111, www.tasrestaurant. com). Southwark tube. **Meals served** noon-11.30pm Mon-Sat; noon-10.30pm Sun. **Main courses** £5.95-£12.90. **Set lunch** £6.95 3 courses. **Set meze** £9.15-£19.95. **Credit** AmEx, MC, V.
They pack 'em in at this branch of Tas. The package deal of tasty stews, promptly delivered meze and savvily chosen wines has proven a hit with commuters, theatregoers and SE1 locals. The best starters are the cold bites: crisp tabouleh, broad beans drenched in olive oil, smoky aubergine purée. For mains, the choice is huge. The casseroles are always peppery, with meats cooked slowly enough to make them tender and allow the

classic Turkish flavourings of wild thyme, coriander and red pepper to ooze in, but portions are small. Alternatively, the mixed grill, fish and meat mains are abundant, flavourful and filling. The minced lamb kebab with pan-fried leek is particularly delicious. A long-standing link with Chile's Veramonte vineyard in the Casablanca valley means the whites are always decent. Desserts of baklava and kazandibi (upside-down milk pudding, made with pine resin and rosewater) make an evening here complete. If you've romance in mind, note that tables are pushed tightly together and neither your squeeze's special words nor the piped Turkish music can be heard above the din of diners and waiters. People come to Tas for value and decent food, not for atmosphere.

Babies and children welcome: high chairs. Booking advisable. Disabled: toilet. Tables outdoors (6, pavement). Takeaway service. Vegetarian menu. **Map 11 N8**.

For branches see index.

North East

Dalston

Mangal II
4 Stoke Newington Road, N16 8BH (7254 7888, www.mangal2.com). Dalston Kingsland rail or 76, 149, 243 bus. **Meals served** 3pm-1am Mon-Thur; 2pm-1am Fri, Sat; 2pm-midnight Sun. **Main courses** £8.45-£15.99. **Credit** MC, V.

When George walked in alone, we were worried something terrible had happened – but Gilbert joined him as soon as he'd been seated. Yes, this fine Turkish ocakbası remains the regular supper spot of unassuming art pioneers Gilbert & George. You can see why. Sweet-natured young waiters in smart black shirts, matching black trousers and bright red ties serve uncomplicated grills to the strains of 'Ain't No Sunshine' – and flavours are punchy. A güveç of aubergine, lamb chunks and big half-cloves of garlic looked unappealing under a layer of skinned, grilled tomatoes and fat kebab-shop chillies, but not a drop of juice was left unmopped by the superb bread. Of the few vegetarian options, zeytin yagli pirasa was an almost fizzily pickled salad that belied its bland description of 'leek and carrot in olive oil' (plus some unmentioned peppers and tomatoes), while simple, light feta and parsley pastries (musga böreği) were fried to crisp perfection. However, the main focus is rightly on what's produced under the metal extractor hood at the back. Star turn on this visit was pirzola: three tender salty lamp chops with their fat cooked perfectly to the point of almost melting away.

Babies and children welcome: high chairs. Booking advisable weekends. Takeaway service. **Map 25 C4**.

Mangal Ocakbasi
10 Arcola Street, E8 2DJ (7275 8981, www.mangal1.com). Dalston Kingsland rail or 67, 76, 149, 243 bus. **Meals served** noon-midnight daily. **Main courses** £9-£13. **Unlicensed**. **Corkage** no charge. **No credit cards**.

The tang of carbonised meat that hangs in the air of Stoke Newington Road is an olfactory reminder you're in ocakbası territory. However, many in-the-know grill-seekers head past the rows of pretenders to this busy restaurant on a quiet side street. You might have a short wait for a table, but keeping appetites sharp is a butcher's-style display cabinet stuffed with an arsenal of metal skewers spearing charcoal-ready lamb,

Menu

It's useful to know that in Turkish 'ç' and 'ş' are pronounced 'ch' and 'sh'. So şiş is correct Turkish, shish is English and sis is common on menus. Menu spelling is rarely consistent, so expect wild variations on everything given here. See also the menu boxes in **Middle Eastern** and **North African**.

COOKING EQUIPMENT
Mangal: brazier.
Ocakbaşı: an open grill under an extractor hood. A metal dome is put over the charcoal for making paper-thin bread.

MEZE DISHES & SOUPS
Arnavut ciğeri: 'albanian liver' – cubed or sliced lamb's liver, fried then baked.
Barbunya: spicy kidney bean stew.
Börek or **böreği**: fried or baked filo pastry parcels with a savoury filling, usually cheese, spinach or meat. Commonest are **muska** or **peynirli** (cheese) and **sigara** ('cigarette', so long and thin).
Cacik: diced cucumber with garlic in yoghurt.
Çoban salatası: 'shepherd's' salad of finely diced tomatoes, cucumbers, onions, perhaps green peppers and parsley.
Dolma: stuffed vegetables (usually with rice and pine kernels).
Enginar: artichokes, usually with vegetables in olive oil.
Haydari: yoghurt, infused with garlic and mixed with finely chopped mint leaves.
Hellim: Cypriot halloumi cheese.
Houmous kavurma: houmous topped with strips of lamb and pine nuts.
Imam bayıldı: literally 'the imam fainted'; aubergine stuffed with onions, tomatoes and garlic in olive oil.
Işkembe: finely chopped tripe soup, an infallible hangover cure.
Kısır: usually a mix of chopped parsley, tomatoes, onions, crushed wheat, olive oil and lemon juice.
Kızartma: lightly fried vegetables.
Lahmacun: 'pizza' of minced lamb on thin pide (qv).
Mercimek çorbar: red lentil soup.
Midye tava: mussels in batter, in a garlic sauce.
Mücver: courgette and feta fritters.
Patlıcan: aubergine, variously served.
Pide: a term encompassing many varieties of Turkish flatbread. It also refers to Turkish pizzas (heavier and more filling than lahmacun, qv).
Pilaki: usually haricot beans in olive oil, but the name refers to the method of cooking not the content.
Piyaz: white bean salad with onions.
Saç: paper-thin, chewy bread prepared on a metal dome (also called saç) over a charcoal grill.
Sucuk: spicy sausage, usually beef. ▸

TURKISH

chicken and vegetables. Further theatre is provided by the Dantean ocakbası itself, which sends volcanic clouds of smoke into the huge extractor while a lone chef expertly manipulates rows of sizzling kebabs. These, along with a few additional grilled dishes, are the biggest draw of Mangal – and there aren't many places that can compete. From loudly spiced beyti kebabs to chunks of tender chicken in garlicky yoğhurtlu tavuk şiş, everything stands up to repeated testing. Meze starters are unobjectionable and fill the time while waiting for mains. BYO and big tables make this an in-and-out sort of place, but service still manages to be cheery and attentive. *Babies and children admitted. Booking advisable. Disabled: toilet. Takeaway service.* **Map 25 C4.**

19 Numara Bos Cirrik I

34 Stoke Newington Road, N16 7XJ (7249 0400). Dalston Kingsland rail or 76, 149, 243 bus. **Meals served** noon-midnight daily. **Main courses** £7.50-£10.50. **Licensed. Corkage** £1-£5. **Credit** MC, V.

There are many reasons to visit this long-standing Hackney favourite, but the decor isn't one of them. Although the furnishings are generally plain, there are some bizarre touches that will leave you scratching your head: Egyptian plaster reliefs on the walls, a year-round miniature Santa above the counter. Still, it offers distraction until the food arrives – and what food! This restaurant has consistently scored top marks over the years. The carved ocakbası dominating the upstairs space provides most of the best dishes on the menu: stridently spiced, tender minced kebabs; skewered chunks of meat with garlicky tomato sauce; lamb chops that demand every morsel of meat is nibbled from the bone. Starters are ordinary, but pass the time while you're waiting for the main events; go easy on them, because efficient staff will bring three complimentary salads (including a punchy grilled onion version with sticky turnip and pomegranate sauce), good bread and buttery rice. The closely packed, long tables mean that the place is regularly crammed, with everyone from hungry couples and local Turkish families to jolly parties taking advantage of the BYO policy. Ridiculously hard to fault. *Available for hire. Babies and children admitted. Booking advisable. Separate room for parties, seats 40. Takeaway service.* **Map 25 C4.** **For branches see index.**

North

Finsbury Park

Petek

94-96 Stroud Green Road, N4 3EN (7619 3933). Finsbury Park tube/rail. **Meals served** 4-11pm Mon-Thur; 11am-11pm Fri-Sun. **Main courses** £7.65-£15.85. **Set meal** £8.85 2 courses. **Set meze** £6.45-£9.85 per person (minimum 2). **Credit** AmEx, MC, V.

A warm welcome, and care to find customers just the right table, has Petek winning friends daily. Set across two shopfronts, it's at once spacious and cosy, with painted crockery, lanterns and colourful fabrics adorning the walls. The gleaming open kitchen sits at the back of one unit, the bar to the rear of the other. Puffy, cider-battered squid (beautifully tender inside) arrived impressively promptly, though mains came before the starter plates had been removed. Yet except for some dry edges to the bread, faults were pleasingly few.

▶ **Tarator:** a bread, garlic and walnut mixture; **havuç tarator** adds carrot; **ıspanak tarator** adds spinach.
Yayla: yoghurt and rice soup (usually) with a chicken stock base.
Yaprak dolması: stuffed vine leaves.

MAIN COURSES
Alabalik: trout.
Güveç: stew, which is traditionally cooked in an earthenware pot.
Hünkar beğendi: cubes of lamb, braised with onions and tomatoes, served on an aubergine and cheese purée.
İçli köfte: balls of cracked bulgar wheat filled with spicy mince.
İncik: knuckle of lamb, slow-roasted in its own juices. Also called **kléftico**.
Karni yarik: aubergine stuffed with minced lamb and vegetables.
Mitite köfte: chilli meatballs.
Sote: meat (usually), sautéed in tomato, onion and pepper (and sometimes wine).

KEBABS
Usually made with grilled lamb (those labelled **tavuk** or **piliç** are chicken), served with bread or rice and salad. Common varieties include:
Beyti: usually spicy mince and garlic, but sometimes best-end fillet.
Böbrek: kidneys.
Çöp şiş: small cubes of lamb.
Döner: slices of marinated lamb (sometimes mince) packed tightly with pieces of fat on a vertical rotisserie.
Halep: usually döner (qv) served over bread with a buttery tomato sauce.
İskender: a combination of döner (qv), tomato sauce, yoghurt and melted butter on bread.
Kaburga: spare ribs.
Kanat: chicken wings.
Köfte: mince mixed with spices, eggs and onions.
Külbastı: char-grilled fillet.
Lokma: 'mouthful' (beware, there's a dessert that has a similar name!) – boned fillet of lamb.
Patlıcan: mince and sliced aubergine.
Pirzola: lamb chops.
Şiş: cubes of marinated lamb.
Uykuluk: sweetbread.
Yoğhurtlu: meat over bread and yoghurt.

DESSERTS
Armut tatlısı: baked pears.
Ayva tatlısı: quince in syrup.
Kadayıf: cake made from shredded pastry dough, filled with syrup and nuts or cream.
Kazandibi: milk pudding, traditionally with very finely chopped chicken breast.
Kemel pasha: small round cakes soaked in honey.
Keşkül: milk pudding with almonds and coconut, topped with pistachios.
Lokum: turkish delight.
Sütlaç: rice pudding.

Ingredients are fresh and healthful, portions generous (you won't need dessert) and the house wines excellent value. Petek's lengthy menu is dominated by chicken and lamb charcoal grills, with variations on the theme – fluffy rice here, crushed new potatoes there. Seafood isn't forgotten, however, with options such as salmon, monkfish and prawns, or perhaps a blackboard special of spicy kingfish steak (a huge grill-striped slab of fish that retained its sweet ozone scent and glistened appetisingly). There's a decent choice of vegetarian dishes too. Complimentary nibbles of olives and chilli-tomato dip mean you may wish to forgo starters, but it's worth sharing a plate of the creamy cheese-stuffed börek.

Babies and children welcome: high chairs. Booking advisable. Tables outdoors (3, pavement). Takeaway service.

Highbury

Iznik

19 Highbury Park, N5 1QJ (7354 5697, www.iznik.co.uk). Highbury & Islington tube/rail or 4, 19, 236 bus. **Meals served** 10.30am-11pm daily. **Main courses** £12.95-£14.95. **Credit** AmEx, MC, V.

Away from the north London Turkish enclaves of Hackney and Harringay, this sweet little restaurant expresses itself with real personality. Initial impressions are of a cosy antique lighting shop, with rows of glass lanterns and chandeliers. Red and pink walls are adorned with carved wooden display cabinets, and every surface is artfully filled with an array of Turkish knick-knacks and curios (including a chain-mail vest). The effect is magnified at night when lights are dimmed and candles cast a seductive glow. İznik is a family-run place, and for 20 years the friendly owners have won plenty of praise for their consistently first-rate cooking. The absence of an ocakbası means that oven-baked dishes stand out on the menu, and there's also room for a few surprises – salads with fruity dressings, grilled fish and neatly presented hot and cold meze. Desserts are a draw too; try Turkish rice pudding with orange, or the unusual ayva tatlısı: quince in syrup. Prices are good value for this salubrious neighbourhood, although diners used to BYO might find drink costs smart a bit.

Available for hire. Babies and children welcome: high chairs. Booking advisable; essential weekends. Takeaway service.

Iznik

Islington

Pasha

301 Upper Street, N1 2TU (7226 1454, www.pasha restaurant.co.uk). Angel tube or Highbury & Islington tube/rail. **Meals served** 11am-11.30pm Mon-Sat; 11am-11pm Sun. **Main courses** £7.95-£14.95. **Set meal** £16.95 2 courses, £19.95 3 courses. **Credit** AmEx, MC, V.

Pasha's contemporary feel makes a refreshing change from the London norm of hectic, wipe-down Turkish caffs or restaurants decked with extravagant Ottoman opulence. Large windows open on to a chic stretch of Upper Street and, inside, shiny banquettes, chandeliers and sparkling candles complement a stylish room. It's a place for impressing your dining companions, rather than a BYO party stop-off. The well-trained and personable staff reflect this, and the wine list and cocktail menu complete the effect. Appropriately, dishes are more sophisticated than you'll find elsewhere, with a lot of thought going into presentation – although critics might say the edges that make this cooking style so vital have been somewhat smoothed off. Also, the extensive menu has made concessions to those who might think of Turkish cuisine as unreconstructed dude food; the appearance of Moroccan spiced salmon or rocket and parmesan salad is unusual. However, ingredients are of a high quality and cooking is consistently excellent. Portions are up to the usual generous Turkish standards too, so take advantage and veer from the standard meze-kebab route.

Available for hire. Babies and children admitted. Booking advisable. Tables outdoors (2, pavement). Takeaway service. **Map 5 O1.**

North West

Belsize Park

Zara

11 South End Road, NW3 2PT (7794 5498). Belsize Park tube or Hampstead Heath rail. **Meals served** noon-11.30pm daily. **Main courses** £9-£15. **Credit** AmEx, MC, V.

Zara's homely vibe and reliable cooking attract a loyal following that ranges from young dating couples to families, expats and serene pensioners. All are welcomed warmly and, were it not for the red London buses idling nearby, you could imagine yourself ensconced in a village restaurant in Turkey, with rustic wooden chairs, coloured glass lanterns and terracotta floor tiles. At the back, where a skylight brightens the dining area, and a fireplace keeps customers warm in winter, is a pile of board games, books and some bongos. The menu reads like a greatest hits of Anatolian cuisine, lamb more than chicken, with plenty of grills. We love the mücver, courgette fritters with a molten centre of creamy cheese, offered as a vegetarian main course or hot meze with kısır. There's more cheesy succulence to be enjoyed in the moussaká, its rich layers of aubergine, lamb mince and béchamel contrasting with a virtuous side salad of crisp leaves and grated carrot. The yoghurt dip with spinach and garlic is nicely balanced if modestly sized – still, there's the kind offer of another basket of bread to accompany, and a simple, keenly priced wine list with some great Turkish bottles to try.

Available for hire. Babies and children welcome: high chairs. Booking essential weekends. Tables outdoors (4, pavement). Takeaway service. Vegetarian menu. **Map 28 C3.**

TURKISH

Vegetarian

It has not been a great year for vegetarian restaurants in London – or has it? We've seen the closure of Marylebone's Eat & Two Veg, and what was the Place Below (now **Café Below**, *see p41*) has begun serving meat. Yet we are also able to welcome **Itadaki Zen**, a Japanese vegan restaurant in King's Cross, which serves healthy home-style (washoku) dishes.

If you want to dress up and enjoy a special-occasion vegetarian meal, the capital can still supply the goods: the Shoreditch cool of **Saf**, the glossiness of **Manna**, the restrained elegance of **Vanilla Black**, and convivial Hammersmith favourite, **The Gate**. You could also splash out at fine-dining restaurants such as **Morgan M** (*see p98*), **Sketch: Lecture Room & Library** (*see p130*) and **Pied à Terre** (*see p126*), all of which offer dedicated vegetarian menus. Prefer to dine casually? Vegetarian choices are dramatically increased when you consider London's profusion of South Indian and Gujarati restaurants (*see pp133-148*) and the extensive offering of vegetarian meze at the city's Middle Eastern eateries (*see pp191-200*).

Central

Chancery Lane

Vanilla Black

17-18 Tooks Court, off Cursitor Street, EC4A 1LB (7242 2622, www.vanillablack.co.uk). Chancery Lane tube. **Lunch served** noon-2.30pm Mon-Fri. **Dinner served** 6-10pm Mon-Sat. **Set lunch** £18 2 courses, £23 3 courses. **Set meal** £24 2 courses, £30 3 courses. **Credit** AmEx, MC, V.
Hidden down a cobbled side street amid the historic buildings near Chancery Lane, Vanilla Black delivers far more than its inconspicuous location would suggest. The subdued decor (muted tones, dark wood chairs, crisp white linen tablecloths) implies a reverential attitude is in order. In stark contrast, the cooking is dazzling. High-concept and creative, it delivers an excitement that marks out the restaurant as an ideal destination when you want to make an impression. The elegantly plated dishes are composed of multiple elements. One elaborate, faultlessly executed main consisted of poached duck egg and ribblesdale pudding, hickory smoked potato croquette and pineapple pickle, each forkful loaded with a new taste to savour. Cauliflower cake with mustard pakora was equally successful, delicately handled to bring out the essence of the humble brassica. Service is faultless: quite formal, but on the ball without becoming overbearing. If we've one caveat, it's the venue's odd layout, which gives the impression of a townhouse or office whose previously separate rooms have been joined by knocking down walls. But when an evening here ends with strawberry crumble trifle with geranium cream and delicately fragrant rosehip macaroons – another outstanding creation – it's easy to forgive minor details.
Babies and children admitted. Booking advisable. Disabled: toilet. **Map 11 N6**.

King's Cross

Itadaki Zen

139 King's Cross Road, WC1X 9BJ (7278 3573, www. itadakizen.com). King's Cross tube/rail. **Lunch served** noon-3pm Mon, Tue, Thur, Sat. **Dinner served** 5-10.30pm Mon, Tue, Thur; 6-10.30pm Wed; 5-11pm Fri, Sat. **Main courses** £6.50-£9.50. **Set menu** £21 4 courses. **Credit** MC, V.
Vegan food has a long and venerable tradition in Japan, notably in the refined and elaborate temple cuisine known as shojin ryori. That isn't what you'll find at Itadaki Zen, though; it's a humbler operation serving more homely dishes. The ideals behind the venture are lofty (there's an emphasis on organic ingredients, sustainable agriculture and the 'healing qualities' of food), but the vegan mission means dishes can be bland.

STREET**SMART**
HELPING THE HOMELESS

"All it takes is one well-fed quid next time you're dining at any of the damned fine establishments taking part in this glorious campaign, and that tiny extra sum will go straight to an excellently worthwhile cause. Go on, it'll make you feel good about that expanding waistband."
Ian Rankin, author

For a list of participating restaurants and details of how to take part, visit
www.streetsmart.org.uk

STREET**SMART**
HELPING THE HOMELESS

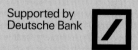

Agedashi dofu – deep-fried cubes of tofu, served with a light soy sauce-based broth called tsuyu – lacked depth, and an udon dish with peanuts and sesame oil tasted mainly of the soft, thick wheat noodles. Western ingredients such as potatoes, capiscum peppers and tomatoes appear, as do some Korean dishes. But there's a lot of tofu and seaweed – neither known for their strong flavour – salt is used minimally and dashi (fish stock), a key taste in much Japanese cuisine, is missing. The small space is calm and simple, with pale wood furniture and ochre walls lined with straw, sand and lime; it was designed and built by volunteers. The short drinks list includes beer (organic), wine, saké and bamboo leaf tea.

Available for hire. Babies and children welcome: high chair. Separate room for parties, seats 14. Tables outdoors (2, pavement). Takeaway service. Vegan dishes. **Map 4 M3**.

Soho

Mildred's

45 Lexington Street, W1F 9AN (7494 1634, www. mildreds.co.uk). Oxford Circus or Piccadilly Circus tube. **Meals served** noon-11pm Mon-Sat. **Main courses** £7-£9.20. **Credit** MC, V.

Now in its twenties, this Soho stalwart acts its age; it's a vibrant venue exuding energy from its chattering customers as they partake of the well-travelled menu. Artichoke crostini with lemon aïoli jostles for space alongside steaming 'mock duck' soup fragrant with star anise and ginger. Portions are generous and flavours unchallenging, yet that's not necessarily a bad thing. There's certainly demand for a central London hangout serving vegetarian versions of easy eats such as chunky burgers with chips, and hearty bangers with mash, as Mildred's consistently packed tables prove. In addition to the sky-lit main space, innocuously decorated in light wood with splashes of colour, there's a bar area at the front for perching, and a couple of outdoor tables for watching the world pass by. Next door, Mrs Marengo's is the takeaway arm of the business, offering breakfast, lunch and afternoon treats. Both establishments are perfectly pleasant, casual spots for a laid-back date with friends. Don't expect fireworks, but for everyday dining that caters for a range of palates, Mildred's hits the mark.

Babies and children welcome: high chairs. Bookings not accepted. Separate room for parties, seats 24. Tables outdoors (2, pavement). Takeaway service. Vegan dishes. **Map 17 A4**.

West

Hammersmith

The Gate

51 Queen Caroline Street, W6 9QL (8748 6932, www. thegate.tv). Hammersmith tube. **Lunch served** noon-2.45pm Mon-Fri. **Dinner served** 6-10.45pm Mon-Sat. **Main courses** £10.50-£13.75. **Credit** AmEx, MC, V.

Just around the corner from the roar of Hammersmith roundabout and behind a wall is a surprisingly bucolic courtyard. The Gate occupies a first-floor hall, its atmosphere part community centre, part refectory. Double-height ceilings accentuate the din over dinner, the hubbub at lunch. It's a friendly spot, however, and rammed with sophisticated diners because the food is generally excellent. A shared meze platter is the ideal starter, as it reflects all the influences on proprietor

chefs and brothers Adrian and Michael Daniel. A Thai salad full of deliciously crunchy slivers of pak choi, beansprouts, mooli and mange tout had been tossed in a hot coriander and mint dressing; broad bean falafel arrived with tasty baba ganoush; a butternut and cashew samosa was light and crisp; Mediterranean tart had a heavenly texture. Sometimes, promised flavours can be lacking: butternut squash, basil and goat's cheese rotolo was a comforting main, but where was the thyme infusion in the potato casing? Similarly imperceptible were the mushroom undertones promised in the polenta underneath a trio of excellent stuffed globe artichoke hearts, and later, the headline flavour in a lavender crème brûlée. Yet with portions this generous and prices that are so reasonable, these are minor complaints.

Available for hire. Babies and children welcome: high chairs. Booking advisable. Tables outdoors (15, courtyard). Vegan dishes. **Map 20 B4**.

Shepherd's Bush

Blah Blah Blah

78 Goldhawk Road, W12 8HA (8746 1337, www.blah vegetarian.com). Goldhawk Road tube or 94 bus. **Lunch served** 12.30-2.30pm Mon-Sat. **Dinner served** 6.30-10.30pm Mon-Thur; 6.30-10.45pm Fri, Sat. **Main courses** £9.95. **Unlicensed. Corkage** £1.45 per person. **Credit** MC, V.

Even before savouring your first mouthful here, you're likely to warm to Blah Blah Blah. Perhaps it's the easy-going welcome from the staff, happy to tailor a meal to your fancies. Perhaps it's the idiosyncratic furnishings: huge TV spotlights (bagged from the nearby BBC, maybe) hanging from the high ceiling; maroon and cream walls sporting wrought-iron artwork; plate-glass windows letting in the street scenery (and some noise) of the Goldhawk Road. From a concise list of multinational dishes, sushi (choice morsels of veg and beancurd) was fridge cold and reasonably fresh, with pickled ginger and wasabi adding a dab of authenticity that was tempered by incongruous mustard-dressed salad leaves. A main course South Indian curry had a preponderance of carrots (as well as broccoli and cauliflower), yet an appealing coconutty flavour. The dish was enhanced by little popadom discs and a dainty side helping of 'cabbage carrot salsa' (in fact, a finely sliced salad pepped up with mustard seeds and curry leaves). Puddings are of the plum crumble or banoffi pie ilk. To drink, there's a choice of teas, coffees, juices and a trio of lagers – or bring your own wine.

Available for hire. Babies and children admitted. Booking advisable. Separate room for parties, seats 35. Takeaway service. Vegan dishes. **Map 20 B2**.

West Kensington

222 Veggie Vegan

222 North End Road, W14 9NU (7381 2322, www.222 veggievegan.com). West Kensington tube or West Brompton tube/rail or 28, 391 bus. **Lunch served** noon-3.30pm, **dinner served** 5.30-10.30pm daily. **Main courses** £7.50-£10.50. **Set lunch** £7.50 buffet. **Credit** MC, V.

Full of bustle and brimming with good vibes on a Tuesday night, 222 Veggie Vegan is the kind of restaurant every neighbourhood would like, but few get. Blond wood and bright surrounds give the deceptively small room a Scandinavian feel. Service is curt yet courteous; if no tables are free, staff will happily take your number and buzz you when one's ready. It's worth the wait. The inventive all-vegan menu is refreshingly free of stuffed red peppers. It covers almost all corners of the globe, with cashew-creamy stroganoff listed alongside chickpea curry and house speciality pancakes (stuffed with everything from black-eye bean and tofu pâté to vegan vanilla ice-cream and chocolate sauce). Generous portions mean you'll get the majority of your five-a-day in any single dish, though the food is certainly not cloyingly wholesome and doesn't leave you feeling unnecessarily stuffed. Fresh juices such as carrot, apple and ginger give a satisfying punch. Diners range from verging-on-raucous birthday parties to first-daters – all enjoying the relaxed, slightly bohemian atmosphere and good-value food. The perfect place for a laid-back midweek meal. *Available for hire. Babies and children welcome: high chairs. Booking advisable. Takeaway service. Vegan menu.* **Map 13 A12.**

East

Shoreditch

Saf

152-154 Curtain Road, EC2A 3AT (7613 0007, www.safrestaurant.co.uk). Old Street tube/rail or 55, 243 bus. **Lunch served** noon-3.30pm, **dinner served** 6.30-11pm Mon-Sat. **Main courses** £13.50-£14.25. **Credit** AmEx, MC, V.

Saf

The provision of vegan, mostly raw food is Saf's raison d'être, and the concept is carried off in style, suggesting California cool instead of stereotypical beard-and-Lennon-glasses hippies. The venue attracts a fashionable crowd thanks to its Shoreditch location, attractive interior and novel menu, but friendly staff rescue it from unapproachable trendiness. A soundtrack of cover versions played during our visit, making an apt simile for Saf's surprising reworkings of the classics: 'fettuccine' consisted of wafer-thin ribbons of salsify rather than pasta; lasagne featured macadamia 'ricotta' (made with pressed nuts). The menu cherry-picks its ethnic cues: flaxseed tacos filled with zingy pineapple salsa; Thai curry. Each artfully presented plate bursts with colour, texture and flavour. A dehydrated tomato slice atop a main course added an intense pop of flavour, pointing to the high-tech methods that created it. The open kitchen provides an animated focus, and in balmy weather a courtyard offers a retreat from the zany-hatted masses. Herbs and edible flowers from the verdant kitchen garden appear in imaginative cocktails, such as a refreshing Botanical Bellini that featured grapefruit and celery alongside prosecco bubbles. Saf now also runs yoga and cooking classes here, and has opened a second branch at Whole Foods Market on Kensington High Street.
Available for hire. Babies and children welcome: high chairs; nappy-changing facilities. Booking advisable weekends. Disabled: toilet. Tables outdoors (10, courtyard). Vegan dishes. **Map 6 R4.**
For branch see index.

North

Camden Town & Chalk Farm

Manna

4 Erskine Road, NW3 3AJ (7722 8028, www.manna-veg.com). Chalk Farm tube or 31, 168 bus. **Dinner served** 6.30-10.30pm Tue-Fri. **Meals served** noon-10.30pm Sat, Sun. **Main courses** £10-£18. **Credit** MC, V.
This luxe, prettily decorated restaurant is somewhat unexpected for those who associate vegetarian food with the hessian-and-sandals movement of the 1960s and '70s, yet Manna has been in business for more than 40 years. The well-groomed yoga bunnies that frequent it – trendy Triyoga is within easy stretching distance – come for the artfully presented dishes, though there's also enough substantial fare (among several options, you can choose fennel and pumpkin seed bangers with mash or spaghetti and meat-free balls) to delight their hunky boyfriends too. Dishes are often vegan, and frequently gluten-free. Even considering the rent and rates in Primrose Hill, prices are high: most main courses cost £13-£18, starters and desserts are mainly priced at £8. Certainly some creations are complex (enchilada casserole features cashew cheese, black beans and mole sauce, layered with soft wheat tortillas and served with green rice, carrot 'salsa' and guacamole), but the kitchen is labouring to add enough perceived value to its raw materials, even if these are 'organic and local products whenever fresh and viable'. In contrast, the range of organic and vegan wines is something of a bargain – look no further than the Buenas Ondas malbec 2008 at £16 a bottle – and service is delightful.
Babies and children welcome: high chairs. Booking essential weekends. Tables outdoors (2, conservatory). Takeaway service. Vegan dishes. **Map 27 A1.**

Vietnamese

East London is the capital's prime destination for authentic Vietnamese cooking. Kingsland Road, affectionately nicknamed the 'pho mile', features a veritable procession of inexpensive places to eat. Our favourites are **Song Que** and **Mien Tay** and, while there hasn't been much action in the Vietnamese restaurant sector this year, the good news is that Mien Tay has opened a branch south of the river, bringing southern Vietnamese cooking and family-run hospitality to the Lavender Hill mob. It will be interesting to see how the restaurant fares in such a middle-class, kids-and-a-big-mortgage neighbourhood after years of catering to the trendsters of Shoreditch. North London has two outposts of the friendly and reliable **Khoai Café** to keep it supplied with bo la lot and goi cuon, but for accomplished Vietnamese cooking in the west of the metropolis, **Saigon Saigon** remains something of a pioneer.

West

Hammersmith

Saigon Saigon

313-317 King Street, W6 9NH (0870 220 1398, www. saigon-saigon.co.uk). Ravenscourt Park or Stamford Brook tube. **Lunch served** noon-2.30pm Mon-Fri; 12.30-3pm Sat, Sun. **Dinner served** 6-10pm Mon, Sun; 6-11pm Tue-Thur; 6-11.30pm Fri, Sat. **Main courses** £5.50-£13.95. **Credit** MC, V.

This highly praised local stands out on an otherwise unremarkable stretch of King Street, its quaint, faintly colonial-era decor lending itself nicely to a romantic meal. The sizeable wine list helps in this respect too, as does the refinement in the kitchen, which sends out dishes that aim to impress. Attentive and efficient service seals the deal. The menu is a lengthy tome, with extensive descriptions of ingredients and preparations. A simple green papaya salad with fresh, crunchy prawns wowed with its punchy flavours, while a small bowl of bun bo hue (spicy beef noodle soup) was delicious, if tame compared to more authentic versions. We couldn't fault a vibrant bowl of bun, made with properly thick, elastic rice noodles topped with bouncy lemongrass pork meatballs and golden-brown spring rolls, and splashed with plenty of nuoc cham. Equally gratifying was a steamed sea bass cloaked in salty fermented soy beans, black fungus, vermicelli and knotted strands of banana flower: a brilliant Vietnamese-Chinese rendition, the fish wonderfully moist and tender. Saigon Saigon's prices are marginally higher than joints along Shoreditch's 'pho mile', but this restaurant is in a different league.
Available for hire (bar). Babies and children welcome: high chairs. Booking advisable. Tables outdoors (4, pavement).
Map 20 A4.

South

Battersea

Mien Tay

180 Lavender Hill, SW11 5TQ (7350 0721, www.mien tay.co.uk). Clapham Junction rail or bus 77, 87, 156, 345. **Lunch served** noon-3pm daily. **Dinner served** 5-11pm Mon-Sat; 5-10pm Sun. **Main courses** £5-£8. **Credit** MC, V.

The original branch on Kingsland Road sent the food community into a lather when it first opened; Mien Tay's fresh approach to Vietnamese cooking clearly struck a chord among those jaded by the near-identical menus along 'pho mile', offering as it did the sweeter, more delicate flavours of south-western Vietnam. Chargrilled quail lightly brushed with honey is a signature dish: all smokiness and spice and deep, gamey flavours. Another highlight is deep-fried sea bream, free of oiliness and served whole under tart slivers of mango and splashes of sour-salty-sweet nuoc cham. These classics are executed with equal aplomb at this newer Lavender Hill outpost. We'd also say that the pho here is marginally better, with an astounding balance of complexity and clarity in the beef broth; bouncy beef balls are a recommended addition. The restaurant is never going to win accolades for outstanding decor – it's the usual plain furniture and paper tablecloths, with colour added by way of cheesy plastic vines and flowers curled around the edge of the ceiling. Service is as hospitable as you might expect in a family-run joint.

Available for hire. Babies and children welcome: high chairs. Booking advisable weekend. Disabled: toilet. Takeaway service. **Map 21 C3**.

For branch see index.

South East

Surrey Quays

Café East

Surrey Quays Leisure Park, 100 Redriff Row, SE16 7LH (7252 1212, www.cafeeast.co.uk). Canada Water tube/rail or Surrey Quays rail. **Lunch served** 11am-3pm, **dinner served** 5.30-10.30pm Mon-Fri. **Meals served** 11am-10.30pm Sat; noon-10pm Sun. **Main courses** £6-£7.50. **Unlicensed** no alcohol allowed. **No credit cards**.

Miles from Hackney and Shoreditch, at the edge of a car park in a depressing 'entertainment' complex – it's not somewhere you'd expect to find some of the best Vietnamese food in London, but here it is. Café East moved from tiny premises in Deptford last year, and its interior doesn't give much away; white walls and rows of plain furniture lend the place a cafeteria feel. You get more of a clue when the menu arrives, its brevity betraying a confidence of execution. There are only six starters (mainly of the rolled sort, including spring rolls and banh cuon), eight soups (with deeply flavoursome broth) and a few curry and noodle dishes. Efficient, affable staff ferry huge bowls and plates to the tables as queues build up outside, and with each mouthful you'll realise why the café is so popular. There's no alcohol, but follow your (largely Vietnamese) fellow diners and slurp a che bam au, a drink made from kidney beans, jelly and coconut. The biggest surprise comes with the bill: it's almost comically cheap. In all, this is one of the closest things to a slice of Hanoi or Saigon we've found in London.

Babies and children welcome: high chairs. Bookings not accepted. Disabled: toilet. Takeaway service.

East

Shoreditch

Cây Tre

301 Old Street, EC1V 9LA (7729 8662, www.vietnamese kitchen.co.uk). Old Street tube/rail or 55, 243 bus. **Lunch served** noon-3pm Mon-Sat. **Dinner served** 5.30-11pm Mon-Thur; 5.30-11.30pm Fri, Sat. **Meals served** noon-10.30pm Sun. **Main courses** £5-£9. **Set dinner** £20 per person (minimum 2) 2 courses. **Credit** MC, V.

Trendy Cây Tre (and its nearby little sister, Viet Grill) is an Old Street success story. Its mix of traditional Vietnamese food cooked with flair, a well-thought-out wine list (and wine pairings) and stylish surroundings has Londoners swooning, not least restaurateur Mark Hix, who on more than one occasion has proclaimed his appreciation for the two eateries. Seafood and beef are the highlights at Cây Tre; the sizzling special of cha ca la vong (a delicious fish dish with intoxicating amounts of turmeric and dill) is a show-stopper, as is the swimmer crab stuffed with rice noodles, minced pork and tree-

Saigon Saigon. See p257.

ear mushrooms in an umami-packed broth. Indochine beef (bo tai chanh) is a classic French-influenced Vietnamese dish where slices of beef fillet are prepared ceviche-style with lemon juice; it makes an appetite-whetting first course. Rarely do Cây Tre's dishes disappoint; most astound with their boldness of flavour and the expertise of their execution. So it's a shame a meal is invariably such a rush. The queues that form nightly mean that staff often reluctantly plonk down your bill as soon as the last noodle has been slurped and the last drop of wine drained. *Babies and children admitted. Booking advisable. Takeaway service.* **Map 6 R4**.
For branch (Viet Grill) see index.

Song Que HOT 50
134 Kingsland Road, E2 8DY (7613 3222). Hoxton rail.
Lunch served noon-3pm, **dinner served** 5.30-11pm Mon-Sat. **Meals served** 12.30-11pm Sun. **Main courses** £4.50-£6.20. **Credit** MC, V.
Song Que is certainly not short of Vietnamese competition on Kingsland Road, but in location (a respectable distance north of the rest) and execution, it stands on its own. Admittedly, the place doesn't look much from the outside (or the inside, for that matter – the sparse, canteen-like decor is relieved only by a few jumble-sale prints, including one of some peculiarly expressive horses). The menu is regulation length for a London Vietnamese: a numbered please-all trawl through the cuisines of the north, the south and Hue. Although we have our favourites, almost every dish we've tried over the years has been brilliant. The Song Que beef pho – something every Vietnamese restaurant has to get right – is exemplary, with deep, complex broth, quality meat and vibrant herbs. Other essential dishes include barbecued quail with an almost effervescent citrus dipping sauce, fresh and fried spring rolls, and ground spiced beef in betel leaf. For years, our guides have rated Song Que as one of the best Vietnamese restaurants in the capital, and we're happy to do so again. *Babies and children welcome: high chairs. Disabled: toilet. Vegetarian menu.* **Map 6 R3**.

North East

Hackney

Green Papaya
191 Mare Street, E8 3QE (8985 5486, www.green-papaya. co.uk). London Fields rail or 26, 48, 55, 277, D6 bus.
Dinner served 5-11pm Tue-Sun. **Main courses** £5-£8. **Credit** MC, V.
Green Papaya makes the most of its proximity to Mare Street's concentration of Vietnamese supermarkets; its unusual menu is more adventurous than some other proponents of the cuisine. As well as the titular unripe tropical fruit, dishes come replete with banana blossom, Vietnamese celery and plenty of purple basil. The restaurant's popularity is evinced by the always-packed dining room (it's open only for dinner): a casual space with Communist-red walls, kitchen-style furniture and serene oil paintings of the homeland. There's a specials blackboard (something of a rarity in London's Vietnamese restaurants) – not always adorned, although diners can also choose from an A4 sheet of 'new dishes'. Here, you'll find some of the more unusual creations that have made this restaurant stand out since its launch in 2000. There might be pert salads, bo nam bo (Hanoi stir-fried beef with peanuts and fried shallots), or

Song Que

silky smoked tofu (a Green Papaya speciality). Friendly service and consistently good cooking make this one of the better restaurants of its type.

Babies and children welcome: high chairs. Booking advisable. Takeaway service.

Tre Viet

251 Mare Street, E8 3NS (8533 7390). London Fields rail or 26, 48, 55, 277, D6 bus. **Meals served** noon-11pm Mon-Thur, Sun; noon-11.30pm Fri, Sat. **Main courses** £4.70-£13. **Credit** MC, V.

Such is the popularity of Tre Viet that the business recently spread into another unit just up the road. Both venues share similar utilitarian decor; both serve the same list of Vietnamese classics alongside a few curiosities. Goat, for example, is eaten all over Vietnam (inevitably, it is said to increase sexual prowess), but isn't often seen in London's restaurants; here it is stir-fried with galangal. Frogs' legs pop up too, cooked in a similar fashion, as does a large choice of fish and seafood, and about 160 other dishes on a menu that doesn't know when to stop. Praise is due for offering diners something approaching the real diversity of cuisine found up and down Vietnam, but the problem is that it doesn't always work. Cha ca la vong is a dish of turmeric-scented fried fish from Hanoi, served with dill and spring onions and assembled at the table – the portion of herbs here was a bit skimpy, though, and there was no fish sauce to complete it. Hit and miss, then, but choose carefully and you'll be rewarded with a distinctive experience.

Booking advisable weekend. Disabled: toilet. Separate room for parties, seats 30. Takeaway service.

For branches (Lang Nuong, Tre Viet) see index.

North

Finchley

Khoai Café

362 Ballards Lane, N12 0EE (8445 2039). Woodside Park tube or 82, 134 bus. **Lunch served** noon-3.30pm, **dinner served** 5.30-11.30pm daily. **Main courses** £5-£9.95. **Set lunch** £5.45 1 course, £7.45 2 courses. **Credit** AmEx, MC, V.

This sister to the Crouch End original doesn't have to try too hard to be the best restaurant in North Finchley, yet at times there's a sense that Khoai Café is resting on its laurels. We're always impressed by the warmth of the welcome and prompt delivery of food, but the service can lack professionalism and cooking and presentation are patchy. The room is spacious and sunny, thanks to a small glass-walled courtyard at the rear. Blond wood furniture is in the sleek Scandinavian style, and there's a cheerful vase of carnations on each table. Do order the chargrilled butterflied prawns with rice vermicelli and sweet mango and cucumber salad – it draws gasps of envy from nearby tables. We also like the thick wedges of succulent aubergine, deep-fried in salty batter then stir-fried with chilli, garlic and spring onions. Beef stir-fried with pickled greens doesn't look much, but has a pleasing vinegary tang. Less appetising were some dry pork ribs marinated with honey and lemongrass. There's a brief wine list, though it's better to opt for Ha Noi beer or a sweet iced Vietnamese coffee.

Available for hire. Babies and children welcome: high chairs. Takeaway service.

For branch see index.

Menu

Banh cuon: pancake-like steamed rolls of translucent fresh rice pasta, sometimes stuffed with minced pork or shrimp (reminiscent in style of Chinese cheung fun, a dim sum speciality).

Banh pho: flat rice noodles used in soups and stir-fries, usually with beef.

Banh xeo: a large pancake made from a batter of rice flour and coconut milk, coloured bright yellow with turmeric and traditionally filled with prawns, pork, beansprouts and onion. To eat it, tear the pancake apart with your chopsticks, roll the pieces with sprigs of herbs in a lettuce leaf, and dip in nuoc cham (qv).

Bo la lot: grilled minced beef in betel leaves.

Bun: rice vermicelli, served in soups and stir-fries. They are also eaten cold, with raw salad vegetables and herbs, with a nuoc cham (qv) sauce poured over, and a topping such as grilled beef or pork – all of which are tossed together at the table.

Cha ca: North Vietnamese dish of fish served sizzling in an iron pan with lashings of dill.

Cha gio: deep-fried spring rolls. Unlike their Chinese counterparts, the wrappers are made from rice paper rather than sheets of wheat pastry, and pucker up deliciously after cooking.

Chao tom: grilled minced prawn on a baton of sugar cane.

Goi: salad. There are many types in Vietnam, but they often contain raw, crunchy vegetables and herbs, perhaps accompanied by chicken or prawns, with a sharp, perky dressing.

Goi cuon (literally 'rolled salad', often translated as 'fresh rolls' or 'salad rolls'): cool, soft, rice-paper rolls usually containing prawns, pork, fresh herbs and rice vermicelli, served with a thick sauce similar to satay sauce but made from hoi sin mixed with peanut butter, scattered with roasted peanuts.

Nem: north Vietnamese name for cha gio (qv).

Nom: north Vietnamese name for goi (qv).

Nuoc cham: the generic name for a wide range of dipping sauces, based on a paste of fresh chillies, sugar and garlic that is diluted with water, lime juice and the ubiquitous fish sauce, nuoc mam.

Nuoc mam: a brown or pale liquid derived from fish that have been salted and left to ferment. It's the essential Vietnamese seasoning, used in dips and as a cooking ingredient.

Pho: the most famous and best-loved of all Vietnamese dishes, a soup of rice noodles and beef or chicken in a rich, clear broth flavoured with aromatics. It's served with a dish of fresh beansprouts, red chilli and herbs, and a squeeze of lime; these are added to the soup at the table.

Rau thom: aromatic herbs, which might include Asian basil (rau que), mint (rau hung), red or purple perilla (rau tia to), lemony Vietnamese balm (rau kinh gioi) or saw-leaf herb (ngo gai).

Wine Bars

London has played a lead role in the wine trade since the 13th century, but since Britain was never a major producer, wine merchants and their customers have traditionally delighted in sampling wines from a variety of countries and regions. Gascony and Bordeaux were the capital's favourites in the 13th and 14th centuries – and while we've been around the world quite a few times since, today you can still enjoy the most interesting Bordeaux wines (a blend of biodynamic merlot and carmenère grapes, say, or the unfiltered Château Chasse-Spleen) at 'natural wine' specialist **Terroirs**, or the finest Gascony has to offer at **Cellar Gascon** (*see p89*). Of course, the capital has myriad places where it's possible simply to drink wine: here we point you in the direction of wine bars that proffer accompanying food with equal seriousness. New this year is the exciting **28°-50° Wine Workshop & Kitchen** from the team behind one of the capital's most original haute-cuisine restaurants, Texture (*see p128*).

Central

Chancery Lane

28°-50° Wine Workshop & Kitchen
140 Fetter Lane, EC4A 1BT (7242 8877, www.2850. co.uk). Farringdon tube/rail. **Open** 11am-11pm Mon-Fri. **Snacks served** noon-10pm, **lunch served** 2-2.30pm, **dinner served** 6-10.30pm Mon-Fri. **Main courses** £12.50-£15.50. **House wine** £17.50 bottle, £3.25 glass. **Credit** AmEx, MC, V.
This wine bar is an offshoot of the acclaimed Texture restaurant, but being a wine bar, it's far more casual and affordable, and the food is simpler. What has not changed is the attention devoted to wine: in this case, available by the smaller, tasting-sized glass, which allows diners to experiment with matching wines to their dishes. There are more than a dozen red and whites by the glass, from good producers and stylistically diverse, from Barossa Valley shiraz to Corsican vermentino. Winemakers of the month are highlighted. The food menu is just as enthusiastically prepared, using ingredients of high quality, but costing City prices. We enjoyed our three little fillets of pan-fried red mullet, served with a bouillabaisse-like sauce of clams and neatly diced veg; and a plate of Spanish and Italian charcuterie, which gave a range of flavours and textures as varied as the wine list.

Available for hire. Booking advisable. Separate rooms for parties, seating 6 and 12. **Map 11 N6.**

Clerkenwell & Farringdon

Bleeding Heart Tavern
Bleeding Heart Yard, EC1N 8SJ (7404 0333, www.bleedingheart.co.uk). Farringdon tube/rail.
Tavern **Open** 7am-11pm Mon-Fri. **Lunch served** noon-3pm, **snacks served** 3-6pm, **dinner served** 6-10.30pm Mon-Fri. **Main courses** £8.45-£14.45.
Bistro **Lunch served** noon-3pm, **dinner served** 6-10.30pm Mon-Sat. **Main courses** £8.45-£15.50.
Restaurant **Lunch served** noon-2.30pm, **dinner served** 6-10.30pm Mon-Fri. **Main courses** £12.95-£24.50.
All **House wine** £16.95 bottle, £4.50 glass. **Credit** AmEx, DC, MC, V.
Part of the sizeable Bleeding Heart enterprise in Hatton Garden, the Tavern is a cross between a wine bar and a gastropub. Access to the big wine list, from the group's more expensive restaurants, lets you choose from a massive selection that wins plaudits on a global scale. Here, in the stripped-wood corner bar on the ground floor, you can happily stick with the house wines from Trinity Hill in Hawkes Bay, one of New Zealand's star producers. Food at lunchtime is of variable quality. Two soups (pea with mint crème fraîche and a daily special of white onion) were silky, creamy and subtle. But a

tasty hot crab toastie had a floury, sticky texture that didn't do justice to the toasted slab of wonderful own-made bread, or to an excellent side salad. The more substantial stuff – lamb burgers and fish cakes with gorgeous onion rings and hand-cut chips, and a popular fish pie – is very inviting. Service from French staff is a pleasure. The Tavern's shortcomings aren't enough to deter us from recommending it to anyone in the vicinity: order food wisely and it should deliver.

Booking advisable. Dress: smart; no shorts, jeans or trainers (restaurant). Separate rooms for parties, seating 12-125. Tables outdoors (10, terrace). **Map 11 N5**.

Vinoteca `HOT 50`

7 St John Street, EC1M 4AA (7253 8786, www.vinoteca. co.uk). Farringdon tube/rail. **Open** noon-11pm Mon-Sat. **Lunch served** noon-2.45pm Mon-Fri; noon-4pm Sat. **Dinner served** 5.45-10pm Mon-Sat. **Main courses** £8.50-£14. **House wine** £13.50 bottle, £2.15 glass. **Credit** MC, V.

We're big fans of this small wine bar and shop, and we're not alone. The no-bookings policy in the evening means it's first come, first served, and such is Vinoteca's reputation for interesting wine and food at very acceptable prices, there's always a queue. Go at lunch if you want a guaranteed seat. The 25 wines by the glass change weekly, but typically traverse

the globe from Austria (a Kurt Angerer 2009 Kamptal grüner veltliner) to Australia (a 2008 shiraz cabernet from One Chain Vineyards). Each dish comes with a wine suggestion. Staff are happy to answer any questions, but wear their knowledge lightly. This lack of pretension combines with excellent dishes (rabbit and pork rillettes; pan-fried hake with broad beans, peas, fregola pasta and Amalfi lemon; or a selection of Spanish cured meats with almonds and olives) to create a winning formula. The punchily flavoured food is produced in full view from a tiny kitchen next to an equally diminutive bar, where there are a few perching stools for those waiting for tables. *Babies and children admitted. Bookings not accepted for dinner. Separate room for parties, seats 30. Tables outdoors (3, pavement).* **Map 5 O5**.

Piccadilly

1707

Fortnum & Mason, 181 Piccadilly, W1J 9FA (7734 8040, www.fortnumandmason.com). Piccadilly Circus tube. **Open/meals served** noon-10pm Mon-Sat. **Main courses** £8-£32. **House wine** from £19.50 bottle, from £6 glass. **Credit** AmEx, MC, V.

Fortnum & Mason has created an improbably lovely niche in its basement. Named after the year of the firm's foundation,

Vinoteca

this wine bar combines modernity and old-fashioned comfort with a vaulted brick ceiling and distressed-wood panelling. Staff welcome you the moment you enter. The menu is unusual, brief and somewhat difficult to navigate – there isn't a conventional starters/main/pudding structure. But the food is good, with an emphasis on outstanding ingredients mostly presented very simply. A small number of 'made' dishes (soups, tarts, a seasonal chicken and asparagus fricassee) compete for attention with the 'degustation' menu (small dishes priced individually or as a set of four). We went the degustation route, with happy results. Everything was impeccable: salmon done three ways (including a sublime tartare), top-quality prosciutto di san daniele, wonderful cheeses from a trolley of a dozen or so, and more besides. To help this merry lot on its way, a selection of wine flights (three 125ml glasses) makes perfect lunchtime drinking for two people. Quality is high, prices reasonable. You can also buy a bottle from the treasure-filled Fortnum retail list and drink it here with £10 corkage. *Available for hire. Babies and children admitted. Booking advisable. Disabled: lift; toilet (ground floor).* **Map 9 J7**.

Let the music play

Fancy a side order of jazz or soul with your dinner? Try one of the following. Admission prices vary.

Blues Kitchen
111-113 Camden High Street, NW1 7JN (7387 5277, www.theblueskitchen.com). Camden Town tube. **Open** noon-midnight Mon-Wed; noon-1am Thur; noon-3am Fri; 10am-3am Sat; 10am-midnight Sun. **Meals served** noon-10.30pm Mon-Fri; 10am-10.30pm Sat; 10am-10pm Sun. **Music** *Bands* 9.30pm Mon-Thur; 10pm Fri, Sat; 7pm Sun. *DJs* 1am-3am Fri, Sat.
Enjoy soul food, blues music and a lengthy selection of bourbons, ryes and Tennessee whiskeys.
Map 27 D3.

Dover Street
8-10 Dover Street, W1S 4LQ (7629 9813, www. doverstreet.co.uk). Green Park or Piccadilly Circus tube. **Open** 5pm-3am Mon-Sat. **Dinner served** 6pm-2am Mon-Thur; 7pm-2am Fri, Sat. **Music** *Bands* 9.30pm Mon; 10pm Tue-Sat. *DJs* until 3am Mon-Sat.
Three bars, a dancefloor, bands playing funk, soul and swing, and French/Mediterranean food until 2am.
Map 9 J7.

Green Note
106 Parkway, NW1 7AN (7485 9899, www.green note.co.uk). Camden Town tube. **Open** 7-11pm Wed, Thur, Sun; 7pm-midnight Fri; 6.30pm-midnight Sat. **Dinner served** 7-10pm Wed, Thur, Sun; 7-10.30pm Fri, Sat. **Music** 9-11pm daily.
Organic and vegetarian dishes and tapas served to the sounds of folk, blues, Americana and jazz.
Map 27 C3.

Jazz After Dark
9 Greek Street, W1D 4DQ (7734 0545, www.jazz afterdark.co.uk). Leicester Square or Tottenham Court Road tube. **Open** 2pm-2am Tue-Thur; 2pm-3am Fri, Sat. **Meals served** 2pm-midnight Tue-Sat. **Music** 9pm Mon-Thur; 10.30pm Fri, Sat.
This unpretentious spot is a hit with the young after-work crowd. Expect a mix of blues, funk, jazz and soul.
Map 17 C3.

Jazz Café
5-7 Parkway, NW1 7PG (7485 6834, www.jazzcafe live.com). Camden Town tube. **Open/meals served** varies. **Music** daily. Phone for details.

There's an international menu in the balcony restaurant, while music ranges from Cuban sosa to 'I love the 80s' nights, but includes some big names along the way.
Map 27 D2.

Pizza Express Jazz Club
10 Dean Street, W1D 3RW (0845 602 7017, www.pizzaexpresslive.com). Tottenham Court Road tube. Restaurant **Meals served** 11.30am-midnight Mon-Sat; 11.30am-11.30pm Sun. *Club* **Meals served** 7-11pm daily. **Music** 9-11pm daily.
This laid-back basement club has a tradition of staging fresh talent, along with more established musicians.
Map 17 B3.

Le Quecum Bar
42-44 Battersea High Street, SW11 3HX (7787 2227, www.quecumbar.co.uk). Clapham Junction rail. **Open** 7pm-midnight Mon-Thur; 6pm-1am Fri, Sat; 6pm-midnight Sun. **Meals served** 7-10pm Mon-Thur; 6-10pm Fri-Sun. **Music** varies Mon, Sun; 8pm Tue-Sat.
A wine bar specialising in gypsy jazz and serving French bistro food. Bring your own instrument for the Gypsy Swing Jam on Tuesdays.
Map 21 B2.

Ronnie Scott's
47 Frith Street, W1D 4HT (7439 0747, www.ronnie scotts.co.uk). Leicester Square or Tottenham Court Road tube. **Open** 6pm-late Mon-Sat; 6.30pm-late Sun. **Meals served** 6pm-1am Mon-Sat; 6-11pm Sun. **Music** 7.30pm-2am Mon-Sat; 8pm-midnight Sun.
Opened in 1959 and one of the most respected jazz venues in the world, attracting all the big names. Fish cakes, burgers and steaks are typical dishes.
Map 17 C3.

606 Club
90 Lots Road, SW10 0QD (7352 5953, www.606 club.co.uk). Earl's Court tube then C3 bus or Sloane Square tube then 22 bus. **Open/meals served** 7.30-11.45pm Mon; 7pm-12.30am Tue, Wed; 7pm-midnight Thur; 8pm-1.30am Fri, Sat; 12.30-11.15pm Sun. **Music** 9pm Mon; 7.30pm Tue, Wed; 8pm Thur; 9.30pm Fri, Sat; 1.30pm, 8.30pm Sun.
A long-running jazz club, with music every night and pasta, salmon and wild boar sausages on the menu.
Map 13 C13.

WINE BARS

Strand

Terroirs

5 William IV Street, WC2N 4DW (7036 0660, www. terroirswinebar.com). Charing Cross tube/rail. **Open** noon-midnight Mon-Sat. **Lunch served** noon-3pm, **dinner served** 5.45-11pm Mon-Sat. **Main courses** £13-£15. **House wine** £15.25 bottle, £4.30 glass. **Credit** AmEx, MC, V.

In this most tourist-clogged of areas, it's a joy to find a brilliant wine bar offering fantastic food, terrific wines and a buzzing Gallic atmosphere – all at reasonable prices. With the opening of the basement restaurant, the appeal of Terroirs has doubled. You can swing by for a pre-theatre white Château Clément-Termes Gaillac with some rich bar snacks, or sit down for a meal proper (booking is essential). The speciality is that curious thing known as 'natural' wine: unfiltered wines with no added acid, sugar or sulphur, made from biodynamically grown organic grapes. These bottles are marked on the menu with a little icon of a horse. There's plenty of choice by the glass and the carafe, which increases the opportunity to indulge in some great vino. Fortunately, the food matches up to the wine list; the menu is a frequently changing list that takes in charcuterie (pistachio and pork terrine was first-class), tapas-style bar snacks (duck scratchings, Marcona almonds) and plats du jour (pot-roasted quail, bavette steak). Decorated in a clean-lined modern style – albeit with a little French ephemera on the white walls – Terroirs has an invigorating vibe, but it can be a touch difficult to flag down staff during peak hours.

Babies and children admitted. Booking advisable. Tables outdoors (3, pavement). **Map 10 L7.**

West

Notting Hill

Kensington Wine Rooms

127-129 Kensington Church Street, W8 7LP (7727 8142, www.greatwinesbytheglass.com). Notting Hill Gate tube. **Open/meals served** noon-11pm Mon-Sat; noon-10.30pm

1707. See p263.

Sun. **Main courses** £13.50-£39. **House wine** £18.20 bottle, £4.30 glass. **Credit** AmEx, MC, V.

It took plenty of courage to launch a serious restaurant within a minute's walk of two Modern European luminaries, Kensington Place and Clarke's, but this 2009 opening has hit on a sound approach. Occupying a low-slung room with a sleek metal bar and stylish decor of burgundy, dark wood and exposed brickwork, KWR is a wine merchant's, wine bar and restaurant all in one – and it does some things very well. Above all, there's an outstanding list including 40 wines served by the glass from Enomatic machines that keep the wine impeccably fresh. The food, which includes both à la carte and authentic Spanish tapas, complements the vinous wonders well, but a quick lunch displayed contrasts in quality. Spicy gazpacho was a marvel: thick, chewy and deeply flavourful. But tuna tartare with green apple, tzatziki and peashoot salad was a let-down: the poorly trimmed fish chunks were overpowered by sun-dried tomatoes. Sometimes the kitchen tries too hard to be original. Much else on the menu is more straightforward, and some careful ordering will allow you to enjoy the excellent wine.

Babies and children welcome: high chairs. Booking advisable evenings. **Map 7 B7.**

Not forgetting...

Don't overlook these terrific operations, which offer platters of deli delights, rather than full-blown meals, alongside their first-rate wine lists.

Green & Blue

36-38 Lordship Lane, SE22 8HJ (8693 9250, www.greenandbluewines.com). East Dulwich rail. **Open/meals served** 9am-11pm Mon-Wed; 9am-midnight Thur-Sat; 11am-10.30pm Sun.
Kate Thal's modern rustic wine bar helped establish Lordship Lane as one of London's leading foodie streets. If you want to discover new wines, it's an excellent destination.
Map 23 C4.

Negozio Classica

283 Westbourne Grove, W11 2QA (7034 0005, www.negozioclassica.co.uk). Ladbroke Grove or Notting Hill Gate tube. **Open/meals served** 3pm-midnight Mon-Thur; 11am-midnight Fri, Sun; 9am-midnight Sat.
It's all Italian at this Notting Hill jewel, where you can people-watch while nibbling on cheeses, salumi or antipasti and enjoying the authoritative selection of wines, plus beer and grappa.
Map 7 N6.

Wonder Bar

Selfridges, 400 Oxford Street, W1A 1AB (7318 2476, www.selfridges.com). Bond Street or Marble Arch tube. **Open/meals served** 11am-9.30pm Mon-Sat; noon-6pm Sun.
Set atop Selfridges wine department (also a good place for spirits), this mezzanine bar has an Enomatic machine that is rather like a jukebox of well-selected wines.
Map 9 G6.

Maps

The following maps highlight London's key restaurant areas: the districts with the highest density of good places to eat and drink. They show precisely where each restaurant is located, as well as major landmarks and tube stations.

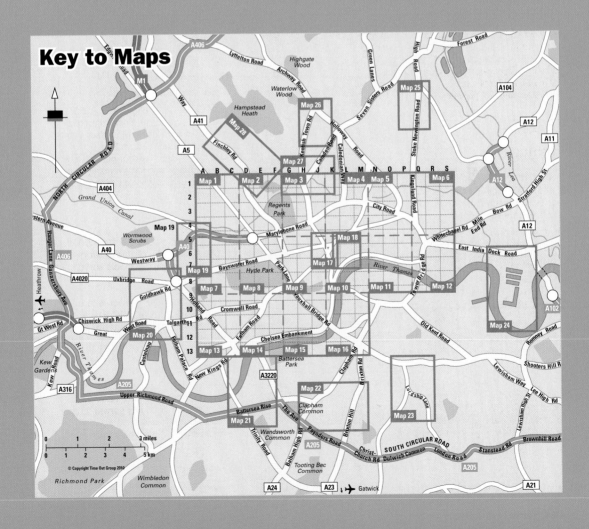

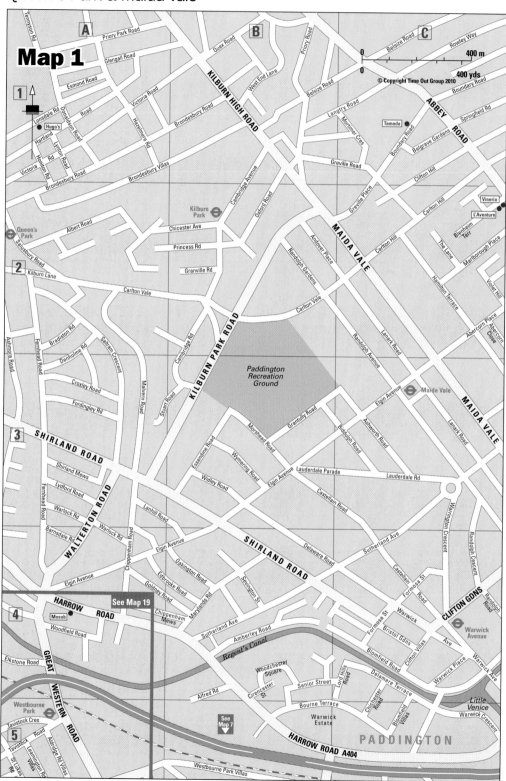

Map 1

Paddington
Recreation
Ground

See Map 19

See Map 7

Little
Venice

PADDINGTON

MAPS

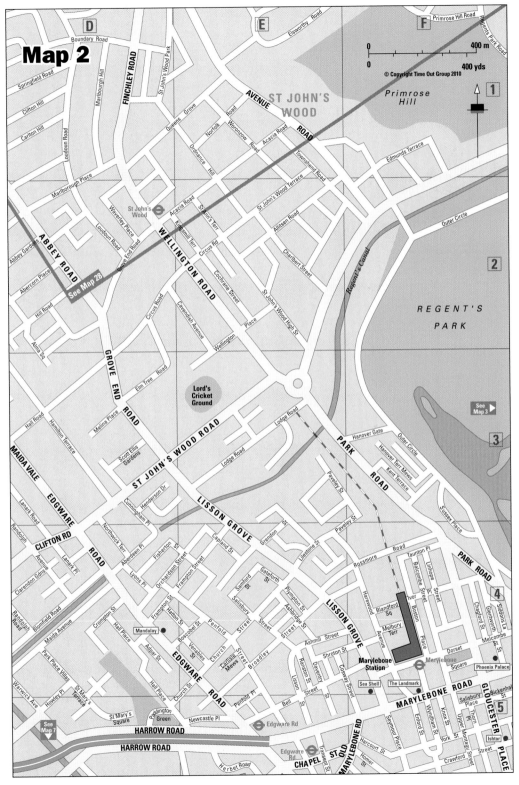

Map 2

MAPS

Camden Town & Marylebone

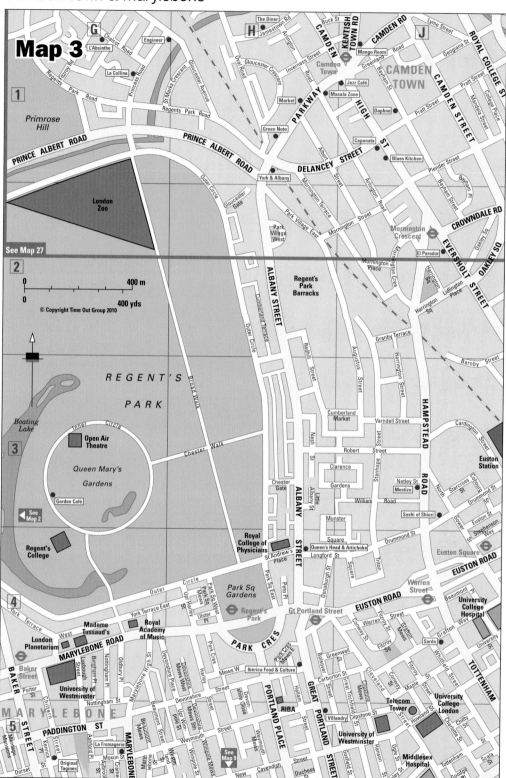

Map 3

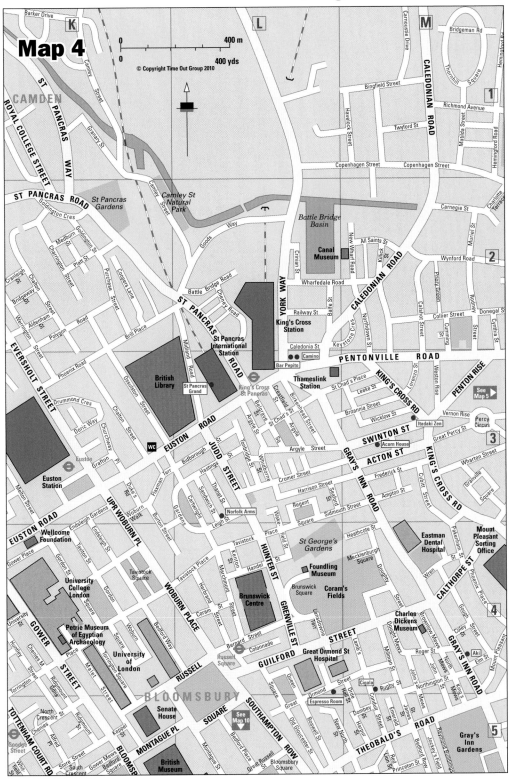

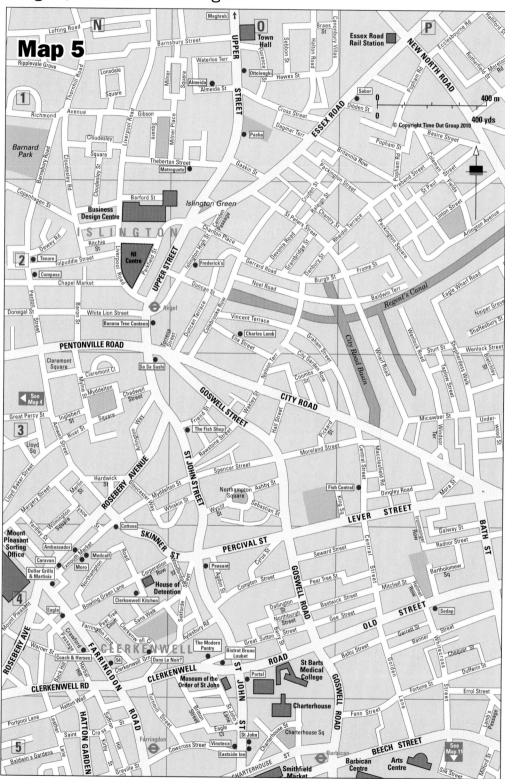

MAPS

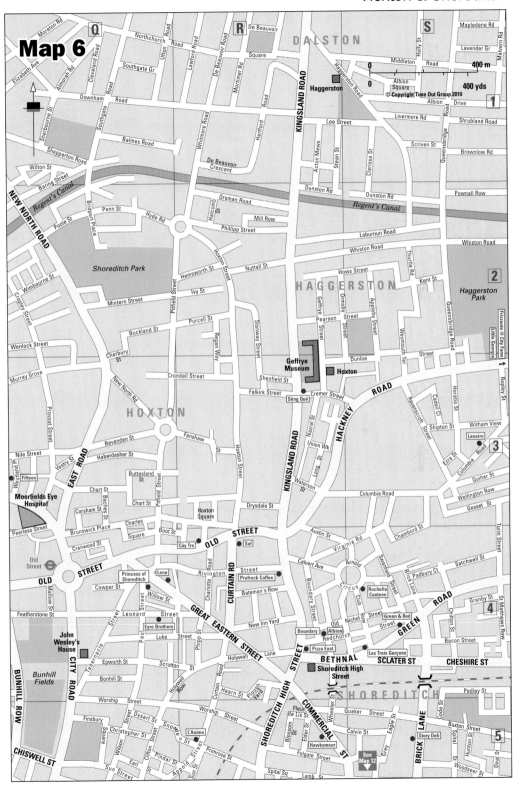

Map 6

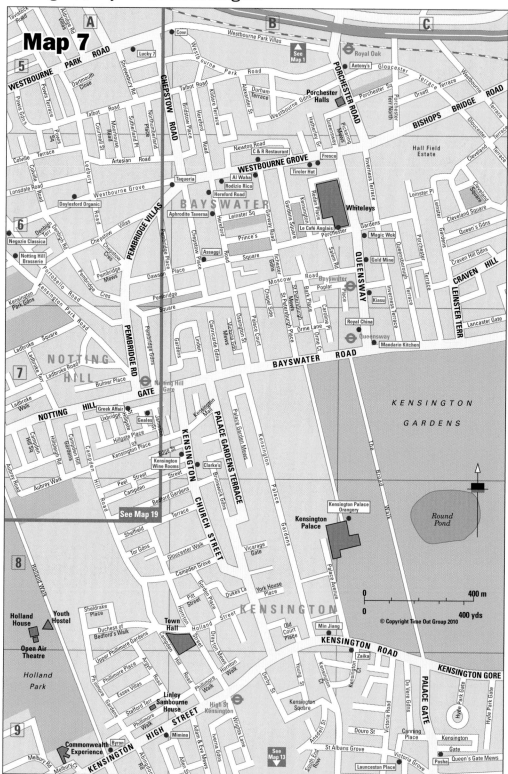

Map 7

MAPS

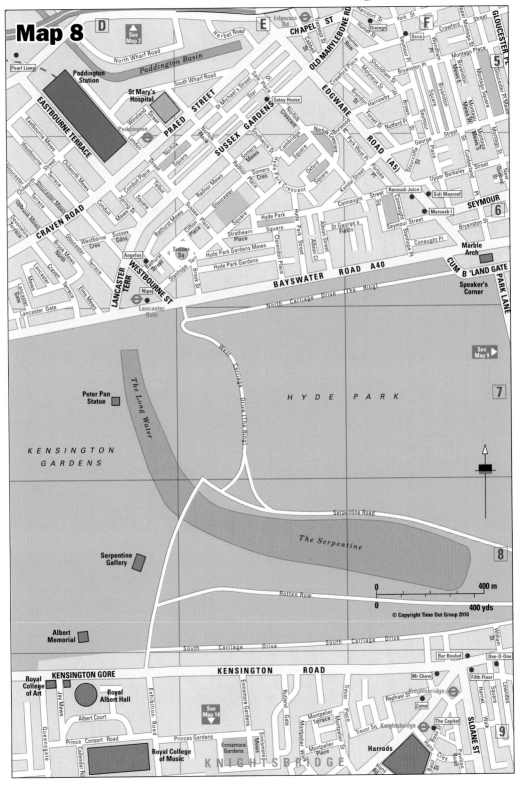

Marylebone, Fitzrovia, Mayfair & St James's

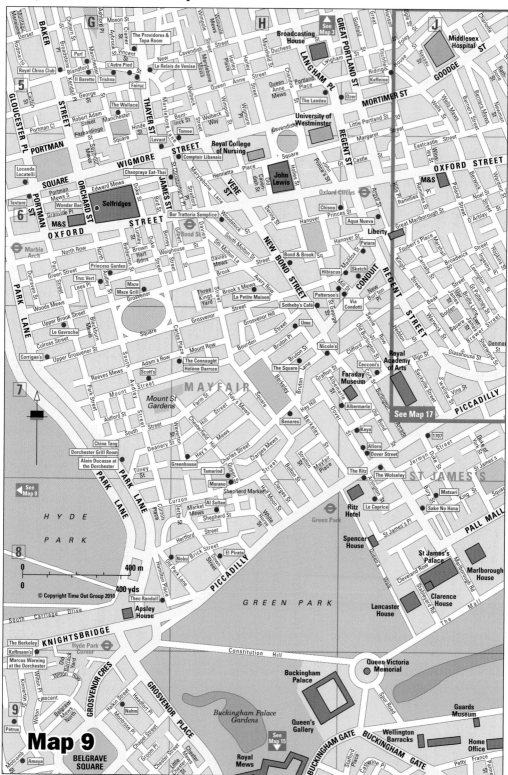

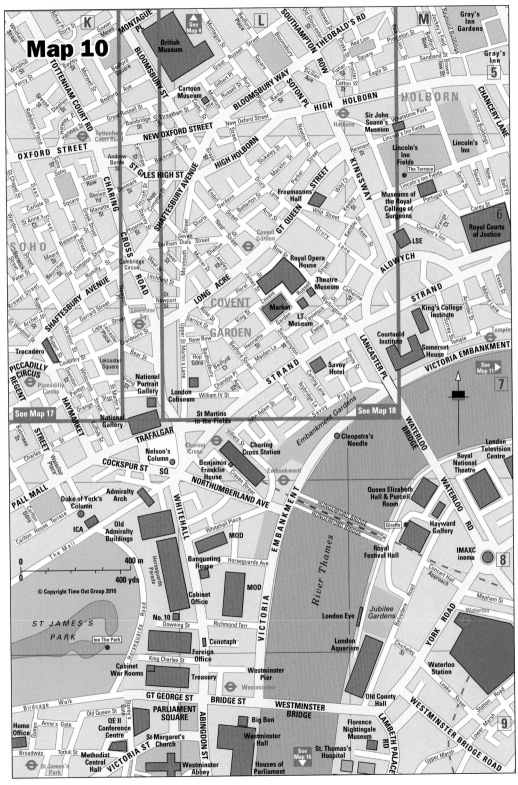

Map 10

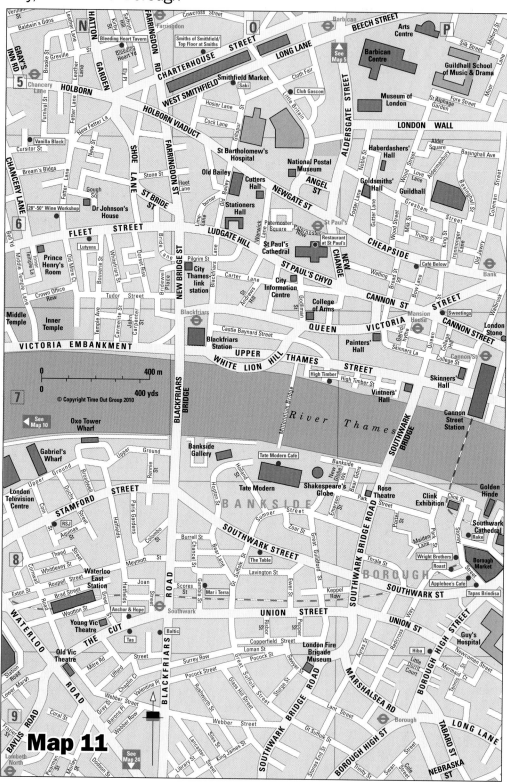

Map 11

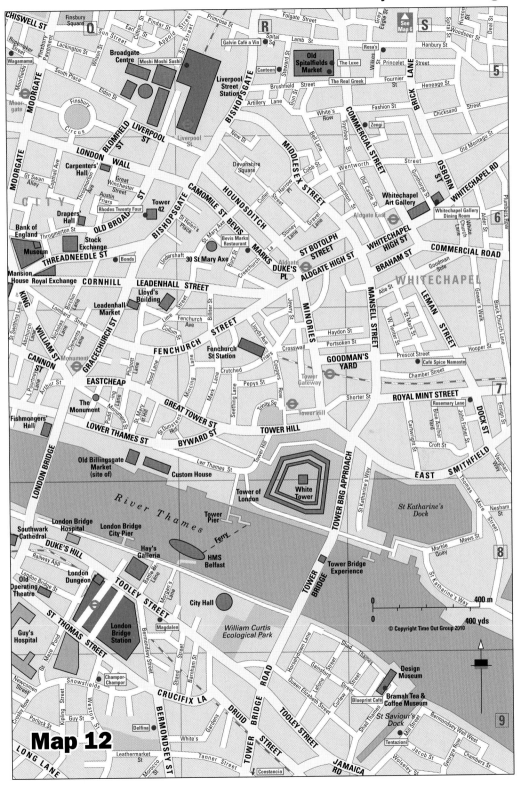

Map 12

Earl's Court, Gloucester Road & Fulham

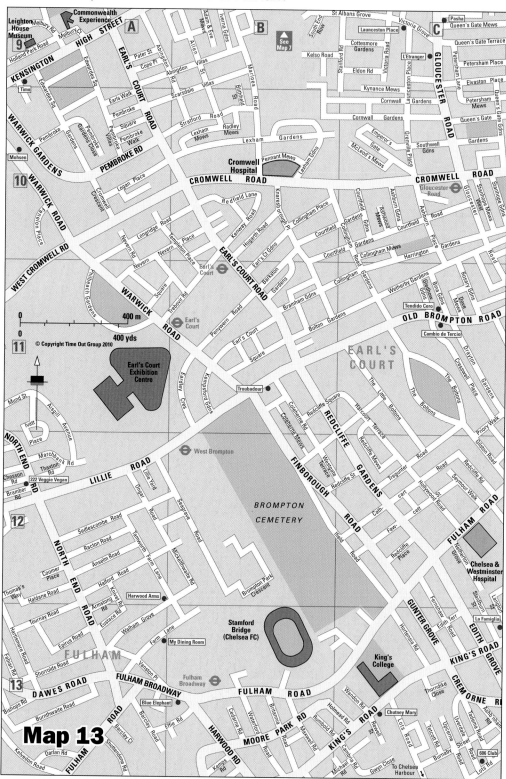

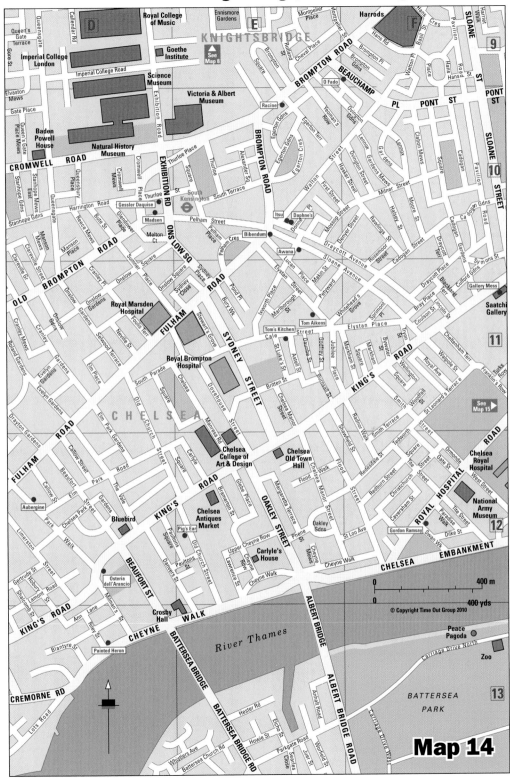

Map 14

MAPS

Belgravia, Victoria & Pimlico

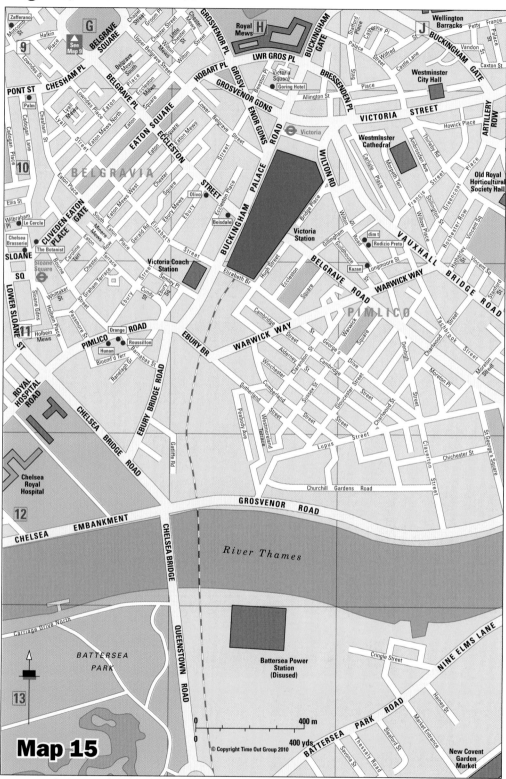

Map 15

0   400 m
0   400 yds
© Copyright Time Out Group 2010

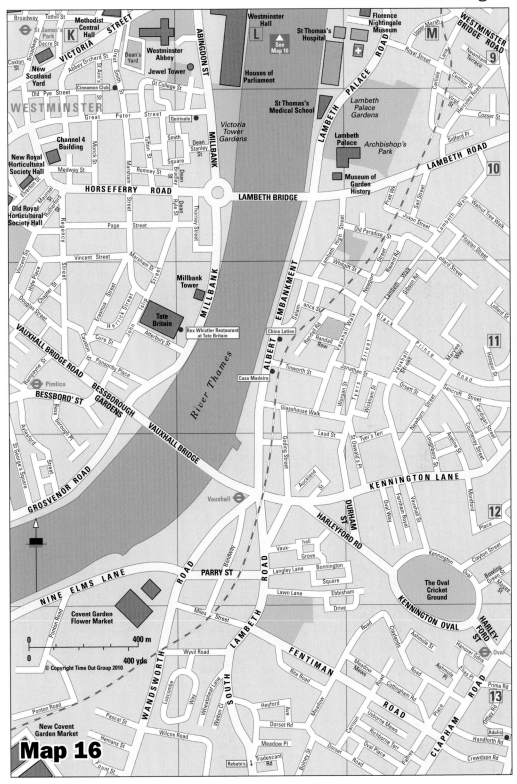

Map 16

MAPS

Fitzrovia, Soho & Chinatown

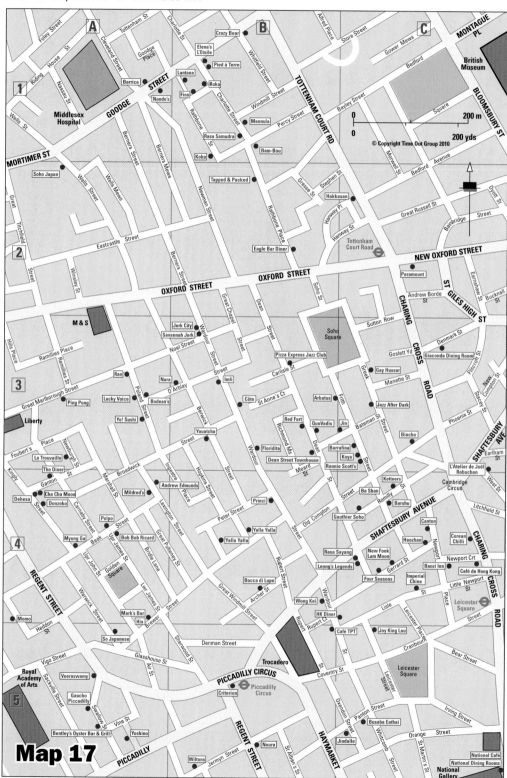

Map 17

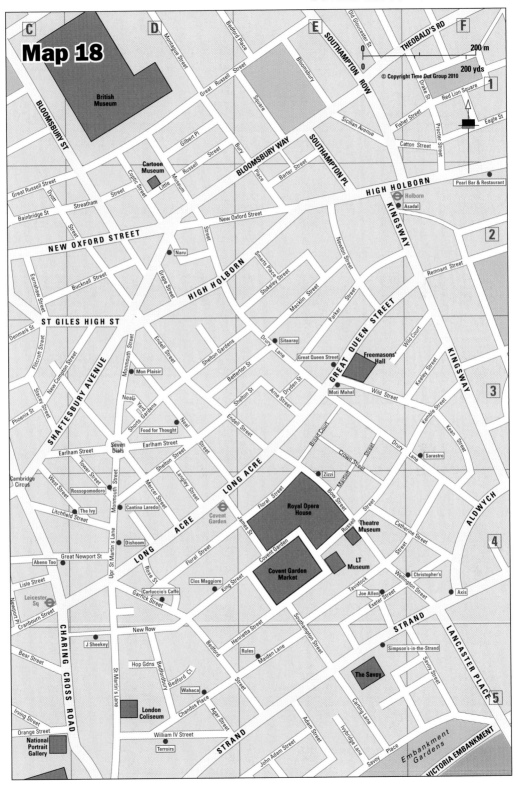

Hammersmith & Shepherd's Bush

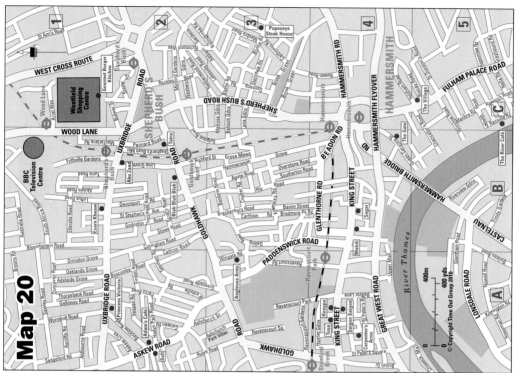

Notting Hill & Ladbroke Grove

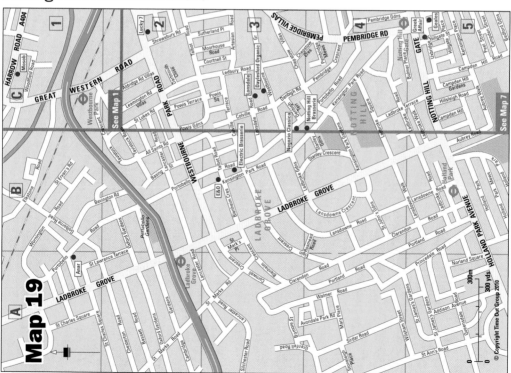

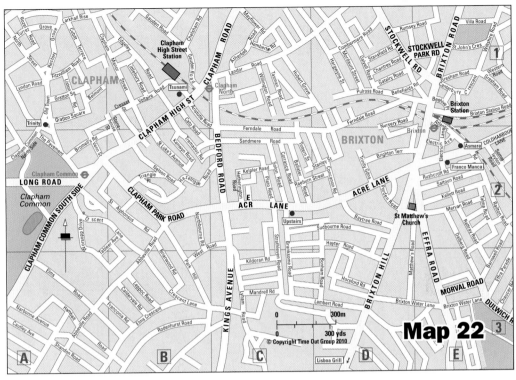

Map 22

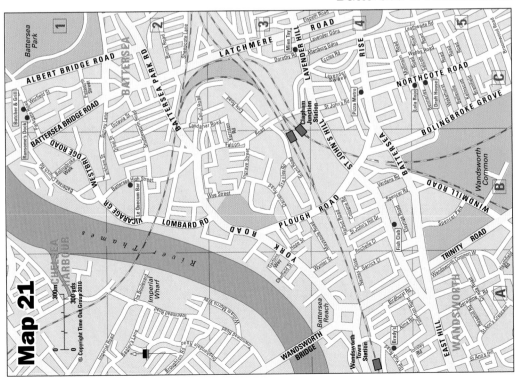

Map 21

MAPS

Docklands

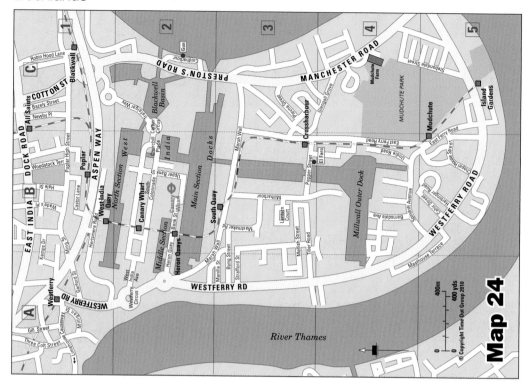

Camberwell & Dulwich

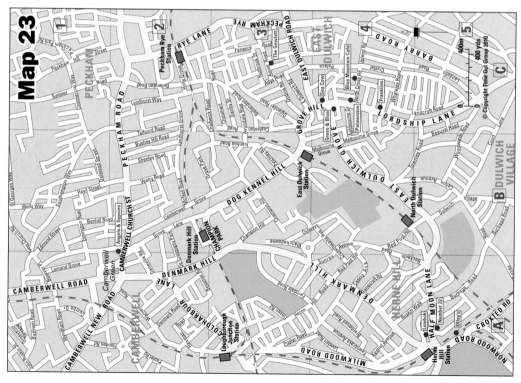

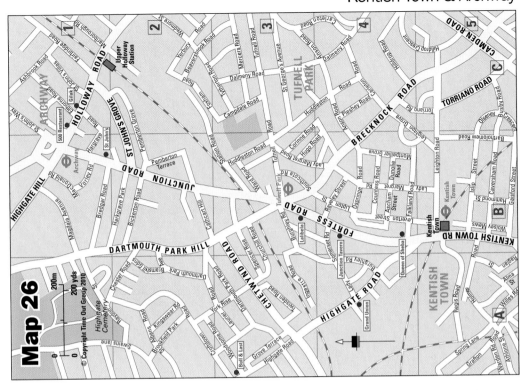

MAPS

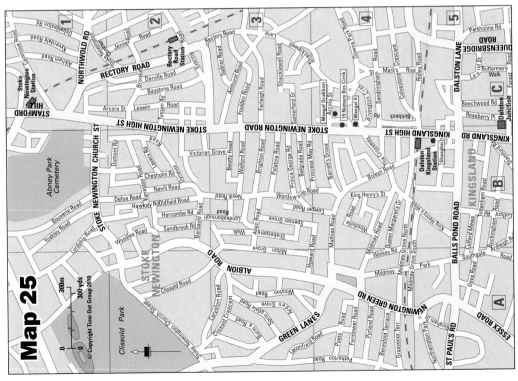

Hampstead & St John's Wood

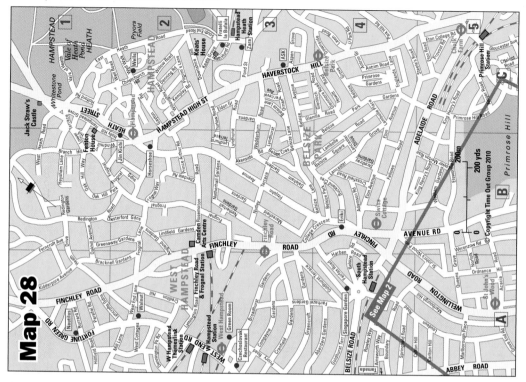

Camden Town & Chalk Farm

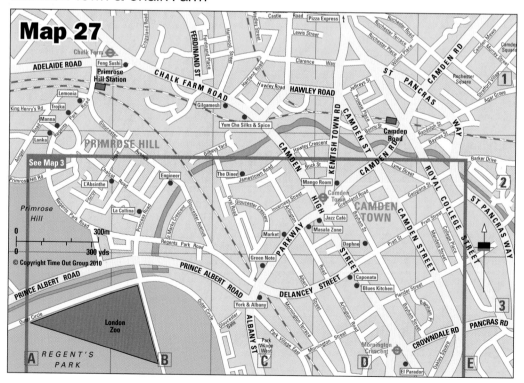

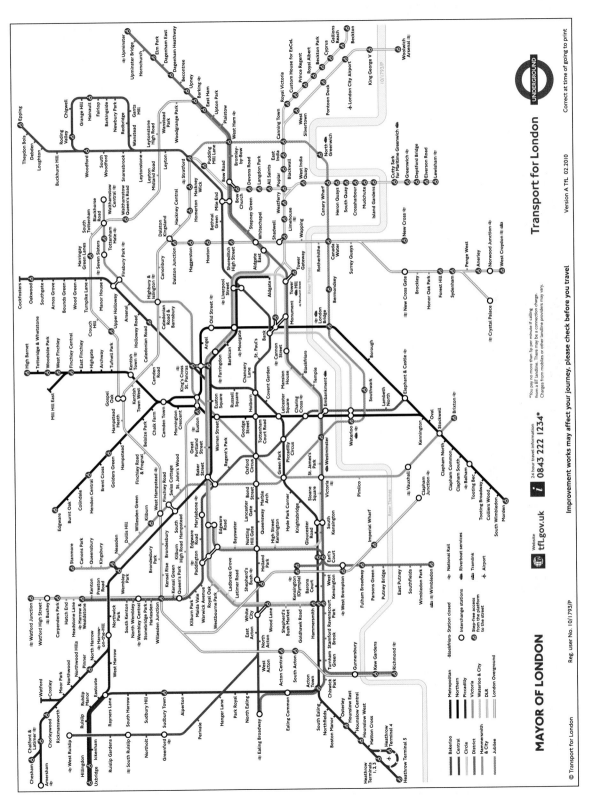

MAYOR OF LONDON

Transport for London

UNDERGROUND

MAPS

Area Index

Zizzi
157 High Street, Beckenham, Kent, BR3 1AE (8658 2050).

Belgravia

Branches
Le Cercle (branch of Club Gascon)
1 Wilbraham Place, SW1X 9AE (7901 9999, www.lecercle.co.uk).
Noura
16 Hobart Place, SW1W 0HH (7235 9444).
Oliveto (branch of Olivo)
49 Elizabeth Street, SW1W 9PP (7730 0074).
Olivomare
10 Lower Belgrave Street, SW1W 0LJ (7730 9022).
Ottolenghi
13 Motcomb Street, SW1X 8LB (7823 2707).
Brasseries & Cafés
Chelsea Brasserie p41
7-12 Sloane Square, SW1W 8EG (7881 5999, www.chelsea-brasserie.co.uk).
Chinese
Hunan p63
51 Pimlico Road, SW1W 8NE (7730 5712, www.hunan london.com).
French
Roussillon p87
16 St Barnabas Street, SW1W 8PE (7730 5550, www.roussillon.co.uk).
Italian
Olivo p149
21 Eccleston Street, SW1W 9LX (7730 2505, www.olivore staurants.com).
Thai
Nahm p239
Halkin Street, SW1X 7DJ (7333 1234, www.nahm.como.bz).
The Americas
Palm p31
1 Pont Street, SW1X 9EJ (7201 0710, www.thepalm.com/london).

Belsize Park

Branches
Giraffe
196-198 Haverstock Hill, NW3 2AG (7431 3812).
Gourmet Burger Kitchen
200 Haverstock Hill, NW3 2AG (7443 5335).
Pizza Express
194A Haverstock Hill, NW3 2AJ (7794 6777).
XO (branch of E&O)
29 Belsize Lane, NW3 5AS (7433 0888).
Pizza & Pasta
ASK p151
216 Haverstock Hill, NW3 2AE (7433 3896, www.ask restaurants.com).
Turkish
Zara p252
11 South End Road, NW3 2PT (7794 5498).

Bermondsey

Italian
Zucca p159
184 Bermondsey Street, SE1 3TQ (7378 6809, www.zuccalondon.com).
The Americas
Constancia p39
52 Tanner Street, SE1 3PH (7234 0676, www.constancia.co.uk).

Bethnal Green

Branches
Nando's
366 Bethnal Green Road, E2 0AH (7729 5783).

British
Palmers p61
238 Roman Road, E2 0RY (8980 5590, www.palmers restaurant.net).
French
Bistrotheque p95
23-27 Wadeson Street, E2 9DR (8983 7900, www.bistrotheque.com).
Pan-Asian & Fusion
Viajante p226
Patriot Square, E2 9NF (7871 0461, www.viajante.co.uk).

Blackheath

Branches
Pizza Express
64 Tranquil Vale, SE3 0BN (8318 2595).
Strada
5 Lee Road, SE3 9RQ (8318 6644).
Brasseries & Cafés
Chapters All Day Dining p49
43-45 Montpelier Vale, SE3 0TJ (8333 2666, www.chapters restaurants.com).
The Americas
Buenos Aires Café p39
17 Royal Parade, SE3 0TL (8318 5333, www.buenos airesltd.com).

Bloomsbury

Branches
Abeno
47 Museum Street, WC1A 1LY (7405 3211).
Carluccio's Caffè
The Brunswick, Marchmont Street, WC1N 1AF (7833 4100).
Giraffe
The Brunswick, Marchmont Street, WC1N 3AG (7812 1336).
Gourmet Burger Kitchen
44-46 The Brunswick, Marchmont Street, WC1N 1AE (7278 7168).
Nando's
The Brunswick, Marchmont Street, WC1N 1AE (7713 0351).
Pizza Express
30 Coptic Street, WC1A 1NS (7636 3232).
Strada
15-17 The Brunswick, Marchmont Street, WC1N 1AF (7278 2777).
Tas
22 Bloomsbury Street, WC1B 3QJ (7637 4555).
Wagamama
4 Streatham Street, WC1A 1JB (7323 9223, www.wagamama.com).
Yo! Sushi
The Brunswick, Marchmont Street, WC1N 1AE (7833 1884).
Brasseries & Cafés
Espresso Room p13
31-35 Great Ormond Street, WC1N 3HZ (07932 137380, www.theespressoroom.com).
Gastropubs
Norfolk Arms p100
28 Leigh Street, WC1H 9EP (7388 3937, www.norfolk arms.co.uk).
Modern European
Giaconda Dining Room p201
9 Denmark Street, WC2H 8LS (7240 3334, www.giaconda dining.com).
Paramount p201
101-103 New Oxford Street, WC1A 1DD (7420 2900, www.paramount.net).
Spanish & Portuguese
Cigala p227
54 Lamb's Conduit Street, WC1N 3LW (7405 1717, www.cigala.co.uk).

Borough

Branches
Pizza Express
4 Borough High Street, SE1 9QQ (7407 2995).
Tas
72 Borough High Street, SE1 1XF (7403 7200).
Tas Café
76 Borough High Street, SE1 1LL (7403 8557).
Wagamama
1 Clink Street, SE1 9BU (7403 3659).
British
Roast p61
The Floral Hall, Borough Market, Stoney Street, SE1 1TL (7940 1300, www.roast-restaurant.com).
Fish
Applebee's Café p81
5 Stoney Street, SE1 9AA (7407 5777, www.applebees fish.com).
Wright Brothers Oyster & Porter House p85
11 Stoney Street, SE1 9AD (7403 9554, www.wrightbros.eu.com).
Middle Eastern
Hiba p197
Maya House, 134-138 Borough High Street, SE1 1LB (7357 9633).
Spanish & Portuguese
Tapas Brindisa p235
18-20 Southwark Street, SE1 1TJ (7357 8880, www.brindisa.com).

Brent Cross

Branches
Carluccio's Caffè
Fenwick, Brent Cross Shopping Centre, NW4 3FN (8203 6844).
Wagamama
Brent Cross Shopping Centre, NW4 3FP (8202 2666).
Yo! Sushi
2nd floor, Brent Cross Shopping Centre, NW4 3FY (8203 7907).

Brick Lane

Pizza & Pasta
Story Deli p161
Old Truman Brewery, 3 Dray Walk, E1 6QL (7247 3137, www.storydeli.com).

Brixton

Branches
Grand Union
123 Acre Lane, SW2 5UA (7274 8794).
Nando's
234-244 Stockwell Road, SW9 9SP (7737 6400).
African & Caribbean
Asmara p25
386 Coldharbour Lane, SW9 8LF (7737 4144).
Modern European
Upstairs p212
89B Acre Lane, entrance on Branksome Road, SW2 5TN (7733 8855, www.upstairs london.com).
Pizza & Pasta
Franco Manca p161
4 Market Row, Electric Lane, SW9 8LD (7738 3021, www.francomanca.co.uk).
Spanish & Portuguese
Lisboa Grill p238
256A Brixton Hill, SW2 1HF (8671 8311).

Bromley, Kent

Branches
Nando's
9 Widmore Road, Bromley, Kent, BR1 1RL (8290 5010).

Pizza Express
15 Widmore Road, Bromley, Kent, BR1 1RL (8464 2708).
Pizza Express
3 High Street, West Wickham, Bromley, Kent, BR4 0LP (8777 7966).
Pizza Express
8 Royal Parade, Chislehurst, Bromley, Kent, BR7 6NR (8295 0965).
Zizzi
11-13 Widmore Road, Bromley, Kent, BR1 1RL (8464 6663).
Zizzi
19 High Street, Chislehurst, Bromley, Kent, BR7 5AE (8467 8302).

Camberwell

Branches
Grand Union
26 Camberwell Grove, SE5 8RE (3247 1001).
Nando's
88 Denmark Hill, SE5 8RX (7738 3808).
Spanish & Portuguese
Angels & Gypsies p235
29-33 Camberwell Church Street, SE5 8TR (7703 5984, www.churchstreethotel.com).

Camden

Branches
Grand Union
102-104 Camden Road, NW1 9EA (7485 4530).
Pizza Express
85 Parkway, NW1 7PP (7267 2600).
Strada
40-42 Parkway, NW1 7AH (7428 9653).
Wagamama
11 Jamestown Road, NW1 7BW (7428 0800).
African & Caribbean
Mango Room p29
10-12 Kentish Town Road, NW1 8NH (7482 5065, www.mangoroom.co.uk).
British
Market p62
43 Parkway, NW1 7PN (7267 9700, www.market restaurant.co.uk).
Eating & Entertainment
Blues Kitchen p265
111-113 Camden High Street, NW1 7JN (7387 5277, www.theblueskitchen.com).
Green Note p265
106 Parkway, NW1 7AN (7485 9899, www.greennote.co.uk).
Jazz Café p265
5-7 Parkway, NW1 7PG (7485 6834, www.jazzcafelive.com).
Greek
Daphne p122
83 Bayham Street, NW1 0AG (7267 7322).
Indian
Masala Zone p147
25 Parkway, NW1 7PG (7267 4422, www.masalazone.com).
Italian
Caponata p163
3-7 Delancey Street, NW1 7NL (7387 5959, www.caponata camden.co.uk).
Modern European
York & Albany p216
127-129 Parkway, NW1 7PS (7388 3344, www.gordon ramsay.com/yorkandalbany).
Spanish & Portuguese
El Parador p237
245 Eversholt Street, NW1 1BA (7387 2789, www.elparador london.com).

AREA INDEX

AREA INDEX

Elephant & Castle

Branches
Nando's
Metro Central, 119 Newington
Causeway, SE1 6BA (7378 7810).
Chinese
Dragon Castle p72
100 Walworth Road, SE17 1JL
(7277 3388).
East European
Mamuska! p77
First floor, Elephant & Castle
Shopping Centre, SE1 6TE
(07986 352810,
www.mamuska.net).

Enfield, Middx

Branches
Nando's
2 The Town, Enfield, Middx,
EN2 6LE (8366 2904).
Pizza Express
2 Silver Street, Enfield, Middx,
EN1 3ED (8367 3311).

Euston

Branches
Nando's
The Piazza, Euston Station,
NW1 2RT (7387 5126).
Pizza Express
Clifton House, 93-99 Euston Road,
NW1 2RA (7383 7102).
Rasa Express
327 Euston Road, NW1 3AD
(7387 8974).
Japanese
Sushi of Shiori p166
44 Drummond Street, NW1 2PA
(7388 9962, www.sushiof
shiori.co.uk).

Farringdon

Branches
Carluccio's Caffè
12 West Smithfield, EC1A 9JR
(7329 5904).
Cellar Gascon
(branch of Club Gascon)
59 West Smithfield, EC1A 9DS
(7600 7561,
www.cellargascon.com).
Le Comptoir Gascon
(branch of Club Gascon)
61-63 Charterhouse Street,
EC1M 6HJ (7608 0851,
www.comptoirgascon.com).
Gaucho Smithfield
93A Charterhouse Street,
EC1M 6HL (7490 1676).
Hix Oyster & Chop House
36-37 Greenhill Rents,
off Cowcross Street,
EC1M 6BN (7017 1930,
www.hixoysterandchophouse.
co.uk).
Morito (branch of Moro)
32 Exmouth Market, EC1R 4QL
(7278 7007).
Pizza Express
26 Cowcross Street, EC1M 6DQ
(7490 8025).
Strada
8-10 Exmouth Market, EC1R 4QA
(7278 0800).
Tas
37 Farringdon Road, EC1M 3JB
(7430 9721).
Yo! Sushi
95 Farringdon Road, EC1R 3BT
(7841 0785).
French
Club Gascon p89
57 West Smithfield,
EC1A 9DS (7796 0600,
www.clubgascon.com).
Japanese
Saki p166
4 West Smithfield,
EC1A 9JX (7489 7033,
www.saki-food.com).

Finchley

Branches
ASK
Great North Leisure Park, Chaplin
Square, N12 0GL (8446 0970).
Nando's
Great North Leisure Park, Chaplin
Square, N12 0GL (8492 8465).
Tosa
152 High Road, N2 9ED
(8883 8850).
Yo! Sushi
O2 Centre, 255 Finchley Road,
NW3 6LU (7431 4499).
Zizzi
202-208 Regent's Park Road,
N3 3HP (8371 6777).
Zizzi
O2 Centre, Finchley High Road,
NW3 6LU (7433 8259).
Fish & Chips
Two Brothers Fish Restaurant p83
297-303 Regent's Park Road,
N3 1DP (8346 0469,
www.twobrothers.co.uk).
Jewish
Olive Restaurant p176
224 Regent's Park Road, N3 3HP
(8343 3188, www.olivekosher
restaurant.co.uk).
Vietnamese
Khoai Café p261
362 Ballards Lane, N12 0EE
(8445 2039).

Finsbury Park

Branches
Old Dairy (branch of Realpubs)
1-3 Crouch Hill, N4 4AP (7263
3337, www.theolddairyn4.co.uk).
Fish
Chez Liline p85
101 Stroud Green Road, N4 3PX
(7263 6550).
Korean
Dotori p184
3 Stroud Green Road, N4 2DQ
(7263 3562).
Turkish
Petek p251
94-96 Stroud Green Road, N4 3EN
(7619 3933).

Fitzrovia

Branches
ASK
48 Grafton Way, W1T 5DZ
(7388 8108).
Busaba Eathai
22 Store Street, WC1E 7DS
(7299 7900).
dim t
32 Charlotte Street, W1T 2NQ
(7637 1122).
Gaucho Charlotte Street
60A Charlotte Street, W1T 2NU
(7580 6252).
Nando's
2 Berners Street, W1T 3LA
(7323 9791).
Ping Pong
48 Eastcastle Street, W1W 8DX
(7079 0550).
Ping Pong
48 Newman Street, W1T 1QQ
(7291 3080).
Pizza Express
4-5 Langham Place, W1B 3DG
(7580 3700).
Pizza Express
7-9 Charlotte Street, W1T 1RB
(7580 1110).
Pizza Express
215-217 Great Portland Street,
W1W 5PN (7580 2272).

Rasa Express
5 Rathbone Street, W1T 1NX
(7637 0222).
Sagar
17A Percy Street, W1T 1DU
(7631 3319).
Salt Yard (branch of Dehesa)
54 Goodge Street, W1T 4NA
(7637 0657, www.saltyard.co.uk).
Yo! Sushi
4 Great Portland Street, W1W 8QJ
(3130 9251).
Zizzi
33-41 Charlotte Street, W1T 1RR
(7436 9440).
Brasseries & Cafés
Kaffeine p13
66 Great Titchfield Street,
W1W 7QJ (7580 6755,
www.kaffeine.co.uk).
Lantana p43
13 Charlotte Place, W1T 1SN
(7637 3347, www.lantana
cafe.co.uk).
Nando's p86
57-59 Goodge Street, W1T 1TH
(7637 0708, www.nandos.co.uk).
Tapped & Packed p13
26 Rathbone Place, W1T 1JD
(7580 2163, www.tappedand
packed.co.uk).
Chinese
Hakkasan p64
8 Hanway Place, W1T 1HD
(7927 7000, www.hakkasan.com).
French
Elena's L'Étoile p45
30 Charlotte Street, W1T 2NG
(7636 7189, www.elenas
letoile.co.uk).
Villandry p91
170 Great Portland Street,
W1W 5QB (7631 3131,
www.villandry.com).
Hotels & Haute Cuisine
The Landau p126
The Langham, 1C Portland Place,
W1B 1JA (7965 0165,
www.thelandau.com).
Pied à Terre p126
34 Charlotte Street, W1T 2NH
(7636 1178, www.pied-a-
terre.co.uk).
Indian
Rasa Samudra p135
5 Charlotte Street, W1T 1RE
(7637 0222, www.rasa
restaurants.com).
Italian
Mennula p150
10 Charlotte Street, W1T 2LT
(7636 2833, www.mennula.com).
Sardo p150
45 Grafton Way, W1T 5DQ
(7387 2521, www.sardo-
restaurant.com).
Japanese
Roka p167
37 Charlotte Street, W1T 1RR
(7580 6464,
www.rokarestaurant.com).
Soho Japan p167
52 Wells Street, W1T 3PR (7323
4661, www.sohojapan.co.uk).
Korean
Koba p181
11 Rathbone Street, W1T 1NA
(7580 8825, www.koba-
london.com).
Pan-Asian & Fusion
Bam-Bou p221
1 Percy Street, W1T 1DB
(7323 9130, www.bam-bou.co.uk).
Crazy Bear p222
26-28 Whitfield Street, W1T 2RG
(7631 0088, www.crazybear
group.co.uk).
Spanish & Portuguese
Barrica p228
62 Goodge Street, W1T 4NE
(7436 9448, www.barrica.co.uk).

Fino p228
33 Charlotte Street, entrance
on Rathbone Street, W1T 1RR
(7813 8010, www.fino
restaurant.com).
Ibérica Food & Culture p229
195 Great Portland Street,
W1W 5PS (7636 8650,
www.ibericalondon.com).
The Americas
Eagle Bar Diner p30
3-5 Rathbone Place, W1T 1HJ
(7637 1418, www.eaglebar
diner.com).
Mestizo p37
103 Hampstead Road, NW1 3EL
(7387 4064, www.mestizomx.com).
Turkish
Özer p247
5 Langham Place, W1B 3DG
(7323 0505, www.sofra.co.uk).

Fulham

Branches
Bodean's
4 Broadway Chambers, Fulham
Broadway, SW6 1EP (7610 0440).
Carluccio's Caffè
236 Fulham Road, SW10 9NB
(7376 5960).
Feng Sushi
218 Fulham Road, SW10 9NB
(7795 1900).
Gourmet Burger Kitchen
49 Fulham Broadway, SW6 1AE
(7381 4242).
Lola Rojo
140 Wandsworth Bridge Road,
SW6 2UL (7371 8396).
Masala Zone
583 Fulham Broadway, SW6 5UA
(7386 5500).
Nando's
Fulham Broadway Retail Centre,
Fulham Road, SW6 1BY
(7386 8035).
Pizza Express
Fulham Broadway Centre, Fulham
Road, SW6 1BW (7381 1700).
Rossopomodoro
214 Fulham Road, SW10 9NB
(7352 7677).
Royal China
805 Fulham Road, SW6 5HE
(7731 0081).
Yo! Sushi
Fulham Broadway Centre, Fulham
Road, SW6 1BW (7385 6077).
Fish & Chips
Fisher's p83
19 Fulham High Street, SW6 3JH
(7610 9808, www.fishers
fishandchips.com).
Gastropubs
Harwood Arms p105
Corner of Walham Grove and Farm
Lane, SW6 1QP (7386 1847,
www.harwoodarms.com).
Modern European
My Dining Room p211
18 Farm Lane, SW6 1PP
(7381 3331, www.mydining
room.net).
Thai
Blue Elephant p244
4-6 Fulham Broadway, SW6 1AA
(7385 6595, www.blue
elephant.com).

Gipsy Hill

Global
Numidie p119
48 Westow Hill, SE19 1RX
(8766 6166, www.numidie.co.uk).

Gloucester Road

Branches
ASK
23-24 Gloucester Arcade,
Gloucester Road, SW7 4SF
(7835 0840).

Ilford, Essex

Branches
Nando's
I-Scene, Clements Road, Ilford,
Essex, IG1 1BP (8514 6012).
Chinese
Mandarin Palace　　　　　　**p73**
559-561 Cranbrook Road, Ilford,
Essex, IG2 6JZ (8550 7661).

Islington

Branches
ASK
Business Design Centre, 52 Upper
Street, N1 0PN (7226 8728).
Byron
341 Upper Street, N1 0PB
(7204 7620).
Carluccio's Caffè
305-307 Upper Street, N1 2TU
(7359 8167).
The Diner
21 Essex Road, N1 2SA
(7226 4533).
Giraffe
29-31 Essex Road, N1 2SA
(7359 5999).
Grand Union
153 Upper Street, N1 1RA
(7226 1375).
Lucky Voice
173-174 Upper Street, N1 1RG
(7354 6280).
Masala Zone
80 Upper Street, N1 0NU
(7359 3399).
Nando's
324 Upper Street, N1 2XQ
(7288 0254).
Pizza Express
335 Upper Street, N1 0PB
(7226 9542).
Rodizio Rico
77-78 Upper Street, N1 0NU
(7354 1076).
Strada
105-106 Upper Street, N1 1QN
(7226 9742).
Wagamama
N1 Centre, 39 Parkfield Street,
N1 0PS (7226 2664).
Yo! Sushi
N1 Centre, 39 Parkfield Street,
N1 0PS (7359 3502).
Brasseries & Cafés
Ottolenghi　　　　　　**p51**
287 Upper Street, N1 2TZ (7288
1454, www.ottolenghi.co.uk).
Fish
The Fish Shop　　　　　　**p86**
360-362 St John Street, EC1V 4NR
(7837 1199, www.thefishshop.net).
French
Almeida　　　　　　**p97**
30 Almeida Street, N1 1AD
(7354 4777, www.dandd
london.com).
Morgan M　　　　　　**p98**
489 Liverpool Road, N7 8NS
(7609 3560, www.morganm.com).
Gastropubs
Charles Lamb　　　　　　**p114**
16 Elia Street, N1 8DE (7837
5040, www.thecharles
lambpub.com).
Compass　　　　　　**p115**
58 Penton Street, N1 9PZ
(7837 3891, www.thecompass
n1.co.uk).
Marquess Tavern　　　　　　**p115**
32 Canonbury Street, N1 2TB
(7354 2975,
www.themarquesstavern.co.uk).
Italian
Metrogusto　　　　　　**p163**
13 Theberton Street, N1 0QY
(7226 9400).
Tenore　　　　　　**p164**
14 Barnsbury Road, N1 0HB
(7278 6955, www.tenore-
restaurant.co.uk).

Japanese
Sa Sa Sushi　　　　　　**p174**
422 St John Street, EC1V 4NJ
(7837 1155, www.sasa
sushi.co.uk).
Modern European
Frederick's　　　　　　**p216**
Camden Passage, N1 8EG
(7359 2888, www.fredericks.
co.uk).
North African
Maghreb　　　　　　**p220**
189 Upper Street, N1 1RQ
(7226 2305, www.maghreb
restaurant.co.uk).
Pan-Asian & Fusion
Banana Tree Canteen　　　　　　**p225**
412-416 St John Street, EC1V 4NJ
(7278 7565).
The Americas
Sabor　　　　　　**p40**
108 Essex Road, N1 8LX
(7226 5551, www.sabor.co.uk).
Turkish
Pasha　　　　　　**p252**
301 Upper Street, N1 2TU
(7226 1454, www.pasha
restaurant.co.uk).

Kennington

Branches
Grand Union
111 Kennington Road, SE11 6SF
(7582 6685).
Pizza Express
316 Kennington Road, SE11 4LD
(7820 3877).
African & Caribbean
Adulis　　　　　　**p25**
44-46 Brixton Road, SW9 6BT
(7587 0055, www.adulis.co.uk).

Kensal

Branches
The Diner
64-66 Chamberlayne Road,
NW10 3JJ (8968 9033).

Kensal Green

The Americas
Sabor Brasileiro　　　　　　**p38**
639 Harrow Road, NW10 5NU
(8969 1149).

Kensington

Branches
Côte
47 Kensington Court, W8 5DA
(7938 4147).
Feng Sushi
24 Kensington Church Street,
W8 4EP (7937 7927).
Giraffe
7 Kensington High Street, W8 5NP
(7938 1221).
Kensington Place
(branch of D&D London)
201-209 Kensington Church Street,
W8 7LX (7727 3184,
www.kensingtonplace-
restaurant.co.uk).
Ottolenghi
1 Holland Street, W8 4NA
(7937 0003).
Randa (branch of Maroush I)
23 Kensington Church Street,
W8 4LF (7937 5363).
Ranoush Juice
86 Kensington High Street,
W8 4SG (7938 2234).
Saf
Whole Foods Market, The Barkers
Building, 63-97 Kensington High
Street, W8 5SE (7368 4500,
www.wholefoodsmarket.com).
Strada
29 Kensington High Street,
W8 5NP (7938 4648).
Wagamama
26 Kensington High Street,
W8 4PF (7376 1717).

Wódka (branch of Baltic)
12 St Alban's Grove, W8 5PN
(7937 6513, www.wodka.co.uk).
Burger Bars
Byron　　　　　　**p86**
222 Kensington High Street,
W8 7RG (7361 1717,
www.byronhamburgers.com).
Chinese
Min Jiang　　　　　　**p71**
10th floor, Royal Garden Hotel, 2-4
Kensington High Street, W8 4PT
(7361 1988, www.minjiang.com).
East European
Mimino　　　　　　**p75**
197C Kensington High Street,
W8 6BA (7937 1551,
www.mimino.co.uk).
Indian
Zaika　　　　　　**p142**
1 Kensington High Street,
W8 5NP (7795 6533, www.zaika-
restaurant.co.uk).
Italian
Timo　　　　　　**p157**
343 Kensington High Street,
W8 6NW (7603 3888,
www.timorestaurant.net).
Modern European
Clarke's　　　　　　**p209**
124 Kensington Church Street,
W8 4BH (7221 9225,
www.sallyclarke.com).

Kentish Town

Branches
Nando's
227-229 Kentish Town Road,
NW5 2JU (7424 9363).
Oxford (branch of Realpubs)
256 Kentish Town Road, NW5 2AA
(7485 3521,
www.theoxfordnw5.co.uk).
African & Caribbean
Queen of Sheba　　　　　　**p26**
12 Fortess Road, NW5 2EU
(7284 3947, www.thequeenof
sheba.co.uk).
Bars
Southampton Arms　　　　　　**p14**
139 Highgate Road, NW5 1LE
(07958 780073, www.the
southamptonarms.co.uk).
Burger Bars
Grand Union　　　　　　**p113**
53-79 Highgate Road, NW5 1TL
(7485 1837, www.gugroup.co.uk).
Gastropubs
Bull & Last　　　　　　**p115**
168 Highgate Road, NW5 1QS
(7267 3641, www.thebulland
last.co.uk).
Junction Tavern　　　　　　**p115**
101 Fortess Road, NW5 1AG (7485
9400, www.junctiontavern.co.uk).
Pizza & Pasta
Pizza Express　　　　　　**p151**
187 Kentish Town Road, NW1 8PD
(7267 0101, www.pizza
express.com).

Kew, Surrey

Branches
ASK
85 Kew Green, Kew, Surrey,
TW9 3AH (8940 3766).
The Glasshouse
(branch of Chez Bruce)
14 Station Parade, Kew, Surrey,
TW9 3PZ (8940 6777, www.
glasshouserestaurant.co.uk).
Pizza Express
10 Station Approach, Kew, Surrey,
TW9 3QB (8404 6000).

Kilburn

Branches
Nando's
308 Kilburn High Road, NW6 2DG
(7372 1507).

Pizza Express
319 West End Lane, NW6 1RP
(7431 8229).
Gastropubs
Salusbury　　　　　　**p116**
50-52 Salusbury Road, NW6 6NN
(7328 3286).

King's Cross

Branches
Carluccio's Caffè
Upper level, St Pancras
International Station, NW1 2QP
(7278 7449).
Madeira Café
279 Gray's Inn Road, WC1X 8QF
(7713 0667).
Nando's
12-16 York Way, N1 9AA
(7833 2809).
Rasa Maricham
Holiday Inn, 1 King's Cross Road,
WC1X 9HX (7833 3900).
Yo! Sushi
The Circle, St Pancras International,
NW1 2QP (7084 7121).
Bars
Bar Pepito　　　　　　**p14**
Varnishers Yard, Regents Quarter,
N1 9FD (7841 7331, www.camino.
uk.com/pepito).
Brasseries & Cafés
St Pancras Grand　　　　　　**p43**
Upper Concourse, St Pancras
International, Euston Road,
NW1 2QP (7870 9900,
www.searcys.co.uk/stpancrasgrand)
.
Modern European
Acorn House　　　　　　**p204**
69 Swinton Street, WC1X 9NT
(7812 1842, www.acornhouse
restaurant.com).
Spanish & Portuguese
Camino　　　　　　**p229**
3 Varnishers Yard, Regents
Quarter, N1 9FD (7841 7331,
www.camino.uk.com).
Vegetarian
Itadaki Zen　　　　　　**p253**
139 King's Cross Road,
WC1X 9BJ (7278 3573,
www.itadakizen.com).

Kingston, Surrey

Branches
Byron
4 Jerome Place, Charter Quay,
Kingston, Surrey, KT1 1HX
(8541 4757).
Carluccio's Caffè
Charter Quay, Kingston, Surrey,
KT1 1HT (8549 5898).
Carluccio's Caffè
Bentalls, Wood Street, Kingston,
Surrey, KT1 1TX (8549 5807).
Gourmet Burger Kitchen
42-46 High Street, Kingston,
Surrey, KT1 1HL (8546 1649).
Nando's
37-38 High Street, Kingston,
Surrey, KT1 1LQ (8296 9540).
Pizza Express
19 Creek Road, East Molesey,
Kingston, Surrey, KT8 9BE
(8941 3347).
Pizza Express
41 High Street, Kingston, Surrey,
KT1 1LQ (8546 1447).
Pizza Express
5 The Rotunda, Kingston, Surrey,
KT1 1QJ (8547 3133).
Strada
1 The Griffin Centre, Market
Place, Kingston, Surrey, KT1 1JT
(8974 8555).
Wagamama
16-18 High Street, Kingston,
Surrey, KT1 1EY (8546 1117).
Zizzi
43 Market Place, Kingston,
Surrey, KT1 1ET (8546 0717).

AREA INDEX

Indian
Eriki p147
4-6 Northways Parade, Finchley
Road, NW3 5EN (7722 0606,
www.eriki.co.uk).
**Malaysian, Indonesian &
Singaporean**
Singapore Garden p190
83A Fairfax Road, NW6 4DY (7624
8233, www.singaporegarden.co.uk).

Teddington, Middx
Branches
Pizza Express
11 Waldegrave Road, Teddington,
Middx, TW11 8LA (8943 3553).

Tooting
Branches
Nando's
224-226 Upper Tooting Road,
SW17 7EW (8682 2478).
Gastropubs
Antelope p107
76 Mitcham Road, SW17 9NG
(8672 3888, www.antic-
ltd.com/antelope).
Indian
Apollo Banana Leaf p145
190 Tooting High Street, SW17 0SF
(8696 1423).

Tottenham Hale
Branches
19 Numara Bos Cirrik IV
665 High Road, N17 8AD
(8801 5566).

Tower Bridge
Branches
ASK
Spice Quay, 34 Shad Thames,
Butlers Wharf, SE1 2YG
(7403 4545).
**Butlers Wharf Chop House
(branch of D&D London)**
Butlers Wharf Building, 36E Shad
Thames, SE1 2YE (7403 3403).
Draft House
206-208 Tower Bridge Road,
SE1 2UP.
Ping Pong
Quayside, Tower Bridge House,
St Katharine Docks, E1W 1BA
(7680 7850).
Pizza Express
Cardamon Building, 31 Shad
Thames, SE1 2YR (7403 8484).
**Le Pont de la Tour
(branch of D&D London)**
Butlers Wharf Building, 36D Shad
Thames, SE1 2YE (7403 8403).
Strada
2 Tower Bridge House, St
Katharine's Way, E1W 1AA
(7702 0123).
Wagamama
Tower Place, Tower Hill, EC3N 4EE
(7283 5897).
Zizzi
Cardamon Building, 31 Shad
Thames, SE1 2YR (7367 6100).
Zizzi
12 Ivory House, St Katharine
Docks, E1W 1AT (7488 0130).
Italian
Tentazioni p159
2 Mill Street, SE1 2BD (7237 1100,
www.tentazioni.co.uk).
Modern European
Blueprint Café p214
Design Museum, 28 Shad Thames,
SE1 2YD (7378 7031,
www.danddlondon.com).

Trafalgar Square
Brasseries & Cafés
National Café p169
East Wing, National Gallery,
Trafalgar Square, WC2N 5DN (7747
2525, www.thenationalcafe.com).

British
National Dining Rooms p169
Sainsbury Wing, National Gallery,
WC2N 5DN (7747 2525,
www.thenationaldiningrooms.co.uk).

Tufnell Park
African & Caribbean
Lalibela p27
137 Fortess Road, NW5 2HR
(7284 0600).

Twickenham, Middx
Branches
ASK
58-62 The Green, Twickenham,
Middx, TW2 5AB (8755 3800).
Grand Union
11 London Road, Twickenham,
Middx, TW1 3SX (8892 2925).
Pizza Express
21 York Street, Twickenham,
Middx, TW1 3JZ (8891 4126).
Sagar
27 York Street, Twickenham,
Middx, TW1 3JZ (8744 3868).
Zizzi
36-38 York Street, Twickenham,
Middx, TW1 3LJ (8538 9024).
French
Brula p99
43 Crown Road, Twickenham,
Middx, TW1 3EJ (8892 0602,
www.brula.co.uk).
Italian
A Cena p164
418 Richmond Road, Twickenham,
Middx, TW1 2EB (8288 0108,
www.acena.co.uk).

Uxbridge, Middx
Branches
Ask
139-140 High Street, Uxbridge,
Middx, UB8 1JX (01895 272799).
Nando's
The Chimes Centre, High Street,
Uxbridge, Middx, UB8 1GE (01895
274277).
Pizza Express
222 High Street, Uxbridge, Middx,
UB8 1LD (01895 2512222).

Vauxhall
Branches
Café 89 (branch of Casa Madeira)
89 Albert Embankment, SE1 7TP
(7587 1999).
**Pico Bar & Grill
(branch of Casa Madeira)**
74 Albert Embankment, SE1 7TL
(7820 1282).
Pan-Asian & Fusion
Chino Latino p224
Park Plaza Riverbank, 18 Albert
Embankment, SE1 7TJ (7769 2500,
www.chinolatino.co.uk).
Spanish & Portuguese
Casa Madeira p238
46A-46C Albert Embankment,
SE11 5AW (7820 1117,
www.madeiralondon.co.uk).
Rebato's p233
169 South Lambeth Road,
SW8 1XW (7735 6388,
www.rebatos.com).

Victoria
Branches
ASK
160-162 Victoria Street, SW1E 5LB
(7630 8228).
Giraffe
120 Wilton Road, SW1V 1JZ
(7233 3303).
Nando's
17 Cardinal Walk, Cardinal Place,
SW1E 5JE (7828 0158).
Pizza Express
154 Victoria Street, SW1E 5LB
(7828 1477).

Pizza Express
85 Victoria Street, SW1H 0HW
(7222 5270).
Wagamama
Roof garden level, Cardinal Place,
off Victoria Street, SW1E 5JE
(7828 0561).
Yo! Sushi
Main concourse, Victoria Station,
SW1V 1JT (3262 0050).
Zizzi
15 Cardinal Walk, Cardinal Place,
SW1E 5JE (7821 0402).
British
Boisdale of Belgravia p53
13-15 Eccleston Street,
SW1W 9LX (7730 6922,
www.boisdale.co.uk).
Goring Hotel p53
Beeston Place, Grosvenor Gardens,
SW1W 0JW (7396 9000,
www.goringhotel.co.uk).

Victoria Park
Branches
**Empress of India
(branch of ETM Group)**
130 Lauriston Road, E9 7LH
(8533 5123, www.theempress
ofindia.com).
Fish & Chips
Fish House p83
126-128 Lauriston Road, E9 7LH
(8533 3327).

Walthamstow
Spanish & Portuguese
Orford Saloon p237
32 Orford Road, E17 9NJ
(8503 6542).

Wandsworth
Branches
Nando's
Southside Shopping Centre,
SW18 4TF (8874 1363).
Pizza Express
198 Trinity Road, SW17 7HR
(8672 0200).
Pizza Express
539-541 Old York Road, SW18 1TG
(8877 9812).
Fish & Chips
Brady's p83
513 Old York Road, SW18 1TF
(8877 9599,
www.bradysfish.co.uk).
French
Chez Bruce p94
2 Bellevue Road, SW17 7EG
(8672 0114, www.chez
bruce.co.uk).

Wanstead
Modern European
Hadley House p216
27 High Street, E11 2AA
(8989 8855).

Wapping
Branches
Pizza Express
78-80 Wapping Lane, E1W 2RT
(7481 8436).
Modern European
Wapping Food p215
Wapping Hydraulic Power
Station, Wapping Wall,
E1W 3ST (7680 2080,
www.thewappingproject.com).
Pizza & Pasta
Il Bordello p161
81 Wapping High Street, E1W 2YN
(7481 9950).

Waterloo
Branches
Canteen
Royal Festival Hall, Belvedere Road,
SE1 8XX (0845 686 1122).

Feng Sushi
Festival Terrace, Royal Festival Hall,
Belvedere Road, SE1 8XX
(7261 0001).
Madeira Café
1 Wootton Street, SE1 8TG
(3268 2127).
**Oxo Tower Restaurant,
Bar & Brasserie
(branch of Harvey Nichols)**
8th floor, Oxo Tower Wharf,
Barge House Street, SE1 9PH
(7803 3888).
Ping Pong
Festival Terrace, Royal Festival
Hall, Belvedere Road, SE1 8XX
(7960 4160).
Pizza Express
The White House, 9C Belvedere
Road, SE1 8YP (7928 4091).
Skylon (branch of D&D London)
Belvedere Road, SE1 8XX
(7654 7800).
Strada
Royal Festival Hall, Belvedere Road,
SE1 8XX (7401 9126).
Wagamama
Riverside Level 1, Royal Festival
Hall, Belvedere Road, SE1 8XX
(7021 0877).
Yo! Sushi
County Hall, Belvedere Road,
SE1 7GP (7928 8871).
Brasseries & Cafés
Giraffe p86
Riverside Level 1, Royal Festival
Hall, Belvedere Road, SE1 8XX
(7928 2004, www.giraffe.net).
East European
Baltic p76
74 Blackfriars Road, SE1 8HA
(7928 1111, www.baltic
restaurant.co.uk).
French
RSJ p94
33 Coin Street, SE1 9NR
(7928 4554, www.rsj.uk.com).
Gastropubs
Anchor & Hope p108
36 The Cut, SE1 8LP
(7928 9898).
Spanish & Portuguese
Mar i Terra p233
14 Gambia Street, SE1 0XH
(7928 7628, www.mariterra.co.uk).
Turkish
Tas p248
33 The Cut, SE1 8LF (7928 2111,
www.tasrestaurant.com).

Wembley, Middx
Branches
Nando's
420-422 High Road, Wembley,
Middx, HA9 6AH (8795 3564).
Indian
Sakonis p148
129 Ealing Road, Wembley,
Middx, HA0 4BP (8903 9601,
www.sakonis.co.uk).
Middle Eastern
Mesopotamia p200
115 Wembley Park Drive,
Wembley, Middx, HA9 8HG
(8453 5555, www.mesopotamia.
ltd.com).

West Hampstead
Branches
Banana Tree Canteen
237-239 West End Lane, NW6 1XN
(7431 7808).
Gourmet Burger Kitchen
331 West End Lane, NW6 1RS
(7794 5455).
Nando's
252-254 West End Lane, NW6 1LU
(7794 1331).
Strada
291 West End Lane, NW6 1RD
(7431 8678).

Advertisers' Index

Please refer to relevant sections for addresses/telephone numbers

A-Z Index

Beirut Express
(branch of Ranoush Juice)
112-114 Edgware Road, W2 2JE
(7724 2700). Branch

Belvedere p93
Holland House, off Abbotsbury
Road, in Holland Park, W8 6LU
(7602 1238, www.belvedere
restaurant.co.uk). French

Benares p136
12A Berkeley Square House,
Berkeley Square, W1J 6BS
(7629 8886, www.benares
restaurant.com). Indian

Bentley's Oyster Bar & Grill p80
11-15 Swallow Street,
W1B 4DG (7734 4756,
www.bentleysoyster
barandgrill.co.uk). Fish

Bevis Marks Restaurant p176
4 Heneage Lane, EC3A 5DQ
(7283 2220, www.bevismarks
therestaurant.com). Jewish

Bibendum p208
Michelin House, 81 Fulham
Road, SW3 6RD (7581 5817,
www.bibendum.co.uk).
Modern European

Bibendum Oyster Bar
81 Fulham Road, SW3 6RD
(7589 1480). Branch

Bincho p171
16 Old Compton Street,
W1D 4TL (7287 9111,
www.bincho.co.uk). Japanese

The Bingham p132
61-63 Petersham Road,
Richmond, Surrey, TW10 6UT
(8940 0902, www.thebingham.
co.uk). Hotels & Haute Cuisine

Bistrot Bruno Loubet p88
St John's Square, 86-88
Clerkenwell Road, EC1M 5RJ
(7324 4455, www.thezetter.com/
en/restaurant). French

Bistrotheque p95
23-27 Wadeson Street, E2 9DR
(8983 7900,
www.bistrotheque.com). French

Blah Blah Blah p255
78 Goldhawk Road, W12 8HA
(8746 1337, www.blah
blahblah.org). Vegetarian

Bleeding Heart Tavern p262
Bleeding Heart Yard, 19 Greville
Street, EC1N 8SJ (7404 0333,
www.bleedingheart.co.uk).
Wine Bars

Blue Elephant p244
4-6 Fulham Broadway, SW6 1AA
(7385 6595, www.blue
elephant.com). Thai

Bluebird
(branch of D&D London)
350 King's Road, SW3 5UU
(7559 1000, www.bluebird
chelsea.com). Branch

Blueprint Café p214
Design Museum, 28 Shad Thames,
SE1 2YD (7378 7031, www.dandd
london.com). Modern European

Blues Kitchen p265
111-113 Camden High Street,
NW1 7JN (7387 5277,
www.theblueskitchen.co.uk).
Eating & Entertainment

Bob Bob Ricard p46
1 Upper James Street, W1F 9DF
(3145 1000, www.bobbob
ricard.com). Brasseries & Cafés

Bocca di Lupo p154
12 Archer Street, W1D 7BB (7734
2223, www.boccadilupo.com).
Italian

Bodean's p33
10 Poland Street, W1F 8PZ
(7287 7575, www.bodeans
bbq.com). The Americas

Bodean's
16 Byward Street, EC3R 5BA
(7488 3883). Branch

Bodean's
169 Clapham High Street,
SW4 7SS (7622 4248). Branch

Bodean's
4 Broadway Chambers, Fulham
Broadway, SW6 1EP (7610 0440).
Branch

Bodean's
57 Westbourne Grove, W2 4UA
(7727 9503). Branch

Boisdale of Belgravia p53
13-15 Eccleston Street,
SW1W 9LX (7730 6922,
www.boisdale.co.uk). British

Boisdale of Bishopsgate
Swedeland Court, 202 Bishopsgate,
EC2M 4NR (7283 1763).
Branch

Bond & Brook p44
2nd floor, Fenwick Bond Street,
63 New Bond Street, W1S 1RQ
(7629 0273, www.fenwick.co.uk).
Brasseries & Cafés

Bonds p126
Threadneedles, 5 Threadneedle
Street, EC2R 8AY (7657 8088,
www.theetoncollection.com).
Hotels & Haute Cuisine

The Botanist p211
7 Sloane Square, SW1W 8EE
(7730 0077, www.thebotanist
onsloanesquare.com).
Modern European

Boundary p95
2-4 Boundary Street, entrance
at 9 Redchurch Street, E2 7DD
(7729 1051, www.theboundary.
co.uk). French

Brady's p83
513 Old York Road, SW18 1TF
(8877 9599, www.bradys
fish.co.uk). Fish & Chips

Brasserie Vacherin
(branch of Le Cassoulet)
12 High Street, Sutton,
Surrey, SM1 1HN (8722 0180).
Branch

Brilliant p148
72-76 Western Road, Southall,
Middx, UB2 5DZ (8574 1928,
www.brilliantrestaurant.com).
Indian

Brown Dog p105
28 Cross Street, SW13 0AP
(8392 2200, www.thebrowndog.
co.uk). Gastropubs

Brula p99
43 Crown Road, Twickenham,
Middx, TW1 3EJ (8892 0602,
www.brula.co.uk). French

Buen Ayre p40
50 Broadway Market, E8 4QJ
(7275 9900, www.buenayre.co.uk).
The Americas

Buenos Aires Café p39
17 Royal Parade, SE3 0TL (8318
5333, www.buenosairesltd.com).
The Americas

Buenos Aires Café & Delicatessen
86 Royal Hill, SE10 8RT
(8488 6764). Branch

Bull & Last p115
168 Highgate Road, NW5 1QS
(7267 3641, www.thebulland
last.co.uk). Gastropubs

Busaba Eathai p239
35 Panton Street, SW1Y 4EA (7930
0088, www.busaba.com). Thai

Busaba Eathai
313-319 Old Street, EC1V 9LE
(7729 0808). Branch

Busaba Eathai
106-110 Wardour Street, W1F 0TR
(7255 8686). Branch

Busaba Eathai
8-13 Bird Street, W1U 1BU
(7518 8080). Branch

Busaba Eathai
22 Store Street, WC1E 7DS
(7299 7900). Branch

Butcher & Grill p31
39-41 Parkgate Road, SW11 4NP
(7924 3999, www.thebutcher
andgrill.com). Brasseries & Cafés

Butcher & Grill
33 High Street, SW19 5BY
(8944 8269). Branch

Butlers Wharf Chop House
(branch of D&D London)
Butlers Wharf Building, 36E Shad
Thames, SE1 2YE (7403 3403).
Branch

Byron p86
222 Kensington High Street,
W8 7RG (7361 1717, www.byron
hamburgers.com). Burger Bars

Byron
2nd floor, Cabot Place East,
E14 4QT (7715 9360). Branch

Byron
4 Jerome Place, Charter Quay,
Kingston, Surrey, KT1 1HX
(8541 4757). Branch

Byron
341 Upper Street, N1 0PB
(7204 7620). Branch

Byron
300 King's Road, SW3 5UH
(7352 6040). Branch

Byron
93-95 Old Brompton Road,
SW7 3LD (7590 9040). Branch

Byron
75 Gloucester Road, SW7 4SS
(7244 0700). Branch

Byron
The Loft, Westfield Shopping
Centre, W12 7GF (8743 7755).
Branch

Byron
97-99 Wardour Street, W1F 0UF
(7297 9390). Branch

Byron
33-35 Wellington Street, WC2E 7BN
(7420 9850). Branch

C

C&R Restaurant p190
52 Westbourne Grove, W2 5SH
(7221 7979). Malaysian,
Indonesian & Singaporean

C&R Café
4-5 Rupert Court, W1D 6DY
(7434 1128). Branch

Cadogan Arms
(branch of ETM Group)
298 King's Road, SW3 5UG
(7352 6500, www.thecadogan
armschelsea.com). Branch

Café 89 (branch of Casa Madeira)
89 Albert Embankment, SE1 7TP
(7587 1999). Branch

Le Café Anglais p208
8 Porchester Gardens, W2 4DB
(7221 1415, www.lecafe
anglais.co.uk). Modern European

Café Below p41
St Mary-le-Bow, Cheapside,
EC2V 6AU (7329 0789, www.cafe
below.co.uk). Brasseries & Cafés

Café de Hong Kong p69
47-49 Charing Cross Road, WC2H
0AN (7534 9898). Chinese

Café East p258
Surrey Quays Leisure Park, 100
Redriff Row, SE16 7LH (7252
1212, www.cafeeast.co.uk).
Vietnamese

Café Japan p174
626 Finchley Road, NW11 7RR
(8455 6854, www.cafejapan.co.uk).
Japanese

Café Spice Namaste p145
16 Prescot Street, E1 8AZ (7488
9242, www.cafespice.co.uk). Indian

Café TPT p69
21 Wardour Street, W1D 6PN
(7734 7980). Chinese

Cah Chi p183
34 Durham Road, SW20 0TW
(8947 1081, www.cahchi.com).
Korean

Cah Chi
394 Garratt Lane, SW18 4HP
(8946 8811). Branch

Cambio de Tercio p232
163 Old Brompton Road, SW5 0LJ
(7244 8970, www.cambio
detercio.co.uk). Spanish &
Portuguese

Camino p229
3 Varnishers Yard, Regents Quarter,
N1 9FD (7841 7331,
www.camino.co.uk).
Spanish & Portuguese

Canteen p62
2 Crispin Place, off Brushfield
Street, E1 6DW (0845 686 1122,
www.canteen.co.uk). British

Canteen
40 Canada Square, E14 5FW
(0845 686 1122). Branch

Canteen
Royal Festival Hall, Belvedere Road,
SE1 8XX (0845 686 1122). Branch

Canteen
55 Baker Street, W1U 8EW
(0845 686 1122). Branch

Cantina Laredo p36
10 Upper St Martin's Lane,
WC2H 9FB (7420 0630,
www.cantinalaredo.com).
The Americas

Canton p69
11 Newport Place, WC2H 7JR
(7437 6220). Chinese

The Capital p127
22-24 Basil Street, SW3 1AT
(7591 1202, www.capital
hotel.co.uk). Hotels & Haute
Cuisine

Caponata p163
3-7 Delancey Street, NW1 7NL
(7387 5959, www.caponata
camden.co.uk). Italian

Le Caprice p207
Arlington House, Arlington Street,
SW1A 1RJ (7629 2239,
www.caprice-holdings.co.uk).
Modern European

Caravan p42
11-13 Exmouth Market, EC1R
4QD (7833 8115, www.caravan
onexmouth.co.uk).
Brasseries & Cafés

Carluccio's Caffè p113
2A Garrick Street, WC2E 9BH
(7836 0990, www.carluccios.com).
Italian

Carluccio's Caffè
25 High Street, SW19 5XD
(8946 1202). Branch

Carluccio's Caffè
The Brunswick, Marchmont Street,
WC1N 1AF (7833 4100). Branch

Carluccio's Caffè
27 Spital Square, E1 6DZ
(7392 7662). Branch

Carluccio's Caffè
Reuters Plaza, E14 5AJ
(7719 1749). Branch

Carluccio's Caffè
12 West Smithfield, EC1A 9JR
(7329 5904). Branch

Carluccio's Caffè
Charter Quay, Kingston, Surrey,
KT1 1HT (8549 5898). Branch

Carluccio's Caffè
Bentalls, Wood Street, Kingston,
Surrey, KT1 1TX (8549 5807).
Branch

Carluccio's Caffè
305-307 Upper Street, N1 2TU
(7359 8167). Branch

Carluccio's Caffè
Upper level, St Pancras
International Station, NW1 2QP
(7278 7449). Branch

Carluccio's Caffè
32 Rosslyn Hill, NW3 1NH
(7794 2184). Branch

Carluccio's Caffè
Fenwick, Brent Cross Shopping
Centre, NW4 3FN (8203 6844).
Branch

Carluccio's Caffè
60 St John's Wood High Street,
NW8 7SH (7449 0404). Branch

Carluccio's Caffè
236 Fulham Road, SW10 9NB
(7376 5960). Branch

Carluccio's Caffè
Brewhouse Street, Putney Wharf,
SW15 2JQ (8789 0591). Branch

A-Z INDEX

A-Z INDEX